these are
my confessions

these are my confessions

Joy King, Electa Rome Parks,
Cheryl Robinson, Méta Smith

red
AVON

An Imprint of HarperCollins*Publishers*

This is a collection of fiction. Names, characters, places, and incidents are products of the authors' imaginations or are used fictitiously and are not to be construed as real. Any resemblance to actual events, locales, organizations, or persons, living or dead, is entirely coincidental.

Interior text designed by Diahann Sturge

ISBN: 978–0–7394–8721–1

Contents

Love B-Ball Style

Joy King

These Are My Confessions is dedicated to all my faithful readers who have shown me so much love in my short span in the literary world. Thank you—your support is greatly appreciated!! Much Love.

First Quarter

Triple Threat

"Once again Glen Goodman has delivered the goods. Like a quiet storm, Goodman came in and stole a pass from an unsuspecting Dexter Jackson, then tiptoed down the sidelines to get loose for a slam dunk," the game's commentator roared. The sound of the crowd put your mind in the state of being at the circus, watching the trapeze artists at work, and watching the greatest show on earth. But instead of being at a Barnum and Bailey production, you were center court for the NBA playoff game between the Chicago Titans and Atlanta Phantoms, with Glen Goodman dominating the scene.

"That's right, baby, work that ball," Sasha screamed, twisting her ample chest to the beat of the team's anthem. All eyes zoomed in on the Beyonce clone because not only did her low-rise skintight jeans and midriff top leave little to the imagination, it was a well known fact that she was Glen's significant other. Sasha had sat in the same courtside seat at every Phantom home game since moving to Atlanta a year ago. Once you got over the pretty face, ten pounds of blond highlighted weave, and the to-die-for body, which included a perfected pair of 34D salines, nobody understood what Glen saw in her. Sasha put the *S* in superficial, with her fake hair, boobs, phony attitude, and, if the rumors were correct, had been an industry groupie before she landed the most sought after bachelor in the NBA.

She blew Glen a kiss as their eyes briefly connected as the crowd stood up and cheered following Glen's slam dunk, the winning shot to seal the deal for the playoff win. Now, only the championship battle was left, and Sasha hoped that not only would her man win the NBA title, but that she in turn would capture the brass ring.

"Girl, let's go," she said to her friend Tracy, who was the girlfriend of one of Glen's teammates. "I want to be right there when Glen exits the locker room. You know all those damn hoochies are going to be swarming him."

"You know it. You better go let those tricks know it's all about you."

"Yeah, that's why I flashed these." Sasha pointed to her bountiful breasts. "To let everybody up in this stadium know what's up." The two ladies clicked their four inch heels on the polished floor as they walked toward the hallway outside the locker room. Some news cameras were waiting for the players to come out, but all hoped to get one of superstar Glen Goodman's classic lines to run with on the eleven o'clock news, ESPN, and tomorrow's newspaper.

"Here he comes now!" one of the reporters yelled.

Glen came out looking like the suave, confident superstar that he was. He paused for a moment and flashed his signature smile, which could brighten even the darkest tunnels.

"Glen, how does it feel to not only hit the winning shot but to score an amazing game high of eighty-five points? You've now beaten Kobe Bryant's record, and are only second to Wilt Chamberlain," the same reporter said.

"Honestly, it's not about the high score it's about my team winning," Glen replied. "I went into overdrive because the Phantoms were lethargic. I had to step it up. I don't believe in losing, especially when I'm on the court," he added in his usual overconfident way.

"Your team—so now the Atlanta Phantoms is your team?" one reporter said sarcastically.

Without missing a beat, Glen countered, "I'm the captain, so yes, it's my team. The players turn to me for leadership, and like the mailman, I always deliver, even on holidays." Then he winked and smiled to his many admirers.

"Okay, no more questions. Mr. Goodman has to go," Glen's personal assistant, Bianca, interceded. Although she'd only been working with Glen for a few weeks, she knew that his arrogance would soon be the centerpiece of every comment he made. No matter how irritating Glen Goodman could be, nobody could deny that he had it all—charisma, talent, and skills that superseded the basketball court. He was definitely a triple threat.

"Glen's new assistant kills me," Sasha snapped as Bianca hurried him away from the thirsty reporters. "She always tries to run everything. You would think she was his agent instead of a lowly assistant. I get so tired of her holding his hand like he's in second grade and she's schoolteacher."

"I feel you," Tracy said. "I'm glad Isaac doesn't have one of those. How did she get that job anyway? I thought he had some older lady as his assistant."

"He did—Ms. Pearl—but the old goose checked out," Sasha said, smacking her lips.

"What? She died? How?"

"Nah, she's not dead. Ms. Pearl had been Glen's father's assistant when he played in the league up until he retired. Then when Glen started playing, she became his assistant. She is damn near sixty years old and had no business being in the hustle and bustle of an on-the-go player like Glen. All those long hours finally got the best of her and she had to take it down. Her niece was a recent college graduate, and I guess couldn't find no job even with her little degree, so Ms. Pearl let her take over the position. It's only supposed to be temporary, but the bitch doesn't seem to be going anywhere."

"That's a trip. You don't mind Glen spending so much time with her?"

"I can't front, it does annoy me. But luckily, she isn't Glen's speed. He's not into those conservative librarian types. He likes sexy divas like myself, so whatever to her."

"Yeah, I feel you," Tracy said, then moved away, to give Sasha some privacy as Bianca led Glen in her direction. Tracy sat on a bench in the corner, watching from the sideline.

A gaggle of cute girls waved at him as he crossed their paths, and Sasha quickly walked forward to claim her property.

"Hi, baby, you played so good tonight," she said before placing a seductive kiss on Glen's lips.

Bianca discreetly rolled her eyes. "Well, Glen," she said, "you seem to be in good hands now, so I'll be heading home."

"Yeah, he is in good hands now, Bianca. Thanks for watching my man for me until I could get to him."

Bianca kept her eyes on Glen, ignoring Sasha's comment, which infuriated her.

"So I'll see you in the morning," Glen said to his assistant. "I want to go over a few things before we start playing the championship games."

"No problem. I'll see you then," Bianca replied, and walked off with Sasha burning a hole in her back.

"Why was miss thing over there playing like she was your publicist or something?" Sasha demanded. "I mean she's only your assistant."

"She's more than my assistant," Glen explained. "Bianca is very skilled. She has a master's degree in marketing, so I feel comfortable giving her more responsibilities. Ms. Pearl was great because she was like a second mother, but Bianca is dope."

"So what, you're thinking of keeping her permanently?"

"That's what I wanted to speak with her about tomorrow. I was hoping she would consider working for me on a long-term basis. I like the way she handles my business, especially with the media. It's hard to find a reliable and proficient assistant. But she has the skills to do multiple jobs."

"She seems a little too boring to work for you."

"I'm looking for someone to handle my business, not go to the clubs with me, I have you for that," Glen said, then kissed Sasha and put his arm around her waist.

"Where's Isaac at?" Tracy inquired, walking up to the couple.

"He should be out any minute. So are we going to celebrate being one step closer to the championship or what?" Glen asked Sasha.

"You know it, baby."

"I'm down, if Isaac would hurry up," Tracy said.

"Cool, let's do this."

When Bianca got home, the first thing she did was pour herself a glass of wine. It was becoming an after-game ritual. The stress of dealing with a high profile athlete was taking a toll on her. She didn't understand how her aunt had survived for so long. She was counting the days down, looking forward to when she would no longer have to play babysitter to an overbearing, egotistical basketball player, but didn't know who was more annoying—Glen, or his bimbo Barbie girlfriend. What she did know was that the sooner she finished her temporary role as Glen's personal assistant, the better.

Bianca kicked off her shoes and sat on the couch, about to unwind, when her phone rang. "Who in the hell could that be, calling me so late?" she mumbled to herself as she picked up the receiver. "Hello."

"Hi, honey, are you sleep?"

Bianca instantly recognized the voice on the other end. "Aunt Pearl, why are you calling so late? It's almost midnight."

"I know, baby, but I need to speak to you."

Bianca eyed the receiver suspiciously. Her aunt sounded so serious, she wondered what was so urgent that she couldn't wait until morning. It made her think about her aunt's health.

"Are you okay?" she asked, worried. "Have you been feeling sick again? Do you need me to come over?"

Bianca's heart was now thumping. Aunt Pearl was like a mother to her, and had been for ten years, since her mother—Pearl's younger sister—had died at the hands of Bianca's abusive father. She'd only been fourteen at the time. After her father was found guilty of murder and sentenced to life in prison, Bianca went to live with her aunt. Both of them were devastated by her mother's death and found comfort in each other. To help ease her grief and not focus on the tragedy, Bianca had thrown all her energy into her schoolwork. When it was time for her to leave for college, her academic skills landed her a full scholarship to a university in Philadelphia. She completed an internship, received a master's degree, then was offered a well-paid marketing position at a top notch advertising firm in New York City. The day she planned to accept the offer, she got the call from her aunt about becoming an assistant to Glen Goodman.

"Calm down," her aunt said. "I'm fine. I just need to speak to you about something very important to me."

"What is it?" Bianca felt a sense of relief as she sat back down, but her curiosity was piquing.

"You know how much I appreciate you taking over my job with Glen. You were truly a lifesaver."

"You don't have to thank me. I would do anything to help you out."

"No, you do deserve a thank-you and so much more. I know you had that great job waiting for you in New York and you turned it down because I needed you. But more important, Glen needed you."

"I understand the Goodmans are like family to you, and I was more than happy to step in and assist you any way I could. Plus, it's only temporary and the job in New York is still waiting for me. They've been great about keeping the position open." There was a long silent pause. "Hello . . . Aunt Pearl, are you there?"

"I'm here." Bianca heard her aunt clearing her throat before continuing. "Bianca, you're like a daughter to me. I never had any kids of my own, but if I did, I would've hoped they all turned out as wonderful as you."

Bianca's gut told her this was a setup for something she wanted no part of. "Umm-hmm."

"So if I ask you for a favor, it's because you're all I have."

"What's the favor?"

"Tomorrow Glen is going to ask you to work for him on a long-term basis, and I want you to say yes." Bianca could hear the subtle pleading in her aunt's voice, but it wasn't enough to garner any sympathy from her.

"You can't be serious? I have one more week to work with that overgrown child and I'm done."

"Bianca, wait. I know Glen can be a bit hard to manage at times, but he means well. You have to understand he's been in the shadow or living the lifestyle of an NBA star all his life. He doesn't know any better."

"Aunt Pearl, not to be rude, but in a week that will no longer be my problem or concern. I've become a borderline alcoholic dealing with him and his slick-with-the-tongue girlfriend. I'm sure there are plenty of hapless souls who would love to be Glen Goodman's assistant, I'm just not one of them."

"But he trusts you. He told me that ever since you started working with him, his professional life has been running smoothly. He said your marketing skills are priceless. He wants you to be more than his assistant. He really does speak highly of you, Bianca. If I thought anyone else could offer him what you can, I wouldn't have agreed to speak to you on his behalf."

"He put you up to this phone call? My goodness, can't he do anything on his own?"

"He simply told me what was on his mind, and I wanted to help him."

"Yeah, that's because everybody wants to save helpless Glen. That's why he's so screwed up now, because everybody kisses his ass, and for the last few weeks I've had to do the exact same thing. I'm sick of it."

"Please, Bianca, reconsider your decision. I've always been there for you and never asked you for much, but I'm begging you to do this for me. Just like you're a daughter to me, Glen is like a son. He has a good heart. If you look past the bravado he throws around, you'll see he's a wonderful young man."

Bianca let out a deep sigh, regretting that she'd ever agreed to take the job in the first place. She felt stuck. There was no way she could refuse a request from her aunt. She had to find another way to get out of her dilemma, one that wouldn't make her the bad guy.

"Okay, Aunt Pearl, if Glen asks me to stay on, then I'll accept his offer."

"I knew you wouldn't let me down. Something wonderful will come out of this for you. You'll see. Now you get some sleep. I know you have to meet Glen early in the morning. Thank you, baby, and good night."

Second Quarter

Position of Power

"Oh Daddy, fuck me harder," Sasha demanded as Glen went deeper inside her with each thrust.

"Damn baby, you feel so good. I'm about to come."

"Come inside of me, Daddy. I want to feel all your warmth."

It was Sasha's way of saying she wanted his baby. She had wanted to get pregnant by Glen from the moment she met him. For the first six months, he wore a condom. When she finally convinced him that she wasn't having sex with anyone else and was on the pill, she maneuvered that condom off his dick. Now, for the last year, she was working to get him to bust off inside of her instead of pulling out. It didn't matter how drunk Glen got, it was as if he was programmed to shoot his seeds in every direction but the inside of her reproductive system.

"Take it in the mouth and swallow it all up for me," Glen directed as he reached his peak and pulled out to explode. Sasha was used to this request, as it was Glen's favorite. She opened her mouth wide and tasted every last drop of his juices. It was getting to the point that she wondered if she should start running to the bathroom, spitting out his come and preserving it so she could have it inserted later on in order to conceive.

"You were wonderful, Daddy."

"So were you," Glen said as he rolled over on his back, feeling exhausted. "Between the game, hitting the club, and the workout you just gave me, I'm tired as hell. I'm going to sleep like a newborn. Good night."

He kissed Sasha on the forehead and fell into a deep sleep within seconds. Sasha glided her gel-tip finger nail up and down Glen's chest, admiring his muscle definition. Out of all the many celebrities she had bedded, none of them had made her feel like Glen. He treated her with respect and made her feel special. She was sure that he had heard some of the rumors that circulated about her, but he didn't seem to either care or believe them, which only made her try harder to get her claws deeper into him. Her past conquests always let it be known that she was nothing more than a great fuck and party girl, but not Glen. That's why she planned on staying with him no matter what.

Beep! Beep! Beep!

Bianca heard the sound of her alarm going off and squeezed the pillow over her head, trying to make the noise fade away. But it didn't help, and she finally dragged herself out of bed to turn it off. The clock said eight-thirty, and she was supposed to meet Glen at ten. It took her forty-five minutes to get to his house because he lived in Buckhead and she lived on the outskirts of Atlanta. That drive alone was enough to make her want to quit.

After a quick breakfast and shower, Bianca threw on her clothes and headed out. She hated to be late, and with morning traffic, there was a very good chance that she would be. She turned up the volume to hear her classical music CD as she thought about what she would say to Glen. Her words had to be executed just right because she had no doubt he would repeat their conversation to her aunt. It was imperative that she seemed cooperative, since her aunt's opinion was extremely important to her. By the time she pulled up to Glen's mansion, it was five after ten.

"I can live with being five minutes late," she said to herself as she approached the front door. She rang the doorbell once, then twice, then three times. By the fifth time, she began banging on the door. She knew Glen was home because the main car he drove was parked in the circular driveway. Just as she was about to pull out her cell phone and dial his house number, the door opened.

"Damn, is somebody attacking you or something?" Sasha spewed as she rubbed her eyes, standing in front of Bianca butt naked.

"No."

"Then what's up with all the banging? People do sleep this time of the morning."

"Your boyfriend and my boss, *soon to be ex-boss,*" Bianca said, mumbling the last part under her breath, "asked me to meet him here this morning so we could discuss some things."

"Oh yeah, that's right. Well, he still sleep, we had a lot of excitement last night. You know, celebrating and stuff."

"I remember, Glen told me he planned on going to the club to celebrate the team's win."

"No honey, I don't mean that celebration. I'm talking about part two, after the club, the excitement that took place in our bed when we got home."

"Speaking of bed, you're no longer in it, so can you please put some clothes on?"

"My fault. Glen is so crazy about my body and loves to see me in my birthday suit. I forget that everyone isn't so blessed."

"Is that what you call—"

The tongue-lashing Bianca had been about to put on Sasha abruptly ended when she noticed Glen coming down the wrap-around stairs in his silk boxers. For the first time, she felt a twinge of lust when she eyed her boss. Never had she seen him in the flesh, except for what he showed in his uniform on the basketball court. His smooth butter-pecan-colored skin glistened against the red silk boxers. Seeing each muscle in his arms connected to his bare chiseled chest had a different effect on her than when she got a glimpse of his biceps in his team jersey.

This is what Sasha is waking up to each morning, she thought. Damn she's a lucky bitch.

"Bianca, I apologize," he said to her. "I had a long night, and as you can see, I just got out of bed." He let out a long yawn.

Bianca noticed Sasha, her arms folded, her hip positioned to the side, as if she were irritated. She wondered if Sasha caught the lustful stare in her eyes. But how could Sasha blame her? Bianca had an inkling that Glen's outside package was just the sprinkles, and nothing compared to the tool in his pants. She hoped that Sasha didn't realize she was getting aroused over her man, because that would be one more thing for Sasha to gloat over. Besides, she knew that Glen would never be attracted to someone like her. Not that she was unattractive, but she just wasn't the obvious kind of pretty that a lot of men like Glen would go for.

In fact, Bianca downplayed her looks by wearing no makeup, pulling her hair in a tight bun, and wearing clothes that didn't accentuate one curve. But if anyone were to look closely, they would have seen that she had tons of potential.

"Would you like to reschedule, since you're obviously not ready for our meeting?" she said. Having snapped out of her lustful mind state, she was now furious that she had gotten out of bed early in the morning and driven over an hour, because of traffic, for a meeting he scheduled and wasn't ready for, due to his bumping and grinding with the still very naked Sasha.

"No, what I need to speak to you about is important," Glen said. "Please don't leave."

Hearing the sincerity in his voice, she was surprised. "Okay, I'll stay."

"Thank you. Come in," he said, moving back so Bianca could step inside. "Sasha, you need to put some clothes on," Glen stated, as if just realizing his girlfriend was naked. "Go make yourself at home," he said to Bianca, "and I'll be back downstairs in a few."

She watched intently as Glen went up the stairs and Sasha sashayed behind him, and was horrified when jealousy consumed her. Could she actually be attracted to Glen? she wondered.

Stop, your mind is simply playing tricks on you! It's just physical. Don't take it so seriously. She could never be attracted to a man that would have a bloodsucker like Sasha as a girlfriend.

She told herself all this and more as she walked toward the living room and waited for Glen to return.

"Baby, don't you want to feel inside of me one more time before getting in the shower?" Sasha propositioned Glen in her most seductive voice.

"You know I do, but I can't keep Bianca waiting. I'm late enough as it is."

"Little Miss Do Good will be fine. I'm sure she understands that a man needs to be gratified when he wakes up in the morning."

Before Glen knew it, Sasha had almost all ten inches of him down her throat. She gave him no teeth, just all wet mouth and tongue. Glen leaned his head back, relishing in her professional skills. When she began massaging his manhood with her hand, the combination of that and her mouth sent his mind spinning. He began fucking Sasha's mouth, and seeing Glen so aroused further turned her on. Sasha scooted her body closer to the bed and gently led him forward with her mouth. He was still in a trance of pleasure and just followed her lead as she continued to work his tool as if auditioning for the lead in a porno movie. When she felt his dick throbbing and the jerk of his body, she knew Glen was about to come.

"Oh shit," Glen groaned, ready to release himself.

At that moment, she took his dick out her mouth, quickly lifted her ass on top of the bed and, as the come poured out like a faucet, with a firm grip still on his cock, Sasha rammed it in her pussy, trying to get every drop inside her. Glen was coming so hard his knees buckled and he found himself lying on top of Sasha with his dick fully inserted. A smiled crossed Sasha's face as she felt his sperm swimming inside her, and she prayed just one would make contact and fertilize an egg.

"What the fuck was that about?" Glen said after getting his mind back right.

"What you mean, baby?" Sasha asked innocently.

"You know what the fuck I mean. Why did you make me come inside of you? I know you're not trying to get a baby out of me."

"Of course not, stop being so paranoid, you know I'm on the pill." It was a straight up lie, but it didn't matter to her. She had to find a way to put herself in a position of power, and a baby would be the perfect start. If her trick worked and she did end up pregnant, it would be too late for Glen to do anything about it.

"Fuck all that pill shit, you know I don't like taking those type of chances. I should've never stopped wearing a condom with you."

"Glen, I can't believe you tripping over this shit. I've been living with you for a year and we've been fucking around for two. If I did end up pregnant, would it really be all that bad?"

Glen stared at Sasha for what seemed like forever. He wasn't quite sure if she was running a game on him or if she'd just gotten caught up in the moment of passion. "Sasha," he finally said, "I made it very clear that I don't want any babies right now. I'm twenty-five and I'm not ready to be a father. So yeah, it would be really bad if you tried some slick shit and ended up pregnant when you know that's not what I want."

"Like I said, I'm on the pill. I'm not trying to trap you, if that's what you're suggesting. Your dick was just feeling so good inside my mouth, I wanted to feel it inside my pussy, that's all." Sasha licked her finger and slowly traced it down her stomach until reaching her clit, and she began playing with it. She let out soft *ohs* and *ahs* and watched as Glen became rock hard again. She knew that sex was the perfect way to divert a man from using his brain.

"Don't do this, Sasha, you know I got to get ready."

"One more time won't hurt."

And just like that, Glen found himself soaking up the warmth of Sasha's insides.

What the hell was taking him so long? After sitting patiently on the couch for forty-five minutes, Bianca was now pacing back and forth wondering what the hell Glen was doing. She couldn't believe he'd had her waiting for so long. When he asked her to stay, he seemed sincere, but his actions were saying something entirely different. "I'm out of here," she said then, grabbing her purse off the couch and heading toward the front door.

"Hold up!" she heard Glen yell, and turning around, saw him hurrying downstairs.

"Glen, not only weren't you ready when I got here for a meeting you scheduled, but then you had me waiting nearly an hour. Your priorities are obviously somewhere else."

"It's not like that. My agent called me and we had some really important business to discuss."

"I didn't hear your phone ring."

"He called on my cell phone. I rarely get calls at home."

Something told Bianca that Glen was lying, but it felt useless to start an argument she couldn't win.

"Fine, so what is this meeting about?" She wasn't sure if her aunt had let Glen know that she'd spoken to her, so she thought it was better to pretend she had no idea what he wanted to ask her.

"Do you mind if we go have a seat in the living room? I really don't want to discuss this here, when you almost have one foot out the door," he said, flashing his signature smile. Bianca couldn't deny that he was a charmer without even trying hard.

"Lead the way."

"Once again I apologize for having you wait so long. Can I get you some water, juice, anything?"

"No, I'm fine."

"Let me just get right to it. I think you're incredible. I love Ms. Pearl, but you bring something to the table that I never expected I would find in a personal assistant. I know this was supposed to be a temporary position until I could find someone else to replace you, but I don't want anybody else, I want you."

"What exactly do you want me to do?"

"Of course I want you to continue on with the duties of being my right hand, but I also want to incorporate more of your marketing skills. You're great with the media, and I want your position to reflect all of your skills."

"I don't know, Glen. To take on so many responsibilities will definitely require an increase in my salary. Working for you on a temporary basis and a permanent one are two totally different things."

"I understand that and I have no problem giving you a raise, just name your price."

Bianca thought about it a moment and figured she would ask for more than double what he was paying her now.

"A hundred thousand dollars, not including work-related expenses that may be incurred, and health benefits." She swallowed hard, and felt her heart was going to leap out her chest. She had already decided she would ask Glen for an absurd amount of money hoping he would show her the door, but wasn't sure she would have the balls to ask for it. Now that she had, she was nervous to hear his response.

"Wow, a hundred thousand. That's more than double what I've been paying you. Plus expenses and benefits. You are not playing. But I will be giving you a lot more responsibilities, and being Ms. Pearl's niece, I do have a certain level of trust with you. Yeah, that's a little steep, but I think you're worth it."

"Excuse me?" Bianca blurted involuntarily, surprised he'd agreed to her terms.

Glen gazed at her with a puzzled look. "Excuse you what?"

"I meant to say, excuse me, I'm not finished." She was trying to find a quick way to save face and get out of what she now considered a bigger jam. She had to find a way to make him say no.

"You want more than the hundred plus expenses?" Bianca could hear the shock in his voice. She took a deep breath, preparing for her last demand, which she was sure he would decline.

"As a matter of fact I do. As you know, I live forty-five minutes away from you. With traffic, it can take me an hour and a half to get here. That is very inconvenient, and let's not forget about the ridiculous gas prices. I want to get an apartment closer to you in the Buckhead area, but I feel you should pay the rent since this area is expensive and I'm only moving so you'll have more access to me for work-related purposes."

Bianca had butterflies in her stomach, but after presenting her latest demand, she stood stoically, as if confident with her request.

Glen put his head down for a moment, and she prepared herself mentally for phrases like "You greedy bitch," "What the fuck are you smokin'?" and "Let the door hit you on your way out" to come from his mouth.

Instead, he said, "You drive a hard bargain but your points are valid. Find a one bedroom apartment that you like and I'll make sure the rent is paid. But you'll be responsible for utilities and cable. I think that's only fair. So do we have a deal?"

Bianca didn't know whether to jump for joy with the sweet paycheck and benefits she'd just landed or scream because if she accepted the offer, she would be stuck being Glen's slave, and around the ignorant Sasha. But remembering the promise she'd made to her aunt, both of them were irrelevant.

"Yes, we have a deal," she said, and the two of them shook hands.

From the top of the stairs, Sasha eyed them, cringing at the fact that miss librarian wasn't going anywhere.

The following evening, Bianca and Glen were still working on the final details for a basketball camp he would be launching in the summer. They started early that afternoon but it was taking much longer than either anticipated.

"I need to eat," Glen said, pushing aside some papers he was reading. "How about we go out for dinner?"

"That's okay, we can order in."

"No," he said, putting his hand on Bianca's shoulder. "We need a break, and I want some fresh air. There's a restaurant not too far from here that has banging food. After we eat, we can come back here and finish up."

"Who am I to argue? Some good food always does the body good." Bianca grabbed her purse and the two headed out.

By the time they reached the restaurant, both of them were famished. Wasting no time, they decided to order a family-size seafood platter and share a bottle of wine.

"I've never had seafood this good before. How long has this place been open?" Bianca asked before taking another bite of her crab cake.

"For a minute now, a lot of people aren't hip to this place, and I hope it stays like that."

"Oh, so it's your little secret?" Bianca purred teasingly.

"You make it sound so naughty."

"Do I? That wasn't my intention, it must be the wine. This is our second bottle."

"Rule number one—always blame unusual behavior on the liquor."

"Unusual behavior?" Bianca gave Glen a confused glare.

"Normally you're a little uptight, but you seem relaxed and carefree tonight. It's very attractive." Bianca didn't know if the wine had her mind playing tricks on her, but she was picking up a flirtatious vibe from Glen. "Here, have the rest," he said, pouring what was left of the wine into her glass.

"No, I really shouldn't. I've had way too much already."

"Then one more glass won't hurt."

Bianca didn't argue; she rather enjoyed the warm, tingly sensation engulfing her body. After swallowing the last drop, she looked down at her watch and realized they had been at the restaurant for over three hours.

"Glen, I can't believe what time it is. We haven't even finished all the paperwork. It's time for us to go."

"I've been enjoying your company so much that the time just flew by."

Bianca was taking pleasure in her time with Glen also, but didn't want to admit it. "I know what you mean," she said. "But it's getting late and I'm sure that Sasha must be wondering where you are."

"Actually, one of her girlfriends that she hasn't seen in a long time is in town, so Sasha's spending the night at the hotel with her. I guess so they can do female stuff. You know, stay up all night, gossiping and shit."

"So that's what you think women like to do?"

"Hell if I know, but right now I don't care. I'm more interested in talking about you."

Their eyes locked then, and without speaking a word, a full-fledged conversation was ensuing between the two of them. Bianca felt as if she was becoming sexually hypnotized. It seemed as if Glen's dick was calling her name. The lips on her pussy began to open as if they could hear it too. The very thought of his mouth tasting her moist insides was making her body temperature rise.

"Glen, I'm tired, let's go," she said abruptly. Even in her intoxicated state, Bianca knew she had to put a stop to the lust that was infecting her mind.

After paying the bill, the two left, and remained silent during the ride back to Glen's house. But it didn't lower the heat mounting between them. When Glen pulled up in his driveway, Bianca didn't even give him a chance to turn off the ignition before getting out and heading toward her car.

"Why are you rushing off?" Glen said as he hurried to get out the car and catch up to her. "We still haven't finished up our work for tonight."

"I told you I was tired, I really need to go." Bianca was now standing face-to-face with him. She put her head down, not wanting Glen to see the craving she had for him in her eyes.

"Look at me." Glen lifted her chin. "Are you tired or are you running away from me?"

"I don't know what you're talking about, I have to go." As Bianca broke away from Glen's embrace, he pulled her in, and she was seduced by the passion of his kiss. Her nipples hardened and her knees became weak. "I really need to go," were the last words she remembered saying.

She went from trying to reject Glen's advances to lying on her back with her long legs wrapped around his neck. He held her ass in the palms of his hands as he stroked her wet pussy with his immense cock. She held onto his shoulders for dear life, trying to endure the pleasure and pain he was unleashing on her.

"Damn, baby, your pussy is like that." Right when Bianca was about to come, he pulled out.

"Don't stop, you feel so good," she panted breathlessly.

"I'm not done. I just want to look at you." Glen ran his hands down every curve on Bianca's body and then flipped her over. Then, with his tongue, he licked from the front of her clit to the insides of her ass cheeks.

"Ahhh," Bianca moaned as her body shivered in ecstasy from his touch.

Glen grabbed her hair, pulling her head back before sliding his dick in and pounding in and out of her dripping wet pussy. Bianca's mind and body escaped to a place of elation that she never new existed. By the time he brought her to her third orgasm, she felt completely drained and fell into a deep sleep.

She was the first to awake early the next morning. It took her a second to focus, but she immediately came to when she saw a naked Glen asleep beside her. Then Bianca began reminiscing over everything that had transpired the night before, which led to her waking up in Glen's bed. Feeling a combination of happiness, confusion, and embarrassment, she slithered out of bed and started to get dressed. The sounds of Bianca scrambling to gather her belongings awoke Glen.

"What time is it?" he asked struggling to open his eyes as he gazed at the clock. "It's early, get back in bed."

"I have so much to do today, I need to go." Bianca nervously buttoned her shirt.

"Here you go again. Do I have to come over there and pull you back into bed? Because I will."

"You're not worried that Sasha could come home any minute?"

"Damn, that's a good point," Glen said, shaking his head, and Bianca felt a stab in her heart when she realized he cared about Sasha walking in on them.

"I'm so stupid," she said. "I should've never let myself get caught up."

"What are you talking about?"

"We had sex last night, and the only thing you're worried about is Sasha coming home."

"What the fuck, you're the one who brought her up," Glen retorted.

"Oh, so now it's my fault that you seduced me?"

"You want to play the blame game?"

"Well, you are the one with the girlfriend."

"Yeah, but you knew that already."

For a moment there was complete stillness between them. Bianca's feelings of shame were written all over her face.

"Listen, last night was incredible," Glen said. "I don't want us to argue."

"No, you're absolutely right. I did know you have a girlfriend, yet I chose to give in to temptation instead of using my head. I made a mistake."

"Don't say that." Glen walked over to Bianca and stroked her cheek. "This wasn't a mistake. What happened last night was incredible, and I don't want it to be a onetime thing."

"You still want us to be intimate?"

Glen nodded his head.

"So what about Sasha?"

"She doesn't have to know."

Bianca's eyes widened. "So you want to see me behind Sasha's back. What type of shit is that?" she said, pushing Glen's hand away from her face.

"I don't understand. You want me to just end things with Sasha just like that? Don't you think we need to see what is going to happen between us? We might decide that we have a better business relationship than a personal one."

"Of course, in Glen Goodman's world there is no such thing as putting all your eggs in one basket when it comes to a relationship. You always need a backup plan. Well, excuse me if I don't want to be it. I think you and Sasha are perfect for each other. I want to forget that last night ever happened."

"Are you sure about that?" From the intense look in Glen's eyes Bianca knew his question was a deal breaker.

"Very. I think we should keep our relationship on a business level." That's what her mouth said, but she knew her heart felt totally different.

"That's cool, business it is."

Glen turned away and headed toward the bathroom. leaving

Bianca with a nauseating knot in the pit of her stomach. She desperately wanted to be back in bed with her legs wrapped around Glen's back, feeling every inch of his dick inside of her, but she had way too much pride to carry on a secret affair with him.

Before leaving, she glanced at the bed that she'd had the best sex of her life in, then walked out the door.

Halftime

I Like the Way You Move

You could hear the sound of a pin drop as the entire arena focused on Glen Goodman's next move down the court. With the championship series tied and only fifty seconds left in the final game, everyone was on edge, including Bianca, who wasn't even a basketball fan.

"It's all up to you, Glen, bring it home," Bianca said to herself. Working closer with Glen and feeling all ten inches of him inside of her, she had officially become a basketball fanatic. Although things had been awkward between them since their sexual tryst, she still secretly cheered every time her boss and lover for one night scored. She loved the way Glen moved, on the court and off. The Los Angeles Falcons were up by two, and the clock was quickly ticking away. If a major play wasn't made in the next twenty seconds, there would be no championship celebration in Atlanta.

"Girl, Isaac need to pass Glen the damn ball and stop wasting time," Sasha barked at Tracy, as if she had any control over what her man was doing.

"I'm with you on that," Tracy said.

Then like a horrible clip from a movie trailer, Isaac dropped the ball and everyone dived to try and retrieve it. The home team crowd erupted in a gasp, wondering what would happen next. When the dust cleared, Glen had stolen the ball and made a crossover fake that freed him up at the three-point line. Everyone zoomed in on the clock as Glen released his shot just before the buzzer sounded—and all they saw was net.

The crowd erupted in a deafening cheer. Glen Goodman had once again come through like a soldier and brought the championship home. Sasha and Tracy ran onto the court along with the crowd, wanting to revel in the victory.

"Damn, there is no way we're getting through this crowd," Sasha said.

"Yeah, ain't no way. We should wait outside the locker room like we normally do."

"Fuck that, it's going to be a zoo over there too. Glen gave me the keys to his Rover, we can just wait there."

"Cool," Tracy said, and the two of them bypassed the crowd and headed for Glen's car.

"Is it me, or does it seem like every ball player got a damn Range Rover with some sick rims?" Sasha asked, walking through the garage, feeling as if she'd stepped into a Range Rover dealership. Then, after getting in the front seat and turning on the ignition, she rolled down the windows, with T.I. blaring out of the speakers. "Let me turn this shit down."

"No, it isn't you, every dude in the league is pushing a Range, with the twenty-four-inch rims," Tracy responded from the passenger side. "It must be some sort of initiation requirement. That was like one of the first things Isaac bought when he went pro."

"Oh shit, you been with Isaac since he first got in the league?"

"That's right. We graduated from the same college, and you know this is only his second year in the pros."

"Were you all together in college?"

"All four years," Tracy said, nodding and feeling proud.

Tracy liked Sasha, but she also felt they were in two different categories. She had been trooping it out with Isaac since before he became an NBA player and the money started flowing. When they were in college, Isaac loved playing ball and wanted to get drafted, and he could have easily dropped out of school and went into the league early. But he wanted that degree. Isaac's dedication to getting an education was one of the reasons Tracy loved him so much. If he wasn't practicing or playing a game, then he was with her, studying for a test, or the two of them were just hanging out.

But since he became cool with Glen, Isaac had been changing. Glen liked to go out every night, and when Sasha moved to Atlanta, she was always right there with him. At first Tracy didn't want to be bothered with Sasha because she'd seen her type come and go with just about every player on the team. But somehow Sasha maneuvered her skills to become a permanent fixture. That didn't sit well with Tracy, but instead of making her the enemy, Tracy decided to make her a friend. She knew girls like Sasha had lots of paper chasing friends, and she wasn't about to let one of them come in and steal her man.

"All four years, huh?" Sasha said. "I didn't know that. So you are definitely trying to be his wife."

"Yeah, I would think," Tracy snapped, put off by Sasha's statement.

"You've been in it for a minute, so why hasn't he married you yet?" Sasha asked sarcastically.

"For one, we're only twenty-three and we both feel we have plenty of time for that. Also, we're committed to one another, so when the time is right we'll be walking down the aisle."

"You sound awfully confident. I guess you be working it out in that bedroom," Sasha said with a playful laugh. She made the comment as if she were joking, but not in a good way. Tracy let it go, however, because she didn't want Sasha to think that she felt her relationship with Isaac wasn't solid. She knew that people like Sasha preyed on any sort of vulnerability, and she wasn't about to hand it to her.

"Yeah, girl, something like that. I was telling the dude we need to install a pole in the crib."

"Speaking of poles, we hitting Magic City or what," Glen said, sneaking up on the two ladies, with Bianca and Isaac right behind him.

"Baby, you won!" Sasha shouted. "I'm so proud of you. We can do whatever you like tonight." She stuck her head out the window to plant a passionate kiss on her man. By now, Tracy had jumped out of the Range Rover and was giving Isaac a huge congratulatory hug. Bianca stood to the side, watching the couples grope each other, and decided this was be the perfect time to make her exit.

"Where do you think you're going, Bianca?" Glen screamed, startling her as she was walking away.

"Home. I know you guys want to go out and celebrate, so I won't keep you."

"Keep us, you coming with us." Everybody looked at Glen surprisingly. It was obvious to them that Bianca wasn't exactly the partying type, so they were shocked that Glen was extending the invitation.

Bianca let out an uncomfortable laugh before responding. "I don't think so. I'm really tired. I just want to go home."

"Bianca, you work for me. Remember that great salary I'm paying you with all the perks. That means you agreed to be a willing participant whenever I need you."

"I don't want to go to a strip club."

"It's not about what you want, it's what I want. Come on, I won my first championship ring tonight. You can at least come out and celebrate with me."

She knew how important this night was for Glen, and he was her boss. At the same time, she didn't want to watch as Sasha kept her paws all over Glen for the duration of the night. It amazed Bianca that Glen was able to act as if they hadn't had the most passionate lovemaking session less than a month ago; it also hurt her feelings. Obviously, it had meant much more to her than it to him. Here, he was carrying on with Sasha and inviting her to a strip club like they'd never seen each other naked. But she steeled herself, decided if he could so easily brush it off his shoulders, then so could she.

"Okay, but if I get tired," she said, "I'm taking a taxi home."

"No problem," he replied. "Now get in."

"I'll follow right behind you, man," Isaac said as he and Tracy moved toward his car.

Sasha moved to the passenger seat and Bianca got in the back. She couldn't believe she was hanging out with Glen and Sasha. But she was curious to see the legendary strip club. Magic City had been open and shut down on a few occasions. but its legions of fans were never far behind. Every African American mover and shaker in the entertainment business had been through the infamous doors at one time or another, and now she would be added to the list.

Upon first entering, Bianca noticed the red, white, and pink baby tees in a glass case to her left. The shirts said MAGIC CITY, with rhinestone decorating the silhouette of a woman's sexy body. She was tempted to purchase the pink one, then decided against it since the tee didn't exactly fit into her uptight wardrobe.

Everybody was shaking Glen's and Isaac's hands as they were led to a booth toward the back of the club. The moment they sat down, the DJ gave a shout. "Glen Goodman, who always delivers the goods, and Isaac Johnson from the Atlanta Phantoms are in the house tonight. Coming off their first championship win, they brought the celebration to Magic City. Now, ladies, you always do it right, but I want yah to perform extra nasty for our special guests."

He put on a Young Jeezy club banger, and all you saw was ass popping and tits jiggling, and then came the bottles of bubbly that would be poured all night. Bianca sat back in shocked awe as women did tricks on stage that she had never envisioned in her wildest dreams. A woman who looked all of six feet tall due to the ten-inch platforms she was rocking, had on a black tank top that cut above her breasts with an itsy bitsy thong, and she glided up the steel pole as if she were a slithering snake. Once she reached the top, the Amazon queen began her descent with hips, thighs, and pussy gyrating the pole as if having consensual sex. Then Bianca turned to the two women who were simulating sex with each other. One was standing on top of her head with her legs spread so wide she was basically doing an in the air split. The other woman was between her legs, humping her pussy.

"Is this what it has come to? Cats only dropping paper if chicks fuck each other," Tracy said to Bianca, since Bianca seemed to be the only person besides her who was disgusted with the sex antics going on around them.

"Seems that way, since those are the girls that have stacks of paper in their garter." Bianca and Tracy stared with their mouths wide open as the men showered the strippers with cash. It was raining nothing but money on the showstoppers.

"Isaac, I'm ready to go," Tracy said, with nothing but attitude in her voice.

"We just got here. The party ain't even got started yet."

"The party been started, and I'm ready to go."

"You need to sit back and relax. Enjoy yourself, like Sasha doing." Tracy eyed Sasha, who was sitting next to Glen, and both had a girl dancing for them. "Why don't you get a lap dance or something?" Isaac suggested.

"You can't be serious? I don't want some girl's coochie all up in my face."

"That's your prerogative. But this is my night to celebrate, so you won't mind if I get one." Isaac waved a hundred dollar bill in the air, summoning a buxom girl in a cheerleading outfit to come over. Tracy slapped his arm down.

"Yes, I do mind you getting a lap dance. I told you I was ready to go, and that means let's leave, *now*!"

Due to the loud music, Bianca couldn't hear the exact words being exchanged between Tracy and Isaac, but from the vexed expression on their faces, she knew neither one was happy. Glen and Sasha were a whole other story. Both seemed like two kids in a candy store. They were enjoying the explicit sex show the strippers were giving them. Sasha even poured the dancers champagne, and they broke out in a toast. Bianca had seen enough and decided it was time to break out. She assumed everyone was so caught up in their own scene that nobody would notice that she went missing, especially not Glen.

She reached the exit relieved that no one had stopped her. Watching Glen get lap dances by the buxom beauties had been about to make her ring the alarm.

"Wait!" she heard; it sounded like a female scream, but she was reluctant to turn around, not wanting anyone to keep her from leaving. "I'll share a taxi with you."

Now she did turn back, and saw Tracy approach, out of breath. "You don't want to wait for Isaac?" she asked.

"Fuck Isaac. He so caught up in all this disease infested pussy he can't even think straight."

Bianca didn't know how to respond, so she remained quiet. Tracy's head was down and she was mumbling like a crazy person as they got into the taxi. Bianca was surprised that she had decided to leave Isaac there. She assumed that since Tracy was always with Sasha, she was also a party girl, and that attending strip clubs was the norm for them.

"If you don't mind me asking, why did you leave Isaac in the club?" she asked as the taxi took off.

At first Tracy just shook her head. Then she started smacking her lips like she had so much to say but couldn't get her words to come out. Finally she spoke.

"Girl, I never thought this would happen, but Isaac has got sucked into this whole NBA lifestyle. Slowly but surely I'm losing him." Tears welled up in her eyes as she spoke. It was obvious to Bianca that the situation was very painful for her.

"I didn't mean to upset you, Tracy. We don't have to discuss it any further."

"No, I need somebody to talk to. Sasha trifling ass doesn't care. She loves the life as an NBA player's girl, even if you're constantly being disrespected. But see, I'm not having that bullshit. I was with Isaac before all this, and I'll be damn if I'm going to sit back and let him sling his dick in other bitches like it's all good in our hood. Fuck that, I'll let him go before I sink that low."

Bianca felt sorry for Tracy. She knew that Tracey meant every word she said, but it was killing her to say them. She obviously loved Isaac very much, but he was beginning to relish the perks of being a basketball star, and Tracy wanted their relationship to continue the way it used to be when it was all about them. Isaac was moving forward and Tracy was still living in the past.

After the taxi dropped Tracy off, Bianca sat back and stared out the window. She'd had no words of encouragement for Tracy, and it bothered her. In the brief time she'd worked for Glen, she had a clear understanding of how difficult it was to deal with a man in the NBA, especially if you truly cared about him. If you were a chick looking for a momentary glimpse into fast cars, endless money, and nonstop parties, then dealing with a basketball player was the place to be. But if you were interested in a committed, monogamous relationship with a man who took pleasure in the simple things in life, you had a better chance of success heading to Vegas and winning at the slot machines. She could only take comfort that her encounter with experiencing love b-ball style was brief, though it was one she'd never forget.

Third Quarter

Sweetest Sin

"I know Isaac ass didn't stay out all night," Tracy said, waking up alone in bed. "This motherfucker better stepped out early this morning to get us some breakfast from McDonald's," she vented, breathing hard as she dialed Isaac's cell phone, but it went straight to voice mail. "Isaac, where the fuck are you? It's obvious that you didn't sleep in this bed last night and your phone is off. My female intuition is telling me you up to no good, but for your sake I better be wrong. If you don't call me right back, I'm coming to look for your ass, and if you up to some trifling shit, it's about to be on," Tracy screamed into the phone before slamming it down.

Bianca was in the middle of a dream that she didn't want to wake up from. A beautifully built six feet four man with muscle tone so defined you would think someone crafted it from a sculpture was gently sprinkling kisses around her breasts and down her stomach.

Her back arched as the tip of his tongue seduced her belly button. As she moaned in pleasure and anticipated his next move, he continued his tongue play, entering her gates to heaven. Her hips swiveled to the rhythm of his strokes, and when she looked down to catch a glimpse of the face of the man who was bringing her so much pleasure, it was Glen, and then the alarm went off snapping her out of her sleep.

Bianca hated that she couldn't stop thinking about that one night of forbidden lust she'd shared with Glen. And how could she when it had been the best sex of her life? But she had no choice but to forget about it, she decided, since it had been a mistake and Glen seemed perfectly content with Sasha. To make matters worse, she now had to head over to Glen's house to discuss a ton of media obligations he had lined up, and would have to pretend it didn't crush her seeing him with Sasha. She prayed that she would be able to bury her feelings for Glen somewhere so deep that the pain of not being with him vanished.

"Isaac, open the damn door!" Tracy screamed. She had been banging on Glen's front door for the last fifteen minutes, and wouldn't stop because she was positive Isaac was inside, since his car was parked in front of the garage. She kept calling his cell phone but it was still turned off. Then she started blowing up Sasha's phone, but it was off too. She was pissed because she didn't know Glen's home or cell phone number, so she just continued banging, waiting for someone to show their face. She was at her wits end and began walking toward the back to bust out the glass doors when someone finally came out. But after Tracy saw who it was, she knew it would've been better if the woman had stayed inside. It was the buxom cheerleader who had been entertaining Isaac before she left Magic City.

"Where's Isaac?" she demanded of the chick who seemed like she was still halfway asleep.

"Who?"

"Don't play with me, bitch. Where is my man?"

"Which one is your man?" the girl asked coyly.

Five seconds later Isaac came walking out the door as if he had no clue Tracy was on the front steps waiting for him. "Oh shit, what are you doing here?"

"Oh shit is right. I've been banging on this damn door for fifteen minutes. I guess you was too occupied fucking with this trick that you didn't hear me."

"Look, ho, don't be calling me no trick because your so-called man wanted to stick his dick up in me all night," the stripper said. "You need to check your man and leave me out of it." Tracy stared at her stripper for a moment, and then, without warning, started going upside her head.

"Tracy, chill. Stop acting crazy out here," Isaac barked as he pulled her off the girl.

Tracy was still swinging her arms and kicking as Isaac held her in the air. "Let me go," she demanded.

"Not until you calm down." The stripper was fixing her hair and patting down the clothes that Tracy had practically ripped off.

"I'm fine," Tracy said as Isaac put her down. "After all the shit we've been through, I can't believe you would play me for some two-bit slut. I hope that pussy was worthwhile because I've done enough crying over your sorry ass."

"Tracy, wait. I fucked up, but don't end it over this." Tracy kept walking as Isaac halfheartedly pleaded his case from the front stairs.

When Bianca pulled up at the house for her meeting with Glen, she saw Tracy going at Isaac's Range Rover Terminator style. She had busted out every window except for the front. She was about to do that one too, but Isaac managed to get to her before she could. And then the two of them were battling as Isaac tried to retrieve the brick from Tracy's hand. It seemed that Tracy's anger had given her superhero strength, because Isaac appeared to have difficulty getting the upper hand, though she was much smaller.

The girl who was watching the mayhem looked awfully familiar to Bianca, who ran up to ask her what was going on.

"Well, that crazy bitch tried to kick my ass because I spent the night with her so-called man," the girl said. "I told her not to get mad at me but to check her man for herself. I guess she took my advice and that's why she fucking up his car."

Bianca wondered if she should try to break up their fight or go inside and get Glen. Before she had a chance to make a decision, Glen and Sasha came outside. Luckily, Sasha had enough sense to put on a bathrobe instead of prancing around butt naked.

"Yo, what the fuck is going on out here?" Glen said as he came off his steps. Isaac and Tracy were still going at it, ignoring him as they continued to fight. Glen walked back in the house, and Bianca couldn't believe he wasn't going to do something. But a minute later he reappeared, and all anyone could hear were gunshots ringing in the air. Everybody froze and looked in Glen's direction. "I got to bust off bullets to get you fools' attention. Now what is all this drama about?"

"You know what the fuck is up," Tracy told him. "You let Isaac bring that trick up in your crib so they could fuck. What type of shit is that?"

"Tracy, on the real, Isaac is a grown-ass man. I don't have anything to do with who he lay down with. And for the record, I'm not saying he laid down with anybody," Glen added.

"Tracy, why don't you come inside so you can calm down," Sasha suggested.

"I'm not going anywhere near that damn house after Isaac stayed up all night fucking some bitch."

"I told you—"

Bianca cut the girl off before she could continue. "Honestly, I think you should just stay out of this."

"That's cool, but I need to get the fuck home. I'm tired of watching all this drama," the girl popped as she rolled her eyes.

"Go wait in my car," Bianca said. "I'll call a cab for you." She took out her cell phone and ordered the car service they used frequently to come as soon as possible. Then she walked toward Isaac and Tracy, who was still breathing like a bull.

"Tracy, let's go home," Isaac pleaded. "We need to sit down and talk. I know we can work everything out."

"I'm not going nowhere with you. You made your bed, now lay in it." Tracy tossed the brick on the ground, walked back to her car and drove off. Five minutes later the car service arrived and the stripper jumped in, not saying so much as a good-bye to anybody. Glen went over and said a few words to Isaac before he pulled off in his window-busted-out Range.

Bianca followed Glen and Sasha back into the house, feeling overwhelmed by the events that had occurred there, in the middle of the afternoon.

"Bianca, I'm sorry you had to arrive in the midst of all that chaos," Glen said.

"Well, maybe if you hadn't brought the chaos home there would be no need to apologize."

"What?" he said, taken aback by Bianca's defiance. They were standing in the foyer, with Sasha behind Glen, straining to hear

Bianca's response. Sasha knew that Glen hated for anyone to talk slick to him, and she hoped Bianca's comment would escalate to an argument, which would mean a curtain call for her. "You're blaming me for what went down between Isaac and Tracy?"

"All I'm saying is if you hadn't allowed Isaac to spend the night with his stripper friend at your house, then Tracy wouldn't have been in front of your crib trying to demolish Isaac's car."

"Baby, before you respond to that, I'm going to get ready," Sasha said to Glen. "Don't forget we have to go dress shopping for the official celebration party you're hosting tomorrow night."

"All right, I'll be up there in a little while."

"Oh, and Bianca, I don't know if you're coming to the party, but I understand dressing up isn't really your thing, so if you need some tips on what to wear, feel free to ask." Without even waiting for Bianca to respond, Sasha strutted upstairs.

Bianca was so irritated by Sasha's obvious diss that she was in no mood to even talk to Glen. But she did, saying, "Glen, I know you have things to do, so let's discuss these interviews you have lined up so I can get out of here."

"Before we go over work-related stuff," he replied, "I want to finish discussing what happened earlier."

"I don't think there's anything left to say."

"I disagree. I can't let you blame me for what other grown folks do and not defend myself."

"Look, I feel that you should accept some of the responsibility too. You know that Isaac lives with Tracy and they're supposed to be in a committed relationship. If he didn't come home last night, it would only make sense that she'd come to your crib looking for him since she left him at the strip club with you. So please don't talk to me as if you're surprised the drama ended in the front of your house when you welcomed it to come in."

"Oh, so what? I should have told Isaac that he and his friend couldn't spend the night?"

"Yeah, you could've told grown-ass Isaac to get a room and fuck his stripper friend on his own premises so none of it would've led back to you."

Glen stood thinking about what Bianca was saying. Even though he wasn't about to admit it, he knew that when Isaac told him he wanted to bring the stripper back to his crib, he should have told him to get a hotel room. Tracy had hung out with him and Sasha on numerous occasions, and he even thought of her as being somewhat of a friend. He should have completely stayed out of whatever dirt Isaac was scheming on.

"I feel what you're saying," he said, "I really do, but you don't have to come off as being so judgmental."

"I'm not trying to judge you, Glen. I guess I feel that no one really takes other people's feelings seriously. Tracy was devastated to see her man coming out of your crib with some stripper he was laid up with all night, and she had every right to be. What if things had turned fatal and somebody ended up dead behind that bullshit? In the heat of passion, shit like that happens all the time. Just think if that brick Tracy was bashing around had been a gun, then the police and ambulance could be parked outside your crib right now, and then what?"

"I can't lie. It wasn't that deep for me. I didn't take Tracy's feelings into consideration. I just wanted everybody to have a good time. Damn, I guess that shows what a fucked-up individual I am."

"You're not a fucked-up individual. If a person doesn't take the time to point something out to you, then it can go right over your head."

"Well, I'm glad you did take the time because I definitely learned something today." Glen gazed into Bianca's eyes, and all the feeling he'd been trying to suppress since she'd told him she only wanted them to have a business relationship resurfaced. He felt an emotional connection toward her. It was a strange bond that he'd never felt with another woman. He couldn't resist walking closer to her and placing his right hand gently on her cheek. "Thank you."

"For what?"

"For being you," he answered sincerely.

"It was nothing." Bianca playfully pushed Glen's hand away, and he knew that was her way of not letting him back in. He was hoping she would let her guard down because she couldn't deny their attraction. He could feel the lust brewing inside her. "We really need to go over these interviews," Bianca said, breaking the silence.

Glen was disappointed that she didn't respond the way he hoped, but decided not to push her. "No problem. But before I forget, you are coming to the party tomorrow night?"

"What party?"

"The one Sasha mentioned."

"Oh, that party. I'm not sure. I think I might have plans."

"Plans like what, a date?" Glen asked, unable to contain his jealousy.

"No, not a date, I might have to do something for Aunt Pearl."

He was relieved it wasn't a man she had plans with. "Don't worry about Aunt Pearl. I'll personally put in a call letting her know I need you at the party I'm hosting tomorrow."

"Don't do that."

"Then that means you're coming."

"Yes, I'll be there."

"Great, now let's get to work." Glen was pleased that Bianca would be in attendance. Even though technically she wasn't his girl, he felt territorial when it came to her.

Fourth Quarter

Showstopper

After leaving Glen, Bianca drove straight to her aunt Pearl's house. Pearl lived in a two-story brick house on a quiet cul-de-sac outside of Atlanta. It was the same house Bianca had lived in after her mother died, and it always gave her a warm, secure feeling. It was the only place she truly considered home. Although she still had a key, she decided to ring the doorbell since her aunt wasn't expecting her.

"If it isn't my favorite girl," Aunt Pearl said, greeting her niece in the endearing motherly nature that Bianca loved so much.

"Hi, Auntie, I hope you don't mind me stopping by without notice."

"Don't be silly. Bring your butt in here. I'm surprised you didn't use your key."

"I didn't want to scare you by just walking in."

"I appreciate that. I don't need no surprises. It might cause me to have some sort of relapse," she said jokingly. "So what brings you out to my neck of the woods?"

"Wanted to see how you were doing."

"You could've called me for that." She gave Bianca the eye, letting her know she knew there was much more to her visit.

"You know me so well. I'm going to just come out and say it. I think I'm falling for Glen, and he's hosting this party tomorrow that I don't want to attend because I don't have anything to wear, and then Sasha . . ." Bianca kept rambling on until her aunt cut in.

"Well I'll be. I was wondering how long it would take before you admitted it," she said, sitting down on the couch.

"What are you talking about? I only recently started developing these feelings."

"That's what your mouth says. But I knew something was up when you were determined not to continue working for him. It was as if you were running away from something, which was those feelings you didn't want to have."

"Maybe because I never thought it was possible for him to reciprocate my feelings. I mean, he obviously loves superficial women like Sasha, and how can I compete with that? The two of us are polar opposites."

"Men go through phases of being attracted to certain types of women. Some of them never outgrow it and others just need the right woman to show them that different can be better. If you really care about Glen, then don't let him slip away."

"If you mean make a total fool out of myself, I'll pass."

"You never know. Glen is like a sweet little boy who just needs guidance in the right direction. He's dated plenty of women and they've all been like Sasha, a tempting piece of candy on the outside with absolutely nothing in the center."

"So obviously that's what he likes, which I'm not."

"Now, who doesn't like candy? Everybody is attracted to something that looks delicious to devour, that's part of being human. But you're the one who chooses not to use what God gave you to further lure Glen in."

"What do you mean by that?"

"You know exactly what I mean. Walking around all the time in ultraconservative clothes, not putting so much as some lip gloss on those luscious lips. I'm not saying you have to be done up all the time, but damn, honey, you got to let your hair down sometimes so a man knows you have a pulse."

"Aunt Pearl, you are so crazy."

"I'm so serious. You have enough assets to give any woman a run for her money. Instead of hiding them under those layers of clothes, flaunt what you were blessed with."

"I know, but it's hard. I always remember how beautiful and vibrant mother was, and out of jealousy my dad just took that away from her in one split second. It seems that in love and life, it leads to nothing but pain and heartache."

"My dear child, I know how deeply your mother's death affected you. My heart hasn't been the same either, but you can't stop living because your mother stopped breathing. Trust me, she would want you to find love and be happy, not to close yourself off and wither away."

"I know, but then falling in love with a man like Glen, I feel I'm destined for a broken heart."

"Nothing in love or life is guaranteed. But I will tell you it's better to have truly loved with all your heart at least once then to never have loved at all."

"You're absolutely right. So what advice would you give me?"

"Well, first you need to attend that party tomorrow, but not just go, go looking so damn good that you erase Sasha out of Glen's mind once and for all. Leave it to your aunt Pearl. When I'm done with you, you'll outshine every female in that entire party, including Sasha."

When Sasha woke up, the first thing she did was take out the dress she was wearing to the party that night. She couldn't help but admire the ocean blue Stella McCartney creation, which guaranteed that she would be the baddest chick at the entire affair. The plunging neckline highlighted her surgically enhanced bodice, and with the blinged-out hello kitty necklace dangling down her chest, all eyes would be on her. As she continued to look over her ensemble, she couldn't believe how far she'd come. A few years ago she had been waiting tables at a diner in a two-bit town in Indiana, and now she was luxuriating in Glen Goodman's mansion and escorting him to an NBA championship party, wearing a dress by a top notch designer, with diamonds decorating her body. Nobody would believe her success. Hitchhiking out of Indiana was the best move she'd ever made.

Once Sasha had arrived in Michigan, she immediately hooked up at Platinum, one of the ritziest strip clubs in Detroit. Soon, she was the most sought after exotic dancer in the club, especially after she got her breast enlargement. The fast cash, and parlaying with the city's biggest ballers, introduced her to the lifestyle she'd always wanted to live. But it wasn't until she met Glen Goodman that things really started looking up for her. While on vacation with another dancer in Miami, she ran into Glen because they were staying at the same hotel when he was in town for a game. In her juicy couture jogging suit and bouncy ponytail, Glen thought Sasha was a sweet girl in town for some fun, and she played that role to a hilt. She told Glen she was a college student, and never mentioned her full-time position as the reigning queen of the stripper pole. With Sasha playing the good girl role, they had been dating ever since.

"Baby, what time are we leaving tonight?" she asked when Glen came out the shower.

"Around eight."

"Is it just going to be me and you or are some of your teammates riding with us too?"

"Nobody else is coming with us, except for maybe Bianca. I have to call her to find out," Glen said while putting on his clothes.

"Bianca's coming to the party?" Sasha asked with astonishment in her voice.

"Of course, she does work with me."

"I don't know why you keep her around, she is so annoying. I just knew you were going to fire her ass after she tried to get fly with you."

"You talking about that discussion we had yesterday about Isaac and Tracy?"

"Hello, yes."

"That was nothing. Bianca has the right to express her opinion, and I actually appreciated her keeping it real with me. She had some very valid points."

Sasha couldn't believe what she was hearing. Glen could be such a hothead, and never liked anyone to step out of line with him, but he was standing there defending little miss goody two shoes. She wanted to vomit. "If you say so," she said.

"I have to run some errands. I'll be back a little later, and then we can head to the party." Glen kissed Sasha good-bye as he walked out, then she sat down on the bed and thought about how miserable she would be if Bianca rode with them to the party that night. The idea of hanging with Bianca made her think about Tracy, and she wondered if Tracy had made up with Isaac yet. She'd tried calling her a few times yesterday, but Tracy didn't pick up. She decided to try again.

Ring ring ring . . .

"Hello."

"Hey girl," Sasha said, trying to sound upbeat.

"What do you want, Sasha?"

"Why you say it like that? I know you not mad at me because of that shit that went down with Isaac."

"Answer this question and I'll let you know. If I hadn't caught Isaac with that stripper bitch, would you have told me he spent the night with her?"

Sasha thought for a moment about what she should say before answering the question. "You my girl, of course I would've let you know. I even told Glen that night it was fucked up he was letting Isaac bring that trick up in our crib. I didn't want that bitch nowhere around me, but you know how these dudes are, they always stick together."

It was a lie. In fact, she'd played a subtle role in what transpired. She'd noticed the cheerleader stripper giving Isaac a lap dance, and afterward became chummy with her, and actually told the girl if she wanted to make some real money she should try and spend the night with Isaac. The stripper took the suggestion to heart and flirted with Isaac for the duration of the night. She promised him a sexual experience of a lifetime if he took her home. Three bottles of bubbly later, they were off to Glen's house, twisting each other out. Sasha never thought Tracy would bust Isaac. She'd only played a role in orchestrating the sexual tryst for her own self-pleasure, since earlier that evening Tracy had acted as if she had Isaac securely in her back pocket, and Sasha wanted to prove that she didn't.

"I appreciate that, Sasha," Tracy said. "I can't even believe Glen let that bullshit go down in his crib. He could've at least told Isaac to get his own damn hotel room. But he don't give a fuck about me. All he cares about is trifling ass Isaac."

"I guess that means you and Isaac haven't made up?"

"Hell no. I'm done with him."

"So where are you staying?"

"Thank goodness my cousin lives in Atlanta. She has a two bedroom, so I'm staying in the guest room."

"So what are you going to do, stay in your cousin's crib forever?"

"What the fuck am I supposed to do? Take Isaac no good ass back so he can continue to cheat on me and think I'll sit around and take it?"

Sasha thought Tracy should do just that. She didn't think Tracy was the flyest chick, and it would be damn near impossible for her to land somebody better than Isaac. Tracy had put mad years in with him. Why let some other girl slide in and reap all the benefits, because they would be flocking to him like bees to honey.

"It's up to you what you want to do," she said. "But all I'm saying is that you been dealing with the cat for a long time. How are you going to go from living with this dude to bunking at your cousin's crib? I guess the next thing you're going to tell me is that you're going to apply for a job and work for a living."

"I do have a degree, Sasha, so I can get a job and take care of myself."

"If you say so, booboo. But listen, I have some errands to run before going to this party tonight."

"What party?"

"You know, the NBA championship party that Glen is hosting."

"Oh yeah, I forgot about that. I'm sure Isaac will be there."

"I'm sure he will be too. If he brings a date, would you like me to tell you?"

"No thanks, because if he does have a date, she must not be keeping him too entertained since he's been blowing up my phone."

"Oh, so you've talked to Isaac?" Sasha was itching to know.

"Nope. I said he called, doesn't mean I answered."

"Whatever works for you. But yeah, like I was saying, I must be going. I'll definitely be in touch, though."

"Okay, have fun," Tracy said dryly before hanging up.

It was two hours before the party, and Bianca was completely nervous. She and Aunt Pearl had spent all day yesterday preparing for the evening's gala, and she'd just gotten back from having her hair and makeup done. When Bianca looked in the mirror, she couldn't believe the reflection staring back at her. It was a transformation she wasn't prepared for. She was gently touching her face, in awe of her newfound beauty, and was jolted out of her trance when the phone rang.

"Hello."

"Hi, there."

"Glen, how are you," Bianca chimed, pleasantly surprised to hear his voice.

"I'm good. So what time do you want me to pick you up?"

"Excuse me?"

"For the party tonight, I know you didn't change your mind?"

"Oh no, I'm definitely coming, but I don't need a ride, I'll meet you there."

"Are you sure? I have no problem picking you up. As a matter of fact, I would prefer it so I would know for sure you were showing up."

"No, I don't need a ride, and yes, I'm showing up."

"You promise?"

"I promise."

"Wonderful, I look forward to seeing you. Oh, and don't forget to save me a dance."

"I will."

Glen looked down at his cell after hanging up with Bianca. He felt excited about seeing her. He wished that Bianca was his date instead of Sasha. Although he cared about Sasha, being with her on an everyday basis made him realize that though her outer package was appealing, there was not a lot to be desired on the inside. He recalled that when he met her she'd said she was a college student, but since moving in with him, he had never even seen her with a book, let alone studying. He'd offered to pay her college tuition, but she said she had grown tired of school and was trying to figure out what she wanted to do with her life. Glen had all the money in the world, but he still wanted his woman to have a life outside of his, and Sasha showed no interest in that. Lately, he'd begun to realize that there was more to a relationship than beauty. Without mutual goals and things in common, how could it last?

When he arrived home, he headed straight to the bedroom. Sasha was stepping out of the shower, still dripping wet.

"Hi, Daddy, I've been missing you all day," she confessed as she dropped her towel. Glen couldn't lie; Sasha's body was flawless. She didn't even have any scars from her breast implants, which were remarkable, but he wasn't interested in having sex with her before leaving for the party. He still had Bianca on his mind, and that erased the temptation dangling before him.

"I really need to get in the shower," he said. "I don't want us to be late for the party."

"Baby, we have time. Lie down and let me give you something to think about until we get back home tonight," Sasha said, licking her lips seductively. Normally, that would be enough for Glen to step out of his pants and give Sasha what she wanted, but things felt different now, and he knew it was his newfound feelings for Bianca.

"Not now, Sasha. Get dressed, we have plenty of time later on for that," he said as he marched passed her.

"Good idea. I need to preserve my sexy for tonight's event," Sasha said, walking into the bedroom-sized closet.

By the time Glen and Sasha arrived at the Ritz-Carlton, the gala was in full swing. To Sasha, it seemed that every rapper, athlete, bigwig politician, and entertainment celebrity was blessing the spot. She did a precise inspection of every chick in the ballroom, and none of them came close to taking her shine away. Her Stella dress was emphasizing every curve just right, so she didn't understand why Glen had been so standoffish in the car. Normally his hands would have been preying on every part of her body, but tonight he seemed to be in another world.

"What's up?" Isaac said, walking up behind Sasha and Glen. When they turned around, Sasha was stunned to see that Isaac had brought the cheerleader stripper as his date.

"Damn, that bitch must let him bust off in her mouth and swallow too," Sasha reasoned, wondering what other reason Isaac would have for keeping her around like she was an official chick.

"Good to see you man," Glen said, giving Isaac a pound.

"Hi," Sasha said in a chipper voice to Isaac's date. "I'm sorry I never got the name you use outside of Magic City. I only know you as Passion, but that couldn't possibly be your government name."

"No problem, it's Penelope. Nice to see you again, but thank goodness under different circumstances."

Sasha replied by giving Penelope a stiff smile. Then out of the blue the whole room transfixed their stares in one direction, and Sasha looked that way too, dying to know what had everybody's undivided attention.

"Who in the world is that?" Isaac asked, being the first in their crew to zoom in on the woman who had mesmerized the room. The gorgeous goddess in a champagne-colored dress glided down the long staircase leading to the center of the ballroom, her long black tousled hair bouncing with each step she took. Her skin was luminous against the silk that draped her statuette body. Sasha studied the woman from the drop emeralds that sparkled in her ears to the diamond-studded Jimmy Choo heels that adorned her feet and had to admit that the lovely specimen was hands down the fiercest chick in the entire room. She hoped that at any moment her date would be at her side, so her man and every other one could stop drooling.

"I think I'm in love," Glen said under his breath, but Isaac heard him.

"You and me both. Who do you think she's here with?"

"I have no idea, but whoever he is, I take my hat off to him."

When the unknown woman reached the bottom stair and made her way through the crowd, every man turned to say hello. Sasha became jittery when it seemed the woman was making a beeline in their direction. It wasn't until the lady got within touching distance that she realized who the dream girl was, and her stomach instantly tightened up in knots.

"Hi, Glen."

"Bianca?" Glen said, as more of a question than a greeting.

"Of course it's me silly."

"Bianca, your assistant?" Isaac asked, not believing his eyes.

"You can't be the same girl that put me in the taxi the other day," Penelope said.

"To answer both of your questions, yes, I'm that girl. It's amazing what a dress and some makeup can do right. I can't believe all the glares and stares I'm getting." She giggled.

"You look absolutely incredible. I didn't even recognize you," Glen admitted.

"I don't know if I should take that as a compliment or be offended," Bianca said with a smile.

"Hi, Bianca. You look lovely tonight," Sasha said, stepping forward and standing between Bianca and Glen.

"Thanks, I guess I didn't need to take you up on your offer for styling tips."

Sasha felt her face turn red after the stinging remark. She didn't know how to respond, so she remained mute. Just when she believed her tension level had reached its limit, one of Glen's teammates approached and asked Bianca to dance.

"She'd love to," Sasha answered quickly, trying to get rid of the woman she never thought she'd consider competition.

The teammate took Bianca's hand and led her to the dance floor, as Glen watched with fire in his eyes.

"Why the fuck did you do that?" Glen asked.

"Do what?"

"Put Bianca off on some stranger?"

"Excuse me, Charlie isn't a stranger, he's your teammate, remember?"

"Still, Bianca doesn't know Charlie. How do you know she wanted to dance with him?"

"I didn't see her putting up a fight. The only person that seems to have a problem with it is you. Why is that?"

"I don't have a problem with it. I'm fine. Excuse me for a minute, I need to go speak to the coach." Sasha turned to where Bianca and Charlie were dancing and was once again astonished that the woman who'd been in their foyer yesterday was the same showstopper who was here tonight. She'd always known that Bianca had potential under those baggy clothes and the plain Jane face, but never did she imagine that Bianca had all that going on.

"Isaac and I are going to dance, you should find Glen and join us," Penelope suggested.

"You two go ahead, we'll join you shortly."

Sasha turned her attention back to Bianca and decided she'd take Penelope's advice. She tracked Glen down at a table, talking to his coach, and lured him to the floor. They slow jammed to an oldie but goody by Jodeci, and as they did, Glen sneaked looks at Bianca and Charlie. It incensed him that his teammate had his arms around Bianca's waist as if they were a couple.

Midway through the song, Sasha couldn't hold her bladder any longer. "Baby, I'll be right back. I have to use the restroom."

"Go ahead. I'll be sitting down at our table waiting for you."

"Okay," Sasha said, and gave Glen a kiss on the lips. Then she hurried away, not wanting to leave him by himself for too long.

Once she disappeared, Glen wasted no time getting to Bianca. "Excuse me, Charlie, but I need to speak to my assistant."

Charlie eyed Bianca, hoping to catch some resistance and not wanting to leave the woman's side, but when she didn't object, he bowed out gracefully.

The second Glen's hands touched her skin, Bianca felt butterflies in her stomach. "So what is it you need to talk to me about?"

"I don't have time to engage in word games since Sasha will be coming back any minute, but I had to tell you that I think I'm falling in love with you."

Bianca's heart felt like it leaped out her chest. That was one confession she didn't expect Glen to make. She was speechless.

"You've been so heavy on my mind, and then when you showed up here tonight, I could no longer deny how strong my feelings are for you."

"What about Sasha?"

"It's hard to let someone go when you allow them to get so close. But I do know I don't want to be with Sasha, I want to be with you."

"Are you sure you're not just overwhelmed from seeing me in a decent outfit?" Bianca joked.

"I've already seen you at your best, naked." Bianca couldn't help but blush. "I want to sit down and really talk to you about how I feel. Do you mind making an early exit?"

"Not at all."

"Then let's go," Glen said as he took Bianca's hand and led the way.

"Are you okay?" Isaac asked, startling Sasha. "Sorry, I didn't mean to scare you, but I noticed that you seemed a little out of it."

"It's that obvious?" Sasha replied angrily, fidgeting with her hair. "I went to the bathroom and when I came out I spotted Glen dancing up close and personal with Bianca. By the time I torpedoed through this crowd, the two of them were ghosts. Have you seen Glen?"

"No, not since earlier with you, but if he is with Bianca, I'm sure it's nothing. They're probably somewhere discussing work-related stuff," he added, trying in vain to ease Sasha's mind.

"Isaac, we're at a party and it's after ten. What type of business would the two of them be discussing?" Sasha shouted.

"Calm down. There's no sense in getting upset."

"I need to stop him." Sasha was now frantic. Isaac firmly put his hand on her shoulder, wanting to make sure he had her attention.

"Listen to me. Chasing Glen down like a madwoman is a waste of time. You can never stop a man from doing what he wants to do. I'm not trying to hurt you, Sasha, but that's the truth. My advice is for you to go home, and if and when Glen's ready, he'll come back."

Glen and Bianca escaped upstairs to a penthouse suite at the Ritz-Carlton. Anticipation filled the air when Bianca stepped into the over 1,400-plus-square-foot suite. The marble entry and panoramic bay windows welcomed her with open arms. "This place is bigger than my apartment," she stated, moving smoothly toward the window as if floating on air. "The view is incredible."

"You're right, it is." Bianca turned back and gazed at Glen, knowing that view he was speaking of was her. "Can I get you something to drink?"

"No thank you." Bianca once again turned her head to absorb the moonlit skyline.

"I guess what's out there is more interesting than me."

"I'm sorry. It's not that at all. I feel like I'm in some incredible dream. I'm so scared I'll wake up and it'll all be gone that staring off into the sky gives me something to hold on to."

"You can hold on to me."

"Glen, the next time I hold on to you, I don't want to ever let go."

"Who said you would have to?"

"I don't want to share you, not with Sasha or any other woman," Bianca stated solemnly.

"You won't have to. After we made love that first time, I knew you were the one, but for a couple of reasons I wasn't ready to take a chance on real love. I want to explain some things to you. Come have a seat."

Bianca sat down on a chair next to the mahogany table.

"Since I can remember, the scrutiny that comes with being a celebrity is all I've been exposed to. My father was a huge NBA star, and by the time I was ten it was expected that I would follow in his footsteps. I know I come off as arrogant and cocky a lot of times, but it's only because I've been living in my father's shadow since the day I was born. The comparisons never stop, and they never will, no matter how much I accomplish. It's made me build this wall to protect myself because there is always that chance that I might fail, and all eyes will be on me if I do. That's difficult for me to deal with, but it's my reality. The people in my life only care about how I play the game. They've never shown any interest on what moves me in my personal relationships."

"Not even your parents?"

"My dad likes to critique my game on the court but not off. The only advice he's ever given me about personal relationships is that if possible, never have a baby with a woman you don't want to be with, and if you do, take care of your responsibilities so you don't have to hear her mouth.

"Growing up, I adored my mother, but she didn't have any backbone when it came to my father. I hate to say it, but she was no more than a trophy wife, and so when I got older, that's all I thought a woman was worth. The idea of falling in love and having a real relationship with a woman was not even something I put much thought into. But when I met you, I knew right away you were unlike any other woman I had ever met. You didn't pretend to be something you weren't because you had an ulterior motive. You told me the truth, whether I wanted to hear it or not, and I respected you for that. I was drawn to your intelligence and how genuine you are. It wasn't about being physical. But when we did make love, it just intensified my feelings even more. Then seeing you tonight, bringing the beauty and sexy back, was an added bonus because you had already captured my heart."

Bianca walked toward Glen and put her finger over his mouth. "Stop talking and make love to me."

He was more than happy to oblige. From the throbbing of his dick, his impulse was to throw Bianca across the table, rip off her clothes, and thrust himself inside of her. Instead, he opted to take his time and make love to her nice and slow. With Bianca's hair sweeping against his face, her fragrance intoxicated him. He gently gripped the nape of her neck and began from the tip of her chin, peppering kisses down her slender neck until he reached her succulent breasts. As the straps on Bianca's dress fell off her shoulders, he cupped her golden brown rounds, letting his tongue rotate back and forth, licking the tip of her sugary nipples. He caressed her voluptuous ass until his hand slid up Bianca's silky smooth inner thigh, touching her sweet, pulsating vagina. His fingers glided with ease on Bianca's clitoris, sending her body into a minor tremor.

"Baby, don't you think I've waited long enough?" she whispered in his ear. "Please give me what my body's been craving since the last time I felt your dick inside of me."

"You'll never have to wait for this dick again. It belongs to you now."

"You promise?" Bianca asked demurely.

"Promise." Glen lifted Bianca up and carried her to the king-size bed. He laid her down with each angle curving to resemble the letter S, and with her long hair spreading out like flowing feathers, she put him in the mind of an exotic black mermaid. He took off his tuxedo, savoring the thought of tasting all of her.

Bianca's eyes widened as she admired the rippling muscles ornamenting Glen's flawless physique. She rose off the bed, yearning to stroke the body that was calling her name. Glen placed his hand on the back of her dress and unzipped it completely down to the arch in her back. He pulled the dress from her body and slipped off her Jimmy Choos, then used her long legs as a map to her inner sanctuary. Bianca pulled him in tight, ready to take all of him, but then he paused.

"Can I taste you first?" His request seemed as innocent as asking for a bite of a delicious piece of cherry pie. He stood still waiting for her to respond.

"Yes," she managed to say under a breathless murmur.

Then all she could do to keep from screaming out in ecstasy was to clench tightly to the bed sheets as Glen's tongue made love to her. He took his erotic pleasuring of her to the next level by tasting her clit and finger fucking her simultaneously. Just as she was about to reach her climax, he stopped his tongue action and replaced it with his rock hard dick. Bianca's juices swallowed his manhood like a sweet coating over an ice cream sundae. She clutched his firm buttocks, pulling him farther in, until she felt as if his manhood was in the pit of her stomach. His width and length filled her up completely. Glen pinned her legs back as he kept each thrust steady, while heightening her arousal by massaging her breast with his mouth. Both were in complete sexual bliss as their bodies became one.

"Baby, I'm about to come," Bianca sighed, holding on tighter to Glen.

"Me too."

"Ahhhhh, ohhhh, I love you, Glen."

"I love you too," he moaned as they reached their climax in unison.

The lovers remained intertwined in each other's rapture all night, the sun shining across their sleeping faces the following morning.

Overtime

I Surrender

Sasha awoke from a nightmare, drenched in sweat. In her dream, Glen and Bianca were married with two kids, living happily ever after, and she was back in Indiana waiting tables at the diner she had escaped from years ago. She turned to the side of the bed Glen slept on, but of course he wasn't there.

"That motherfucker spent the night with that bitch!" she screamed, picking up the lamp on the nightstand and throwing it across the room, crashing it against the plasma television. Then she picked up the phone and dialed both Glen's cell phones and his car phone, but got no answer. She tried to calm herself down but was overtaken by rage. Bianca had come along and stolen her man without even brandishing a weapon.

She prayed that it would end up being a one-night stand, and that afterward, Glen would see the pussy wasn't that great and come crawling back to her.

***

"Rise and shine, my beautiful princess," Glen said, kissing Bianca on her forehead.

"What time is it?"

"Two in the afternoon."

"Are you serious? I never sleep this late. It must be because I was lying in your arms."

"Lying next to you did feel so right. I've never been so mentally and physically connected to a woman before. You have to be the person I was meant to spend the rest of my life with."

"Do you really mean that?"

"Yes, I put that on everything I love."

"Glen, I'm scared," she admitted.

"Why?"

"Because you represent everything I thought could never work in a relationship. Superstar athlete with fame, money, an endless choice of women, plus the one you already have."

"I know. I can't front that seriously settling down seemed way off for me. But being with you makes me ready for the wedding, kids, white picket fence—okay, make that gated mansion," he chuckled.

"Are you sure you want that life with me?"

"That, and so much more."

"How are you going to explain that to Sasha?"

"I'll handle it. I know she's been feeling that the vibe is off, but I'll let her know you're the one I want to be with."

"You know she's going to lose it."

"Yeah, at first, but Sasha is a survivor, she'll bounce back. I'd rather tell her the truth now then lead her on. She can move on with her life and find happiness the way I have with you." Glen bent down and kissed Bianca, and the two began making love once again.

***

Isaac woke up for the third morning in a row with Penelope by his side. After trying every sexual position known to mankind with the cheerleader stripper, he'd become increasingly bored with her. He realized just how much he missed Tracy, and decided he would do anything possible to get her back. "Penelope, wake up," he said, shaking the still sleeping girl.

She slowly started coming out of her sex and liquor induced coma. "What is it?"

"I need you to get up, get dressed, and leave."

"Huh, I don't understand."

"I'll call you a cab, but I'm ready for you to go now."

Isaac's demand woke Penelope right up. "What happened? I thought it was all good between us."

"It was, but we've had enough fun. It's time for me to get back to reality."

Penelope wasn't stupid, she'd played this game many times. She knew exactly what Isaac meant. "So you're going back to your girlfriend?"

"Yeah, if she'll have me."

"She'd be crazy not to. I can tell you're a really great guy, even if you did fuck around on her."

"I hope she's as understanding."

After Penelope got dressed, Isaac walked her downstairs to the waiting taxi. He handed her a fist-sized knot of one hundred dollar bills totaling ten thousand dollars. He felt it was the least he could do for her services.

"You have real class, Isaac," she told him. "If you ever need to talk, you know where to find me."

Back in his apartment, Isaac sat down and called Tracy. For the first time since all the drama went down, she answered the phone.

"Baby, I want you to come home," were the first words out of Isaac's mouth.

Sasha ran to the top of the stairs when she heard the front door opening. "Glen, I was so worried about you. I'm glad you're home." After going through every emotion, from crying to screaming to contemplating murder, she had decided to use a different approach. Instead of flipping out and calling Glen every name in the book, she pretended that Bianca wasn't even part of the equation, hoping that after today she wouldn't be.

"No, I'm fine. I was with—" Sasha cut him off.

"You don't have to explain. We don't need to discuss what happened last night. It's the past, and we should focus on the present. What we have is so much stronger than whatever meaningless dalliance you had last night."

Glen stared up at Sasha and started feeling guilty. He'd expected her to come at him with all sorts of four letter words and maybe even objects to go upside his head with, but her demeanor and attitude were surprisingly calm. Sasha walked down the stairs wearing a subtle terry-cloth sundress, another surprise. He figured she would be sashaying down the stairs with tits and ass jiggling, trying to seduce him into bed.

"How about we go in the kitchen and I make you something to eat?"

Glen started to wonder if he had walked into the right house. It damn sure looked like his crib, and the woman in front of him was an excellent replica of Sasha, but her actions were those of a stranger. "Okay, I am hungry." More than that, he was curious as to what Sasha planned in the way of food. He didn't even know she could cook. In their whole time of dating she had never served him so much as a drink of water. He sat down at the table and watched as she began whipping up a meal.

"Would you like a snack while I'm preparing your food?"

"I'll just take a glass of juice."

As he requested, Sasha poured him a glass of juice, and set it down on the table with a smile on her face. Glen started getting antsy about the discussion he was about to have with her, but knew he had to get it over with.

"Sasha, as I was saying when I got home, I have to talk to you about something."

"I told you it wasn't necessary."

"But it is because I'm in love with Bianca and I want to be with her." As soon as the words were out of his mouth, he felt relieved. He waited to hear the tongue lashing Sasha would give him.

"Glen, because you fell up in some new, untouched pussy, now you're in love," she said coolly.

"It's more than sex. I've been developing feelings for Bianca for some time now."

"During the same time you were falling asleep and waking up making love to me, during that time?" Glen felt a lump in his throat as he struggled to answer Sasha's questions. He hadn't planned on the conversation going like this. Somehow, Sasha had managed to turn the tables and make him question himself.

"I'll admit that I care about you, Sasha, and we shared some good times together, but what I have with Bianca is different. I want to spend the rest of my life with her."

"You mean like marriage, family—that type of life?"

"Yes," he answered, not wanting to crush Sasha, but since she'd asked, he wanted to be honest.

"I see. Well, how do you think Bianca will take being a step-mother?" Sasha said, continuing to cook Glen's meal as if she hadn't just dropped a bombshell.

"What are you talking about?"

"I'm talking about the child I'm carrying, your child." Glen stood up and then sat back down, getting a migraine as if a hammer was knocking on his head.

"You're on the pill and I always pull out."

"Not a little over a month ago when I gave you the best head of your life and then we had sex before you got in the shower, I unfortunately misplaced my pills and didn't take them that month."

Glen wasn't sure what had him reeling more, remembering the one time he got so caught up in Sasha's dick-sucking that when she pulled him in, he did in fact explode inside of her, or how confident her declaration of being pregnant was.

Sasha knew she had Glen by the balls, and she planned on squeezing them until he couldn't breathe. "And don't even think about asking me to have an abortion. Even though you're leaving me for Bianca, I still love you very much, and the child I'm carrying is a reflection of that." As if nothing had changed, she added, "Your food is ready, so relax and enjoy your meal."

Bianca was still on cloud nine, relishing her time with Glen. She never knew love would feel this good. She'd only been with one other man her whole life, and that ended up being a summer fling that left her with a broken heart. It was after her first year of college, and instead of going home, she opted to stay and take extra courses during the summer break. She met a handsome football player who was taking courses to get caught up so he would be able to play for the upcoming season.

First, he asked Bianca to tutor him, which she agreed to do. But then he showed a romantic interest, which totally surprised her.

Bianca was a bookworm, not the kind of girl she'd seen the football player on campus with. They soon began a passionate love affair that lasted throughout the summer. With Bianca doing all his schoolwork and studying with him for his tests, her lover aced his summer classes. Meanwhile, during their time together, he confessed his undying love and promised to remain committed to her. Being young and naive, Bianca believed every word. She had given her virginity to the football stud, and in her heart wanted to marry him. It wasn't until a week before school was about to start and he stopped answering her calls that she became alarmed. When she finally ran into him in the student lounge the first week of school, holding hands with a beautiful sorority sister, she realized he had just used her for the summer and then tossed her away like a dirty napkin. He gave her no explanation as to why he stopped seeing her, just simply stated that their relationship was over.

From that day on Bianca had never trusted men and refused to date any of them. She continued to study hard and focus on doing great in school, but that experience made her petrified to ever take a chance on love again—until now. Glen gave her the self-assurance she needed to open her heart and fall in love. A smile crept across her face, knowing that at that moment Glen was ending his relationship with Sasha and they would soon enjoy exploring their newfound love.

Glen hadn't moved from the kitchen table. The plate of Cuban cuisine Sasha had prepared was still sitting in front of him, untouched. The sun had gone down hours ago, but he couldn't tear himself away from his chair. Sasha's pregnancy bombshell was tearing him up. It threw a monkey wrench into his plans with Bianca. They were in the beginning of their love affair, and he wasn't sure if they could endure the unexpected arrival of a baby he was having with another woman. In his heart, he knew that he wanted to give their love a try, but he wasn't confident that Bianca would come to the same conclusion. Of course, the only way to know for sure was to give her the choice, so he grabbed his car keys and headed for the door.

"Where are you going?" Sasha had been sitting in the living room patiently waiting for feedback from Glen after she gave given him her news. He'd been speechless.

"I'm going to see Bianca."

"Do you plan on telling her about the baby?"

"Of course, she has the right to decide whether she wants to continue things knowing that you're pregnant with my child."

"What if she doesn't, then what?"

"I don't know, Sasha. I don't even want to think about that. I'm hoping she'll decide we can get past this."

"So what, you all can continue on your love affair and then you just throw me out in the streets and forget about your child?"

"Of course not. I'm going to be a father to my child. You don't ever have to second-guess that."

"What about me?"

"Sasha, I'll make sure you're provided for throughout your pregnancy and after. Honestly, I don't want you stressing right now. You need to take care of yourself for the baby's sake."

"I appreciate that. Good luck with Bianca."

Sasha sat in the dark preparing her next move as if playing a game of chess. Ideally, as far as she was concerned, Bianca would bow out, not wanting to be bothered with a baby mama, especially one as treacherous as her. But landing a man like Glen was incredibly tempting, and Bianca might decide the battle was worthwhile. If Bianca decided to ride it out, Sasha knew she would have to find another way to lure Glen back. For now, Sasha could tell that the calm, cool, collective approach was pushing the right buttons with him. As badly as he wanted to be mad and flip out on her because she wasn't pulling the normal card, "If you're not with me I'll make your life a living hell attitude," her calm approach had caused Glen to be cordial, which was exactly what she wanted. That meant all she would have to do was catch him at the right time, when he was vulnerable, and she'd be back in his bed.

As Glen drove to Bianca's apartment, he struggled with how he would break the news to her about Sasha. This was no way to start a new relationship, but he hoped it would make their bond stronger instead of ripping them apart. He got out of his car and slowly walked to Bianca's front door. He never thought he would come to a place in his life when he would fear losing a woman, and realized now that's what happened when you fell in love. He rang the doorbell, and within seconds Bianca answered.

"Hi, baby," she said. "I've been missing you since the moment I left you."

Glen wrapped his arms tightly around Bianca, never wanting to let go. "I missed you too. I've been waiting to hold you again all day. You feel so good," he said, hoping it wouldn't be the last time he would hold her in his arms like this.

"Would you like me to get you anything?"

"No, you're all I need." Glen's words sounded sweet, but his body language was saying something else.

"What's wrong? You seem a little edgy. I guess things didn't go so well with Sasha?"

"It's a little more complicated than that."

"What's so complicated? I'm sure Sasha got extra dramatic and probably threatened to ruin your life and mine, but that was her anger talking. She'll cool down."

"Actually, she was extremely calm."

Bianca did a double take. "Calm. That isn't a word I thought I'd ever hear used to describe Sasha."

"Me neither. But she was. And she shared some interesting news with me."

"What news?"

Glen was building up the courage to spill his guts as he paced back and forth.

"Glen, what's wrong? You're scaring me."

"I'm not trying to. The news is still fresh in my mind, and finding the right words is difficult."

"Stop trying to figure out the right words and just say it." Bianca was becoming frustrated, trying to read Glen's mind. She wanted to know what had him walking on eggshells.

"Sasha is pregnant with my child."

Bianca's heart dropped. When she finally found true love, once again the beautiful sorority sister was coming along and taking away her happiness. She stood up and held her stomach as the pain of rejection captured her. "And of course she's going to have it, and what you've decided is to leave me and go back to her?"

"Yes, I mean no. I mean yes, she's going to have the baby, but no, I'm not going to leave you. I love you. I want to spend the rest of my life with you, Bianca."

Bianca wanted to believe Glen, but a baby put a whole new spin on things. "But she's carrying your child. I can't compete with that."

"I'm not asking you to. I want you to be a part of my life and my child's. This baby doesn't change the love I have for you. I just hope it doesn't change how you feel about me."

"Nothing can change how I feel about you, and of course I would love your child. But what about Sasha? She'll use that baby to try to get you back every chance she gets. Every time you go visit your child, I know Sasha will be plotting and scheming to make her move on you." Glen reached out and held Bianca's face in the palm of his hands. "Do you love me?" he asked, staring into her eyes.

"Of course I love you. Why would you even ask something like that?"

"Because I need to know that for better or worse you'll stand by my side no matter what."

"Always."

"Then not Sasha or anyone one else will be able to come between us. No matter how many tricks she may try to pull out her bag, our unity will keep our love intact. You have to truly believe that. You can't allow your insecurities to destroy what we have. The only people that can ruin what we have are us."

"You make it sound so simple. But love is far from simple, Glen. My heart was broken once before, and I never thought I would be able to trust another man with my love until you. If you hurt me, it would be too devastating." Tears began falling down Bianca's face, and Glen kissed each of them away. He wanted her to be secure with the feelings they shared. It was imperative for her to believe his love would never waver.

"Baby, your heart is safe in my hands. I will protect it because now it belongs to me. The only tears I want you to cry are those of happiness, not pain. Now let me make love to you so we can create and bring our own child into this world."

"You're ready for us to have a baby together?"

"Nothing would make me happier, except for you being my wife, but we can discuss that at a later time. But, Bianca it's okay to surrender your love to me," Glen said, flashing his signature smile.

Looking into his eyes, Bianca finally believed that Glen wasn't like the football player who had stolen her heart and then broke it. She was no longer the young girl who didn't understand the difference between love and infatuation. Glen was all man, and she was now a mature woman who could follow her heart. Yes, with love you'd always be taking a chance that the other person might hurt or disappoint you. But what was the sense in living if you weren't willing to take the biggest gamble of all, experiencing love b-ball style?

JOY KING was born in Toledo, Ohio, and raised in California, Maryland, and North Carolina. She represents a new genre of young, hip, sexy novels that take readers behind the velvet rope of the glamorous but often shady relationships in the entertainment industry.

Joy attended North Carolina Central University and Pace University, where she majored in journalism. Emerging onto the entertainment scene in the late nineties, Joy accepted an internship position, and immediately began to work her way up the ranks, at the Terrie Williams Agency. She worked hands-on with Johnnie Cochran, the Essence Awards, The NBA Players' Association, Moët & Chandon, and other entertainment executives and celebrities.

In 1999, Joy attended the Lee Strasburg Theater Institute before accepting a job as Director of Hip Hop Relations at Click Radio, where she developed segments featuring the biggest names in hip hop. Joy pushed her department to new levels by creating an outlet that placed hip hop in the forefront of the cyber world.

Joy made her debut in the literary world with *Dirty Little Secrets*, a novel that is loosely based on her life. The sequel, *Hooker to Housewife,* will be in released in April 2007.

A prolific writer, Ms. King also writes street novels under the pseudonym Deja King. With the debut of *Bitch*, Ms. King garnered a loyal urban following who are eagerly anticipating the sequel, *Bitch Reloaded*, which will be released in 2007.

These Are My Confessions

Electa Rome Parks

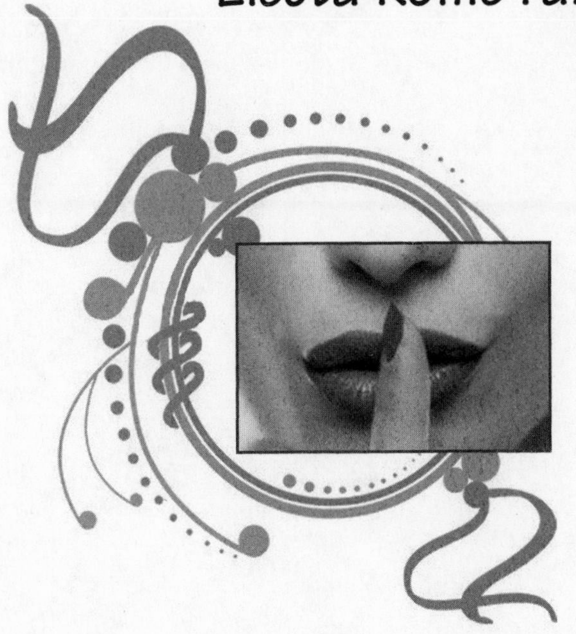

This is dedicated to all the keepers of secrets . . . know that the truth heals.

The Beginning . . .

"Oooh yeah, baby! That's right! Don't stop doing what you're doing!" Drake was in heaven.

"Okay, babe. Anything you say. You sure you can handle this?" I teased in between licks.

Starting in small circles, I twirled my tongue up and down his shaft, and with each flick reached farther and farther down. When I placed all of him inside my warm mouth, I thought Drake was going to collapse in a heap in the middle of the floor.

"Damn, Kennedy. You do that shit too good," he exclaimed as his eyes rolled back in his head like he was going into convulsions.

"Who do you love?" I asked, momentarily pausing to look up at Drake. I needed to hear him say it, again.

"Don't stop now! Put it back in. I was almost there. Put it in," Drake moaned, trying to place his stiff, massive organ back in the comfort, wetness, and warmth of my eager, accommodating mouth.

"Not until you answer my question," I stated, shyly looking up at him from beside the sofa in my living room.

"Damn, Kennedy, you can't tease a man like this," he exclaimed, pushing my long hair back out of my flushed face. Unsuccessfully, he tried to force my head back down with his other hand.

"Who do you love?"

I took the opportunity to suck down on his tip, just like he had taught me. Not too hard, but with enough pressure to cause him to involuntarily shudder and close his eyes. Drake had patiently and expertly instructed me on everything he liked for me to do to him in bed. The things I didn't care for, I did them anyway. Just to please him. *Cosmopolitan* magazine articles revealed what you wouldn't do for your man, another woman would. Women should learn to be accommodating in the bedroom. I went above and beyond for Drake.

Tonight was costume night. Sometimes Drake and I played games where I'd dress up in costumes and live out his fantasies. It kept the sex exciting and interesting, is what Drake said. I had no complaints. Tonight, I had on a red and blue cheerleading uniform minus my panties and bra. I even sported long socks and tennis shoes to complete the look. As I squatted on the floor with my open, bent legs, Drake manually stimulated me and squeezed my breasts through the thin fabric while I pleased him. My wetness was all over his fingers. I think I was addicted to his dick; it was beautiful, just like him, and I could suck him for hours.

"Kennedy, baby. You know I love you. From the first day I saw you, I've loved you," he exclaimed, rubbing some more on my spot. I felt my knees getting weak.

I let out a slow, sensual moan, closed my eyes and bit down on my bottom lip. "Yeah, right there." I opened my legs even wider, granting Drake full access.

He reached to push my head back down, and I searched his face for the truth. I knew Drake sometimes told me what he thought I wanted to hear. His confessions, sometimes, didn't hold an ounce of truth.

"Come on, baby. Work my dick. Do it like I taught you. Suck that lollipop."

"Hmm, you taste sweet," I cooed, licking my lips.

"It was love at first sight when you walked through my door. I knew you were the one."

Drake had told me all I needed to hear. His words were music to my soul. I went to work, harder and faster than before. How many licks does it take to get to the center of the tootsie roll pop? Slurping, wet sounds echoed throughout the stillness of the moment. We never made love with any background music or noise. Drake was turned on by the sensual, raw sounds and smells of our lovemaking.

"Ohhh yeah! That's it! That's my girl! Damn!" he screamed out in ecstasy as I moved just in time before he spewed all over me. With his eyes still closed and a big smile on his gorgeous face, Drake collapsed against my sofa, pulled me to him, and caressed my hair and face over and over. He loved to run his hands through my long, wavy locks. Drake despised when I wore my hair pulled up in a ponytail, and he expected me to take it down when I was with him. I obliged. Always accommodating.

"You're getting better. Go get a warm washcloth for your man," he said, pulling up my skirt and smacking me on the ass two times, leaving a light red mark.

I stared at him from my spot on the floor. Getting better? I thought he'd enjoyed that. I knew he did. I was on point with all he had taught me. I made a mental note to do better the next time. I had finally gotten my gag reflex under control. Maybe, next time I'd surprise him by swallowing.

"Go on, baby. Hurry up," he demanded, bending down and taking one of my throbbing nipples in his mouth like he possessed it and absently playing between my quivering legs. "I'm ready to eat some honey because your pussy always tastes sweet."

I quickly jumped up to retrieve a towel because I knew what was in store for me. My kitty twitched. Twitched again. Drake was off the chain when it came to sexing me. He had turned me out; inside and out.

Ring. Ring. Ring.

In my daze, I glanced around and surveyed my surroundings. In my bed, safe and sound in my tiny apartment. The ringing telephone woke me from my flashback of events that had transpired several months earlier, during happier times. The tingling between my legs was present day and very real. My coochie was having some serious dick withdrawals and feeling like an addict for a piece of Drake. However, that would happen only over my dead body.

Present Day . . .

Drake.

Drake, I never want to set my eyes on him for the rest of my life. If I never, ever see him, that would be too soon. I don't know what led me to believe that I'd make a difference in his life and he'd fall hopelessly and helplessly in love with me. What made me think that I'd possess him someday? Drake could never be possessed by a mere woman. I think he secretly hates the female population and only tolerates and uses us for his enjoyment and pleasure.

Snuggling deeper under my comforter and adjusting my pillows, I glanced at the digital clock that sat on my nightstand. It read 7:35 A.M. I had tossed and turned for most of the night with fretful dreams when I did dose off for a few restless minutes. There was definitely no sleeping now; I was wide-awake and antsy. For a second I had forgotten it was a Saturday morning, no work. I reached down beside my bed, retrieved, and once again examined my brand-new leather journal and thought, Why not? It had tons of blank, lined pages to write on. Maybe if I wrote some of my jumbled thoughts down, I could make some sense of the turn my life had taken. But where to begin?

I remember a college professor telling his creative writing class that every story has a beginning, middle, and ending. Simple enough. I'll start at the beginning. Maybe in the process I'd answer the million-dollar question: What makes a woman want to end her life over a man? These are my confessions:

Dear Journal,

I guess I should start by telling you something about myself. Let's see. There's really not much to tell, that's interesting anyway. I'm pretty average in most ways and live a relatively tame lifestyle. That is until recently. I'm twenty-eight years old. Work as a customer service representative for a telecommunications company in Midtown. By the way, it's a job I don't particularly care for, but I do my best nevertheless. It could be a cool job, but there is always so much drama going on with the women there. Trivia stuff at that. Why can't women just get along?

Oh, I'm adopted. Mother and Daddy adopted me when I was two months old. I was born to a teenage, crack-addicted biological mother who gave me up at birth. Signed over her maternal rights. Just like that. With the snap of two fingers. In the blink of an eye. She signed over her maternal rights, and I became a ward of the state of Georgia. She wasn't even sure who my biological father was. That line on my birth certificate was left blank.

I don't get it. And believe me, I've tried. How can a

mother, any mother, give birth to a child that she has carried for nine months, felt her moving around inside her, bonded with, and then, then . . . just give her up like she's dumping the trash? Me, I could never do that in a million years. It's actually ironic, my life didn't mean anything to my biological mother and I guess it didn't mean anything to me either since I tried to take it over a month ago. Thirty days ago.

Luckily for me, Mother and Daddy came into my life when I was two months old. Mother said she took one look at me lying all alone in the hospital crib, underweight because I was born premature, and knew she had to have me to love, shield, and nurture. Mother said she'd never forget how small, fragile, and vulnerable I appeared. Like I was calling out for her to love and protect me. And she did and hasn't stopped loving me in all my twenty-eight years.

What else? I guess you could say I'm a loner. I don't have very many friends, male or female. That's fine with me. I've halfway attempted to be friends with women at work, but in the end, there are always too many jealousies, insecurities, and backstabbing going on for me. Mother said I shouldn't stress or worry about it. She claims these women are jealous of my good looks. I don't know, I think I have average looks. I'm about five-seven. Very fair skinned, long, naturally wavy brownish-red hair, hazel eyes, and a slim frame. Strangers are always saying I could easily be a model with my long legs, slim waist, and exotic looks.

Anyhow, whatever the reason, I choose to go to work, perform my job duties, and leave. My coworkers assume I'm a snob since I won't get involved in their gossip, after-work activities, and petty ways. Until a year ago, most weekends found me at home curled up with a good book. Occasionally, Taylor, a college friend, would convince me to hit a local night spot. I'd tag along, to please her, even though the club scene wasn't really me. Clubbing wasn't my thing. Typically, I'd sit in a corner for most of the night, nurse one drink and turn down dances left and right. Taylor, on the other hand, lived on the dance floor and loved the attention men showered her with.

I've never been good with men either. I can count on one hand the number of boyfriends I've had. I've never had problems attracting men, only attracting the right ones. I honestly think I have an invisible sign posted on my forehead that reads: Use and Abuse Me. Please. The wrong ones flock to me like bees to honey.

After I met Drake, I thought all that had changed. Was all in my past. I felt like I had won the lottery and I had the chance for love, marriage, and a family. How wrong I was. Love is so blind, it feels right even when it's wrong.

Life After the Incident . . .

Gloomy and bleak, just like me, most of Monday morning found me answering and returning client calls, researching existing problems, and completing follow-up items. This was my first week back at work—after my incident. I had made it halfway down my "to do" list when the phone rang again.

"Hello, Kennedy Logan speaking."

"Yeah. Yeah. Yeah. Save it, save it. Sweetie, what's going on? You got a minute? I'm seriously stressing on my end. What are you doing?"

It was Taylor. As usual, she was talking a mile a minute, showed no signs of stalling, and I couldn't get a word in edgewise.

"Working," I replied sarcastically.

"I'm so glad you're back at work, because your mother wouldn't let me within one hundred feet of you. I think she set up guard duty next to your phone. I get the impression she thinks I'm a bad influence on you or something."

"Taylor, be for real. You know Mother loves you like a second daughter. She's always asking about you and how you're doing."

"Well, I wouldn't have known it the way she has treated me the last couple of weeks. Every time I called, you were always busy or resting, according to her. I didn't feel the love. Not at all."

"Taylor, you know how Mother is, and I didn't know she was screening my calls. I thought I hadn't heard from you because you were out of town on business."

"Well, now you know. Plus, when has being out of town ever stopped me from calling you?"

"True. Well, I apologize."

"Plus, I'm so mad at you. I had to go to the club by myself that night you promised you'd hang out."

"Oh, I'm sorry. I've had so much on my mind that I completely forgot all about that," I lied.

"I know you forgot. Of course, when I called to remind you, your mother wouldn't put me through. Said you were resting and still not feeling well."

"Did she?"

"Yes, K."

"Ump."

"Kennedy, what's going on? For real."

"What do you mean?"

"I mean just what I asked, what's really going on? Why did you stay out from work this long? A month? And why had Mrs. Logan moved in with you and was acting like your personal bodyguard? Who or what does she have to protect you from?"

"Taylor, I've already told you what happened. Mother was nursing me back from the flu. Even now, my body hasn't fully recovered. I'm always tired and I've lost weight. Mother's back at her house now." I wondered silently, how did you inform your best friend that you almost overdosed on prescription pills because of a man? And Mother found me.

"Kennedy, come on now. This is me you're talking to. I've known you for a minute. I know how you act when you try to lie."

Silence.

"You are not very good at it."

To calm down, I breathed deeply through my nose. "Taylor, I don't feel like talking about this right now. Okay?" I felt a headache coming on.

"Knowing what a private person you are, I'm going to respect your request, but soon you gotta let me know what's really going on."

"Yeah, soon."

"I'm going to hold you to that," Taylor quirked with determination in her voice.

"Yeah, whatever."

"Whatever, my ass. I am. I'm always in your corner and don't you forget that."

"I know."

"Anyway, I'm supposed to be on a self-imposed twenty minute break. My coworkers have gotten on my last nerve; everybody is tripping, so I had to take a breather. I'm gonna have to go, but I have to know one thing," Taylor said in a near whisper.

"What?"

"Have you seen him yet?"

"Seen who?"

"K, what is wrong with you today? Who do you think? Drake."

"You know we broke up. I wish you'd stop worrying about me and Drake with your nosy self. No, I haven't seen him, and I'm not looking for him either."

"I'm not nosy!"

"Yes, you are. You are the nosiest person I know besides Mother."

"Well, I'm in good company," she laughed.

"Whatever."

"K, you'll have to see him sooner or later. For God's sake, you work for the same company. I still can't believe, you of all people, got caught up in an office romance."

"That's right. Pour more salt on my wounds."

"I'm sorry, but you're usually so practical about everything. This office romance was so uncharacteristic of you."

"I guess Drake was very persuasive."

"Just don't let him sweet-talk you, change your mind, and draw you back into his life and his bed. His dick is not gold."

"I won't, Mother. Now stop bugging me," I laughed, but the laugher never reached my eyes.

"Kennedy, I know you, and you didn't stop loving that man overnight. You don't give your love away frivolously. You're vulnerable right now and Drake knows that. So, be weary of that slimy snake in the grass."

"Okay, I will. I promise. Now, enough."

"Drake doesn't deserve you."

"That's what you and Mother keep telling me," I cited, playing with the phone cord, wrapping it around my thin fingers.

"Well, it's true. You're too good for him. Always was."

Deadly silence.

"Hello?"

"I'm here."

"I have to run; we have our weekly meeting in a few minutes. I'll talk to you later. Maybe we can do lunch one day this week and play catch-up."

"Cool. Let me know," I answered as we said our good-byes and hung up the phone. My mind was reeling back to what Taylor had said, the exact same thing Drake had stated in what seemed like eons ago. I would have to see him sooner or later. Hopefully, it would be later, much later. Like when hell froze over.

First Encounter . . .

Dear Journal,

The first time I laid eyes on Drake was a year, two months, and a day ago. I can break it down to the hours, minutes, even seconds if you asked me to because I recall it just like it was yesterday. If only I had known or sensed in some way that he'd be trouble. Trouble with a capital T. It's true, if it's too good to be true, then it probably is. All that glitters isn't gold. Drake was more like fool's gold.

I was hand delivering business reports and correspondence, up on the sixth floor, to one of the managers, Bill Walker. Mr. Walker managed some of the top tier clients that I serviced. We were engaged in the usual, cordial, how's the weather chitchat in his spacious office. Not much of anything was really being said. Just polite conversation. Then

Mr. Walker asked me the question that changed my entire life–for the worse.

"Kennedy, have you met our new manager, Drake Collins? He came to us by way of California roughly two weeks ago."

"No, I haven't."

"Well, come and let me introduce the two of you. You'll probably work with him periodically on accounts and assist in getting him up to speed."

We walked out of Mr. Walker's corner office and strolled four doors over. I envied management. They all had large, stately offices that had floor-to-ceiling windows and were privileged to a spectacular view of Atlanta and could see as far away as Stone Mountain. Me, I had a tiny cubicle that didn't have a door I could conveniently close for privacy, and I definitely didn't have a view of the city. My view was the grayish walls of my cubbyhole.

With my degree in business administration, I could be in management within a few years, but I didn't have the desire to work my way up the ladder. Sometimes I felt that corporate America was not for me. I didn't know what I wanted to do. Whenever I complained to Mother, she encouraged me to go back to school for my MBA. Sometimes I thought it was a good idea, but other times I wasn't feeling like another two or more years of professors, studying, and exams. With a full-time job, when would I have the time or energy?

As we walked into Mr. Collins's office, sitting with his back to us and talking on the phone was an African-American male who I hadn't seen before. He signaled with his finger that he'd be just a moment. We patiently waited for him to end his phone call, and I quickly checked out his office space with curiosity. Everything was neat, in place, and very efficient-looking. There weren't a lot of personal items such as photos or anything of that nature. So I wasn't sure if he was married or had any children. This new manager had a few colorful framed prints and affirmations on his wall and credenza. I still hadn't gotten a good look at this Mr. Collins yet. I was secretly thinking about all the work piled up on my desk.

Finally, he turned around and stood up to address us and I stumbled head first into his soulful eyes. Standing before me was the absolute most gorgeous man I had ever seen in my entire life. My breath caught in my throat. He was almost flawless; almost too perfect. Drake was the perfect specimen of a strong, black man, on the outside anyway. The only imperfection I saw was a small scar, barely noticeable, right below his perfect bottom lip. I wanted to reach out, touch his cheek and see if he was real because the man standing before me had to be an illusion.

With close-cropped, slightly wavy hair, light brown eyes with specks of green, a thin mustache, and smooth dark brown skin, he was a god. And to top it all off, he had a beautiful smile to match his six feet, two inch frame. Even through his business jacket, I could make out the six-pack that was beneath his blue dress shirt. It was obvious he worked out at a gym because he was too tight. I figured he was around thirty, no older than thirty-three. Yes, this was all man because just his presence was affecting me.

I was truly shocked I hadn't heard the women on my floor talking, gossiping, and placing claims on this manly specimen. You couldn't miss Drake. When he walked in a room, he was the kind of man who made you pause in whatever you were doing and just drool. He commanded attention. I had simply blocked out my coworkers' comments regarding him, or maybe they didn't bother to inform me about him. I know they didn't consider me competition, not because of my looks, but because they knew I didn't date on the job.

I didn't believe in office romances. I had witnessed what messing with the boss could do for you—give you your walking papers when the relationship went south, or just an internal black ball followed you out the door. The termination of office affairs had ended some promising careers at my company.

"Kennedy, Kennedy?" Mr. Walker repeated, giving me an odd look with a slight smile on his pale face. Mr. Walker was forever in need of a few hours of sun, but he was pretty decent. He always treated me with respect and valued my opinion regarding clients. Recently, he personally called and asked me why I hadn't interviewed for one of the management positions that was open. Internal associates always received first priority over external candidates. Mr. Walker thought I was a perfect candidate to interview for the position.

"Oh, I'm sorry," I said, swallowing the lump that had suddenly formed in my throat. "I spaced out for a moment. I guess I was thinking about the workload waiting on my desk downstairs."

"Well, yes. You guys have been swamped with a high volume of calls lately, since we installed the new software. Don't worry, Drake and I won't keep you long."

Drake and I awkwardly stared at each other. I longed to hear what his voice would sound like directed toward me. I thought it would be rich, deep and sexy. Suddenly, images of him whispering sweet nothings in my ear clouded my brain. What was going on?

"As I was saying, Kennedy, I'd like for you to meet Drake Collins. Drake, this is Kennedy Logan. She's one of our best customer service representatives. Kennedy has helped me out on numerous occasions and has an excellent rapport with many of our top tier clients. She's a great asset to the company."

As I tried unsuccessfully to stop the huge blush that had assaulted my face, I held out my slightly shaky right hand. I was pretty light-skinned, so I knew that Drake and Mr. Walker noticed the redness that flushed my cheeks, neck and face.

"Nice to meet you, Mr. Collins. Welcome aboard."

"Same here, nice to meet you too," he stated as his huge hand swallowed mine. I couldn't help but notice the contrast of our skin tones as they meshed in a handshake. I observed that Drake had perfectly manicured nails. And his hands were smooth and soft to the touch. I knew then that this man took care of himself and hadn't done any hard labor a day in his life. He had been pampered and catered to.

Even though we were in a professional setting, I saw Drake quickly take me in from head to toe. Starting at my feet, he swiftly admired my long legs, paused at my hips, made his way up to my chest, and finally took in my glowing face. All in a matter of seconds. When I went out with Taylor, this was the same look that I typically received from the men in the clubs. In the clubs, it turned me off because I always felt like I was being sized up like a piece of raw meat by the hungry lions. For some reason, with Drake, my heart gave a quick flutter. This completely caught me off guard.

"Kennedy. What a lovely name." My name just flowed off his tongue like a fine wine poured into expensive crystal glassware.

"Thank you."

"Are you originally from Atlanta, Kennedy?"

"Yes, born and raised here. A Georgia peach."

"I can't believe it. I'm finding it's rare to find a true Atlanta native. Everyone here seems to be a transplant from New York, Florida, or someplace up North."

"Well, you've found me."

"Indeed I did."

He smiled.

I smiled.

"Maybe you can suggest some good restaurants for lunch and dinner, for that matter. I just relocated here from Los Angeles, and I'm still learning my way around and finding the hot spots in the city."

"I'm afraid I'm the wrong one to ask. I usually eat lunch at my desk, I'm a diehard brown bagger," I explained, Drake's eyes never left mine. I could get lost in them. Drown. When the sunlight from his open window blinds hit them just right, the specks of green in his eyes danced around in merry circles.

When we heard Mr. Walker politely clear his throat, we came back to reality. As I brushed my wild hair out of my face, I quickly blushed again and looked down at the floor. Suddenly, I wished I had worn my nice black Donna Karan suit and put on some makeup. Plus, I was in dire need of a manicure. I quickly balled my fingers into tight fists at my sides and hoped he hadn't noticed.

"Well, Miss Kennedy . . . it is Miss, isn't it?"

"Yes." I wanted to scream out, Yes, I'm single. Single and available. It had been a while since I'd been in a long-term relationship. Any relationship.

"It's a pleasure to meet you, and I may have to call you so you can explain some of these reports you guys generate in your department. And if Bill recommended you, then you must be great," he said, holding my hand again—a bit too long. I shuddered. Felt a moistness that surprised me.

"Nice meeting you too. And sure, I'll be glad to explain the client reports. They can be a bit confusing to someone not used to reviewing them. Just give me a call. I'm in the directory, extension 3–5123."

"I may certainly do that," he said, finally releasing his hand and eyes from mine. My heart stopped fluttering then, slowly returned to near normal.

As Mr. Walker and I walked out, I felt Drake's eyes as they seductively caressed my butt. When I discreetly glanced back, our eyes meshed, I was lost, and he smiled. I offered a weak one in return and kept walking, faster. Somebody was a lucky woman because I knew that man had a woman. And if she was smart, she was a woman who kept a close eye on him. Drake could almost make a woman go back on her promise to never date someone she worked with. As Taylor would say, "Don't shit where you eat."

Approximately a week after I was introduced to Drake at work, I picked up my ringing phone to find him on line two.

"Miss Logan?"

"Yes. Speaking."

"This is Drake Collins."

"Hi. How are you?"

"Good. And yourself?"

"I'm great. How are you adjusting to the company and your new role?"

"I can't complain. Everything is going well both on and off the job. Everybody that I've met in Atlanta has extended true southern hospitality to me. Strangers actually speak to you in the streets and everyone is super friendly and laid back. I really think I'm going to enjoy living here."

"That's good."

"Listen, I don't know what your schedule looks like today, but would you have a few minutes, maybe an hour, to walk me through some of these reports? I know you service most of the clients on this list."

I looked around at the pile of paperwork on my desk, but found myself agreeing to come up to his office in twenty minutes.

"Sure, I can squeeze you in."

"It won't be a problem?" Drake questioned in that deep voice of his.

"No, not at all. See you in twenty."

"Great. You're a sweetheart, Miss Logan. I owe you one."

Exactly twenty minutes later, after making a quick trip to the restroom, brushing my teeth, and combing through my thick mane of hair, I was softly knocking at Mr. Collins's closed door.

"Come in."

I slowly opened the door and strolled in. Drake was working with an Excel spreadsheet on his PC. He looked up and smiled in my direction. Perfect white teeth. Again, I couldn't get over how utterly gorgeous he was. I simply stared. And he was all man. Solid. Drake carried himself like a man definitely in charge of any situation. I admired that.

"Hi, Kennedy. You're right on time," he stated, looking down at his gold wristwatch.

I still stood near the open door.

"Come on in and close the door because it's been pretty hectic and noisy on the floor today. I don't want us to be disturbed."

"Okay. Sure." I shut the door and was enveloped into his space.

Standing up, he said, "You can take my chair. I'm going to be walking back and forth and pulling files, et cetera. It'll be easier for you to sit and for me to stand."

"Sounds like a plan." I smiled.

I took a seat in his black, soft leather, swivel chair and felt his alluring fragrance and aura completely overtake me. As I made myself comfortable, Drake pulled out a stack of computer printouts and laid them in the center of his elegant cherrywood desk and deposited himself on the edge of the desk, right next to me. With his suit jacket off and the sleeves to his white starched shirt rolled up, it was obvious that he was ready to get down to some serious business.

"Miss Kennedy, what is this mess? I can't make heads or tales out of most of it. There are all these acronyms for everything. Where is a list that explains all the codes?"

I picked up a stack of the paperwork that he was referring to, reviewed them briefly, and started to explain what we were looking at in reference to our clients, their demograph-

ics, bundles, etc. The entire time, I was very aware of Drake being very near me. So close. I could feel the heat rising from his body. I could see the tiny hairs standing up on his arms. Too close for comfort. Definitely.

When he was reviewing the printouts, I used that time to secretly check him out, closer. He had the smoothest brown skin, and his hands were so large, yet smooth. His haircut was perfect, like he had just stepped out of a barber's chair, and the way his eyelashes swooshed over his eyelids was super sexy.

At one point, he stopped looking at the printouts and glanced over at me. For a moment I thought he had caught me staring. I panicked. Coughing, I quickly looked down at the report in front of me.

"What is that delicious perfume you're wearing? It smells wonderful."

"Ellen Tracy."

"Smells nice on you," he said, and went back to examining the trail of paperwork he had laid out in neat stacks on his desk and credenza.

"Thank you."

A couple of times I thought I felt him staring down the low-cut silk blouse that I wore with a straight black skirt and black pumps. From Drake's point of view, he could clearly see my black lace bra and probably could see the swell of my breasts as they rose and fell in his presence with a desire and mind of their own.

"Where is that list of codes?" he asked, looking around at the stacks of reports on his desk.

"There they are, third stack from your right," I explained as we reached for the code sheet at the same time. When his

hand touched my fingers, I experienced cool chills run up and down my arms. I quickly placed my hands back in my lap to steady them.

"Good. This is exactly what I need. Thank you."

"You're welcome."

Running his hand across his head, Drake absently glanced down at his wristwatch.

"You know what? I've kept you long enough today. I didn't realize it was so late, and you haven't even eaten lunch."

"No, but I'm glad to help out any way I can."

"Miss Logan, you've been an incredible help. Unfortunately, we only made it through a quarter of the reports. Can we meet again next week? Say, next Friday at ten o'clock?" he asked, looking at me expectantly. "Is that asking too much?"

"No. That shouldn't be a problem."

"How about penciling in two hours on your calendar?"

"I'll see what I can do."

"If you'd like, I can check with your manager to make sure she's cool with it. Your manager is Peggy Hunt, isn't she?"

"Yes."

"Good. That'll give me the chance to put in a good word for you as well. Let her know what a great asset you've been to me."

"You don't have to do that."

"I know, but I want to," Drake volunteered, with that smile shining bright.

"Thanks, that'll be wonderful."

"Okay then, next week it is. Take care, Miss Logan."

"You too," I said, retrieving my belongings, then opening

the door and heading out with a warm tingling coursing between my legs.

Wednesday of the following week I ran into Drake in the lobby, down by the security desk. He was talking with someone that I vaguely recalled meeting at an interdepartmental business meeting. Drake abruptly ended their conversation, came up behind me and fell in pace with me. The fluttering began again.

"Hi, Miss Logan." He smiled. I loved that smile.

"Hi, Mr. Collins." I grinned back, looking up at him.

"Please. Call me Drake."

"Well, in that case, please call me Kennedy." We grinned at each other again.

"Where are you headed?"

I held up my lunch bag. "Since the women on my floor are seriously tripping today, I decided to sit in the cafeteria with my leftovers from last night and read."

Drake reached to check out the cover of the book I held in my other hand. "Is it good?"

"So far it's excellent. It's by a local Atlanta author."

"Cool, maybe I'll check her out. I love supporting our own local talent."

I nodded.

"I'm headed to lunch as well, but I hate eating alone. Could you do me the honor of joining me?"

"I don't know. I was—"

"I'll even buy. Come on. Say yes. I owe you for all your hard work last week."

"Really, it's not necessary. I was just doing my job."

"I'm not taking no for an answer."

"Okay, sure. Since you put it that way. Why not?" I said as

I left my bagged lunch at the security desk for safekeeping.

"Where would you like to eat, Kennedy?"

"I've overheard my coworkers talking about this recently opened Italian restaurant that's not far from here; it's within walking distance and has delicious lunch specials."

"Excellent. Lead the way," he said, opening the door that led to the busy street.

As we walked the couple of blocks, I noticed the women checking Drake out. He walked with a confident stride.

An hour later, an hour that flew by, I couldn't believe I had laughed, talked, and had such a wonderful time. The food was mouth-watering and the conversation even better. Our conversation wasn't forced; it came natural and easy. As I ate my seafood pasta and Greek salad, Drake had me in stitches over some of his tales of growing up in Los Angeles. His descriptions were so vivid; I felt like I was right there with him. I found myself opening up in ways I never expected. I surprised myself by confiding in him about my dissatisfaction with my current position. He really seemed to understand, and even offered suggestions and advice. A few times I'd look up and find him staring at me. I'd look down and play with a strand of my hair in order to avoid his eyes, which appeared to reach within my soul and seek out my deepest desires.

"May I ask you a personal question?" he asked, suddenly serious.

"Sure, why not? Ask away."

"Are you seeing or dating anyone in particular?"

I paused for only a moment. "No and no."

"That's hard to believe. A beautiful lady like yourself. I'd think you'd have men beating down your front door."

"I'm afraid not," I said, twirling another strand of my hair around and through my middle fingers.

"Why is that?"

"I'm afraid I'm too picky and selective."

"What are you saying? There aren't any good men in Atlanta?"

"If there are, I'm not meeting them."

"Is it true that there's a large and growing gay and lesbian population?"

"That's what I've been told. Atlanta isn't called the new San Francisco for no reason."

"Interesting. You know, you remind me so much of my first love. She was kinda quiet, with your smothering, alluring beauty and innocent sexiness."

I blushed. "Really?" I asked, breaking our eye contact.

"I'm sorry. I shouldn't have said that. That was inappropriate. I apologize if I made you uncomfortable in any way."

"No. I'm fine."

Drake glanced down at his watch. "Man, look at the time. I guess we'd better be getting back before they come looking for us and while we still have jobs." He signaled for the waiter and the check.

"You're absolutely right. My manager demands promptness from our team. I wouldn't want to get on her black list because of tardiness."

He winked conspiratorially. "Don't worry. I'll handle her. If she asks, I'll say we were on a boring business lunch that dragged on."

Drake and I made it back to the building and waited at the first bank of elevators to go up to our floors. The elevator doors opened and a stream of people rushed out. As we stepped in, surprisingly, he and I were the only two people in the elevator. I stood to one side and Drake on the other. There was a comfortable silence that only we could truly appreciate.

"Drake, thanks for the lunch. I see what I'm missing by eating at my desk all the time. I have to get out more and enjoy the Midtown restaurants."

"I definitely enjoyed the meal and the company. See you Friday, Kennedy," he said as we arrived at my floor and I stepped off. "Kennedy?" he called, holding the elevator door open.

"Yes?" I stopped walking and turned around.

"Don't worry. You'll meet that special man soon."

"If you say so."

"I know so." The door shut with me still staring at it and trying to figure out his hidden message.

On Friday, I was back in Drake's office, behind closed doors again. Since Fridays were casual, I was dressed down in a cotton, long-sleeve, button-down shirt and dark navy blue slacks, with my hair pulled back in a ponytail. I was looking more like a college student than a professional businesswoman. But at least I didn't overdo it, like some of the women on my floor who obviously thought Casual Friday meant Nightclub Friday.

Drake had on a tennis shirt embossed with our corporate logo and khaki pants. Even dressed down, the man was all that. He probably looked sexy wearing a sweaty T-shirt and holey shorts while he scratched his butt. Now that I had gotten a better view of those abs, I had an overwhelming urge to reach out and squeeze them. I couldn't deny it—the man was making me crazy.

"Let me get up so you can claim your seat," he laughed, showing those straight white teeth that reminded me of the sexy actor Taye Diggs.

I smiled, somewhat shyly. "Thank you, sir. Good afternoon."

"Oh, let's not go back to that formality. We had a great lunch the other day and I thought all those barriers came down with the meal. Deal?"

"Deal."

As I moved into my assigned seat, we briefly brushed against each other, and my nipples instantly hardened like never before. Drake smelled divine.

"Excuse me," I said, catching my breath.

"Sure. You look nice today. But you always look good."

"Thanks. Are you ready to get started?"

"Yes. But first I want to ask you something."

"Okay." I looked up at him expectantly.

"This is totally not business related, but I feel comfortable around you. I hope you feel the same about me."

I stared at him and searched his face, unsure of what he was going to ask me. I guess he saw uncertainty reflected in my eyes.

"Really, my question is nothing major. I went to Vision nightclub the other night and almost got mobbed by the women there. Are Atlanta women always that aggressive?"

I laughed and exhaled. "I don't know, I guess so, from what I've heard. I don't do the club scene much, but the women in Atlanta are pretty bold. The women-to-men ratio is pretty high, so the competition is fierce and no holds barred."

"I see. Well, curious minds wanted to know. That's all. It's cool. I had women asking me to dance. Wanting to buy me drinks and take me home."

"Welcome to Atlanta."

He didn't say anything, just stared at me.

"What?"

"Nothing. I probably shouldn't say this again, but you are a beautiful woman."

"And thank you again," I said, looking off before Drake saw how flustered he was making me.

"No really, you are gorgeous. Are my comments making you uncomfortable?" he asked, searching my face for answers.

"Of course not. I love being told I'm beautiful by a handsome man," I said, laughing my nervous giggle. I found myself searching for strands of my hair to twist between my fingers. I forgot it was up in a ponytail. So my hand clung and lingered in the air, making me feel foolish.

"You should be used to it by now, Kennedy." His eyes never left my face. Was he still searching for a reaction?

There was an awkward, uncomfortable silence as I felt my face heat up. I shuffled the paperwork on his desktop.

"Well, I guess we need to get to work and earn our paychecks. I only have two of your precious hours, and we still have a lot to cover."

"Let's dig in," I stated, eager to get back to business-related matters. I was more comfortable discussing clients and their needs.

Drake and I worked steadily for over an hour. I typed codes into his PC, and my neck was getting stiff, so I found myself massaging it with my free hand. Without expecting it, Drake came up behind me.

"Got a kink?"

I nodded my head and kept typing.

"Here, let me fix that." He proceeded to firmly but gently knead the muscles of my neck with his large hands. It felt so good that I found myself closing my eyes and reclining back against his expert hand.

"How's that? Better?"

"Much better." I didn't want him to stop.

"Good," he said as his hand inched farther down. I could feel the heat of his fingertips through my thin cotton shirt. He hesitated.

I froze too, stiff as a board. I didn't breathe. Didn't dare to.

"Kennedy, I know this sounds crazy, but I have this overwhelming urge to touch you."

I didn't say anything. I didn't know what to say or do. This man was my superior. With my back to him, I kept staring at the computer screen like it held all the answers. The secret to life. My mind was screaming, Yes, yes, yes, touch me, but my tongue wouldn't verbalize it. I was in conflict because I would be going against my self-imposed work policy. Yet, I'd never had such a strong sexual attraction to any man before. Drake was the complete package: handsome, professional, financially secure, from the looks of it, well-rounded, and sexy. Drake had it all; he was every woman's dream. Even Mother would approve.

"Kennedy?" he said, pressing his hand firmly against my shoulder.

I didn't utter a word. I couldn't. By now my chest was heaving up and down. My mind was screaming for me to stop this madness before it went too far. However, for once in my life I wasn't thinking with my brain.

"Kennedy?" Every time Drake spoke my name, his right hand went down a little farther. Almost there.

"Kennedy, talk to me. Do you want this?" This time his hand made contact. I tensed up and immediately found myself relaxing as his fingers skillfully began caressing my breasts and hard, throbbing nipples. Without realizing it, I leaned into his hand. I embraced his touch.

"Hmmm. You feel so good. Just like I imagined. I dreamed about you the other night." His fingers were kneading firmly, but gently. When he tweaked a nipple between his thumb and forefinger, I swooned.

"Turn around, let me see you." He proceeded to swirl my chair around, and I was flushed. I looked down at the floor.

Drake slowly, gently, lifted my chin back up. "Look at me." His eyes never left mine as he proceeded to unbutton the tiny buttons on my shirt. He took his time. Drawing the anticipation out. I was breathing so deeply, I thought I would hyperventilate and need a brown paper bag to breathe into.

"Drake? I'm not sure about this."

"Sssh. It's okay," he softly whispered, rubbing his index finger sensually across my lips. So light, it felt like a feather.

"Somebody might walk in."

"Kennedy, take a chance. Trust me. They are all at lunch now. Besides, my associates know not to disturb me when my door is closed.

"Beautiful," he said, proceeding to lift up my lacy bra and push it out of the way. My breasts were fully exposed, sitting high, and my nipples were already proudly erect. On display. Beckoning him.

There wasn't any more talking. Drake bent down in

front of me, without my permission, and proceeded to suck my breasts like a starving man. He was definitely a breast man because this went on for about thirty minutes with him sucking, touching, licking, and squeezing them until I moaned out loud several times. Perfect care was given to each breast.

Drake made me feel so good. I held onto the side of my chair and gave into the wonderful sensations as he pulled me near. The only sounds were our breathing, moaning, and his sucking. My nipples were as hard as they had ever been, and every time he tweaked them, I moaned out loud. He didn't touch me anywhere else. Drake didn't even kiss me, only my neck. Showered me with light, delicate kisses. Whispered in my ear. Sucked my breasts some more and tenderly bit down on my nipples. He was on a mission. Finally, he stopped abruptly and stood back up. I couldn't read the blank expression on his face.

"Kennedy, you're a sweet lady. So sweet," he stated, gently cupping my face.

I didn't respond.

He leaned back down and stroked my nipples between his fingers one more time. Had a nipple in each hand, pulling. Again, an involuntary moan of pleasure escaped me as I saw a small smile of victory grace his face.

"That should take the edge off," he said with a sparkle in his eyes. "Listen, why don't we knock off for today. We've accomplished a lot. Let's meet again next week."

"I don't know," I said, swiftly attempting to button up my shirt. Awkward. Tense.

"I've already talked with your manager, and she said I could have you for as long as I need you."

"Did she?" I questioned.

"So, it's settled. Same time next week," he said, sitting on the edge of his desk and intensely watching me as I clumsily fastened the last button on my shirt. My breasts were straining to be free again. To be handled by him.

"Same time, then."

"Sure."

"How you feeling?" he asked, teasing my breasts through the fabric of my blouse and making me light-headed.

"Okay."

"Just okay? Well, I haven't done my job effectively."

"I'm feeling great," I volunteered too eagerly.

"That sounds better. Much better."

Drake was still caressing. Probing. Feeling me up.

"Well, I'd better go." I stood up on weak knees.

"Are you sure?" he asked, towering over me. Still touching me. Hand underneath my shirt. Squeezing. Fondling. Tweaking.

"I'd better get back; I only allocated two hours for this project," I barely managed to get the words out.

Drake had sat back on the edge of his desk, and he stared at me with lust-filled eyes as he gently pulled me to him, within his open legs. I clearly saw the outline of his hard, thick dick. He saw me looking and grinned. I quickly looked away, feeling like I'd been caught by the teacher doing something naughty.

Pressing my hand against his erection, he lowered his head and bit down on each nipple through my shirt, then stated, "If you're sure."

"I'm sure," I managed to mutter. "I have to go." A lump had formed in my throat.

Palming my butt cheeks and pulling me into him, he said, "You have pretty breasts."

"I really have to go."

"Take care, then," he said, pulling down and smoothing out my shirt.

I proceeded to gather my pen, purse, and other belongings. I was totally confused as to what had just happened. I knew what had occurred, but Drake was now acting like nothing was out of the ordinary. He was seated at his desk and writing something on a Post-it note. Oblivious to my departure.

"See you next week," I said, for lack of anything better to say. My trembling hand was on the doorknob.

"And Kennedy?" Drake stated right before I opened the door. He didn't even look up.

"Yes?"

"Next Friday, wear a skirt."

The Seduction Continues . . .

Dear Journal,

After what transpired in Drake's office, I should have run for the high hills. I've never, ever, done anything like that in my life. I can't believe I let it happen. Maybe it was the thrill and excitement, perhaps it was doing things that were not in my character, maybe it was because Drake was my superior, or perhaps it was because Drake brought out a level of sexuality in me that I didn't know existed.

To my credit, I will admit that during the preceding week, I debated back and forth whether I'd show up at the appointed time. To be honest, I could have easily gotten out of it by telling my manager that my workload was too heavy. I purposely avoided Drake by not venturing into our lobby area during lunch, not even to take care of personal mat-

ters. I literally camped out in my cubicle and hoped that he wouldn't call. Every time an internal call came through, I prayed it wasn't Drake.

I was totally confused over what happened. My feelings flip-flopped back and forth. One minute I was flattered that he liked me, the next I wondered did he really like me or did he think I was some sort of whore for what I let him do to me. One thing I was sure of, I was very attracted to Drake. Probably more attracted to him than any other man I had ever met. It didn't help that word had gotten out about him on my floor and my coworkers were constantly making comments about the sexy new manager upstairs and what he could do for them.

Basically, for seven days my mind was in a total state of chaos. My emotions bounced back and forth like a tennis match. When Friday finally arrived, I still wasn't sure what my final decision would be. I had picked up the phone several times to cancel our appointment and make up some excuse as to why I needed to. However, there was just something about Drake that drew me to him. I couldn't stay away until I learned and experienced more.

At my designated time, I found myself taking the elevator up to his floor. As requested, I was dressed in a casual skirt and top. I don't know why Drake made that particular request, but I obliged him. As usual, I knocked on the closed door, heard Drake's sexy voice requesting that I come in. I took two deep breaths, because it was now or never, and stepped into the office of the man who, in the months that followed, I'd blindly love and follow.

"Hi." I smiled timidly. Being in Drake's presence brought out all my insecurities. I always wondered if I looked pretty

enough or was intelligent enough. After all, he could have his pick of women. Why choose me?

"Hey, Kennedy. Give me a minute," he stated in a direct, professional tone. He hadn't even looked up from his paperwork.

"Take your time." In my nervousness, I found myself playing with a strand of my hair and biting down on my bottom lip.

Drake, dressed in a pair of linen pants and button-down shirt, looked very serious today. There was no indication of what had gone down only a week earlier. This day, he was Mr. Professional. I was beginning to think that I'd imagined the entire incident; maybe it was an erotic dream.

He proceeded to pull out the final stack of reports and place it next to me on the desk. We were in our usual position: me sitting at his desk, in his chair, and Drake sitting on the edge of his desk or standing up behind me.

"Looks like we can finally see the light at the end of the tunnel," he said.

"Looks that way."

"Kennedy, you've been a great help."

"Really, I'm just doing my job."

"I must say I'm going to miss your company. Where have you been keeping yourself this week?" Finally. He was giving me his undivided attention.

"What do you mean?" I asked as he walked up behind me and glanced out his window, overlooking the city. Without turning around in my chair, I sensed him checking me out.

"I usually see you in the elevator or catch a glimpse of you in the lobby, but this week I didn't run into you. I looked for

you. Hoped to see you. Seeing you, even for a few seconds, always makes my day. You're a breath of fresh air."

I blushed. "Oh, I've had a lot of paperwork to catch up on and not to mention my growing to-do list."

"Well, I hope I haven't put you behind schedule."

"No, we are unusually busy for this time of the year; this is not the norm."

"This makes me appreciate you helping me out all the more." There was that perfect smile again. I shivered when I thought of those lips nibbling on my neck.

"You're welcome."

By now he had moved and was sitting in the chair across from his desk. The one usually reserved for visitors. For a moment the only sound in the room was our breathing. Self-conscious, I looked down. Drake continued to stare intensely at me.

"I really like you Kennedy Logan. You know that? I could get into you."

I didn't comment; didn't know what to say.

"I know this could be complicated for both of us, but I'd love to see you outside the office. I don't typically mix business and pleasure, but there's something about you that's different, worth breaking the rules for. I can't get you off my mind. I'm seriously feeling you."

"Me either . . . I don't mix business with pleasure."

"Well, we are adults. We can handle this. There are exceptions to everything. Right? Rules are made to be broken."

I didn't respond. My thoughts were racing, bumping, colliding into each other at rapid speed.

"And I'm sure we could be discreet. No one has to know."

I glanced down at my Fossil watch. "We'd better get started. Don't you think?"

Drake glared at me for a few seconds and then he smiled that fabulous, one hundred watt smile. The one that made my heartbeat speed up, my pulse race, and my legs quiver.

"Don't say another word. I understand. Lets get started . . . on this paperwork."

Drake and I worked diligently for the next forty-five minutes or so. I didn't want to see another stack of printouts for a long, long time. We had accomplished quite a bit in a short span. Now, he was joking around and telling me about some of his encounters since coming to work for our company. He had the diction and movements of some of the senior managers down to a science. He had me in stitches with his imitations. I'd never laughed so hard. I told him he missed his calling, he should have been a stand-up comedian on BET. Our mood had quickly switched from business to playful in a matter of minutes. He took me totally off guard when he asked, "Why haven't you mentioned what happened between us?"

I hesitated and crossed my legs. "I don't know, I thought maybe I had imagined the entire thing."

"No, it definitely was real," he stated, looking at me from his spot back on the edge of the desk.

"Oh," was all I could say.

"You are too funny, Kennedy. You've never done anything like that before, have you?" he asked, amused.

"No, I can't say that I have, not in a professional setting anyway."

"See, that's what so refreshing about you. There is so much you haven't experienced. You've lived a sheltered life, Kennedy Logan."

"Well, I don't know if that's good or bad."

"It's not bad. You just need to loosen up and let go sometimes. Don't freak out over everything. Life is too short not to try to experience all it has to offer."

"That's funny, you sound just like my friend, Taylor."

"Well, she's right. We're right," Drake proclaimed proudly.

"I'm not sure I know how to let loose. I'm pretty boring."

"Don't worry. Stick with me. I can show you things, Miss Logan, that you wouldn't believe or couldn't perceive before."

"I bet you can, Mr. Collins," I stated, boldly flirting with him now.

"How old are you?"

"I'm twenty-eight, with a June birthday."

"Oh, so that makes you a Gemini. Y'all love hard–give your all in relationships. See, I'm up to par on astrology."

"You are crazy," I laughed, forgetting where we were.

"Am I? I think I'm a thirty-year-old man who speaks his mind and goes after what he wants. And I want you," he stated, only inches from my face now. I smelled the mint he had only a few minutes earlier popped into his mouth. "I typically get what I want."

"Really?"

"Yes. Really."

With that, Drake came and kneeled down in front of my chair. I noticed the muscles of his thighs expand and bulge against the fabric of his pants. Seconds later, while he cupped my chin and looked deep into my eyes, he moved his other hand from my ankles up to my thighs, taking my skirt with him in one swift swoosh. I instantly closed my eyes and let out a surrendering sigh. I couldn't fight this. When I opened them again, he had my skirt pulled up, showing off my silky red panties as his large hand rubbed and massaged between my open thighs. Already I experienced a warmness spreading and radiating within.

"Pull those off," Drake demanded.

"Pardon me?"

He laughed and repeated himself, "You heard me. Pull those off." Whispering now. "Take off your panties."

"I don't know, Drake, somebody might walk in." I could barely think with him opening my legs and touching me.

"They won't. Trust me. You do trust me, don't you?" His middle finger found my spot, as it slid underneath my panties. Dove in deep. Pulled out and pushed in with two fingers.

I nodded my head. With my eyes never leaving his face, I took a deep breath, stood up and slipped my panties off and dropped them to the floor, then just stood there, not knowing what to do next. With his hands on my shoulders, Drake slowly pushed me back down into his chair. He spread my legs as wide as they'd go and went to work. I allowed him to do whatever with me. I didn't fight him. I didn't protest. I didn't say no. I . . . simply . . . surrendered.

First, he placed his gorgeous face down there and gently rubbed it around. Then his tongue proceeded to do things to me that my mind had only imagined. At one point he had to put his free hand over my mouth to muffle my intense moans. Drake was relentless with his mouth and fingers. He knew exactly what to do to get my body to respond. I was putty in his hands. Mere molding clay. I couldn't move. I couldn't think. I couldn't breathe. I couldn't do anything but come.

For thirty minutes, yes thirty minutes, Drake took me to heaven with his oral pleasure. When he added his fingers to the equation, I thought I'd go out of my freaking mind. Added to the surrealness and excitement was the fact that there was an entire floor of associates and managers, just on the other side of that door, just beyond his closed door, and they had no idea what was going on.

Later, Drake had me wide open, sprawled across his desk, on my back, with my private parts and breasts exposed, in full view for the world to see. At one point I thought I'd die of fright and embarrassment. There was a soft knock at his door, his secretary. I froze. Drake was cool and actually kept pushing his three fingers in and out of my womanhood. Ever so slowly. In and out. Deeper. Slowly.

"Yes?" He pushed in.

"Mr. Collins, I wanted to remind you that I'm leaving early today."

"See you Monday. Have a great weekend, Brenda." He pulled out. His fingers were glistering with my wetness.

"You too."

"I will," he said, inserting another finger, now four. He had me moving up and down to his finger motion as he took me to yet another orgasm while he coaxed me through.

"Yeah. That's it. Let yourself go. That's my girl," he whispered. "Tell me you love the way I make your pussy feel."

I lay back against the desktop, half on, half off, totally exhausted. Waiting for my breathing to return to normal. My chest rapidly heaving up and down.

"Tell me," he whispered near my ear. "It feels good, doesn't it?" His warm breath tickled my ear. I shivered in anticipation over his skillful fingers.

"I love the way you make me feel," I said in a monotone voice.

Drake laughed and said, "I know you do. You are so wet right now. Dripping. You enjoy me eating your pussy? Don't you?"

I remained silent. His fingers were still inside me, moving, teasing me.

"Let me hear you say pussy."

"Nooo," I squeeched.

"Come on," he said, moving his fingers around a bit, exploring. Opening me up.

As another spasm shook my body, I closed my eyes and shook my head.

"Just say, 'I want you to eat my pussy again, Drake,' and I'll leave you alone."

He leaned in closer. Whispered in my ear, "Say, 'Shove your tongue up my wet pussy and make me come.'"

I couldn't say it. He laughed and pulled out his fingers. He held up his index finger, showing it to me, which was drenched with my wetness.

"I bet you've never tasted yourself either, have you?"

He didn't wait for an answer. "Come here," he stated, guiding his finger into my mouth before I could protest. "Lick it off." His eyes held mine. Waiting on me to comply.

I didn't move.

Drake pushed his fingers back inside me and pulled out. "Lick it off, Kennedy."

He gently opened my mouth with his fingers, and I did what he told me. I proceeded to taste myself.

"That's right. Get it all," he demanded, using his free hand to play with my pussy some more, gently squeezing my clit.

"I'm going to enjoy turning you out," he whispered as he caressed my face.

"What?"

"Nothing, baby. Nothing."

With a big smile on my face, I left his office fifteen minutes later. Drake had my phone number, home address, and confirmation for a date on Saturday evening.

Lustful Ways . . .

Dear Journal,

After Drake turned me out orally, it was on. My body had never felt that way before. And we hadn't even had actual sexual intercourse. Imagine that. Yes, I was already whipped. You see, I'm one of those unfortunate women who doesn't have orgasms easily. Sure, I've had small ones before, with a lot of hard work on my partner's part, but never the mind blowing, earth-shattering ones that I hear women talk about all the time.

According to Taylor, she is multiorgasmic and she'll have orgasm on top of orgasm if a man so much as blows in her right ear. It has to be her right ear, not her left one. Well, maybe I'm exaggerating, but she doesn't have a problem. If I can have just one, I am doing great.

When I came in Drake's office chair from just his mouth and fingers, I was like "Damn!" I jumped at the chance to see him over the weekend and find out more about this exciting, mysterious, and sexy man.

Our first date was beyond unbelievable. I felt like Cinderella at the ball with her black prince charming in tow. If I didn't think I was in lust with the man before, by the end of our first date, I knew I definitely was seeing stars and hearing sweet violins playing our song; I was sprung. A night out on the town turned into a two-day date. That was one thing I would learn about Drake, he never did anything halfway. He did everything in a big, dramatic way. Drake was very passionate about everything: his career, his hobbies, his woman.

I thought we were simply going out to the movies and then dinner. Therefore, I dressed in a nice but casual dress and heels. We ended up going to an early dinner out in Buckhead, catching a play at the Fox Theater, and capping the night off by going for a horse and carriage ride through Midtown. It was magical. It was perfect. And then to top off all that excitement and my natural high, Drake had reserved a room for us at the Georgian Terrace Hotel, directly across from the theater. I was totally speechless.

I simply adored this man who was able to so easily take control of any given situation. Drake was a man who took charge, and that excited me in the beginning. I noticed the envious looks women gave me when I went out with him. I didn't care, Drake was my man. And I was his woman . . . or so I thought.

* * *

Our room came complete with a Jacuzzi, king-size bed, colorful flowers, expensive champagne, and a great view of the city. Drake didn't forget anything; he attended to the smallest of details. That was impressive. Of course, I hadn't packed an overnight bag, but he came prepared. The man was amazing. He had secretly packed a small suitcase for both of us that he had hidden in the trunk of his car. He bought a toothbrush, toothpaste, and other essentials for me. He even purchased a sexy purple teddy, his favorite color, for me to sleep in. Not that it stayed on very long.

That night, Drake and I ordered room service after deciding to have a midnight snack of assorted cheese and crackers, and we sipped on chilled champagne. Drake gave what I thought was a heartfelt toast to having me in his life. Afterward, he didn't rush to get me in bed or attempt to get intimate with me. We actually cuddled on the cozy bed and talked. With my head on his stomach, I learned quite a bit about his upbringing.

Drake had been given a lot on a silver platter. Don't get me wrong. He worked hard for everything he received, but his parents owned a sports apparel manufacturing plant in Los Angeles. Money wasn't an issue for them. He grew up with his mother, father, and a brother. He attended private schools, excelled academically and in sports, and dated girls from affluent families. His family even owned a summer home. After graduating from an Ivy League college and working for the family-owned business for a few years, he wanted to branch out on his own for a change. Be his own man. Test his wings. He'd heard so much about the A-T-L that it was his first choice.

Literally, as the sun was rising over the city, he made the most delicious, sweetest love. Slow and easy. I felt Drake down to my soul. He made me understand and appreciate the meaning of feeling like a woman. With every touch, I grew to crave him. He made love to my entire body, mind, and soul. Drake didn't rush; he reveled in loving and caressing every inch of me. He asked what felt good. He watched to gauge my reaction to things he did to me. Drake wanted to possess me. I wanted him to love me. And love and possession don't mix . . .

By Saturday morning we were so tired that we slept, wrapped in each other's arms, until almost noon. I never imagined being so safe and protected. After I woke up to tender kisses, we made love two more times, took our showers, and had a light lunch in one of the restaurants downstairs. The salmon salad with iced tea was excellent. After checkout, we weren't ready to part company, so we rode out to Lenox Mall and shopped for a couple of hours. We giggled, held hands, and French kissed like two teenagers. Drake bought me a gorgeous Coach bag. It didn't matter that the price tag was almost $750; he didn't bat an eye at the price. When he declared that he had to have his woman dressed to the nines, I beamed because I knew he was claiming me as his woman. He had already claimed and tamed my pussy.

Yeah, that was the best date ever! It was perfect. Unfortunately, Drake wasn't. Not by a long shot. However, it took months for me to discover that tidbit of information. That revelation would have saved me so much heartache and pain. Looking back, the signs were there. Hindsight really is twenty-twenty.

Before the Storm . . .

Dear Journal,

"Kennedy, I could stay like this forever," Drake whispered, leaning down and kissing me on the forehead. His body was warm and solid. I felt protected, secure, and wanted.

"Me too," I barely answered with closed eyes. I was still coming off my high. We had made love and I was relishing the moments before the sweetness fled into the darkness and cover of night. Candlelight flickered off the walls in my bedroom, creating strange shadows in their wake. And there was a strong and strange mixture of berries and sex that clung to the air.

Drake was slowly tracing his fingers up and down my arm. Each touch sent shivers throughout my being. And lying, wrapped in his arms, I felt happy.

"How you feeling?" he asked.

"Great, babe, as always. You?"

"Satisfied."

"I love you, babe."

"Ditto."

"Ditto? What does that mean?"

"You're special to me. You know that, Kennedy." Still tracing patterns on my arm.

"Special?" I questioned with a pout.

"I've dated a lot of women in my past, but you—you are, by a long shot, different and very special."

"How many are a lot of women?" I asked jokingly, but curious at the same time. I rose up on one elbow so I could see his face.

"Oh, come on, Kennedy, I've told you of my past. I've never had a problem meeting women. Women are always throwing themselves and their pussy at me. You are with me now. So, it doesn't matter how many," he said, slightly agitated. The candlelight cast dark, contorted shadows across his face.

"You're right, babe," I crooned, relaxing back into his arms.

"Wait a minute. Different? Is that good or bad?" I laughed, pulling myself up to look into his eyes again. Drake had the sexiest eyes. A woman could get lost in them, and before she knew it, she could simply drown. Sometimes I felt like I was drowning in his presence. I couldn't breathe or catch my breath.

"Baby, of course, different in a good way. It couldn't possibly be in a bad way."

"How am I different, babe?"

"You really want to know?" he asked, absently cupping my breast in his hand.

"Yes. I really want to know," I laughed on a natural high. The moment was perfect. A light rain had started to fall outside, and my apartment was warm and cozy on the inside.

"Well, for one, you don't try to be the man."

"What?" I laughed. "You're joking."

"You know what I mean. There are so many women who are kidding themselves and thinking that they can do it all, have it all, all without a man."

"What is wrong with that?"

"Baby, a man wants his woman to need him. He doesn't want to feel like he's not wanted or appreciated or needed. There can only be one leader in a relationship. The man."

"I see." I was hearing this theory for the first time.

"Women in Atlanta are notorious for that type of bullshit, feminist attitude. I don't need a man; a man can't do anything for me that I can't do myself . . . Bullshit! Then why are they at the club with a dress on two sizes too small showing all their ass, leaving absolutely nothing to the imagination? Why are they always in search of some dick? Answer that. Well, you aren't like that."

"Are you saying I'm not independent?"

"No, baby. I'm saying you act like a woman. You are content with letting me be your man. Your girl Taylor could learn from you too."

"What? How did Taylor get brought into this conversation?"

"I don't care for Taylor, and it's obvious that she doesn't care for me either. Taylor thinks her shit don't stink."

"I wish the two of you would try to get along. She's my best friend and you're my man. I don't want to be caught in the middle."

"I don't like her putting crazy ideas into your pretty head. I like the way things have gone with us these last few months, and I just don't want anyone to destroy that."

"Oh really now?" I said as Drake planted a kiss, then another, on my neck. He knew that was one of my weak spots. The meltdown began.

"Definitely. I like how you let me order for you in restaurants, how you accept my advice and opinions, surrender to me in the bedroom."

"Do you?" I asked while he traced a line up my arm.

"Yes, Miss Logan, I do." He tweaked a nipple between his thumb and forefinger. I moaned loudly.

"And a woman shouldn't be vocal and proactive in achieving her goals?"

"I'm not saying that. I'm simply stating that a real woman should make an effort to please her man and take care of his needs. If I tell you to get down on your knees and suck my dick, I expect you to do it. No questions asked. Again, there can only be one leader in a relationship. That's why Taylor can't keep a man; she thinks she's one."

"You are sounding like a male chauvinist, babe."

For a moment this angry look crossed Drake's face, and just as quickly disappeared. Then he broke into a huge, mischievous grin. He reached for me.

"Call it what you want, now come here and surrender to me again," he said as his hand found the warm place between my legs. "Dance for me."

"What? Dance for you? Are you serious?"

"Yeah. Don't I look serious? Stand up and do a strip tease for your man."

"No, I don't think so."

"Come on, just a small one," he said, tugging on my arm to pull me into a standing position.

"I don't know," I said, pulling the sheet tighter around me.

"I thought you loved me."

"I do."

"Well then, do this for me. Kennedy, it's just you and me here. We are behind closed doors, and I thought you were my woman."

"Okay, but just a little one," I said, motioning with my fingers.

"Just a little one, then," Drake stated, assaulting my neck with kisses.

I hesitated.

"Okay, let's see what you got," he said, placing his hands behind his head and leaning back against his pillow, waiting for the show.

I shyly released the sheet and stood up in all my glory. Slowly, I started moving around, doing a belly dancer type routine. Drake was taking it all in.

"That's it. Lower your hands so I can see those gorgeous tatas. You know I'm a breast man."

I continued to dance as I slowly lowered my hands, then raised them above my head, twirling my fingers in midair.

"Yeah. Nice. Show me my titties. Turn around, slowly. Tease me . . . Not too fast. Now, touch yourself for me, baby."

"What?"

"Touch yourself. Play with your breasts and nipples. Real slow. We got all night."

I paused for just a moment. Drake's lust-filled eyes never left mine.

"Yeah, squeeze your nipple. A little harder. The other one. Harder. Make 'em stand at attention for me. Salute me."

"Drake?"

"Shhh, you're doing great. Now, keep one hand on your breast and move your other hand down between your thighs."

"I don't know."

"Come on. Right now, you are sexy as hell. You got my dick hard as bricks . . . That's right. Don't stop; touch yourself. Stick two of your fingers in. Deeper. Pull 'em out. Back in. In. Out.

"Look at you. Yeah, you're getting good and wet for me.

"Moan for me.

"Keep stroking. Stick your fingers all the way in. Do it harder. Faster. Open your legs wider."

With my eyes closed, head thrown back, my breathing was getting more erratic.

"That's my girl. Get yourself off. Get yours.

"Come here, let me taste you," he said, sticking my fingers in his mouth and sucking. "Hmm, finger lickin' good. Delicious. Come here," he said again, this time pulling me down onto the bed, on top of him.

Drake entered me quickly and roughly, a sigh of surprise escaping me. Tonight we weren't making love; tonight was fuck night. We had those too, just like costume night. Drake was going to fuck me unmercifully as he frantically gripped and maneuvered my hips up and down to the steady, rhyth-

mic beat of his relentless dick. With every thrust of his rod, my womanhood eagerly anticipated and accepted the next.

Later, still not sated, he smacked my butt as he leaned me over a chair and entered me from behind, pulling me into him as he bit down on my neck and gave me all he had. Over and over.

Smack! *"Work that ass."*

Smack! *"Take this dick."*

Smack! *"Open that pussy up for me. That's right." Pushing my legs open with his knees.*

Ohhh. Ahhh. Ohhh.

"Yeah. You like this dick, don't you?"

Smack! *"Don't you?"*

"Ohhh, yes, babe."

"You ready to come? You almost there?"

"Ohhh. Yeah."

"Come on this dick."

"Ohhh. Ohhh. Oh . . . my . . . God."

"Yeah, this is mine. My pussy."

It's Over . . .

Dear Journal,

Sometimes I close my eyes and dream of the day when Drake will love me. However, it's just that, a dream . . . a carefully crafted illusion. I used to think I needed him next to me. Sometimes, I craved him so much I couldn't sleep at night. Thoughts of him kept me at full alert. Drake was my natural high.

Now, that's never going to happen–Drake loving me. There are situations and events that occur in one's life that never allow you to go back. There aren't any "what ifs," "buts," or "ands." Some things are totally unforgettable, unacceptable, and unforgivable. In some situations saying "I'm sorry" is simply not enough. Not good enough. The only feasible solution is to go your own, separate ways because hate is your constant companion.

We were once happy, though, at least I was. I'll admit that. Drake, I think he was happy with me. At first anyway. There were many smiles, gentle moments in time, sincere mutterings of truths. I hope everything wasn't a lie. However, I know, once you tell one lie, you have to continue to keep up with the first one. Eventually, your reality becomes based on myriad lies on top of lies, and that's no way to live. You're simply existing under an illusion of untruths.

I figured out, much too late, that Drake is all about the chase. The thrill of the game. He gets off making women love him. That gives him an adrenaline rush. Once that's accomplished, he's gone . . . like a thief in the night. Game over. He is very competitive by nature. Love, just like business, is all about dividing, conquering, and winning. Once it's accomplished, it's another notch on his belt. Another line or two on his glorious résumé. Broken hearts his souvenir.

Drake realizes he is a very attractive, gorgeous, charming man, and most women's fantasy. He uses that to his advantage. He has cultivated it to an exact science that turns women to putty in his strong hands, and then he attempts to mold and sculpture that clay to his heart's desire.

So yes, in the beginning we were happy. Very happy. Drake wouldn't have had it any other way. It was all part of the illusion he expertly crafted. In order to love him, you have to be happy first. And believe me, Drake knows how to make a woman feel special and desired. Special, intimate dinners, weekly deliveries of fresh fragrant flowers, luxurious weekend getaways, whispered promises during midnight phone calls, "just because" cards that speak of love and devotion; these were all part of that total facade to make one love him. He succeeded.

I thought Drake was the one who could make my life complete. Now, I think that whole concept is totally ludicrous and I was crazy for thinking it. Neither Drake nor anyone else can make my life complete. I have to do that for myself. I didn't come to this realization overnight; I won't give myself that much credit. It took a near fatal mistake, reflecting, and growing up.

Looking back, I was at Drake's beck and call. I'd drop everything to be with him. My family, friends, even myself, played second fiddle to Drake. I used to upset Taylor so much when I'd break an outing with her to be with Drake. All Drake had to say was jump, and I'd ask how high. I had no shame. Drake became my entire world, and that's when he became dangerous to my soul and well-being. Never make a man your entire world! Don't give him that power.

The Aftermath . . .

"Hey, I'm in the lobby. Come on down, girl. I'm starving," Taylor screamed into the phone, hanging up before I could manage more than a simple greeting.

"I'll be right down," I said to a dead line.

Today was Valentine's Day, and I almost didn't come to work. I seriously contemplated calling in sick. I didn't feel like seeing my coworkers' cubicles overflowing with beautiful red roses or hearing them boast about what their boyfriends or husbands were doing for them or taking them for Valentine's Day. It seemed everyone was in a relationship or had that special someone in their life to love and adore them, but me. I had no one. I was all alone. Drake was history. After what went down.

Even Taylor, who went through men like ruined and discarded stockings, had been dating this one guy on a regular basis. Regular for Taylor meant for more than a month. I have to admit, I was more than a bit jealous. Sometimes, I wished I were more like her. Taylor was outgoing, chipper, and gorgeous. I don't think she ever met anyone who wasn't a friend. She was the type of person who would strike up a conversation in an elevator with a complete stranger, while most of us would stare at the ceiling or the doors and wait for them to open. She'd walk out of the elevator with a phone number and plans to hook up later at happy hour.

After making it down to the lobby, stepping off the elevator and glancing toward the gold and black security desk, I spotted Taylor right away. She wasn't hard to miss. With a dress that was fierce, but not too sexy for work, she was dressed from head to toe in red. She had on red shoes with straps that enclosed her ankles, which I'm sure cost her a small fortune.

Her long brown hair was pulled back off her face and cascaded in waves down her back. Taylor would tell you in a minute that her hair wasn't a weave either. Don't even think it. Resembling a young Janet Jackson, she looked gorgeous. However, Taylor always looked great, like she just stepped off the pages of a fashion magazine or perhaps a catwalk in Paris.

The thin and very married security guard closest to her was trying to check her out without being too obvious. Taylor was so busy checking her lipstick and hair in her small compact that she didn't even notice him. Yet, all the men passing by noticed her and gave admiring stares and no doubt wished they'd be lucky enough to spend even one night with her.

After putting her compact away, she looked up and spotted me. Instantly, a huge smile spread across her face. A smile that lit up her deep dimples. Her happiness made me grin, and I momentarily forgot my situation. Taylor met me halfway and linked her left arm through my right one.

"Hey, sweetie," she said, giving me a quick kiss on the cheek. "Happy Valentine's Day."

"Is it? I wouldn't know."

"Oh, Kennedy, come on. It's not that bad. Today is just another day. A day for big corporations to make money off of the buying public who get caught up in yet another holiday. Next month it will be Easter."

"That's easy for you to say. I bet your new boyfriend, what's his name, hooked you up."

Taylor didn't say anything, just continued confidently walking toward the revolving doors to the outside.

"Well?" I asked, stopping halfway out the door.

"Okay, Kennedy, I did receive some flowers. But so what?"

"Someone in the world cares about you. That's what."

"I care about you, and so do your parents."

"Thanks, but it's just not the same," I declared, walking outside.

"Well, I'm going to put a smile on that pretty face of yours if it kills me. What do you want to eat?"

"I don't care. Food is food. I'll go wherever you want to."

"See what I mean? K, you have to start making decisions. Quit being so indecisive. That's why Drake bossed you around."

"Whatever."

"I'm treating you to lunch. I haven't seen you in weeks, and here you are, acting funky. Snap out of it."

"Well, thanks a lot. We can't all be the charming, sexy lady in red," I stated sarcastically.

"What am I going to do with you?"

I rolled my eyes upward. Before I could answer, Taylor was off on another tirade.

"Since you can't decide, I'll choose for us. Let's do Mick's for lunch. I've been feening for some of their chocolate chip cheesecake; I haven't had any in months."

"It doesn't matter. Sounds good to me."

"Okay, cool. Let's do it. Ooh, I'm so happy to see you," she declared, squeezing me into a gentle hug.

As we walked the couple of blocks up to Mick's, Taylor was a complete chatterbox. I couldn't help but notice the appreciative glances and outright stares that were directed our way. Whenever Taylor and I hung out, men seemed to come out of the woodwork like roaches. I couldn't remember a time we'd ever had to buy ourselves drinks in the clubs. As for Taylor, I couldn't recall when she didn't have a man she was dating or one or two waiting in the wings. I met plenty of men, but I guess my personality spoke volumes for me. Men saw me as standoffish, and I wasn't into dating every Jamal, Brandon, and Malik who asked me out. I was looking for quality, not quantity. Taylor, on the other hand, was following her mother's example. By the time I met her, Taylor's mother had already gone through four husbands.

"Here we are. Crowded as usual, just as we expected," Taylor said, opening the door for us to enter. The noise level, as always, was in maximum overdrive. We had to nearly scream to hear what each other was saying.

"Table for two, nonsmoking," she requested of the friendly waiter dressed in black and white.

Taylor and I were in luck because we were immediately led to a booth, near the kitchen, over in the corner of the busy restaurant. I didn't have to study the menu since I had eaten at Mick's on numerous occasions, but I pretended to check out the selections to shield myself from her scrutiny and pending questions. As I pretended to peruse the menu, I could feel her eyes on me.

"Well, friend, what's up? Looks like you've lost some weight," Taylor said, carefully looking me over.

"Have I? I haven't noticed." Actually, I had, since my clothes were too loose, but Taylor didn't need to know all that. I knew it was only a matter of time before the fifty questions began.

"And don't tell me nothing's up because I know better."

"I'm sorry to disappoint you, but nothing is up."

"Kennedy, I've been your best friend for how many years? I know when something is bothering you," she said, squeezing my hand across the table. "I love you. When you hurt, I hurt."

After hearing the sincerity in her voice, I had to close my eyes shut because I longed to tell her everything that was wrong in my world. I wanted to inform her of my unhappiness with myself and my failed relationship with Drake. I longed for her to know of my attempted suicide and how Mother was smothering me with her unwavering love and devotion. Living down in Florida, after their divorce, Daddy was not aware of what happened.

I ached to ask why I couldn't find love, only sorrow, and to ask why my life wasn't going the way I wanted it to go. I yearned to tell her how I daydreamed about finding my birth mother and asking her why she gave me up. There was so much I desperately needed to share with Taylor as she sat there with her perfect manicure, expertly lined MAC lips, beautifully coiffed hair. But, I didn't; I couldn't.

I lied and told her half-truths because the real truth hurt too deeply. My truths weren't pretty, and I wanted to be pretty in her eyes. I didn't want to disappoint Taylor or take the smile from her lips. Her smile let me know that there was joy in life. It wasn't impossible.

"Taylor, so much is going on. It would take three lunches to discuss everything."

"I have time. I have all the time in the world for you, K."

"I know and I appreciate it."

"Girl, is Drake still bothering you?"

At first I didn't speak. I just looked ahead of me and stared at the wall. I hated that I had shared details the other night on the phone of how he'd harassed me after our breakup. Driving by, calling me. Making my life a living hell . . . after all that happened.

"Well, is he?" Taylor asked impatiently.

I had to let some of my confusion out. "Not lately. But I can't get him off my mind. I have a love-hate relationship playing out in my head and heart. I despise how he treated me, which is what caused our relationship to end; yet I still love him when I think of all the good times we shared. And yes, Taylor, we did share many wonderful times," I declared, staring at her and praying that she'd understand where I was coming from.

"I know, sweetie. I'm sure you did. I know you are hurting now, but there are more fish in the sea if you'd only give them a chance. Drake wasn't the one. He wasn't right for you. He was more like a piranha. I sensed that. I don't know what happened to permanently end your relationship, but I assume you will tell me in time. I'm just glad he's out of your life. For good."

"Yeah, you're right."

"What can I do? What can I do to help?"

"Nothing. I just need time to see where I wanna be."

"Take it. Take that time."

I didn't say anything, just looked up as our waiter approached the table with pen and pad in hand.

"Are you lovely ladies ready to order?"

Taylor answered for us. "Yes. I think we are."

We placed our orders and settled into a comfortable silence, as friends do.

"Kennedy, you know I don't usually get involved in your love life."

"Since when?"

"I want to discuss Drake. You know I don't like how he treated you."

"Here we go again."

"Yes, here we go again. When you love someone, you just don't treat them bad."

"He is no longer in my life. Between you and Mother, y'all are driving me crazy over Drake Collins."

"Well, maybe you should listen to us. Underneath all that bullshit charm and good looks, he is an arrogant, conniving, good for nothing, lowlife. I think he secretly hates women," Taylor exclaimed in her usual animated way, with hands and hair flying all over the place.

"You really don't like him do you?" I asked with a genuine smile on my face.

"No, I don't, and I don't feel that you—" Taylor stopped in midsentence when she realized I was making fun of her.

We laughed for a good two minutes.

For the remainder of lunch my mood soared. It was good to be back in Taylor's presence. Her aura was so positive and full of intoxicating energy. She was perfect for her role as an account executive over at Coca-Cola.

"Are we still going away in June?" she asked out of the blue.

"I don't know."

"What do you mean you don't know? We can't break with tradition."

"Well, yeah, I guess you're right. I'm going."

"Oh, oh. And we have to go shopping for swimwear."

"I'll wear my suit from last year."

"No. We have to pick out something new and sexy. Something

that will make the men fall out of their lounge chairs with their tongues dragging the ground."

"Maybe I don't want them falling out of their chairs over me."

"K, you are no fun. That's the thrill—to see how stupid and juvenile they act just to see a little ass and cleavage."

"That's your idea of fun?"

"Yes. I'm seriously thinking about writing a book called '1001 Stupid Men Tricks.' I've seen enough dumb shit at the clubs to fill up two books."

"I wouldn't have enough material for a quarter of a book."

"K, you've got to get out more and be more observant. You've never noticed how you can bat your long eyelashes, toss your hair, and just look at men with those big innocent eyes, and they'll be at your beck and call . . ." With that, Taylor was into chatterbox mode again. I listened for a few more minutes before my attention span floated away.

For as long as I could remember, Taylor and I always went away the second week in June. It was a tradition we started right after college. We'd do the girl thing, pack our swimsuits and sunscreen, and head off for a wonderful week full of fun and sun. We always rebond during those times, and I realize what a true and real friend Taylor is to me. We have some really deep conversations, and of course, we party!

Our waiter brought our meals and drinks to the table and went to greet new customers who were seated at his other stations.

"Sweetie, how's your salad?" Taylor asked, digging into her lunch with gusto.

"It's good."

"Well, you're not eating like it's good. You are barely touching your food. We've got to get those pounds back on you."

"Yes, Mother."

"Men don't like twigs. A sistah got to have some meat to hold onto."

"Yes, Mother. I hear you, Mother."

Taylor gave me this look like she wanted to say something but then stopped.

After taking a long lunch, I was actually feeling better. Taylor is good for me. She had me cracking up with her antics and good nature. At one point she was feeding me pieces of my grilled chicken Caesar salad with her fork.

"Come on, open up. Here comes the choo choo. Oh, I forgot to ask you, how's your Coke?"

"Delicious, ice cold, and packed full of caffeine."

"Good. Well, let's make a toast to Drake."

We held our glasses up and clicked. Taylor had witnessed Drake's tirades on me drinking Cokes. I'd come to realize it wasn't an issue of my health; it was an issue of control with Drake.

"Good riddance."

"Ditto."

We were laughing our heads off. Being silly. It felt good to laugh. In passing, our waiter asked if we'd slipped some liquor into our cherry sodas. We giggled some more. But like they say, all good things must come to an end. I glanced down at my watch and realized I had overstayed my lunch hour, and my desk held tons of paperwork that was calling my name.

Suddenly, I noticed the atmosphere at our table had changed. It became ice cold. I looked up at Taylor and saw her staring toward the entrance. Since my back was to the door, I turned in my seat to see what had stolen her attention and evidently her good mood as well.

I froze and my hands literally started shaking as Drake's eyes met mine. I could see the familiar specks of green dancing in his pupils. Taylor sensed my immediate distress.

"Calm down, Kennedy. Be cool. We can leave," she whispered between clenched teeth.

"Yeah, let's go. Now," I barely muttered.

"Shit. His ass showing up made me miss getting my slice of cheesecake," Taylor nearly screamed in anger.

As she attempted to pay the check and leave a tip, Drake approached our table with a huge smirk on his face. He was looking as handsome as ever in his gray pin-striped suit, and it looked like he had gotten some sun because his skin tone was radiant. He didn't look like a man who was pining over his woman or the loss of a doomed relationship.

"Hello, ladies. You two are a sight for sore eyes. Two beautiful ladies at one table."

Taylor answered. "I wish I could say the same because my eyes have seen enough."

"Taylor, how are you? Good to see you too," he said sarcastically. "I see your attitude hasn't changed."

"No. Still not willing to let you treat me like a second-class citizen."

Drake ignored her and directed his full attention on me.

"Happy Valentine's Day, Kennedy. I started to send you some flowers, but then I remembered how you kicked me to the curb. You and I must talk," he stated, reaching over to touch my left shoulder.

"Don't! Don't touch me! Don't you ever place your hands on me again!" I managed to utter through clenched teeth as I pulled away.

"You heard the lady!" Taylor screamed, pushing Drake out of the way and making her way from our table.

Following her, I sideswiped people in my path and was almost out the front door when I barely heard Drake call out, "Kennedy, we will talk. You can't run from me forever." When I glanced back, our waiter and Drake were staring at us. There was amusement on Drake's face and disbelief on our waiter's.

On our walk back to my building, Taylor managed to calm me down a little.

"K, don't give that man your power. I don't know what went down with you guys, but Drake is obviously getting joy out of your pain. Don't let him. Don't give him the satisfaction."

"All I did was love that man. That's all."

"I know, sweetie, but sometimes love isn't enough. He'll miss you one day. He'll realize what he lost in you, and you'll understand what you have to offer a *real* man. In time your heart will heal and you won't feel so sad."

We made it back to the front of my building, and all I wanted to do was walk the two blocks to my car and drive home.

"Listen, K," Taylor said. "Call me if you need me. I have a two o'clock meeting, but I should be at my desk after three o'clock, no later than three-fifteen."

"I will."

"I mean it. Call me."

"Thanks for lunch."

"K, you are gonna be all right. Time heals all wounds. That and a new man with a big dick." She laughed. I didn't.

As I headed into the building, I didn't look back. I tried to walk tall and confident. If I turned around, Taylor would see the beginnings of tears forming in my eyes. I didn't want her to see how weak I was. I used the ride up in the elevator to mentally compose myself. I somehow made it through work for the rest of the day and managed to make it safe and sound through rush hour traffic.

All I could think about was my bed; it was my single focus. As soon as I entered my apartment, I left a track of clothes down the hallway. I stayed up long enough to write an entry in my journal before I was in bed with the covers pulled tightly over my head. I wrote:

Dear Journal,

Today was not a very good day. In fact, today was one of the worst in a while. When I saw Drake at Mick's, I wanted to die again. With him standing there, gloating down at me, I felt smaller than minuscule. I hate that man. I despise him so much. What does he want to talk about? There's nothing more to say. We are history, kaput, done! After what he did, there's nothing more to discuss. I hate him for that.

Happy Valentine's Day. Yeah, right.

I recalled another holiday season. It's amazing how a day that started out so normal would turn into my worst nightmare. It was a few days before New Year's Day, a Friday night, and Drake and I had attended a post-Christmas party with some of his friends. I swear, the man had been in Atlanta only briefly, yet he had more friends than I did, and I had lived here all my life. People were naturally drawn to him.

Drake and I had a great time. It was a small, intimate affair. There were about six couples total and we sat around and sipped wine, ate delicious food, played board games, and talked. A real low-key event; just my speed. Drake was very relaxed and especially attentive to my needs.

I drank a bit too much, which was anything over two glasses, but I'd noticed that whenever I was with Drake, he encouraged me to let loose. I knew if I were with him, he'd take care of me and not let anything horrible happen.

I truly enjoyed myself, and no one could have told me that would be the last time Drake and I were together as a couple. We laughed, we cuddled, and we kissed under the live mistletoe. It was a magical evening, and there were even a few snow flurries in the crisp air that added to the magical spell. We left the party around midnight and I convinced him to drive around to look at Christmas lights and decorations before they were taken down.

Drake and I drove around, listened to Christmas music on the radio, laughed and had a great time in the sanctity of his car. It was like it was just he and I in our own little world. We sipped on some hot cider, taken from the party, that was laced with liquor, and I was feeling no pain. I was buzzed, but I didn't care. I felt free and in love. I knew Drake had his imperfections, but I knew he'd change for me. Love could do that . . . change a person. It was almost a new year, with new beginnings.

We arrived back at my apartment a little after one A.M. The apartment was nice and cozy. Without turning on the lights in the living room, I asked Drake to turn on the Christmas lights on my tree while I took a hot shower. I wanted to slip into something sexy, this Frederick's of Hollywood outfit I'd purchased complete with Santa boots. It was Drake's last present that he had to open. Ho! Ho! Ho!

After I couldn't convince him to join me in the shower, I slipped in alone. I turned the water to as hot as I could stand it and placed my face under the shower head and enjoyed the feel of the water streaming down my face. I relived our night together and smiled because it wasn't over yet.

I vaguely heard Drake rambling around in the bedroom and kitchen. He had said that he was going to get the rest of the champagne out of the fridge. We had a leftover bottle from a few days earlier that he'd spent an enormous amount of money on. I stepped out of the shower, layered myself with body lotion and spritz, and slipped on my sexy lingerie. I pinned my hair up on top of my head, pulled on my black and red Santa boot slippers, and walked back into the bedroom.

Drake was already under the covers, completely nude and waiting for me. He reached out his hand, pulled back the covers, and I slipped under after tossing my boots to the floor.

"You are so beautiful. You know that," he stated, propped up on his elbows, caressing my cheek.

"You are too."

He gave me a funny look.

"What? Men can't be beautiful. Well, you are, babe."

"I think you have definitely had too much to drink," he declared.

"You think so?"

"I know so," he said, pulling down my red spaghetti strap and pouring some chilled champagne, from the nightstand, on my nipples.

He proceeded to lick it off, and I proceeded to melt.

"Oh, you like that, huh, Miss Claus?" he asked, searching between my legs to see if I was ready.

I nodded my head.

"Well, Santa has more where that came from."

"Oh really?"

"Have you been a naughty girl? Or a good girl?"

"Good."

"Come here. We'll have to correct that." Drake flipped me over on my stomach and discarded my gown. So much for the $125 I'd spent. He poured champagne in the arch of my back and proceeded to lick and suck it off, all the way down to my buttocks.

That night it was all about me. Drake pleased me from the tip of my toes to the top of my head, and I got to ride his reindeer. Afterward, we lay wrapped in each other's arms with our legs entwined. I let out a pleased, satisfied sigh.

"I could get used to this, babe."

Drake had his eyes closed and his arms wrapped protectively around me.

Silence.

"Did you hear what I said?"

"Shhh. Just relax. Go to sleep," he murmured in a drowsy voice.

Cradled in his arms, the man I loved, I did just that. I dosed off into a peaceful, dream-filled sleep while visions of family, children, and marriage danced through my head. In my sleep-induced state, I vaguely remember Drake getting up to go to the restroom. He was soon back, claiming his rightful spot. Nestled next to me. I quickly dosed back off.

I don't know how much time passed; I was disoriented and shrouded in the throes of deep slumber. I felt Drake gently nudging me and kissing my neck. His hardness pressed against me.

"Babe, go back to sleep," I whispered, reaching behind me to stroke his cheek.

Drake didn't say anything. He continued to spoon with me and caress my breasts. As usual, he knew my nipples were one of my weak spots. He started playing with them, squeezing them between his thumb and forefinger, and I started moaning. Sleep was quickly slipping away. We were still naked from earlier, and I felt the heat rise from his body. I reached back to stroke his erection.

"Oh, I thought you'd like that. I see Rudolph the red-nosed reindeer is awake and ready to drive his sleigh," I teased.

I still had my eyes closed as I continued to stroke him up and down. Fast and then slow. Just like he liked. At some point Drake reached around and inserted three of his fingers inside me. I was already wet and very excited. I turned on my back and spread my legs wider so he could continue to do what he was doing so well. My hand pressed down on his to encourage him not to stop.

I wanted him then. He could forget foreplay. I needed to feel him inside me, again. Drake had other ideas, because when I tried to mount him, he stopped me and pulled my head down near his lap. Through the darkness of the room, he looked at me and smiled. I knew what he wanted. I went to work with a passion. I licked, sucked, squeezed, and sucked some more. Taking it all in. I'd glance up and see him trying to hold his moans in.

"That's enough for you, you greedy boy," I joked, coming up for air. "It's time for you to eat your supper," I teased.

Through the eerie shadows of my room, Drake looked at me with this strange glow in his eyes.

"Come on babe, go down on me. You know I love that."

Drake went to work; it was his best performance ever. The man had a true talent for going downtown. When I was on the verge of coming, I pushed him off me. I wanted to feel that delicious dick inside me before I came.

Drake was more than ready to oblige. He eased me onto all fours and slowly eased himself inside me. I was taken back for a moment because he felt larger or wider or something that I couldn't quite put my finger on. His thrusts felt like they were coming out my stomach. They had never felt that way before, and he smelled different too. I assumed it was the new cologne he had purchased at Belk's.

"Oh, babe. You feel so good."

Drake didn't say anything. He continued to ram me with no mercy. His fingers were clawing at my breasts.

"Babe, slow down. There's more where this came from. Quit being so greedy."

I looked back, and Drake had his undivided attention focused on the task at hand. By now he was usually saying all kinds of nasty shit to me. He loved to talk dirty to me during sex. Instead of turning me off, I'd get super hot. I was pretty verbal now myself, and initially that surprised me, but Drake preferred it that way. That early morning, he was uncharacteristically quiet. Too silent. All I heard from him was his heavy panting.

"Oh babe, your dick is making my pussy feel sooo good. You've got me so hot."

He was still ramming me with no sign of slowing down.

"That's right. Take what's yours. Oh God! You've got me coming! I'mmmmm coming, babe!"

We both came at the same time in hard, forceful, spastic shudders. I felt him shoot hot squirts up inside me. At the exact moment that was happening, I heard a cell phone go off in my closet.

Without an ounce of energy left, I collapsed down on the

bed. At first I thought I was imagining things. I dismissed the sound. But then I heard movement.

"What? What is that? Did you hear that," I asked, crouching on my bed, ready to flee.

Sprawled out on the bed, Drake looked at me in surprise and stared at the closed closet door. Then the door swung wide open and there stood Drake. I looked from one to the other in amazement. There were two Drakes.

"What the hell?" I said, jumping up and trying to hide my nakedness.

Then Drake spoke. The one from the closet entrance. "Calm down, Kennedy."

"What do you mean calm down?" I asked, glancing from him to the Drake on the bed. The one on the bed whose dick was now erect and pointing wickedly at me. "Drake, what's going on?" By now I was crying as the realization of what had occurred was slowly sinking in.

The Drake from the closet closed the gap between us.

"That's my identical twin brother, Blake," he said, pointing to the man now hurriedly pulling on his pants.

"What? Your twin? You let your twin brother fuck me? You bastard! I can't believe this! My God, you're sick!"

"Calm down, Kennedy!" Drake was saying, walking toward me with outstretched hands . . .

The Confrontation . . .

Monday morning came before I knew it or was ready for it. I absolutely hate Monday mornings. They are a constant reminder that I'm a slave to corporate America for at least the next five days. Ugh.

I awoke sweaty and tangled in my sheets, with my comforter on the floor. I had tossed and turned all night in my lonely apartment. Every sound was elevated tenfold. I witnessed every creak and groan of the walls settling. I heard my upstairs neighbor when he arrived home and attended to various household duties. I swear the man is a night owl or a vampire. Who vacuums at ten o'clock at night? Faintly, I could even pick up traffic sounds two streets over, on a major bypass. Around six o'clock A.M., just as I was finally dosing off into a deep, restless sleep, the alarm clock blazed me awake. I lay there for another ten minutes, unable to move the few feet to my bathroom.

I felt horrible, and I didn't look any better, with the heavy, puffy bags concentrated under my eyes. I didn't feel like going into work, but if I didn't, I knew I'd mope around the apartment all day. For some reason, I was afraid to be alone with my random thoughts. So, off to work I went, grumpy and all. If I had known what was coming, I would have stayed at home, in bed.

Around nine o'clock, after I'd finished off my first can of soda, I felt much better. I could feel the caffeine and sugar surging through my veins giving me an instant high. It gave me renewed energy to tackle the never-ending phone calls and pile of work sitting on my desk. In need of a diversion from my issues, I dove in.

At ten o'clock my manager informed me there was an emergency meeting upstairs that I was to attend in her absence. She had another client meeting that couldn't be missed, and since she couldn't be in two places at once, I was her stand-in. My stomach immediately fell to my knees because I knew Drake would be a part of the mandatory meeting. I'd have to be in the same room with him for at least an hour or more. That realization frightened me and made me sick to my stomach.

At first I debated faking illness and leaving for the day, but I couldn't run from him forever. Besides, my manager believed in me and confirmed that I was an asset to the company by sending me to represent our department at an important meeting. Today was the day I'd make a stand and prove I was strong. Drake wanted me to bow down and surrender. I refused.

I arrived upstairs ten minutes before the meeting was to begin. I figured I'd need the additional minutes to pull myself together and psych myself out. Plus, I needed to review the agenda. The friendly administrative assistant informed me where the meeting was to be held. I was one of the first to arrive in the large conference room at the end of the hallway. I spoke to the two other women who were already there and made sure I secured a seat near the middle of the table. I didn't want to be up front, where I knew Drake would be. Yet, I didn't want to entirely disappear at the very back either.

Slowly, different managers started drifting in with cups of freshly brewed coffee and pens and notepads in hand. Drake was one of the last to arrive. For just a quick second, I saw the surprise flash across his face when he saw me seated at the massive table. I looked down at my yellow legal pad and pretended to read my briefing. As always, his presence intoxicated and overwhelmed me.

"Okay, people, let's go ahead and get this meeting started," Drake said, chairing the meeting and looking from one to the other of us. "We all have a lot on our plates today, and I apologize for taking you away from other matters. However, we have a small crisis that needs to be addressed and handled as promptly as possible."

He stood tall and confident as he went on to inform us that one of our major clients was threatening to pull out once their contract ended in a couple of months. This company's bigwigs had complaints of inferior service and poor customer service, among other things, and said they could obtain lower pricing elsewhere. They had been a client for many, many years and brought in an enormous amount of revenue. Everyone seated at the table knew there was no way in hell we could afford to lose them. We had to handle them with kid gloves and come up with a planned resolution; our jobs depended upon it.

Drake skillfully went over the history of our client, revenue figures, and then addressed each complaint. When he came to the customer service piece, he looked directly at me for guidance.

"It appears we have Miss Logan in our presence today. For those of you who don't know her, she's a CSR and very familiar with this particular client. Maybe she can be so kind as to address some of these issues concerning customer service." Then he looked at me again and smiled, knowing he'd put me on the spot. I wasn't prepared. I was simply sitting in for my manager. He knew that.

All eyes turned in my direction for clarification and understanding. I felt my face flushing. I swallowed the lump in my throat and gulped.

"Mr. Collins, this is the first time that I've been made aware of these complaints concerning our department. As you know, I'm sitting in for my manager, who had a conflicting appointment. I'll be happy to tag this as a take-away item, investigate, and report back to everyone ASAP."

Drake sat there with this smirk on his face. I wanted to slap it off. Honestly, I just wanted to slap him, period. "Miss Logan, as you know, this is of a most urgent nature. Time is of the utmost importance. Can you shed any light at all on the current situation? And when can we expect to receive your report?"

"Today, by five o'clock."

Not trying to shift blame, I proceeded to explain what little I knew of the situation, starting with high turnover ratios in our department contributing to unusually heavy workloads. Until very recently, several different reps had handled the client's account.

"Very good. Thank you, Miss Logan, for your input," Drake stated, as his eyes looked me up and down. "I'll expect to have that report in my office, in more detail, by five o'clock sharp. Please copy everyone in this room as well."

"Thank you, Mr. Collins," I responded. I was pleased with my comeback in his effort to make me look stupid in front of my colleagues.

"Well, unless there are any more questions or concerns, I suggest we all get back to work, and with your take-aways in hand, be prepared to meet again on Wednesday, same time and place. I'll have my administrative assistant send out an agenda. I would like a manager's meeting scheduled with them by next week. Thank you."

Everyone rose to leave.

"Miss Logan, may I speak with you for a minute, please?"

I wanted to scream out *Hell no,* but controlled myself.

"Sure," was all I said. Drake was now seated at the head of the table. He hadn't looked up again and was reading his notes. By now mostly everyone had filtered out of the room.

"Do you mind closing the door, Miss Logan, so that we may speak privately?"

As I got up to close the door, I could feel his eyes taking me in. Caressing my body. At one time I enjoyed knowing that my man was watching me. Now it made my skin crawl. I stopped myself from scratching. I turned slowly around, didn't make eye contact, walked and sat two seats down from him.

"You did great today. I put you on the spot, but you were quick on your feet. I like the way you didn't tolerate everyone placing total blame on your department for the mess we are in. You are very loyal."

"Loyal to those who deserve it."

Drake laughed and stared at me for a few seconds.

"You look very nice today."

"What do you need to speak with me about?"

"Oh, so now you don't have any manners?"

"You look very nice today."

"Thank you."

Drake reached for my hand. "I've missed you, Kennedy."

I pulled my hand from his reach. "Is that all, Mr. Collins?" I acted as if I hadn't heard his previous comment.

"Did you hear me?"

"Yes, I did. Is that all?"

He chose that moment to move and sit directly next to me. I instantly felt a powerful combination of uneasiness and desire rise from the pit of my stomach. Despite my feelings for him, he was still a very handsome and sexy man. No one could take that away from him. And today, dressed in a black suit with a crisp white shirt, his hair freshly cut and him smelling divine, I couldn't help but notice and wonder how he could look so good on the outside and be so messed up on the inside.

"You are so beautiful. You're all I think about lately. When are you going to forgive me and let bygones be bygones?" He reached over and caressed my face and hair. I froze.

I couldn't believe what he was saying. Let bygones be bygones. Like we'd had a simple argument over something trivial. He was either in denial or totally insane; maybe both.

"How about never? Is that clear enough?"

"You can't mean that. I promise, what happened will never happen again. It was a test."

"If that's all, I have to get back to my desk. I have a report to deliver by five. Sharp." I stood to leave.

He roughly grabbed my arm and pushed me back down into the chair. "This meeting isn't over. I am your superior, Kennedy, and don't you forget that. I can make your life a living hell. With the economy the way it is, now isn't a good time to search for a new job. Do you understand me?" Then he reached down, boldly placed his hand inside my blouse and fondled my left breast, first gently, then rougher as I attempted to pull away.

I jerked away like I'd been burnt. "What are you doing? Take your hands off me!" I screamed through gritted teeth.

Drake grabbed me by the wrist. "We'll continue this conversation later. Believe that."

"Don't hold your breath!"

"Good day, Miss Logan. Like I said, we'll talk later. Real soon."

"Stay away from me. I mean it or . . ."

"Or you'll what? Go to your manager, who is seriously sweating me, by the way, and tell her that I've been fucking you silly and that you've loved every damn minute of it? I don't think so. Kennedy, you don't air your dirty laundry like that. You're too much of a lady. Well, that's what everyone thinks anyway. I've seen the real Kennedy. The real freak."

"Stop!" I screamed, placing my hands over my ears to block out his words.

"Kennedy, you should know by now that I get what I want. One way or the other. And I want you. And I will have you," he stated, tracing a circle around my nipple through the sheer silk of my blouse.

I slapped his hand away. "Why are you doing this to me?"

"Because I can. If I wanted to, I could have you down on your knees doing what you do best. You want to suck my big dick, Kennedy? You're one of the best; I taught you well. I bet I can even get you to sleep with my brother again. It was a trip watching my twin brother handle his business."

I started to cry softly. "You are sick."

"Don't cry now. You were not crying when Blake was hitting it from behind."

"What man would want to watch another man screw his woman, let alone his own brother?"

"A man who can control his woman. Why not my twin brother? It was like watching myself get busy."

"You're sick," I said again.

"Join the club. When my brother Blake was hitting it right, I didn't see any complaints. You were all into that shit. All over his dick."

"I thought he was you. I didn't even know you had a twin."

"You don't know how your own man moves and feels inside you?" Drake asked with disgust in his eyes.

I shook my head sadly. "I can't believe I thought I loved you. You don't even know the meaning of the word. How could I have been so blind? So misled?"

"At some point in time, y'all all do . . . think you love me. Women always confuse a good fuck with love. I, on the other hand, know that good pussy is just that . . . good pussy. Fix yourself up and get back to work."

With that, Drake turned and readied himself to walk out of the room. Not another word was spoken, but the tension in the air could slice through steel.

After I had composed myself enough to walk out of the conference room, I found the administrative assistant sitting at her desk looking at me curiously. I turned away and kept walking. As I stifled a sniffle, I could feel her eyes boring into my back.

The Finale . . .

It was a little over a week later, after our first impromptu business meeting, that I found myself riding the elevator back upstairs for yet another meeting. My manager had asked me to finish it up, since I started the process, and to report back to her. She claimed that this would be good experience for me. The previous week, I had turned in my findings in a detailed, comprehensive ten-page report. Today was to be a follow-up meeting for all concerned and to tie up loose ends.

As before, I arrived early. Again, I wasn't sure what to expect from Drake after the fiasco last time. I knew I wouldn't and couldn't allow myself to be alone with him. I had thought long and hard about filing sexual harassment charges, but I wasn't sure. I had no doubt Drake would drag our so-called secret affair into the spotlight, and I definitely wasn't ready for that. I was totally confused. I had no clue what I should do or how I should proceed. I just knew my life was in shambles and I had to do something to move forward and reclaim it.

This time when I arrived on the floor, the conference room wasn't empty. Apparently, another meeting was going on, which was expected to end shortly. I stood just outside the door and chatted with the administrative assistant. She was an older black woman, with salt and pepper hair, who I heard had started out as a temp and eventually moved into a permanent position.

"How are you today, Miss Logan?"

"I'm okay, and yourself?" I asked.

"I can't complain. I'm here, I'm alive, and I'm kicking. That's a blessing in itself, wouldn't you say?"

I laughed. That sounded like something Mother would say.

"True."

"Sometimes you young people forget to count your blessings." She winked.

"You might be right."

"I know I am. I have a daughter about your age."

I smiled and looked toward the conference room door. I didn't want a lecture on religion or the state of the younger generation.

"If I may say, you're smart, gorgeous, and seem like a wonderful person who was brought up right."

"Thank you."

"I mean it. Your mother should be very proud of you. I noticed you months ago. You stand out around here because of the way you carry yourself with such grace. You don't gossip and be all up into everyone's business. You have class."

"Thank you," I stated, again glancing back at the conference room.

I noticed the other meeting was ending, as associates walked out the conference room, scattering in different directions. I saw a few familiar faces and I waved.

"I like conversating with young people, and I think they like talking to me because I call it as I see it. I'm real, as you say. For you, I have just one simple piece of advice. Remember, what looks good isn't always pretty," she said, raising her eyebrows.

I opened my mouth to ask her what that meant, but just then Drake and a very lovely woman with legs from here to eternity and a Halle Berry short hairstyle came around the corner. I'd never seen her on the floor before, and I knew all the managers.

"Excuse me," the mystery woman said in a condescending tone as she stuck her nose up at me and walked around me.

I moved out of the way. Drake barely acknowledged me.

"Miss Logan, the meeting is starting in just a few minutes," he stated, looking down at his watch as if I was running late.

I delivered a half smile to the administrative assistant. "I guess that's my clue to go."

"Sure, darling. You take care of yourself," she replied.

"By the way, who was the woman with Mr. Collins?" I asked.

"Oh, that's Miss Reynolds. She started a week ago. Replacing the management slot that was vacated by Mr. Stephenson."

"Umm. I see."

By the time I made it into the conference room, I had to sit closer to the front and to Drake. I vaguely noticed Miss Reynolds glaring at me out of the corner of my eye. I couldn't figure out for the life of me why I was getting strong vibes that she didn't care for me. This from a woman I hadn't even had the opportunity to be formally introduced to or knew existed until a few moments ago.

"Good morning everyone. Today's meeting should be short and

sweet," Drake announced, his eyes lingering on me for a few additional seconds. I noticed Miss Reynolds catching him and openly glaring at me.

"Before we go any further, for those of you who haven't had the opportunity to meet her yet, I'd like to introduce you to Miss Brittany Reynolds. She's one of our new managers."

She waved and stood briefly. "Thank you, Mr. Collins. I look forward to meeting everyone and fostering a productive and meaningful working relationship."

"Okay, let's get down to business. The first item on the agenda is . . ."

The meeting went by quickly, and the good news was that we were able to pacify our client with some modifications on how we handled their account. Bottom line, they were no longer pulling out and our working relationship would continue, hopefully, into infinity.

Throughout the meeting, I noticed a silent communication going on between Drake and Miss Reynolds. It was very subtle, but there nevertheless. I knew it wasn't my imagination because it was how we used to interact with each other in public. I immediately picked up on the vibes.

Finally, the meeting ended and I couldn't wait to get off that floor. I retrieved my notes, purse, and pen, and was trying to slip quietly away. Of course, that wasn't in Drake's plan.

"Miss Logan, have you been formally introduced to Miss Reynolds?" he inquired. He was trying to be funny, and I hated him for it. I knew what was going on. He was messing with me.

I turned around with a plastered smile on my face. Drake and Brittany were standing side by side, looking at me expectantly. "No, I haven't." I reached out my hand. "Good to meet you. I'm Kennedy Logan."

"Brittany Reynolds. Kennedy, what a lovely name."

"Thank you."

"You're one of those customer service reps, aren't you?"

"Yes, I'm one of those." I immediately didn't like her condescending tone.

"I must come down there and check out the team. I haven't been in the trenches in a while." Then she laughed, a shrill, irritating cackle.

"You do that."

"I told Brittany what a wonderful team you and I made behind closed doors, *working* on our project," Drake injected, emphasizing working.

"Did you?" I said, knowing what he was insinuating.

"Well, Drake and I have spent an enormous amount of time behind closed doors as well," Brittany said. "So, your services won't be needed anytime soon. He now has me to handle that role."

"Good for him."

"Drake is showing me the ropes, so to speak," she laughed, daring me to read between the lines.

Heifer! I silently screamed.

"Well, it was nice meeting you. Take care."

"You too, Kendall."

"That's Kennedy."

"Oh, I'm sorry. Of course, Kennedy."

I bet you are. Heifer!

With them not too far behind me, I started to make my exit and escape. I could hear them whispering and laughing behind my back and having too much fun. Yes, they were very comfortable with each other. As much as I despised Drake, I still felt a tinge of jealousy.

Free at Last . . .

Two months later . . .

I prayed. Prayed some more. Then, I called Drake. Called him for the last time. I pushed each digit of his number like I had done hundreds of times before, but slowly. The phone rang and rang and rang with no pickup other than his voice mail. It didn't matter. It was probably for the best. I wanted to get this off my chest and it didn't matter if I told Drake face-to-face, over the phone, or in an impersonal voice mail. Who knew when he would arrive home? He was probably still out partying from the night before or laid up with somebody. I listened to his voice. Closed my eyes to commit it to memory. He always had such a sexy, deep voice. One day he'd miss me and realize how wrong he was. One day he'd be sorry.

My message, which took two phone calls, went like this:

"Drake, I want to inform you that you are not going to intimidate, harass, or threaten me anymore. I'm sick of running. I've prayed about you. Today, I made the decision to fight. If you ever call me, drive by or come by my apartment again, I swear I will call the police and report you. Everything will come out. Everything!

"One day, you'll get yours, because we really do reap what we sow! I deserved so much more from you. I loved you. Thought you were the one. The man of my dreams. Now, I just pity you. I pity you. Don't ever contact me again. I realize you tried to shape me into someone I wasn't, tried to strip away my integrity, but it doesn't matter. You almost succeeded, but not quite, because I'm still standing! Goodbye, Drake."

After hanging up, I felt free. Free like a bird gliding through the sky. I felt like a burden had been released from my shoulders, and when I turned the car radio back on, guess what was playing? "Jesus Walks With Me," by Kanye West. For the remainder of my drive I felt confident that no matter what went down, I knew I could handle it. I was stronger than I thought. I was humiliated, and had almost sacrificed my soul for a man, but I was still standing! A calmness settled over me and I sensed a shroud of protection and love surrounding me. I was at peace.

These are my confessions. . .

ELECTA ROME PARKS, one of the rising stars in contemporary fiction, is the author of the best-selling novels *The Ties That Bind* and *Loose Ends*, which were originally self-published through her own company, Novel Ideal Publishing and Editorial Services Company, a company now dedicated to quality editorial services.

After successfully self-publishing her debut novels, New American Library, a division of Penguin Group, bought the rights. Mrs. Parks signed a three-book deal with New American Library. Her first novel, *The Ties That Bind*, was rereleased in October 2004, and *Loose Ends* was rereleased in November 2004. Both books were immediately chosen as Black Expressions Book Club selections and embraced as Books of the Month by book clubs across the country. A third manuscript, *Almost Doesn't Count*, which was immediately chosen as the main selection for Black Expressions Book Club, was released in August 2005.

Recently, Electa signed her *second* and *third* book deals with Penguin Group/New American Library and HarperCollins/Avon Red. Her upcoming projects are: *Ladies' Night Out* (NAL, January 2007) and *These Are My Confessions* (Avon Red, July 2007).

Electa Rome Parks has been a frequent guest on radio shows. She's been interviewed by newspapers, *Vibe Vixen*, *Upscale Magazine*, *Rolling Out*, and *Booking Matters*, to name just a few. Parks lives outside Atlanta, Georgia, with her husband and two children. With a B.A. degree in marketing and a minor in sociology, she is following her true passion and working on her next novel.

Please contact Electa at *www.electaromeparks.com*.

Strapped

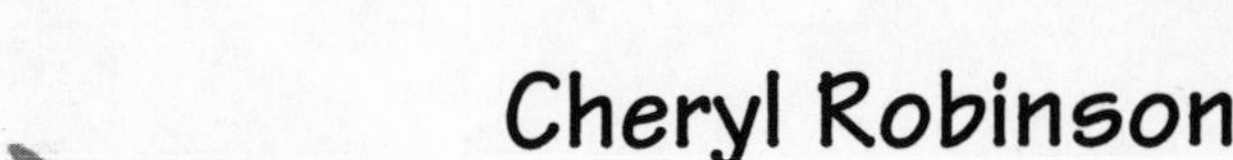

Sex Games

The first man I killed was by accident.

I'd been chatting with him online nearly the entire summer before finally arranging to meet him at Sambuca's, a popular jazz club in the uptown section of Dallas. In his profile, he wrote: I'M INTO PLAYING GAMES, BUT I'M NOT TALKING ABOUT MONOPOLY. During our first of a series of phone conversations, he shared with me that his fantasy was more of a fetish. He wanted to be choked as he was getting ready to come. He said that a woman could use her hands, but he preferred a thin black leather belt to be tightened around his neck for a few seconds just until he went unconscious. To me, it sounded like a dangerous game, but he'd had this done to him before . . . many times . . . and the sensation, he said, was indescribable.

Initially, I had my reservations, which is why I'd decided to meet another man instead, but when things didn't work out with him, I called Lester. I hated his name but I loved his deep and sexy voice. Something as simple as the way he said my name made my pussy wet, and the things he said to me while I was on my way to meet him almost caused me to have an accident.

"You want me to fuck you deep and hard, don't you? I just hope you can handle my big dick, otherwise I might bust your juicy pussy wide open."

I started squirming in the seat of my car from the anticipation. "Are you really strapped?"

"Strapped?" he asked, laughing. "I got a ten inch dick. How big do you need it?"

"The bigger, the wetter; the bigger your dick is the wetter my pussy will be."

Neither of us had a picture attached to our online profiles, so the mystery of how he'd look in person, wondering whether or not he'd truly have what I wanted, and whether he'd find me sexy, quickly turned into my own fantasy. I wanted to know if it was really true that *everything* was bigger in Texas, and was bigger really better.

Quiet as I've always kept it, I do think about having sex just as much if not more than most men. But the men I'd been with didn't have what I wanted. I wasn't asking for a dick that was so big it could be confused with being a third leg; a solid seven inches would do just fine, I'm sure. But if I lucked up on more, like ten inches, I definitely wouldn't turn it down. So after my devastating breakup with my fiancé of three years, I set myself on a mission while on my summer vacation—to find just that, a big dick. Better to get loose in Dallas, a city where I'm completely unknown and detached, than in my hometown of Detroit, where I live and work.

For nearly an hour, I waited at the bar for Lester, sipping on chocolate martinis that were being generously supplied to me by a secret admirer whom I had yet to see. My mind started to drift into a fantasy of being loved, just not with the heart. I'd had that many times before, or so I thought. Words—I couldn't trust. But could I make love to a man without being in love? Could I fuck him? I thought so. I wanted to be someone other than who I'd always been, someone other than a stiff middle school teacher who pulled her hair back into a puffy ponytail and hid behind a pair of granny glasses and ruffled blouses buttoned all the way to the top. But I had to change, not just how I looked, but how I received pleasure. The next time I slept with a man, I wanted him to make my body feel what his words couldn't express. I wanted the truth, and an orgasm never lies; a good fuck, no one can take away. Something like that can stay in your consciousness forever.

After accepting the fact that Lester was a no show, I stood to leave the bar, and that's when a man who was not attractive in the least—or at least not to me—walked toward me. He was stuck in the eighties, still wearing his hair in a curl with a skinny leather tie and a pair of penny loafers with a nickel in the slit. But I was willing to sacrifice good looks and style for some good dick any day, and so I smiled and sat back down.

"Are you Lester?" I asked, assuming he was the man I'd been waiting for.

"Lester?" he questioned.

"Is that your name?"

He shook his head. "No, I'm sorry. My name is Eugene." He sat on the bar stool beside me. "But it can be Lester tonight if you'd like."

"Well, it depends," I said as I placed my hand on his leather tie and then slid it down between his legs to feel his dick. "How big is Lester?"

"Pardon me?" he said, before becoming stunned into silence.

I could have played it off by pretending to be buzzed and then apologize, but why should I? His reaction provided me with my answer—the one I wasn't looking for—that it wasn't big enough.

When I started to remove my hand, he grabbed hold of my wrist and placed his other hand on top of mine, pressing it down firmly. That's when I felt his pants balloon. "Does that answer your question?"

"Part of it."

"And the other part?"

"How's it going to feel when it's inside of me?"

"Would you like to find out?"

I nodded, and this is where it all started to go wrong.

We stood from the bar holding hands. Neither of us said a word, but I knew what was going to happen next. I followed him out of the club into the parking lot, cautiously walking toward his car, and then I stopped suddenly.

"I'd rather follow you in my car."

"Don't get lost," he said with a wink.

I followed behind his convertible Mustang for several miles, ignoring my cell phone, which had been vibrating all night with calls from my friend Melony. Finally I pulled into the parking lot of a luxury hotel, where we parked side by side. After he let his top up, he got out of his car and walked over to the passenger side of my car. I unlocked the door so he could get in.

"You look good enough to eat." He didn't waste any time sliding my dress halfway up my thighs and sticking his head between my legs, but I held him back, wiping the Jheri curl juice from my thighs.

"There's a time and a place for everything," I told him. "I'd rather my car not be the place."

"You have to learn to let go. I prefer to be teased a little and fucked a lot." He took his forefinger and shoved it inside of my pussy. The quickness of his jab made me gasp. He pulled me over the center console with his finger stuck deep inside of me and let the seat go back as far as it could. "Ride this," he said as he inserted two more fingers inside my pussy, "like it's the biggest, juiciest dick you've ever had."

"Fingers annoy me."

"If they annoy you, why are you so wet?"

"I'm naturally lubricated."

He slid his fingers out, sniffed them, and then put them in his mouth to suck my pussy juices. "I love the smell and taste of sex. That's why I like to finger fuck. It gets me in the mood." He started rubbing between his legs. "Are you ready for me to let the beast out?" I looked down at his bulge and didn't hesitate to grab it. "Let's do a quickie right here in the car. I'll still have more for you when we get to the room."

"I'm ready to go up right now and then take it from there," I said, and opened the passenger door. We both tumbled out of the car. I stood, repositioning my dress, pulling my thong from the crack of my ass.

He grabbed me by the wrist and we started walking in the direction of the hotel.

"You ain't never had it like I'm going to give it to you," he whispered in my ear.

"I hope you're not all talk. I've had that type before . . . several times."

He ignored my comment, which caused me major concern. It was bad enough I was getting ready to fuck a man that I didn't know, but it would be even worse if the sex turned out to be a disappointment.

"When you go inside, head straight for the elevator, get on and take it to the tenth floor. I don't want it to seem like we're together. I don't think my wife would follow me, but you never know."

I was slightly offended, but I had to remind myself that I wasn't looking for a relationship. So I did what he said and waited close to fifteen minutes for him to join me on the tenth floor. I'd pressed the down button to the elevator, ready to leave, assuming I'd been stood up a second time, when the elevator door opened and he slid out.

"Sorry it took so long. I had to make a call. The room number is 1027."

I followed behind him without any reservation as to what I was doing, but rather with anticipation of what the two of us would be doing very shortly. When we entered the small but quaint room, he immediately started taking off his tie and shirt.

"Are you in a rush?" I asked.

"Just anxious." He sat on the edge of the bed. "How much?"

"How much what?"

"If I want oral and possibly some anal. How much for all that?"

"What do you mean by how much?"

"You're a call girl, right? Come on. I know that's what you are. I can always tell you high class hoes. You come to a nice club alone and you dress real seductively. You pretend to be into the music, but every so often you look around to see who might be looking at you. I guess it's better than walking the streets, huh?"

"And I can always tell a John. You come to a club alone with that deranged look in your eyes like you need a fix bad and pussy is your drug. What's wrong, you can't get what you need at home?"

"Every now and then I get tired of home cooking and I need to eat out." He pulled two hundred-dollar bills from his wallet. "For this," he said, as he tossed the money at my feet, "I should be able to get all I can eat."

I picked the bills up one at a time and looked over at him. "For this? I guess you're eating fast food, or better yet you might as well go on a fast. For this, I might as well walk the street." I threw the money back to him.

"What, that's not enough?"

"Not for this." I sat on the window ledge, hiking up my dress, and with my legs spread open began rubbing my pussy. His eyes zoomed toward my chest. "Is that all you?" he asked.

"Who else's would it be?"

He shrugged. "I don't know, but why don't you come out of your dress so I can see what you're working with, and I only hope it's not a miracle bra."

"Do you have on miracle briefs?" I walked over to him and turned so that my back was facing him. "Unzip me."

"Look at that fat ass," he said as he squeezed my butt cheeks. I closed my eyes when I realized my fantasy was about to finally come true. He unzipped his pants, and a few seconds later I felt two rock hard taps against my hip.

"Try to imagine how good my dick is going to feel once it's inside of you," he said as he bent down and used his teeth to pull my thong down. "I'm about to give you something you can feel."

I felt a few more taps, but this time they were even harder.

I opened my eyes, looked between his legs, and lay down on the bed with my legs spread wide, "Jump in."

"Am I strapped?" he asked as he stood naked at the foot of the bed, holding his dick in one hand. It was so thick that his hand barely fit around the shaft. He wasn't much to look at in the face, but in the flesh his body looked just as chiseled as Terrell Owens's, and that's who I pretended he was—the NFL player I've always wanted to fuck.

"You still haven't answered my question. Is this what you mean when you say you want a man that's strapped?" I hadn't mentioned anything to Eugene about wanting a man who was strapped, but I had talked about what I was looking for with Lester. "Surprised? No, I didn't forget."

"You said you weren't Lester."

"I say a lot of things. I said I was ten inches when in reality I'm a foot long. I'm into playing games, remember?" he asked as he picked his leather belt from the floor and snapped it in the air.

The crackling sound of the leather both frightened and intrigued me. I felt naughty and nasty, like the tramp that I'd always wanted to become. I'd never seen a dick that big. Correction, I'd never seen a big dick period. "I want to suck on your fat dick head," I said, "until you come in my mouth."

I started crawling toward him with my tongue wiggling. His dick was so perfectly shaped, not just long, but thick also. Even his Jheri curl started to look good. I'd reached the tip of his head and swirled my tongue up and down his slit. I opened my mouth and started sucking his dick, moving up the shaft inch by inch. He wanted his balls tickled with my tongue, and I was more than willing to accommodate. His toes curled, his head fell back, but then when it seemed like he was going to make a deposit, he pulled out of my mouth suddenly.

"I don't want to come that way. I want you to ride me, and then when I'm getting ready to come, I want you to take the belt and strangle me."

"But it tastes so good that I was ready for more. I wanted to swallow." I stood from the bed and pushed him against the wall. He held his hands out and snatched me toward him by my nipples. He was into pain—giving and receiving. That much was obvious.

When he let go of my nipples, I had to feel them to make sure they were still there. My breasts were tender and my pussy was wet and tight. "Can't you be gentle?" I asked as I took one of his hands and rubbed it along my hairy slit.

He pushed me back down on the bed and yanked me toward him by my ankles. "I like it rough." He knelt between my legs and ate my pussy like he was drilling for gold, and before long he struck it. I closed my eyes and thought of Terrell Owens. That's who was eating me . . . not Lester. Every inch that he went deeper caused me to wonder about him. Every swirl he made inside of me had me question his true intentions, but then there was the presence of the black leather belt and knowing what he wanted me to do with it. I should have refused, but instead, when he turned on his back and gestured for me to straddle him, I did. It could have stopped there. I was in control, riding his dick like a bull and taking in as much of it that I could stand. And then he handed me the belt.

"When do you want me to use it?" I asked, still on top of him, enjoying the ride.

"I'll let you know. Just keep going. Keep doing what you're doing, baby. I don't come quickly." It was hard to imagine how I survived for so many years with so much less. "Your fat pussy was made to take a big juicy dick. Look how good you're handling me."

The more he talked, the harder I rode him and the more of his dick I took in, until I'd swallowed him whole.

"Now," he said, "right now. I'm getting ready to come. Do it now!"

Reluctantly, I placed the belt around his throat and then tightened it. It felt powerful, mixing pain with pleasure. At first I didn't think I could do it, but I kept thinking about the men who'd done me wrong, and somehow strangling him with that belt wasn't so difficult. He smiled for a second and I continued choking him until I saw foam oozing from the side of his mouth. His eyes rolled in the back of his head and I knew that I'd killed him . . . accidentally, of course.

Last Day of School

Here is how it all began.

On the last day of school I told my students to enjoy their summer vacation and to be sure to come back next year with plenty of stories to share. Little did I know that I'd be the one with the stories, but none that I'd be able to share. Even though it was the last day of school for the students, teachers had to stick around for an extra week, but on this day I had a half day, and instead of going straight home after work, I decided to check on my best friend. She was on vacation, and since I had to pass her house to get to mine, I figured I might as well swing by there and see how she was doing. Catch up on old times, since it had been a few months since we really talked, and nearly a year since we hung out. But that wasn't the real reason I went to see her. I needed to put my suspicions to rest.

With less than thirty minutes before the bell would ring, I sat at my desk and allowed my students to goof off while I thought about my fiancé Edward. First, I was pretty sure that he was cheating on me. And I was almost positive that I knew with whom—my best friend Nancy, which was the reason I had to confront her. Edward never bit his tongue when it came to assessing a woman's attributes. He always thought Nancy had a nice body, and didn't mind telling me. And Nancy had broken up with her man and suddenly stopped coming around me. It didn't take a rocket scientist to figure out what was going on.

Edward and I had been together for nearly three years. In the beginning, our relationship progressed very quickly, but soon I discovered through calling certain numbers from his Sprint bill that he was still seeing his ex. I should have left him then. To know that he told some other woman that he missed her touch tore my insides apart. I thought Edward and I were close. I honestly thought he loved me, but now I knew that he didn't know how or who to love. And it wasn't just his ex. It was a flight attendant and a female police officer, both of whom he'd met online. I'd talked to all three ladies and couldn't get mad at them, especially not his ex, who was in his life before I was. But my best friend Nancy was a different story. I was furious with her, and she was going to find out just how much.

"Class," I said as I stood. I had to raise my voice. "Please settle down. We only have ten more minutes." What did I expect on the last day of school? There was no work to do . . . just a countdown until the bell rang. I walked down the middle aisle of desks and noticed one girl cover her mouth with laughter as she looked down at my low-heeled Ecco shoes. Maybe in wearing them I wasn't as stylish as I could have been. I hated to admit that in some ways I'd started letting myself go. Several months ago I'd lost a contact, and instead of getting a new pair, I went back to wearing my glasses. The year before, I started letting my hair grow out of the stylish layered cut, and when it became too unruly, I pulled it back in a ponytail and have worn it that way ever since. And now I could barely get my fiancé to take a second look at me, but he stared down every attractive woman he saw on the street.

"Monica, get out of his lap and sit in your own chair. One day maybe you'll learn it's better to keep it to yourself," I said, shaking my head.

"So when *you* gonna learn when to let some go?" Monica asked.

I ignored her comment. I taught seventh grade, yet so many of my students acted as if they were grown, especially Monica, who already had a reputation for being easy.

"What you doing for the summer, Miss Cartwright?" Toy, whose reputation didn't far precede Monica's, asked.

I shrugged. "Not sure yet, but I'm going to try and do something a little different this summer."

"You and your man," Toy said.

"Miss Cartwright don't have no man," Monica said.

"Miss Cartwright, you should come back next year with a whole new look," Scottie, the class clown, said.

"What's wrong with my look?" I asked as I surveyed my students' expressions and the many smirks across their faces. But before anyone responded, the bell rang and they jumped from their desks and flooded through the door.

"You cute, Miss Cartwright," Scottie said, "you just need to loosen up a little. Let your hair down. Listen to some Shawna and learn a little somethin' 'bout satisfying your man."

"Listen to some who, so I can learn how to do what?"

"Listen to Luda's girl, Shawna from Disturbing Tha Peace. You know," Scottie rapped, "I was getting some head."

"Okay, Scottie, I get the point. Enjoy your summer."

"You too, Miss Cartwright. I hope you really enjoy yours too. I really mean that."

I watched as Scottie ran from my class, sneaking behind a female student to grab her ass. She screamed, pushed him, and then he put his arm around her shoulder and they strolled out of the building.

I rushed out of the school and headed for Nancy's house. When I arrived, I pulled into her driveway behind a black 5-series BMW—Edward's. He worked at a BMW dealership and had also sold Nancy's ex-fiancé a preowned 5-series that had the older body style. I walked around to the back of the car to look at the license plate: 1OF2. I guess his car wasn't the only thing that was one of two. I was also one of two, and Nancy, who I thought was my best girlfriend at one time and would never do something like this to me, was a back-stabbing bitch. I ran onto the porch and started ringing the doorbell. Of course, no one answered. So I called Edward on his cell phone as I sat on the hood of his car jingling my keys, fully prepared to use one all over his ride if need be.

"Be a man and come outside and bring that bitch with you," I said.

"What are you talking about? And why are you talking like that? I'm at work."

"You're at work, but your car is at Nancy's house."

"My car is at Nancy's house because I let Floyd borrow it since his is in the shop and we were out of loaners. He's probably over Nancy's house, so please don't start tripping."

"So if I call Floyd right now, he'll confirm that."

"Yes he will."

"Okay, 'bye," I said, and hung up. Edward was the type who would lie until the bitter end. He probably figured that I wasn't going to call Floyd. For one, I didn't like him. We never saw eye-to-eye on anything, and we'd gotten into it a few times in the past over Nancy and the way he did her. But all that aside, I needed to know the truth, and that was just a phone call away.

"Floyd, this is Alexis. I just talked to Edward and he claimed that he let you use his car, but I know that's probably not true. Call me back when you get this message. Don't worry about it. The more I say it out loud the dumber it sounds."

I pressed the End button. Looked at my key and got to writing. I wrote: I'M NOT GOING TO BE 1 OF 2 across the driver's side of his car.

Nancy's front door swung open and Nancy shouted, "What are you doing?"

I turned with evil in my eyes and said, "Me, what about you? What are you doing with . . . Floyd?" I asked as Floyd walked out of the house. "Edward really did let you use his car?"

"Yeah, so why did you do that? Maybe she already knows," Floyd said as he turned to walk back into the house.

Nancy grabbed the tail of his shirt. "She doesn't know. She thought he was over here with me," Nancy said, then looked at me. "And for the record, I would never do some low down shit like that to one of my girls. But don't worry about what you just did to his car because he deserves it. Tell her why he deserves it, Floyd."

"Look, I'm not in all this."

"You in it if you want me to take you back. Tell her."

"What do you want me to say?"

"Tell her what you told me."

Club Flirt

Well, Floyd told me. And the only thing that I could think about was that all school year while I was busy planning what Edward and I were going to do over the summer, what trip we were going to take—a three-day cruise to Jamaica, which was one of his favorite places to visit, or a leisurely drive to Toronto, which was something he'd always talked about doing—he'd had other things on his mind.

I wanted to do something different. Something that could possibly help reignite our dying relationship, and Edward, well, I found out he was already doing something different, or should I say doing someone different. Her name was Black Exotica, and it wasn't too hard for me to figure out what she did for a living. My fiancé had, like the song said, fallen in love with a stripper. It would have been so much better for all involved if Edward had just told me himself. I would have been upset, but I would have had to deal with it. At least, I would've been able to tell myself that he finally decided to be honest. But no, he wanted to continue to play me like a fool, and of all the people I had to find the truth out from, it had to be from one of my least favorite ones, my best friend's man, who was trying to get Nancy off his ass when he admitted that he'd gone to the strip club but only stayed an hour . . . but guess who was there and who seemed more than a little comfortable with the star stripper—Edward.

I really didn't feel like going all up in Club Flirt to front him and Black Exotica. What would I, a woman with a master's degree in education from the University of Michigan, an educator, a member of one of the largest black sororities, and a volunteer with Big Brothers/Big Sisters, look like going into a strip club? But that didn't stop me from storming in there to confront my man and his new woman. I felt like I didn't have a choice. Edward forced me to pull out my ghetto card. And I didn't go alone. I took Nancy and her half sister Veronda along for moral support. So there the three of us were at Club Flirt, looking just as lost as ever.

As we approached the door, there was a bouncer seated on a stool in front of the roped-off entrance. His massive muscular arms were folded and his eyes were concealed by dark shades. And even though I had come there on a mission to catch my man in the act, I couldn't help but notice the bulge in the center of the bouncer's pants. Oh, how I wanted so badly to take his dick out and get some pleasure for a change, because Edward sure hadn't given me any, and not just in a long time . . . never.

"Ladies, the club's closed," he said.

"Closed," Veronda said. "It's just eleven o'clock. The club ain't closed."

"Who you going in there to see?" the bouncer asked.

"What you mean who we going to see?" Veronda responded. "Is

that a question you asked all those horny men who came through here?"

"Are you coming in here to see women or you coming in here to find your horny man, because we don't want nothing jumping off tonight."

"The sign outside was blinking girls . . . girls . . . girls. So let us in so we can see some."

"All right, shorty," he said as he removed the rope from the entrance. "I was just making sure."

Veronda winked as she led us into the club. We wanted to sit at a table in the back because Floyd had already confirmed that Edward was going to be there and I definitely didn't want him to see me before I saw him, but even more importantly, before I saw her. It was standing room only, so we stood along the side in front of two large red neon hearts. We knew that Black Exotica was the last stripper to dance, and we didn't have long to wait because she was up next. We'd walked in on the tail end of Skin Tight's routine.

"I wonder how many of these men are married?" Nancy asked.

"Mmm," I said as I looked around at the faces concealed in darkness. For those who were, I wondered where their wives thought they were that night. I started thinking once again that I was with a man that I really didn't know, a man I would have sworn wouldn't be caught dead in a strip club. But I guess that was a naive way of thinking. I know men like to see naked women. I guess most men would love to see nude females sliding down poles and to get a lap dance from them, but why did my man have to be one of them?

"Half these women are lesbians," Veronda said.

"How do you know?" I asked.

"I don't know. I'm just talking. Got to find something to say about these bitches since they're packing 'em in like this."

When Skin Tight left the stage, the table in front of us became available, so we quickly filled the empty seats. During the half hour delay between sets while the stage was being changed before Black Exotica came out, we started drinking. I could feel myself getting buzzed right when Black Exotica's theme music began playing. I was so anxious to see her that I was practically bouncing in my seat.

"By the looks of all the money they make on an average night, I might need to consider stripping. At least I wouldn't have to worry about layoffs," Veronda said.

The men went wild as soon as Black Exotica hit the stage in her fishnet outfit. She had a small chest with very large nipples that were poking through the holes. She was wearing a black half mask over her eyes and a platinum blond ponytail that hung to the middle of her back. Even I, as a woman, had to shake my head. She had a tiny waist and the biggest ass I'd ever seen. I wondered why she'd picked my man. I could see why he picked her. I mean, if I were a man, I'd be interested in that. She was an exotic looking black woman with a body that I'd love to have as my own. But why did she want him? Out of all these men, there had to be one with more to offer, and I wasn't talking about money. My man's thing was barely five inches. So it must have all boiled down to money. My man was generous when he wanted to be, and more importantly, when he wanted something. At one time it was me he chased because I was a hard one to get, but once he had me, my good times were over.

"Maybe this was a bad idea," I said to Nancy. "I've seen all I need to."

"I thought you wanted to talk to her? We didn't drive all the way over here just to leave."

The whole idea of going to the strip club to confront her seemed so ridiculous to me now. Black Exotica was in that place handling her business, and to be honest, the more that I watched her on stage, the more I started to desire her lifestyle. How nice it would be to have the full attention of a room full of men with hard dicks.

As I was heading for the door, I bumped into Edward as he walked in. Our eyes met, but he tried ignoring me until I said. "I guess you're surprised to see me here, huh?"

"Not really," he said as he attempted to brush pass me. "You're doing what you do best—stalk. And if I wasn't on probation, I'd kick your ass right here for fucking up my car."

I grabbed his arm and dug my acrylic French tip nails into his shirt. "I wish you would."

He turned to face me. "I wish I could," he said as he snatched my hand away from his arm.

"Enjoy your life because I'm moving on to bigger and better things." I looked down at his crotch. "Much bigger and honey so much better." My girls walked passed him and giggled.

"That's fine, because I've already done the same."

"Go to hell, Edward."

"I left there when I left you."

My girls pushed me out of the club when they saw the rage in my eyes and the bouncer in our path.

"Did you hear what he said?" I asked Nancy and Veronda as I stepped out of the door. "He left me? No, I left him. He had nothing when I met him. Not even a decent job. Now, just because he sells cars and has a BMW, he thinks his shit doesn't stink."

"Let's go," Nancy said as we stood in the parking lot.

"I'm not going anywhere until I can confront the two of them."

The three of us waited in the car for nearly an hour, exchanging relationship horror stories, until finally Edward stormed out of the club alone and sped off. After another thirty minutes or so with still no sign of Black Exotica, I decided to walk to the side door and knock until someone answered. One of the dancers let me in.

"I'm outside waiting for Black Exotica. I'm her ride."

"You seen Exotica?" she asked a dancer who walked down the hallway topless.

"She's in the champagne room with a customer."

"Oh, she might be a while," the dancer who let me into the building said. "You can wait in her dressing room," she added, standing in front of a door that had a large red star plastered to it with the name BLACK EXOTICA written on it, "or in your car, and I'll tell her you're out there. I thought for sure she drove," she said as a baffled look came over her face.

"I'll wait in her room," I said, then walked inside and sat on the vanity stool. When the dancer walked into another room, I started looking around. There were pictures of Black Exotica with men—some prominent figures—local politicians, athletes, and famous entertainers.

"You a new girl?" Black Exotica asked as she glided into her dressing room with the smell of sex hovering over her naked body. She had a tattoo of a rainbow above her hipbone.

"No, I'm just here to talk."

"Talk? Do I need to call Security?" she said as she stood by the open door, holding the handle.

"No, please don't call Security. I'm just here to talk. I'm Edward's fiancé. Did you know that he had one?"

"Who's Edward?" she said as she remained standing. "Security!" she yelled.

"You don't need to call Security. I just want to talk." I closed the door. "Please."

"I don't know any Edwards. And if he's one of these perverts who come to gawk at me, I can't help that."

"He's in love with you and you don't even know who he is?"

"Do you know how many of these fools are in love with me? Narrow it down."

"He has a small dick."

"Keep narrowing."

"A real small one. He sells BMWs at Euro World."

"Itty," she said, twisting her nose. "How did you manage to work with that little string bean dick? It just slips right out of me." She locked the door.

"A lot of faking."

"I make a living from performing, but with Itty it's only so much acting I can do," Black Exotica said as she walked over to the sofa, where she plopped down and crossed her shapely legs while eyeing me seductively. "Besides, I'm more into women." She patted the empty spot beside her. "And it's nothing better than getting some pussy after I've just had some dick. Come over her and let me show you."

"Oh, I'm not like that."

"No one said you had to be. All I want you to do is sit beside me."

I hesitated before reluctantly walking over to her.

"The only way a man is going to see my body is if he pays me. If he wants to touch me, he's going to pay even more. And if he wants to put his slimy worm inside my precious hole," she said as she used two fingers to spread open her pussy, "then I'm getting his whole damn paycheck because I don't even want a man." She picked up my index finger and inserted it deep inside of her, guiding it in and out. My finger was soaked with her juices. "Your hands are so soft and your fingers are so delicate. Men just want to stab me with theirs." When she let her hand go, I continued to wiggle my finger inside of her. She dropped her head back and then turned to face me. She caressed the side of my face with the back of her hand. "I don't want your man; I'd rather have you." I pulled out my finger. "Don't be frightened. Be open to new experiences." She put my finger back, and I continued wiggling it inside of her. She leaned toward my face in an attempt to kiss me but I drew back.

"I'm not like that."

"You're not?" she asked with laughter as she looked between her legs. "Are you sure? You seem to be enjoying it just as much as I am. Have you ever been with a woman?" I shook my head. "Because once you do that . . . you really won't go back."

"I just came here to talk about Edward." I took my finger out again.

"I don't want your little man. Girl, I only messed with him for the money. For me, it's all about money. And we could make a lot of it if we did a porno together. We could call it—the schoolteacher learns a new lesson."

"He told you that I was a teacher?"

"He didn't have to," she said, pulling my hair from its bun, then taking off my glasses. "You have long, pretty hair that's perfect for tugging." She ran her fingers through my strands as she slid over closer to me. Her hands crept underneath my top, unsnapped the front fasten to my 38D cups, and started juggling them. "Wouldn't you love to go back and tell your man that you got with me? That you'd done something that he couldn't, which was made me come?" She got onto her knees on the sofa then, in front of me, grinding her "precious hole" over my nipples while she squeezed both of my breasts together. "Are you going to let me eat your pussy?"

"I have to go," I said as I stopped her from using my breasts to jack off with.

She slid her knees off the sofa onto the floor and began kissing the fabric between my legs. Her long stiff tongue rode up my zipper and struck a nerve that caused me momentary pleasure. She untied the drawstring to my linen pants, pulled down my zipper with her teeth and began fingering me through the material of my panties until they became soaking wet. She snatched off my pants and panties.

How did this evening turn out this way? I wondered. I'd come to Club Flirt to confront my man, but now I was in Black Exotica's dressing room sitting on her sofa with my bra unfastened and my top pulled up, exposing my bare breasts. I was completely naked from the waist down, and the star stripper had just started drilling her long pierced tongue inside of me, her head bobbing up and down. This was wrong and I knew it. It went against everything I morally believed in, yet I couldn't stop her because she was making me feel too good to end it.

She stopped for a second and looked up at me. Her lips were dripping wet with my pussy juices. "I'm not going to stop until I turn you all the way out," she said.

I pushed her head back down between my legs so she could continue doing what Edward never would . . . at least not to me. My eyes closed for a minute. I felt in control and realized that was how men must have felt when they were getting head. My cell phone started ringing from inside my purse. It stopped after several rings and then started back up again. That's when I struggled to come to my senses. "I have to go. I have people waiting for me outside in the car." I stood, pulled up my soaking wet panties and my pants, fastened my bra, pulled down my top, and started pinning my hair up.

"But we were just getting started. I have so much more in store for my virgin."

"I'm sorry. I don't know what I was thinking. It was a big mistake," I said as I made my way to the door.

"Mistakes don't taste that good. You'll be back."

I unlocked the door, rushed out of her dressing room and the club to get back to my car.

"Well, what happened?" Nancy asked.

"Did you tell her ass off?" Veronda asked.

My heart was pounding a million miles a second. I shook my head. I was too afraid to talk because I wasn't good at lying. I pulled out of the parking lot.

"What's that smell?" Veronda asked. "Smells like fish." Both Veronda and Nancy let their windows down.

"I don't smell anything." I tried to focus on the road but my mind was back in Black Exotica's dressing room wondering what it would have felt like if I had let her go all the way.

"He left hell when he left me," I said aloud as I entered the house and slammed the door leading from the garage. I tossed my purse on the sofa and walked through our bedroom to the bathroom. I had to take a shower and wash that fish smell away. I stepped out of my clothes and put on a shower cap. I turned on the shower, adjusting the setting so the water would run out warm, then stepped in. I watched as the water beaded on my dark skin.

Black women hate to get their hair wet, so I decided to prove to myself that water was not our kryptonite. I pulled off the shower cap, removed the bobby pins from my hair, and stepped underneath the shower head with my eyes closed. I smiled. This wasn't so bad, especially since I was getting my hair done the next day. I was feeling sexy and free. My man wasn't all that, and now our breakup was going to allow me to look for one that was. I cupped my breasts and squeezed them tightly as I slid my hand between my precious hole. The hair down there had gotten long enough to braid; it was time to shave again—time to become a bare naked lady. My index finger wiggled inside my opening. In and out . . . in and out . . . the way I'd done Black Exotica. But that only frustrated me because it wasn't nothing like the real thing.

I felt soap suds on my back, but I didn't know where they were coming from. Then two hands were placed firmly on my shoulder, turning me around to face a tall muscular man who had to be a figment. He had a tattoo on his chest of a long red arrow pointing down to his dick. He didn't have a "slimy worm." He had a dangerous python that was hissing for me.

"Are you real?" I asked.

"Do I look real?"

I nodded.

"Jump on me and see if I feel real."

We started kissing passionately, and then he sat on the shower bench and pulled me toward him. I started to climb on him but he turned me around so I sat on his snake while he spread my ass apart. I began bouncing on him. It was what I had needed. There was no way I was gay. I'd had too much to drink and so I let Black Exotica take advantage of me. But who was this man who suddenly appeared in my shower, strapped. Had he followed me from the strip club?

"Where did you come from?" I asked right before my home phone rang. I bounced off his dick, and on the way back down my ass fell flat against the marble shower seat. He'd vanished. I shook my head. This was why I didn't go out drinking.

My phone was still ringing. I didn't bother with an answering machine, figuring if a call was important enough, they'd call back, but this person wouldn't hang up. I rushed into the bedroom and picked up the phone, hoping it was Edward calling to tell me that he'd come to his senses and that he was on his way home, because even though he had a little one, little ones were better than none at all.

"I got your message about wanting to come visit me for the summer," my sister said. "But what about Edward?"

"What about him? He's history."

"Are you serious? You finally took your garbage out. I hope you dumped him on the side of the road."

I sighed. "Can I come for a visit and stay with you?"

"Girl, I been begging you to come visit me for years. Of course you can."

"I'll be there next week. I just need to go the salon for a touch-up and to Vision Matters for my contacts."

New Girl in Town

I arrived at Dallas–Fort Worth airport on a Saturday with nothing but the clothes on my back, because the ones I left behind in my closet weren't fit for the adventure I was going on. My sister and her boyfriend were a little late picking me up, which didn't surprise me because my sister was late for most things except her job with the Dallas Police Department. She'd made detective a few years back and had the exciting task of investigating murders. I sat outside the terminal reading the *Dallas Morning News*. On the front page was a story about the Black Widow serial killer. She'd killed five men in Texas over the last two summers, mostly in Dallas.

After about a twenty minute wait, my sister and her boyfriend pulled up. He was driving a black Escalade with fancy rims. I didn't know much about my sister's man . . . just that his name was Tony. I was shocked when I saw his physique because usually my sister's men were fit like her. But Tony had a little more than a few extra pounds. But even though he was wide, he didn't have a big stomach. He was wearing shorts and showing off his chicken legs, which I found to be hilarious, but I could tell he was nice, and doubted that it was his personality that hooked my sister. Had to be something I couldn't see.

On the ride to her home, I couldn't stop thinking about Black Exotica. It bothered me that I could still feel her tongue swirling around my pussy.

"I'm taking you to my book club meeting tonight," my sister said to me. "You'll have fun. The girls are so crazy, and the book we're discussing is off the chain."

"What's the name of it?" I asked.

"*In Too Deep*. It's erotic."

"*In Too Deep*," Tony said, looking over at my sister. "What's that about?"

"Men like you . . . men who are well-endowed."

"And women say men have a one-track mind," Tony said. "You women are no different."

"Some of us aren't. You're right, baby," my sister said.

My sister and I made a detour and went shopping for some sexy clothes to wear to Club Knubian Fantaciez, a male strip club, where the book club members were all going later that evening, and because I hadn't brought any clothes, I picked up several outfits. By the time we left the mall in our new outfits and headed to the book club meeting in someone's home, we were late. On the ride there, my sister filled me in on some of the members. Most, but not all, were DPD officers, and a few, like my sister, were detectives. The meeting was only supposed to last for a couple of hours, and then we were hitting the strip club to follow along with the theme of the book.

"I'm too ready to discuss this book," my sister said, clutching her copy as we entered. In so many ways my sister and I were night and day. She'd always been the life of the party, while I'd been the shy one.

"You're an hour late," one of the ladies said as she walked from the kitchen into the living room carrying a bowl of chips. "We already started talking about the book, finished talking about the book, and now we're on to something else and almost ready to go to the strip club."

"Well, start over," my sister said. "I was the one who was supposed to introduce the damn book, and you already started talking about something else . . . let me guess . . . why are men such dogs?"

"No matter what book we discuss, don't they always find a way to ease that topic back into our discussion?" one of the other ladies said. "I see you brought along a friend." She smiled in my direction.

"I brought my sister."

"Hi, sis," the same young lady said.

"Hello," I said with a smile.

"I'm Melony. Your sister and I go way back. We were in the academy together."

"What did I miss?" my sister asked as she hurried to take her seat on the sofa next to Melony. I stood, since there were no available seats, but another young lady rushed from the kitchen and handed me a bar stool.

"Karen was telling us about that man she met online—the excop who she asked us about a while back."

"Oh, yeah, I didn't know him when he was with the department," my sister said. "Whatever happened with him?"

Funny, when you're going through the heartbreak and pain of

losing someone you truly loved, it's always a little easier to handle when you know you're not alone.

"Let me get your sister caught up. I met this man on the Internet about a year and a half ago. That was my first mistake. Never go online to meet a man for anything other than sex because that's what those cyberspace men are looking for. While they're dating you, they keep their profiles up, and still meet women. I would wake up at three o'clock in the morning just to find him surfing the Net."

"What did he say he was doing?" I asked.

"He said he was doing research . . . as much research as he did at that time every morning he needed to have a damn doctorate degree."

"So you think he was still meeting women online?" I asked.

"Do I think? He *was* meeting women online and visiting porno sites. He was doing a little bit of everything. I knew something wasn't right about him. First of all, the photo he had was of him standing in a real nice kitchen with stainless steel appliances and a large island in the center. The profile said he lived in Plano, and usually that means you have a little money, am I right?" The ladies nodded. "Well, I never got to see his house in Plano because as soon as we started talking on the phone, he told me that he had to move out of that house because he was renting and the owner decided to sell."

"In other words, he got evicted," Melony said.

"Pretty much. First red flag, but I looked past all that because by that time we'd met in person and I was really attracted to him, things were all good, or so I thought. He rented a U-Haul truck and wanted me to help him move. Now, if you're just now moving out of your house, why was all your shit already in storage? Second red flag."

"Stop," said one of the other ladies, who was milling in and out of the kitchen. "Did he fuck you so good that you lost all sense of reason? Did you let him get in too deep?" We all laughed at her play on the book title.

"Girl, we hadn't even had sex yet, which was why I thought this man was not like all the others. And he wasn't. He was worse."

"Karen, can you make a long story short?" Melony asked.

"Not this one . . . no. I want all the women in here to beware of him and men like him. This man did things differently. He took me to Shreveport to meet his parents. We spent the holidays together. He cooked for me, fixed the viruses on my computer, but he was also online on several dating Web sites with about twenty aliases, trying to meet other women."

"And if the woman is fool enough to fall for it, is that his fault?" Melony asked. "I'm tired of women crying that men have done them wrong. You all are the fools that mess with the men who you already know aren't shit."

"Well, Melony, maybe you're being a little impatient because you're not a woman who has to worry about something like that ever happening to you," Karen said.

"You damn straight I don't."

I figured she told Melony that she never had to worry about that happening to her because Melony was very attractive. Not that pretty women don't get hurt—look at Halle Berry—but I guess when they do, it might not take them as long to bounce back into another relationship.

"You've already told half of us this at least a dozen times. It's time to move on. What is our motto, ladies?"

"Move on to bigger and better things," we all said; I'd heard that motto from my sister.

"Let me help you get to the punch line," Melony continued,

"He convinced you to put a car in your name for him and he never paid one note. The two of you built a house. Once again, it was in your name, he lived there, and never paid a dime, but was telling people it was his house. The utilities were getting shut off every other month."

"I worked my ass off, had to borrow from my 401(k), take out a home equity loan just to keep us afloat. He kept saying he was about to close on this house or that house, and never closed on one, or if he did, I never saw any money come through."

"And was he cheating too?" I asked.

"What do you think? That part goes without saying. Yes, he was cheating on me with a twenty-five-year-old who told me that he drove to her job and picked her up in the car I financed when it still had the temporary tag on the window."

"Mmm," I said, shaking my head, because oh how I could relate.

"He didn't have any male friends," Karen continued. "Every last one of his friends was female. And he used to say, 'I need to tell you in advance that in my line of work I mainly deal with women because most of the real estate agents are females, so don't get jealous if I'm talking to a woman from time to time because it's business.'"

"If you didn't know that was game, shame on you," Melony said, shaking her head. "I'm so glad I don't have to worry about that shit. I've never been treated like that, and I would never treat a woman like that."

"Man," I said, correcting her.

"What, sweetie?"

"You said woman, and I was just correcting you with what you meant to say . . . you'd never treat a man like that."

Several of the other women in the room began laughing. "No, she said what she meant to say," my sister said.

"That's right, I meant to say woman. I don't date men," Melony said.

"Oh, I see."

"Well, was the sex at least good?" my sister asked. "Shit, was he at least strapped?"

"Yeah, he was strapped . . . financially. Owed child support from a previous marriage and everybody else."

"So the sex wasn't even good," Melony said, still shaking her head.

"I didn't say that the sex wasn't good, because I'd be lying if I said all that. It was damn good and he was big enough for me. I mean he wasn't strapped, but he wasn't itty bitty either. But I know one thing, though—he was a little too much into anal sex for my taste."

Melony started laughing. "That's because he was probably bi."

"No . . . no . . . no," my sister said, "there are a lot of men that like that."

"Listen," Melony said, "it's nothing like some pussy. I don't get with a woman and ask her to strap on a dick. When I strap on a dick, that's because I'm with a woman who is bi and she needs that to achieve her climax. If you're with a so-called straight man and he's always trying to poke you in the other hole, he's a bisexual, and I'm not debating that shit with anyone because I know too much about that. He may not have ever been with a man . . . may not even know that's why he wants it so much, but I guarantee you, you get that punk behind closed doors with one of my gay male friends, and when they stick their ass in his face, guess what he's going to stick in their ass?"

"Oh, my," I said.

"That's right, oh, my," Melony said. "I mean, Karen, you can't be mad at that man, because deep down you knew what he was about from day one. As far as a man cheating on you, a man who isn't married isn't cheating. I don't even care if he's living with someone. You have to know what's out there. Sex is plentiful. Cheating is abundant. Pick yourself up, brush your shoulders off, and keep it movin'."

"Yeah," my sister said, "instead of looking for a man you can get into a relationship with, look for a man you can have great sex with. A man who can fill you up. How long it is really doesn't matter. Just as long as it's fat. The thicker his shaft, the better the sex will be. Trust me. And don't have him top it off with a big head too, girl, please. Why do you think I'm with Tony?"

"Personally, I believe that it all boils down to not just the man's size, but how it's shaped," Karen said. "I have a preference for a penis shaped like a lollipop. You know what I'm talking about. You have a big knob for the head and a thinner shaft. That's the perfect shape for sucking."

I looked over at Melony, who had just turned up her nose and shook her head.

"See, I'm the opposite of you," another woman said, "because I like the ones where that head is a little smaller than the shaft because, I'll admit it, I'm one of those naughty girls that like to be poked in that other hole, my little brown eye, and that's when a small head comes in handy."

I was trying my best to stop staring over at Melony, whose nose couldn't stop twitching from disgust of what the other ladies were saying, but it was difficult because I assumed that a woman who was a lesbian would look, act, and dress like a man. But Black Exotica and Melony were two very attractive and feminine females, so my perception was all wrong, and it freaked me out. The other reason I found myself looking over at Melony was because I could feel her eyes climbing my bare legs before stopping at my plunging neckline.

"Okay, I have a question," Melony said, standing with a glass of wine in her hand. "How many of you have been with a woman? Raise your hand."

No hands went up, but I was tempted to raise mine and then explain that even though I'd been with a woman, it had only been once and I didn't take it as far as it could go. But I couldn't say much since my sister was there.

"It's obvious you didn't read the book," my sister said to Melony, "but did you at least read the back cover? The author's not talking about women. This book is about men. Men with big dicks. It got me so hot while I was reading last night that now I'm ready to go to the strip club and feel on some. I brought my dollars with me." My sister pulled out a bank envelope stuffed with one dollar bills.

"We're getting ready to go to the club now," a woman named Belinda said.

"I'm not going," Melony said, then sat back down. "I wouldn't waste my dollars on some dicks."

"Just come on," my sister said as she stood and snatched up Melony. "You're going. We're all going. I can't wait to see Miami Splash, Black Thunder, Hardcore, Sexy L, Orgazm, Hurricane, Flight 69, Playboy, Just Enuff, Mr. Biggs—"

"Damn, just say that you know them all," Karen said. "You must be a regular. Does Tony know about that?"

"Let's just say I've been to my fair share of bachelorette parties. And if you want to talk about men who are strapped . . . you'll get an eyeful in there, especially if it still becomes all nude after midnight. Oh, and grab a few bottles of wine because it might still be BYOB."

***

I'd never been to a male strip club before . . . well, once before, but it was so long ago that I couldn't remember much. There was definitely a difference with how men behaved at a strip club versus women. The women were actually louder when the acts came on stage, and they were more aggressive with touching the dancers. I never thought I could get personally wrapped up into watching men strip, but after a couple of drinks and a few overly inflated G-strings flopping in my face, I lost it, especially when they started taking it all off.

One of the dancers came to our table and started giving me a lap dance. He stood in front of me flapping his red elephant G-string in my face, and before I knew what had come over me, I'd grabbed hold of his long trunk and didn't want to let go. I placed a ten dollar bill between the string that was flossing the crack of his ass, and if not for the fact that Melony had started to squeeze my thigh under the table, I probably would have rubbed on his big round ass, but she'd shocked me still. I tried to move her hand away, but her grip was too tight.

"What are you doing?" I asked her.

She leaned over and whispered in my ear, "I'm not interested in what's going on in here." I looked at the other ladies, who were too focused on the dancers to pay Melony and me any mind. "I'm more interested about what's going on in here," she said as she slid her hand under my dress and inside my thong. I gasped loudly. That's when all of the ladies at our large table turned to look over at me.

"What's wrong?" a few asked in unison.

Melony discreetly snatched her hand away.

"Look at the size of Mr. Biggs," I said, trying to play it off. They all turned back toward the dancers. I rolled my eyes at Melony.

I won't tell, she mouthed.

I turned my chair away from her and started waving my dollars in the air so the men would come my way, and a couple of them did. Several minutes later, when I looked back in Melony's direction, she was gone.

Swingers

After being in Dallas for a couple weeks, my patience level was at an all-time low. I'd see them on the street—attractive men that I wanted to get with. But I had no idea how to go about meeting them. Maybe if I was into flirting, but I wasn't; in fact, I could barely make eye contact. I'd gone online and met a few male friends that I chatted with. One man, named Lester, I'd given my number and we talked every day, but I wasn't interested in meeting him. Something about him and his name seemed creepy.

My sister said that a lot of her friends had met men in grocery stores, so I decided why not see if the same could happen to me. I drove downtown to Urban Market and walked around for a little less than an hour before I met a man in the frozen foods section. I was wearing a white T-shirt, but even with my black bra, you could still see my nipples protruding, especially after I opened the freezer door and they became frozen stiff.

"You look cold," the man said as I closed the door. He was slender, so light he was almost white, with red low-cut hair and deep dimples. Above average looking, but far from the drop dead gorgeous men I'd seen in Dallas. Besides, I wasn't much for yellow men.

I placed the pot pie in my basket. "I'm actually hot," my ultra-sexy alter ego said.

"Are you?" He extended his hand. "I'm Bates."

"Is your first name Master?" I said with a giggle. "It was a joke."

"Oh," he said as he put his hand down before I could shake it.

"I'm Alexis. Nice to meet you."

After a few minutes of small talk, we exchanged numbers, and by that evening he was already calling me. He seemed like a normal guy, so I agreed to meet him at a get-together in Deep Ellum. The street leading to the warehouse where the get-together was being held was packed with cars all moving at a snail's pace. Bates had given me the code for the underground garage structure that was attached to the building where the party was. I could see the building less than a block ahead of me, but I wondered how long it would take me to make my way over there. Twenty minutes later I was punching in the five-digit code, with Bates in the car directly behind me.

I parked and waited for him by the elevator. I noticed several people with half masks and long trench coats walk onto the elevator. The women were all wearing high heels, and most of the men had on hiking boots.

"Is this a masquerade party?" I asked Bates as he walked up to me.

"Not really, but most people prefer to partially cover their faces," he said as he handed me a black half-face mask.

"Why do I need to wear this? What's really going on?"

"Nothing, as long as you have an open mind."

"Why do I need one of those?"

"This is Dallas, and in this city you can find almost anything you want."

"All I'm trying to find is a man with a big dick."

"And that's all I'm trying to find."

"What?" I said, convincing myself that I couldn't have heard what I thought I had.

"There'll be plenty of those upstairs."

The elevator door opened and we walked inside. He pressed the button to the top floor. "I know I told you a lot about myself over the phone, but what I didn't tell you is that I'm a swinger."

"A what?"

"A swinger. I'm into group sex. I don't sexually hold myself back from too much of anything."

"But you're black."

"There a lot of black swingers, baby."

"So this get-together is for swingers?"

"Yes," he said, and seemed to grow impatient.

"Wait, you can't just spring something like this on me and expect me to be all down for it. How did you get into this? How do you all find each other?"

"The Internet. That's how I got connected. Relax, everything's going to be fine. I'm sure you're going to enjoy yourself."

I shook my head. "This is too freaky for me. I'm not into all that. Don't you worry about diseases? I mean, I am looking for a man with a big dick, but not one he's been swinging all over town."

"Just go inside and judge for yourself. The beauty for you is that nobody in there knows you and you're not from here."

He was right, and that was the whole point of this summer to sexually explore, but swinging?

The elevator stopped and the door opened. "Put on your mask. And don't be frightened. Just be open," When we walked through the door, there were two big burly men standing behind it. "You'll need to take off your clothes so they can check you."

"Check me for what?"

"You have to be naked in here. They want to make sure that no one is hiding cameras. None of us want to end up on a *Dateline* or *20/20* special," Bates said as he started to undress. "And besides, you don't need to be dressed for what goes on in here."

One of the men started searching Bates, but he was stroking his dick a little too long, and judging by how hard he'd gotten, it was turning him on. Next thing I knew, the body checker got on his knees and put Bates's dick in his mouth and started sucking it like his life was depending on it. Bates extended his arms out and started grabbing hold of the wall.

"You need to get undressed, sweetie," my body checker said to me as I stood in shock, watching the other body checker continue to perform oral sex on Bates. "Take it all off."

I unbuttoned my blouse while I watched Bates begin pounding his dick inside that big burly man's ass. Made me think about what Melony said at the book club meeting about gay men. I was nervous when I stripped down to my birthday suit. Nervous, as I stood in front of my body checker trying not to eye him as he rubbed his hands over my silhouette.

"You're not hiding anything in here, are you?" he said as he rubbed the light fuzz on my pussy.

"No, I'm not," I said as I jerked his hand away from me. Then I walked to a dark corner in the house so I could observe and hopefully not be forced to participate.

A man came up to me—a man who had just finished slipping off a rubber after having sex with some other woman—and for his introduction, he rubbed his stiff dick on my thigh. This wasn't right. Not the kind of scene I was into. I wanted to explore, but not with a house full of freaks. "Let's fuck," he said to me.

"No, I don't want to," I said firmly.

"Isn't that what you're here for?"

"You just finished doing that other woman. Why would you think I'd now want you?"

"Well, in case you haven't noticed, that's what we're all in here doing." He tried moving his dick from my thigh to my pussy.

"Get off of me," I said as I pushed him away.

I moved to another corner. Now, I was standing beside a man who was sitting on an ottoman jacking off with a red spotlight shining on him, while a very thin, blond white woman danced in front of him. He took my hand and squeezed it while he climaxed. I couldn't do this. I didn't bother to find Bates to tell him I was leaving, I just left.

The next night, while my sister was at work, I did a Google search, typed in *swingers* and *Dallas*, and came up with a site that was full of thousands of posts. From the search results I found a sex site that announced: ENTER THE WORLD OF ANONYMOUS SEX. But it wasn't too anonymous because many of them included their picture. I started to put up my own profile, but decided instead to reply to a few. I wasn't looking for much. I just wanted to be fulfilled by one man, if possible. Hopefully someone would respond. Someone I could have my summer fling with.

Nice-N-Wet Looking for a Girlfriend to Play With

A few men responded to me from the Web site, but when I logged back on, I kept clicking on the women seeking women category. I had to get whatever had entered my system out so I could focus on my mission at hand, which was to have fun with some men who were strapped. There were plenty of them on the site, but first I needed to fulfill a fantasy that I'd never known existed before my encounter with Black Exotica, and that was to be with a woman. There were two pages of ads and over two dozen women with pictures showing off their best assets.

I was torn between Nice-N-Wet, who was the same age as me, thirty-one, and lived in Cedar Hill, which wasn't too far from my sister. Her ad read:

> ***I'm looking to meet an attractive female for a serious relationship. I'm very ladylike and I wish***

> *to find a woman who is the same. I have my own place and all the essentials. I'm professionally employed with no kids or responsibilities other than pleasing me and the woman who I decide to let enter my life. I'm tired of men so you need not continue to respond hoping you'll change my mind. I have a preference for a woman with a big fat ass like mine and long hair, no weaves please and no strippers.*

The other ad had the heading, LOOKING FOR A GIRLFRIEND TO PLAY WITH:

> *I am a black female, 30, seeking a companion to hang out with that can meet my sensual needs. I would like to go out for drinks, shop, and eat more than good food, and of course play. I am in a relationship with a man, but I need the touch of a woman every now and then. I am sexy, 5'6, 130 pounds, and uninhibited. My man knows of my preference and will not interfere. If you are a slim female, race unimportant, d/d free slim with big breasts. E-mail a picture of your best assets and I will do the same.*

It was a toss-up, so I decided to write both names on a tiny slip of paper, mix them up and pull one. And the winner was . . . LOOKING FOR A GIRLFRIEND TO PLAY WITH.

I used my sister's digital camera and snapped a few pictures of my breasts, legs, and feet, which I felt were my best assets, and I waited for her response. Every day for over a week, I checked my e-mail. Finally I received an e-mail from *sxyblkldy* with an attachment. She wrote:

> hey got your picture and i definitely like what i see. love those pretty toes and sexy legs. everything you sent was all good. sorry it took me so long to respond but my schedule with work and school is real hectic. i'd love to meet you face to face asap. take down my number and give me a call if you like what i have to offer. here's a picture i recently took to let you see what you could be holding on to real soon.
>
> —tricia

I scribbled her number on a Post-it and proceeded to cautiously open the attachment, since my sister had complained that her computer had recently gotten a virus and her e-mail was filled with porn, but I was curious and so I took the risk. The file opened a picture of Tricia bending over a chair, with her large butt and thighs nearly filling the nineteen-inch screen. When I heard the doorbell ring, I quickly closed all my open screens, logged out of the Internet, and then rushed to the front to see who was there.

"Hello again," Melony said when I opened the door.

"My sister isn't home."

"Do you really think I'm here to see your sister? I came by to see you. I thought that you might want to go out to eat."

"I have some company on *his* way."

"Listen, Alexis, I'm not one to bite my tongue. I prefer to do other things with it, and I'm sure it's probably pretty obvious what those other things are and who I'd like to do them with. I can tell when a woman's interested in me . . . and I can tell that you are. Don't worry, this isn't something that your sister has to find out about."

I was attracted to her, and thought that maybe it was better to meet a woman for my first experience this way then over the creepy Internet, where anyone can be lingering.

"Let me just take you out for some drinks so we can talk," she said.

"Where are you going to take me to, some gay club?"

She laughed. "No, guess what? We go to Ruby Tuesday also."

"I hate Ruby Tuesday."

"I wouldn't take you to a chain restaurant while you're visiting Dallas. Have you been to Pappadeaux yet?" I shook my head. "You'll love it. I don't think I've tasted anything better, but I haven't tasted your pussy yet either."

My eyes widened and my mouth partially opened from the shock of her statement. Looking back on it, if there was ever a turning point, something that caused me to go over to the dark side, it had to be the day I met Melony. Aside from the fact that she was a police detective who carried a gun and a stern look, she was a very feminine woman whom I was drawn to in some way. She had plenty of curves to her body, pretty light brown eyes, and extremely long golden brown hair. Seeing the two of us together, no one would have thought that we were anything other than girlfriends.

Men flirted when we walked into the restaurant during happy hour, and they bought us drinks all night. Before long the two of us had an obvious buzz.

"What are you thinking about right now?" I asked, hoping to break her stare.

"Eating you. I bet you taste so sweet. Don't you?"

"I don't know, I never tasted myself."

"Oh, yes you have. I'm sure you've had a man eat you out and then kiss you."

"I've had them try. But I'm not down for that. I don't want to taste my own or anyone else's."

"Well, I'm a firm believer that it's better to give than receive, anyway. So, when are you going to let me give some to you?"

I shrugged. "I enjoyed our talk, and I know that you're attracted to me, right?"

"I want to take you home and show you just how attracted to you I am. Is that okay with you?"

"Melony, listen to me," I whispered. "You're pretty. If I was leaning that way, I'd jump all over you."

"I'd let you."

"And I'm sure to a certain extent you might be able to satisfy me, but then, there would come a point when I'd need something to finish it off, and you don't have that something else."

"Oh, I do have something that can finish it off. Don't you worry about that."

"Oh, really, what, you're going through a sex change?"

She smirked. "Not quite."

"Then you don't have what I'm looking for. I came down here to find a man who's strapped."

"And you found yourself a woman who can strap one on and work it better than any man can."

"So you're the dominant one?"

"I carry a gun, don't I? Look . . ." She stood from the table, walked over to my side and bent down to whisper in my ear, "I'm ready to take you back to my place and fuck the shit out of you. How is that for honesty?"

One of the men who'd been buying us piña coladas all evening walked up and introduced himself to Melony and me as we were getting ready to leave.

"Thank you for the drinks," Melony said, "but we're not interested in getting to know you. We're trying to get to know each other. This is our first date. We're gay."

"Oh, shit, okay. They said there were a lot of lesbians in Dallas, so I guess they were right."

"Who ever they are . . . they were," she said as she took my hand, then walked out of the restaurant holding it.

"Why did you tell that man we were gay?" I asked, intentionally slurring my words. "You're gay. I'm not."

"You will be after I get finished with you. Get in the car."

"I'm not getting in your car," I said, still slurring.

She pushed me inside her convertible Saturn Sky. "And stop acting like you're drunk. You had one and a half drinks . . . piña coladas at that. You're fully aware of what's going down, so don't try to detract from my fun."

"How did you turn so gay, as pretty as you are?" I asked. "You couldn't have had any problems getting a man."

"Getting men wasn't my problem. Having them satisfy me has always been." She started rubbing my thighs while she drove down I–20 with the top up. "I like women—sexy, brown women. And I have a breast fetish, and you have some nice big round ones that I can do plenty with."

"They're not that big," I said.

"Let me see."

"See," I said, pulling down the top half of my tube dress.

"They're bigger than mine, which means they're big enough."

"Don't you want to be with a man, Melony? A man with a nine inch dick? There are plenty of them online."

"I'm a woman with a ten inch dick at home, and as soon as we get there, I'm going to use it on you."

"I'm sleepy," I said, struggling to keep my eyes open.

"You're not sleepy, you're faking it."

"I am sleepy."

"Close your eyes. I'll wake you when we get to my place."

When I opened my eyes, I was lying in her bed fully clothed and Melony was sitting beside me with the sheet concealing her bottom half. "How did I get in here?"

"I carried you."

"You must be strong."

"It's not like you're that big. You probably only weigh about a hundred and twenty with your pretty petite self," she said.

"I weigh a hundred and twenty-seven pounds, and you can't weigh much more than that yourself."

"One thirty-five." She smiled.

I sat up and glanced at the clock sitting on her nightstand. "I've been sleeping for almost two hours. And what have you been doing?"

Again she smiled. "Watching you."

I tugged at the peak in the center of her sheet. "What's that?"

She pulled the sheet off and revealed her strapless strap on. At first glance it appeared real. It was the same color as her flesh, and it even had veins and testicles. She inched her way over to me, brushing her thin lips against my full ones, and then gently bit my top lip before placing her tongue inside my mouth. She pulled my tube top down and caressed my breasts, swirling her tongue around my nipples and nibbling on them. I stood to wiggle out of my dress.

"Keep your heels on," she said, lying on her back with her head resting against two pillows.

I straddled her, leaned backward and supported myself with the palms of my hands as she used upward thrusts to penetrate me. Her strap-on was vibrating inside of me while her hands continued to cup my breasts. She rolled me onto my back and pulled off the strap-on. She began sucking my left nipple while squeezing my right breast and fingering me, all at the same time. She was gentle with every movement, and I kept coming over and over again. Her lips gradually traveled down my stomach until her tongue was wiggling inside my pussy. I spread my legs so her long wet tongue could get even deeper. Her long silky hair was resting on my thighs. I was a long way from my mission of finding a man who was strapped, but at least, so far, I had managed to find a woman who was.

My juices were covering her face. Melony spread her legs open and started playing with her clit. I was lying on my side next to her, resting my head in my hand. Her breasts were right in my face. "Yours are bigger than mine," I said as I took one in my mouth and started sucking.

"My breasts aren't bigger than yours," she said, "my nipples are."

While she was playing with her clit, I scooped my hand underneath her bottom half and stuck a finger inside her ass.

"You're getting kind of dominant, don't you think?" she said. "That's supposed to be my job."

She used a little unnecessary force to get me to lie on my back before sitting on my face and telling me to "Lick it like you love it." She was on my face, and I had no other choice but to insert my tongue inside of her, and the minute I did, she came. She came so many times, I lost count. When I was riding her and she had the strap-on, she came, saying that the sight of my breasts flapping in the air was what did it for her.

"Now, are you ready for me to make love to you?" she asked.

"I thought that's what we were doing."

"No, baby, that was foreplay. This is the real deal. This is the way I'm going to take your virginity and you're going to feel your cherry burst."

While I was lying on my back, she straddled me. "Aren't you going to put on that strap-on?" I asked.

Melony shook her head. "For what? I don't need one. I only did that to warm you up since you still think a dick is what you need. I know you've heard the saying that size doesn't matter. Well, it doesn't."

Our pussies began tongue kissing. She yelled out at the height of her climax and then became angry at me when she thought I was holding back. My clitoris couldn't stop vibrating from pleasure, but when I wouldn't scream out and express it, she flattened her body over mine and grinded while she filled my ear with her dirty talk. "You're not looking for a big dick. You're not looking for a dick at all. You want my pink pussy. Tell me what you want and how you want me to give it to you." She used her hand to gather the strands of my hair into a ponytail and then yanked my head back and proceeded to kiss and bite on the side of my neck while she continued rubbing our bodies together, causing so much friction I thought we were ready to ignite. She screamed out again, another climax, and this time her fluids were running down both her legs and mine. "Why are you fighting this when you know you want me?"

"I want a man with a big dick and plenty of veins protruding from it," I said, to piss her off, because I was ready to stop.

My statement made her do just that.

"Fine, go out and get you one," Melony said, rolled off me and sat on the edge of the bed.

"I told you at dinner what I came to Dallas to find."

"How could I forget what you came down here for, as much as you keep reminding me? But if you play with fire, you're bound to get burned."

"*You* seem more like fire than anything," I said.

"I'm not the fire, but those men you're out looking for . . . one of them might be. Don't you know that I'm looking for a serious relationship, and with this HIV epidemic, now is not the time to be searching for big dicks."

"I'm not gay and I know how to use protection."

"You can pretend with yourself but not with me. Tell me the last time a man has ever made you feel as good as I just did."

"Never. But all the men I've been with had little ones, so I'd rather answer that question after I've been with a man with a big one."

She shook her head. "I hate men. And I'd kill one before I'd let one put his hands on you and his nasty thing inside of you. You're mine now, and you're going to do what I say."

"I'm going to what?"

"Do what I say," she repeated with a smile, and then pushed me down on the bed and buried her head in my pussy for a few seconds before raising it. "Starting with growing some hair down here."

"Use your strap-on," I pleaded. "I need to feel something hard in my pussy."

"I'm not using anything," she said as she got up. "You need to come to grips with who you are and what you want. I'm not getting hurt again."

"Who hurt you?"

Melony left the room without answering, and I sat on the bed more confused than ever about my sexuality.

Two for the Price of One

When I returned to my sister's house the next afternoon, she had left for work and Melony had already called a few times to let me know how much she enjoyed having me over. While I was talking to Melony on the phone, I logged on to the sex site that I'd joined, to check my messages.

"And I know you liked it too," she said, "especially when I twirled my tongue all around the inside of your pussy and tickled your clit. I felt it throbbing. Are you going to let me lick you every day? A lick a day can keep those fucking men away."

"I don't see how that's possible."

"Anything's possible. Either I can make a detour while I'm at work to get a quick taste or you can meet me at my house when I get off."

"Melony," I said firmly, because it was time to set the record straight. "I hope you're not the possessive type."

"I can be if I have reason to. So just don't give me any reason to."

"Well, that's really too bad because I was just experimenting. In a few weeks my vacation will be over and I'll be in Detroit teaching."

"With my credentials, I could easily get a job on the Detroit Police Department."

"Whoa, slow down. No need to do all that."

"You weren't telling me to slow down last night when I was eating your pussy, so why are you telling me to slow down with the way I'm trying to love you?"

There was one new message waiting in my fantasy mail box. The e-mail was sent by asexymarriedcouple and read:

> hi, my wife and i like what we read and she'd like for you to be her first. this isn't the sort of thing we'd planned on doing, but we need someone to help us add a little spice in the bedroom. i know you didn't mention a preference for women but if you're open to the experience i'm sure my wife won't disappoint and all i want to do is watch. can you send us your photo? you can check out ours on the home page . . . we just joined and we're featured this week.

I clicked on the couple's photo that opened up to their profile and a gallery of over twenty photographs. I looked at every one, mostly full body shots that were taken while they were having sex. They were very careful not to expose their faces. The profile said that they were both thirty-five and had been married for five years. No children. His wife was "bi-curious," and he said that he just liked to watch. NO BUTCHES PLEASE. MUST BE FEMININE.

"I'll do anything just to be with you," Melony said to me while I read. "I'll even let you have a man from time to time as long as you don't get pregnant."

"What about a threesome? Would you ever be with a man if I wanted you to?"

"Never. And don't ever bring that shit up again."

"So your anything has limits?" I continued focusing on the online photo of the nude couple in the midst of a sex act. The caption underneath one of the pictures read, SOMEONE PLEASE HELP ME. I'M CHOKING ON THIS FOOT LONG COCK.

"As long as I don't have to be with a man, I will do anything."

When I ended my conversation with Melony, I typed a quick response to the married couple's e-mail.

> i'd luv to meet w/you especially . . . and as for your wife i have a special request. i'd like for my girlfriend to be with your wife and i desperately need to be with you. trust me, neither you nor your wife will be disappointed. think of it as getting two for the price of one.

The Web site indicated that asexymarriedcouple were online, so it didn't take long for a response.

> do you have a webcam?

> don't have a webcam but i can buy one today.

> ever had cybersex?

> no, but i'm up to trying new things.

not sure if you could tell from the photos but we are an interracial couple. i'm black and my wife is white. although race is not important, my wife would like to be with a black woman. she thinks their dildos are bigger.

well i'm black and my girlfriend is mixed. and she does have a pretty big dildo.

while i'm sitting at my desk responding to you she's under the desk orally satisfying me. it doesn't get much better than that, and not sure if you can bring it the way my wife does. can you?

most of the pictures i see you in she seems to be doing just that . . . sucking . . . how is she when it comes to fuckin'? she can continue to take you in her mouth . . . i want to put all twelve inches of you inside a different hole.

yeah, it's hard for her to handle me beyond oral . . . she can take some of me but not all . . . i haven't met a woman yet who could.

allow me to introduce myself . . . i'm the one woman who can and gladly will.

i'm getting excited. only one catch . . . my wife said i could only watch . . . and not participate. so we might have to figure a way to work around that . . . if i like what i see.

you will.

what's your best asset?

my juicy titties that get bigger every day.

yum . . . i'm a breast man. are they juicier than my wife's? she's a d.

so am i . . . but a full d, meaning i pop out of my bra . . . whenever i decide to wear one.

let's not chat the day away. go out and get the cam so we can get the ball rolling.

speaking of balls rolling . . . [I typed]

lol. get the webcam and maybe the rest can be arranged. my wife and i are really into role playing. can you and your girlfriend act something out for us?

don't see why not.

Melony called me while I was standing in line buying the webcam. "You are just the person that I wanted to talk to," I said. "My sister's staying over Tony's tonight. Can you come over and keep me company?"

"I can be there in a couple hours."

"Do you mind if we role-play tonight?"

"Why would I mind that? Anything for my baby," she said.

"I'll be waiting for you. Oh, don't ring the doorbell. Take down the code to the garage door. I want to start our role-play as soon as you enter the house."

"Okay, but who am I playing?"

"The sexy nurse coming for a house call."

"Mmm, there's a few things I can bring over."

I had set up the webcam to record the guest bedroom. I tested the picture quality with asexymarriedcouple to make sure they could see the room. The show was going to start in less than thirty minutes, I assured them, and our show ran without advance previews so their early request for me to reveal myself was denied.

When I heard the garage door open and the alarm chime to indicate someone had opened the door leading from the garage to the kitchen, I immediately went into action and started crying real tears, a gift I'd acquired from childhood.

Melony rushed through the bedroom door and found me sitting on the side of the bed with a thin sheet draping my naked body. "What's wrong, Alexis?"

My eyes popped open when she walked through the door in white lace-up and Oxford platform high-heeled pumps with a red cross on the toe, and holding a doctor's bag. She was wearing a naughty red and white nurse's outfit with red rubber gloves and a stethoscope hanging around her neck that had a purple penis dangling at the end.

"Why couldn't the doctor come?" I asked.

"Well, the hospital has rules about treating patients who don't have insurance, but I could tell from our phone conversation that you were in real need of some emergency medical treatment."

"Nurse Melony, thank you so much for coming over. I'm really worried that I may be sick. I fucked a man with a twelve inch dick and I haven't felt right ever since." Both Melony and I sounded like a couple of B actresses.

"I'll need to give you an exam to make sure everything is still intact down there."

"But I'm so sore I can barely move. My pussy feels like it's on fire."

"A burning sensation could mean a venereal disease. I'll need to take a culture swab. Lie on the table flat on your back so I can take a look."

I did what she'd asked. "Now put your legs in these stirrups," she said, pulled out a pair of wrist and ankle cuffs and tied me to the bed with the straps that were attached. "Slide your lower body toward me so I can take a look."

Melony sat on the bar stool that I'd taken from the kitchen. She pulled the sheet away from my body so she could see my lower half in full view. "I'll need to do a pelvic."

She stood from the chair, walked closer to me and bent down. She opened her doctor's case and removed a metal speculum that she inserted inside of me so she could spread my pussy open. She put her latex-gloved finger inside of me, and it began vibrating while she pressed her other hand down on my stomach. "Everything feels normal. Is that painful?"

"Not at all," I moaned.

She removed her finger, took off the fingertip vibrator and the glove, and then reinserted her bare finger inside of me. "Does that feel any better?"

"Yes," I moaned.

"This is better for me to gauge how wet your pussy is getting. Now let me take some cultures to make sure that big dick didn't give you an STD." She stuck her head between my legs and covered her head with the sheet, and within seconds her tongue was licking my clit.

"That sure doesn't feel like a Q-tip," I said.

She stopped licking and said, "Our clinic is in short supply so I had to improvise."

I held her head between my legs and tossed the sheet off of my body so the webcam could catch Melony in action.

"There are just a few more procedures I need to perform and then I should be on my way."

"Okay, and those are?"

"I need to do a full breast exam, and then a pap smear."

"The pap smear hurts so much."

"I'll try to be gentle. Which do you want me to do first?"

"The pap smear, since I'm already in the stirrups."

She walked over to the light switch and flicked it off. Her purple stethoscope was glowing in the dark. "I need to check your vaginal beat."

"What kind of nurse are you?"

"A nurse that wants your pussy. You said you had twelve inches inside of you. Well, this is eighteen inches long and two inches wide."

"I can't handle all of that."

"I know. That's why we're going to share."

I realized that with the light off, the webcam couldn't record the action. "Can you turn the light back on? I want to see you gettin' some too."

She flipped the light switch on, slid one end of the dildo inside of her, and then stood between my legs. "Do you want me to take it fast or slow?"

"Do whatever you feel."

"I feel like fucking," she said as she rammed the other end inside me.

My moans became so loud, I was afraid my sister's next door neighbors, who were sitting on their back porch, might hear me. She climbed on top of me and I wrapped my legs around her back and enjoyed every second of the vibration her lower half was causing mine to have.

Melony left before morning, afraid that my sister might come home early. A few hours later I logged on to check my e-mail.

Asexymarriedcouple wrote:

> we'd like to meet you and the nurse asap. my wife is also in need of some emt.

"Explain all of this to me again," Melony said on the phone the next day, after I tried telling her about the married couple and how his wife wanted to meet her for sex. She didn't seem to fully understand how I was willing to share her with another woman. She appeared hurt and offended. "I thought your feelings for me were genuine."

"They are, Melony, but I still need to get this urge of mine out of my system."

"And you want to do that by having me screw some man's wife so you can screw her husband? How did you even meet these people?"

"Online."

"Online, Alexis? You met them online, and now you're going to their house to have sex with them? Do you know how dangerous that is? Why would you even want to do that?"

"I'm not sure why, but one thing I don't feel like is being judged.

All my life I've played it safe, and all that got me was a bunch of men who didn't want to do anything for me, just wanted to use me for whatever I was worth. Now, I want to be the one in control for a change. I want to be the person using someone for what they're worth. I'm tired of faking my orgasms . . . I want to have one."

"I don't make you come?" Melony asked.

"Yes, you do, but I want to have an orgasm with a man, Melony." I walked into the garage and got in my sister's car. "I'm on my way to their house."

"Don't go over to someone's house that you don't know. Are you out of your mind?"

I started the engine. "Don't let me go by myself. Meet me there so nothing will happen. You don't want to be the lead detective investigating my murder, do you?" I said as I pulled out of the garage.

"Like I keep telling you, you're playing with fire, and one day, Alexis—"

"I'm going to get burned. I know, but I thought my woman would protect me."

She laughed. "Amazing how I conveniently became your woman when you want me to do something." There was a few seconds of silence. "There is no way I would go to a stranger's house for sex."

"Forget it. I won't go either, but I'm getting some big dick tonight somehow," I said before ending the call.

Later, I spent a couple hours milling through e-mails, looking at the attachments of penises that were locking up my in-box. One e-mail in particular caught my eye. Anaconda said he needed someone to suck the venom from his huge snake, and he sent over a picture of himself sucking his own. That's when I realized that I was dealing with some real freaks. I didn't want that anymore. I'd been talking on the phone to Lester all summer. The only thing that prevented me from meeting with him was when he told me he wanted to be choked. But I'd rather choke a man out of play than watch a man choke on himself for pleasure, so I called Lester and finally arranged a face-to-face meeting.

We arranged to meet at Sambuca's, a jazz club in uptown Dallas. I went and waited for a while, but when it appeared that I'd been stood up, I left with a different man, whom I'd met that evening, and the two of us went to a hotel. I thought he was a complete stranger, only to discover that he was Lester, the man I'd been chatting with, doing what he said he did best—playing games. But things went terribly wrong that night. I'd finally gotten what I wanted—almost. At the height of his climax, it was time for me to strangle him, even though I hadn't come yet. I strapped the belt around his neck, but maybe I did it a little too firmly and held on longer than I should have. It was an accident, I kept trying to convince myself.

"Melony, where are you?" I whispered through my cell phone.

"I'm at work. Where do you think I am? You finally decided to answer your phone."

"Melony, I need your help. I got burned . . . badly. I can't say too much over the phone."

"Is it serious?"

"Very. Things got out of hand."

"Don't say any more. Just tell me where you are and I'll be there."

The Black Widow Strikes Again

I was in tears when I opened the door. Melony was standing there dressed all in black and wearing a pair of leather gloves.

She stepped inside the hotel room. "What happened?"

"I've been playing with fire and I got burned, just like you told me I would."

"Well, maybe you'll listen to me from now on." She walked around the room. "What did you touch?"

"Nothing," I said.

"You had to touch something," she said as she walked across the room and looked down at the dead body. "You touched the doorknob when you let me in. I'll have to remove it before I leave. There's too much of your DNA in this room. We're going to have to burn it."

"Cause a fire? I've already killed one person. I don't want to kill any more."

"You won't kill any more. These hotels have sprinklers. I just need a little fire to get rid of the DNA and to make it look like this is the workings of the Black Widow."

She removed a tube of red lipstick from her bag and wrote across the mirror:

The Widow Black has struck again
XXX

"You write just like her," I said with concern. "I watched the news special. Her writing is very distinctive."

"Okay, well, I'm a detective and I've worked the case so I've seen a lot of the evidence."

"Are you sure that's all it is?"

"Who killed this man, me or you? There's a party going on in the second floor ballroom. It's a public party. I need you to take the elevator to the second floor, pay whatever they're charging. Don't sign a guest book, just walk around and be seen—that way, if someone remembers you from this evening, you can always say you were there for the party. When I'm getting ready to set the fire, I'll call you. Don't answer. That's when I want you to leave and go to my house. I'll meet you there."

It took nearly an hour for Melony to call me. I wondered what she'd been doing up there for all that time, but as soon as my cell phone rang and I saw her name on my caller ID, I did as she instructed. I didn't answer, but I did leave the hotel and headed to her house. I had the key she'd given me weeks earlier and so I let myself in. I wanted to look around. See if there was any evidence that could link Melony to the Black Widow, but then there was that part of me that didn't really want to know. Perhaps it was just a coincidence that her writing matched exactly, or maybe it wasn't exact. The only thing I did remember the news special saying was that the Black Widow most likely used the Internet to meet her victims, which put me at ease because Melony didn't even own a computer.

I curled up in her bed and went to sleep.

In the morning, I woke up to the smell of pancakes and bacon. Melony had come home and cooked me breakfast.

"Good morning," she said, as she set the tray of food on the bed. "I took care of everything. You don't have anything at all to worry about. They linked the murder to the Black Widow. There's no DNA and they're just as baffled by this case as they are by all the rest."

"I'm so drained."

She started rubbing her fingers through my hair. "Well, you probably just need to get some more rest. You had a crazy night. I won't disturb you."

"You just got off work. Don't you want to take a nap?" I asked.

"No, not now. I'm kind of wired up."

"But I want you to take one with me. Are you going to turn me in?"

She shook her head. "I'm an accessory so I can't turn you in, but even if I wasn't, I still wouldn't turn you in, because I'm in love with you."

"You're still in love with me even though I killed someone?"

"We all make mistakes," she said as she walked to the closet and pulled out a black bag.

"What's in the bag?"

"My lap top. I have some work to do."

"You have a lap top? I didn't know that. I've never seen you use it before. Is it new?"

"No, I've had this for a little while. I just don't use it that often."

"So why are you using it now?"

"Like I said, I have some work to do. Go to sleep, baby. I'll join you soon enough."

When she left the room, I sprung up from the bed, but I was too afraid to leave the room. I didn't want her thinking that I suspected her, but now it was starting to come together. Now I could link her to a computer, which was a means for the Black Widow to meet her victims. Why had Melony been in the hotel room so long? Was she recreating the crime scene to make it look even more like the work of the Black Widow? Or was I just tripping because I'd killed someone and I didn't want to be the only murderer in the household. I climbed back in the bed, under the sheets, and closed my eyes trying to put the past well behind me. My entire summer vacation was a waste, not just of time, but also of a life. I'd come here because everything was supposed to be bigger in Texas, and I was hoping the same held true when it came to the men. But the only person I was able to find who was truly strapped and could satisfy me was a woman—a woman who had to strap one on—a woman who just might be the Black Widow serial killer.

I couldn't get back to sleep, but I did manage to eat some of the food Melony had brought. After a few hours she joined me in the bed, but turned her back toward me while she lay there. I asked if something was wrong and she said nothing so I left it alone.

"When are you going back to Detroit?" she asked a few minutes later.

"Next week. Why, are you going to miss me?"

"Well, honestly, I was thinking about going back with you."

"But what about your job? You're going to quit it? And what about your house?"

"I'm sure I can get on with the Detroit Police Department. Just like I'm sure I can sell this house. But I'll only come if you want me to. Do you?" I hesitated. I mean, did I? That was a good question. Even if I was stretching my imagination and she wasn't the Black Widow, would I want her to follow me home? In Dallas, I could act out a few fantasies and no one would be the wiser. But in Detroit, I'd have to answer to some folks who would be all in my business. Like Nancy, for one.

"I guess you don't," Melony said, waiting on my answer. "I guess I was just your summer fling."

"The summer isn't over yet," I said as I snuggled up next to her to initiate our lovemaking. She wasn't expecting that, but I felt that I at least owed her that much. She'd gotten me out of a jam, and since sex was a stress reliever, we had might as well relieve some.

"Do you feel bad about what you did to that man?" she asked as I was playing in her long locks.

"Not really." I kissed her soft lips.

"I can tell. So why don't you?"

"I'm not sure. The way I look at it, if he had a choking fetish, he was probably going to get killed sooner or later. The only thing I'm upset about is that the sex wasn't even worth it. I didn't even have an orgasm."

"Do you realize that less than twenty-four hours ago you killed a man, and now you're still thinking about sex?"

"It was an accident. I mean, I wasn't the one playing with fire . . . he was. In fact, in some ways, I wish that I really was the Black Widow," I said, hoping to bait her in, but it didn't work. She didn't say a word, except to tell me she wasn't in the mood for sex that evening.

The First Day of School

"Did you hear my story, Miss Cartwright?" one of my students asked, snapping me from my thoughts of the summer I'd had; a summer that I couldn't share with my students the way they were doing with me and the rest of the class on their first day of school. While some of my students could boast of a trip to Disney World or a summer they spent out of state with relatives, many others remained in Detroit the entire summer highlighting a concert they attended at the Fox Theatre of a famous urban or hip hop artist like Kanye West, or a day at the State Fair.

I sat behind my desk and pretended to be interested in what Kenya, one of my students, said about her weekend spent at the Indianapolis Black Expo, when in actuality my mind was hundreds of miles away back in Dallas, where I'd unintentionally left a deadly mark. It was easier for me not to think about what I'd done while I was there. Even though it was an accident, I'd still killed someone. And the part that concerned me more was whether I'd be caught for running away from the scene of the crime.

Knowing that Melony was going to join me permanently made me wonder if I'd ran at all. We had arrived in Detroit a week before school started, but she was going back to Dallas in a few days to take care of some business. I was purposely avoiding my best friend Nancy, who'd left dozens of messages on my answering machine in a one week period, demanding to know how my summer went.

"Welcome back, Miss Cartwright," Scottie, one of my students from last year, said as he passed by my classroom, snapping me from my daze. I turned and gestured and then watched as he stopped dead in his tracks.

"Dang, Miss Cartwright, what happened to you?" The classroom fell out in laughter as if it were an inside joke. Had I changed that much in two and a half months? I guessed so. Gone were the glasses and down went my hair. I'd turned in the flats for some stilettos and my buttoned-up blouse for plunging necklines.

"I wish I could tell you, Scottie," I said with a wink, "but you're just a little too young."

"A summer fling . . . a summer fling. I got you," he said as he disappeared down the hallway.

If I were to write my own paper about my most memorable event of the summer, I doubt if I could pen it down to just one. And first I'd have to start with the moment that changed my life, which wasn't the murder but my encounter with Black Exotica. This past summer was a wild ride from the last day of the school year to the first day back. And what happened in between was simply unforgettable.

I stood from my desk. "Well, it's been a great first day and I'm excited about the upcoming school year. No homework today but come prepared because you'll have plenty tomorrow."

The last bell for the day rang and all of my students scattered out of the classroom. I gathered my belongings and stood at the window, watching the school kids rushing to their buses or the cars that waited.

I walked down the hall to the teacher's lounge to spend the last hour doing my lesson plans for the week. When I entered, all eyes were on the television screen mounted to the wall and blasting the twelve o'clock news.

"Girl," LaShandra, one of the teachers, said, "did you bring that serial killer back with you?"

"What are you talking about?"

"The Black Widow . . . they think she's in Detroit. They found a dead man in a motel room and there were those markings left on the mirror. The room was set on fire. They say it's the work of the Black Widow, the same serial killer that was murdering those men in Texas."

"It's probably just a copycat," I said.

"I doubt that," LaShandra said, "I really doubt that. You're not the Black Widow, are you?"

"Me?" I said, shaking under my skin. "I couldn't kill a fly." I took a seat by the window and stared out at the rain that had just started to fall.

"That's strange, though, isn't it?" LaShandra asked.

The door creaked open and in walked Jamal, the gorgeous math teacher I'd fantasized about last school year. He was carrying a Pizza Hut box. He was my type of man; well-groomed, cleanly shaven, with a bald head and a clear chocolate brown complexion. I could tell he worked out regularly by the way his clothes hugged his body.

"Would you like some, Mrs. Cartwright?" Jamal asked.

"I do, but not pizza," I mumbled.

"What was that?" he asked as he sat beside me.

"Well, my little break is over," LaShandra said, then stood and walked out of the door, the rest of the room following behind her, with the exception of Jamal.

He opened the pizza box and pulled apart a slice. "Do you want some?" he asked again.

"Yes," I said, looking directly into his eyes, "I do want some . . . just not some pizza."

"Well, what do you want, Mrs. Cartwright?"

"Just call me Alexis. And I'm not a Mrs." I moved my chair closer to his. "I have a lot on my mind and I need to do something that will reduce my stress level. Any suggestions?"

"Working out usually helps me."

"Really?" I said, leaning into him. "I've been telling myself that I needed to start working out, but I hate to do it alone. Would you mind training me?" I rested my hand on his thigh and rubbed my way up and over until I had his belt buckle in my hand. "We don't need to go to a gym. We can do it all right here."

We both scrambled—I for the door and he for the window shade. The lights stayed on, so I could see just what I'd be working with. And as he stripped down to his birthday suit, I stood in awe of not only his perfectly sculpted body, varnished with tattoos and fraternity brands, but also the biggest muscle of them all—his ten-inch weight. "I had no idea you were that muscular," I said, eyeing the weight between his legs. "I better change into my workout clothes." I dropped my dress, removed my bra, and stepped out of my panties.

"Before you begin any exercise, you should start off stretching the muscles you plan to work," he said, tugging on his big muscle.

"I need to stretch my pelvic muscles, and I want you to use your big muscle that you're tugging on to help me." I sat on the table on the open lid of his pizza box, spread my legs apart as far as they could go and started to Kegel. He walked over to me and without saying one word rammed his ten inch muscle inside of me. My muscles quickly tightened around his hard as steel dumbbell.

"We're going to do three sets of ten. Make sure you inhale and exhale," he said between the heavy breathing.

Within minutes I'd come. And to think I went all the way to Dallas to find something I had right here at home.

He kissed me on the forehead. "How was that for a stress reliever?"

"It helped," I said as I stood from the table and got dressed. "Now we just need to establish a regular workout schedule—three days a week."

"I'll see you again on Wednesday, then. I got something you can work your lip muscles on."

I walked out of the teacher's lounge with a big smile plastered to my face and fresh thoughts of the best first day of school I'd ever had. The news report wasn't far from my mind either. LaShandra called the news strange, but it was more than strange. It was obvious. Now I had a dilemma. The first man I killed was by accident. The second man I killed was on purpose. And even though I wasn't the original black widow, I was trained by the best. Now that Jamal had sex with me, as good as it was, he had just become my next target.

Native Detroiter **CHERYL ROBINSON** is the author of three novels: *If It Ain't One Thing*, *It's Like That*, and *When I Get Free*. She is a graduate of Wayne State University with a degree in Marketing. She resides in central. Florida and is working on her fourth novel, which will be published in late 2007. To learn more, please visit www.cherylrobinson.com.

Divas Need Love Too

Méta Smith

Acknowledgments

I'd like to thank my muse for inspiring me to write this story. You know who you are, Spock, and you know I love you.

Thanks to my family and friends, especially my girls Angela Allen, Tracey Smith, and Dinora Lozano, for being there when I needed you. I swear I'd be in the loony bin without you. Or in jail! And once again, thanks Linda Duggins for keeping me sane, even when it's not in your job description. I love you guys.

Thanks to Marc Gerald for hooking this up, a million thanks to May Chen for your flexibility and patience while I worked on this project, and many thanks to HarperCollins for the opportunity. I've loved every minute of it.

And of course I'd like to acknowledge the talented and beautiful women who join me in this anthology: Electa Rome Parks, Cheryl Robinson, and my girl Joy King.

Prelude

A musky, exotic scent and the sound of soft music wafted through the air. I sipped my glass of Opus One and crossed my legs demurely, but I was feeling anything but demure. I repositioned myself in order to appear more alluring. There was no need to beat around the bush or pretend that I wanted anything besides an intense, passion-filled, uninhibited, buck-wild fuck session. My lover sipped a little more of his wine, allowed me to do the same, and then gently removed the glass from my hand and put it on the cocktail table. I lowered my lids and leaned forward, exposing maximum cleavage while parting my lips in expectation of a kiss. My lover allowed me to get inches away from his lips before running his hand through my hair, then slowly but firmly tightened his grip until he was almost painfully pulling my hair. I gasped in pain and delight.

"You are so fucking beautiful," he said, turning my head to face him and looking at me as if I were the sexiest woman alive.

A soft moan escaped my lips. I licked them and tried to kiss him. He firmed his grip on my hair and yanked a little.

"We have all night," he told me. "There's no reason to rush this." His tongue darted across my lips and I strained to kiss him again.

"But I want you so bad," I begged.

"Good, Songbird. Good."

He licked and nipped and nibbled at my lips, at times kissing me, at others allowing only his breath to tickle my lips as he hovered above me. I flicked my tongue outward in an attempt to taste any part of him. I caught the softly scented area beneath his chin and licked down to his Adam's apple. He felt scratchy, where the coarse hairs of his beard where growing in. I inhaled his smell; just a whiff of his cologne made me wet. He released his hold on my hair, gave me a little shove onto the couch and stood in front of me.

"Don't move," he ordered. I did what he wished.

He slowly unbuttoned his shirt and peeled it from his body. Then he unbuckled his belt and let his trousers fall to the floor before stepping out of them. I could see his hard-on bulging through the fabric of his boxer briefs, and I reached out to touch it.

"Not yet," my lover commanded. He approached me and stroked my cheek before letting his hardness brush against my face. His underwear was a little wet where drops of lubrication must have been oozing from the tip of his penis.

"I want to suck it," I told him. I needed to feel him inside of every part of me.

"I want you to suck it," he replied. I reached for him but he stopped me. He took both my slender wrists into one of his large hands.

"I want you to suck it," he repeated, "but you can't touch it. Put your hands behind your back."

Kinky, I thought, and did what I was told.

He lowered his briefs, a centimeter at a time, until his rock hard cock sprung forth and was throbbing right before my lips. I opened my mouth and leaned forward, growing excited as I tasted the faint saltiness of his pre-come. I looked up at him, and he was staring right back at me. I sucked the tip a little harder, using gentle suction to draw him farther into my mouth.

"That's right," he said. "I want you to get it wet."

I slurped and sucked away, gradually engulfing more of his dick, until I was nearly gagging and saliva was dripping from the corners of my mouth and onto my breasts. I could tell my lover was growing more excited, which turned me on a great deal. He told me that I couldn't touch him and ordered my hands behind my back, but I was going to break the rules. As he thrust himself in and out of my mouth, I caressed my breast and pinched my nipple with one hand, while slowly stroking between my legs with the other. Very soon my fingers were covered with my own juices as they slid in and out of me.

"You're cheating," he said.

I would have answered him, but my mouth was full. He pushed me away from his body.

"You're a naughty girl," he said. "I'm going to have to punish you."

"I'd like to see you try," I said, full of bravado. "Are you going to spank me?" I asked provocatively.

"I could just keep this dick to myself," he said.

Damn, I hadn't thought of that form of punishment.

"Don't do that," I said quickly.

"I won't," he replied. "I have something more devious in mind."

My lover's hands moved slowly and deliberately as he let his fingertips dance lightly over my skin. I wanted him to grab me, embrace me, fuck my brains out. I couldn't take the anguish of his slow seduction. I writhed and wiggled, arching my back and thrusting my pelvis, trying to increase our body contact, but he continued to take his time.

My desire burned hotter as my lover's hands caressed every inch of me. Articles of clothing fell from my body like a snake shedding its skin until I lay naked, shivering beneath his touch. He allowed me to touch him now, and my hands roamed over his taut, muscular shoulders. God, he had the perfect body, and I told him so. His skin was smooth and perfect, and he wasn't too big or too small. As he gently sucked my nipples, his hands never ceased kneading my flesh between his strong fingertips, causing me to tingle.

"Please," I begged him. "You're driving me crazy. I need you."

"Not yet," he replied.

He began to move lower across my torso, kissing a trail down my chest and over my abdomen until I felt his hot breath and the hairs of his goatee tickle the sensitive skin between my thighs. I sighed in anticipation, parted my legs and closed my eyes. I felt his fingertips as they spread my lips apart, and moaned when he began to taste me, flicking his tongue around my clitoris. And just as I was about to explode, he stopped. I thought he was giving me a break in an attempt to prolong my climax and that he would continue and eventually finish what he started, but he was gone.

I sat up and looked around, searching for him through the dim light of the scented candles that illuminated the room.

"That is so not fair," I pouted.

He reappeared, his erection standing out from his body in an intimidating arch. I hummed in approval.

"I wanted to be ready," he said. He'd put on a condom. Responsible . . . I can never hate that.

He dropped back to his knees and began to lick me again. I threw my head back and began to sing in ecstasy, grinding my hips eagerly against his face. As my body tensed and I felt a wave of pleasure radiate from the inside out, he stopped eating me and entered me. I throbbed around him as he plunged inside me. I hit high notes that Minnie Ripperton and Mariah Carey could never achieve.

"That's right, Songbird," he said, "sing for me," he breathed into my ear, intensifying my climax.

I moaned and sighed and screamed until my voice began to sound harsh and shrill. Then things got weird. I shut my mouth but I could still hear the shrill sound getting louder and louder. My body felt lighter and lighter, until finally I slipped from unconsciousness into the land of the living.

Damn it! Another wet dream. Literally. I ran my hand over the four-hundred-thread count sheets that were now wrinkled and damp.

I really, really need to get laid. I am hornier than a twelve-year-old boy who just discovered his father's stash of skin mags. Maybe if I get laid, I'll stop dreaming about *him*. My dream lover and I are over, and have been for some time, and moreover, there is absolutely no good reason for me to be wasting time thinking about him, my *ex*-boyfriend. He was the one who lost out on a good thing, not me! He should be in bed dreaming about me!

I'm everything a man could want and then some. A few years ago I was a thirty-year-old college grad who was waiting tables and struggling to make ends meet, chasing the dream of being a star long after what most folks said was an appropriate age to make it big. Friends and family, though they may have meant well, totally discouraged my aspirations to sing, even though there was no question that I could not just sing, but *blow*, plus I write songs that stir the soul. But they thought that because I was "smart" and had a degree, I should get serious and get a "real job" and stop pining after my "childhood fantasies." But I couldn't give up on myself like that.

I couldn't take the easy road out just because things got tough. I've known since the first day I opened my mouth in the choir of the First Chicago Missionary Baptist Church that I was born to be a singer. I knew there was no expiration date on my talent. Now I live in a mansion in Miami and have a platinum album and a trio of number one hits to my songwriting credits because of my hard work, perseverance, and uncanny ability to say "Fuck the world, I'm going for mine." Now I have everything that I ever dreamed of . . . except someone to share it all with.

God, I know that sounds pathetic! But trust me, I'm not one of those women who simply because I'm a member of the "Dirty 30 Club" feels so desperate that I'm willing to jump on anything that shows an interest. And I certainly don't subscribe to the bullshit theory that my life isn't complete without a man. But a man would be nice! Lately I've been spending more time in the studio than out looking for Mr. Right or in the bedroom getting my freak on, and the lack of action is starting to take its toll on my peace of mind and my vibrators!

It seems like the more successful I get, the harder dating becomes. I never thought that Waiting to Exhale stuff would happen to me, but here I am, thirty-something and still no better at relationships than when I was twenty-something. I'm simply no good at affairs of the heart. Either my judgment sucks or I think with the wrong part of my body or a little bit of both, but that just seems so . . . stupid. And I'm pretty sure I'm not stupid; I mean, would I have gotten this far if I was?

Maybe there's some kind of crazy generational love curse on me. None of my sisters are married, and my mother and aunts—and there are nine of them—never could stay married for long or are married to the wrong-ass men. My mom and aunts are smart; all of them have good careers and are making a decent living, and they're all fine. Nine dimes. They should have it all together. But they don't. My grandmother is the big dime. She was a straight-up fox back in the day: big legs, nice figure, with beautiful skin and hair, and a sweet disposition that hid an evil streak that struck fear in the boldest and most courageous of men. She married five times, but each of her husbands died strange and mysterious deaths at a young age. Needless to say, she's the subject of many rumors, and there has even been some speculation that Tyler Perry's character Madea's penchant for killing men with sweet potato pies was inspired by my nana!

But curse or no curse, I just can't seem to get the hang of what almost everyone else acts as if it's so simple: finding the man, hooking the man, and keeping the man until you die or kill each other. The real irony here, though, is that my name is Lucky. Straight up, it's my real name, and yes, my mother named me that. She said it was because she loves to read those books by that chick Jackie Collins, about some ballsy mafia daughter named Lucky. But those books came out *after* I was born. My aunt told me the real deal—that my mom used to date a dude in high school named Lucky—but he's not my dad, at least not to my knowledge. But with my crazy ass family, nothing would surprise me.

I've come to respect love, not just desire it, I really and truly have. I've remained open to all the possibilities of finding that special someone, staying optimistic and not becoming bitter, but now my patience is starting to wear thin. I'm not old by any means, and I know I've got some time left before I become a spinster with no one but her cats to show her love. But I'm not getting any younger. In the meantime, I keep on believing, hoping that one day, as far as my love life is concerned, I'll live up to my name.

Verse 1

I curled up under the fat, goose-down comforter and tried to go back to sleep. Despite the fact that my alarm clock had gone off, I could get in another thirty minutes before I had to get up and officially start my day, but nothing doing; the phone rang and destroyed any hope of catching more z's.

"Hey Lucky girl, are you up?" It was my publicist, Leslie. In my line of work you really need someone around that cares about what happens to you, and not just because your paycheck pays the note on their snappy little Jag, but because they have a conscience and ethics and integrity and a heart. Leslie is that someone in my life. She isn't just my publicist, she's my friend, and she helps keep me sane. She was also keeping me from the possibility of getting some extra sleep.

"I'm up," I told her.

"Are you sure?"

"I'm up."

"I'm on my way and I'm going to use my key. If I come up there and your butt is still in the bed, I'm going to drag you out by your hair extensions," she warned me.

"I'm not in bed, I'm up!" I lied.

"Good. See you in a minute," she said, and hung up.

I peeked at the alarm clock at my side, which read 3:30 A.M. Time to make the doughnuts. I reluctantly got out of the luxurious bed at my suite at the Peninsula Hotel in downtown Chicago, threw the curtains back, and took in the most magnificent skyline in the world. Sweet home, Chicago, my kind of town! I was the prodigal daughter who returned home a big success, and I planned on reveling in the glory of my accomplishments. I wanted all the naysayers and nonbelievers who thought I'd never make it to bow down and recognize the diva. I also wanted my ex-boyfriends to eat their collective hearts out.

True to her word, Leslie breezed into my suite looking totally pulled together and chic in a cropped denim jacket, capris, and a funky T-shirt. She greeted me with a hug and got right down to business. Her curly hair bounced as she pushed back her glasses and spoke to me a mile a minute in her mellow voice tinged with a New York accent.

"You ready to do this?" she asked, full of enthusiasm. I looked at her with wonder. Her copper skin was practically glowing and she seemed so organized. How she managed to be so fucking chipper, so focused, and look so good so early in the morning, was beyond me.

"Yeah, I'm ready," I said, looking longingly at the bed. Those Egyptian cotton sheets were calling my name.

"Well move, girl, like your ass is on fire. We've got a schedule to keep!" Leslie clapped her hands at me. Any minute, the "glam squad"—the hair stylist and makeup artist dedicated to making me fly—would arrive. It was going to take them at least an hour to get me appearance ready, and my itinerary was crammed full of appointments, interviews, and the like.

"Are you rested? You've got a busy day ahead of you, and tomorrow's the big night, your CD's platinum party!"

"I slept all right, I guess," I told her, thinking about my erotic dream. "But you know I'm a night owl. It's too early to be waking up. I should be just now going to bed!"

"Sleep is for the weak, so get moving. Take a shower."

I didn't move.

"What's wrong with you?" she asked, putting her hands on her hips. We spent so much time together that Leslie could easily read my moods, even when I tried to disguise them.

"I'm a little nervous," I admitted. I was a tad bit worried about how my homecoming was going to go over. Hometown artists have it hard in the Windy City. Talented cats like Common and Twista still don't get the love they deserve at the crib. I was afraid that I wouldn't be respected by my hometown, afraid that the haters would take over. *She's not all that . . . I remember when she was a nobody . . . I hope she doesn't think she's special now.* I could just hear the envious people saying all that about me.

"You've got nothing to be worried about," Leslie reassured me, grabbing my hand and leading me into the bathroom.

"What if nobody comes?" I asked in an uncharacteristic moment of self-doubt.

"Stop tripping. People are going to come. Your friends will come." She turned on the shower.

"I don't have any friends," I told her.

"Well, your enemies are going to come too," Leslie said.

"I don't have any enemies."

Leslie rolled her eyes at me and laughed. "Yes you do!" she kidded.

"Haters but not enemies," I corrected her, punching her lightly on the arm.

"Whatever," she said. "People are going to be curious. You're already a big star. And the buzz around you is phenomenal. You have nothing to worry about. When you see me worry, then you should worry."

"Okay," I said, hesitantly. "You're from New York. Chicago is not like New York. Chicago never supports its own people. This is the city of hate. Folks might not come just so they can see me fall on my face."

"Well, if they don't come, they can't see you fall, now can they?" Leslie quipped.

"Shut up," I said dryly.

"Get naked, get in, get clean, and get out," she ordered like a drill sergeant. "You've got fifteen minutes."

I saluted her, and she left me in peace. I took off my clothes, looking at my body in the mirror as I did so. My full breasts were still firm, my waistline was still tiny, and my hips hadn't spread to the point of no return. I was holding up very well. No, fuck that! I'm sexier than a motherfucker! I turned around to look at my ass and the back of my thighs for signs of cottage cheese. Not a ripple! My body was definitely tight. My finances were tight. I was talented and a nice person. There was no reason I could think of as to why I hadn't found the man I'd spend the rest of my life with or why he hadn't found me.

I stepped into the shower and closed my eyes as I let the water run over my face in an effort to wake up and get energized. I tried to get focused on business, but found my thoughts drifting back to the ex-boyfriend who haunted my dreams. I wished that things had worked out with him. It was his fault I was alone. No one could compare to him. Dating other men after him seemed like a step down.

The warm water rained down on my skin, and I began to soap my body absentmindedly with a bath pouf, imagining how my former lover's hands felt. When the sponge glided across my nipples, they hardened, and I shivered as bubbles of cucumber-melon soap dripped around my areolas. I dropped the sponge and replaced it with my hands, touching my nipples, squeezing and caressing my breasts, not thinking about how long I'd been in the shower or who might come in and catch me. I wasn't going to be able to do anything—I'd think of my ex all day—unless I released my sexual frustration.

My hands traveled lower, across my stomach, until I reached my mound, and I slipped the tip of my index finger between the lips of my vagina. I wiggled my finger around until I found what I was looking for. My knees buckled slightly as my fingertip brushed across the hood of my clitoris, and I held onto a rail in the shower for balance. I rubbed my finger in slow circles, imagining that it was my lover's tongue. I threw my head back and opened my legs a little wider as the water pelted my body, continuing to stroke myself, increasing the speed and intensity.

I was on the brink of an orgasm when I stopped touching myself and detached the removable shower head from its base. I changed the setting on it so the water gushed forth in one powerful stream and directed the spray toward my clit. Then I inserted two fingers inside my vagina and felt the muscles contract as my fingers looked for and found my G-spot. I stroked it, slowly increasing the pressure, while pretending that my fingers were my ex's hard cock.

The heat from the water pounding on my clitoris, coupled with the stimulation of my sweet spot and my fantasy, sent me over the edge, and I bit my lip to keep from crying out. Wave after wave of pleasure shook my body in violent spasms as I came once and then again as the water mixed with my juices and flowed down my leg. I debated whether to go for a third orgasm but realized that my fifteen minutes were probably almost up. Deciding against it, I gasped for breath, composed myself, and hurriedly finished my shower.

When I emerged from the bathroom, ensconced in a fluffy terry robe with a towel wrapped around my hair, the glam squad had arrived and lined up what had to be a thousand little jars, bottles, containers, and tubes of war paint, pomade, gel, and hair spray to prep me for the day's activities. Leslie and I chatted as I sat in a chair and the glam squad pulled and tugged at my hair and face from every direction.

"You feeling better?" she asked. "Refreshed?"

"Yeah," I said. She had no idea how much better I felt.

"Good," she said.

"Girl, all of Chi-town is talking about your party tomorrow night," the hairstylist Karl told me as he pulled sections of my hair through a ceramic flat iron.

"For real?" I asked.

"Oh hell yeah," the makeup artist, Bonita, chimed in.

"This girl was worried that no one would come," Leslie informed them.

"That won't happen," Karl said. "You know any guy you gave the time of day to is going to show up professing his love, trying to find a way to get back in."

"What would make you say that?" I asked him, hoping it was true, at least in the case of the ex from my dream.

"I've seen it a million times," he said. "Anytime a young entertainer comes up—especially a fine one, but hell, the ugly ones too—every time a woman blows up, all the men that fucked up and missed the boat start crawling out the woodwork!"

"Well I hope not. I went out with some crazy motherfuckers," I said jokingly. "I hope they stay well within the woodwork!"

"Do I need to get extra security?" Leslie asked me, arching her eyebrow. I'm sure she was only half kidding.

"Nah. There was nobody dangerous. A little touched, yes, but nothing the bouncers can't handle."

"Sounds juicy," Bonita said, digging for details.

"Your nosy ass," Karl said, teasing her.

"Hell, I'm nosy too," Leslie said with a giggle. "What kind of men should we be expecting to show up at your soiree?"

"Well, if your theory is right and some of the guys I used to date are going to show up, then you'll be expecting all kinds," I said, rolling my eyes and sighing. The faces of the men I'd dated shuffled through my mind. "I've got more exes than the Nation of Islam! You wouldn't know from the state of my love life now, but once upon a time, I dated so much that the chicks on *Sex and the City* looked like nuns in comparison."

"Yeah, well, that well's run dry," Leslie teased me.

"Yeah, but when it was full, it was full. And I dated some fine-ass men. But most of them were just a little off," I told them, traveling down memory lane. "Like there was this hotboy named Harley I used to kick it with. He was tall, a smooth almond complexion, and had muscles on top of muscles," I said with a shiver.

"He had a bangin' body, but his fashion sense was wack. He used to wear sleeveless shirts and leather pants and motorcycle jackets and sunglasses all the time. No matter how hot, no matter how cold. He wanted everybody to know he rode a bike. But despite all that he was a good fuck, so you know we kicked it a minute.

But outside of bed, his ass bored me to death. All he ever said was, 'And stuff, you know, whatever.' That was his way of answering damn near every question you asked." I wrinkled up my nose and shuddered.

"The men a woman will put up with just for some good dick!" Karl said with a smirk.

I laughed and thought about another nut job I kicked it with.

"It's not always even about the dick, though. There was this guy Jeffery," I said. "I met him at an art gallery and he was sprung. He sent me flowers and poetry; he e-mailed me, called me, you name it."

"You must have put it on him," Bonita said, giggling.

"Nope, not at all. We hadn't even been on a date, he was just chasing it."

"Sounds like a stalker to me," Karl said with a laugh.

"No, that's not what was wrong with him, but I'm getting to that. It wasn't creepy or anything, I just thought he was really, really sweet. He was a gentleman, you know? It was cool he wasn't pressuring me for some ass because I just wasn't feeling him that much. He was a little on the short side, and he was too old for me, but I began to develop a kind of soft spot for him. Eventually, I let him take me for coffee, and we went to museums and stuff like that. Finally he stepped up his game and asked me out for dinner and dancing.

"We went to Gibson's and had filet mignon and champagne and talked and laughed, and I was feeling so relaxed and comfortable that I was thinking that I might even give him some. Then we went club-hopping after dinner, and I thought we were having a good time but I drank too much that evening,"

"Please tell me you did not throw up on the man," Leslie said.

"No, I did not throw up on him. I wasn't drunk, but I would have gotten drunk if I knew what I was in for. I'm going to the bathroom constantly, and after my third trip, the mood of the date shifted. Jeffery started bugging the fuck out and accused me of trying to 'escape.' He said that I was using the bathroom breaks as an opportunity to flirt with other guys. Then he started crying, right there in the middle of the dance floor. I mean bawling. Dude had rolled up in a ball on the floor!"

"Oh my God, what did you do?" Leslie asked.

"I hope you left his ass right there on that floor," Karl said.

"At first I didn't know what to do. I asked him to get up off the floor. I told him to get ahold of himself. That just made things worse. He went into this rant about why he didn't date in America anymore and preferred the brothels of Thailand, because at least then you knew what you were getting."

"All that fool was getting in Thailand was a transsexual and a trip to the STD clinic!" Karl hooted.

We all cackled with laughter as they put the finishing touches on and I squeezed into a dress that was illegally tight. Leslie pulled out a black velvet bag and smiled as she unveiled the contents; a local jeweler was letting me borrow a couple of fabulous pieces from his pink diamond collection. Oh, the perks of showbiz! We oohed and aahed at the carats upon carats of pastel-colored ice set in platinum. Diamonds truly are a girl's best friend, and I switched into diva mode the instant the jewels touched my body.

The glam squad was rolling with us to make sure I looked my best during the long day ahead of us, and the four of us piled into a Hummer limo and headed off to my media appearances. I munched on a blueberry muffin and drank juice as we headed out toward the Dan Ryan Expressway, everyone still laughing at my crybaby ex.

"If you think Jeffery sounds like a piece of work, let me tell you about this other cat I kicked it with named Jodeci," I told them. They started cracking up again.

"You gotta be fucking kidding me," Leslie said.

"I wish I was. This fool had his name legally changed because he loved them so much."

"And you went out with him knowing this?" Karl asked me. "What the hell was wrong with you?"

"Look, he was fine as hell, okay! And he had a dick down to his knees. I was blinded by the dick; I'm not going to even front. He used to roll off Ecstasy, and that shit made him a big time freak who would do anything, and I mean anything that I asked him to do in bed, so hell, it was kind of working for me. But I got over that shit real quick when this fool stood outside my building unsolicited and uninvited in the pouring rain, singing 'Cry for U' by who else, Jodeci. I'm serious! He was howling at the top of his lungs! 'Laaaaadddy, I-I-I-I, will cryyyy for youuuu, tooniiiiight!' He may have been crying for real, but it was raining, so I couldn't really tell. Plus I was slumped down on the floor in embarrassment with the lights out, praying he would take his crazy ass home. I guess he was high or something, but that didn't explain the sweatshirt with my picture on the front and him holding a huge, neon pink sign that said he loved me. Don't worry about him, though. It was easy to get a restraining order for him."

"Now I know I'm calling for extra security," Leslie said, and we laughed until we arrived in Hammond, Indiana, an industrial suburb about thirty minutes south of downtown Chicago.

I visited the radio stations Power 92 and Soul 106.3, then we headed back into the city to my alma mater, where I did a concert and gave away CDs and posters and things. Finally, we headed back downtown, where I received the key to the city. All of this was accomplished by early afternoon. It's like that army commercial: I do more by 9:00 A.M. than most folks do all day.

We took a well deserved food and champagne break at Tavern

on Rush, gorging ourselves on platters of food that would take weeks to work off, and drinking more than our share of Veuve Cliquot Rosé.

"Did you have any boyfriends that weren't crazy?" Leslie asked me.

I wanted to mention the ex I'd dreamt about, but I didn't. In every woman's life there is at least one man that she just can't shake. He gets so deep down into her soul that no matter what, she'll always use him as the guide by which she measures every other man she meets. He's the man a woman will play herself for over and over again, leading her friends and family to think that she's on drugs or lost her mind. He's the man who can get you to get out of bed at two in the morning and drive across town in the pouring rain just to get a little loving. He's the one who causes aftershocks to rumble through your body at the mere memory of his bedroom antics. My dream lover was that man.

But instead of telling them about him, I went for shock value and gave them one last tale.

"Yeah, sure," I told them. "I dated some normal guys. But most of them were crazy. One almost drove me crazy too. My college sweetheart gone sour, Cali stressed me so much I almost had a nervous breakdown. We met in Spanish class and fell in love and dated for three years, but they were not a good three years. He was possessive and jealous and had a very short temper. People used to call us Ike and Tina because we argued so much, and because he thought he was a producer who was going to make me famous. It was a trip. But what folks didn't realize was how close to the truth they were. On top of all his obvious problems, he had a drinking problem, and he used to yell at me a lot. A couple of times he got violent and we fought. It was . . . ugly. I stayed in it because I loved him and I thought that I could help him. He basically kept treating me like shit in return, finally cheating on me with a stripper, getting her pregnant, and marrying her."

"Dayum," was the collective response at the table.

Then I changed the subject. Thinking about Cali put a damper on my mood that I hadn't expected; I thought I'd look back at my experiences with him and laugh, but I didn't. Whoever said that when you're a success you look back on the painful parts of your life and laugh, didn't know what the hell they were talking about. I'd had enough of talking about my pathetic love life, so I talked about the part of my life that didn't suck: my career. I chattered away about how I wanted my hair, nails, and makeup at my platinum party, and we argued over what I was going to wear until the table fell silent and I felt a tap on my shoulder. Everyone was staring at the person I felt standing behind me.

"Songbird, is that you?" a baritone voice boomed. I didn't have to turn around to see the face in order to recognize the voice. Only one man called me Songbird. It was *him*, the lover from my dreams, my ex-boyfriend, Spock. I was taken aback and clearly shaken, and I almost knocked the bottle of champagne over. *Get it together*, I scolded myself.

"Well, well, well, Spock. Imagine running into you here," I said coolly, extending my hand for him to kiss. I was the definition of a diva.

There was crazy chemistry between the two of us, and it was obvious to anyone by my feigned indifference and the grin on his face that we had history. Everyone was staring at me now and looked like they wanted to explode with questions. Spock smiled and played along, gallantly lifting my hand to his lips and kissing it, maintaining a steady gaze directly in my eyes. He has amazing, soft, light brown eyes that aren't quite hazel, and long lashes, a fact a lot of people miss because he always wears his glasses.

"You look beautiful as usual," he said, still grinning.

"Yes," I replied, turning away from him.

"Aren't you going to introduce us to your gentleman friend?" Leslie asked.

"This is no gentleman," I said with a little attitude, then laughed to cover any trace of bitterness. As much as I loved him, he'd hurt me, and I wasn't really over it. Everyone laughed with me. "I'm sorry. Leslie, Karl, Bonita, this is Spock." He shook hands with them and stood beside the table awkwardly. They looked him over from head to toe, eyes scrutinizing every inch. He looked immaculate in his Hugo Boss suit, shiny dress shoes, and crisp dress shirt with monogrammed French cuffs fastened with gold cuff links, but I could tell he felt uncomfortable.

"Well, it was good seeing you," he finally said, clearing his throat and straightening his tie. He placed his business card on the table in front of me. "In case you forgot," he said, and excused himself.

I pretended not to, but I watched him walk out of the restaurant and down the street, growing smaller and smaller until he disappeared. Back in the limo, I acted like the exchange didn't happen, but of course my crew wasn't going to let it die.

"That sure was a handsome brother back at the restaurant," Leslie said. I could tell she was waiting for me to elaborate.

"He's all right."

"So what's the deal with him?" Karl asked.

"An ex," I said casually.

"We figured as much," Bonita said knowingly. "But what's the *deal*?"

"He's a liar and a cheater and he's too wrapped up in his work. Nuff said." I dug into my purse, found my iPod, slipped the headphones into my ears, and stared blankly out the window all the way back to the hotel.

I was tripping off the fact that I literally dreamed Spock up. I wasn't expecting to see him, at least not until the party if at all. I was full of mixed emotions. Spock was a brother who took my body to heaven and my mind through hell. Things were great for us in the beginning, as they almost always are in any relationship. We were set up by mutual friends, and it seemed that we had everything in common. He loved music like I loved music, maybe even more, but he was an engineer by trade, and a very successful one at that. He had a big muckety-muck job with the city, a great loft in the West Loop, and a convertible BMW, not to mention he was very, very well-endowed.

He was also a University of Chicago graduate, was in a fraternity, and he was a gentleman. He was pretty cute too. He looked good in person and on paper, and I really cared about him. I did everything I could think of to please him, including cleaning his house and cooking for him and leaving meals in his freezer to be reheated later so he wouldn't spend so much money on junk food and eating out. Things were perfect. Too perfect.

Of course, Spock wasn't perfect, he was a cheater. I found out that he had another girlfriend, some lawyer chick, whom he neglected to tell me about. That's when his ugly side reared its head. His punk ass wasn't even man enough to face the music. He pulled a straight up bitch move and wouldn't answer my calls or texts when I wanted to get to the bottom of things. That instantly turned me off. And when we broke up, that was when I got the idea to leave Chicago, because if he was the best that Chicago had to offer, I was better off somewhere else.

I moved to Miami and didn't look back. Everything fell into place once I moved. I got a job bartending at this restaurant called Mango's on South Beach, where the staff all did sexy dances on top of the bar. We weren't strippers but wore these skimpy little animal print catsuits and bodysuits and shook our maracas and poom-pooms to salsa, reggeaton, reggae, you name it. I learned a gang of Latin dances plus I met all the movers and shakers in Miami and high-profile tourists, including plenty of people in the music biz. I scored gigs singing and dancing backup for Latin artists, which paid the rent and bills and led to writing songs in both English and Spanish, which led to my getting a record deal of my own. I guess I should thank Spock for being a man-whore. If I hadn't found out what a lying dog he was, I might have still been in Chicago chasing dreams and him.

Leslie tapped me on the shoulder, and I removed my earplugs.

"One last question. Why do you call him Spock?" she asked. "I know that isn't his given name."

"Because he's a nerdy know-it-all that is only half human. The other half is a cold, emotionless Vulcan, just like Spock on *Star Trek*. Remember how women used to dig him but he'd remain detached and aloof? That's Spock for you. He's great with facts and figures, and his mind and body go through the motions of life, but I'm not sure if he has a heart."

I replaced the earplugs and stared out the window. The undisputable truth that stared back at me in the darkly tinted glass was that I was still in love with Spock, even if he was heartless and manipulative. It disgusted me to want someone who had hurt me so, and disgusted me more that not only did I want him, but my body craved him and I dreamt of him. I felt a pull in my midsection every time he was near, and I know that he felt it too. I might sound delusional to you, but I know what I know. We just had it like that. And it wasn't just because we had amazing sex. It was something more. The fact that he cheated on me didn't change that.

I felt my purse vibrating from the ringing phone inside. I pulled out my Treo and saw that there was a text message.

> Great running into u. I know ur busy, but think u can meet me 4 a drink 2nite? I'd luv 2 show u my nu crib.

I stared at the phone until the display faded to black and then pushed a few buttons to look at it some more.

"Just go," Leslie said. She'd peeped the message over my shoulder.

I furrowed my brow and pursed my lips crossly. I sighed and thought about it. What did I have to lose? I had the upper hand. I was rich and famous. Yes, he'd broken my heart, but he still wanted me. I saw it in his eyes. Then a more sinister thought crossed my mind. I'd finally have the chance to pay him back for breaking my heart. What could be better than dangling myself like a carrot in front of his nose and letting him chase me? I would tease him, drive him crazy with lust, and then I would reject him cold. He'd be left with the angst of seeing my image every time he turned on the television, and the torture of hearing my voice every time he turned on the radio, but he wouldn't have me. And I'd finally have a sense of satisfaction and closure and be able to move on with my life.

I texted back:

> Let's meet at Ruth's Chris. Maybe I'll go see your crib later.

I thought about my dream, the reality that inspired it, and the effect he had on me then and now. He was the best lover I'd ever had. The things he made me feel, both physical and mental, were dangerous. He pushed me to the limit and challenged me in every aspect, and I had an insatiable appetite when it came to him. He had me so twisted out of shape when we dated; I went through a ton of ups and downs because of him.

Willpower, girl, I told myself. I had to have willpower. And I had to remember that I had the upper hand. *I'm the star! He's just a groupie.* We arranged to meet at nine.

Once we reached the hotel, Leslie and I let the glam squad use the limo to go shopping, and we went upstairs to my room. The smell of flowers hit us as soon as we opened the door to the suite.

"Right on cue," Leslie said. "I told you this was going to happen, didn't I?"

"What the hell?" I asked, looking around at the forest that had been transported into the room.

"Someone's making their move," Leslie said, nudging me with her elbow.

"These are not from Spock," I told her.

"Well no, not all of them, silly. But I bet he had an arrangement sent."

"What makes you think that?" I asked her.

"He seems like such a classy guy."

"He is classy, but flowers aren't his style. Vulcans think flowers are a frivolous gift. To buy something that will undoubtedly die is illogical," I said, doing my best Leonard Nimoy imitation, which wasn't that good. "Besides, they couldn't have gotten here that quickly."

"Only one way to find out," Leslie said. I could tell her curiosity was getting the best of her.

"I don't care. You look," I said, and nodded my approval. She ran about, collecting the cards from the various bouquets placed around the room. She rifled through them, scanning each one.

Wondering what to wear on my date with Spock, I began to sift through outfits, trying to decide if I should roll with something I already owned or wait to see what the glam squad brought me back from their shopping trip.

"Ah ha!" Leslie said with excitement. "I knew it!"

"Knew what?" I asked. Could it be? Could Spock have found a true romantic bone in his body and sent me a bouquet?

"Oh, I was just looking at this card for these flowers, but you don't care, do you?"

I rolled my eyes. "Who are they from?" I tried to conceal it, but I was a little eager to know who'd sent them.

"They're from . . . the label," she said, laughing. "Gotcha!"

"Good Lord!" I said, rolling my eyes. "I'm going to take a shower. Are we done here?" I asked her.

Leslie was staring at a card with a concerned expression on her face.

"Who's that one from?" I asked.

"Huh?" she said, looking up, then smiling a tight-lipped smile.

"You were staring at that card kind of hard. Who were the flowers from?" I asked her.

"Oh, girl, just the hotel. I couldn't understand the handwriting," she explained, then tore the card into little pieces.

Chorus

This may sound a little vain, but I had Karl and Bonita ride in the limo with me on the way to my date with Spock. I wanted to make sure I looked devastatingly beautiful when I saw him so that I'd be impossible to resist, but I planned on resisting the hell out of him. After what he did to me and how he hurt me, there was no way in hell any woman with any self-worth would give up the goodies. Right? Naturally! Still, I knew that I was going to be very, very tempted.

I was working my bright red wrap dress as I strolled into the restaurant, aware of how the silky fabric hugged every curve and moving my body in a way that would ensure that everyone else was aware of it too. I looked like I stepped off a magazine cover, with my perfectly applied makeup and not a hair out of place. I looked around to locate Spock, but he was nowhere to be seen. I took a seat at the bar and looked at my Rolex. I was giving him fifteen minutes, the same amount of time it would take for me to down a glass of single-barrel Jack on the rocks with just a splash of tonic and a twist of lime and not look like a total lush.

I felt a little conspicuous. My grand entrance was wasted on Spock, but not on the patrons who, upon recognizing me, began to murmur and point and ask for autographs. I was definitely starting to get pissed off, but kept a fake smile plastered across my face. It was nearing the fifteen minute mark and Spock was nowhere to be found. I couldn't be rude and just get up abruptly and walk out the door and leave people hanging, but I didn't want to be there if he arrived a half hour late, or worse, if he never showed up.

Finally, I excused myself from my fans to go to the ladies' room. I was going to reapply my lipstick and then hot-tail it out of there. I had to stop myself from looking at my cell phone to see if he'd called. What did it matter if he had some excuse? I was Lucky! I didn't have to wait for any man. He should have been early, if anything! I checked myself out in the mirror, and with my fake smile still in place and my head held high, walked confidently out the bathroom and toward the front door.

"Going somewhere?" Spock asked. He was standing at the hostess station, arms folded across his chest and smiling.

"You better know it, buddy. You're late! I'm outta here!" I said, moving to the side to step around him. He reached out and grabbed me, pulling me into an embrace.

"I wasn't late, Songbird," he breathed into my ear. "I just didn't want to disturb your groove. You were surrounded by fans."

"Yeah right," I said doubtfully, pulling away from him.

"I'm serious. I was here early. I stepped into the men's room. I had to make sure I looked my best, you know," he said, still grinning.

"Mmm-hmm," I replied. I wasn't buying it for a minute.

"Honestly, you can ask the hostess," he said. I pursed my lips and rolled my eyes.

"How much did you pay her to lie?" I asked.

"What? You don't believe me?" He shook his head in disbelief.

"We all know how you lie," I said sourly.

"Don't be that way," he said.

"I'm not being any way," I said quickly. I hadn't been with him for five minutes and already I was playing myself. I couldn't let him know how much our past relationship had hurt me. That would be giving him the upper hand.

Conveniently, the hostess interrupted us. "Your table is ready," she said.

"I thought we were having cocktails," I said to Spock.

"You're not hungry?" he asked. "Don't tell me you've gone all Hollywood and stopped eating. The Lucky I know will eat anything at any given hour."

"I haven't changed," I said with a laugh as we were ushered to our seats in the private dining room. I nodded approvingly and told him, "You know I want a filet Oscar, and a bunch of appetizers."

"I know, that's why I took the liberty of calling ahead to make sure they could prepare it for you," he said. "Songbird, you don't even have to look at the menu. Anything you could want is already on its way." Damn, he was as debonair as ever. That was a classic Spock move, not something he was doing just because I got famous and he was kissing up. He always took care of the smallest details and made sure that each and every single time we were together he did something small but big to show me that I was special and appreciated. Spock's only flaw was that I couldn't trust him, and that's a pretty big flaw.

I honestly don't know how he could have had two girlfriends. I know I wore his ass out, and I got plenty of his time and money. We had to have truly drained him, though I suspect that she wasn't putting it down in any department, especially not the bedroom, and he had been with her for the business connections and appearance of being with a lawyer. It damn sure wasn't for her personal appearance, because I saw her picture once, and she certainly wasn't cute. She was downright matronly.

Just thinking about it made me heated all over again. What had been so wrong with me that I didn't look good enough on paper? I had a degree and I was smart, plus I had talent and was fine and a freak. I just wasn't pulling in the big dollars nor was I well known. But I made sure he was satisfied in every way that I could. I could never understand what she gave him that I didn't. Especially since I knew that his "side counsel" was getting sloppy seconds; there's no way in hell they could have had the kind of physical connection we did. I couldn't help but wonder if she was still in his life, but I wasn't going to ask. What did it matter anyway? We were just two old friends sharing a meal.

We talked about music, one of great shared loves, and the industry. As his lips moved, I fantasized about how they would feel, nipping at my neck, licking my clavicle, and sucking my nipples. I shifted uneasily in my chair and felt my La Perlas getting moist. And I know the sexual attraction was mutual. Spock found reasons to touch my hand, rub my shoulder, and he even brushed a stray lock of hair from my eyes. I know it sounds innocent, but it was suggestive as hell. He wanted me too.

Dinner was perfect, and we finished up with key lime pie for dessert and coffee. It wasn't the coffee that had me feeling warm, though, it was Spock. I was burning up inside with uncontrollable desire, although I maintained the illusion of composure. I excused myself to go the ladies' room while Spock settled the tab. My hands shook lightly as I reapplied my lipstick, dusted my face with a sweep of powder, and washed my hands. The moment of truth was coming. The games were about to advance to the next round.

The time had come for us to decide if I would go back to see his new house. I knew that if I went, the only room I would see was his bedroom. I wanted so badly to go, but I knew that would destroy my entire plan. I wanted to tease him, torture him, and make him want me. But the plan was backfiring. I wanted to jump his bones. I didn't want to tease or beat around the bush, I wanted to fuck.

"I'm sure you have a long day ahead of you," he told me as he looked at his watch. It was around midnight.

"Yeah, I do," I said, and it was true.

"Did your car wait, or can I do the honor of escorting you back to your hotel?" he asked. I was glad he didn't ask if I wanted to see his house, because I didn't want to be tempted, but I was disappointed at not having the chance to turn him down.

"You still got that big, pretty quarter-to-eight?" I asked, referring to his BMW 745.

"Yeah. I've got a Porsche Cayenne too."

"Big baller," I teased.

"Nah, that's you."

"Yeah, it is me," I said with a laugh. He laughed too.

I don't know what came over the both of us once we got in his car. I don't know if it was the music from the smooth jazz and R&B station that was playing, or the wine we drank at dinner, but something overwhelmed us. At the first red light, we caught each other's eye, fell into each other's arms and started kissing. Not a simple, chaste peck either. I'm talking about straight-up busting slob. It was like we were two high school kids getting in last minute gropes while trying to make curfew; we were all over each other, touching every body part within reach. A horn blared from behind us and Spock reluctantly broke our embrace and drove through the intersection, but that didn't break the mood.

As soon as we pulled into a space in the hotel parking garage, we picked up where we'd left off. We kissed and touched each other urgently, pulling at each other's clothes. I unbuttoned his shirt and ran my hands across his chest. He reached inside my dress and squeezed my breasts, stroking my nipples until I was moaning and squirming.

Spock must have paid the programming director at the radio station, because every song that played seemed like it was meant just for us. I looked into his soft brown eyes as Mint Condition sang "Pretty Brown Eyes," and felt the lyrics deep down inside when the lead singer Stokely begged, "Quit breaking my heart." The next song hit me just as hard when Kem asked, "How did you find your way back in my life?" Tina Marie's "Out on a Limb" told just what was in my heart: "I've never felt so sure and yet I feel so insecure, what am I gonna do?"

"You still want me, don't you, Songbird?" Spock asked me in between kisses.

"Yes," I gasped, grabbing his crotch. "And you want me too."

His hands found his way under my dress and beneath my panties. He began to explore me, his fingers expertly stroking all the spots that made me purr.

"You're so wet," he said, plunging his fingers inside of me. He knew exactly what buttons to push and how I would respond. He teased my clit, bringing my body higher and higher, until I was about to explode. He ran his fingers along my inner lips, causing me to arch my back and spread my legs. It wasn't the most comfortable position, sitting in the front seat with the console between us, so I suggested that we move to the back seat. He ignored me, instead using the controls by his side to maneuver my seat until it lay flush against the back seat. He crawled over the console and got on top of me, kissing me deeply. Our tongues danced and intertwined and we moaned, pulling at each other's bodies in an effort to get even closer.

"You want me to fuck you, don't you?" he asked.

"Yes!"

"Say it!"

"I want you to fuck me," I moaned. "Please fuck me, baby."

He inserted his fingers into my pussy again and wriggled them around a bit while circling my clit with his thumb.

"I've got to feel that dick. Please give it to me." I was begging now. Fuck pride; I had none left. My plans for stringing him along were aborted. All I had left was desire. He prolonged the torture, continuing to finger fuck me. Finally, he pulled his fingers out, brought them to his lips, and then licked them.

"You taste so good," he told me. Then he dipped back into my pussy, this time bringing his fingers to my lips.

"Taste," he ordered. I sucked his fingertips into my mouth slowly, imitating fellatio.

"Is that how you want to suck my dick?" he asked.

"Yes," I gasped, then flipped him over like a Sumo wrestler and straddled him. Our eyes locked as I pulled his jacket off and grabbed his shirt by the collar. I kissed him deeply before pulling the fabric of his shirt until I could feel the buttons pop off and knew his chest was exposed. I licked my way down his body before yanking off his belt and opening his pants. I didn't bother to take them all the way off; I couldn't in the cramped space, so I just pushed them down around his ankles.

His throbbing dick greeted me, erect and at least ten inches long. I slid it into my mouth, savoring the taste of him. Flicking my tongue along the shaft, I looked up at him to gauge his reaction. He was definitely enjoying it. I moved my mouth up and down slowly, caressing his balls with one hand and stroking his hardness up and down with the other.

"Damn, woman," he muttered. "I missed you."

My hand pumped like a piston as I sucked harder and harder. He was on the brink of losing control and pulled me away from him by my hair, looked at me with animalistic passion and growled, "I need to feel you."

The windows of the Cayenne were all fogged up, and it wasn't the most comfortable situation, but none of that was on my mind. I needed to feel him the way he needed to feel me. I dug in my purse for a condom, rolled it on, and then lowered myself onto his monster cock. We rocked together in perfect rhythm, looking into each other's eyes, moaning, grunting, and sighing, making a melody all our own.

I rode him with all my might, thrashing and winding my hips in ecstasy. He made me feel so good, but at the same time, I started to feel so bad. The pain of the memories of how badly he'd hurt me mingled with the pleasure of him inside me, and tears started to roll down my cheeks.

"It's okay, baby," he said. "Let it out."

I didn't break down and cry, though. I gritted my teeth, grabbed him by the throat and squeezed. I was choking him, riding him furiously, and before I could stop myself, I slapped him. I thought he was going to freak out, or worse, slap me back, but he didn't. It excited him, and he thrust himself hard against my body in an attempt to match my maniacal pace. I slapped him again and again until he grabbed my hands. But he didn't stop fucking me. Instead he pulled my body against his and told me he was about to come.

"Come with me baby," he whispered in my ear, and I did.

Afterward, I felt weak in every sense of the word. He held me in his arms and stroked my hair, kissing my forehead and cheeks. He sang softly to me and told me all the little things a woman loves to hear. You're so beautiful. Your skin is so soft. Your hair is so pretty. You make me feel so good. I could feel my emotions getting caught up; the love I used to have for him had come rushing back. I was doomed.

Verse 2

I was just about to turn in and go to sleep when my cell phone rang. I almost broke my neck running to get it, and it was exactly who I'd hoped it would be.

"Hey," he said. It was Spock.

"Hey," I replied, trying to disguise the fact that I'd been anxious to answer.

"I was just calling to tell you good night. Or good morning. You know what I mean."

"Thanks. I had a good time this evening, or this morning. You know what I mean," I said. We laughed a little.

"Good . . . me too," he said, sounding a bit distracted.

There was an awkward silence.

"Can I see you again before you leave town?" he asked suddenly.

I thought about it. Was he asking me if we could fuck again before I left? That's what would happen if we saw each other again. But I wanted to fuck him again, so it didn't really matter.

"That would be nice," I told him. "Will you come to my party tomorrow night?"

"Are you sure that I won't be in the way? I saw how many fans you had tonight at dinner. You're going to be mobbed."

"I wouldn't ask if you would be in the way."

"And I wouldn't miss your party for anything in the world. I'm flattered that you invited me."

"Cool. I guess I'll see you tomorrow night. You know where it is?"

"Everyone knows where it is," he said. "It's all the city is talking about. Lucky is back in town with her platinum album and her golden voice. You did it, girl. I'm proud of you."

"Thank you, baby," I told him.

"I'm serious. Your CD is hot. You did a good job."

"It means a lot, coming from you. I guess all my hard work paid off."

We sat there a second holding the phone until he cleared his throat.

"That was good tonight, wasn't it?" He went ahead and brought up what we'd both been thinking about and pretending not to.

"Mmm-hmm. Better than good."

"I can't stop thinking about being inside of you," he said. My pussy started to juice up again from his statement. The richness of his voice was always enough to get me going, and the mere thought of how we felt together made me horny. I was satisfied, but my sexual appetite wasn't satiated. I needed to feel him, but in the meantime I'd feel myself.

"I can't stop thinking about it either," I confessed. I slid my hand beneath my panties.

"I don't want you to think that it's just about sex with you and me. You know it isn't like that," he explained.

"I know," I told him. But none of that mattered at that moment. The sex is what mattered to me.

"But the sex is so good," he said.

"I agree," I whispered.

More silence before he asked, "Are you thinking about it now? And are you doing what I think you're doing?"

"Yes. You know me so well." I wasn't just thinking about it, and he knew it. As I lay there in my bed, my free hand was stroking my pubic hair and massaging the lips of my vagina.

"What are you thinking about?" he asked.

"I'm thinking about how thick your dick is, and how good it feels inside of me," I told him.

"Mmm. And what are you doing?"

"I'm touching my clit. I wish you were here to do it for me. What are you doing, now that you know what I'm doing here?"

"I've got my dick in my hand."

"Good. I want you to stroke it for me. I want you to remember how good my pussy felt this evening, how wet it was, how tight it was. Can you do that for me?"

"I'm doing it. I'm stroking it. And I'm pretending that my hand is your pussy. It feels so tight when I first stick it in. It feels so good that I want to come right then. But I could never be that selfish. I need to make you feel good too. And I need you to stick your fingers in your pussy and rub your clit with your thumb at the same time, the way I did to you earlier tonight. Imagine that I'm there."

"Ooh, I'm doing it. You're here with me, baby, and I'm so wet for you. You don't know what you do to me, baby, you just don't know."

"I know, Songbird, I know," he told me as I whimpered and moaned. "That's right, girl, do it," he encouraged me. "Take it there."

I cut loose like I was all alone, my fingers exploring every part of me. I moaned and panted and grunted and squealed with delight. His sexy baritone voice encouraging me, telling me what to do.

"I want you to lick your fingers," he told me. "Lick them like you licked mine tonight. I want to hear it," he instructed, and I was an attentive and obedient student. I sucked the juices of my fingertips noisily and hungrily. I began to rub my clit again.

"You're gonna make me come," I told him.

"Come, girl, and keep on making yourself come. I know you can do it. I know that pussy. You know I know that pussy."

He knew my pussy, all right. It was no problem for me to reach as many orgasms as I wanted, provided I had the right mental stimulation and the right stimulation of my G-spot. It was a gift he fully appreciated and took advantage of in the past. I shook and screamed as the first orgasm hit me.

"Work that spot, girl. You remember how I used to love to watch you masturbate? You were such a showoff. I used to get so hard, just looking at you. Remember how I used to stroke my dick in front of you while you made yourself come over and over?"

"I remember. You know I remember. Do you remember how much I used to love it when you came all over me? Do you remember—" I screamed as my second orgasm washed over me. I wondered if anyone could hear me; I have a naturally loud and powerful singing voice, and even when I don't try, it carries pretty far. I kept on screaming, though. I didn't care who heard me as long as my guy was getting an earful.

"I love to hear you moan, girl. Nobody but me knows the kind of music you can make. Sing for me, baby. One more, girl, make yourself come, girl, and I'm going to come with you," he told me. That was all I needed to hear.

"I'm coming again, baby," I told him. "I need you so bad. I'm going to fuck the hell out of you tomorrow."

"I'm there, Songbird, I'm coming," he told me. I heard him shout and could imagine the look on his face. For a moment I felt as if our souls met on some other plane, some parallel universe, because our connection was so strong. I felt him inside of me, inside my heart, my body, and my mind all at once as our heavy breathing carried across the telephone line.

"I guess I ought to let you get some rest," he finally said.

"Yeah. I've got a big day ahead of me. But, uh, that was nice too," I said.

He laughed, and I could tell he felt just as silly as I did for having phone sex, but hell, we both enjoyed it, and we'd both sleep well and have pleasant dreams.

The next day, Spock was all I could think about. He didn't call, but I didn't really expect him to; we'd been on the phone half the night. And it wasn't like I could have talked to him if he had because I was so busy getting ready for my special night. I did a couple of radio satellite interviews and an online Internet chat for my fans. I love doing stuff like that, so I was on a high. Leslie was on her BlackBerry nonstop, handling last minute details and cursing anyone out who didn't meet her standards. I promised her I'd take her to the Turks and Caicos for a week when this was all over.

"Brazil, baby, you've got to take me to Brazil. You owe me bigtime!" she said, and I agreed.

"We can go wherever you want. I need a vacation!" I told her.

"Well, maybe your boy Spock can take you somewhere romantic."

"Nothing happened. We're just friends, you know. We had a good time," I lied.

"Yeah right," Leslie said. She wasn't buying it. I started giggling. I couldn't help it.

"Okay, I fucked him," I admitted. "And it was good."

"You go, girl," she said, giving me a high-five.

"But this was not supposed to happen," I explained. "He hurt me. I was supposed tease him and leave him hanging."

"But you needed to get laid."

"Yeah, but now what?"

"I don't know. That's up to you guys."

"I want some more dick. It's like he's all I can think about," I admitted.

"Then get some more, girl! Who knows when you'll get the chance again?"

"That's just it. I think I kind of want to get back with him. You know, be a couple again, but I'm not sure."

"Well, I can't tell you what to do about that. Only the two of you know if that's a chapter of your lives worth revisiting. But remember, no matter what happens with this guy, you're fabulous," Leslie said. I smiled and was going to say something, but her phone started ringing again and things shifted back to business.

More flowers came to the suite. Not a lot of them, but enough to seem a little strange. I let Leslie do the honors again of collecting all the cards and seeing who they were from. None were from Spock, but I didn't care. I generally like flowers, but there is such a thing as overkill, and my allergies were starting to act up. It was also starting to feel like a damn funeral. I donated most of them to the cleaning staff and hotel employees and didn't bother to ask who they were from. Leslie didn't tell me either, she just kept her BlackBerry plastered to her ear.

The glam squad arrived, and after the obligatory hours of primping and preening, the big moment had finally arrived. It was time to head to the party. Leslie radioed the security guards she hired for the night, who were stationed outside my door. Three burly guys came lumbering into the suite, facial expressions gruff and mean.

"What's with all the bodyguard stuff?" I asked her. Usually one guy was enough.

"I just want to make sure that you're safe. You're a lot more famous than you seem to realize sometimes. It's part of your life now," she explained.

"I don't think all this is necessary. It feels weird," I said.

"Get used to it," she told me.

I went along with it even though it seemed like the bodyguards were a bit much. It made me seem like I was trying too hard to look like I was a star, but Leslie was steadfast in her decision. The bodyguards escorted us into a private elevator and then into a waiting Bentley. Two of them rode in the car with us and another rode in a separate car that trailed behind us. I felt like the President or something, and the whole thing was making me nervous.

"You're going to knock them dead," Leslie assured me, rubbing me on the back. I took a deep breath and poured myself a glass of champagne.

"To me!" I exclaimed.

"To you!" Leslie said, toasting me.

"And to you too," I said, leaning over and hugging her. "You're the best publicist a diva could have."

"I am, aren't I?" she said, laughing, as we drank our bubbly.

Spotlights flooded the sky and Hummers painted with my image and CD cover patrolled the streets around the club. There were traffic cops out making sure things went as smoothly as possible. There was a line around the corner of the club. People were dying to get inside to kick it with me. I was dripping in diamonds and looking flawless, and thanks to about two hours of preparation, it looked as if it were natural and effortless. My makeup and my hair were perfect, and my dress by Chicago designer Barbara Bates fit me like a second skin.

I tore that red carpet up. The photographers were already clicking away at the celebs who came to celebrate my success and were in the house, but they really went crazy when I showed up, pushing and shoving each other and calling my name. I posed and twirled and showed off my dress and body, knowing precisely what angles to position my limbs and hips in order to accentuate my hourglass shape. And when I stepped inside, everything was exactly as I imagined it would be. Every detail had been attended to, the club looked amazing and everyone seemed to be having a fantastic time.

I greeted my fans and the press and my guests with enthusiasm and appreciation. Chicago had come through for me, after all, and the athletes and entertainers who showed up added to the star factor. The DJ was off the hook and had everybody dancing until they were dripping in sweat.

"I told you that you had nothing to worry about," Leslie screamed over the blaring music.

"Who was worried?" I kidded her.

"Think you can handle yourself?" she asked. "I love you, but I want to mix and mingle."

"Do your thing," I encouraged her.

"Security will roll with you," she informed me.

"I'm good," I told her.

"I insist," Leslie said. "Don't let her out of your sight," she told my bodyguards. "Not even to go to the bathroom," she added, and then disappeared into the crowd.

Leslie was being overprotective. There was nothing but love there. I surveyed the room. I saw a lot of people from high school, girls who didn't like me and guys who ignored me, and I ran into a couple of guys I used to date, and oddly enough I didn't feel like throwing my success in their faces like I thought I would. I was happy; there was no reason to make anyone else miserable.

After an hour or so of getting reacquainted with old friends and hanging out, I decided to seek refuge from the crowd in my private VIP room. It was more like an oversized booth with a huge bed in it and heavy silk curtains that could be pulled shut to shield you from the crowd. It was perfect for what I had in mind. I looked in my purse to check my phone and see if I had missed calls or texts. Of course I was checking to see if Spock had called, but he hadn't. I sent him a text.

When r u coming to my party?

A little while later I received his reply:

Already here. Where r u?

I gave him directions to my private booth and instructed one of the bodyguards to make sure he got to me with no problem and to make sure we wouldn't be disturbed once he did. I was all smiles when he slipped inside.

"Hello, Songbird," he said, hugging me and holding me tight. Even over the deafening noise of the party, I could hear the desire in his voice.

"Hello," I said. "I ordered a bottle of your favorite." I motioned to the huge bottle of Bombay Sapphire sitting on the cocktail table.

"Damn, that's a big bottle."

"Well, I want to get you pissy drunk so I can take advantage of you and make you my sex slave," I told him with a wink.

"You don't have to get me drunk in order to get that," he replied.

"Oh yeah?" I asked him.

"No doubt. Your wish is my command. You know there's nothing I wouldn't do to please you." He leaned forward and kissed me. Then he put my hand on his crotch and whispered, "I jacked my dick this morning thinking about the taste of your pussy. My dick has been hard all day thinking about you."

My body shivered.

"But I don't just want your body. I want all of you. I need all of you, Lucky. I want it to be right this time. Can we take it slow and get it right? I can't let you walk out of my life again."

I thought about how much his infidelity hurt me, and how he didn't in my opinion try hard enough to make things up to me when he got busted. He was ruining the mood.

"Why talk about this all of a sudden? You didn't want to talk to me when you got caught cheating. Let's just forget about that and enjoy each other." It didn't matter who else he was or wasn't fucking. I was horny. I hiked up my dress and spread my legs. "Don't tell me how you feel. Show me," I said.

Whatever had been on his mind before was pushed aside. He stared at me, shaking his head.

"What are you waiting for?" I asked him.

He pushed me back onto the bed and pulled the straps of my dress from my shoulders, exposing my breasts.

"I want you so much," he said.

"Don't talk," I told him. I guided his mouth to my nipples. He sucked them attentively, making sure to increase and decrease the pressure, wetness, and suction, according to my body's response.

"You were always so good at that," I whispered before pushing him away. "But you were always good at something else too." I carefully removed the dress and laid it neatly on the corner of the bed.

"Take my panties off," I requested, and he did as I wanted, slowly and deliberately.

"Now, take off my shoes." He slid each of my shoes off and cradled my feet in his hands. "Suck them," I told him, lifting my toes to his mouth. He smiled and did as I asked. His tongue glided between my toes as he sucked each one gently in his mouth. He licked my instep and kissed my ankle. Then he repeated his actions with my other foot.

"I want you to eat it." I spread my legs wide so there'd be no doubt as to what I was referring to.

He licked his way up my calf and up my inner thigh in little circles. Then he spread my lips and swirled his tongue slowly around my clitoris.

"That's right," I told him. "Like that." He licked me softly and I squeezed his head between my thighs.

"Give me more," I sighed.

He nibbled and sucked at my clit, applying more pressure, and then inserting his fingers inside me and stroking my G-spot. I came almost instantly, but still wanted more.

"Now take your clothes off. I want to look at you," I ordered breathlessly.

He hesitated. "What if someone sees me?" he asked.

"You're worried about that *now*?" I asked back. "Look, my security isn't going to let anyone in. Now get naked," I ordered. I could tell he wanted to protest, but I spread my legs and began to play with my clit and he got back on track.

The sounds of hardcore gangsta rap blared through the club's speakers as he slowly peeled off his clothes until he had nothing on. I could tell by the way he was walking toward me—like a man on a mission—that he wanted and expected me to give him head. I wasn't going to, at least not now, not because I didn't want to, but because I was getting off on the feeling of being in control. Plus I had a special treat in store for him if he could follow instructions.

"Get a condom," I said, and he did even though I could tell he was a little disappointed that he wouldn't be getting a blowjob. Once the condom was on, he mounted me, entering me slowly. We both groaned as he filled me up and began to move slowly inside of me.

"You like that pussy, don't you?" I asked him.

"You know I love that pussy, girl."

"You missed this pussy, didn't you?"

"You know I missed it. I missed it so much, I can't let you go again," he said as he pushed himself deeper and deeper and I got wetter and wetter.

"Ooh, you don't want to let me go, do you?" he asked. "I can feel you gripping my dick. I know you don't want to let me go."

I squeezed and clenched my muscles, gripping him so tightly that I could feel him throbbing inside of me. He gave a few thrusts before pulling out and flipping me over onto all fours. Inch by inch he entered me from behind, working my clit with one hand and caressing my breast with the other. Every stroke made my body shake and twitch as I threw my hips at him. I needed him deeper and deeper inside of me.

"Mmm, fuck me harder," I pleaded. "Give me all of that big ass dick."

He pounded and pounded me from behind to the rhythm of the thumping bass pulsating through the club.

"I want you to fuck me, baby," I told him again. "And when you come, I want you to come in my mouth."

This comment sent Spock into overdrive, and he fucked me harder, spanking me on the ass hard. He slapped and slapped until my skin was sore and I begged him to stop and to come in my mouth. Finally he pulled out of me, yanked the rubber off, and shot a forceful load of semen into my awaiting mouth. I swallowed every drop.

"I want more," I said, smiling at him.

"Oh my God," he said, out of breath. "You're a nympho!"

"Yep," I agreed with him. I reached for his penis and he pulled away.

"I think we should continue this in another venue," he suggested, and began pulling his clothes back on. "I've got some things I want to do to you." I pouted and reluctantly pulled my clothes back on. I was so horny I could have fucked him all night in that VIP booth. And I wanted him so bad that I couldn't wait the time it would take to get to his house; my hotel was closer. Besides, we'd already wasted an opportunity to utilize my gorgeous suite with our tryst in the parking lot. I wasn't going to let another one go by the wayside.

"I've got a great suite. You didn't get a chance to see it the other night. Let's go," I suggested.

We caught up to Leslie and I informed her of my plans.

"Looks like you already got started," she said, smoothing my hair, which was probably standing out all over my head. "Go on and get out of here before somebody sees you looking crazy!"

"I don't look that bad," I said to her.

"You don't look that good either."

"Well I feel good," I said, raising my eyebrows at her. She laughed and gave me a hug. "I'm out."

"Take Security with you," she told me.

"We're just going to the hotel," I told her. If anyone was going to need a bodyguard, it was going to be Spock. I was going to tear his ass up.

"Have them follow you."

"I don't want to. I might want to do something freaky to him in the car. It's not that serious, Leslie, I'll be okay. Spock is with me." I grabbed his bicep. "He'll guard my body."

Leslie looked like she was debating, but there would have been no point in her doing so. I was going to do what I wanted, which was get the hell out of the crowded club and somewhere more private.

"Go straight to the car and straight to the suite. Don't sign any autographs. Got it?" she asked.

"Got it."

Spock and I made our way outside the club, holding hands as we waited for the attendant to pull his car around to the valet stand.

"Which whip are you in tonight, Mr. Big Stuff?" I asked him.

"The Cayenne," he said. "Why, you wanna repeat of last night?" He pulled me close to him, and as we were about to kiss, we were interrupted by someone calling my name.

"Lucky! Luuuuuccckkkkaaaayyyyy! Lucky, Lucky, Lucky!" the voice screamed. I tried to ignore the voice and kissed Spock. Then I heard the scream again. It was the most irritating sound ever.

"I know you hear me, Lady Luck! Hey, Ms. Singer Lady! I know you're not going to leave the party without saying 'bye to me!" I turned around with a practiced but gracious smile on my face. I'd deal with this fan quickly and then get back to the real business at hand.

In front of us stood a man who looked like stir-fried shit. He was so broke down he made Old Dirty look like a high fashion model. His hair was matted and hung down his back in unkempt, ill-formed, oddly shaped dreadlocks. A couple of his front teeth were missing, and the remaining ones were yellow, brown, or black with rot and decay. His Sean John sweatsuit was torn and dirty, and he stank with the funk of forty thousand years. A crackhead, no doubt.

"Have a good night," I said with a cheery wave and a smile. I looked him directly in the eyes because I think that it's disrespectful not to make eye contact with someone just because they're homeless or have issues. You never know who could be an angel in disguise. I studied the dirty face a little harder and recoiled in shock. It looked like my ex-boyfriend Cali. It couldn't be!

"Don't tell me you forgot your first love?" the grizzled man asked.

Holy Golden Gate Bridge, Batman! It was *Cali!*

"Did you get my flowers?" he asked.

"Fl-fl-flowers?" I stammered.

"I went through a whole lot to get you those flowers. I got your favorite: tulips. I stole a credit card to get you all those goddamned flowers." Cali's voice began to escalate.

"Thank you," I said, nervously looking around. Where was that damned valet? I tightened my grip on Spock's hand.

"Are you okay?" Spock asked me.

"Yeah, she's okay," Cali said to him. "I'm her first love. She gonna always be okay when she's with me. Ain't that right?" he asked me.

"What happened to you?" I asked. It wasn't that I cared about him so much as that I was curious. He had clearly fallen all the way off.

"As you can see, I'm a little down," he said. "I invested in a record company with these hustlers and to make a long story short I lost everything. But it can all be different now. We can get back together and pick up where we left off. I wrote some new stuff for you to sing. It's gonna be hot. So why don't you leave this clown and come on with me where you belong."

"You've got to be fucking kidding," I told him. "This ain't 'What's Love Got to Do with It?' You can't just come into my life after all this time. Not like this."

"But I need your help," he said, looking helpless. I felt a little sorry for him. I took a deep breath and thought about what I saw. I exhaled, hoping I wouldn't regret what I was about to say.

"Okay, well that's different. I can get you into rehab or something. I can help get you cleaned up and get your life back on track, but I can't be with you again, and we aren't going to work together. You need to focus on you," I said gently, walking toward him. "You deserve better than this."

"Lucky." Spock spoke my name but nothing else. He grabbed my hand to prevent me from getting any closer to Cali.

"Who is this clown?" Cali asked, hocking and spitting at the ground just short of Spock's Gucci loafers.

"I'm her man," Spock said.

"Uh, you are?" I asked Spock.

"Lucky baby. Why are you even talking to this corny motherfucker? It took a lot of hustling for me to get all the way here. You see I don't have shit. I got here all the way from Atlanta. I had to steal a car to stalk your ass to figure out where you were. I come all this way just for you baby, to show you that I love you, and you're hooked up with this guy? You's a selfish bitch!"

"That's enough," Spock said to Cali. "I believe the lady has had enough. I suggest that you move along."

Cali laughed so hard that he farted. Loud. And it stunk like four-day-old garbage that's been sitting in the sun.

"I suggest you move along," Cali said, mocking Spock. He

reached in his jacket pocket and pulled out a switchblade. He danced around, jabbing at the air with the knife in an attempt to intimidate us. It was working, as far as I was concerned, but Spock was cool and collected. I hid behind him, shaking.

"You don't want to try anything," he said to Cali. "You'll regret it."

"Oh, I'll regret it?" Cali scoffed. "Nigga, puh-lease! I'm gonna whoop your ass and then I'm gonna whoop this bitch's ass. Hmm, should I beat her ass before or after I fuck her? I know, I'll beat her ass while I fuck her!" Cali lunged at us. Spock pushed me aside, managing to remove me from harm's way but barely missing the swipe of the blade.

"Oh God!" I shrieked. I looked around and saw that my very big bodyguards from the club were headed our way, but before they got a chance to do shit, Spock regulated things. He started doing karate or jujitsu or something like his ass was Jet Li. By the time Security got to us, Cali was lying in a ball on the cement.

"What the fuck?" I asked Spock.

"Remember I told you I took tae kwon do growing up? I was a big-time nerd in the hood. I needed something to defend myself," he said.

I remember him telling me something of that nature but had written it off as him just trying to impress me.

"Are you okay?" he asked me.

"Yes, I'm fine," I told him.

Leslie came running up to me, hysterical, while my bodyguards grabbed Cali. Then Leslie, Spock, and I went back into the club's office, where we called the police and waited for them to arrive.

"Oh my God. This is too crazy!" Leslie said, shaking her head in disbelief. "I feel responsible. I should have had your security go wait with you. I just thought you'd be safe."

"I was safe. Spock didn't let anything happen to me," I told her. That didn't seem to matter. She still seemed riddled with guilt. "This isn't your fault, Leslie. Cali is crazy. That's obvious. He always has been, but nobody could have predicted this insanity."

"I knew you were too big to go without security," she said. "Not at an event like this. And then . . ." Leslie said, tears rolling down her face.

"What?" I asked her gently.

"There were a few cards that came with the flowers yesterday and today . . . they must have come from him."

"What did they say?"

"The cards said stuff like, 'Always watching. Always wanting. Always connected. It's me or no one.' It was creepy, but it just seemed like run-of-the-mill overzealous fan stuff. I was going to tell you, just after your big party. I didn't want you to worry about anything. So I hired the extra security and had them stick with you. I just figured you'd be safe with Spock and needed some privacy. It was a dumb move. What if something would have happened to you because I was slipping? Oh God, I'm so sorry." Leslie was crying and I could tell she was really shaken up. I felt like I needed to be strong for her.

"It's not your fault," I said. "You did what I wanted you to do. You wanted to see me happy. It was an honest mistake." I wrapped my arms around her and hugged her.

We ran down the whole episode to the police.

"I think that drugs are an issue," the officer filling out the report said. "We found a crack pipe and quite a few rocks in his pocket. You press charges, we'll make sure he does the maximum, and he'll be out of your hair for a long time."

"Oh, I intend to," I told him. "I'll take this as far as it needs to go."

The officer handed me some paperwork and left.

"Are you okay, Songbird?" Spock asked me.

"Hell no," I told him. "I can't believe that fool showed up here and tried to . . ." My voice cracked as I broke down. It all hit me at once. My ex-boyfriend had basically stalked me and had planned on doing who knows what.

"I am not going back to that hotel," I announced. "I know I probably have nothing to worry about, but who knows what other sickos are waiting for me. It just feels creepy. I won't feel better until I talk to the police again."

"We'll check you into another hotel," Leslie said. "I'll get right on it." She pulled out her cell phone, but her hand was shaking so much that it fell to the floor.

"You can stay with me," Spock offered. "I have more than enough room."

Leslie and I looked at each other.

"I think that would be a good idea," she said. "You don't mind if a bodyguard sits outside the house? You know, to keep an eye on things of course."

"He can wait inside. Like I said, I have more than enough room, and a state of the art alarm. He's more than welcome. In fact, I insist that you come too," he said to Leslie. "You're in no condition to be at the hotel alone."

"I'll get room service, pour a good, stiff drink, take a bubble bath and lose myself in my work," she said, attempting to compose herself. "I'll be fine. I'll have a bodyguard come with me."

"Are you sure?" Spock asked her.

"I'm sure. Tell him, kid," Leslie said.

"Leslie lives for her work. Keeping her from it for the night would drive her crazier than staying at the hotel. She's from New York, she's tough," I said, trying to lighten things up. It was the truth. Leslie was a professional, the best publicist in the biz. If anyone could handle this kind of drama, it was her.

"Queensbridge, baby," she said, smoothing her clothes and wiping her face. "No doubt."

"Make sure to let him comfort you," Leslie whispered in my ear as she gave me a hug and we parted.

Chorus

The bodyguard, Spock, and I rode in silence from downtown to Spock's new house in a recently gentrified neighborhood called Bronzeville on the south side. The area had changed so much from my childhood. Dilapidated buildings were now replaced with condos and renovated brownstones. The asking prices still seemed a little steep, though; an uneasy feeling crept over me as we rolled through the streets. The buildings might have changed, but the unsavory characters still remained. Crackheads lurked with heads down, their eyes frantically scouring the cement for a dropped rock. Transients begged on corners. It reminded me of what had transpired with Cali earlier. I just wanted to get away from it all.

"Where do you live?" I asked impatiently.

"Just around the corner, on St. Lawrence," Spock informed me. "Don't worry, Songbird, we're almost there. Besides, no one can hurt you when you've got us around looking out for you. Ain't that right, man?" he asked the bodyguard.

"No doubt," he agreed.

We pulled into Spock's garage, he deactivated the alarm with a remote, and we entered the house through the back door. It was a breathtaking, tastefully decorated, updated graystone with lots of the original finishes and trim. A woman had to have helped him with it.

"Look, we may as well get this out of the way," I blurted. "If you've got a girl, you may as well tell me. I appreciate what you're doing for me, but I don't want any drama."

"Lucky, chill. I don't have a girlfriend. My mother and sister helped me decorate. You remember my sister, the artist, right?"

"Yeah I remember," I admitted.

"That's the girl who helped me pull this all together. I know that's what you're thinking. Calm down, okay. I want you to relax. Let me take care of you."

The bodyguard looked at me and then at Spock. I'm sure he felt awkward as hell. Spock let him off the hook. He fixed me a glass of wine, told me to sit on the couch, and gave me the remote control. Then he showed the bodyguard how the alarm worked and set him up in a guest bedroom.

"Come upstairs Lucky," Spock told me, and I followed him up a winding staircase. We went into his bedroom, which was dark, but he didn't turn on the lights.

"Just relax," he said, guiding me to the bed. I kicked off my shoes and squinted to make him out. He lit candles placed around the room. I couldn't help but wonder who else he'd lit those candles for, but shooed the thought from my mind and gulped down my wine.

Spock went into the bathroom, where I heard him running water in the tub. He came out and told me to get undressed and get in. I hesitated.

"Don't get shy on me now," he teased.

"It isn't that. It's just that I'm really questioning my judgment when it comes to men. You see what happened earlier. I seem to be a really bad judge of character. I attract all the wrong men. Why are we here, Spock?" I asked. My mind was spinning from the incident outside the club with Cali. I felt like I couldn't trust myself when it came to who I loved.

"I am nothing like that man. Songbird, I still love you. Is that what you need to hear?" he asked. I could tell he was trying not to get frustrated.

"Only if you mean it," I admitted.

"I do. Lucky, this isn't about you being famous, or me just trying to get some ass or whatever you might be thinking. I love you, and everything was fine before the night went wrong, but I'm trying to change it. Will you let me do that?" he asked. I sighed and took off my clothes.

"I'll will," I said. I stepped into the warm, sudsy water, and Spock activated the jets that sent powerful and relaxing bursts of water onto my weary body.

"Want some music?" he asked.

"Sure," I told him.

"What do you want to hear?" he asked.

"You're so good at telling me what I want to hear. Why don't you choose?" I snapped. I couldn't help it. I knew I'd been though a lot, but a part of me couldn't trust why he was being so nice to me and was so frustrated that I lashed out on the person closest to me.

"I'm going to ignore that comment," he said. "I'll play you some of my stuff. But don't worry; I'm not trying to work you over to help me get a deal. And if you hate it, you can feel free to tell me. But I don't think you will." I did believe that he just wanted to share his music with me, no strings attached. That was one of the things that made our relationship in the past so special. We collaborated on lots of songs, just fooling around in his home studio, and it always seemed to just fit. To borrow a corporate term, there was a synergy between us.

He cued up a couple of tracks he'd been working on, and I hummed quietly along, freestyling and improvising lyrics here and there. My tension dissolved into the water, and soon I was totally at ease, singing softly while I lounged in the luxurious bath.

"I want to hear you better," he said. He knelt beside the tub and turned the water jets off. I smiled and sang a little louder.

"We sound good together," he commented.

"We always did," I replied.

"How's the water?" he asked. I gazed up at him, thinking about what we had done earlier, and what we were on our way to do before we were interrupted by Cali's foolishness.

"Why don't you find out for yourself?" I asked him. Spock was disrobed and in the tub with me in less than sixty seconds. We were like two little kids in the soapy water, splashing each other and putting bubble beards and hats on each other. You know I had to be feeling good to let him mess up my hair and makeup. The glam squad would be thoroughly pissed when they saw what I'd done with all their hard work.

"Come here," he said. Luckily, the tub was large enough for me to move around easily. He opened his arms and I slid in between them. We sat there, soaking, and every now and then he'd caress my body or kiss me on the cheek or neck.

"You're going to turn into a raisin," he teased me, lifting my hand and inspecting my wrinkled fingertips. "Let's get out."

I pouted, splashing my hands on the water's surface and poking out my bottom lip like an impudent toddler.

"Come on, you big baby," he said. "Lay down on the bed."

I got out of the water quickly and cocked my eyebrow at him suggestively.

"I'm going to give you a massage," he said. "Get your mind out of the gutter."

"I like my mind in the gutter, and you like it too!"

"We're getting to that," he said. "You're always in such a rush. You always try to make things happen. Calm down. Enjoy the journey," he said.

He spread a bath towel on his king-sized bed and I laid down on it. I buried my face into his down comforter, not caring if I smeared what remained of my makeup on it. Hell, I wanted to leave a reminder of myself behind in case any chicks came over. Besides, if he didn't like it, he had a good job—he could pay to get it cleaned or buy another one. I could smell a stick of incense burning as Spock squeezed some oil between his palms and rubbed them together. They were warm when he placed them on my body and began to rub and knead my shoulders.

"You have such a beautiful body," he told me as he caressed my skin with what smelled like almond oil. He took his time while working on my lower back, hips, ass, and thighs. I was weak beneath his touch, and I knew that my inner thighs were going to be particularly slippery, and not from the oil. He made his way slowly down my calves and finally to my feet, working on my strained insteps, massaging the damage from the stilettos I adore. I moaned and sighed as he worked out every bit of stress I had, and I was ready to take the rubdown to the next level. I think he was too, because he stopped rubbing my backside, flipped me over and made that face men make when what they see what looks real good to them.

But he didn't jump my bones. He poured oil directly on my

breasts and looked into my eyes as he began to rub it in, his hands gliding and sliding over my nipples. I returned his stare, biting my lip and thrusting my chest upward. I know he liked to drag things out and savor every moment, and I loved that about him, but I could rarely wait when I was near him.

"Kiss me," I whispered. He leaned down and kissed me, and I could feel the hairs on his chest sliding over my breasts. I wrapped my legs around his and kissed him deeply, hungrily sucking his tongue into my mouth as we squished and slid against each other.

He pulled away. "Not yet," he said.

"Come on, baby. Why do you torture me like this?" I asked.

"I told you, you need to appreciate the journey. You know you're going to get there . . . a bunch of times," he said, and chuckled softly. He continued his rubdown, making me squirm beneath his fingertips.

"I want to feel your cock inside of me right now," I said forcefully. I needed him to take me to the place that only he knew, and I needed it right then. He stopped touching me and just looked at me. He looked like he was going to say something, but he didn't. I couldn't wait anymore. "Please, please, I need you now," I whimpered.

"Shh," he said, putting his finger to my lips. I stuck my tongue out and licked it before quickly drawing it into my mouth and sucking. He pulled it out and I nipped it gently with my teeth. His hand drifted between my legs, and I eagerly spread them, giving him full access. His nimble fingers rubbed my clit until I was at a fever pitch.

"You're such a freak," he told me.

"Yeah," I panted. "And you love it."

"I do," he replied.

"Stop all that talking and put your mouth to work," I said. Our relationship and our lovemaking were like tug of war, a constant battle of will and strength. I always lost, but I put up a good fight.

"You always tell me that," he said.

I grabbed him by the back of the neck and pulled him down to my crotch, but instead of him diving in the way I wanted, he rained soft kisses across my mound. He gently opened me up with his thumbs and forefingers and licked slowly, teasingly, around my pearl. He brought me to three orgasms, kissing me and stroking my face, giving me a few minutes to rest after each one before beginning again.

At last he reached into the nightstand and got a condom; he put it on quickly and pulled my body to meet his. He entered me forcefully, and I could feel him grow even harder as I engulfed him in my wet sweetness. He pumped powerfully on top of me for what felt like an hour until he could barely move and we switched positions.

He lay down on the bed and I sat on top of him again and rode him, this time turning my back to him and facing the mirror that sat perched atop his dresser. We both watched our reflections illuminated by the flickering candlelight as I reached down and gently played with his scrotum, bouncing up and down his pole, my breasts bouncing up and down with me.

Spock spread my ass cheeks apart and gently wiggled a finger inside. I gasped, tensed, and then relaxed as he reached around with his other hand and massaged my clitoris. Before long he had three fingers inserted in my ass, and the sensation of the three different kinds of stimulation sent me soaring. I screamed his name over and over, not caring if I woke the whole damn neighborhood.

Soon he exploded as well, and I watched the expression on his face in the mirror with sensual satisfaction. We curled up in each other's arms and held each other tight. We didn't speak. We didn't dare break the perfect silence between us, and soon drifted off to sleep.

Bridge

The next morning, Spock treated me to breakfast in bed. He slipped pieces of fresh tropical fruit between my lips, kissing me after each bite and savoring the sweet taste of nectar on my lips.

"How do you feel?" he asked me, nibbling on my neck.

"Much better," I told him.

"Well I'm about to make you feel even better."

Spock slid beneath the sheets and began to lick and suck at my nipples, gently biting each one before going lower and lower until he was nestled between my legs. He parted his lips and sucked my clit between them before plunging his tongue in and out. I was shivering, bucking my hips upward, straining to meet his tongue.

"You taste like fruit," he said, before throwing my legs back over my shoulders and fucking my moist slit with his tongue. He gazed into my eyes with a look of pure mischief, before grinning, and then he licked the puckered opening of my anus.

"What are you doing?" I gasped.

"You know what I'm doing," he said, grinning, and continued to lick the crack of my ass, teasing me before inserting his tongue inside the tight crevice. I let out a small yelp and squirmed to change position.

"Oh no you don't," he said. "I'm going to lick it, get it nice and wet, and then I'm going to stick my cock inside of you."

My eyes widened in fear.

"I won't hurt you, baby," he promised. "I'm going to go nice and slow. And you're going to love it."

I held my breath and my body tensed, but soon I was relaxed and gave in to the sensation of him giving slow, seductive licks to my backside. Spock stopped, put on a condom, and lifted me up, flipping me on all fours. He held onto my shoulder firmly.

"I'm going to put it in now. I want you to relax. If you don't like it, we'll stop. But I know you're going to like it. I warmed you up with my fingers last night, and now I'm going to give it all to you and you're going to take it. You're going to take it and give it back to me."

Millimeter by millimeter, I felt my rectum expand. There was pain intermingled with pleasure and I felt dizzy and weak from the sensation. Spock reached around to work my clit, heightening my pleasure, and before long he was at least halfway inside me, which was good enough for both of us, because we came soon after, him clutching me and muttering my name and that I was beautiful in my ear as we did.

As we lay there in the bed, spent, I wondered what it was about Spock that made me so willing to give every part of my body to him. Was I sexually addicted to him? Was it because I loved him? And more important, did he feel the same way for me, or was this just a fling? Sure, he'd tried to verbally reassure me, but didn't all men say what they felt they had to in order to get what they wanted?

The sound of Spock's BlackBerry vibrating snapped me out of my thoughts, as he untangled his arms and legs from my body and got up to retrieve it. He frowned as he read a text message.

"Don't hate me," he said.

"Don't tell me," I told him. "You have to go to work."

"There's a massive computer outage at the mayor's office. Everything's screwed up around there."

"But can't you just delegate the work?" I asked. I wanted to spend as much time with Spock as I could before I had to leave. Who knew what would happen between us once I was out of sight? No matter what our fate, I wanted to remain in the bliss of the present for as long as possible.

"Not if I want things to be done right, and not if I don't want the mayor to tear me a new asshole." We looked at each other and cracked up laughing at the new asshole reference.

"You're a pervert," I teased him.

"So are you."

I spent most of the day lounging around, watching TV, something I never get a chance to do. Then I went into Spock's home studio and messed around with equipment and listened to the stuff he'd been working on. While I was fooling around, experimenting with making beats, the phone in the studio rang. I should have ignored it, but I couldn't. I looked at the caller ID. It read: JURIS PRESCOTT. I knew that name. It was his other ex-girlfriend, the one he had when we dated before. That motherfucker! Nothing had changed! I was going to kill him, but not until I handled one bit of important business. I did something I never did before, but that I should have done years ago when Spock's little love triangle first became apparent. I picked up the phone and pressed the Talk button.

"Hello?"

"Uh, hello? Who is this?" Juris asked, surprised.

"This is Lucky, Juris," I told her. There was silence. "Do you remember me?"

"Of course," she said. "How could I forget? I just wasn't expecting to hear your voice."

An awkward silence.

"Can I speak to him?" she asked.

"No, you can't," I said.

Another silence.

"Why are you calling him, Juris?" I asked.

"Why are you there?" she asked back. She didn't say it with a funky attitude; in fact, she seemed amused, which just pissed me off even more.

"You know what?" I asked. I was about to read her from A to Z when I realized that it wouldn't solve anything. "Never mind," I said and hung up.

This was stupid. I didn't need to ask her why she was calling. I already knew why. He was still playing the both of us. I was getting the fuck out of there. If I didn't by the time Spock came home, there would be a bloodbath. I had way too much going for me to ruin my life over some jerk. I'd just pulled on my clothes when my cell phone rang. It was Spock, of course.

"What do you want?" I barked into my cell phone.

"I just spoke to Juris."

"So did I," I said.

"Oh good," he said, sounding relieved. "So then you know that nothing is going on."

"No, I don't know that," I told him. "In fact, I'd say the opposite is true. I should have known better. You're still the same lying motherfucker you were before. Nothing's changed."

"Songbird—" he said. I cut him off.

"Don't Songbird me! Don't call me that stupid name! Don't say shit to me!" I screamed.

"Lucky, damn it, listen. I don't want you to leave. Promise me that you won't leave before I get there. I can't make it home just yet, but I'll be there around eight." I looked at the clock. It was six. "Lucky, please? I hope you're still there when I get there. We need to talk about this because it really isn't what you think."

I hung up my cell. Damn it! Was I going to stick around to hear whatever lame excuse he was going to offer? I was. But I wasn't going to let him know that. I was going to make him wonder until he brought his ass home. But I knew that I was going to stay, even though I tried to convince myself a million ways that I shouldn't. There was one thing that overruled all my arguments: I loved him. There was no escaping it. And it was because I loved him that I told myself that maybe there was a reasonable explanation for her call.

My bodyguard must have heard me screaming because he came busting into the room. I screamed in shock.

"You okay, Lucky?" he asked, looking around. I placed my hand over my chest, where I could feel my heart racing like Seabiscuit.

"Yeah," I told him. "I was on the phone."

"Oh," he said. "Well, are you sure everything is all right?"

"Yeah," I told him.

"Do you want to stick around here?" the bodyguard asked. "We can go back to the Peninsula if you want. We can move your things, but since you're leaving tomorrow, you don't have to if you don't want. I'll make sure you have nothing to worry about."

"No, that's all right," I said. "I have some unsettled business to take care of."

I didn't have any more work-related business to do for the remainder of my stay. I just wanted to hit Michigan Avenue for some shopping. But I checked in with Leslie while I waited for Spock to return. She pressed me for details of the night, which I kept to myself. And I didn't tell her about the phone call from Juris. I just told her that I'd fill her in later, which I would undoubtedly do. I just hoped I wouldn't be weaving another tale of woe.

Spock finally made it in, and my bodyguard and I both eyeballed him with sour looks on our faces. I excused the bodyguard, and Spock and I went into the kitchen. He fixed us a couple of cocktails and then we slipped outside to sit on his deck.

"Okay," I said. "You've had enough time to come up with a good-ass story. So let's hear it."

"There's no story. Juris and I are just friends. That's all," he said.

"Why was she calling you?" I asked him.

"Do you really want to know why?" he asked.

"Hell yeah!"

"She saw on some entertainment show the story about your ex-boyfriend pulling a knife on you. She wanted to know if I'd talked to you and if you were okay."

"That's bullshit and you know it," I said.

"For real. Juris and I are over. We never belonged together in the first place. Who do you think encouraged me to go for another chance with you?"

"Damn sure not her!" I said.

"Well, it's true," he said. "I wanted to move on after you left, but I couldn't. Not with her, not really with anyone. I didn't stay at home knitting, but no one could take your place. Nothing compares to you. Juris and I stayed friends and, well, I used to talk about you to her sometimes."

"I wish I believed that."

"Well, you should. Her husband even knows how I feel about you," he said.

"Her husband?" I said, shocked.

"Yeah. She got married a few months ago. To my frat brother."

"How the hell did that happen?" I asked.

"He always liked her. And when things fell apart—"

"When you got busted," I said, correcting him.

"Whatever. He stepped to her, and she liked what he had to say. She told me she wasn't going to wait for me to make up my mind. They're expecting a baby."

I felt stupid, but not really. I was just looking out for myself and for my heart. I was glad that I stuck around, though, because if I hadn't over a misunderstanding, then I really would have felt stupid.

"I love you, Lucky. You're the one for me. No one else," he told me. I didn't know what to say, which was cool, because he kept talking. "Call her back if you want to. You didn't give her a chance to tell you. She was just surprised to hear you answer the phone. Talk to her husband. Look, I'm going to prove to you that I'm sorry I ever let you go. And I know that I wasn't the man you needed me to be. But I can be now. Don't give up on me yet. I really care about you and I need you in my life."

I took a moment to look up at the night sky for stars, as if they could guide me, but I didn't see any. The night sky was either too cloudy or maybe stars don't shine as bright in Chicago. Since I couldn't find what I was looking for, I went on ahead and said what was on my mind.

"I love you too. But I don't want you to hurt me again. I will not be your fool again."

"I'm not going to make a fool out of you."

He said those words with what appeared to be earnest sincerity, and yet I still wasn't sure.

"What am I going to do with you?" I asked.

"Just love me," he said.

"Loving you is easy," I told him. "Being in love with you is what's hard."

We sat there on the deck, holding hands, saying nothing. Although many questions lingered between us, we sat in peaceful silence. Time would be the answer.

Repeat Chorus

I can't explain why I love him, why I can't move forward without him. I guess I just like having him along for the ride, although I'm afraid that one day I'll look over on the passenger's side and it will be empty. But for now, he's there, right where I need him to be. What the future holds for us, the uncertainty of it, all scares me. I still have issues with trusting Spock. Fool me once, shame on you, fool me twice, shame on me and all that shit. Maybe one day the past will truly be buried and we can live happily ever after. But I'm happy right now, and that's what counts.

Fade Out

MÉTA SMITH was born in Philadelphia and raised on the south side of Chicago. She is a graduate of Spelman College, where she received her bachelor's degree in English. She is a DJ, a creative writing teacher, lecturer, and the author of two novels, *The Rolexxx Club* and *Queen of Miami*. She lives in Miami and Chicago with her son, Jordan.

Glory Be to the Father
GLORIA PATRI
H. W. Greatorex
Glo-ry be to the Fa-ther, and to the Son, and to the Ho-ly Ghost; As it
was in the beginning, is now, and ever shall be, world without end. A-men, A - men.
(Second Tune)
GLORIA PATRI
Charles Meineke
Glo-ry be to the Fa-ther, and to the Son, and to the Ho-ly Ghost; As it
was in the be-gin-ning, is now, and ever shall be, world without end. A-men, A-men.
All Things Come of Thee
OFFERINGS
Arranged from Beethoven
All things come of Thee, O Lord, and of Thine own have we giv-en Thee. A-MEN.

Favorite Hymns of Praise

1970
Printed in U.S.A.

TABERNACLE PUBLISHING COMPANY
Corner Lake St. and Waller Ave.
Chicago, Illinois 60644

I will sing unto the Lord
As long as I live:
I will sing praise to my God
While I have my being.

—*Psalm 104:33*

Favorite Hymns of Praise

When Morning Gilds the Skies

1

FROM THE GERMAN
TR. BY EDWARD CASWALL

JOSEPH BARNBY

1. When morn - ing gilds the skies, My heart a - wak - ing cries:
2. When sleep her balm de - nies, My si - lent spir - it sighs:
3. Does sad - ness fill my mind, A sol - ace here I find:
4. In heav'n's e - ter - nal bliss The love - liest strain is this:
5. Be this, while life is mine, My can - ti - cle di - vine,
May Je - sus Christ be praised; A - like at work and prayer . .
May Je - sus Christ be praised; When e - vil thoughts mo - lest, . . .
May Je - sus Christ be praised; Or fades my earth - ly bliss, . .
May Je - sus Christ be praised; The pow'rs of dark - ness fear, . . .
May Je - sus Christ be praised; Be this th' e - ter - nal song, . .
To Je - sus I re - pair: . . May Je - sus Christ be praised.
With this I shield my breast: . May Je - sus Christ be praised.
My com - fort still is this: . . May Je - sus Christ be praised.
When this sweet chant they hear: . May Je - sus Christ be praised.
Thro' all the a - ges on: . . . May Je - sus Christ be praised.

2
Holy, Holy, Holy
Reginald Heber
John B. Dykes
1. Ho-ly, Ho-ly, Ho - ly, Lord God Al - might - y! Ear - ly in the
2. Ho-ly, Ho-ly, Ho - ly! All the saints a - dore Thee, Cast-ing down their
3. Ho-ly, Ho-ly, Ho - ly! Tho' the dark-ness hide Thee, Tho' the eye of
4. Ho-ly, Ho-ly, Ho - ly, Lord God Al - might - y! All Thy works shall
morn - ing our song shall rise to Thee; Ho - ly, Ho - ly, Ho - ly!
gold-en crowns a-round the glass-y sea; Cher-u-bim and ser-a-phim
sin - ful man Thy glo - ry may not see, On - ly Thou art ho - ly;
praise Thy name, in earth, and sky, and sea; Ho - ly, Ho - ly, Ho - ly!
Mer-ci-ful and Might-y! God in Three Per-sons, bless-ed Trin-i - ty!
fall-ing down be-fore Thee, Which wert, and art, and ev - er-more shalt be.
there is none be-side Thee Per - fect in pow'r, in love, and pu - ri - ty.
Mer-ci-ful and Might-y! God in Three Per-sons, bless-ed Trin-i - ty!
3
Breathe on Me, Breath of God
Edwin Hatch
Robert Jackson
1. Breathe on me, Breath of God, Fill me with life a-new, That I may
2. Breathe on me, Breath of God, Un - til my heart is pure, Un - til with
3. Breathe on me, Breath of God, Till I am whol - ly Thine, Un - til this
4. Breathe on me, Breath of God, So shall I nev - er die, But live with

Breathe on Me, Breath of God

love what Thou dost love, And do what Thou wouldst do.
Thee I will one will, To do and to en - dure.
earth-ly part of me Glows with Thy fire di - vine.
Thee the per-fect life Of Thine e - ter - ni - ty. A - MEN.
Come, Thou Almighty King 4
AUTHOR UNKNOWN
FELICE DE GIARDINI
1. Come, Thou Al - might - y King, Help us Thy name to sing,
2. Come, Thou In - car - nate Word, Gird on Thy might - y sword,
3. Come, Ho - ly Com - fort - er, Thy sa-cred wit - ness bear
4. To the great One in Three E - ter-nal prais - es be
Help us to praise: Fa - ther, all glo - ri-ous, O'er all vic -
Our prayer at - tend: Come, and Thy peo - ple bless, And give Thy
In this glad hour: Thou who al - might - y art, Now rule in
Hence ev - er - more. His sov'reign maj - es - ty, May we in
to - ri - ous, Come, and reign o - ver us, An - cient of Days.
word suc-cess: Spir - it of ho - li-ness, On us de - scend.
ev - 'ry heart, And ne'er from us de-part, Spir - it of pow'r.
glo - ry see, And to e - ter - ni - ty Love and a - dore.

5 Fairest Lord Jesus

From the German, 17th Century
4th Verse Tr. Joseph A. Seiss

Silesian Folk Song
Arr. by Richard S. Willis

1. Fair - est Lord Je - sus! Ru - ler of all na - ture!
2. Fair are the mead - ows, Fair - er still the wood - lands,
3. Fair is the sun - shine, Fair - er still the moon - light,
4. Beau - ti - ful Sav - ior! Lord of all the na - tions!

O Thou of God and man the Son! Thee will I cher - ish,
Robed in the bloom - ing garb of spring; Je - sus is fair - er,
And all the twin - kling star - ry host; Je - sus shines bright-er,
Son of God and Son of Man! Glo - ry and hon - or,

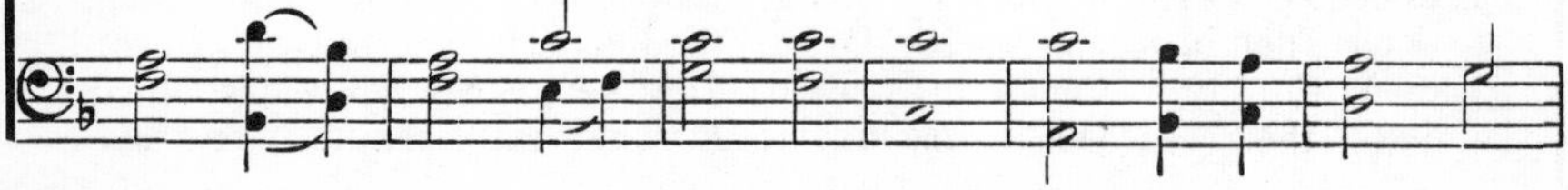

Thee will I hon - or, Thou, my soul's glo-ry, joy, and crown!
Je - sus is pur - er, Who makes the woe-ful heart to sing!
Je - sus shines pur - er, Than all the an - gels heav'n can boast!
Praise, a - dor - a - tion, Now and for - ev - er - more be Thine! A-MEN.

6 O, for a Faith That Will Not Shrink

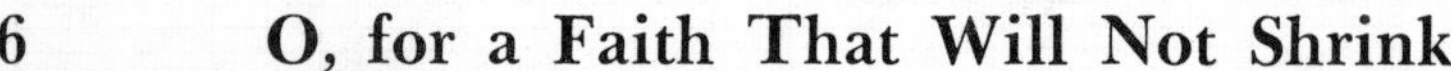

William H. Bathurst

John B. Dykes

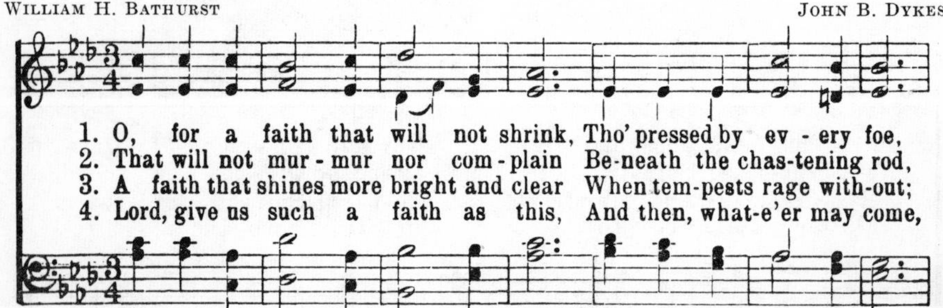
1. O, for a faith that will not shrink, Tho' pressed by ev - ery foe,
2. That will not mur - mur nor com - plain Be - neath the chas - tening rod,
3. A faith that shines more bright and clear When tem - pests rage with - out;
4. Lord, give us such a faith as this, And then, what - e'er may come,

O, for a Faith That Will Not Shrink

That will not trem - ble on the brink Of an - y earth - ly woe!—
But, in the hour of grief or pain, Will lean up - on its God;—
That when in dan - ger knows no fear, In dark-ness feels no doubt.—
We'll taste, e'en here, the hal - lowed bliss Of an e - ter - nal home.
Rejoice, Ye Pure in Heart
7
EDWARD H. PLUMPTRE
ARTHUR M. MESSITER
1. Re - joice, ye pure in heart, Re - joice, give thanks, and sing:
2. With all the an - gel choirs, With all the saints on earth,
3. Still lift your stand - ard high, Still march in firm ar - ray;
4. Yes, on through life's long path, Still chant - ing as ye go;
5. Then on, ye pure in heart, Re - joice, give thanks, and sing;
Your fes - tal ban - ner wave on high, The cross of Christ your King.
Pour out the strains of joy and bliss, True rap - ture, no - blest mirth!
As war-riors through the dark - ness toil Till dawns the gold - en day.
From youth to age, by night and day, In glad - ness and in woe.
Your fes - tal ban - ner wave on high, The cross of Christ your King.
REFRAIN
Re - joice, re - joice, Re - joice, give thanks, and sing! A-MEN.
Re - joice, re - joice,

8 All Hail the Power of Jesus' Name

(CORONATION)
EDWARD PERRONET
ALT. BY JOHN RIPPON
OLIVER HOLDEN
1. All hail the pow'r of Je - sus' name! Let an - gels pros - trate fall;
2. Ye cho - sen seed of Is - rael's race, Ye ran-somed from the fall,
3. Let ev - 'ry kin - dred, ev - 'ry tribe On this ter - res - trial ball,
4. O that with yon - der sa - cred throng We at His feet may fall!
Bring forth the roy - al di - a - dem, And crown Him Lord of all,
Hail Him who saves you by His grace, And crown Him Lord of all,
To Him all maj - es - ty as - cribe, And crown Him Lord of all,
We'll join the ev - er - last - ing song, And crown Him Lord of all,
Bring forth the roy - al di - a - dem, And crown Him Lord of all!
Hail Him who saves you by His grace, And crown Him Lord of all!
To Him all maj - es - ty as - cribe, And crown Him Lord of all!
We'll join the ev - er - last - ing song, And crown Him Lord of all!
9 All Hail the Power of Jesus' Name
(MILES LANE)
EDWARD PERRONET
WILLIAM SHRUBSOLE
1. All hail the pow'r of Je - sus' name! Let an - gels pros - trate fall; Bring forth the roy - al
di - a - dem, And crown Him, crown Him, crown Him, Crown Him Lord of all!

All Hail the Power of Jesus' Name

(DIADEM)

EDWARD PERRONET
ALT. BY JOHN RIPPON

JAMES ELLOR

1. All hail the pow'r of Je - sus' name! Let an - gels pros-trate fall,
2. Ye cho - sen seed of Is - rael's race, Ye ran-somed from the fall,
3. Let ev - 'ry kin - dred, ev - 'ry tribe, On this ter - res - trial ball,
4. O that with yon - der sa - cred throng We at His feet may fall,
Let an - gels pros-trate fall; Bring forth the roy - al di - a - dem,
Ye ran - somed from the fall, Hail Him who saves you by His grace,
On this ter - res - trial ball, To Him all maj - es - ty as - cribe,
We at His feet may fall! We'll join the ev - er - last - ing song,
And crown . . . . Him, Crown Him,
And crown Him, crown Him, crown Him, crown Him, And crown Him Lord of
And crown . . . . Him, Crown Him,
And crown Him, crown Him, crown Him, Crown . . . .
crown Him, crown Him;
all, crown Him; And crown Him Lord of all!
crown . . . . . . Him;
. . . . Him; And crown Him Lord of all!

11 Still, Still with Thee

HARRIET BEECHER STOWE — FELIX MENDELSSOHN-BARTHOLDY

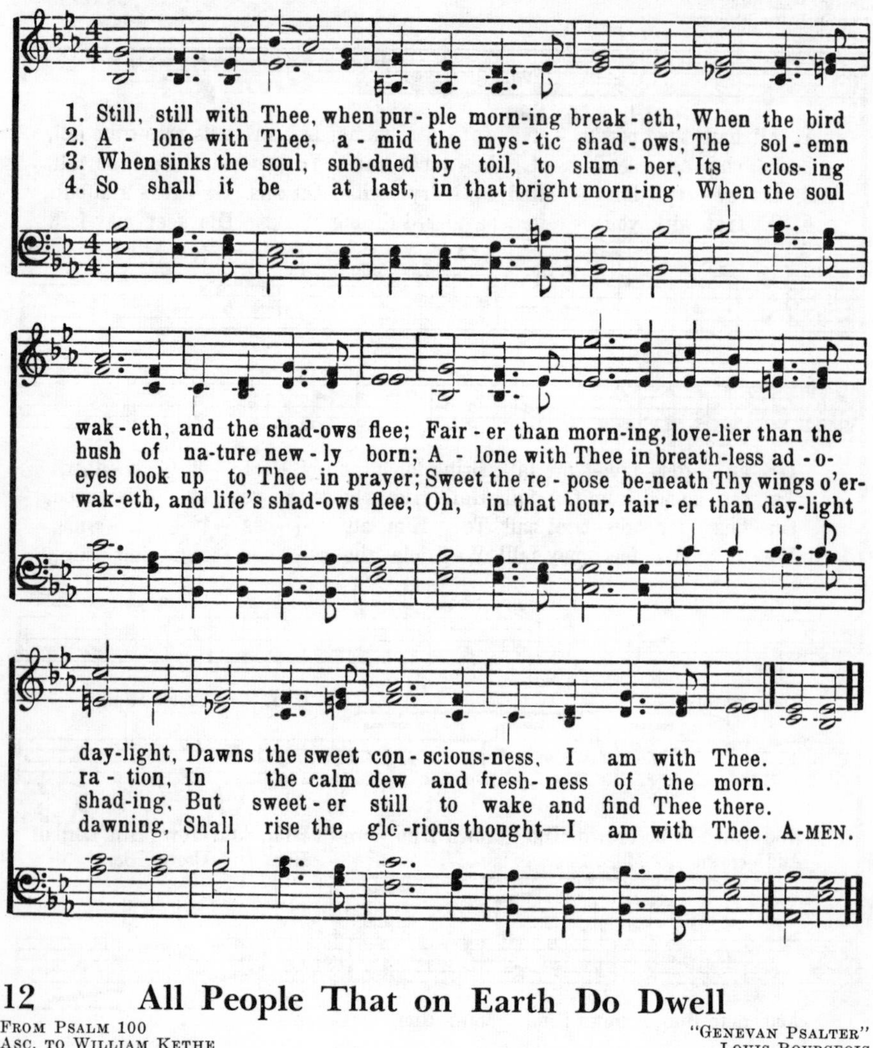
1. Still, still with Thee, when pur-ple morn-ing break-eth, When the bird
2. A - lone with Thee, a - mid the mys-tic shad-ows, The sol-emn
3. When sinks the soul, sub-dued by toil, to slum - ber, Its clos-ing
4. So shall it be at last, in that bright morn-ing When the soul
wak-eth, and the shad-ows flee; Fair - er than morn-ing, love-lier than the
hush of na-ture new-ly born; A - lone with Thee in breath-less ad - o-
eyes look up to Thee in prayer; Sweet the re - pose be-neath Thy wings o'er-
wak-eth, and life's shad-ows flee; Oh, in that hour, fair - er than day-light
day-light, Dawns the sweet con - scious-ness, I am with Thee.
ra - tion, In the calm dew and fresh - ness of the morn.
shad-ing, But sweet - er still to wake and find Thee there.
dawning, Shall rise the glo-rious thought—I am with Thee. A-MEN.

12 All People That on Earth Do Dwell

FROM PSALM 100
ASC. TO WILLIAM KETHE

"GENEVAN PSALTER"
LOUIS BOURGEOIS

1. All peo - ple that on earth do dwell, Sing to the Lord with cheerful voice; Him
2. The Lord, ye know, is God in-deed; With-out our aid He did us make; We
3. O en-ter then His gates with praise, Ap-proach with joy His courts un-to: Praise
4. For why? the Lord our God is good, His mer - cy is for - ev - er sure; His

All People That on Earth Do Dwell

serve with fear, His praise forth tell; Come ye be - fore Him and re-joice.
are His flock, He doth us feed, And for His sheep He doth us take.
laud and bless His name al-ways, For it is seem-ly so to do.
truth at all times firm - ly stood, And shall from age to age en-dure. A-MEN.
O Worship the King
13
FROM PSALM 104
ROBERT GRANT
ADAPTED FROM J. MICHAEL HAYDN
1. O wor-ship the King, all - glo-rious a - bove, And grate-ful - ly
2. O tell of His might, and sing of His grace, Whose robe is the
3. Thy boun-ti - ful care what tongue can re - cite? It breathes in the
4. Frail chil-dren of dust, and fee - ble as frail, In Thee do we
sing His won-der-ful love; Our Shield and De-fend - er, the An-cient of
light, whose can-o - py space; His char - iots of wrath the deep thunder-clouds
air, it shines in the light, It streams from the hills, it de-scends to the
trust, nor find Thee to fail; Thy mer - cies how ten - der! how firm to the
days, Pa - vil-ioned in splen-dor, and gird-ed with praise.
form, And dark is His path on the wings of the storm.
plain, And sweet-ly dis - tills in the dew and the rain.
end! Our Mak - er, De - fend - er, Re - deem-er, and Friend. A - MEN.

14 Praise Ye the Lord, the Almighty

Joachim Neander
Tr. by Catherine Winkworth

"Stralsund Gesangbuch"
Arr. in "Praxis Pietatas Melica"

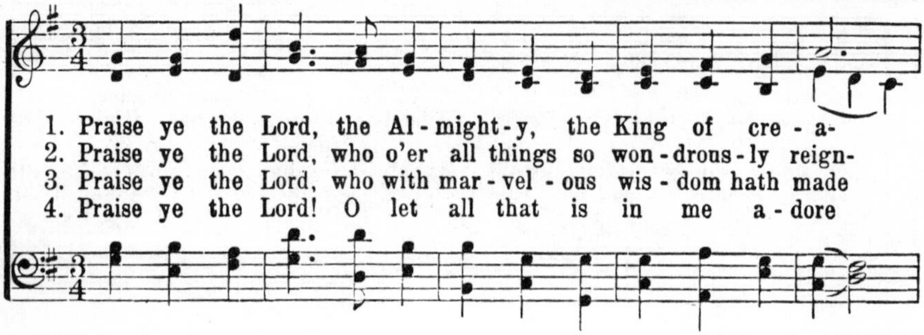

1. Praise ye the Lord, the Al - might - y, the King of cre - a-
2. Praise ye the Lord, who o'er all things so won - drous - ly reign-
3. Praise ye the Lord, who with mar - vel - ous wis - dom hath made
4. Praise ye the Lord! O let all that is in me a - dore

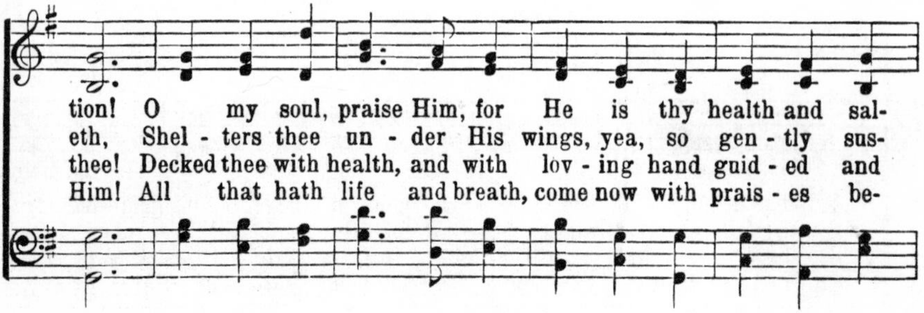

tion! O my soul, praise Him, for He is thy health and sal-
eth, Shel - ters thee un - der His wings, yea, so gen - tly sus-
thee! Decked thee with health, and with lov - ing hand guid - ed and
Him! All that hath life and breath, come now with prais - es be-

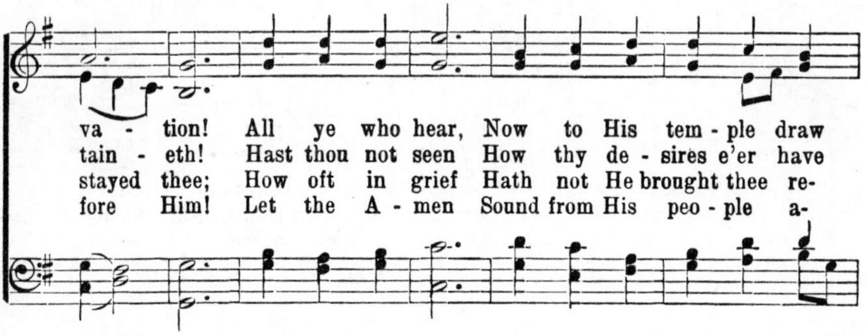

va - tion! All ye who hear, Now to His tem - ple draw
tain - eth! Hast thou not seen How thy de - sires e'er have
stayed thee; How oft in grief Hath not He brought thee re-
fore Him! Let the A - men Sound from His peo - ple a-

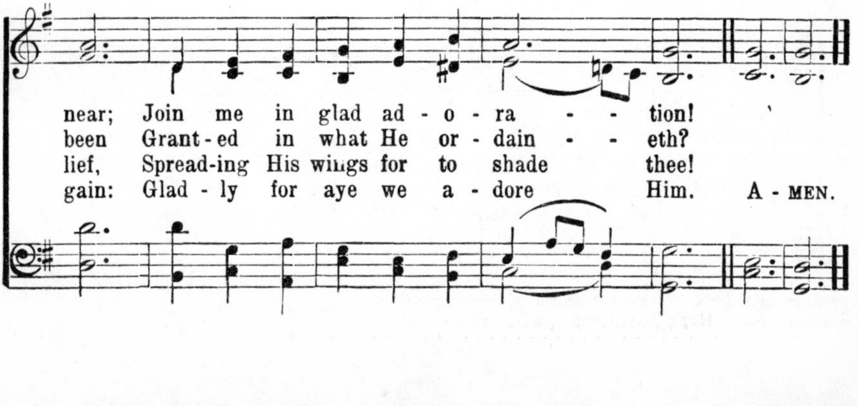

near; Join me in glad ad - o - ra - - tion!
been Grant - ed in what He or - dain - - eth?
lief, Spread - ing His wings for to shade thee!
gain: Glad - ly for aye we a - dore Him. A - men.

O Thou God of My Salvation

15

THOMAS OLIVERS — DANIEL B. TOWNER

1. O Thou God of my sal - va - tion, My Re-deem-er from all sin;
2. Though un-seen, I love the Sav - ior, He hath brought sal-va - tion near;
3. While the an - gel choirs are cry-ing, "Glo - ry to the great I Am,"
4. An - gels now are hov-'ring round us, Un - per-ceived a - mong the throng;
Moved by Thy di - vine com - pas - sion, Who hast died my heart to win;
Man - i - fests His pard-'ning fa - vor; And when Je - sus doth ap - pear,
I with them will still be vy - ing—Glo - ry, glo - ry to the Lamb!
Won-d'ring at the love that crowned us, Glad to sing the ho - ly song;
I will praise Thee, I will praise Thee, Where shall I Thy praise be - gin?
Soul and bod - y, soul and bod - y, Shall His glo - rious im - age bear;
Oh, how pre-cious, oh, how pre-cious Is the sound of Je - sus' name!
Hal - le - lu - jah, hal - le - lu - jah, Love and praise to Christ be - long!
I will praise Thee, I will praise Thee, Where shall I Thy praise be-gin?
Soul and bod - y, soul and bod - y, Shall His glo-rious im-age bear.
Oh, how pre-cious, oh, how pre-cious Is the sound of Je - sus' name!
Hal - le - lu - jah, hal - le - lu - jah, Love and praise to Christ be-long! A-MEN.

16 Blessed Be the Name

W. H. Clark
Refrain, Ralph E. Hudson

Ralph E. Hudson
Arr. by William J. Kirkpatrick

1. All praise to Him who reigns a - bove In maj - es - ty su - preme,
2. His name a - bove all names shall stand, Ex - alt - ed more and more,
3. Re - deem - er, Sav - ior, Friend of man Once ru - ined by the fall,
4. His name shall be the Coun - sel - or, The might-y Prince of Peace,

Who gave His Son for man to die, That He might man re - deem!
At God the Fa - ther's own right hand, Where an - gel - hosts a - dore.
Thou hast de - vised sal - va - tion's plan, For Thou hast died for all.
Of all earth's king-doms Con-quer - or, Whose reign shall nev-er cease.

Chorus

Bless-ed be the name, bless-ed be the name, Bless-ed be the name of the Lord;

Bless-ed be the name, bless-ed be the name, Bless-ed be the name of the Lord.

Come, Thou Fount

17

ROBERT ROBINSON JOHN WYETH

1. Come, Thou Fount of ev - 'ry bless - ing, Tune my heart to sing Thy grace;
2. Here I raise mine Eb - en - e - zer; Hith - er by Thy help I'm come;
3. O to grace how great a debt - or Dai - ly I'm con-strained to be!

Streams of mer - cy, nev - er ceas - ing, Call for songs of loud-est praise.
And I hope, by Thy good pleas-ure, Safe - ly to ar - rive at home.
Let Thy good-ness, like a fet - ter, Bind my wan-d'ring heart to Thee:

Teach me some me - lo-dious son - net, Sung by flam - ing tongues a-bove;
Je - sus sought me when a stran-ger, Wand'ring from the fold of God;
Prone to wan - der, Lord, I feel it, Prone to leave the God I love;

Praise the mount—I'm fixed up - on it—Mount of Thy re - deem-ing love.
He, to res - cue me from dan - ger, In - ter-posed His pre-cious blood.
Here's my heart, O take and seal it; Seal it for Thy courts a - bove.

18 **O to Be Like Thee!**

THOMAS O. CHISHOLM — WILLIAM J. KIRKPATRICK

1. O to be like Thee! bless-ed Re-deem-er, This is my con-stant
2. O to be like Thee! full of com-pas-sion, Lov-ing, for-giv-ing,
3. O to be like Thee! low-ly in spir-it, Ho-ly and harm-less,
4. O to be like Thee! Lord, I am com-ing, Now to re-ceive th' a-
5. O to be like Thee! while I am plead-ing, Pour out Thy Spir-it,
long-ing and prayer; Glad-ly I'll for-feit all of earth's treas-ures,
ten-der and kind, Help-ing the help-less, cheer-ing the faint-ing,
pa-tient and brave; Meek-ly en-dur-ing cru-el re-proach-es,
noint-ing di-vine; All that I am and have I am bring-ing.
fill with Thy love; Make me a tem-ple meet for Thy dwell-ing,
Je-sus, Thy per-fect like-ness to wear.
Seek-ing the wan-d'ring sin-ner to find.
Will-ing to suf-fer oth-ers to save.
Lord, from this mo-ment all shall be Thine.
Fit me for life and heav-en a-bove.
CHORUS
O to be like Thee!
O to be like Thee, Bless-ed Re-deem-er, pure as Thou art; Come in Thy
sweet-ness, come in Thy full-ness; Stamp Thine own im-age deep on my heart.

Praise Him! Praise Him!

Fanny J. Crosby — Chester G. Allen

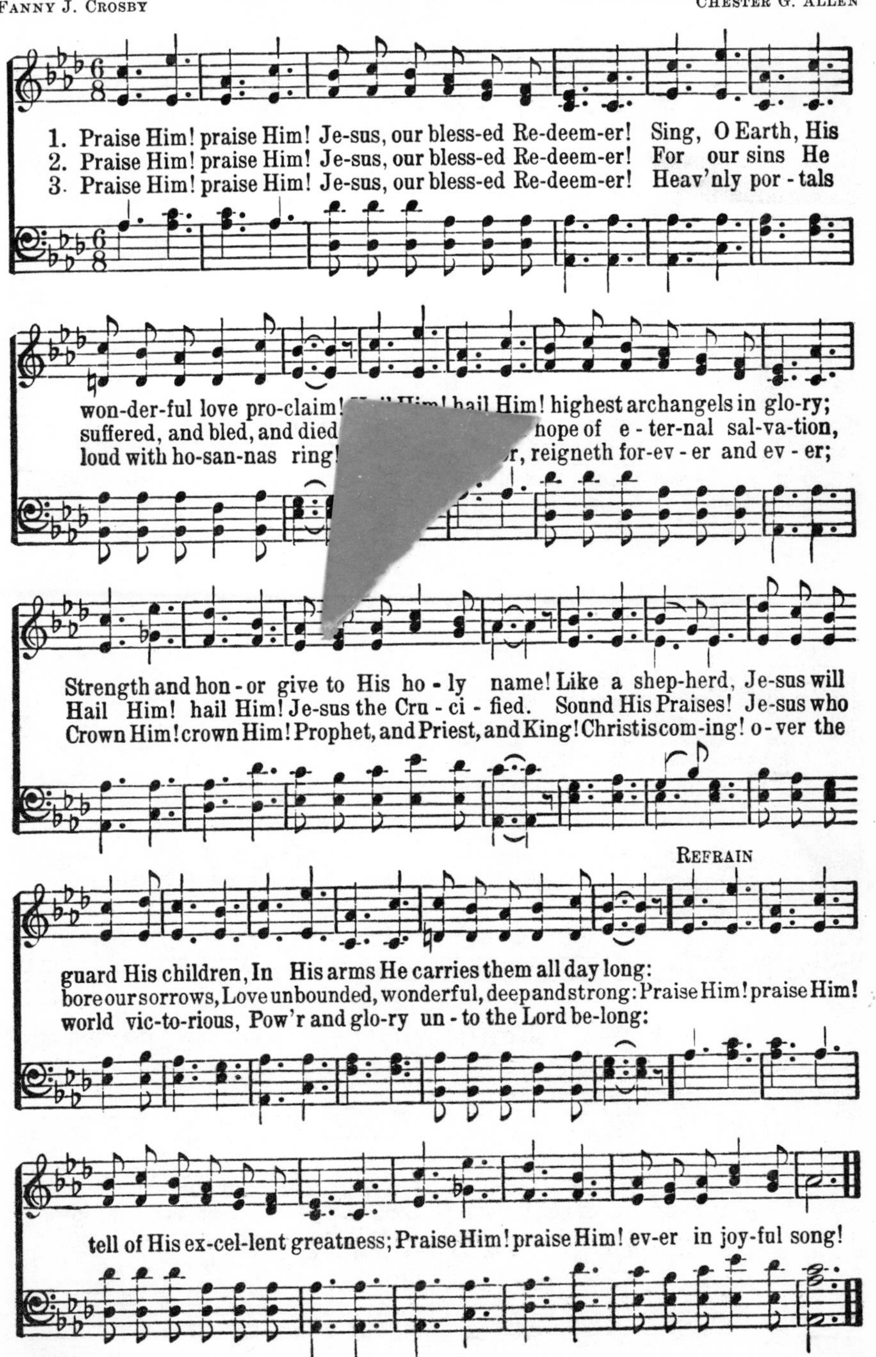
1. Praise Him! praise Him! Je-sus, our bless-ed Re-deem-er! Sing, O Earth, His
2. Praise Him! praise Him! Je-sus, our bless-ed Re-deem-er! For our sins He
3. Praise Him! praise Him! Je-sus, our bless-ed Re-deem-er! Heav'nly por-tals
won-der-ful love pro-claim!
hail Him! highest archangels in glo-ry;
suffered, and bled, and died
hope of e-ter-nal sal-va-tion,
loud with ho-san-nas ring!
reigneth for-ev-er and ev-er;
Strength and hon-or give to His ho-ly name! Like a shep-herd, Je-sus will
Hail Him! hail Him! Je-sus the Cru-ci-fied. Sound His Praises! Je-sus who
Crown Him! crown Him! Prophet, and Priest, and King! Christ is com-ing! o-ver the
Refrain
guard His children, In His arms He carries them all day long:
bore our sorrows, Love unbounded, wonderful, deep and strong: Praise Him! praise Him!
world vic-to-rious, Pow'r and glo-ry un-to the Lord be-long:
tell of His ex-cel-lent greatness; Praise Him! praise Him! ev-er in joy-ful song!

20 O Could I Speak

Samuel Medley

Wolfgang A. Mozart
Arr. by Lowell Mason

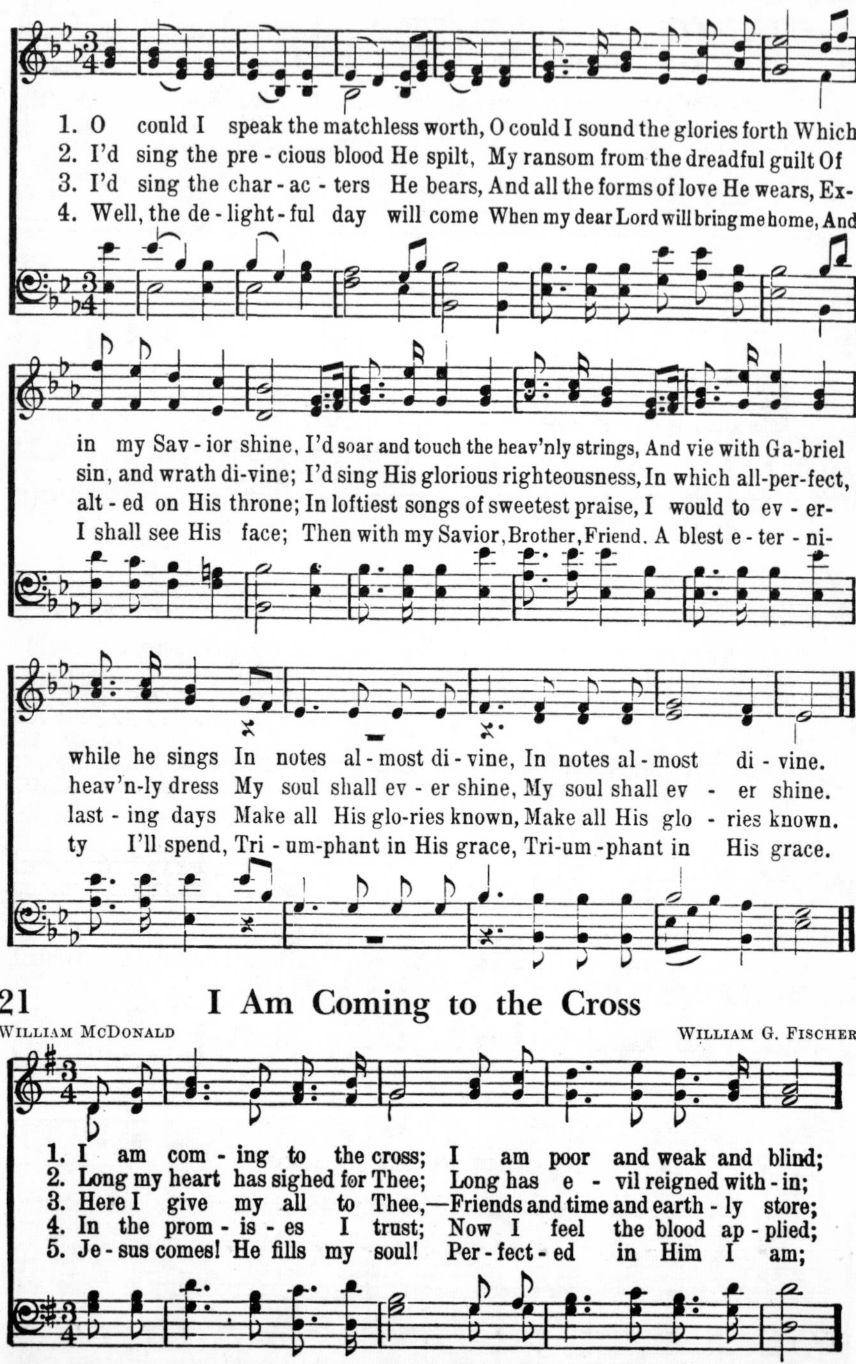
1. O could I speak the matchless worth, O could I sound the glories forth Which
2. I'd sing the pre - cious blood He spilt, My ransom from the dreadful guilt Of
3. I'd sing the char - ac - ters He bears, And all the forms of love He wears, Ex-
4. Well, the de - light - ful day will come When my dear Lord will bring me home, And
in my Sav - ior shine, I'd soar and touch the heav'nly strings, And vie with Ga-briel
sin, and wrath di-vine; I'd sing His glorious righteousness, In which all-per-fect,
alt - ed on His throne; In loftiest songs of sweetest praise, I would to ev - er-
I shall see His face; Then with my Savior, Brother, Friend, A blest e - ter - ni-
while he sings In notes al - most di - vine, In notes al - most di - vine.
heav'n-ly dress My soul shall ev - er shine, My soul shall ev - er shine.
last - ing days Make all His glo-ries known, Make all His glo - ries known.
ty I'll spend, Tri - um-phant in His grace, Tri-um -phant in His grace.
21 I Am Coming to the Cross
William McDonald
William G. Fischer
1. I am com - ing to the cross; I am poor and weak and blind;
2. Long my heart has sighed for Thee; Long has e - vil reigned with - in;
3. Here I give my all to Thee,—Friends and time and earth - ly store;
4. In the prom - is - es I trust; Now I feel the blood ap - plied;
5. Je - sus comes! He fills my soul! Per - fect - ed in Him I am;
Cho.—I am trust - ing, Lord, in Thee. Bless - ed Lamb of Cal - va - ry;

I Am Coming to the Cross

D. C. Chorus
I am count - ing all but dross; I shall full sal - va - tion find.
Je - sus sweet - ly speaks to me,—"I will cleanse you from all sin."
Soul and bod - y Thine to be,— Whol-ly Thine for - ev - er - more.
I am pros - trate in the dust; I with Christ am cru - ci - fied.
I am ev - 'ry whit made whole: Glo - ry, glo - ry to the Lamb!
Hum - bly at Thy cross I bow, Save me, Je - sus, save me now.
Bring Them In
22
Alexcenah Thomas
William A. Ogden
1. Hark! 'tis the Shepherd's voice I hear, Out in the des - ert dark and drear,
2. Who'll go and help this Shepherd kind, Help Him the wand'ring ones to find?
3. Out in the des - ert hear their cry, Out on the mountains wild and high;
Call - ing the sheep who've gone a-stray Far from the Shepherd's fold a - way.
Who'll bring the lost ones to the fold, Where they'll be sheltered from the cold?
Hark! 'tis the Mas - ter speaks to thee, "Go find my sheep wher - e'er they be."
Chorus
Bring them in, bring them in, Bring them in from the fields of sin;
Bring them in, bring them in, Bring the wand'ring ones to Je - sus.

23 Joyful, Joyful, We Adore Thee

HENRY VAN DYKE — ARR. FROM LUDWIG VAN BEETHOVEN

1. Joy-ful, joy-ful, we a-dore Thee, God of glo-ry, Lord of love;
2. All Thy works with joy sur-round Thee, Earth and heav'n re-flect Thy rays,
3. Thou art giv-ing and for-giv-ing, Ev-er bless-ing, ev-er blest,
4. Mor-tals, join the might-y cho-rus Which the morn-ing stars be-gan;

Hearts un-fold like flow'rs be-fore Thee, Hail Thee as the sun a-bove.
Stars and an-gels sing a-round Thee, Cen-ter of un-bro-ken praise;
Well-spring of the joy of liv-ing, O-cean-depth of hap-py rest!
Fa-ther love is reign-ing o'er us, Broth-er-love binds man to man.

Melt the clouds of sin and sad-ness; Drive the dark of doubt a-way;
Field and for-est, vale and moun-tain, Flow-'ry mead-ow flash-ing sea,
Thou our Fa-ther, Christ our Broth-er, All who live in love are Thine:
Ev-er sing-ing, march we on-ward, Vic-tors in the midst of strife;

Giv-er of im-mor-tal glad-ness, Fill us with the light of day!
Chant-ing bird and flow-ing foun-tain, Call us to re-joice in Thee.
Teach us how to love each oth-er, Lift us to the Joy Di-vine.
Joy-ful mu-sic lifts us sun-ward In the tri-umph song of life.

All Creatures of Our God and King 24

St. Francis of Assisi
Tr. by William H. Draper

"Geistliche Kirchengesange"

IN UNISON
1. All crea-tures of our God and King, Lift up your voice and with us
2. Thou rush-ing wind that art so strong, Ye clouds that sail in heav'n a-
3. And all ye men of ten-der heart, For-giv-ing oth-ers, take your
4. Let all things their Cre-a-tor bless, And wor-ship Him in hum-ble-
*Praise God from whom all bless-ings flow, Praise Him all crea-tures here be-
sing, Al-le-lu-ia! Al-le-lu-ia! Thou burn-ing sun with gold-en
long, O praise Him! Al-le-lu-ia! Thou ris-ing morn, in praise re-
part, O sing ye! Al-le-lu-ia! Ye who long pain and sor-row
ness, O praise Him! Al-le-lu-ia! Praise, praise the Fa-ther, praise the
low, Al-le-lu-ia! Al-le-lu-ia! Praise Him a-bove, ye heav'n-ly
beam, Thou sil-ver moon with soft-er gleam! O praise Him, O
joice, Ye lights of eve-ning, find a voice! O praise Him, O
bear, Praise God and on Him cast your care! O praise Him, O
Son, And praise the Spir-it, Three in One! O praise Him, O
host, Praise Fa-ther, Son and Ho-ly Ghost, Al-le-lu-ia, Al-le-
praise Him! Al-le-lu-ia! Al-le-lu-ia! Al-le-lu-ia! A-MEN.
lu-ia!

* Sometimes called the "Keswick Doxology"

25 The Spacious Firmament on High

JOSEPH ADDISON | FRANZ JOSEPH HAYDN

1. The spa-cious fir - ma - ment on high, With all the blue, e-
2. Soon as the eve-ning shades pre - vail, The moon takes up the
3. What though, in sol - emn si - lence, all Move round the dark ter-

the - real sky, And spangled heavens, a shin - ing frame, Their great O-
won-drous tale; And night - ly, to the lis - tening earth, Re - peats the
res - trial ball? What though no re - al voice nor sound A - mid their

rig - i - nal pro - claim: Th'un-wea - ried sun, from day to day,
sto - ry of her birth; While all the stars that round her burn,
ra - diant orbs be found? In rea - son's ear they all re - joice,

Does his Cre - a - tor's power dis-play; And pub - lish - es to
And all the plan - ets in their turn, Con - firm the ti - dings
And ut - ter forth a glo - rious voice, For - ev - er sing - ing

ev - ery land The work of an al-might - y hand.
as they roll, And spread the truth from pole to pole.
as they shine, "The hand that made us is di - vine." A-MEN.

In My Heart There Rings a Melody

ELTON M. ROTH — ELTON M. ROTH

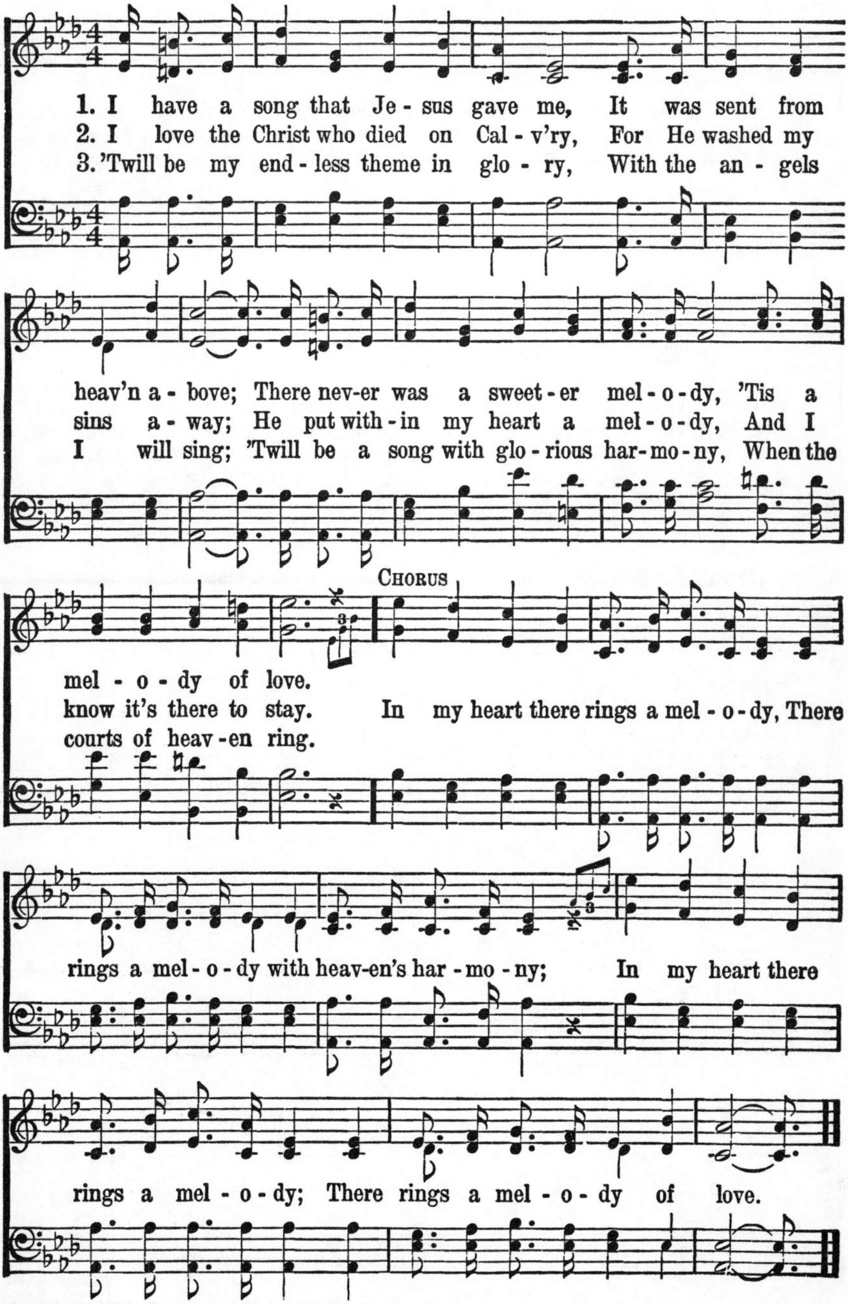

1. I have a song that Jesus gave me,
It was sent from heav'n above;
There never was a sweeter melody,
'Tis a melody of love.

2. I love the Christ who died on Cal-v'ry,
For He washed my sins away;
He put within my heart a melody,
And I know it's there to stay.

3. 'Twill be my endless theme in glory,
With the angels I will sing;
'Twill be a song with glorious harmony,
When the courts of heaven ring.

CHORUS

In my heart there rings a melody,
There rings a melody with heaven's harmony;
In my heart there rings a melody;
There rings a melody of love.

27

Heavenly Sunlight

H. J. ZELLEY

GEORGE H. COOK

1. Walk-ing in sun - light, all of my jour - ney; O - ver the moun-tains,
2. Shad-ows a - round me, shad-ows a - bove me, Nev-er con - ceal my
3. In the bright sun-light, ev - er re - joic - ing, Press-ing my way to

thro' the deep vale; Je - sus has said "I'll nev - er for - sake thee,"
Sav - iour and Guide; He is the light, in Him is no dark - ness;
man-sions a - bove; Sing-ing His prais - es glad - ly I'm walk - ing,

Prom-ise di - vine that nev - er can fail.
Ev - er I'm walk - ing close to His side.
Walk-ing in sun - light, sun-light of love.

CHORUS

Heav-en - ly sun - light,

heav-en - ly sun - light, Flood-ing my soul with glo - ry di - vine: Hal-le-

lu - jah, I am re - joic - ing, Sing-ing His prais-es, Je - sus is mine.

Ring the Bells of Heaven 28

William O. Cushing George F. Root

1. Ring the bells of heav-en! there is joy to-day, For a soul re-
2. Ring the bells of heav-en! there is joy to-day, For the wan-d'rer
3. Ring the bells of heav-en! spread the feast to-day, An-gels, swell the
turn-ing from the wild; See! the Fa-ther meets him out up-on the way,
now is rec-on-ciled; Yes, a soul is res-cued from his sin-ful way,
glad tri-um-phant strain! Tell the joy-ful ti-dings, bear it far a-way!
Chorus
Wel-com-ing His wea-ry, wan-d'ring child.
And is born a-new a ran-somed child. Glo-ry! glo-ry! how the
For a pre-cious soul is born a-gain.
an-gels sing; Glo-ry! glo-ry! how the loud harps ring! 'Tis the ran-somed
ar-my, like a might-y sea, Peal-ing forth the an-them of the free.

29 Since Jesus Came into My Heart

Rufus H. McDaniel — Charles H. Gabriel

1. What a won - der - ful change in my life has been wrought Since Je-sus came
2. I have ceased from my wand'ring and go - ing a-stray, Since Je-sus came
3. I'm pos-sessed of a hope that is stead-fast and sure, Since Je-sus came
4. There's a light in the val - ley of death now for me, Since Je-sus came
5. I shall go there to dwell in that Cit - y, I know, Since Je-sus came
in - to my heart! I have light in my soul for which long I had sought,
in - to my heart! And my sins, which were man-y, are all washed a - way,
in - to my heart! And no dark clouds of doubt now my path - way ob-scure,
in - to my heart! And the gates of the Cit - y be-yond I can see,
in - to my heart! And I'm hap-py, so hap-py, as on-ward I go,
Chorus
Since Je - sus came in - to my heart! Since Je-sus came in - to my
Since Je - sus came in, came
heart, Since Je-sus came in - to my heart, Floods of joy o'er my
in - to my heart, Since Je-sus came in, came in - to my heart,
soul like the sea bil-lows roll, Since Je - sus came in - to my heart.

Sunlight

JUDSON W. VAN DEVENTER — WINFIELD S. WEEDEN

1. I wan-dered in the shades of night, Till Je - sus came to me,
2. Tho' clouds may gath - er in the sky, And bil - lows round me roll,
3. While walk-ing in the light of God, I sweet com-mun - ion find;
4. I cross the wide ex - tend - ed fields, I jour - ney o'er the plain,
5. Soon I shall see Him as He is, The light that came to me;
And with the sun - light of His love Bid all my dark-ness flee.
How - ev - er dark the world may be I've sun - light in my soul.
I press with ho - ly vig - or on, And leave the world be - hind.
And in the sun - light of His love I reap the gold - en grain.
Be - hold the brightness of His face, Thro'-out e - ter - ni - ty.
CHORUS
Sun - light, sun - light in my soul to - day,
to-day, yes,
Sun - light, sun - light all a - long the way;
nar - row way;
Since the Sav - ior found me,
Took a-way my sin.
load of sin,
I have had the sun-light of His love with - in.

31 Sunshine in the Soul

ELIZA E. HEWITT — JOHN R. SWENEY

1. There's sun-shine in my soul to-day, More glo-ri-ous and bright
Than glows in an-y earth-ly skies, For Je-sus is my light.

2. There's mu-sic in my soul to-day, A car-ol to the King,
And Je-sus, lis-ten-ing, can hear The songs I can-not sing.

3. There's springtime in my soul to-day, For, when the Lord is near,
The dove of peace sings in my heart, The flow'rs of grace ap-pear.

4. There's glad-ness in my soul to-day, And hope and praise and love,
For bless-ings which He gives me now, For joys "laid up" a-bove.

REFRAIN

O there's sun - - - shine, bless-ed sun - - - shine,
O there's sun-shine in the soul, bless-ed sun-shine in the soul,
When the peace-ful, hap-py mo-ments roll;
hap-py mo-ments roll;
When Je-sus shows His smil-ing face, There is sun-shine in the soul.

I Will Praise Him

32

Mrs. M. J. Harris — Mrs. M. J. Harris

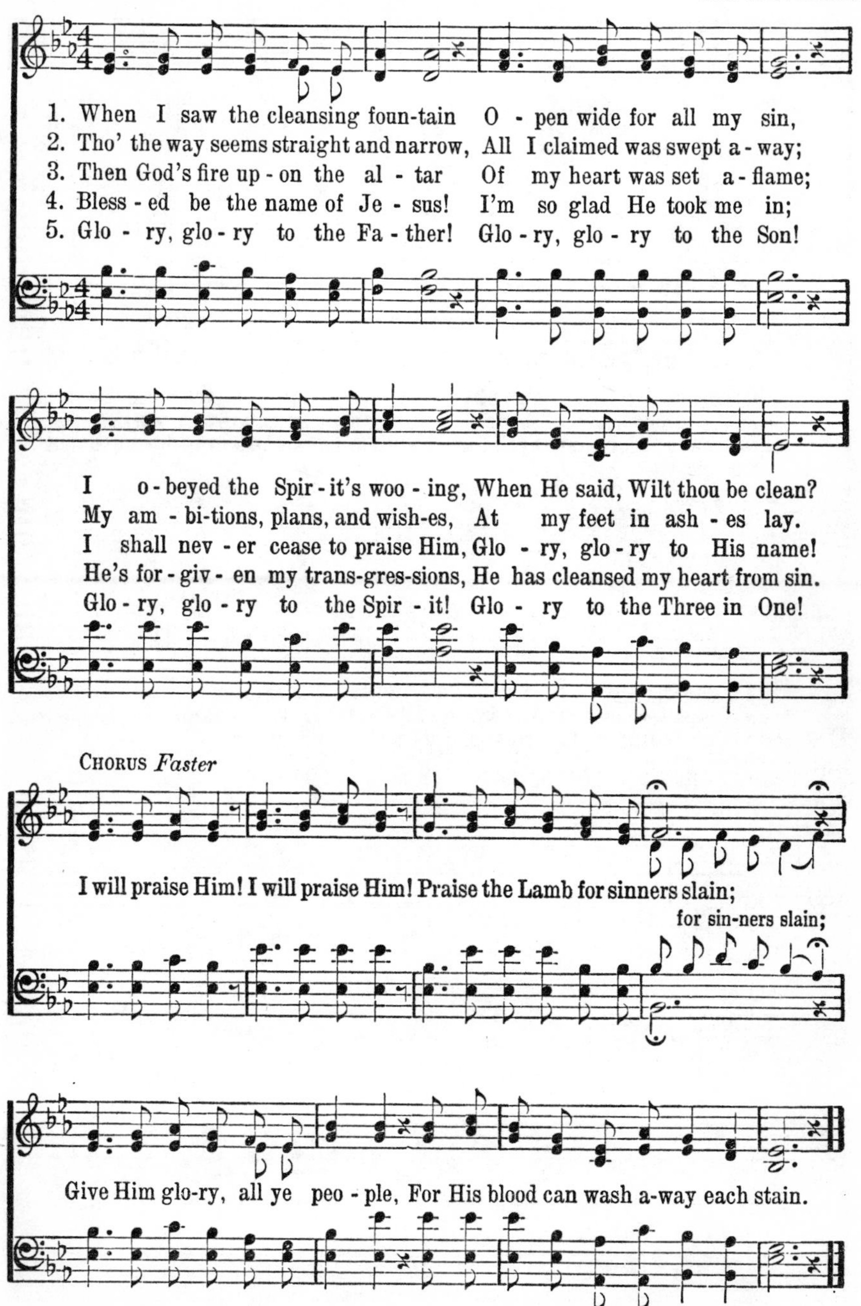

1. When I saw the cleansing foun-tain O - pen wide for all my sin,
2. Tho' the way seems straight and narrow, All I claimed was swept a - way;
3. Then God's fire up - on the al - tar Of my heart was set a - flame;
4. Bless - ed be the name of Je - sus! I'm so glad He took me in;
5. Glo - ry, glo - ry to the Fa - ther! Glo - ry, glo - ry to the Son!
I o - beyed the Spir - it's woo - ing, When He said, Wilt thou be clean?
My am - bi-tions, plans, and wish-es, At my feet in ash - es lay.
I shall nev - er cease to praise Him, Glo - ry, glo - ry to His name!
He's for - giv - en my trans-gres-sions, He has cleansed my heart from sin.
Glo - ry, glo - ry to the Spir - it! Glo - ry to the Three in One!
Chorus Faster
I will praise Him! I will praise Him! Praise the Lamb for sinners slain;
for sin-ners slain;
Give Him glo-ry, all ye peo - ple, For His blood can wash a-way each stain.

33 Nailed to the Cross

CARRIE E. BRECK — GRANT C. TULLAR

1. There was One who was will - ing to die in my stead, That a
2. He is ten - der and lov - ing and pa - tient with me, While He
3. I will cling to my Sav - ior and nev - er de - part—I will
soul so un - wor - thy might live; And the path to the cross He was
cleans - es my heart of the dross; But "there's no con - dem - na - tion"—I
joy - ful - ly jour - ney each day. With a song on my lips and a
will - ing to tread, All the sins of my life to for - give.
know I am free, For my sins are all nailed to the cross.
song in my heart, That my sins have been tak - en a - way.
REFRAIN
They are nailed to the cross,
pp
They are nailed to the cross, O how much He was will - ing to bear! With what
rit.
an - guish and loss Je - sus went to the cross! But He carried my sins with Him there.

How Great Thou Art! 34

CARL BOBERG
TR. BY STUART K. HINE

SWEDISH FOLK MELODY
ARR. BY MANNA MUSIC, INC.

Slowly

1. O Lord my God! When I in awe-some won-der Con-sid-er
2. When through the woods and for-est glades I wan-der And hear the
3. And when I think that God, His Son not spar-ing, Sent Him to
4. When Christ shall come with shout of ac-cla-ma-tion And take me

all the worlds* Thy hands have made, I see the stars, I hear the roll-ing*
birds sing sweet-ly in the trees; When I look down from loft-y moun-tain
die, I scarce can take it in;— That on the cross my bur-den glad-ly
home, what joy shall fill my heart! Then I shall bow in hum-ble ad-o-

thun-der, Thy pow'r through out the un-i-verse dis-played,
gran-deur And hear the brook and feel the gen-tle breeze;
bear-ing, He bled and died to take a-way my sin;—
ra-tion And there pro-claim, my God, how great Thou art!

REFRAIN

Then sings my soul, my Sav-ior God to Thee; How great Thou art, how great Thou art! Then sings my soul, my Sav-ior God to Thee; How great Thou art, how great Thou art!

*Translator's original words are "works" and "mighty"

He Is Able to Deliver Thee

William A. Ogden — William A. Ogden

1. 'Tis the grand-est theme thro' the a-ges rung; 'Tis the grandest theme for a mor-tal tongue; 'Tis the grandest theme that the world e'er sung, "Our God is a-ble to de-liv-er thee."
2. 'Tis the grand-est theme in the earth or main; 'Tis the grandest theme for a mor-tal strain; 'Tis the grandest theme, tell the world a - gain, "Our God is a-ble to de-liv-er thee."
3. 'Tis the grand-est theme, let the ti-dings roll, To the guilt - y heart, to the sin - ful soul; Look to God in faith, He will make thee whole, "Our God is a-ble to de-liv-er thee."
Chorus
He is a - - - - ble to de-liv-er thee,
a - ble, He is a - ble
He is a - - - - ble to de-liv-er thee;
a - ble, He is a - ble
Tho' by sin op-prest, Go to Him for rest; "Our God is a-ble to de-liv-er thee."

Jesus Is the Sweetest Name I Know

Lela Long — Lela Long

1. There have been names that I have loved to hear, But nev - er has there been a name so dear To this heart of mine, as the name divine, The pre-cious, precious name of Je - sus.
2. There is no name in earth or heav'n a-bove, That we should give such hon - or and such love As the blessed name, let us all acclaim, That wondrous, glorious name of Je - sus.
3. And some day I shall see Him face to face To thank and praise Him for His wondrous grace, Which He gave to me, when He made me free, The bless-ed Son of God called Je - sus.

CHORUS.

Je - sus is the sweetest name I know, And He's just the same as His love - ly name, And that's the reason why I love Him so; *rall.* Oh, Je - sus is the sweet - est name I know.

37 My Hope Is in the Lord

NORMAN J. CLAYTON NORMAN J. CLAYTON

1. My hope is in the Lord, Who gave Him-self for me, And paid the price of all my sin at Cal-va-ry.
the Lord, for me,

2. No mer-it of my own, His an-ger to sup-press, My on-ly hope is found in Je-sus' right-eous-ness.
my own, suppress,

3. And now for me He stands, Be-fore the Fa-ther's throne, He shows His wounded hands and names me as His own.
He stands, the throne,

4. His grace has planned it all, 'Tis mine but to be-lieve, And rec-og-nize His work of love and Christ re-ceive.
it all, be-lieve,

CHORUS

For me, He died, For
For me, He died,

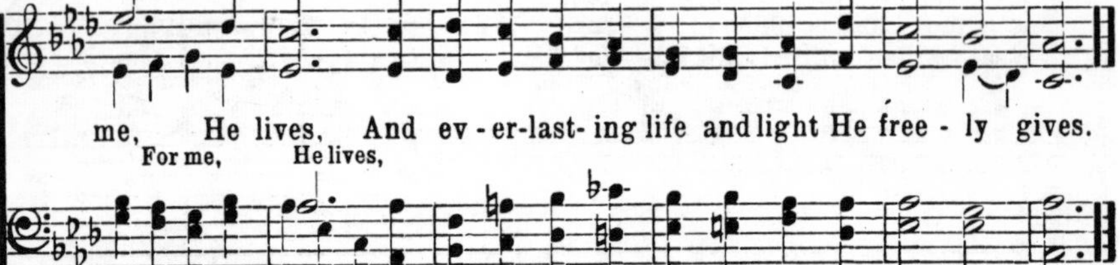
me, He lives, And ev-er-last-ing life and light He free-ly gives.
For me, He lives,

38 How Firm a Foundation

(FOUNDATION)

AUTHOR UNKNOWN EARLY AMERICAN MELODY

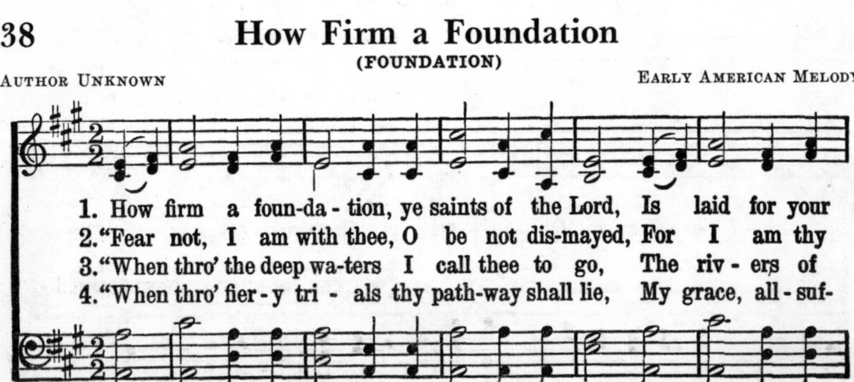
1. How firm a foun-da-tion, ye saints of the Lord, Is laid for your
2. "Fear not, I am with thee, O be not dis-mayed, For I am thy
3. "When thro' the deep wa-ters I call thee to go, The riv-ers of
4. "When thro' fier-y tri-als thy path-way shall lie, My grace, all-suf-

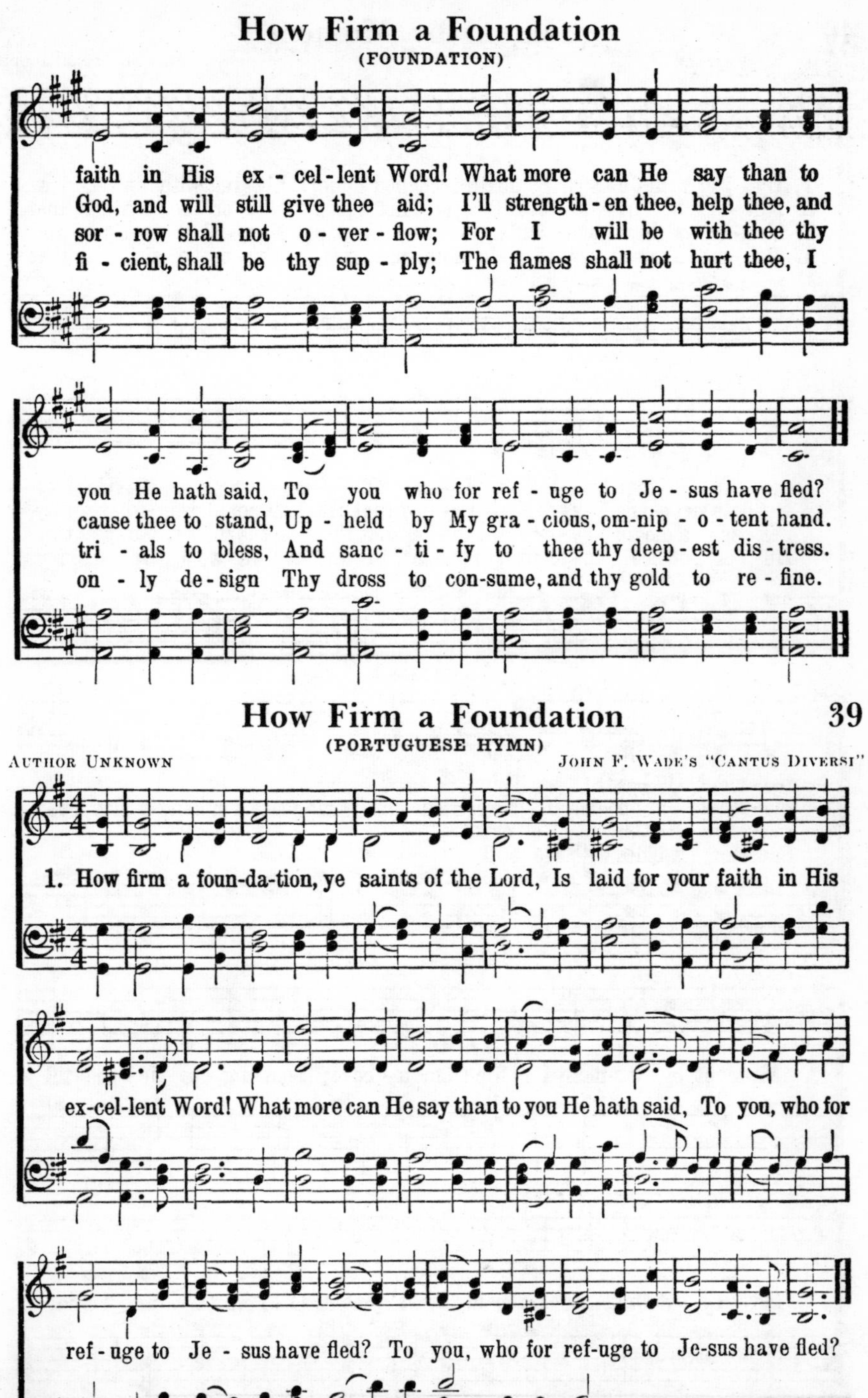
How Firm a Foundation
(FOUNDATION)
faith in His ex - cel - lent Word! What more can He say than to
God, and will still give thee aid; I'll strength - en thee, help thee, and
sor - row shall not o - ver - flow; For I will be with thee thy
fi - cient, shall be thy sup - ply; The flames shall not hurt thee, I
you He hath said, To you who for ref - uge to Je - sus have fled?
cause thee to stand, Up - held by My gra - cious, om - nip - o - tent hand.
tri - als to bless, And sanc - ti - fy to thee thy deep - est dis - tress.
on - ly de - sign Thy dross to con - sume, and thy gold to re - fine.
How Firm a Foundation
39
(PORTUGUESE HYMN)
Author Unknown
John F. Wade's "Cantus Diversi"
1. How firm a foun-da-tion, ye saints of the Lord, Is laid for your faith in His
ex-cel-lent Word! What more can He say than to you He hath said, To you, who for
ref - uge to Je - sus have fled? To you, who for ref-uge to Je-sus have fled?

40

Moment by Moment

DANIEL W. WHITTLE — MAY WHITTLE MOODY

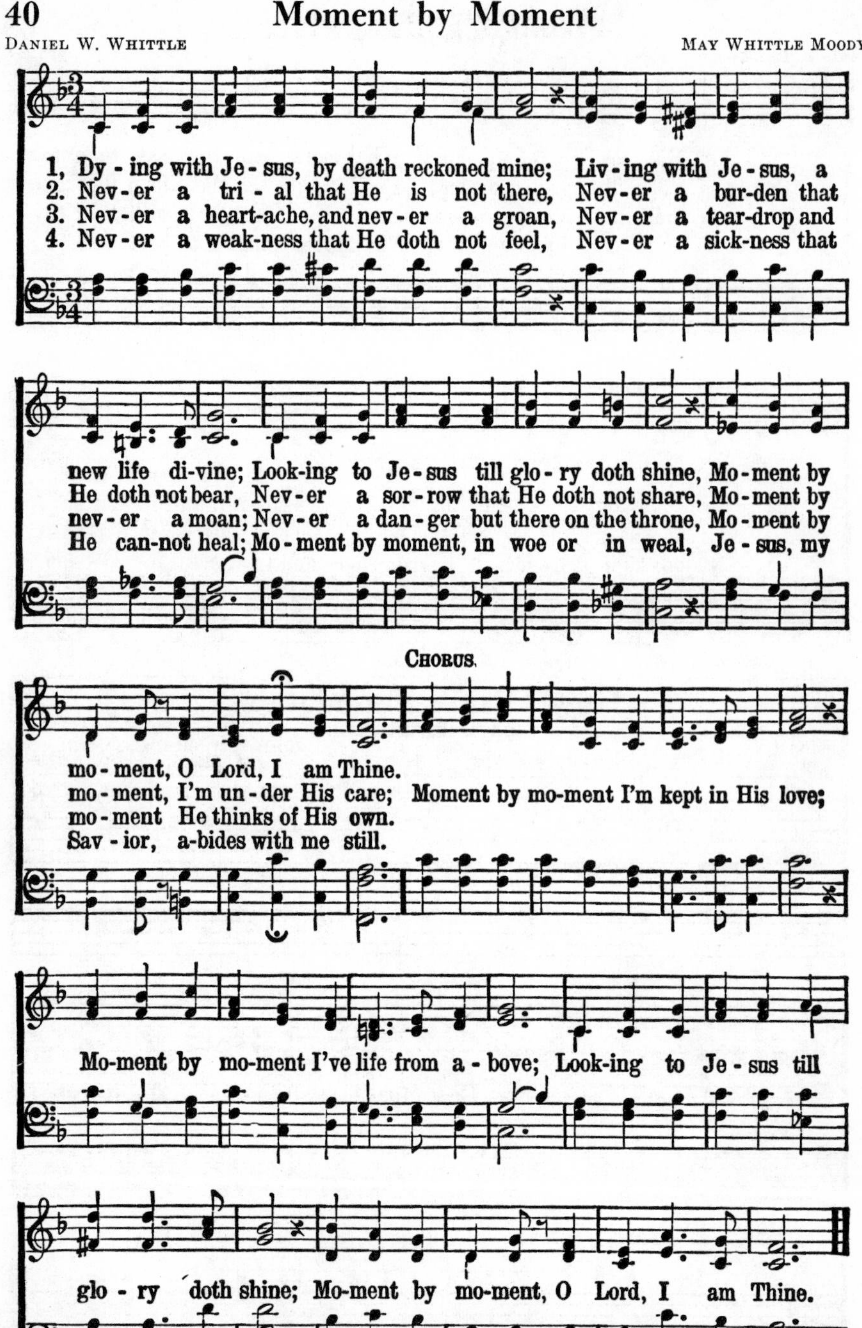
1, Dy - ing with Je - sus, by death reckoned mine; Liv - ing with Je - sus, a new life di-vine; Look-ing to Je - sus till glo - ry doth shine, Mo-ment by mo - ment, O Lord, I am Thine.
2. Nev - er a tri - al that He is not there, Nev - er a bur-den that He doth not bear, Nev - er a sor - row that He doth not share, Mo - ment by mo - ment, I'm un - der His care;
3. Nev - er a heart-ache, and nev - er a groan, Nev - er a tear-drop and nev - er a moan; Nev - er a dan - ger but there on the throne, Mo - ment by mo - ment He thinks of His own.
4. Nev - er a weak-ness that He doth not feel, Nev - er a sick-ness that He can-not heal; Mo - ment by moment, in woe or in weal, Je - sus, my Sav - ior, a-bides with me still.
CHORUS.
Moment by mo-ment I'm kept in His love;
Mo-ment by mo-ment I've life from a - bove; Look-ing to Je - sus till glo - ry doth shine; Mo-ment by mo-ment, O Lord, I am Thine.

Precious Hiding Place

AVIS B. CHRISTIANSEN

WENDELL P. LOVELESS

1. I was straying when Christ found me In the night so dark and cold;
2. With His nail-scarred hand He bro't me To the shel - ter of His love;
3. Tho' the night be dark a - round me, I am safe, for He is near;
Ten - der - ly His arm went round me And He bore me to His fold.
Of His grace and will He taught me, And of heav'n-ly rest a - bove.
Nev - er shall my foes con - found me, While the Sav-ior's voice I hear.
CHORUS
Pre - cious hid - ing place, . Pre - cious hid - ing place, In the
shel - ter of His love; Not a doubt or fear, Since my
rit.
Lord is near, And I'm shel - tered in His love.

42 Constantly Abiding

Mrs. Will L. Murphy — Mrs. Will L. Murphy

1. There's a peace in my heart that the world nev-er gave, A peace it can
2. All the world seemed to sing of a Sav - ior and King, When peace sweetly
3. This treas-ure I have in a tem - ple of clay, While here on His
not take a - way; Tho' the tri - als of life may surround like a cloud,
came to my heart; Troubles all fled a - way and my night turned to day,
foot-stool I roam; But He's coming to take me some glo - ri - ous day,
I've a peace that has come there to stay!
Bless-ed Je - sus, how glorious Thou art!
O - ver there to my heav - en - ly home!
Chorus
Con - - - stant-ly a-
Con-stant-ly a-bid - ing,
bid - - - - ing, Je - - - sus is mine;.........
con - stant - ly a - bid - ing, Je - sus is mine, yes, Je - sus is mine;
Con - - - stant-ly a - bid - - - - ing, rap - - ture di-
Con-stant-ly a - bid - ing, con-stant-ly a - bid - ing, rap - ture di-vine, O

Constantly Abiding
vine; He nev - er leaves me lone - - - - ly, whis-pers,
rap - ture di-vine; He nev - er leaves me, nev - er leaves me lone - ly, whis-pers,
O, so kind:— "I will nev- er leave thee," Je - sus is mine.
whis-pers, O so kind:— nev-er leave thee," Je-sus, Je - sus is mine.
My Jesus, as Thou Wilt!
43
Benjamin Schmolck
Tr. by Jane L. Borthwick
Carl M. Von Weber
Arr. by Joseph P. Holbrook
1. My Je - sus, as Thou wilt! O may Thy will be mine; In - to Thy
2. My Je - sus, as Thou wilt! Tho' seen thro' man-y a tear, Let not my
3. My Je - sus, as Thou wilt! All shall be well for me; Each changing
hand of love I would my all re - sign. Thro' sor - row, or thro' joy,
star of hope Grow dim or dis-ap - pear. Since Thou on earth hast wept
fu - ture scene I glad-ly trust with Thee. Straight to my home a - bove
Conduct me as Thine own; And help me still to say, My Lord, Thy will be done.
And sorrowed oft a - lone, If I must weep with Thee, My Lord, Thy will be done.
I trav - el calm-ly on, And sing, in life or death, "My Lord, Thy will be done."

44 Safe in the Arms of Jesus

FANNY J. CROSBY WILLIAM H. DOANE

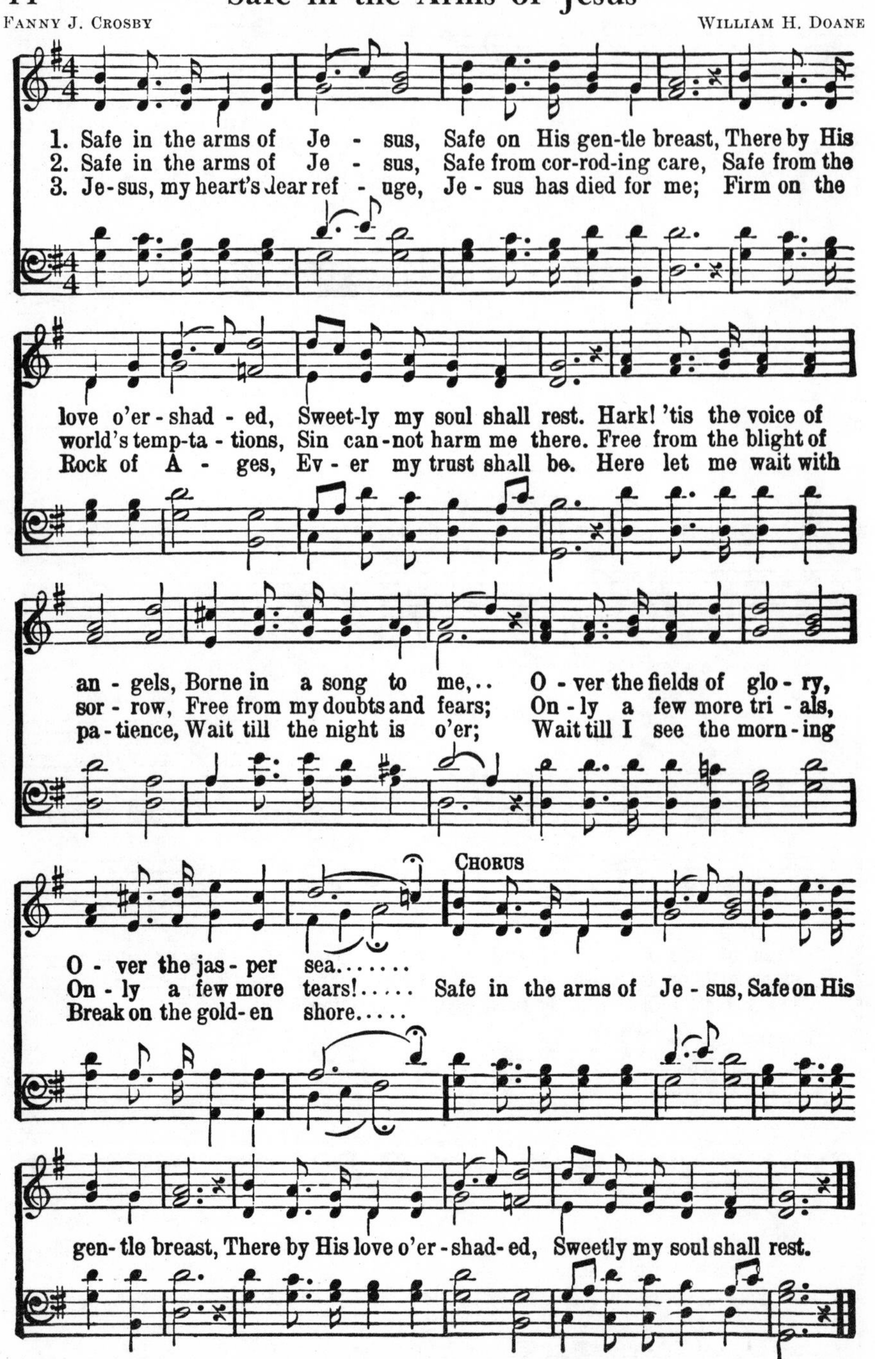
1. Safe in the arms of Je - sus, Safe on His gen-tle breast, There by His
2. Safe in the arms of Je - sus, Safe from cor-rod-ing care, Safe from the
3. Je-sus, my heart's dear ref - uge, Je - sus has died for me; Firm on the
love o'er-shad - ed, Sweet-ly my soul shall rest. Hark! 'tis the voice of
world's temp-ta - tions, Sin can-not harm me there. Free from the blight of
Rock of A - ges, Ev - er my trust shall be. Here let me wait with
an - gels, Borne in a song to me,.. O - ver the fields of glo - ry,
sor - row, Free from my doubts and fears; On - ly a few more tri - als,
pa - tience, Wait till the night is o'er; Wait till I see the morn - ing
CHORUS
O - ver the jas - per sea.......
On - ly a few more tears!..... Safe in the arms of Je - sus, Safe on His
Break on the gold - en shore.....
gen - tle breast, There by His love o'er - shad - ed, Sweetly my soul shall rest.

Love Divine, All Loves Excelling

CHARLES WESLEY JOHN ZUNDEL

1. Love di - vine, all loves ex - cel-ling, Joy of heav'n, to earth come down;
2. Breathe, O breathe Thy lov-ing Spir - it In - to ev - 'ry troub - led breast!
3. Come, Al-might - y to de - liv - er, Let us all Thy life re - ceive;
4. Fin - ish then Thy new cre - a - tion; Pure and spot - less let us be;
Fix in us Thy hum - ble dwell - ing; All Thy faith - ful mer - cies crown.
Let us all in Thee in - her - it, Let us find that sec - ond rest.
Sud-den - ly re - turn, and nev - er, Nev - er - more Thy tem - ples leave:
Let us see Thy great sal - va - tion Per - fect - ly re-stored in Thee:
Je - sus, Thou art all com-pas-sion, Pure, un-bound-ed love Thou art;
Take a - way our bent to sin-ning, Al - pha and O - me - ga be;
Thee we would be al - ways blessing, Serve Thee as Thy hosts a - bove,
Changed from glo - ry in - to glo - ry, Till in heav'n we take our place,
Vis - it us with Thy sal - va - tion; En - ter ev - 'ry trem - bling heart.
End of faith, as its be - gin-ning, Set our hearts at lib - er - ty.
Pray, and praise Thee with- out ceas- ing, Glo - ry in Thy per - fect love.
Till we cast our crowns be - fore Thee, Lost in won-der, love, and praise.

46 Holy Spirit, Faithful Guide

MARCUS M. WELLS — MARCUS M. WELLS

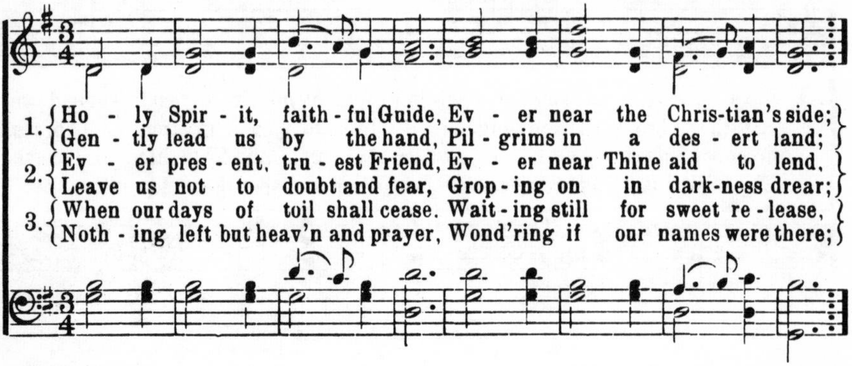

1. Ho - ly Spir - it, faith - ful Guide, Ev - er near the Chris-tian's side;
Gen - tly lead us by the hand, Pil - grims in a des - ert land;
2. Ev - er pres - ent, tru - est Friend, Ev - er near Thine aid to lend,
Leave us not to doubt and fear, Grop - ing on in dark-ness drear;
3. When our days of toil shall cease, Wait - ing still for sweet re - lease,
Noth - ing left but heav'n and prayer, Wond'ring if our names were there;

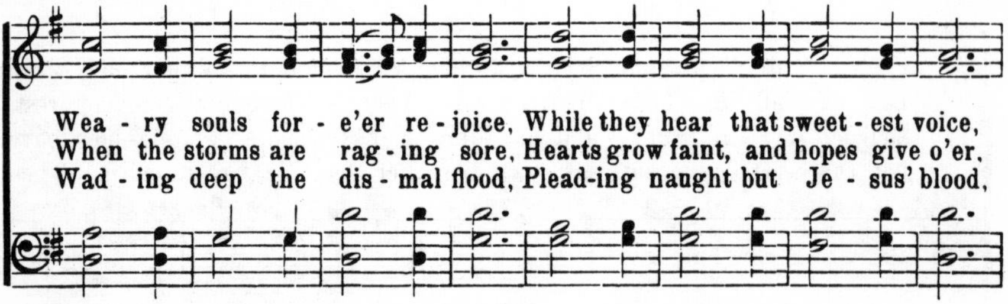

Wea - ry souls for - e'er re - joice, While they hear that sweet - est voice,
When the storms are rag - ing sore, Hearts grow faint, and hopes give o'er,
Wad - ing deep the dis - mal flood, Plead-ing naught but Je - sus' blood,

Whis-p'ring soft-ly, "Wand'rer, come! Fol - low Me, I'll guide thee home."
Whis - per soft - ly, "Wand'rer, come! Fol - low Me, I'll guide thee home."
Whis - per soft - ly, "Wand'rer, come! Fol - low Me, I'll guide thee home." A-MEN.

47 Holy Ghost, with Light Divine

ANDREW REED — LOUIS M. GOTTSCHALK, ARR. BY EDWIN P. PARKER

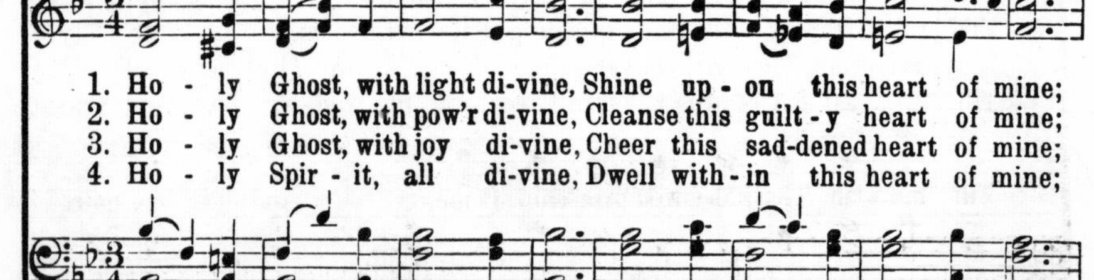
1. Ho - ly Ghost, with light di-vine, Shine up - on this heart of mine;
2. Ho - ly Ghost, with pow'r di-vine, Cleanse this guilt - y heart of mine;
3. Ho - ly Ghost, with joy di-vine, Cheer this sad-dened heart of mine;
4. Ho - ly Spir - it, all di-vine, Dwell with - in this heart of mine;

Holy Ghost, with Light Divine

Chase the shade of night a - way, Turn my dark-ness in - to day.
Long has sin, with-out con-trol, Held do - min- ion o'er my soul.
Bid my man-y woes de - part, Heal my wound-ed, bleed-ing heart.
Cast down ev - 'ry i - dol-throne. Reign su-preme, and reign a - lone. A-MEN.
Fill Me Now
48
ELWOOD H. STOKES
JOHN R. SWENEY
1. Hov - er o'er me, Ho - ly Spir - it, Bathe my trem-bling heart and brow;
2. Thou canst fill me, gra-cious Spir - it, Though I can - not tell Thee how;
3. I am weak-ness, full of weak-ness, At Thy sa - cred feet I bow;
4. Cleanse and com-fort, bless and save me, Bathe, O bathe my heart and brow;
Fill me with Thy hal-lowed pres-ence, Come, O come and fill me now.
But I need Thee, great-ly need Thee, Come, O come and fill me now.
Blest, di - vine, e - ter - nal Spir - it, Fill with pow'r, and fill me now.
Thou art com-fort - ing and sav - ing, Thou art sweet - ly fill - ing now.
CHORUS
Fill me now, fill me now, Je - sus, come and fill me now;
Fill me with Thy hal-lowed pres-ence, Come, O come and fill me now.

The Comforter Has Come

FRANK BOTTOME — WILLIAM J. KIRKPATRICK

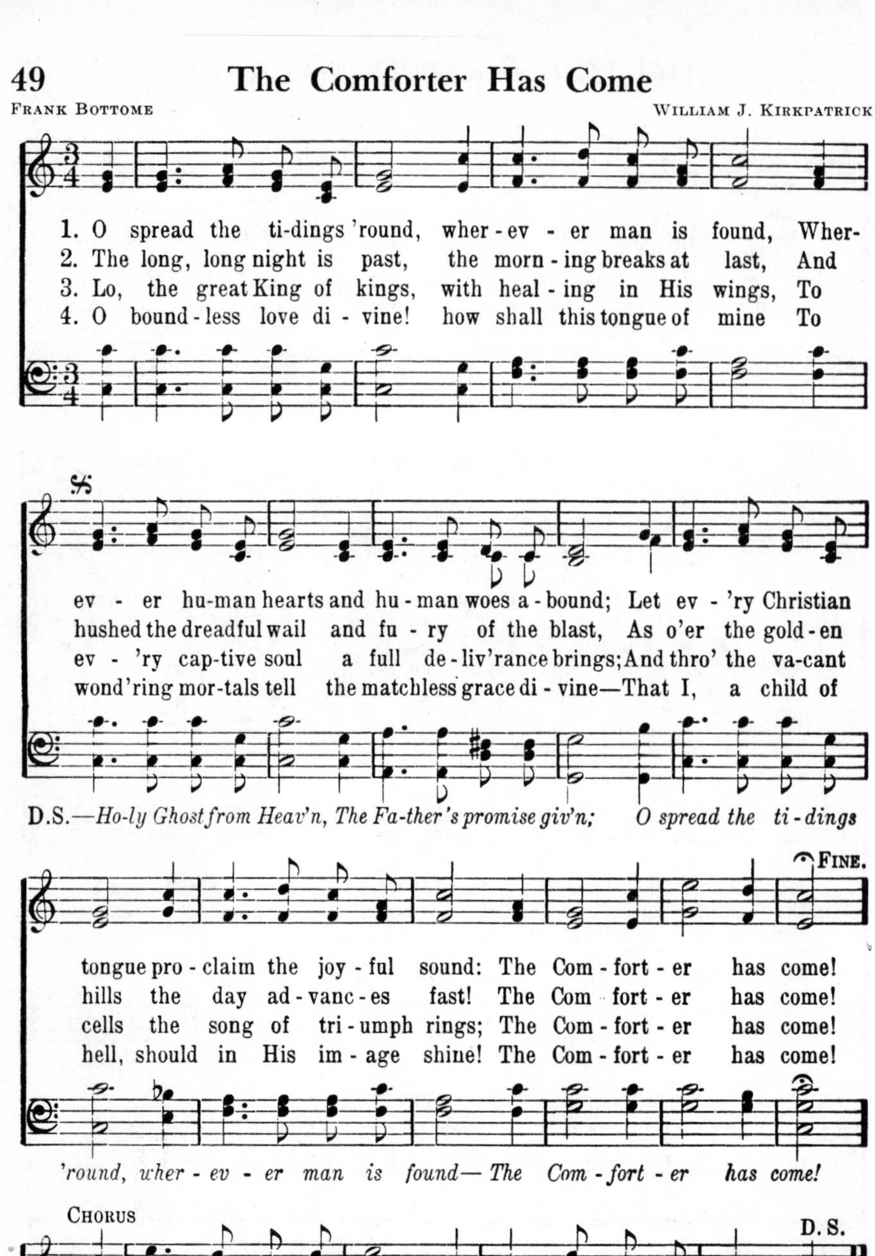
1. O spread the ti-dings 'round, wher-ev - er man is found, Wher-
2. The long, long night is past, the morn - ing breaks at last, And
3. Lo, the great King of kings, with heal - ing in His wings, To
4. O bound-less love di - vine! how shall this tongue of mine To
ev - er hu-man hearts and hu - man woes a - bound; Let ev - 'ry Christian
hushed the dreadful wail and fu - ry of the blast, As o'er the gold - en
ev - 'ry cap-tive soul a full de - liv'rance brings; And thro' the va-cant
wond'ring mor-tals tell the matchless grace di - vine—That I, a child of
D.S.—Ho-ly Ghost from Heav'n, The Fa-ther's promise giv'n; O spread the ti - dings
FINE.
tongue pro - claim the joy - ful sound: The Com - fort - er has come!
hills the day ad - vanc - es fast! The Com fort - er has come!
cells the song of tri - umph rings; The Com - fort - er has come!
hell, should in His im - age shine! The Com - fort - er has come!
'round, wher - ev - er man is found— The Com - fort - er has come!
CHORUS
D. S.
The Com - fort - er has come, The Com - fort - er has come! The

Spirit of God, Descend upon My Heart

George Croly — Frederick C. Atkinson

1. Spir - it of God, de - scend up - on my heart;
2. Hast Thou not bid us love Thee, God and King?
3. Teach me to feel that Thou art al - ways nigh;
4. Teach me to love Thee as Thine an - gels love,

Wean it from earth, through all its puls - es move;
All, all Thine own, soul, heart and strength and mind;
Teach me the strug - gles of the soul to bear,
One ho - ly pas - sion fill - ing all my frame;

Stoop to my weak - ness, might - y as Thou art,
I see Thy cross— there teach my heart to cling:
To check the ris - ing doubt, the reb - el sigh;
The bap - tism of the heav'n - de - scend - ed Dove,

And make me love Thee as I ought to love.
O let me seek Thee, and O let me find.
Teach me the pa - tience of un - an - swered prayer.
My heart an al - tar, and Thy love the flame. A - men.

51 Pass Me Not, O Gentle Savior

FANNY J. CROSBY — WILLIAM H. DOANE

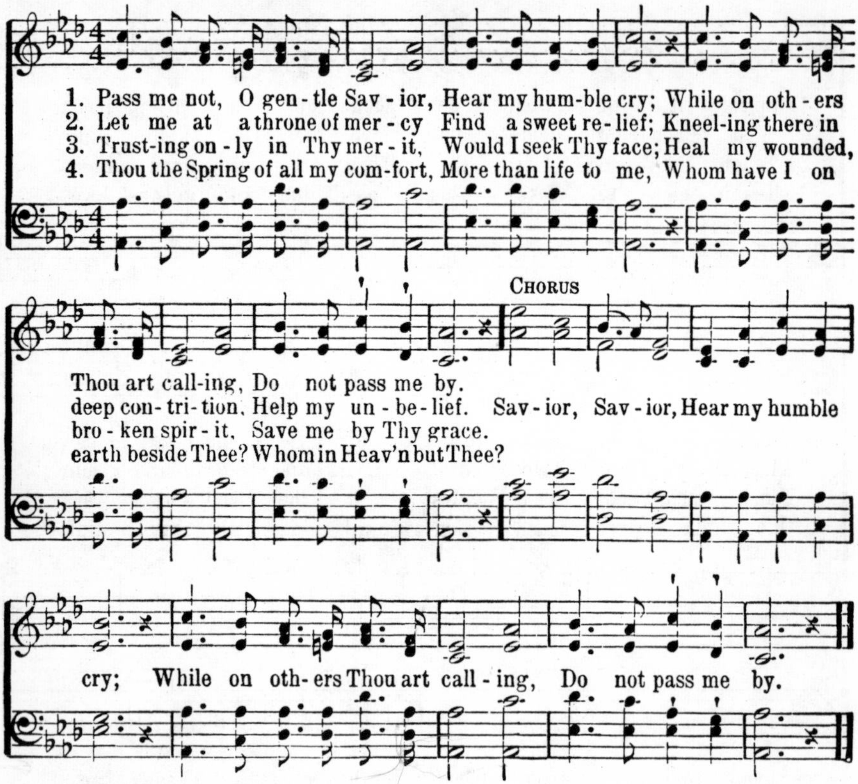

1. Pass me not, O gen-tle Sav-ior, Hear my hum-ble cry; While on oth-ers Thou art call-ing, Do not pass me by.
2. Let me at a throne of mer-cy Find a sweet re-lief; Kneel-ing there in deep con-tri-tion, Help my un-be-lief.
3. Trust-ing on-ly in Thy mer-it, Would I seek Thy face; Heal my wounded, bro-ken spir-it, Save me by Thy grace.
4. Thou the Spring of all my com-fort, More than life to me, Whom have I on earth beside Thee? Whom in Heav'n but Thee?

CHORUS

Sav-ior, Sav-ior, Hear my humble cry; While on oth-ers Thou art call-ing, Do not pass me by.

52 I Am Coming, Lord

LEWIS HARTSOUGH — LEWIS HARTSOUGH

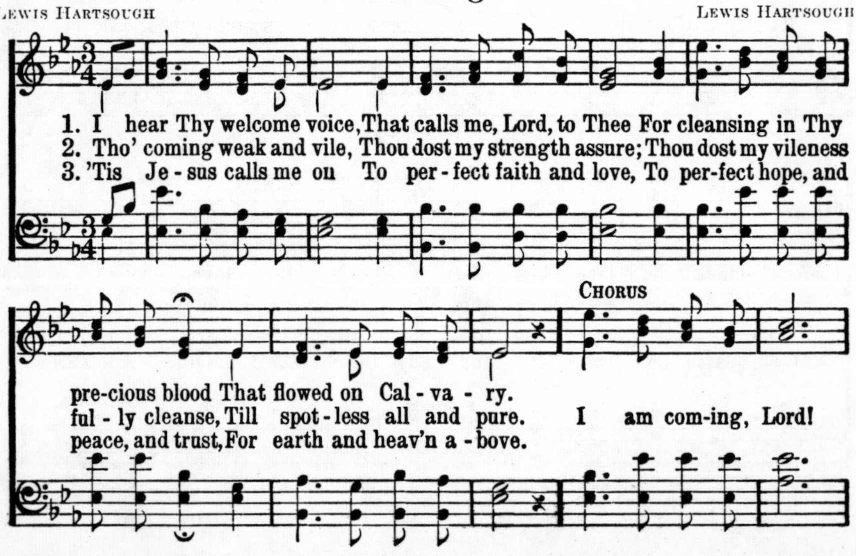

1. I hear Thy welcome voice, That calls me, Lord, to Thee For cleansing in Thy pre-cious blood That flowed on Cal-va-ry.
2. Tho' coming weak and vile, Thou dost my strength assure; Thou dost my vileness ful-ly cleanse, Till spot-less all and pure.
3. 'Tis Je-sus calls me on To per-fect faith and love, To per-fect hope, and peace, and trust, For earth and heav'n a-bove.

CHORUS

I am com-ing, Lord!

I Am Coming, Lord

Look to the Lamb of God

H. G. Jackson — James M. Black

Com-ing now to Thee! Wash me, cleanse me in the blood That flowed on Cal-va-ry!
1. If you from sin are long-ing to be free, Look to the Lamb of God;
2. When Satan tempts, and doubts and fears assail, Look to the Lamb of God;
3. Are you a-wea - ry, does the way seem long? Look to the Lamb of God;
4. Fear not when shadows on your path-way fall, Look to the Lamb of God;
He, to re-deem you, died on Cal - va - ry, Look to the Lamb of God.
You in His strength shall o-ver all pre-vail, Look to the Lamb of God.
His love will cheer and fill your heart with song, Look to the Lamb of God.
In joy or sor - row Christ is all in all, Look to the Lamb of God.
Chorus
Look to the Lamb of God, Look to the Lamb of God,
the Lamb of God, the Lamb of God,
For He a - lone is a - ble to save you, Look to the Lamb of God.

54

I Heard the Voice of Jesus Say

HORATIUS BONAR

JOHN B. DYKES

mf
1. I heard the voice of Je - sus say, "Come un - to Me and rest;
2. I heard the voice of Je - sus say, "Be - hold, I free - ly give
3. I heard the voice of Je - sus say, "I am this dark world's Light;
Lay down, thou wea - ry one, lay down Thy head up - on My breast."
The liv - ing wa - ter; thirst - y one, Stoop down, and drink, and live."
Look un - to Me, thy morn shall rise, And all thy day be bright."
p
cresc.
I came to Je - sus as I was, Wea - ry, and worn, and sad;
I came to Je - sus, and I drank Of that life - giv - ing stream;
I looked to Je - sus, and I found In Him my Star, my Sun;
cresc.
f
I found in Him a rest - ing-place, And He has made me glad.
My thirst was quench'd, my soul re - vived, And now I live in Him.
And in that Light of life I'll walk, Till trav'l-ing days are done.

Let Jesus Come into Your Heart

Leila N. Morris — Leila N. Morris

1. If you are tired of the load of your sin, Let Je - sus come
2. If 'tis for pu - ri - ty now that you sigh, Let Je - sus come
3. If there's a tem - pest your voice can - not still, Let Je - sus come
4. If you would join the glad songs of the blest, Let Je - sus come
in - to your heart; If you de - sire a new life to be - gin,
in - to your heart; Fountains for cleans-ing are flow - ing near by,
in - to your heart; If there's a void this world nev - er can fill,
in - to your heart; If you would en - ter the man-sions of rest,
Let Je - sus come in - to your heart.
Chorus
Just now, your doubt-ings give o'er; Just now, re - ject Him no more; Just now, throw o - pen the door; Let Je - sus come in - to your heart.

56 O Jesus, Thou Art Standing

William W. How — Justin H. Knecht, Edward Husband

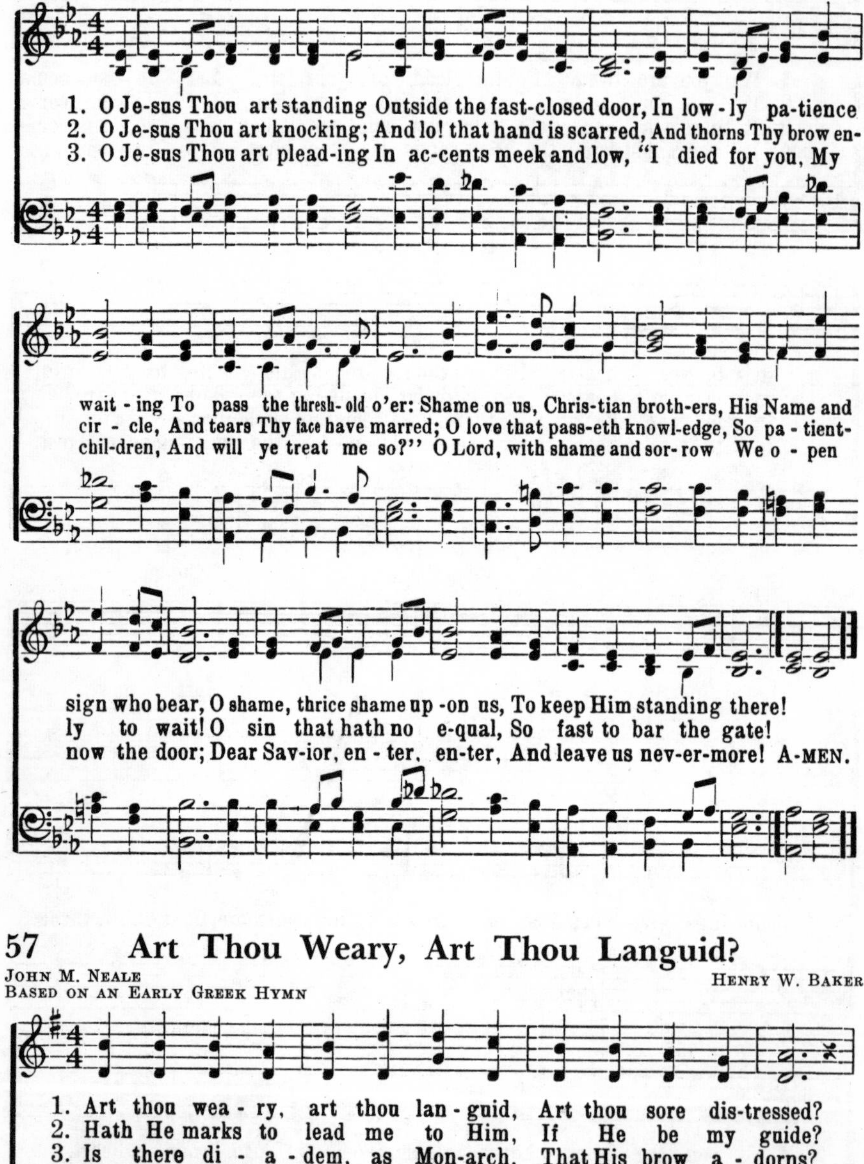
1. O Je-sus Thou art standing Outside the fast-closed door, In low - ly pa-tience
2. O Je-sus Thou art knocking; And lo! that hand is scarred, And thorns Thy brow en-
3. O Je-sus Thou art plead-ing In ac-cents meek and low, "I died for you, My
wait - ing To pass the thresh- old o'er: Shame on us, Chris-tian broth-ers, His Name and
cir - cle, And tears Thy face have marred; O love that pass-eth knowl-edge, So pa - tient-
chil-dren, And will ye treat me so?" O Lord, with shame and sor-row We o - pen
sign who bear, O shame, thrice shame up -on us, To keep Him standing there!
ly to wait! O sin that hath no e-qual, So fast to bar the gate!
now the door; Dear Sav-ior, en - ter, en-ter, And leave us nev-er-more! A-MEN.

57 Art Thou Weary, Art Thou Languid?

John M. Neale — Henry W. Baker
Based on an Early Greek Hymn

1. Art thou wea - ry, art thou lan - guid, Art thou sore dis-tressed?
2. Hath He marks to lead me to Him, If He be my guide?
3. Is there di - a - dem, as Mon-arch, That His brow a - dorns?
4. If I ask Him to re - ceive me, Will He say me nay?
5. Find-ing, fol-l'wing, keep - ing, strug-gling, Is He sure to bless?

Art Thou Weary, Art Thou Languid?

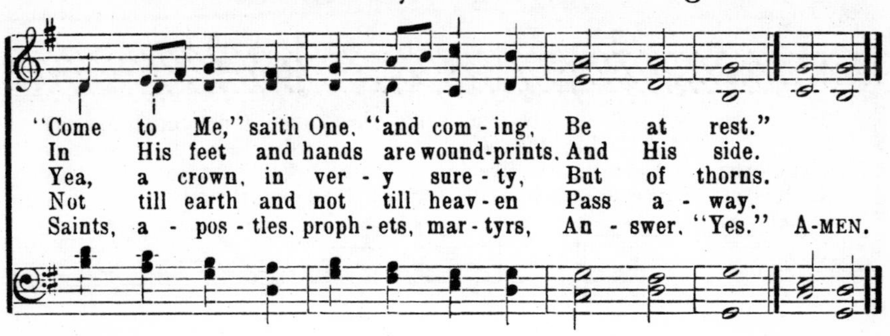

"Come to Me," saith One, "and com - ing, Be at rest."
In His feet and hands are wound-prints, And His side.
Yea, a crown, in ver - y sure - ty, But of thorns.
Not till earth and not till heav - en Pass a - way.
Saints, a - pos - tles, proph - ets, mar - tyrs, An - swer, "Yes." A-MEN.

I Gave My Life for Thee 58

FRANCES R. HAVERGAL PHILIP P. BLISS

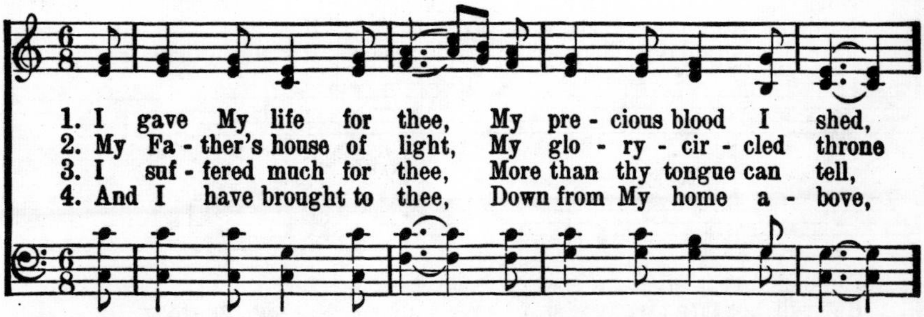

1. I gave My life for thee, My pre - cious blood I shed,
2. My Fa - ther's house of light, My glo - ry - cir - cled throne
3. I suf - fered much for thee, More than thy tongue can tell,
4. And I have brought to thee, Down from My home a - bove,

That thou might'st ran - somed be, And quick - ened from the dead;
I left for earth - ly night, For wan-d'rings sad and lone;
Of bit - t'rest ag - o - ny, To res - cue thee from hell;
Sal - va - tion full and free, My par - don and My love;

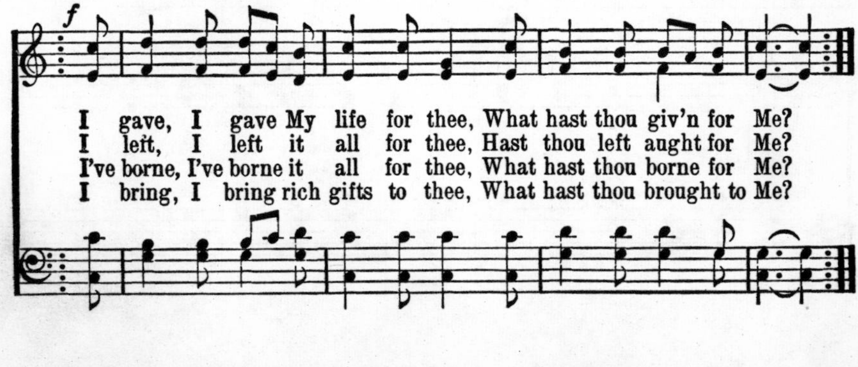

f

I gave, I gave My life for thee, What hast thou giv'n for Me?
I left, I left it all for thee, Hast thou left aught for Me?
I've borne, I've borne it all for thee, What hast thou borne for Me?
I bring, I bring rich gifts to thee, What hast thou brought to Me?

59 Jesus Is Calling

FANNY J. CROSBY — GEORGE C. STEBBINS

1. Je - sus is ten - der - ly call - ing thee home— Call - ing to - day,
2. Je - sus is call - ing the wea - ry to rest— Call - ing to - day,
3. Je - sus is wait-ing; O come to Him now— Wait-ing to - day,
4. Je - sus is plead-ing; O list to His voice: Hear Him to - day,
call - ing to - day; Why from the sun - shine of love wilt thou roam
call - ing to - day; Bring Him thy bur - den and thou shalt be blest:
wait - ing to - day; Come with thy sins; at His feet low - ly bow;
hear Him to - day; They who be - lieve on His name shall re - joice;
REFRAIN
Far-ther and far-ther a - way?
He will not turn thee a - way. Call - - ing to - day, ...
Come, and no lon-ger de - lay.
Quick-ly a - rise and a - way. Call - ing, call - ing to - day, to - day,
Call - - ing to - day, ... Je - - - - sus is
Call - ing, call - ing to - day, to - day, Je - sus is ten - der - ly
call - - - - ing, is ten - der - ly call - ing to - day.
call - ing to - day,

Is My Name Written There?

Mary A. Kidder Frank M. Davis

1. Lord, I care not for rich-es, Nei-ther sil-ver nor gold; I would make sure of heav-en, I would en-ter the fold. In the book of Thy king-dom, With its pa-ges so fair, Tell me, Je-sus, my Sav-ior, Is my name writ-ten there?
2. Lord, my sins they are man-y, Like the sands of the sea, But Thy blood, O my Sav-ior, Is suf-fi-cient for me; For Thy prom-ise is writ-ten, In bright letters that glow, "Tho' your sins be as scar-let, I will make them like snow."
3. Oh! that beau-ti-ful cit-y, With its man-sions of light, With its glo-ri-fied be-ings, In pure gar-ments of white; Where no e-vil thing com-eth To de-spoil what is fair; Where the an-gels are watching, Yes, my name's written there. Yes, my name's, etc.
Refrain.
Is my name writ-ten there, On the page white and fair? In the book of Thy king-dom, Is my name writ-ten there?
Yes, my name's writ-ten there.

61 Why Do You Wait?

George F. Root — George F. Root

1. Why do you wait, dear broth-er, Oh, why do you tar-ry so long?
2. What do you hope, dear broth-er, To gain by a fur-ther de-lay?
3. Do you not feel, dear broth-er, His Spir-it now striv-ing with-in?
4. Why do you wait, dear broth-er? The harvest is pass-ing a-way;

Your Sav-ior is wait-ing to give you A place in His sanc-ti-fied throng.
There's no one to save you but Je-sus, There's no other way but His way.
Oh, why not ac-cept His sal-va-tion, And throw off your burden of sin?
Your Sav-ior is long-ing to bless you, There's danger and death in de-lay.

Chorus

Why not? why not? Why not come to Him now? now?

62 Just As I Am

Charlotte Elliott — William B. Bradbury

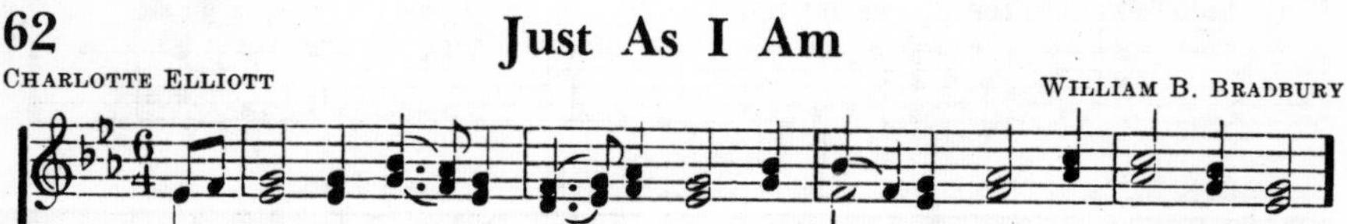

1. Just as I am, with-out one plea, But that Thy blood was shed for me,
2. Just as I am, and wait-ing not To rid my soul of one dark blot,
3. Just as I am, tho' tossed a-bout With many a con-flict, many a doubt,
4. Just as I am, poor, wretched, blind; Sight, riches, heal-ing of the mind,
5. Just as I am, Thou wilt re-ceive, Wilt welcome, pardon, cleanse, relieve;

Just As I Am

And that Thou bidd'st me come to Thee, O Lamb of God, I come! I come!
To Thee whose blood can cleanse each spot, O Lamb of God, I come! I come!
Fight-ings and fears with-in, with - out, O Lamb of God, I come! I come!
Yea, all I need, in Thee to find, O Lamb of God, I come! I come!
Be - cause Thy prom-ise I be-lieve, O Lamb of God, I come! I come!
Lord, I'm Coming Home
63
William J. Kirkpatrick
William J. Kirkpatrick
1. I've wan-dered far a - way from God, Now I'm com - ing home;
2. I've wast - ed man - y pre - cious years, Now I'm com - ing home;
3. I've tired of sin and stray - ing, Lord, Now I'm com - ing home;
4. My soul is sick, my heart is sore, Now I'm com - ing home;
Fine
The paths of sin too long I've trod, Lord, I'm com-ing home.
I now re - pent with bit - ter tears, Lord, I'm com-ing home.
I'll trust Thy love, be - lieve Thy word, Lord, I'm com-ing home.
My strength re - new, my hope re - store, Lord, I'm com-ing home.
D. S.—O - pen wide Thine arms of love, Lord, I'm com - ing home.
Chorus
D. S.
Com - ing home, com - ing home, Nev - er - more to roam,

64 Springs of Living Water

JOHN W. PETERSON JOHN W. PETERSON

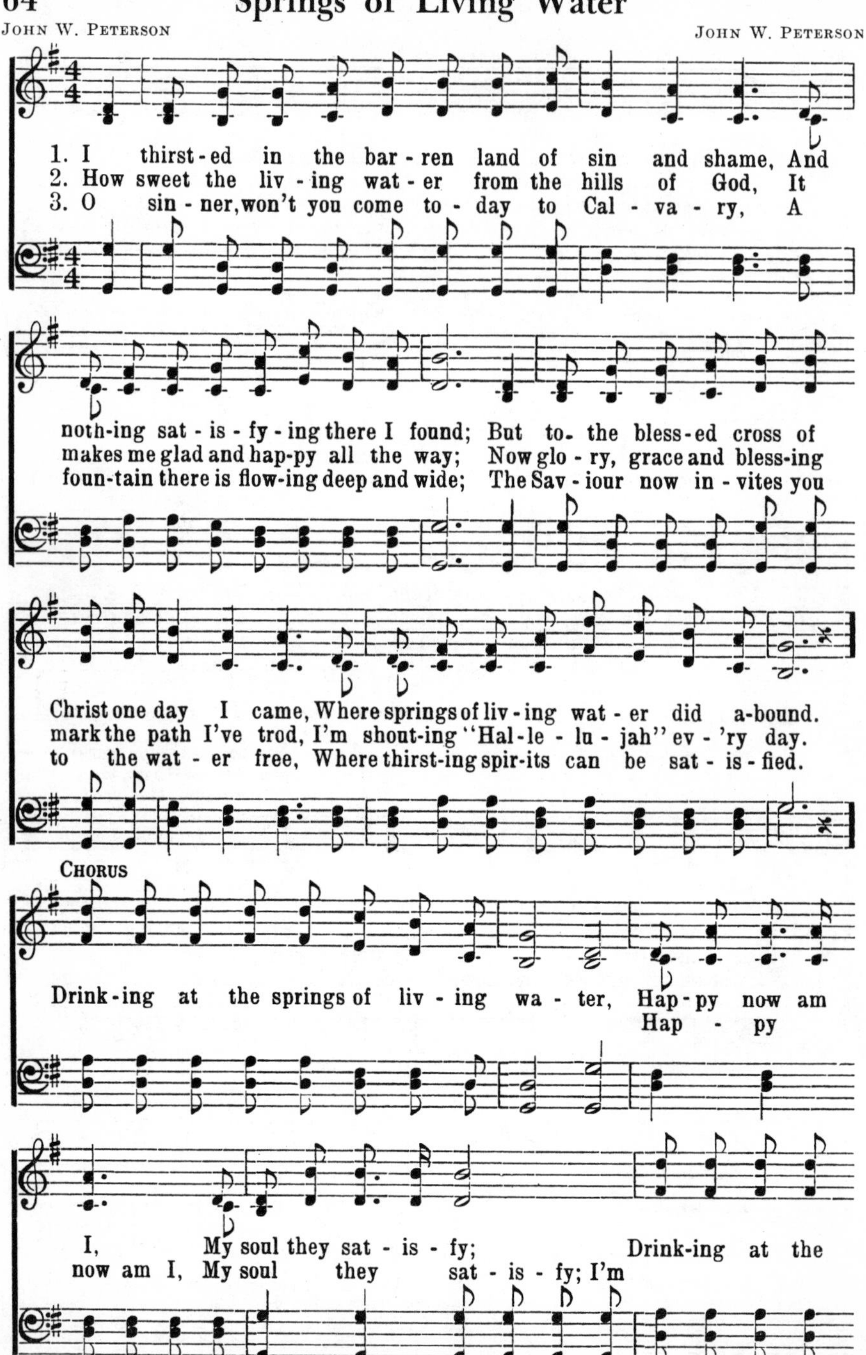
1. I thirst-ed in the bar-ren land of sin and shame, And
2. How sweet the liv-ing wat-er from the hills of God, It
3. O sin-ner, won't you come to-day to Cal-va-ry, A
noth-ing sat-is-fy-ing there I found; But to the bless-ed cross of
makes me glad and hap-py all the way; Now glo-ry, grace and bless-ing
foun-tain there is flow-ing deep and wide; The Sav-iour now in-vites you
Christ one day I came, Where springs of liv-ing wat-er did a-bound.
mark the path I've trod, I'm shout-ing "Hal-le-lu-jah" ev-'ry day.
to the wat-er free, Where thirst-ing spir-its can be sat-is-fied.
CHORUS
Drink-ing at the springs of liv-ing wa-ter, Hap-py now am
Hap-py
I, My soul they sat-is-fy; Drink-ing at the
now am I, My soul they sat-is-fy; I'm

Springs of Living Water

springs of liv-ing wa-ter, O won-der-ful and boun-ti-ful sup-ply.
All That Thrills My Soul
65
Thoro Harris
Thoro Harris
1. Who can cheer the heart like Je - sus, By His pres-ence all di - vine?
2. Love of Christ so free - ly giv - en, Grace of God be - yond de - gree,
3. What a won - der - ful re - demp - tion! Nev - er can a mor - tal know
4. Ev - 'ry need His hand sup - ply - ing, Ev - 'ry good in Him I see;
5. By the crys - tal flow - ing riv - er With the ran-somed I will sing,
True and ten - der, pure and pre - cious, O how blest to call Him mine!
Mer - cy high - er than the heav - en, Deep - er than the deep - est sea.
How my sin, tho' red like crim - son, Can be whit - er than the snow.
On His strength di - vine re - ly - ing, He is all in all to me.
And for - ev - er and for - ev - er Praise and glo - ri - fy the King.
Refrain
All that thrills my soul is Je - sus, He is more than life to me (to me);
And the fair - est of ten thou - sand In my bless - ed Lord I see.

66 'Twas a Glad Day When Jesus Found Me

ALBERT S. REITZ ALBERT S. REITZ

1. I was lost in sin when Je - sus found me, But He res - cued me, all
2. O the bells of heav - en now are ring - ing, For I hear their tones with -
3. O the joy when we shall meet in glo - ry, In the man - sions of my
glo - ry to His name! And the cords of world - ly pleas - ure bound me,
in my ran - somed soul; And my heart is filled with joy - ful sing - ing
Father's home a - bove; And thro' end - less a - ges tell the sto - ry
Till He saved me from sin and shame.
Since the Sav - ior hath made me whole.
Of the Sav - ior's re - deem - ing love.
CHORUS
'Twas a glad day when Je - sus
found me, When His strong arms were thrown around me; When my sins He buried
in the deep - est sea, And my soul He filled with joy and vic - to - ry, 'Twas a

'Twas a Glad Day When Jesus Found Me
glad day, O hal-le-lu-jah! 'Twas a glad day He claimed His own; I will
shout a glad ho-san-na in glo-ry When I see Him up-on His throne.
Ye Servants of God, Your Master Proclaim 67
Charles Wesley
Arr. from J. Michael Haydn
1. Ye serv-ants of God, your Mas-ter pro-claim, And pub-lish a-
2. God rul-eth on high, al-might-y to save; And still He is
3. "Sal-va-tion to God who sits on the throne," Let all cry a-
4. Then let us a-dore, and give Him His right— All glo-ry and
broad His won-der-ful name; The name all-vic-to-rious of
nigh— His pres-ence we have; The great con-gre-ga-tion His
loud and hon-or the Son; The prais-es of Je-sus the
pow'r, and wis-dom and might; All hon-or and bless-ing, with
Je-sus ex-tol; His king-dom is glo-rious, He rules o-ver all.
tri-umph shall sing, As-crib-ing sal-va-tion to Je-sus our King.
an-gels pro-claim, Fall down on their fac-es. and wor-ship the Lamb.
an-gels a-bove, And thanks nev-er ceasing, and in-fi-nite love. A-MEN.

68 Let Him In

JONATHAN B. ATCHINSON — EDWIN O. EXCELL

1. There's a Stran-ger at the door, Let Him in;
2. O - pen now to Him your heart, Let Him in;
3. Hear you now His lov - ing voice? Let Him in;
4. Now ad - mit the heav'n-ly Guest, Let Him in;
Let the Sav-ior in, Let the Sav-ior in;
He has been there oft be - fore, Let Him in;
If you wait He will de - part, Let Him in;
Now, oh, now make Him your choice, Let Him in;
He will make for you a feast, Let Him in;
Let the Sav-ior in, Let the Sav-ior in;
Let Him in, ere He is gone, Let Him in, the Ho - ly One, Je - sus
Let Him in, He is your Friend, He your soul will sure de - fend, He will
He is stand-ing at your door, Joy to you He will re - store, And His
He will speak your sins for-giv'n, And when earth ties all are riv'n, He will
Christ, the Fa - ther's Son, Let Him in.
keep you to the end, Let Him in.
name you will a - dore, Let Him in.
take you home to heav'n, Let Him in.
Let the Sav-ior in, Let the Sav-ior in.

69 You May Have the Joy-bells

J. Edward Ruark — William J. Kirkpatrick

1. You may have the joy-bells ring-ing in your heart, And a peace that
2. Love of Je-sus in its full-ness you may know, And this love to
3. You will meet with tri-als as you jour-ney home; Grace suf-fi-cient
4. Let your life speak well of Je-sus ev-'ry day; Own His right to
from you nev-er will de-part; Walk the straight and nar-row way,
those a-round you sweet-ly show; Words of kind-ness al-ways say,
He will give to o-ver-come; Tho' un-seen by mor-tal eye,
ev-'ry serv-ice you can pay; Sin-ners you can help to win
Fine
Live for Je-sus ev-'ry day, He will keep the joy-bells ringing in your heart.
Deeds of mer-cy do each day, Then He'll keep the joy-bells ringing in your heart.
He is with you ev-er nigh, And He'll keep the joy-bells ringing in your heart.
If your life is pure and clean, And you keep the joy-bells ringing in your heart.
Chorus
D. S.—He will keep the joy-bells ring-ing in your heart.
Joy - - - bells ring-ing in your heart, Joy - - - - bells
Ring-ing in your heart,
You may have the joy-bells
D.S.
ringing in your heart; Take the Sav-ior here below With you ev'rywhere you go;

70 There's a New Song in My Heart

John W. Peterson — John W. Peterson

1. Once my life was filled with dis-cord, Sad-ness reigned with-in,
2. What a won-drous trans-for - ma-tion In my life was wrought,
3. Some day I will go to Heav-en Where the an-gels sing,
4. I shall nev - er cease in prais-ing Je - sus Christ my Lord,
For my heart was heav - y - lad - en With a weight of sin.
When I trust - ed Christ as Sav-ior And His par - don sought.
And I'll join their hap - py cho - rus Prais-ing Christ the King.
For the won-der - ful sal - va - tion That He did ac - cord.
CHORUS
MEN
Faster
There's a new song in my heart Since the Sav-ior set me free;
WOMEN
There's a new song in my heart— 'Tis a heav'n-ly har-mo - ny!
ALL
All my sins are washed a - way In the blood of Cal-va - ry; O what

There's a New Song in My Heart
PARTS
peace and joy Noth-ing can de-stroy, There's a new song in my heart.
Some Day!
71
(BEAUTIFUL ISLE OF SOMEWHERE)
JESSIE B. POUNDS, 1
AVIS B. CHRISTIANSEN, 2, 3, REF.
J. S. FEARIS
1. Some-where the sun is shin - ing, Some-where the song-birds dwell;
2. Soon will earth's night be o - ver, Soon will the morn-ing dawn;
3. There a-mid Heav-en's beau - ties They shall be-hold His face,
Hush, then, thy sad re - pin - ing, God lives, and all is well.
Soon will the Christ of Glo - ry Call His re-deemed ones home.
And through e-ter - nal a - ges Sing of His won-drous grace.
REFRAIN
Some day! Some day! We shall be - hold His glo - ry!
Com-ing a-gain, ev - er-more to reign, All will be won-drous glo - ry!

Safely Through Another Week

JOHN NEWTON

LOWELL MASON

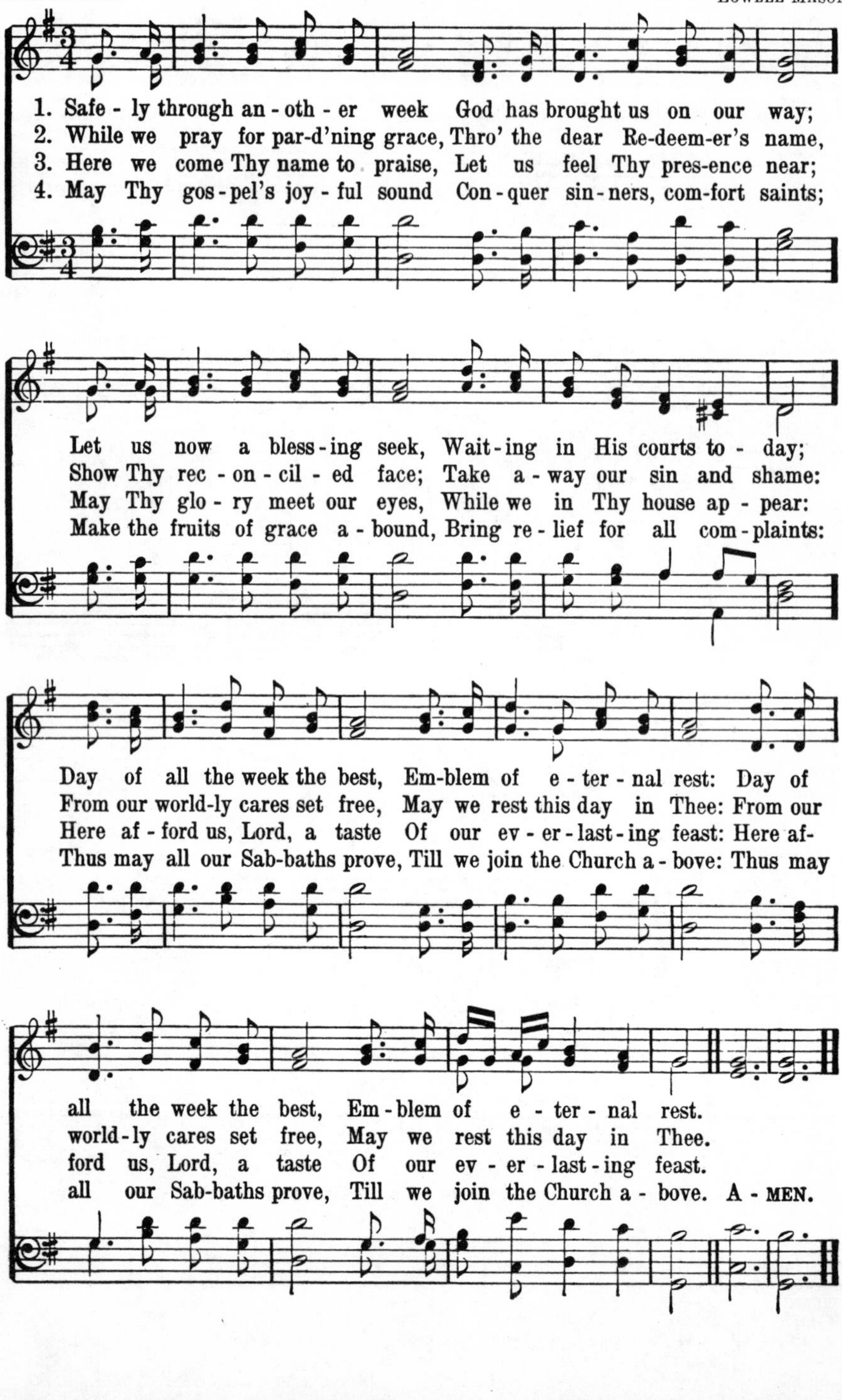

1. Safe - ly through an - oth - er week God has brought us on our way;
2. While we pray for par-d'ning grace, Thro' the dear Re-deem-er's name,
3. Here we come Thy name to praise, Let us feel Thy pres-ence near;
4. May Thy gos - pel's joy - ful sound Con - quer sin - ners, com-fort saints;

Let us now a bless - ing seek, Wait - ing in His courts to - day;
Show Thy rec - on - cil - ed face; Take a - way our sin and shame:
May Thy glo - ry meet our eyes, While we in Thy house ap - pear:
Make the fruits of grace a - bound, Bring re - lief for all com - plaints:

Day of all the week the best, Em-blem of e - ter - nal rest: Day of
From our world-ly cares set free, May we rest this day in Thee: From our
Here af - ford us, Lord, a taste Of our ev - er - last - ing feast: Here af-
Thus may all our Sab-baths prove, Till we join the Church a - bove: Thus may

all the week the best, Em - blem of e - ter - nal rest.
world - ly cares set free, May we rest this day in Thee.
ford us, Lord, a taste Of our ev - er - last - ing feast.
all our Sab-baths prove, Till we join the Church a - bove. A - MEN.

It Is Well with My Soul 73

Horatio G. Spafford — Philip P. Bliss

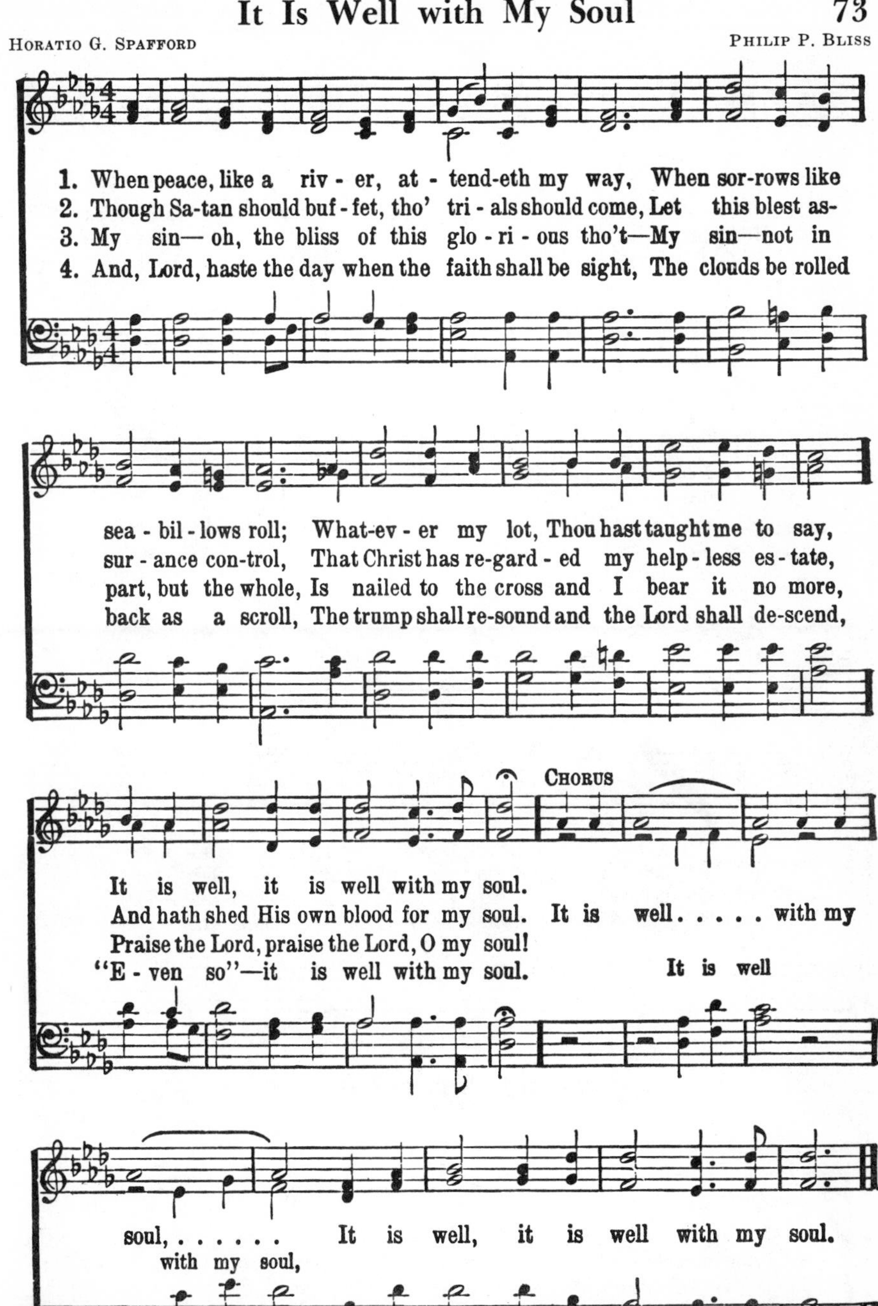
1. When peace, like a riv - er, at - tend-eth my way, When sor-rows like sea - bil - lows roll; What-ev - er my lot, Thou hast taught me to say, It is well, it is well with my soul.
2. Though Sa-tan should buf - fet, tho' tri - als should come, Let this blest as-sur - ance con-trol, That Christ has re-gard - ed my help - less es - tate, And hath shed His own blood for my soul.
3. My sin— oh, the bliss of this glo - ri - ous tho't—My sin—not in part, but the whole, Is nailed to the cross and I bear it no more, Praise the Lord, praise the Lord, O my soul!
4. And, Lord, haste the day when the faith shall be sight, The clouds be rolled back as a scroll, The trump shall re-sound and the Lord shall de-scend, "E - ven so"—it is well with my soul.
Chorus
It is well . . . . . with my soul, ... It is well, it is well with my soul.
It is well with my soul,

74 O Love That Wilt Not Let Me Go

GEORGE MATHESON — ALBERT L. PEACE

p
1. O Love that wilt not let me go, I rest my wea - ry soul on Thee; I give Thee back the life I owe, That in Thine o-cean depths its flow May rich - er, full - er be.
2. O Light that fol-low'st all my way, I yield my flick-'ring torch to Thee; My heart re-stores its bor-rowed ray, That in Thy sun-shine's glow its day May bright-er, fair - er be.
3. O Joy that seek-est me thro' pain, I can - not close my heart to Thee; I trace the rain-bow thro' the rain, And feel the prom-ise is not vain That morn shall tear - less be.
4. O Cross that lift-est up my head, I dare not ask to hide from Thee; I lay in dust life's glo - ry dead, And from the ground there blossoms red Life that shall end - less be.
75
Jesus Shall Reign
ISAAC WATTS
JOHN HATTON
1. Je-sus shall reign wher-e'er the sun Does his suc-ces-sive jour-neys run;
2. From north to south the prin-ces meet To pay their hom-age at His feet;
3. To Him shall end-less prayer be made, And end-less prais-es crown His head;
4. Peo-ple and realms of ev - 'ry tongue Dwell on His love with sweetest song,

Jesus Shall Reign

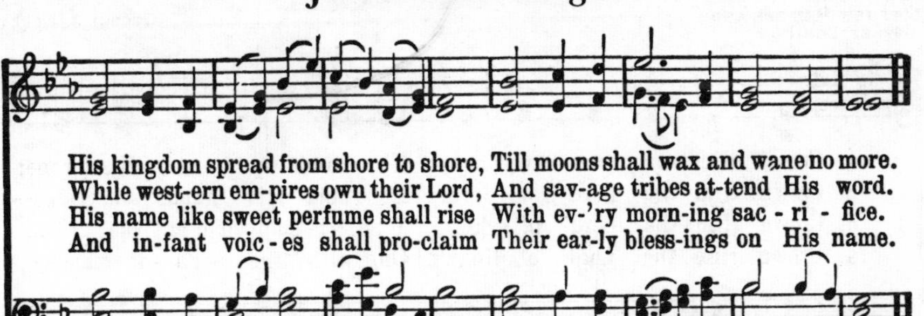
His kingdom spread from shore to shore, Till moons shall wax and wane no more.
While west-ern em-pires own their Lord, And sav-age tribes at-tend His word.
His name like sweet perfume shall rise With ev-'ry morn-ing sac - ri - fice.
And in-fant voic-es shall pro-claim Their ear-ly bless-ings on His name.

Lead On, O King Eternal 76

ERNEST W. SHURTLEFF HENRY SMART

1. Lead on, O King E - ter-nal, The day of march has come; Henceforth in fields of
2. Lead on, O King E - ter-nal, Till sin's fierce war shall cease, And ho-li-ness shall
3. Lead on, O King E - ter-nal, We fol-low, not with fears; For gladness breaks like

con-quest Thy tents shall be our home. Thro' days of prep - a - ra - tion Thy
whis - per The sweet A - men of peace; For not with swords loud clashing, Nor
morn - ing Where'er Thy face ap-pears; Thy cross is lift - ed o'er us; We

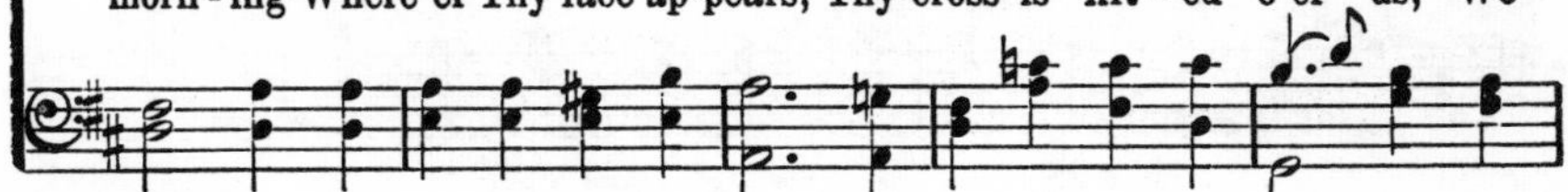

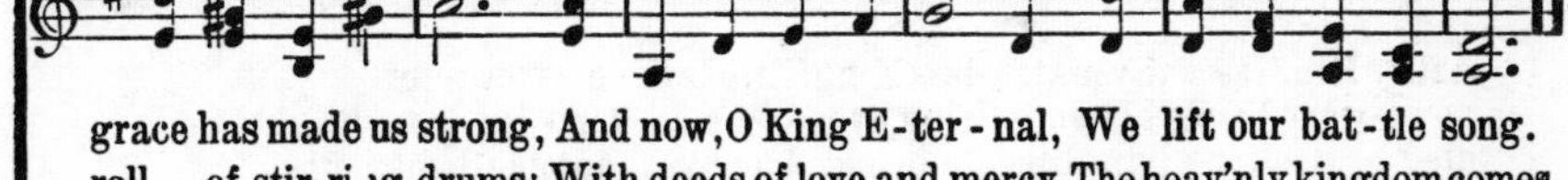

grace has made us strong, And now, O King E - ter - nal, We lift our bat - tle song.
roll of stir-ring drums; With deeds of love and mercy, The heav'nly kingdom comes.
jour - ney in its light: The crown awaits the conquest; Lead on, O God of might.

77 Crown Him with Many Crowns

Matthew Bridges and Godfrey Thring

George J. Elvey

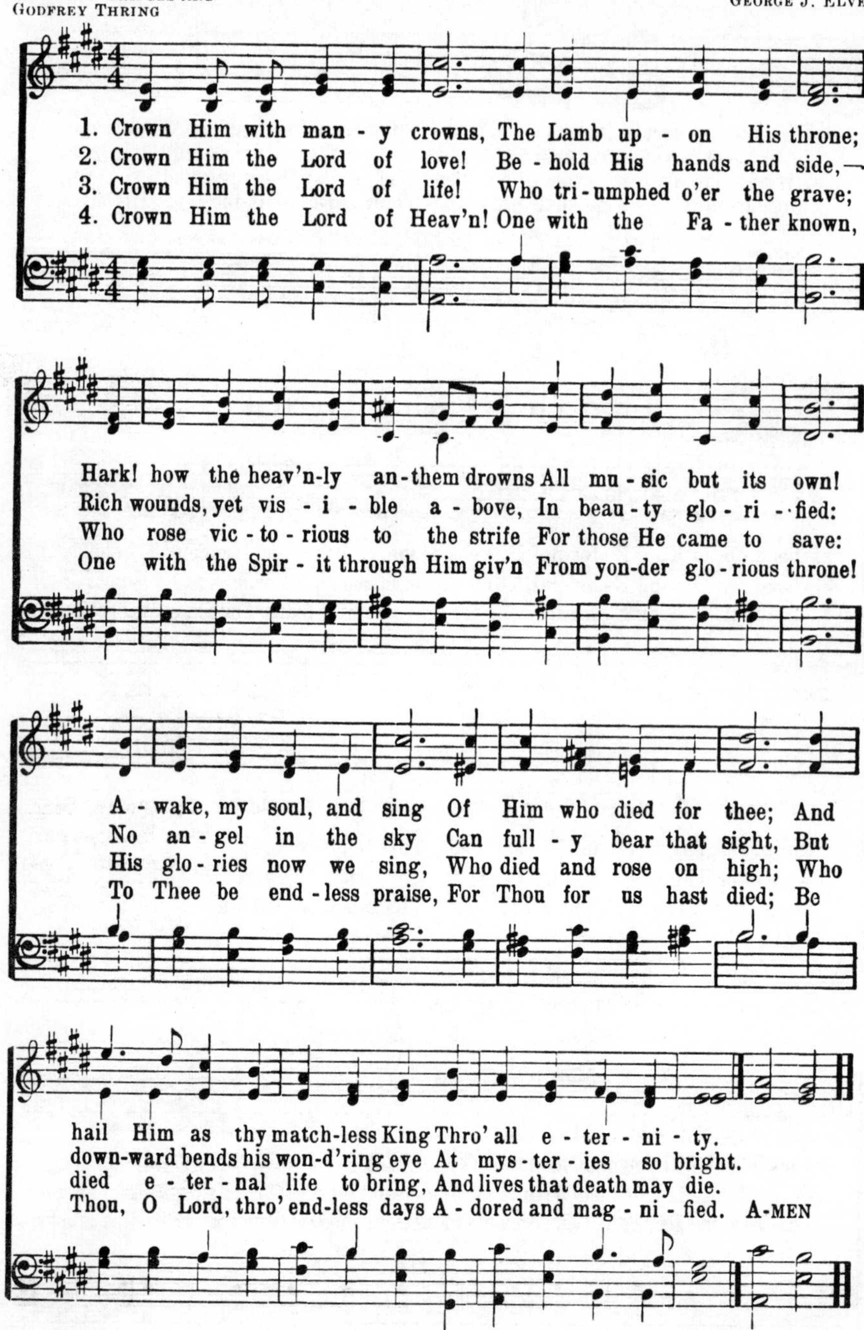
1. Crown Him with man - y crowns, The Lamb up - on His throne;
2. Crown Him the Lord of love! Be - hold His hands and side,—
3. Crown Him the Lord of life! Who tri - umphed o'er the grave;
4. Crown Him the Lord of Heav'n! One with the Fa - ther known,
Hark! how the heav'n-ly an - them drowns All mu - sic but its own!
Rich wounds, yet vis - i - ble a - bove, In beau - ty glo - ri - fied:
Who rose vic - to - rious to the strife For those He came to save:
One with the Spir - it through Him giv'n From yon - der glo - rious throne!
A - wake, my soul, and sing Of Him who died for thee; And
No an - gel in the sky Can full - y bear that sight, But
His glo - ries now we sing, Who died and rose on high; Who
To Thee be end - less praise, For Thou for us hast died; Be
hail Him as thy match - less King Thro' all e - ter - ni - ty.
down - ward bends his won - d'ring eye At mys - ter - ies so bright.
died e - ter - nal life to bring, And lives that death may die.
Thou, O Lord, thro' end - less days A - dored and mag - ni - fied.
A - MEN

O Day of Rest and Gladness

Christopher Wordsworth

Old German Melody
Arr. by Lowell Mason

1. O day of rest and glad - ness, O day of joy and light,
2. On thee, at the cre - a - tion, The light first had its birth;
3. To - day on wear - y na - tions The heav'n-ly man - na falls;
4. New gra - ces ev - er gain - ing From this our day of rest,
O balm of care and sad - ness, Most beau - ti - ful, most bright;
On thee, for our sal - va - tion, Christ rose from depths of earth.
To ho - ly con - vo - ca - tions The sil - ver trump-et calls,
We reach the rest re - main - ing To spir - its of the blest.
On thee, the high and low - ly, Bend - ing be - fore the throne, Sing,
On thee our Lord vic - to - rious The Spir - it sent from Heav'n; And
Where gos - pel light is glow - ing With pure and ra - diant beams, And
To Ho - ly Ghost be prais - es, To Fa - ther and to Son; The
Ho - ly, Ho - ly, Ho - ly, To the great Three in One.
thus on thee most glo - rious A tri - ple light was given.
liv - ing wa - ter flow - ing With soul - re - fresh-ing streams.
Church her voice up - rais - es To Thee, blest Three in One. A - men.

79 Tell Me the Old, Old Story

A. CATHERINE HANKEY — WILLIAM H. DOANE

1. Tell me the Old, Old Sto - ry, Of un-seen things a - bove, Of Je - sus
2. Tell me the sto - ry slow - ly, That I may take it in— That won-der-
3. Tell me the sto - ry soft - ly, With ear-nest tones and grave; Re - mem-ber
4. Tell me the same old sto - ry, When you have cause to fear That this world's
and His glo - ry, Of Je - sus and His love; Tell me the sto - ry
ful re - demp-tion, God's rem - e - dy for sin; Tell me the sto - ry
I'm the sin - ner Whom Je - sus came to save; Tell me the sto - ry
emp-ty glo - ry Is cost - ing me too dear; Yes, and when that world's
sim - ply, As to a lit - tle child, For I am weak and wea - ry,
oft - en, For I for-get so soon, The "ear - ly dew" of morn-ing
al - ways, If you would real-ly be, In an - y time of troub-le,
glo - ry Is dawn-ing on my soul, Tell me the Old, Old Sto - ry:
And help - less and de - filed.
Has passed a - way at noon.
A com - fort - er to me.
"Christ Je - sus makes thee whole."
CHORUS
Tell me the Old, Old Sto - ry, Tell me the
Old, Old Sto - ry, Tell me the Old, Old Sto - ry Of Je - sus and His love.

We Three Kings of Orient Are

John H. Hopkins — John H. Hopkins

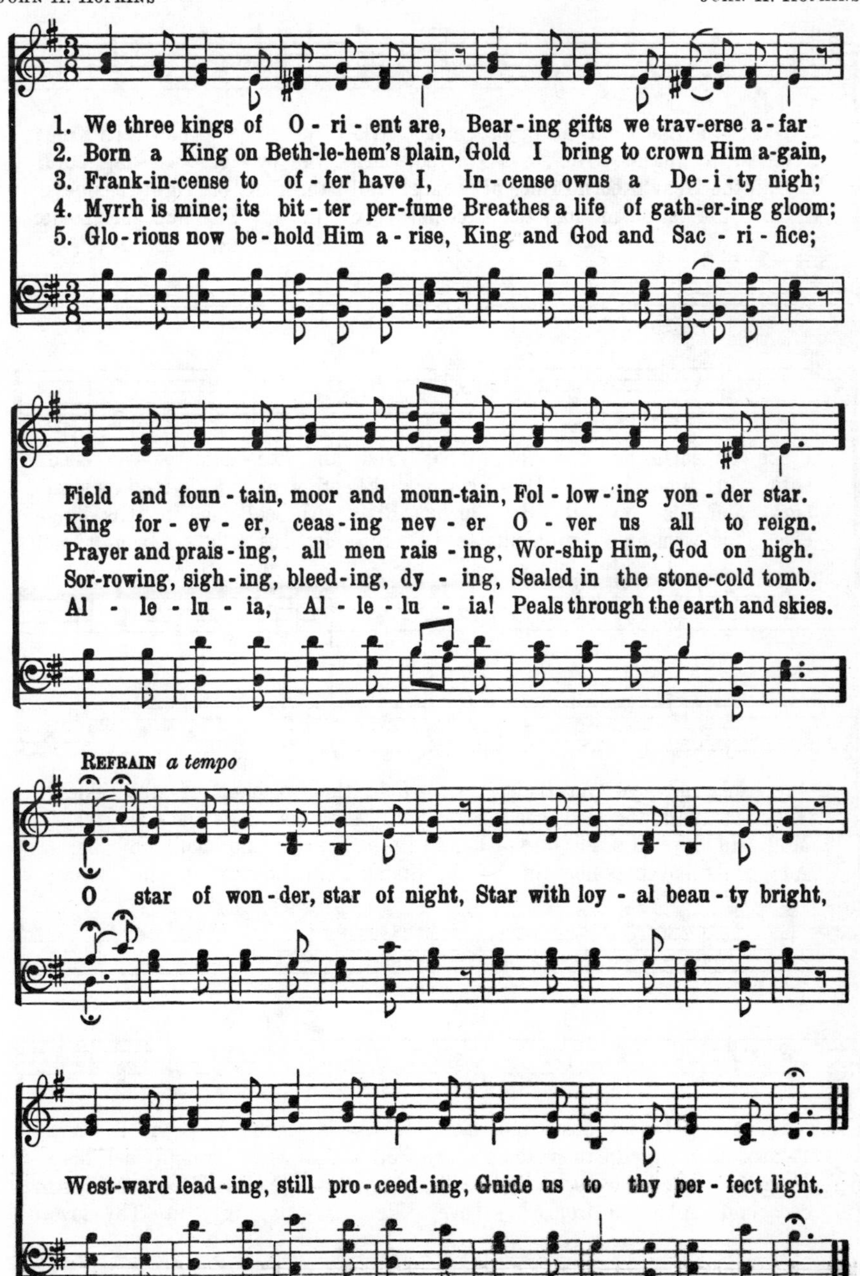
1. We three kings of O - ri - ent are, Bear - ing gifts we trav-erse a - far
2. Born a King on Beth-le-hem's plain, Gold I bring to crown Him a-gain,
3. Frank-in-cense to of - fer have I, In - cense owns a De - i - ty nigh;
4. Myrrh is mine; its bit - ter per-fume Breathes a life of gath-er-ing gloom;
5. Glo - rious now be - hold Him a - rise, King and God and Sac - ri - fice;
Field and foun - tain, moor and moun-tain, Fol - low - ing yon - der star.
King for - ev - er, ceas - ing nev - er O - ver us all to reign.
Prayer and prais - ing, all men rais - ing, Wor-ship Him, God on high.
Sor-rowing, sigh - ing, bleed-ing, dy - ing, Sealed in the stone-cold tomb.
Al - le - lu - ia, Al - le - lu - ia! Peals through the earth and skies.
Refrain a tempo
O star of won - der, star of night, Star with loy - al beau - ty bright,
West-ward lead - ing, still pro-ceed-ing, Guide us to thy per - fect light.

81 Hark! the Herald Angels Sing

CHARLES WESLEY

FELIX MENDELSSOHN-BARTHOLDY
ARR. BY WILLIAM H. CUMMINGS

1. Hark! the her - ald an - gels sing, "Glo - ry to the new-born King;
2. Christ, by high-est Heav'n a - dored, Christ, the ev - er - last - ing Lord:
3. Hail the Heav'n-born Prince of Peace! Hail the Sun of right-eous-ness!
4. Come, De - sire of na - tions, come! Fix in us Thy hum - ble home:
Peace on earth, and mer - cy mild; God and sin - ners rec - on - ciled."
Late in time be - hold Him come, Off - spring of a vir-gin's womb.
Light and life to all He brings, Ris'n with heal - ing in His wings:
Rise, the wom-an's con-qu'ring seed, Bruise in us the ser - pent's head;
Joy - ful, all ye na - tions, rise, Join the tri - umph of the skies;
Veiled in flesh the God - head see, Hail th' in - car - nate De - i - ty!
Mild He lays His glo - ry by, Born that man no more may die;
Ad - am's like - ness now ef - face, Stamp Thine im - age in its place:
With an - gel - ic hosts pro - claim, "Christ is born in Beth - le - hem."
Pleased as man with men to ap - pear, Je - sus our Im - man - uel here.
Born to raise the sons of earth; Born to give them sec - ond birth.
Sec - ond Ad - am from a - bove, Re - in - state us in Thy love.

Hark! the Herald Angels Sing

Hark! the her- ald an-gels sing, "Glo - ry to the new- born King!"

O Little Town of Bethlehem 82

PHILLIPS BROOKS | LEWIS H. REDNER

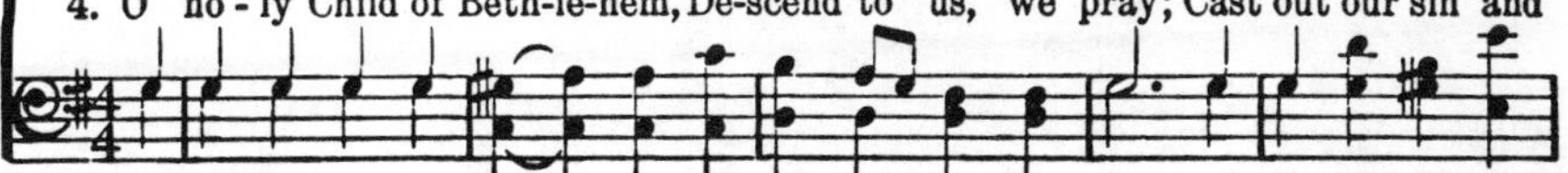

1. O lit-tle town of Beth-le-hem, How still we see thee lie! A-bove thy deep and
2. For Christ is born of Ma - ry; And gath-ered all a-bove, While mortals sleep, the
3. How si-lent-ly, how si - lent - ly The wondrous Gift is giv'n! So God im-parts to
4. O ho - ly Child of Beth-le-hem, De-scend to us, we pray; Cast out our sin and

dreamless sleep The si - lent stars go by; Yet in thy dark streets shin-eth The
an - gels keep Their watch of wond'ring love. O morn-ing stars, to-geth - er Pro-
hu- man hearts The bless-ings of His Heav'n. No ear may hear His com - ing; But
en - ter in, Be born in us to - day. We hear the Christmas an - gels The

ev - er-last-ing Light; The hopes and fears of all the years Are met in thee to - night.
claim the ho - ly birth, And prais-es sing to God the King, And peace to men on earth.
in this world of sin, Where meek souls will receive Him still, The dear Christ enters in.
great glad tidings tell,—O come to us, a-bide with us, Our Lord Em-man-u - el.

83 O Come, All Ye Faithful

LATIN HYMN
TR. BY FREDERICK OAKELEY

JOHN F. WADE'S "CANTUS DIVERSI"

1. O come, all ye faith - ful, joy - ful and tri - um - phant,
2. Sing, choirs of an - gels, sing in ex - ul - ta - tion,
3. Yea, Lord, we greet Thee, born this hap - py morn - ing,
O come ye, O come ye to Beth - le - hem;
O sing, all ye bright hosts of heav'n a - bove;
Je - sus, to Thee be all glo - - ry giv'n;
Come and be - hold Him born the King of an - gels;
Glo - ry to God, all glo - ry in the high - est;
Word of the Fa - ther, now in flesh ap - pear - ing;
REFRAIN
O come, let us a - dore Him, O come, let us a - dore Him,
O come, let us a - dore Him, Christ, the Lord. A - MEN.

It Came upon the Midnight Clear 84

EDMUND H. SEARS RICHARD S. WILLIS

1. It came up - on the mid-night clear, That glo-rious song of old,
2. Still thro' the clo - ven skies they come, With peace-ful wings un - furled,
3. And ye, be - neath life's crushing load, Whose forms are bend-ing low,
4. For lo, the days are has-t'ning on, By proph-et bards fore-told,

From an - gels bend-ing near the earth To touch their harps of gold:
And still their heav'n-ly mu - sic floats O'er all the wea - ry world:
Who toil a - long the climb-ing way With pain-ful steps and slow,
When with the ev - er - cir - cling years Comes round the age of gold;

"Peace on the earth, good-will to men, From heav'n's all-gracious King:" The
A - bove its sad and low - ly plains They bend on hov-'ring wing: And
Look now! for glad and gold - en hours Come swift-ly on the wing; O
When peace shall o - ver all the earth Its an-cient splen-dors fling, And

world in sol - emn still-ness lay To hear the an - gels sing.
ev - er o'er its Ba - bel sounds The bless - ed an - gels sing.
rest be - side the wea - ry road, And hear the an - gels sing.
the whole world give back the song Which now the an - gels sing. A-MEN.

85 There's a Song in the Air
Josiah G. Holland
Karl P. Harrington
Adante con moto
1. There's a song in the air! There's a star in the sky! There's a moth-er's deep
2. There's a tu-mult of joy O'er the won-der-ful birth, For the Vir-gin's sweet
3. In the light of that star Lie the a-ges im-pearled; And that song from a -
4. We re-joice in the light, And we ech-o the song That comes down thru the
ritard.
piu mosso
prayer, And a ba-by's low cry! And the star rains its fire while the
boy Is the Lord of the earth. Ay! the star rains its fire while the
far Has swept o - ver the world. Ev-'ry hearth is a-flame, and the
night From the heav-en-ly throng. Ay! we shout to the love-ly e -
ritard.
beau-ti-ful sing, For the man-ger of Beth-le-hem cra-dles a King!
beau-ti-ful sing, For the man-ger of Beth-le-hem cra-dles a King!
beau-ti-ful sing In the homes of the na-tions that Je-sus is King!
van-gel they bring, And we greet in His cra-dle our Sav-ior and King!
86 While Shepherds Watched Their Flocks
Nahum Tate
George F. Handel
1. While shep-herds watched their flocks by night, All seat - ed on the ground, The
2. "Fear not!" said he; for might-y dread Had seized their trou-bled mind, "Glad
3. "To you, in Dav-id's town this day, Is born of Dav-id's line, The
4. "The heav'n-ly Babe you there shall find To hu - man view dis - played, All
5. "All glo-ry be to God on high, And to the earth be peace: Good

While Shepherds Watched Their Flocks

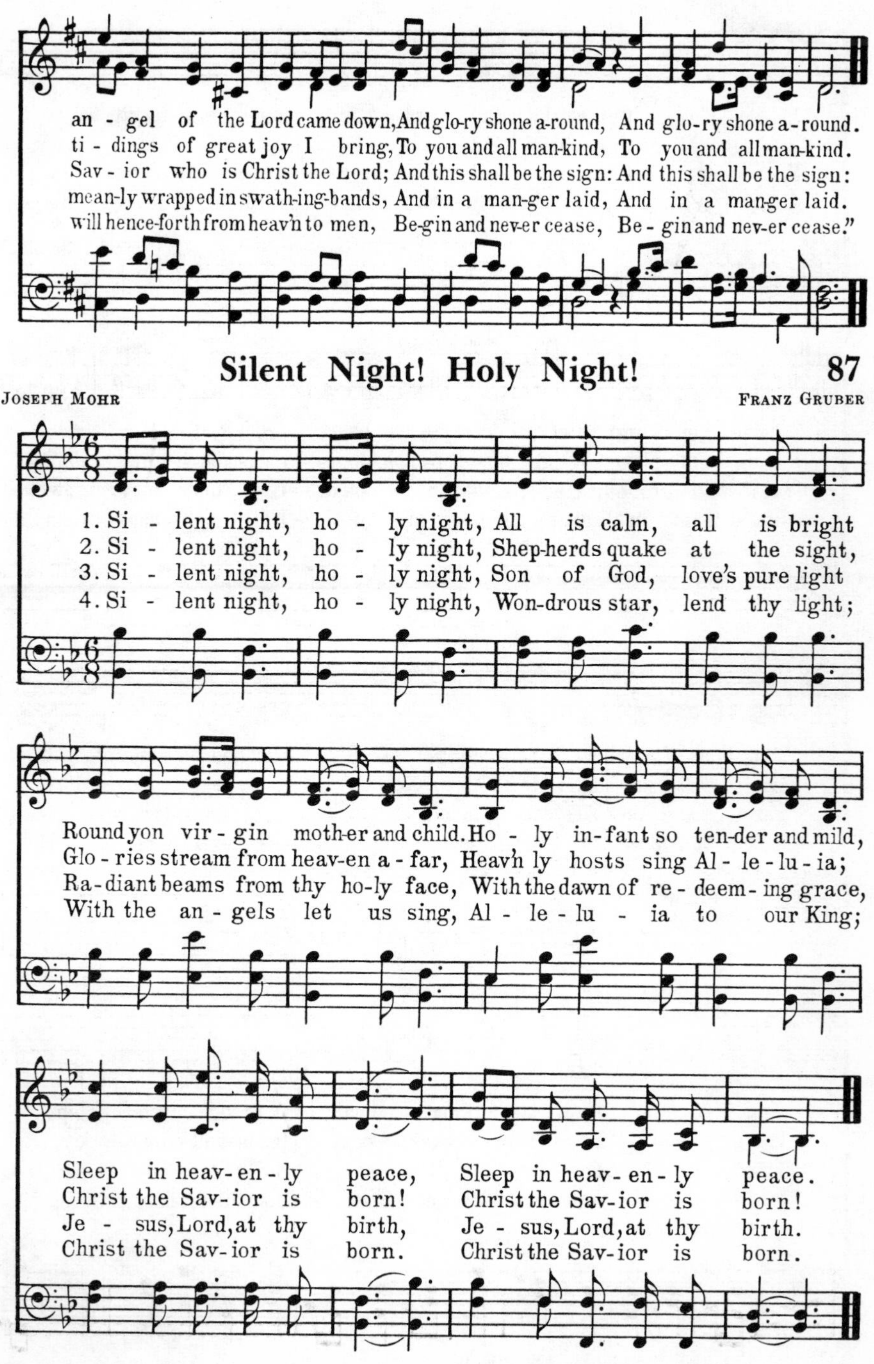
an - gel of the Lord came down, And glo-ry shone a-round, And glo-ry shone a-round.
ti - dings of great joy I bring, To you and all man-kind, To you and all man-kind.
Sav - ior who is Christ the Lord; And this shall be the sign: And this shall be the sign:
mean-ly wrapped in swath-ing-bands, And in a man-ger laid, And in a man-ger laid.
will hence-forth from heav'n to men, Be-gin and nev-er cease, Be - gin and nev-er cease."
Silent Night! Holy Night!
87
JOSEPH MOHR
FRANZ GRUBER
1. Si - lent night, ho - ly night, All is calm, all is bright
2. Si - lent night, ho - ly night, Shep-herds quake at the sight,
3. Si - lent night, ho - ly night, Son of God, love's pure light
4. Si - lent night, ho - ly night, Won-drous star, lend thy light;
Round yon vir - gin moth-er and child. Ho - ly in-fant so ten-der and mild,
Glo - ries stream from heav-en a - far, Heav'n ly hosts sing Al - le - lu - ia;
Ra - diant beams from thy ho-ly face, With the dawn of re - deem - ing grace,
With the an - gels let us sing, Al - le - lu - ia to our King;
Sleep in heav-en-ly peace, Sleep in heav-en-ly peace.
Christ the Sav-ior is born! Christ the Sav-ior is born!
Je - sus, Lord, at thy birth, Je - sus, Lord, at thy birth.
Christ the Sav-ior is born. Christ the Sav-ior is born.

88 Joy to the World!

FROM PSALM 98
ISAAC WATTS

ARR. FROM GEORGE F. HANDEL

1. Joy to the world! the Lord is come; Let earth re-
2. Joy to the world! the Sav - ior reigns; Let men their
3. No more let sins and sor - rows grow, Nor thorns in-
4. He rules the world with truth and grace, And makes the
ceive her King; Let ev - 'ry heart pre - pare Him room,
songs em - ploy; While fields and floods, rocks, hills and plains
fest the ground; He comes to make His bless - ings flow
na - tions prove The glo - ries of His right - eous - ness,
And heav'n and na - ture sing, And heav'n and na - ture
Re - peat the sound - ing joy, Re - peat the sound - ing
Far as the curse is found, Far as the curse is
And won - ders of His love, And won - ders of His
1. And heav'n and na - ture sing,.......... And
sing, And heav'n, and heav'n and na - ture sing.
joy, Re - peat, re - peat the sound - ing joy.
found, Far as, far as the curse is found.
love, And won - ders, and won - ders of His love.
heav'n and na - ture sing,

Thou Didst Leave Thy Throne

Emily E. S. Elliott — Timothy R. Matthews

1. Thou didst leave Thy throne And Thy king - ly crown When Thou
2. Heav-en's arch - es rang When the an - gels sang, Pro - -
3. The fox - es found rest, And the birds their nest In the
4. Thou cam - est, O Lord, With the liv - ing word That should
5. When the heav - ens shall ring, And the an - gels sing, At Thy
cam - est to earth for me; But in Beth - le - hem's home
claim - ing Thy roy - al de - gree; But of low - ly birth
shade of the for - est tree; But Thy couch was the sod,
set Thy peo - ple free; But with mock - ing scorn,
com - ing to vic - to - ry, Let Thy voice call me home,
Was there found no room For Thy ho - ly na - tiv - i - ty:
Didst Thou come to earth, And in great - est hu - mil - i - ty:
O Thou Son of God, In the des - erts of Gal - i - lee:
And with crown of thorn, They bore Thee to Cal - va - ry:
Say - ing, "Yet there is room, There is room at My side for thee:"
Refrain
1-4. O come to my heart, Lord Je - sus, There is room in my heart for Thee.
5. My heart shall rejoice, Lord Je - sus, When Thou comest and call-est for me.

90 The First Noel

Old English Carol

Traditional Melody from W. Sandy's "Christmas Carols"

1. The first No - el the angel did say Was to certain poor shepherds in fields as they lay;
2. And by the light of that same Star, Three wise men came from country far;
3. This Star drew nigh to the northwest, O'er Beth - le-hem it took its rest,
4. Then enter-ed in those wise men three, Full rev-'rent-ly up-on their knee,

In fields where they lay keeping their sheep, On a cold winter's night that was so deep.
To seek for a King was their in - tent, And to follow the Star wherever it went.
And there it did both stop and stay, Right o-ver the place where Jesus lay.
And of - fered there in His pres-ence, Their gold, and myrrh, and frank-incense.

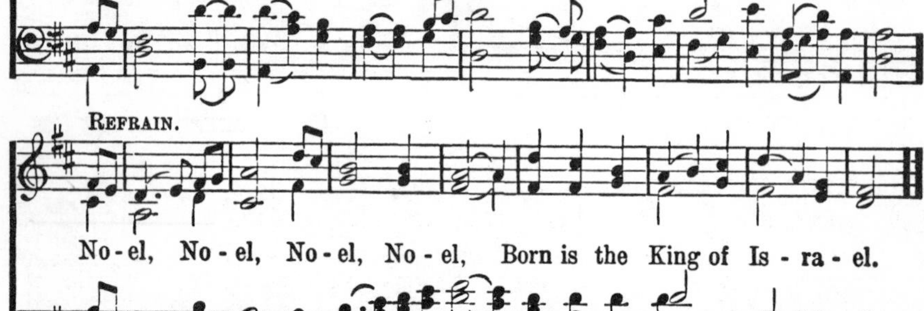

Refrain.

No - el, No - el, No - el, No - el, Born is the King of Is - ra - el.

91 I Heard the Bells on Christmas Day

Henry W. Longfellow

J. Baptiste Calkin

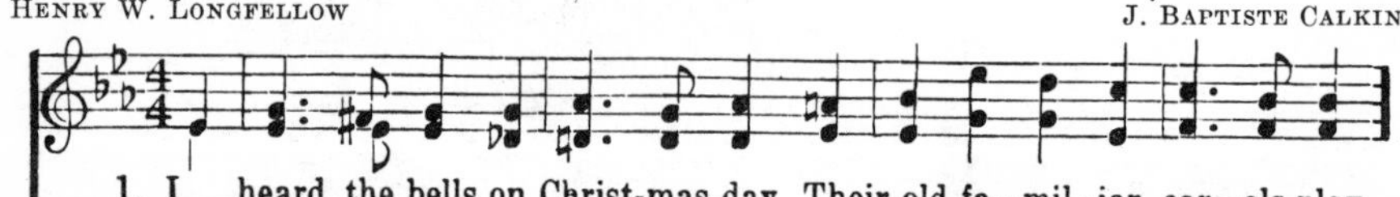

1. I heard the bells on Christ-mas day Their old fa - mil - iar car - ols play,
2. I thought how, as the day had come, The bel-fries of all Chris-ten-dom
3. And in de-spair I bowed my head: "There is no peace on earth," I said,
4. Then pealed the bells more loud and deep: "God is not dead, nor doth He sleep;
5. Till, ring - ing, sing-ing on its way, The world revolved from night to day,

I Heard the Bells on Christmas Day

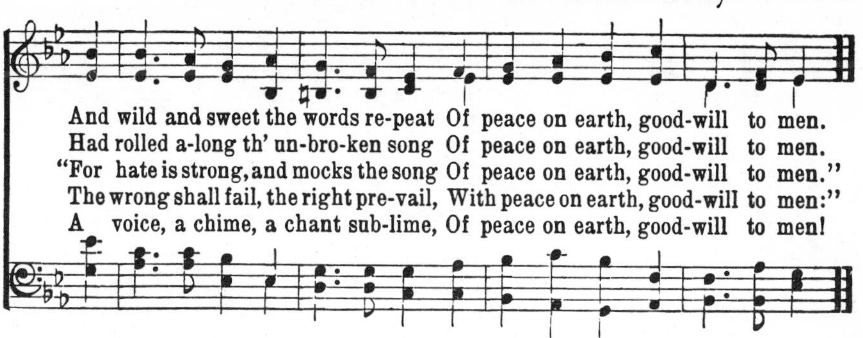
And wild and sweet the words re-peat Of peace on earth, good-will to men.
Had rolled a-long th' un-bro-ken song Of peace on earth, good-will to men.
"For hate is strong, and mocks the song Of peace on earth, good-will to men."
The wrong shall fail, the right pre-vail, With peace on earth, good-will to men:"
A voice, a chime, a chant sub-lime, Of peace on earth, good-will to men!

Angels, from the Realms of Glory 92

JAMES MONTGOMERY | HENRY SMART

1. An - gels, from the realms of glo - ry, Wing your flight o'er all the earth;
2. Shep-herds, in the field a - bid - ing, Watching o'er your flocks by night,
3. Sa - ges, leave your con - tem-pla-tions, Bright-er vi - sions beam a - far;
4. Saints, be - fore the al - tar bend-ing, Watching long in hope and fear,

Ye, who sang cre - a - tion's sto - ry, Now pro-claim Mes - si - ah's birth:
God with man is now re - sid - ing, Yon-der shines the In - fant-Light;
Seek the great De - sire of na - tions, Ye have seen His na - tal star;
Sud-den - ly the Lord, de - scend-ing, In His tem - ple shall ap - pear;

Come and wor-ship, come and wor-ship, Wor - ship Christ, the new-born King.

93 Away in a Manger

MARTIN LUTHER — MARTIN LUTHER

1. A-way in a man-ger, No crib for a bed, The lit-tle Lord Je-sus Laid down His sweet head; The stars in the sky.... Looked down where He lay,—The lit-tle Lord Je-sus, A-sleep on the hay.

2. The cat-tle are low-ing, The poor ba-by wakes, But lit-tle Lord Je-sus, No cry-ing He makes; I love Thee, Lord Je-sus! Look down from the sky, And stay by my cra-dle To watch lul-la-by.

94 Alas! and Did My Savior Bleed?

ISAAC WATTS — HUGH WILSON

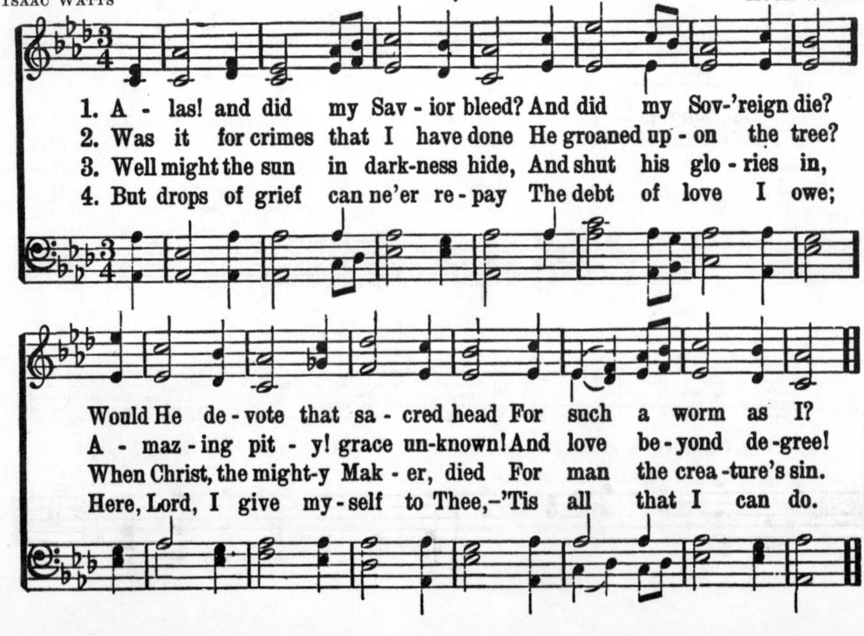

1. A-las! and did my Sav-ior bleed? And did my Sov-'reign die? Would He de-vote that sa-cred head For such a worm as I?

2. Was it for crimes that I have done He groaned up-on the tree? A-maz-ing pit-y! grace un-known! And love be-yond de-gree!

3. Well might the sun in dark-ness hide, And shut his glo-ries in, When Christ, the might-y Mak-er, died For man the crea-ture's sin.

4. But drops of grief can ne'er re-pay The debt of love I owe; Here, Lord, I give my-self to Thee,—'Tis all that I can do.

At the Cross

Isaac Watts
Ref., Ralph E. Hudson

Ralph E. Hudson

1. A - las, and did my Sav - ior bleed? And did my Sov-'reign die?
2. Was it for crimes that I have done, He groaned up - on the tree?
3. Well might the sun in dark-ness hide, And shut his glo - ries in,
4. But drops of grief can ne'er re - pay The debt of love I owe:
Would He de - vote that sa - cred head For such a worm as I?
A - maz - ing pit - y! grace unknown! And love be - yond de - gree!
When Christ, the might-y Mak - er, died For man the crea-ture's sin.
Here, Lord, I give my - self a - way, 'Tis all that I can do!
Chorus
At the cross, at the cross where I first saw the light, And the
bur - den of my heart rolled a - way, (rolled a-way,) It was there by faith
I re-ceived my sight, And now I am hap - py all the day!

96 Heaven Came Down and Glory Filled My Soul

JOHN W. PETERSON | JOHN W. PETERSON

1. O what a won-der-ful, won-der-ful day — Day I will nev-er for - get;
2. Born of the Spir-it with life from a-bove In-to God's fam-'ly di - vine;
3. Now I've a hope that will sure-ly en-dure Aft-er the pass-ing of time;
Af-ter I'd wan-dered in dark-ness a-way, Je-sus my Sav-ior I met.
Jus-ti-fied ful-ly thru Cal-va-ry's love, O what a stand-ing is mine!
I have a fu-ture in heav-en for sure, There in those man-sions sub-lime.
O what a ten-der, com-pas-sion-ate friend, He met the need of my heart;
And the trans-ac-tion so quick-ly was made, When as a sin-ner I came,
And it's be-cause of that won-der-ful day When at the cross I be - lieved;
Shad-ows dis-pel-ling, with joy I am tell-ing, He made all the dark-ness de - part!
Took of the of-fer of grace He did prof-fer, He saved me, O praise His dear name!
Rich-es e-ter-nal and bless-ings su-per-nal From His pre-cious hand I re - ceived.
CHORUS
Heav-en came down and glo-ry filled my soul,
filled my soul,

Heaven Came Down and Glory Filled My Soul

When at the cross the Sav-ior made me whole; made me whole; My
sins were washed a - way And my night was turned to day –
Heav-en came down and glo-ry filled my soul! filled my soul!
Thy Holy Spirit, Lord, Alone 97
Henrietta E. Blair
William J. Kirkpatrick
1. Thy Ho-ly Spir-it, Lord, a-lone Can turn our hearts from sin; His pow'r a-lone can sanc-ti-fy And keep us pure with - in.
2. Thy Ho-ly Spir-it, Lord, a-lone Can deep-er love in - spire; His pow'r a-lone with - in our souls Can light the sa-cred fire.
3. Thy Ho-ly Spir-it, Lord, can bring The gifts we seek in pray'r; His voice can words of com-fort speak, And still each wave of care.
4. Thy Ho-ly Spir-it, Lord, can give The grace we need this hour; And while we wait, O Spir-it, come In sanc-ti-fy-ing pow'r.

98 Be Still, My Soul

FROM PSALM 46
KATHARINA VON SCHLEGEL
TR. BY JANE L. BORTHWICK

JEAN SIBELIUS

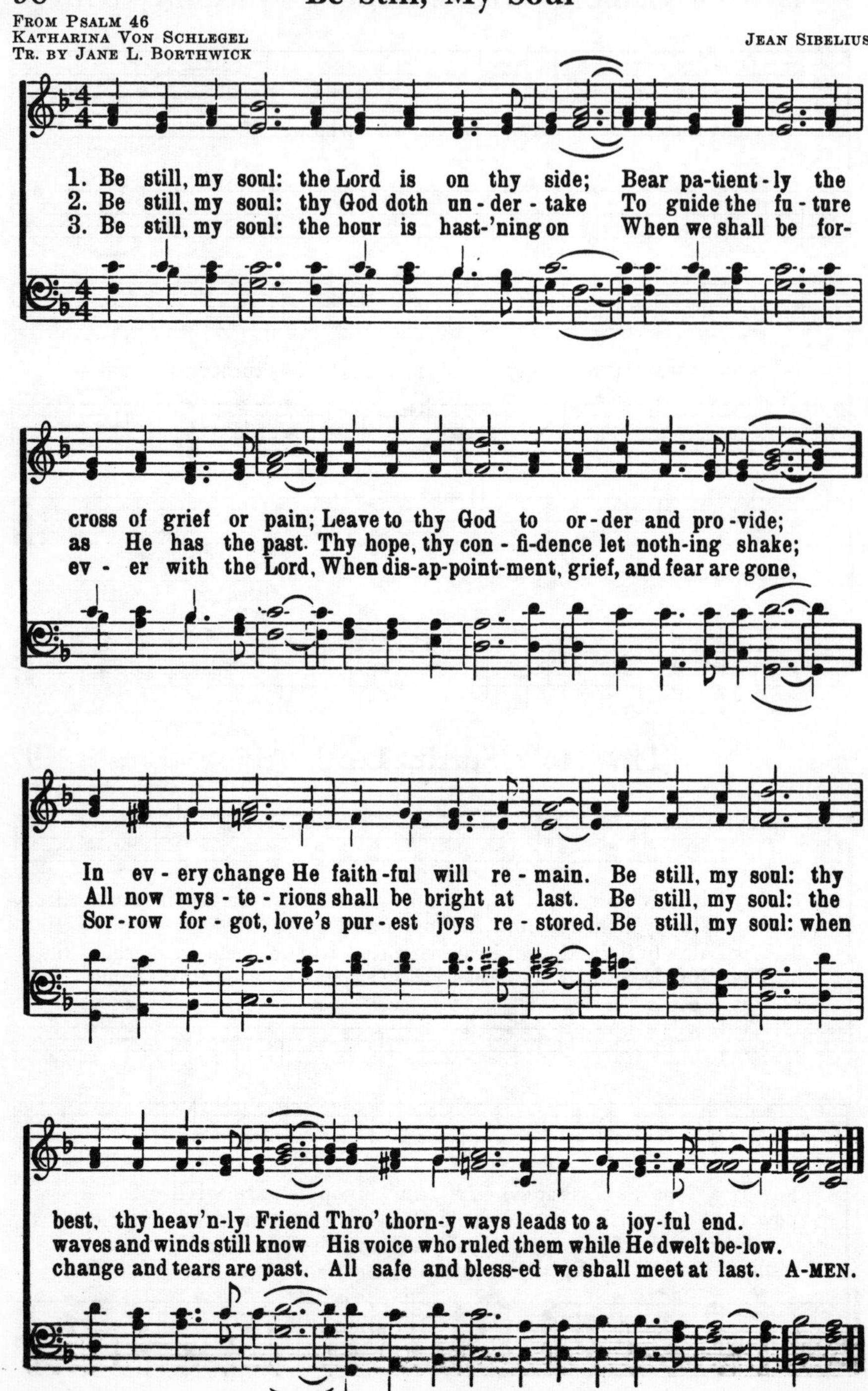

1. Be still, my soul: the Lord is on thy side; Bear pa-tient-ly the
2. Be still, my soul: thy God doth un-der-take To guide the fu-ture
3. Be still, my soul: the hour is hast-'ning on When we shall be for-
cross of grief or pain; Leave to thy God to or-der and pro-vide;
as He has the past. Thy hope, thy con-fi-dence let noth-ing shake;
ev-er with the Lord, When dis-ap-point-ment, grief, and fear are gone,
In ev-ery change He faith-ful will re-main. Be still, my soul: thy
All now mys-te-rious shall be bright at last. Be still, my soul: the
Sor-row for-got, love's pur-est joys re-stored. Be still, my soul: when
best, thy heav'n-ly Friend Thro' thorn-y ways leads to a joy-ful end.
waves and winds still know His voice who ruled them while He dwelt be-low.
change and tears are past. All safe and bless-ed we shall meet at last. A-MEN.

Sweet Peace, the Gift of God's Love

Peter P. Bilhorn — Peter P. Bilhorn

1. There comes to my heart one sweet strain, (sweet strain,) A glad and a joyous refrain; (re-frain;) I sing it again and again, Sweet peace, the gift of God's love.
2. Thro' Christ on the cross peace was made, (was made.) My debt by His death was all paid; (all paid;) No other foundation is laid For peace, the gift of God's love.
3. When Jesus as Lord I had crowned, (had crowned,) My heart with this peace did abound; (a-bound;) In Him the rich blessing I found, Sweet peace, the gift of God's love.
4. In Jesus for peace I abide, (a-bide,) And as I keep close to His side, (His side,) There's nothing but peace doth betide, Sweet peace, the gift of God's love.

Chorus

Peace, peace, sweet peace! Wonderful gift from above! (a-bove!)
cres.
Oh, wonderful, wonderful peace! Sweet peace, the gift of God's love!

100 Wonderful Peace

W. D. Cornell, Alt. W. G. Cooper

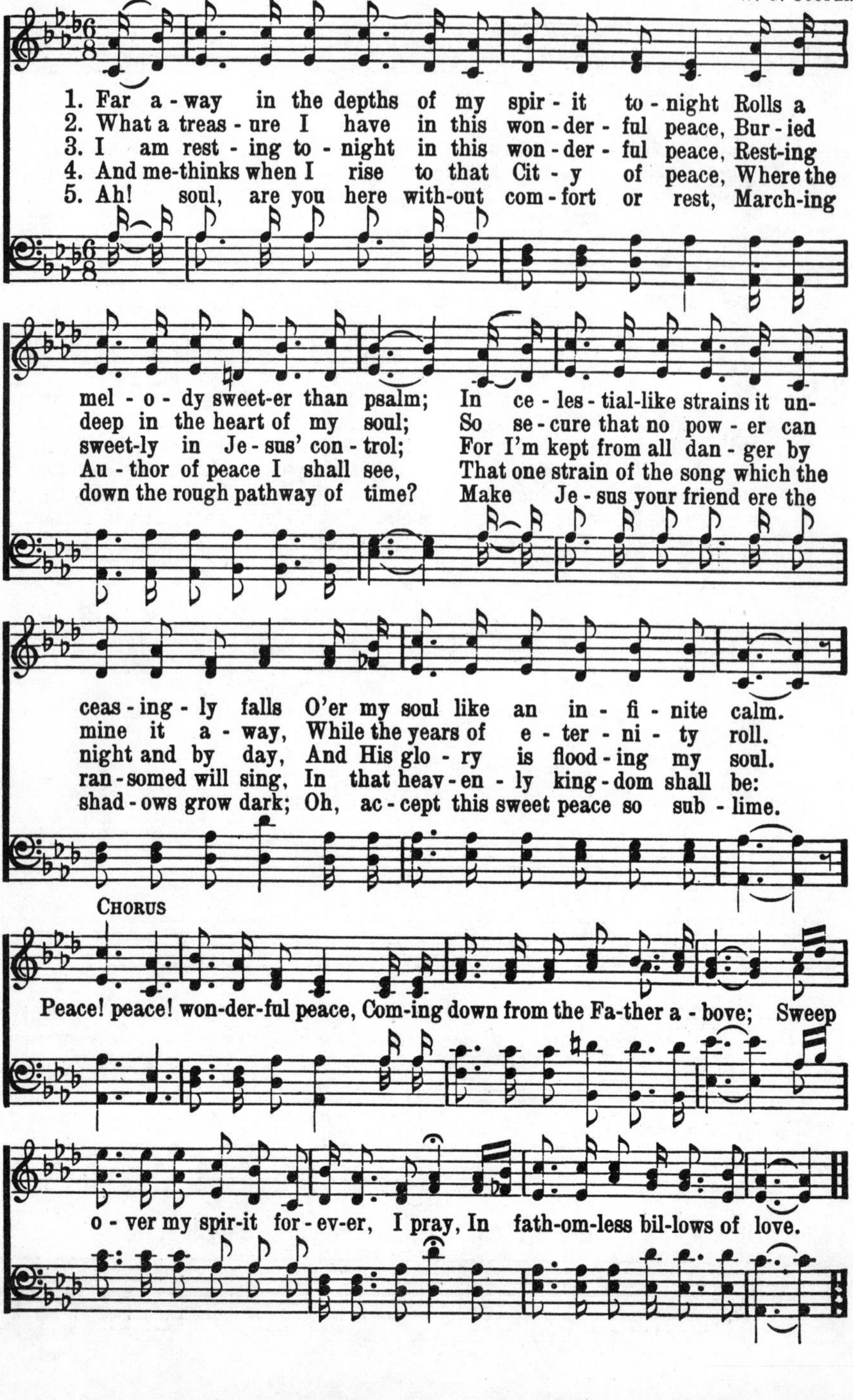

1. Far a - way in the depths of my spir - it to - night Rolls a
2. What a treas - ure I have in this won - der - ful peace, Bur - ied
3. I am rest - ing to - night in this won - der - ful peace, Rest-ing
4. And me-thinks when I rise to that Cit - y of peace, Where the
5. Ah! soul, are you here with-out com - fort or rest, March-ing

mel - o - dy sweet-er than psalm; In ce - les - tial-like strains it un-
deep in the heart of my soul; So se - cure that no pow - er can
sweet-ly in Je - sus' con - trol; For I'm kept from all dan - ger by
Au - thor of peace I shall see, That one strain of the song which the
down the rough pathway of time? Make Je - sus your friend ere the

ceas - ing - ly falls O'er my soul like an in - fi - nite calm.
mine it a - way, While the years of e - ter - ni - ty roll.
night and by day, And His glo - ry is flood - ing my soul.
ran - somed will sing, In that heav - en - ly king - dom shall be:
shad - ows grow dark; Oh, ac - cept this sweet peace so sub - lime.

Chorus

Peace! peace! won-der-ful peace, Com-ing down from the Fa-ther a - bove; Sweep
o - ver my spir-it for - ev-er, I pray, In fath-om-less bil-lows of love.

Wonderful Peace

Haldor Lillenas | Haldor Lillenas

1. Coming to Jesus, my Savior, I found Wonderful peace, wonderful peace; Storms in their fury may rage all around, I have peace, sweet peace.
2. Peace like a river, so deep and so broad, Wonderful peace, wonderful peace; Resting my soul on the bosom of God, I have peace, sweet peace.
3. Peace like a holy and infinite calm, Wonderful peace, wonderful peace; Like to the strains of an evening psalm, I have peace, sweet peace.
4. Gone is the battle that once raged within, Wonderful peace, wonderful peace; Jesus has saved me and cleansed me from sin, I have peace, sweet peace.
Refrain
Peace, peace, wonderful peace, Peace, peace, glorious peace; Since my Redeemer has ransomed my soul, I have peace, sweet peace. . . . . . .
wonderful peace.

102 Master, the Tempest Is Raging

MARY A. BAKER

HORATIUS R. PALMER
ARR. BY FRED JACKY

1. Mas - ter, the tem - pest is rag - ing! The bil - lows are toss - ing high!
2. Mas - ter, with an - guish of spir - it I bow in my grief to - day;
3. Mas - ter, the ter - ror is o - ver, The el - e-ments sweet - ly rest;

The sky is o'ershadowed with blackness, No shel - ter or help is nigh;
The depths of my sad heart are trou-bled; O wak - en and save, I pray!
Earth's sun in the calm lake is mir-rored, And heav-en's with-in my breast.

"Car - est Thou not that we per - ish?" How canst Thou lie a - sleep,
Tor - rents of sin and of an - guish Sweep o'er my sink - ing soul!
Lin - ger, O bless - ed Re - deem - er, Leave me a - lone no more;

When each moment so mad - ly is threat'ning A grave in the an - gry deep?
And I per - ish! I per - ish, dear Mas - ter; O has - ten, and take con - trol!
And with joy I shall make the blest har - bor, And rest on the bliss - ful shore.

Master, the Tempest Is Raging

Chorus
Solo
p Parts
pp
(Hum)
"The winds and the waves shall o - bey My will. Peace. . . be still!
Peace, be still! peace, be still!
(Hum)
Solo p cres - - - cen - - - do
(Hum)
Wheth-er the wrath of the storm-tossed sea, Or de - mons, or men, or what-
(Hum)
mf cres - Parts cen - - - do f
ev - er it be, No wa - ter can swal-low the ship where lies The Mas-ter of
ff f dim. p
o-cean and earth and skies; They all shall sweetly o - bey My will; Peace, be still!
pp f dim. pp ppp
Peace, be still! They all shall sweet-ly o - bey My will; Peace, peace, be still!"

103 Like a River Glorious
Frances R. Havergal
James Mountain
1. Like a riv-er glo-rious Is God's per-fect peace, O-ver all vic-to-rious In its bright in-crease; Per-fect, yet it flow-eth Full-er ev-ery day, Per-fect, yet it grow-eth Deep-er all the way.
2. Hid-den in the hol-low Of His bless-ed hand, Nev-er foe can fol-low, Nev-er trai-tor stand; Not a surge of wor-ry, Not a shade of care, Not a blast of hur-ry Touch the spir-it there.
3. Ev-ery joy or tri-al Fall-eth from a-bove, Traced up-on our di-al By the Sun of Love. We may trust Him ful-ly All for us to do; They who trust Him whol-ly Find Him whol-ly true.
Chorus.
Stayed up-on Je-ho-vah, Hearts are ful-ly blest; Find-ing, as He prom-ised, Per-fect peace and rest.
104 From Every Stormy Wind
Hugh Stowell
Thomas Hastings
1. From ev-'ry storm-y wind that blows, From ev-'ry swell-ing tide of woes,
2. There is a place where Je-sus sheds The oil of glad-ness on our heads;
3. There is a scene where spirits blend, Where friend holds fellowship with friend:
4. There, there on ea-gles' wings we soar, And sin and sense mo-lest no more,

From Every Stormy Wind

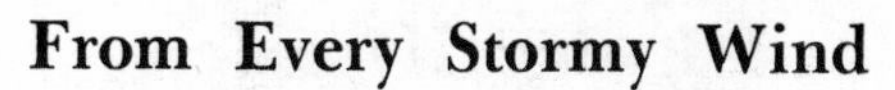

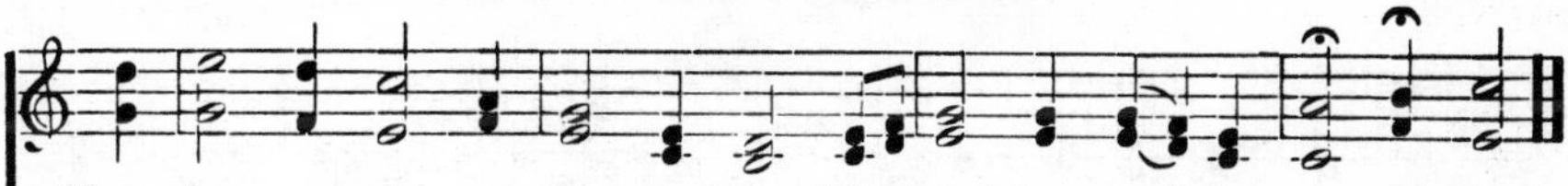

There is a calm, a sure re-treat: 'Tis found be-neath the mer-cy seat.
A place than all be-sides more sweet: It is the blood-bought mer-cy seat.
Tho' sun-dered far, by faith they meet A-round one com-mon mer-cy seat.
And heav'n comes down our souls to greet, When glo-ry crowns the mer-cy seat.

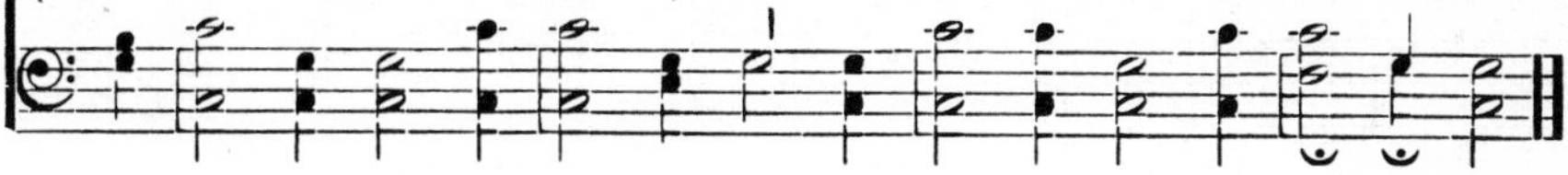

O Thou in Whose Presence 105

JOSEPH SWAIN FREEMAN LEWIS

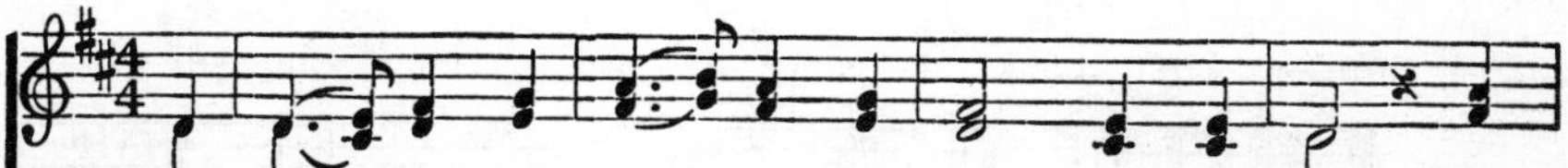

1. O Thou in whose pres-ence my soul takes de-light, On
2. Where dost Thou, dear Shep-herd, re-sort with Thy sheep, To
3. O why should I wan-der an a-lien from Thee, Or
4. Ye daughters of Zi-on, de-clare, have you seen The

whom in af-flic-tion I call, My com-fort by day, and my
feed them in pas-tures of love? Say, why in the val-ley of
cry in the des-ert for bread? Thy foes will re-joice when my
star that on Is-ra-el shone? Say, if in your tents my Be-

song in the night, My hope, my sal-va-tion, my all!
death should I weep, Or a-lone in this wil-der-ness rove?
sor-rows they see, And smile at the tears I have shed.
lov-ed has been, And where with His flocks He is gone.

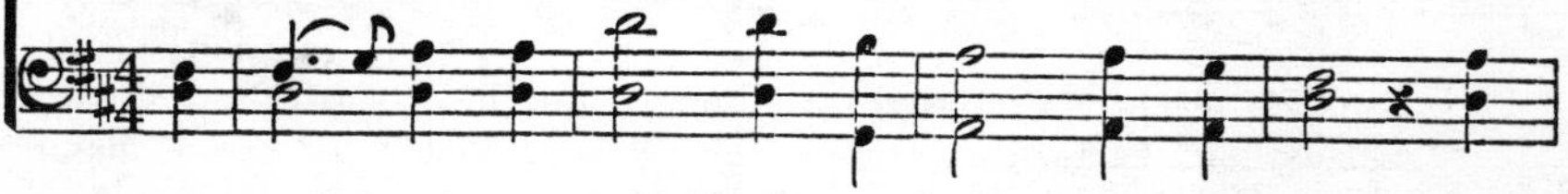

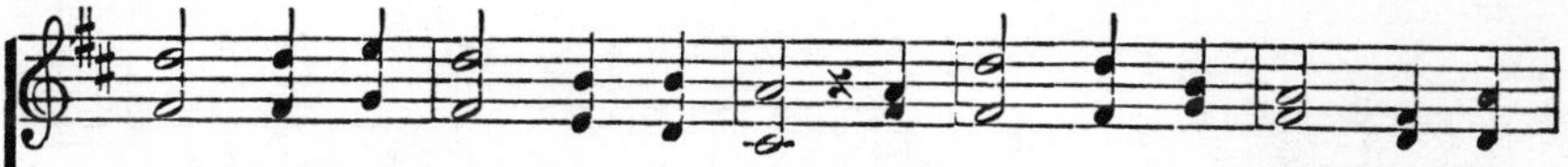

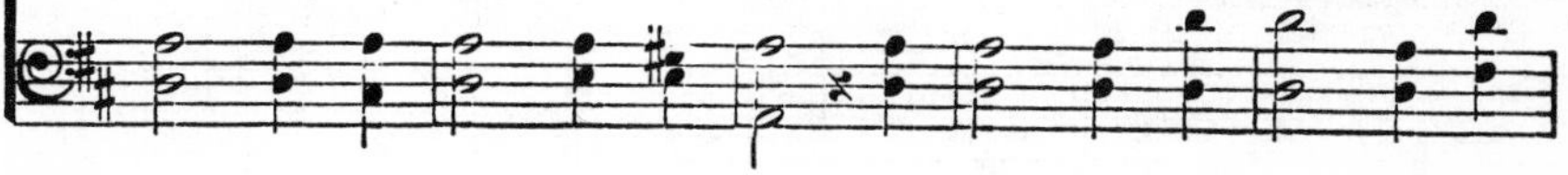

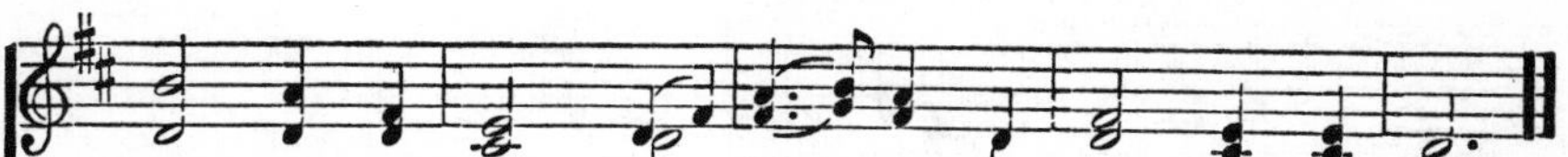

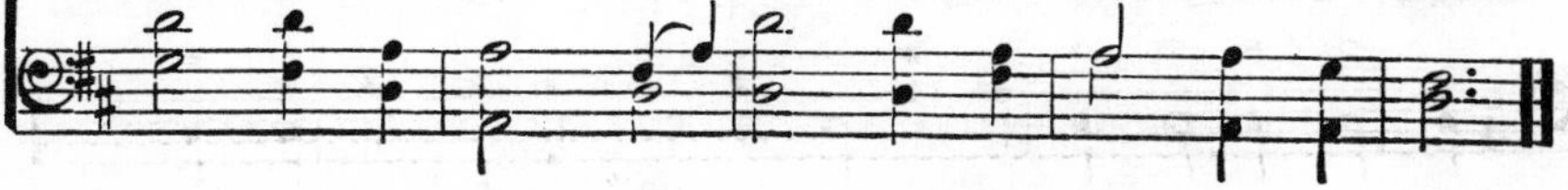

106 I'd Rather Have Jesus

RHEA F. MILLER — GEORGE BEVERLY SHEA

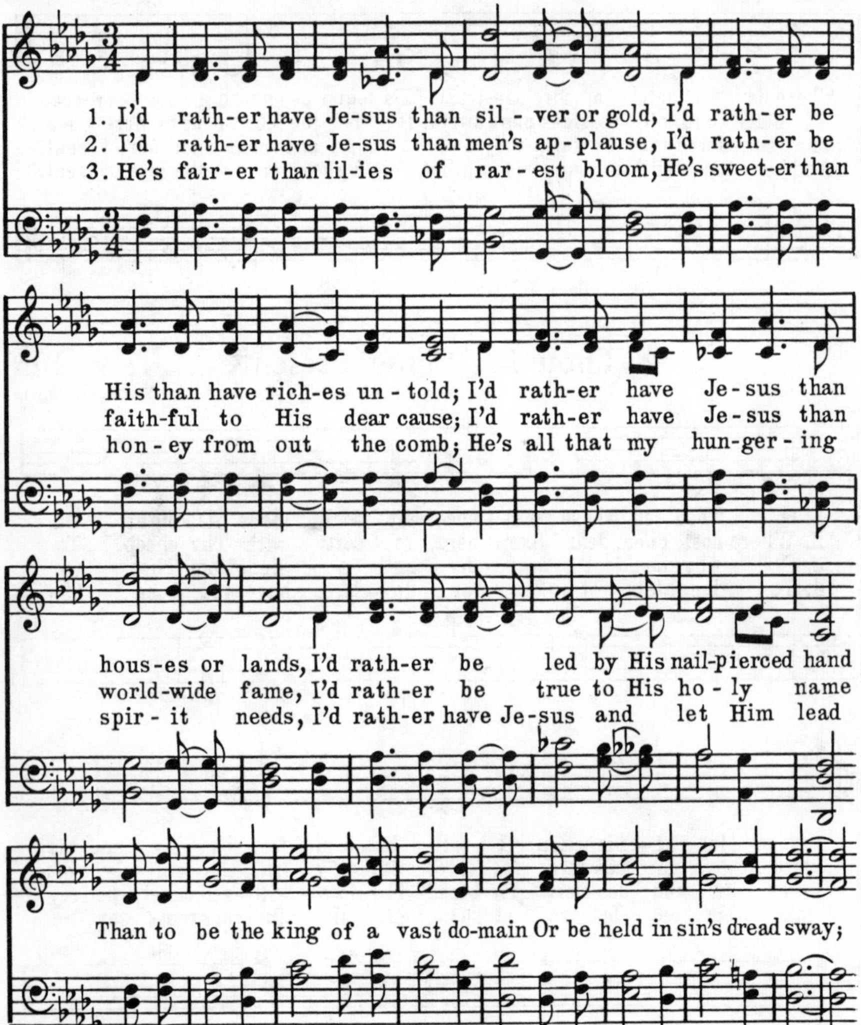

1. I'd rath-er have Je-sus than sil - ver or gold, I'd rath-er be
2. I'd rath-er have Je-sus than men's ap-plause, I'd rath-er be
3. He's fair-er than lil-ies of rar - est bloom, He's sweet-er than

His than have rich-es un - told; I'd rath-er have Je - sus than
faith-ful to His dear cause; I'd rath-er have Je - sus than
hon - ey from out the comb; He's all that my hun-ger - ing

hous-es or lands, I'd rath-er be led by His nail-pierced hand
world-wide fame, I'd rath-er be true to His ho - ly name
spir - it needs, I'd rath-er have Je-sus and let Him lead

Than to be the king of a vast do-main Or be held in sin's dread sway;

I'd rath-er have Je-sus than an-y-thing This world af-fords to-day.

107 And Can It Be That I Should Gain?

CHARLES WESLEY
THOMAS CAMPBELL
1. And can it be that I should gain An interest in the Saviour's blood? Died He for me, who caused His pain? For me, who Him to death pursued? Amazing love! how can it be That Thou, my God, shouldst die for me?
2. He left His Father's throne above, So free, so infinite His grace; Emptied Himself of all but love, And bled for Adam's helpless race; 'Tis mercy all, immense and free; For, O my God, it found out me.
3. Long my imprisoned spirit lay Fast bound in sin and nature's night; Thine eye diffused a quick'ning ray, I woke, the dungeon flamed with light; My chains fell off, my heart was free; I rose, went forth, and followed Thee.
REFRAIN
Amazing love! how can it be That Thou, my God, shouldst die for me.
Amazing love! How can it be That Thou, my God,

108 Blessed Quietness

Manie P. Ferguson

W. S. Marshall
Arr. by James M. Kirk

1. Joys are flow-ing like a riv - er, Since the Com - fort - er has come;
2. Bring-ing life and health and glad-ness, All a - round this heav'nly Guest,
3. Like the rain that falls from heav - en, Like the sun-light from the sky,
4. See, a fruit - ful field is grow-ing, Bless - ed fruit of right-eous-ness;
5. What a won - der - ful sal - va - tion, Where we al - ways see His face!

He a - bides with us for - ev - er, Makes the trust - ing heart His home.
Ban-ished un - be - lief and sad-ness, Changed our wea - ri - ness to rest.
So the Ho - ly Ghost is giv - en, Com - ing on us from on high.
And the streams of life are flow-ing In the lone - ly wil-der-ness.
What a per - fect hab - i - ta - tion, What a qui - et rest-ing place!

Refrain

Bless-ed qui - et - ness, ho - ly qui - et - ness, What as-sur - ance in my soul!

rit.

On the storm-y sea, He speaks peace to me, How the bil-lows cease to roll!

I Am Praying for You

109

S. O'Malley Cluff

Ira D. Sankey

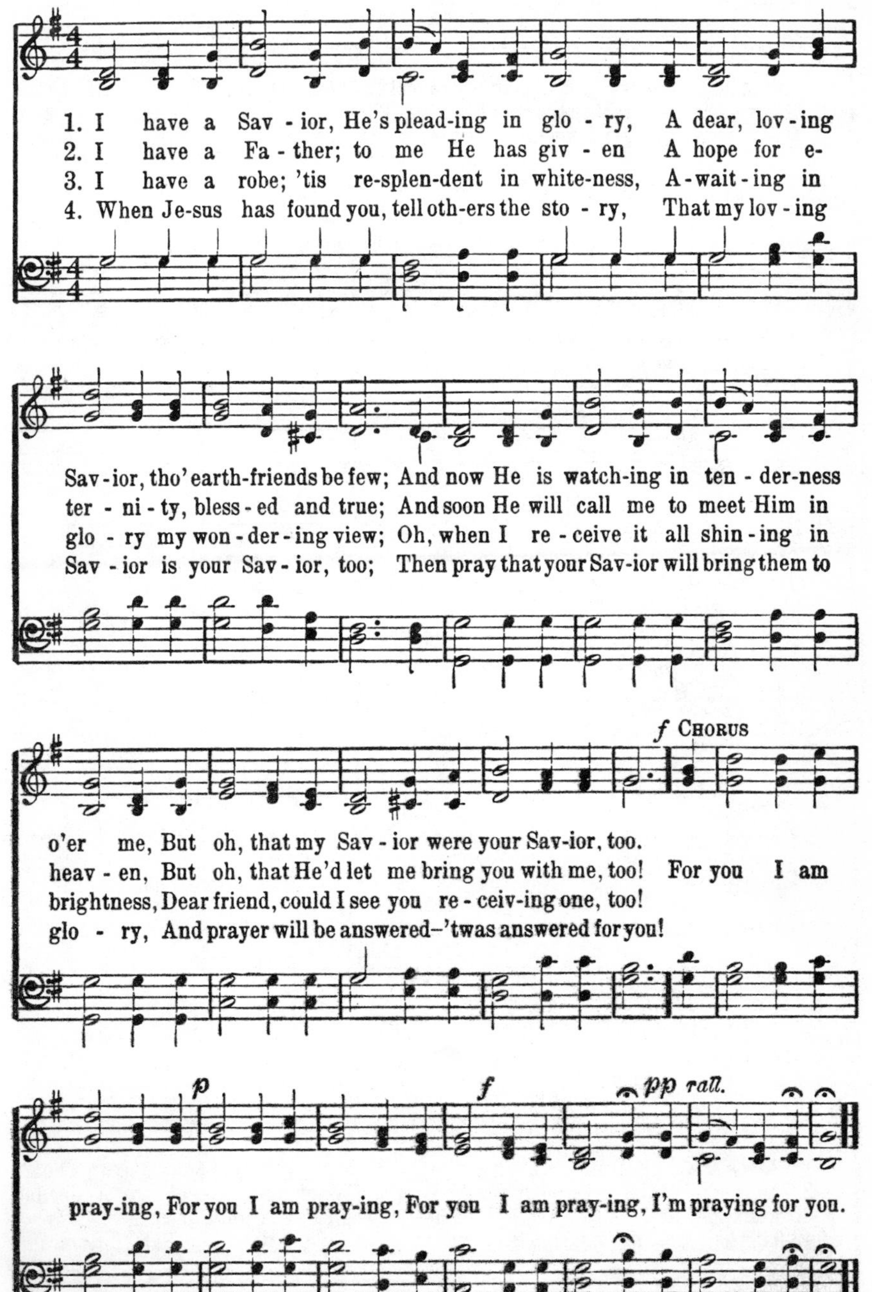
1. I have a Sav - ior, He's plead-ing in glo - ry, A dear, lov - ing
2. I have a Fa - ther; to me He has giv - en A hope for e-
3. I have a robe; 'tis re-splen-dent in white-ness, A-wait - ing in
4. When Je-sus has found you, tell oth-ers the sto - ry, That my lov - ing
Sav - ior, tho' earth-friends be few; And now He is watch-ing in ten - der-ness
ter - ni - ty, bless - ed and true; And soon He will call me to meet Him in
glo - ry my won - der - ing view; Oh, when I re - ceive it all shin - ing in
Sav - ior is your Sav - ior, too; Then pray that your Sav-ior will bring them to
f Chorus
o'er me, But oh, that my Sav - ior were your Sav-ior, too.
heav - en, But oh, that He'd let me bring you with me, too! For you I am
brightness, Dear friend, could I see you re - ceiv-ing one, too!
glo - ry, And prayer will be answered—'twas answered for you!
p
f
pp rall.
pray-ing, For you I am pray-ing, For you I am pray-ing, I'm praying for you.

110 Sweet Hour of Prayer
William W. Walford
William B. Bradbury
1. Sweet hour of prayer! sweet hour of prayer! That calls me from a world of care,
2. Sweet hour of prayer! sweet hour of prayer! Thy wings shall my pe - ti - tion bear
3. Sweet hour of prayer! sweet hour of prayer! May I thy con - so - la - tion share,
And bids me at my Fa-ther's throne Make all my wants and wish - es known;
To Him whose truth and faith-ful-ness En-gage the wait-ing soul to bless;
Till, from Mount Pisgah's loft - y height, I view my home, and take my flight:
In sea - sons of dis-tress and grief, My soul has oft - en found re - lief,
And since He bids me seek His face, Be-lieve His word and trust His grace,
This robe of flesh I'll drop, and rise To seize the ev - er - last - ing prize;
And oft es - caped the tempter's snare By thy re-turn, sweet hour of prayer.
I'll cast on Him my ev - 'ry care, And wait for thee, sweet hour of prayer.
And shout, while passing thro' the air, Farewell, farewell, sweet hour of prayer.
111 Jesus, and Shall It Ever Be?
Joseph Grigg
Alt. by Benjamin Francis
Henry K. Oliver
1. Je - sus, and shall it ev - er be, A mor - tal man a-shamed of Thee?
2. A-shamed of Je - sus! that dear Friend On Whom my hopes of heav'n depend!
3. A-shamed of Je - sus! yes, I may, When I've no guilt to wash a - way;
4. Till then—nor is my boast-ing vain— Till then I boast a Sav - ior slain;

Jesus, and Shall It Ever Be?

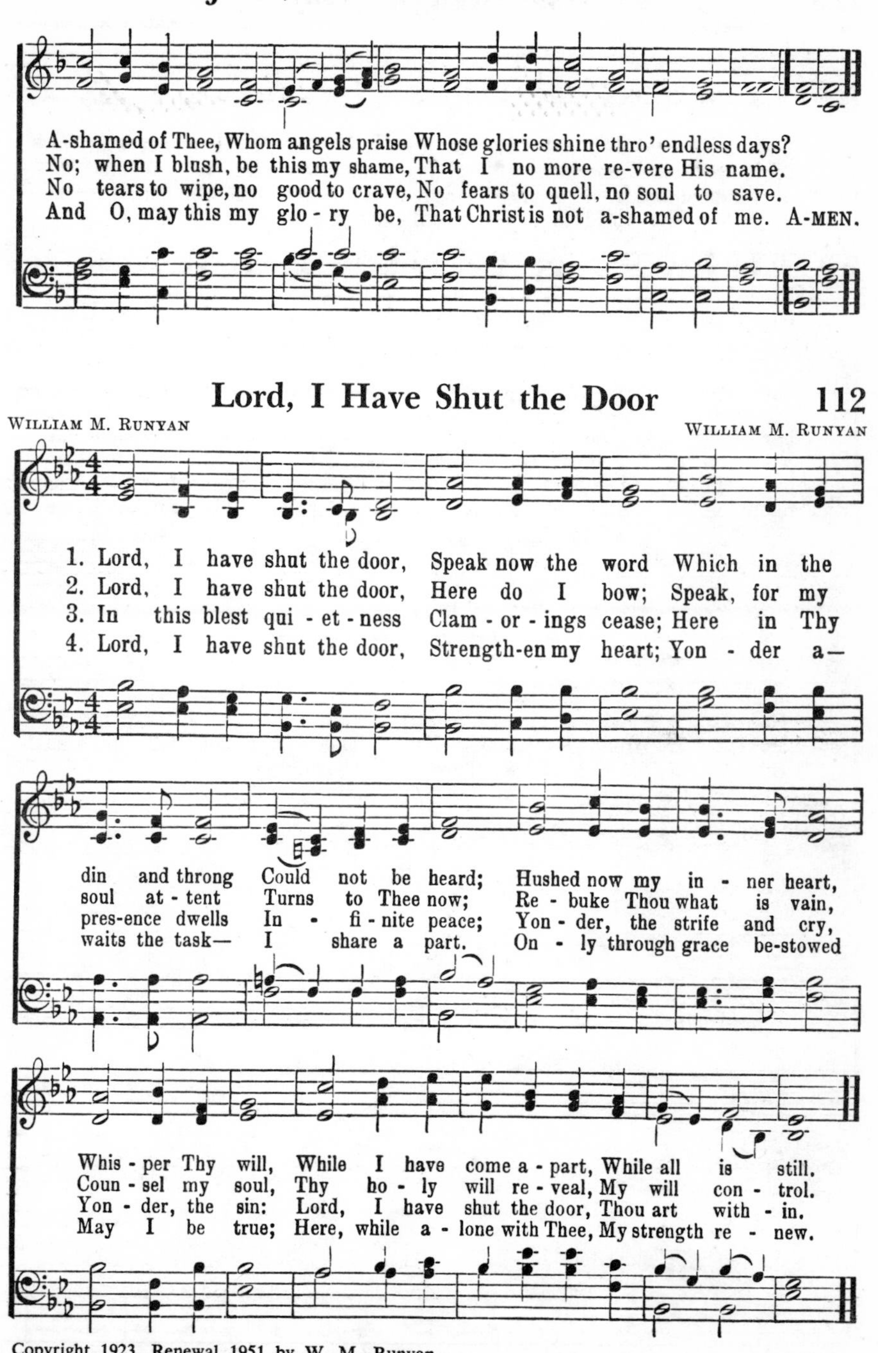
A-shamed of Thee, Whom angels praise Whose glories shine thro' endless days?
No; when I blush, be this my shame, That I no more re-vere His name.
No tears to wipe, no good to crave, No fears to quell, no soul to save.
And O, may this my glo - ry be, That Christ is not a-shamed of me. A-MEN.
Lord, I Have Shut the Door
112
WILLIAM M. RUNYAN
WILLIAM M. RUNYAN
1. Lord, I have shut the door, Speak now the word Which in the
2. Lord, I have shut the door, Here do I bow; Speak, for my
3. In this blest qui - et - ness Clam - or - ings cease; Here in Thy
4. Lord, I have shut the door, Strength-en my heart; Yon - der a—
din and throng Could not be heard; Hushed now my in - ner heart,
soul at - tent Turns to Thee now; Re - buke Thou what is vain,
pres-ence dwells In - fi - nite peace; Yon - der, the strife and cry,
waits the task— I share a part. On - ly through grace be-stowed
Whis - per Thy will, While I have come a - part, While all is still.
Coun - sel my soul, Thy ho - ly will re - veal, My will con - trol.
Yon - der, the sin: Lord, I have shut the door, Thou art with - in.
May I be true; Here, while a - lone with Thee, My strength re - new.

113 I Must Tell Jesus

ELISHA A. HOFFMAN — ELISHA A. HOFFMAN

1. I must tell Je - sus all of my tri - als; I can - not bear these bur - dens a - lone; In my dis - tress He kind - ly will help me; He ev - er loves and cares for His own.
2. I must tell Je - sus all of my troub - les; He is a kind, com - pas - sion - ate Friend; If I but ask Him, He will de - liv - er, Make of my troub - les quick - ly an end.
3. Tempted and tried I need a great Sav - ior, One who can help my bur - dens to bear; I must tell Je - sus, I must tell Je - sus; He all my cares and sor - rows will share.
4. O how the world to e - vil al - lures me! O how my heart is tempt - ed to sin! I must tell Je - sus, and He will help me O - ver the world the vic - t'ry to win.
CHORUS
I must tell Je - sus! I must tell Je - sus! I can - not bear my bur - dens a - lone; I must tell Je - sus! I must tell Je - sus! Je - sus can help me, Je - sus a - lone.

Revive Thy Work

ALFRED MIDLANE JAMES MCGRANAHAN

1. Re - vive Thy work, O Lord! Thy might - y arm make bare;
2. Re - vive Thy work, O Lord! Dis - turb this sleep of death;
3. Re - vive Thy work, O Lord! Cre - ate soul-thirst for Thee;
4. Re - vive Thy work, O Lord! Ex - alt Thy pre - cious name;
Speak with the voice that wakes the dead, And make Thy peo - ple hear.
Quick - en the smoul-d'ring em - bers now By Thine al - might - y breath.
But hun-g'ring for the bread of life, Oh, may our spir - its be!
And, by the Ho - ly Ghost, our love For Thee and Thine in - flame.
CHORUS
Re - vive! . . . re - vive! . . . And give re - fresh-ing show'rs;
Re - vive Thy work! re - vive Thy work! And give, oh, give re - fresh - ing show'rs;
The glo - ry shall be all Thine own; The bless-ing shall be ours.

115 Teach Me to Pray

ALBERT S. REITZ — ALBERT S. REITZ

1. Teach me to pray, Lord, teach me to pray; This is my heart-cry, day unto day; I long to know Thy will and Thy way; Teach me to pray, Lord, teach me to pray.
2. Power in prayer, Lord, power in prayer, Here 'mid earth's sin and sorrow and care; Men lost and dying, souls in despair: O give me power, power in prayer!
3. My weakened will, Lord, Thou canst renew; My sinful nature Thou canst subdue; Fill me just now with power anew. Power to pray and power to do!
4. Teach me to pray, Lord, teach me to pray; Thou art my Pattern, day unto day; Thou art my Surety, now and for aye; Teach me to pray, Lord, teach me to pray.
CHORUS
Living in Thee, Lord, and Thou in me; Constant abiding, this is my plea; Grant me Thy power, boundless and free: Power with men and power with Thee.

Tell It to Jesus 116

Jeremiah E. Rankin — Edmund S. Lorenz

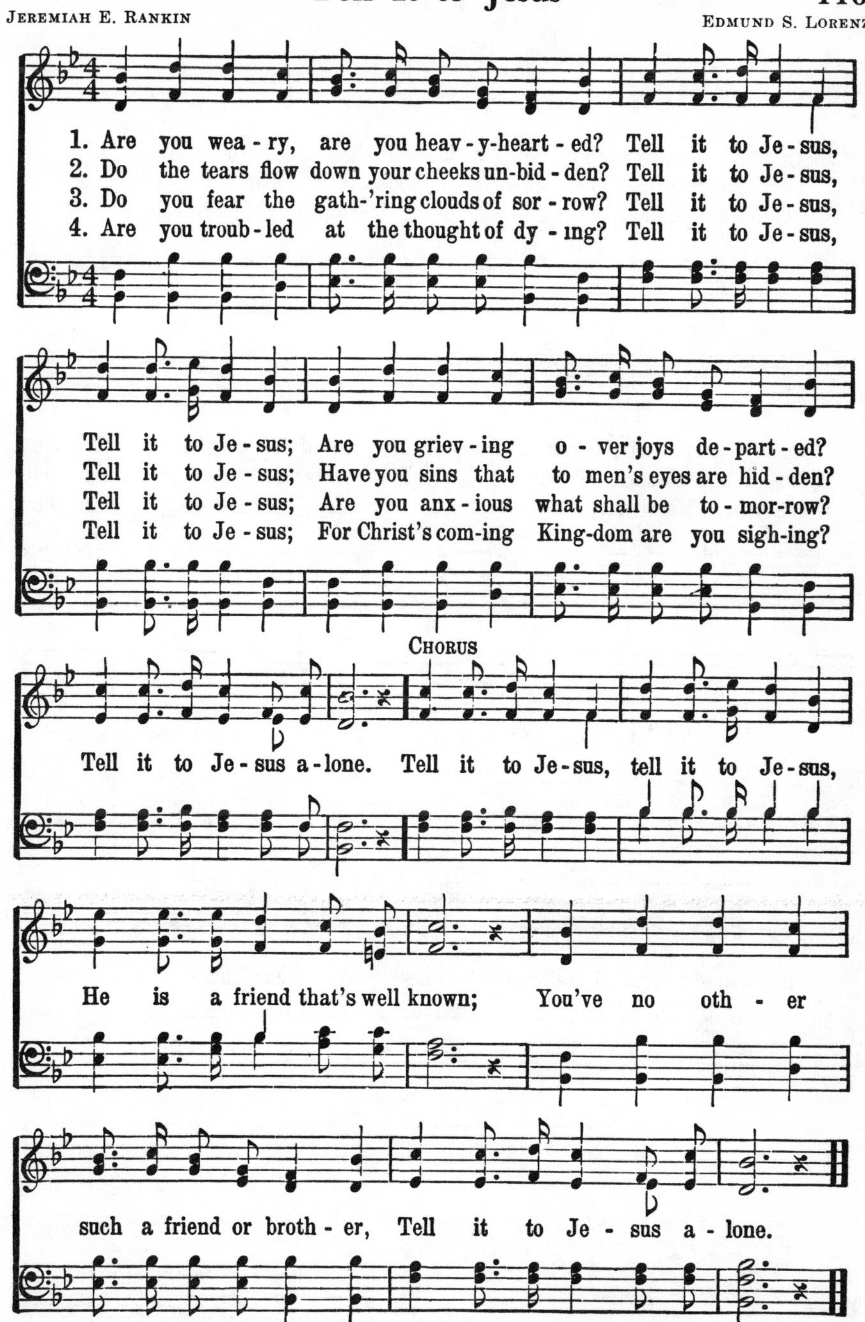
1. Are you wea - ry, are you heav - y-heart - ed? Tell it to Je - sus,
2. Do the tears flow down your cheeks un-bid - den? Tell it to Je - sus,
3. Do you fear the gath-'ring clouds of sor - row? Tell it to Je - sus,
4. Are you troub - led at the thought of dy - ing? Tell it to Je - sus,
Tell it to Je - sus; Are you griev - ing o - ver joys de - part - ed?
Tell it to Je - sus; Have you sins that to men's eyes are hid - den?
Tell it to Je - sus; Are you anx - ious what shall be to - mor-row?
Tell it to Je - sus; For Christ's com-ing King-dom are you sigh-ing?
CHORUS
Tell it to Je - sus a - lone. Tell it to Je - sus, tell it to Je - sus,
He is a friend that's well known; You've no oth - er
such a friend or broth - er, Tell it to Je - sus a - lone.

117 The Beautiful Garden of Prayer

ELEANOR A. SCHROLL | JAMES H. FILLMORE

1. There's a gar-den where Je-sus is wait-ing, There's a place that is
2. There's a gar-den where Je-sus is wait-ing, And I go with my
3. There's a gar-den where Je-sus is wait-ing, And He bids you to

won-drous-ly fair; For it glows with the light of His pres-ence, 'Tis the
bur-den and care, Just to learn from His lips words of com-fort In the
come meet Him there; Just to bow, and re-ceive a new bless-ing, In the

beau-ti-ful gar-den of prayer.

REFRAIN

O the beau-ti-ful gar-den, the gar-den of prayer, O the beau-ti-ful gar-den of prayer; There my Sav-ior a-waits, and He o-pens the gates To the beau-ti-ful gar-den of prayer.

'Tis the Blessed Hour of Prayer

FANNY J. CROSBY — WILLIAM H. DOANE

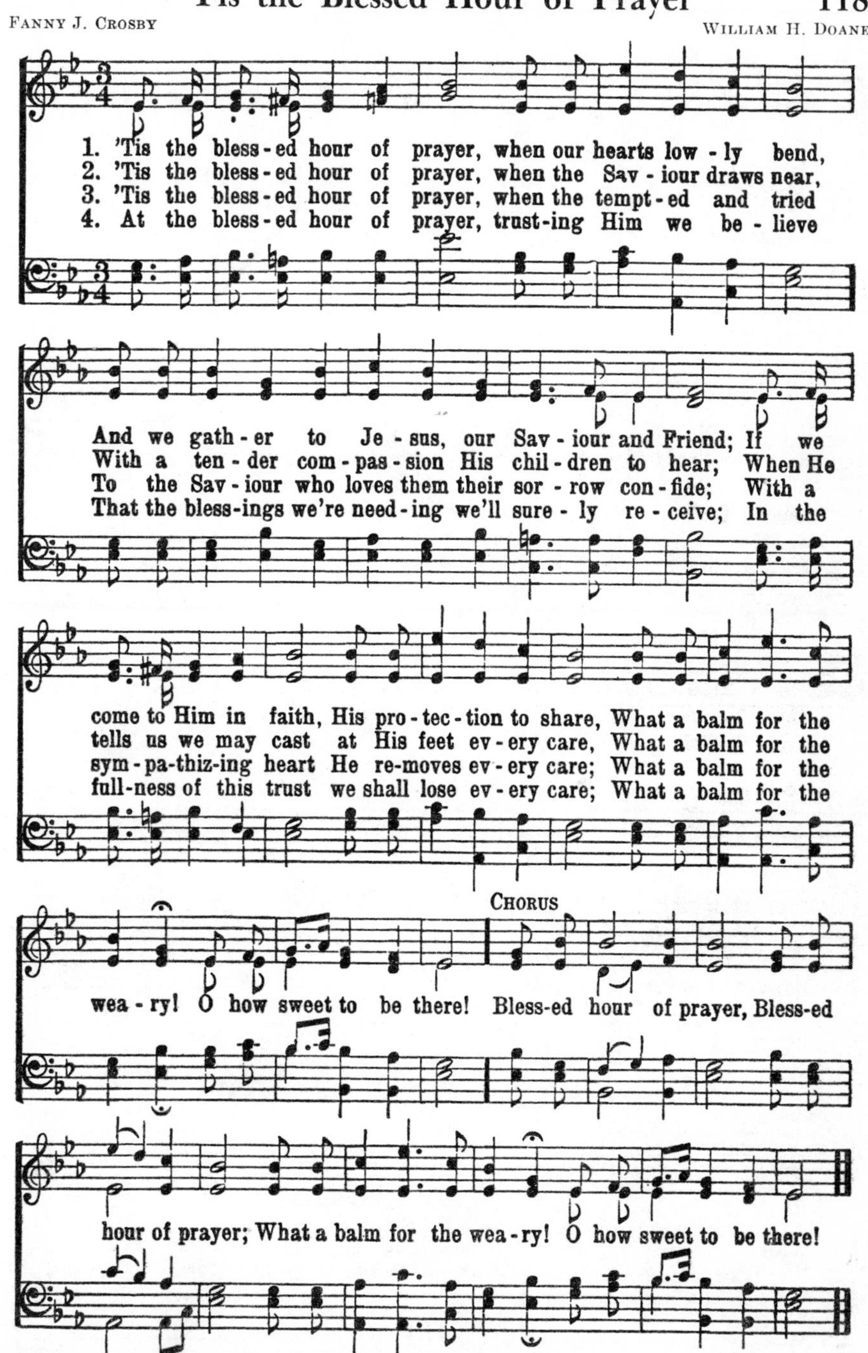
1. 'Tis the bless-ed hour of prayer, when our hearts low-ly bend,
2. 'Tis the bless-ed hour of prayer, when the Sav-iour draws near,
3. 'Tis the bless-ed hour of prayer, when the tempt-ed and tried
4. At the bless-ed hour of prayer, trust-ing Him we be-lieve
And we gath-er to Je-sus, our Sav-iour and Friend; If we
With a ten-der com-pas-sion His chil-dren to hear; When He
To the Sav-iour who loves them their sor-row con-fide; With a
That the bless-ings we're need-ing we'll sure-ly re-ceive; In the
come to Him in faith, His pro-tec-tion to share, What a balm for the
tells us we may cast at His feet ev-ery care, What a balm for the
sym-pa-thiz-ing heart He re-moves ev-ery care; What a balm for the
full-ness of this trust we shall lose ev-ery care; What a balm for the
CHORUS
wea-ry! O how sweet to be there! Bless-ed hour of prayer, Bless-ed
hour of prayer; What a balm for the wea-ry! O how sweet to be there!

119 Did You Think to Pray?

MRS. M. A. KIDDER — W. O. PERKINS

1. Ere you left your room this morning, Did you think to pray? In the name of
2. When you met with great temp-ta-tion, Did you think to pray? By His dy - ing
3. When your heart was filled with an-ger, Did you think to pray? Did you plead for
4. When sore tri - als came up - on you, Did you think to pray? When your soul was

Christ our Sav - ior, Did you sue for lov - ing fa - vor, As a shield to - day?
love and mer - it, Did you claim the Ho-ly Spir - it As your guide and stay?
grace, my broth-er, That you might forgive an-oth - er Who had crossed your way?
bowed in sor - row, Balm of Gil-ead did you bor - row, At the gates of day?

D. S.—*So in sor-row and in glad - ness, Don't for-get to pray.*

CHORUS

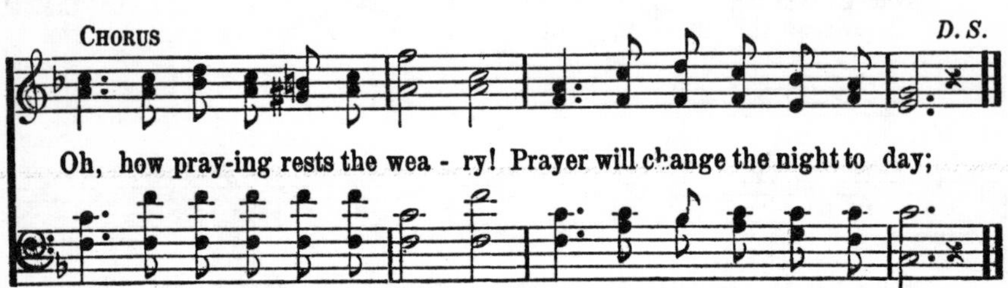

Oh, how pray-ing rests the wea - ry! Prayer will change the night to day;

120 Work, for the Night Is Coming

ANNA L. WALKER — LOWELL MASON

1. Work, for the night is com-ing, Work thro' the morning hours; Work while the dew is
2. Work, for the night is com-ing, Work thro' the sun-ny noon; Fill brightest hours with
3. Work, for the night is com-ing, Un - der the sun - set skies; While their bright tints are

Work, for the Night Is Coming

sparkling; Work, 'mid springing flow'rs. Work, when the day grows bright-er,
la - bor, Rest comes sure and soon. Give ev - 'ry fly - ing min - ute
glow - ing, Work, for day-light flies. Work till the last beam fad - eth,
cres.
Work in the glow-ing sun; Work, for the night is coming, When man's work is done.
Something to keep in store; Work, for the night is coming, When man works no more.
Fad-eth to shine no more; Work, while the night is dark'ning, When man's work is o'er.
Praise Ye the Father
121
Author Unknown
Friedrich F. Flemming
1. Praise ye the Fa - ther! for His lov - ing kind-ness, Ten - der - ly
2. Praise ye the Sav - iour! great is His com - pas - sion, Gra - cious - ly
3. Praise ye the Spir - it! Com-fort - er of Is - rael, Sent of the
cares He for His err - ing chil - dren; Praise Him, ye an - gels,
cares He for His cho - sen peo - ple; Young men and maid - ens,
Fa - ther and the Son to bless us; Praise ye the Fa - ther,
praise Him in the heav-ens, Praise ye Je - ho - vah!
ye old men and chil - dren, Praise ye the Sav - iour!
Son and Ho - ly Spir - it, Praise ye the Tri - une God! A-men.

122 Unto the Hills

JOHN D. S. CAMPBELL
FROM PSALM 121 CHARLES H. PURDAY

1. Un - to the hills a - round do I lift up My long-ing eyes;
2. He will not suf - fer that thy foot be moved: Safe shalt thou be.
3. Je - ho - vah is Him-self thy keep-er true, Thy change-less shade;
4. From ev-ery e - vil shall He keep thy soul, From ev - ery sin;
O whence for me shall my sal-va-tion come, From whence a-rise? From God, the
No care-less slum-ber shall His eye-lids close, Who keep-eth thee. Be-hold, He
Je-ho-vah thy de-fense on thy right hand Him-self hath made. And thee no
Je-ho-vah shall pre-serve thy go-ing out, Thy com-ing in. A-bove thee
Lord, doth come my cer-tain aid, From God, the Lord, who heav'n and earth hath made.
sleep-eth not, He slumbereth ne'er, Who keep-eth Is-rael in His ho - ly care.
sun by day shall ev-er smite; No moon shall harm thee in the si - lent night.
watch-ing, He whom we a-dore Shall keep thee hence-forth, yea, for-ev-er - more.

123 Come, We That Love the Lord

ISAAC WATTS AARON WILLIAMS

1. Come, we that love the Lord, And let our joys be known; Join
2. Let those re-fuse to sing Who nev - er knew our God; But
3. The hill of Zi - on yields A thou-sand sa - cred sweets Be -
4. Then let our songs a - bound, And ev - ery tear be dry; We're

Come, We That Love the Lord
in a song with sweet ac-cord, And thus sur-round the throne.
chil-dren of the heaven-ly King May speak their joys a-broad.
fore we reach the heaven-ly fields, Or walk the gold-en streets.
march-ing thro' Em-man-uel's ground To fair-er worlds on high. A-MEN.
Teach Me Thy Will, O Lord
124
KATHERINE A. GRIMES
WILLIAM M. RUNYAN
1. Teach me Thy will, O Lord, Teach me Thy way; Teach me to
2. Teach me Thy won-drous grace, Bound-less and free; Lord, let Thy
3. Teach me by pain Thy power, Teach me by love; Teach me to
4. Teach Thou my lips to sing, My heart to praise; Be Thou my
know Thy word, Teach me to pray. What-e'er seems best to Thee, That be my
bless-ed face Shine up-on me. Heal Thou sin's ev-ery smart, Dwell Thou with-
know, each hour, Thou art a-bove. Teach me as seem-eth best In Thee to
Lord and King Through all my days. Teach Thou my soul to cry, "Be Thou, dear
ear-nest plea; So that Thou draw-est me Clos-er each day.
in my heart; Grant that I nev-er part, Sav-iour, from Thee.
find sweet rest; Lean-ing up-on Thy breast, All doubt re-move.
Sav-iour, nigh, Teach me to live, to die, Saved by Thy grace." A-MEN.

125 Sweet Will of God

LEILA N. MORRIS

LEILA N. MORRIS

DUET

1. My stub-born will at last hath yield-ed; I would be Thine, and
2. I'm tired of sin, foot-sore and wea-ry, The dark-some path hath
3. Thy pre-cious will, O con-qu'ring Sav-ior, Doth now em-brace and
4. Shut in with Thee, O Lord, for-ev-er, My way-ward feet no

Thine a-lone; And this the prayer my lips are bring-ing,
drear-y grown, But now a light has ris'n to cheer me;
com-pass me; All dis-cords hushed, my peace a riv-er,
more to roam; What pow'r from Thee my soul can sev-er?

rit.

"Lord, let in me Thy will be done."
I find in Thee my Star, my Sun.
My soul a pris-oned bird set free.
The cen-ter of God's will my home.

CHORUS

Sweet will of God, still fold me clos-er, Till I am whol-ly lost in Thee; Sweet will of God, still fold me clos-er, Till I am whol-ly lost in Thee.

We're Marching to Zion

Isaac Watts — Robert Lowry

Spirited
1. Come, we that love the Lord, And let our joys be known, Join
2. Let those re - fuse to sing Who nev - er knew our God; But
3. The hill of Zi - on yields A thou - sand sa - cred sweets Be-
4. Then let our songs a - bound, And ev - 'ry tear be dry; We're
in a song with sweet ac - cord, Join in a song with sweet ac-cord, And
chil-dren of the heav'n-ly King, But chil-dren of the heav'n-ly King, May
fore we reach the heav'n-ly fields, Be - fore we reach the heav'n-ly fields, Or
marching thro' Immanuel's ground, We're marching thro' Immanuel's ground, To
thus sur - - round the throne, And thus sur-round the throne.
speak their joys a - broad, May speak their joys a - broad.
walk the gold - en streets, Or walk the gold - en streets.
fair - - er worlds on high, To fair - er worlds on high.
thus sur-round the throne, And thus sur - round the throne.
Chorus
We're march - ing to Zi - on, Beau-ti - ful, beau-ti - ful Zi - on; We're
We're march-ing on to Zi - on,
march-ing up-ward to Zi - on, The beau-ti - ful cit - y of God.
Zi - on, Zi - on,

127 To God Be the Glory

FANNY J. CROSBY WILLIAM H. DOANE

1. To God be the glo-ry — great things He hath done, So loved He the world that He
2. O per - fect re-demp-tion, the purchase of blood! To ev - 'ry be-liev - er the
3. Great things He hath taught us, great things He hath done, And great our rejoicing thro'
gave us His Son, Who yield-ed His life an a-tone-ment for sin And o-pened the
prom-ise of God; The vil - est of-fend-er who tru-ly be-lieves, That moment from
Je - sus the Son; But pu - rer and higher and greater will be Our won-der, our
CHORUS
Life-gate that all may go in.
Je - sus a par-don receives. Praise the Lord, praise the Lord, Let the earth hear His
transport, when Jesus we see.
voice! Praise the Lord, praise the Lord, Let the peo-ple re - joice! O come to the
Fa-ther thro' Je-sus the Son, And give Him the glo-ry — great things He hath done.

Blessed Redeemer 128

Avis B. Christiansen | Harry D. Loes

1. Up Cal-vary's mountain one dreadful morn, Walked Christ my Saviour, weary and worn;
2. "Fa-ther, forgive them!" thus did He pray, E'en while His life-blood flowed fast a-way;
3. O how I love Him, Sav-iour and Friend, How can my prais-es ev - er find end!
Fac-ing for sin-ners death on the cross, That He might save them from endless loss.
Pray-ing for sin-ners while in such woe— No one but Je - sus ev - er loved so.
Thro' years un-num-bered on heaven's shore, My tongue shall praise Him for-ev-er-more.
Chorus
Bless-ed Re-deem - er! pre-cious Re-deem - er! Seems now I
Bless-ed Re-deem-er! bless-ed Re-deem-er!
see Him on Cal-va-ry's tree; Wound-ed and bleed - ing, for sin-ners
Wound-ed and bleed-ing,
plead - ing— Blind and un-heed - - ing— dy-ing for me!
for sin-ners plead-ing— Blind and un-heed - ing—

129 Arise, My Soul, Arise!

Charles Wesley — Lewis Edson

1. A - rise, my soul, a - rise, Shake off thy guilt-y fears; The bleed - ing
2. He ev - er lives a - bove, For me to in - ter - cede, His all - re-
3. Five bleeding wounds He bears, Re-ceived on Cal - va - ry; They pour ef-
4. My God is rec - on - ciled; His par-d'ning voice I hear; He owns me

Sac - ri - fice In my be - half ap-pears; Be- fore the throne my Surety stands,
deem-ing love, His pre-cious blood to plead; His blood a - toned for all our race,
fectual prayers, They strongly plead for me: "For-give him, O for-give," they cry,
for His child; I can no lon - ger fear; With con-fi - dence I now draw nigh,

Be-fore the throne my Surety stands: My name is writ-ten on His hands.
His blood a-toned for all our race, And sprinkles now the throne of grace.
"For - give him, O forgive," they cry, "Nor let that ransomed sin - ner die!"
With con -fi-dence I now draw nigh, And, "Father, Ab-ba, Fa - ther," cry. A-MEN.

130 Majestic Sweetness Sits Enthroned

Samuel Stennett — Thomas Hastings

1. Ma - jes-tic sweetness sits enthroned Up - on the Sav-ior's brow; His head with
2. No mor-tal can with Him compare, A-mong the sons of men; Fair-er is
3. He saw me plunged in deep distress, And flew to my re - lief; For me He
4. To Him I owe my life and breath, And all the joys I have; He makes me

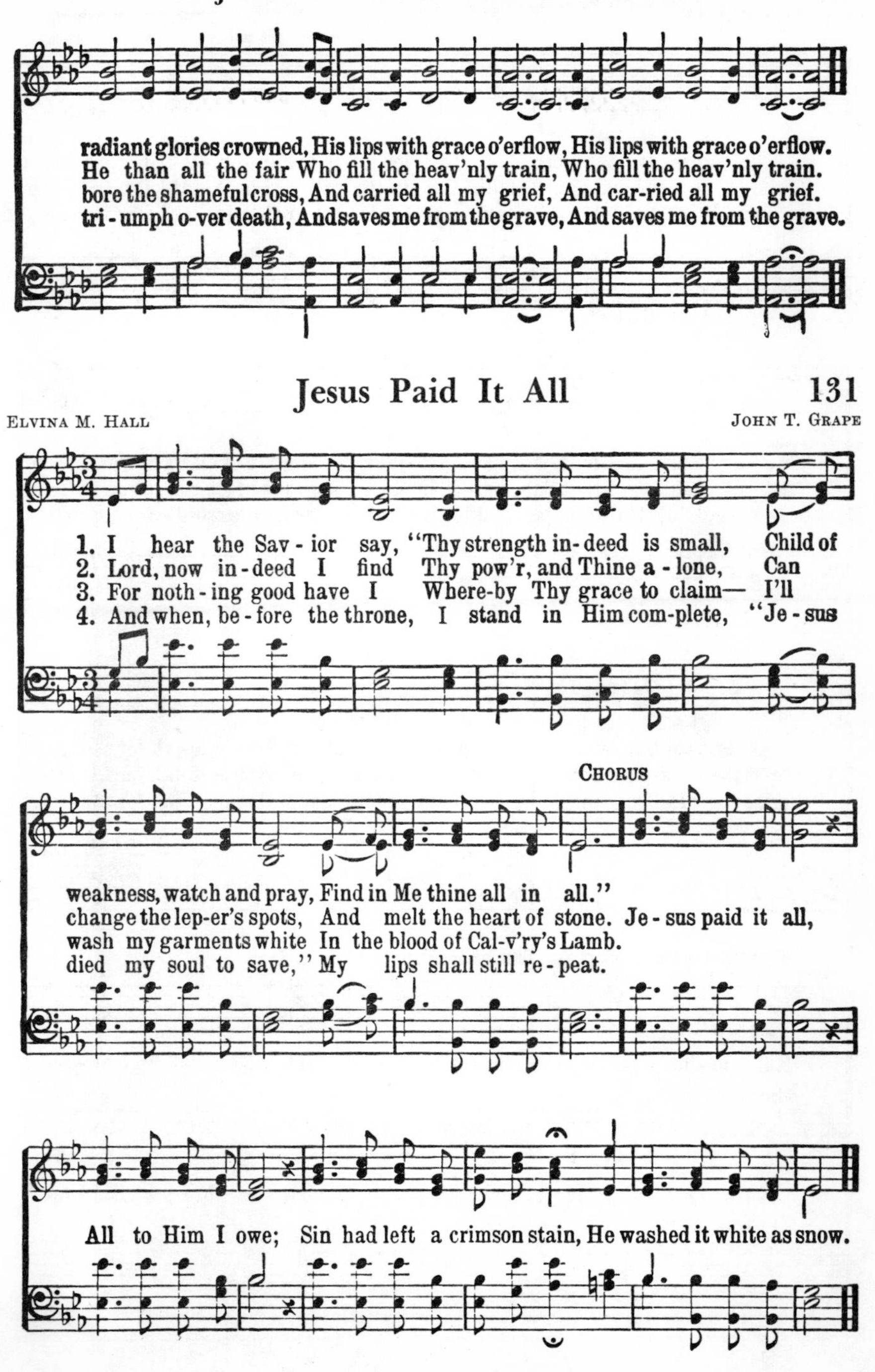
Majestic Sweetness Sits Enthroned
radiant glories crowned, His lips with grace o'erflow, His lips with grace o'erflow.
He than all the fair Who fill the heav'nly train, Who fill the heav'nly train.
bore the shameful cross, And carried all my grief, And car-ried all my grief.
tri - umph o-ver death, And saves me from the grave, And saves me from the grave.
Jesus Paid It All
131
Elvina M. Hall
John T. Grape
1. I hear the Sav - ior say, "Thy strength in-deed is small, Child of
2. Lord, now in-deed I find Thy pow'r, and Thine a - lone, Can
3. For noth - ing good have I Where-by Thy grace to claim— I'll
4. And when, be - fore the throne, I stand in Him com-plete, "Je - sus
Chorus
weakness, watch and pray, Find in Me thine all in all."
change the lep-er's spots, And melt the heart of stone. Je - sus paid it all,
wash my garments white In the blood of Cal-v'ry's Lamb.
died my soul to save," My lips shall still re - peat.
All to Him I owe; Sin had left a crimson stain, He washed it white as snow.

132 Hallelujah for the Cross!

Horatius Bonar, Arr. | James McGranahan

1. The cross it stand-eth fast, Hal-le-lu-jah, hal-le-lu-jah! De-fy-ing
2. It is the old cross still, Hal-le-lu-jah, hal-le-lu-jah! Its tri-umph
3. 'Twas here the debt was paid, Hal-le-lu-jah, hal-le-lu-jah! Our sins on
ev-ery blast, Hal-le-lu-jah, hal-le-lu-jah! The winds of hell have blown, The
let us tell, Hal-le-lu-jah, hal-le-lu-jah! The grace of God here shone Thro'
Je-sus laid, Hal-le-lu-jah, hal-le-lu-jah! So round the cross we sing Of
cres.
world its hate hath shown, Yet it is not over-thrown, Hal-le-lu-jah for the cross!
Christ the bless-ed Son, Who did for sin a-tone, Hal-le-lu-jah for the cross!
Christ our of-fer-ing, Of Christ our liv-ing King, Hal-le-lu-jah for the cross!
Obbligato Duet Sop. (or Ten.) and Alto
Hal-le-lu-jah, hal-le-lu-jah, Hal-le-
Soprano & Alto*
Chorus mp Hal-le-lu-jah, hal-le-lu-jah, Hal-le-
Tenor & Bass

*If desired, the Soprano and Alto may sing the upper staff, omitting the middle staff.

Hallelujah for the Cross!

lu - jah for the cross! Hal - le - lu - jah,
lu - jah for the cross, hal-le - lu-jah for the cross! Hal - le - lu - jah,
hal - le - lu - jah, It shall nev - er suf - fer loss!
hal - le - lu - jah, It shall nev-er suf - fer, nev - er suf - fer loss!
FULL CHORUS
f
*Hal - le - lu - jah, hal - le - lu - jah, Hal - le - lu - jah for the cross!
cres.
ff
Hal - le - lu - jah, hal - le - lu - jah, It shall nev - er suf - fer loss!

*For a final ending, all the voices may sing the melody in unison through the last eight measures—the instrument playing the harmony.

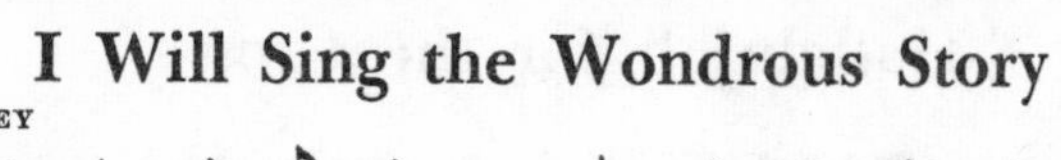

133 I Will Sing the Wondrous Story

Francis H. Rowley · Peter P. Bilhorn

1. I will sing the won-drous sto - ry Of the Christ who died for me,
2. I was lost, but Je - sus found me, Found the sheep that went a - stray,
3. I was bruised, but Je - sus healed me; Faint was I from many a fall;
4. Days of dark-ness still come o'er me, Sor - row's paths I oft - en tread,
5. He will keep me till the riv - er Rolls its wa - ters at my feet;

How He left His home in glo - ry For the cross of Cal - va - ry.
Threw His lov - ing arms a-round me, Drew me back in - to His way.
Sight was gone, and fears possessed me, But He freed me from them all.
But the Sav - ior still is with me; By His hand I'm safe - ly led.
Then He'll bear me safe - ly o - ver, Where the loved ones I shall meet.

Chorus

Yes, I'll sing..... the won-drous sto - - - ry Of the
Yes, I'll sing the won-drous sto - ry

Christ.... who died for me,....... Sing it with.... the saints in
Of the Christ who died for me, Sing it with

glo - - ry, Gath-ered by...... the crys-tal sea.........
the saints in glo - ry, Gath-ered by the crys-tal sea.

Love Led Him to Calvary

George O. Webster — Charles H. Gabriel

1. Love led the Sav-ior, in days long a - go, Down to earth's dark-ness, its sin and its woe; Seek-ing the lost ones, His mer-cy to show,
2. Love, for a man-ger, a-ban-doned a throne, Seek-ing the sin-ful, the sad and the lone; Yearn-ing to win them and make them His own,
3. See-ing the soul in its in-fi-nite worth, Stoop-ing, in love, to the low-li-est birth, Seek-ing the lost in the by-ways of earth,
4. Long-ing, in pit-y, the lost ones to save, Brav-ing the Gar-den, the Cross and the Grave, Seek-ing this on-ly, the sin-ful to save,
Love led Him to Cal-va-ry.
Chorus faster
Love led Him to Cal-va-ry, Love led Him to Cal-va-ry; Seek-ing the lost, at the ut-ter-most cost, Love led Him to Cal-va-ry.

135 It Took a Miracle

JOHN W. PETERSON JOHN W. PETERSON

1. My Fa - ther is om - nip - o - tent, And that you can't de - ny;
2. Tho here His glo - ry has been shown, We still can't ful - ly see
3. The Bi - ble tells us of His pow'r And wis-dom all way thru,
A God of might and mir - a - cles—'Tis writ - ten in the sky.
The won-ders of His might, His throne—'Twill take e - ter - ni - ty.
And ev - 'ry lit - tle bird and flow'r Are tes - ti - mo - nies too.
CHORUS
It took a mir - a - cle to put the stars in place, It took a
mir - a - cle to hang the world in space; But when He saved my soul,
Cleansed and made me whole, It took a mir - a - cle of love and grace!

My Sins Are Blotted Out, I Know!

Merrill Dunlop | Merrill Dunlop

1. What a won-drous mes-sage in God's Word! My sins are blot-ted out, I know! If I trust in His re-deem-ing blood, My sins are blot-ted out, I know!
2. Once my heart was black but now what joy, My sins are blot-ted out, I know! I have peace that noth-ing can de-stroy, My sins are blot-ted out, I know!
3. I shall stand some day be-fore my King, My sins all blot-ted out, I know! With the ran-somed host I then shall sing: "My sins are blot-ted out, I know!"

Chorus

My sins are blot-ted out, I know! I know! My sins are blot-ted out, I know! I know! They are bur-ied in the depths of the deep-est sea: My sins are blot-ted out, I know! I know!

137 Nor Silver Nor Gold

JAMES M. GRAY DANIEL B. TOWNER

1. Nor sil - ver nor gold hath ob-tained my re-demp-tion, Nor rich - es of earth could have saved my poor soul; The blood of the cross is my on - ly foun - da-tion, The death of my Sav - ior now mak - eth me whole.
2. Nor sil - ver nor gold hath ob-tained my re-demp-tion, The guilt on my con-science too heav - y had grown; The blood of the cross is my on - ly foun - da-tion, The death of my Sav - ior could on - ly a - tone.
3. Nor sil - ver nor gold hath ob-tained my re-demp-tion, The ho - ly com-mand-ment for - bade me draw near; The blood of the cross is my on - ly foun - da-tion, The death of my Sav - ior re - mov - eth my fear.
4. Nor sil - ver nor gold hath ob-tained my re-demp-tion, The way in - to heav - en could not thus be bought; The blood of the cross is my on - ly foun - da-tion, The death of my Sav - ior re-demp-tion hath wrought
CHORUS
I am re - deemed, ... but not with sil - ver;
I am re-deemed, I am re-deemed, but not with sil - ver;
I am bought, . but not with gold; Bought with a
I am bought, I am bought, but not with gold;

Nor Silver Nor Gold
price...... the blood of Je - sus, Pre-cious price of love un-told.
Bought with a price— the precious blood of Je-sus,
3
Nothing but the Blood
138
Robert Lowry
Robert Lowry
1. What can wash a - way my sin? Noth-ing but the blood of Je - sus;
2. For my par - don this I see— Noth-ing but the blood of Je - sus;
3. Noth - ing can for sin a - tone— Noth-ing but the blood of Je - sus;
4. This is all my hope and peace—Noth-ing but the blood of Je - sus;
What can make me whole a - gain? Noth-ing but the blood of Je - sus.
For my cleans-ing, this my plea—Noth-ing but the blood of Je - sus.
Naught of good that I have done—Noth-ing but the blood of Je - sus.
This is all my right-eous - ness—Noth-ing but the blood of Je - sus.
Refrain
Oh! pre - cious is the flow That makes me white as snow;
No oth - er fount I know, Noth-ing but the blood of Je - sus.

Once for All

PHILIP P. BLISS PHILIP P. BLISS

1. Free from the law, O hap-py con-di-tion, Je-sus hath bled, and there is re-mis-sion; Cursed by the law and bruised by the fall, Grace hath redeemed us once for all.
2. Now are we free—there's no con-dem-na-tion, Je-sus pro-vides a per-fect sal-va-tion; "Come un-to Me," O hear His sweet call, Come, and He saves us once for all.
3. "Chil-dren of God," O glo-ri-ous call-ing, Sure-ly His grace will keep us from fall-ing; Pass-ing from death to life at His call, Bless-ed sal-va-tion once for all.
CHORUS
Once for all, O sin-ner, re-ceive it, Once for all, O broth-er, be-lieve it; Cling to the Cross, the bur-den will fall, Christ hath re-deemed us once for all.

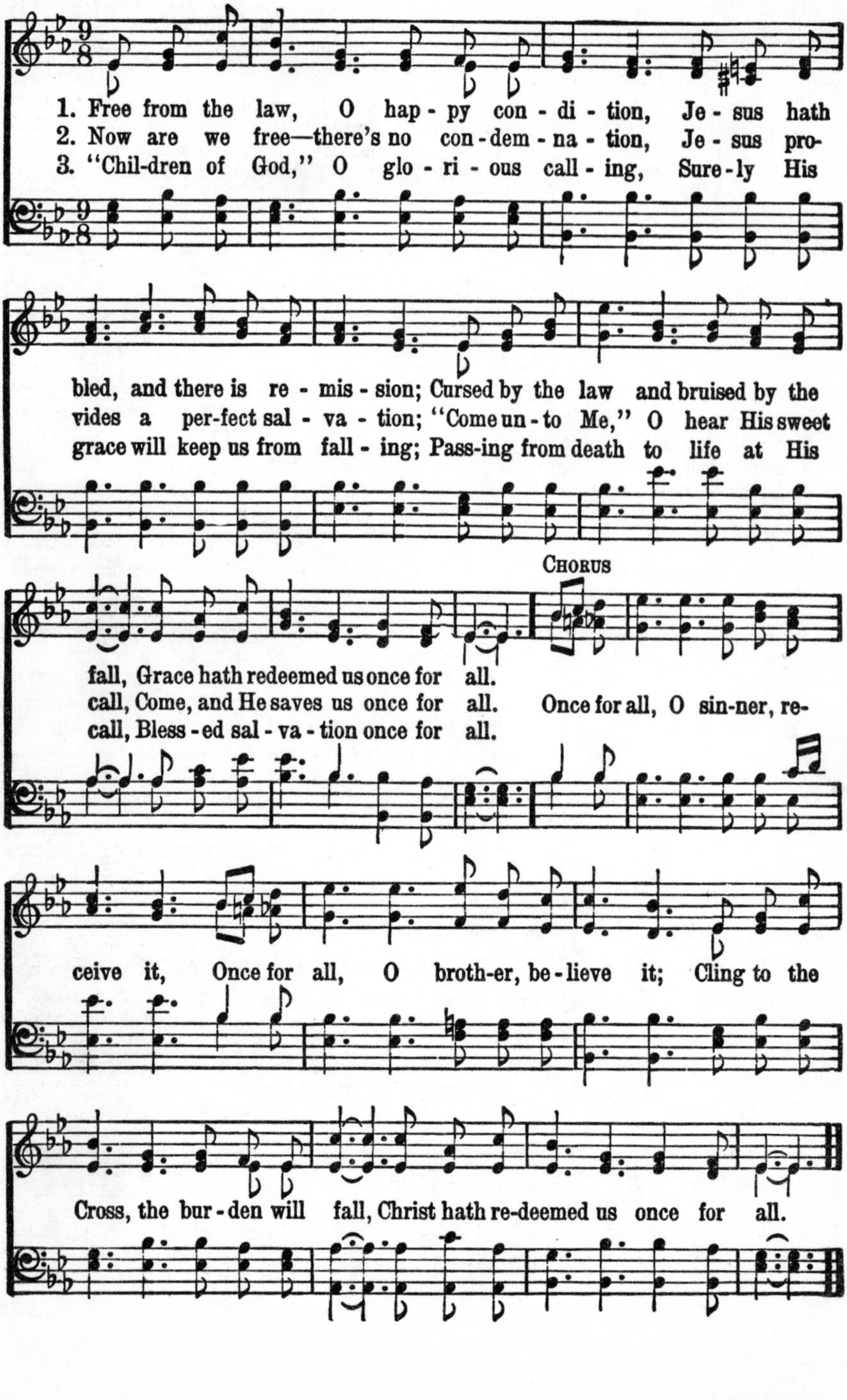

Redeemed

Fanny J. Crosby

William J. Kirkpatrick

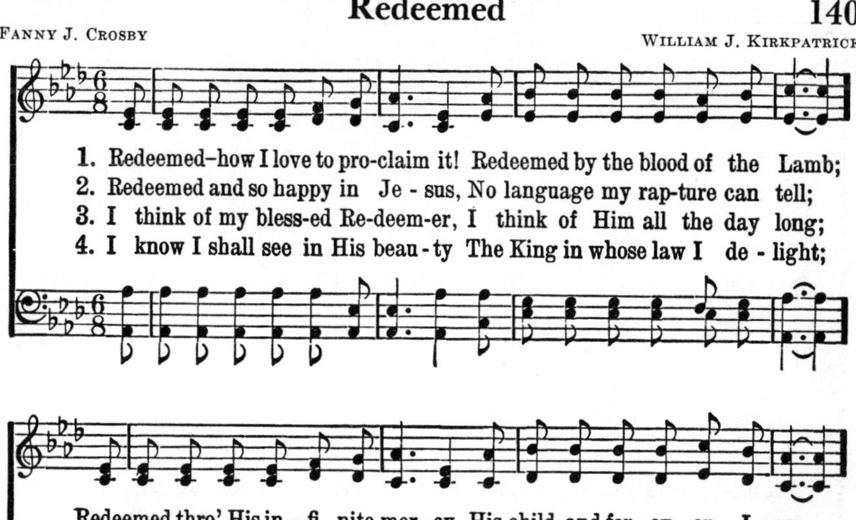
1. Redeemed–how I love to pro-claim it! Redeemed by the blood of the Lamb;
2. Redeemed and so happy in Je - sus, No language my rap-ture can tell;
3. I think of my bless-ed Re-deem-er, I think of Him all the day long;
4. I know I shall see in His beau - ty The King in whose law I de - light;

Redeemed thro' His in - fi - nite mer - cy, His child, and for - ev - er, I am.
I know that the light of His presence With me doth con-tin - ual - ly dwell.
I sing, for I can-not be si - lent; His love is the theme of my song.
Who lov - ing - ly guardeth my footsteps, And giv-eth me songs in the night.

Chorus

Re - deemed, . . re - deemed, . . Redeemed by the blood of the Lamb;
re-deemed, re-deemed,

Re - deemed, . . re - deemed, . . His child, and for - ev - er, I am.
re-deemed, re-deemed,

141 There Is a Fountain

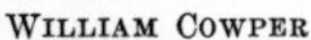

WILLIAM COWPER — EARLY AMERICAN MELODY

1. There is a foun-tain filled with blood Drawn from Im-man - uel's veins;
2. The dy - ing thief re - joiced to see That foun - tain in his day;
3. Dear dy - ing Lamb, Thy pre-cious blood Shall nev - er lose its pow'r,
4. E'er since, by faith, I saw the stream Thy flow - ing wounds sup - ply,
5. Then in a no - bler, sweet - er song, I'll sing Thy pow'r to save,

And sin - ners, plunged be-neath that flood, Lose all their guilt - y stains:
And there may I, though vile as he, Wash all my sins a - way:
Till all the ran-somed Church of God Be saved, to sin no more:
Re - deem - ing love has been my theme, And shall be till I die:
When this poor lisp - ing, stamm'ring tongue Lies si - lent in the grave:

Lose all their guilt - y stains, Lose all their guilt - y stains; And
Wash all my sins a - way, Wash all my sins a - way; And
Be saved, to sin no more, Be saved, to sin no more; Till
And shall be till I die, And shall be till I die; Re-
Lies si - lent in the grave, Lies si - lent in the grave; When

sin - ners, plunged be - neath that flood, Lose all their guilt - y stains.
there may I, though vile as he, Wash all my sins a - way.
all the ran-somed Church of God Be saved, to sin no more.
deem-ing love has been my theme, And shall be till I die.
this poor lisp - ing, stam-m'ring tongue Lies si - lent in the grave.

142 Though Your Sins Be As Scarlet

FANNY J. CROSBY — WILLIAM H. DOANE

DUET *Gently*

1. "Tho' your sins be as scar-let, They shall be as white as snow;
2. Hear the voice that en-treats you, O re-turn ye un-to God!
3. He'll for-give your trans-gres-sions, And re-mem-ber them no more;

Tho' your sins be as scar-let, They shall be as white as snow;
Hear the voice that en-treats you, O re-turn ye un-to God!
He'll for-give your trans-gres-sions, And re-mem-ber them no more;

QUARTET

Tho' they be red . . . . . like crim-son, They shall be as wool!"
He is of great . . . . compas-sion, And of won-drous love;
"Look un-to Me, ... ye peo-ple," Saith the Lord your God!

1. Tho' they be red

DUET *p* — QUARTET *f*

"Tho' your sins be as scar-let, Tho' your sins be as scar-let,
Hear the voice that en-treats you, Hear the voice that en-treats you,
He'll for-give your trans-gres-sions, He'll for-give your trans-gres-sions,

p rit.

They shall be as white as snow, They shall be as white as snow."
O re-turn ye un-to God! O re-turn ye un-to God!
And re-mem-ber them no more, And re-mem-ber them no more.

143 When Love Shines In

Mrs. Frank A. Breck — William J. Kirkpatrick

1. Je-sus comes with pow'r to gladden, When love shines in, Ev-'ry life that woe can sad-den, When love shines in. Love will teach us how to pray, Love will drive the gloom away, Turn our darkness in-to day, When love shines in.
2. How the world will grow with beauty, When love shines in, And the heart re-joice in du-ty, When love shines in. Tri-als may be sanc-ti-fied, And the soul in peace a-bide, Life will all be glo-ri-fied, When love shines in.
3. Dark-est sor-row will grow brighter, When love shines in, And the heav-iest bur-den light-er, When love shines in. 'Tis the glo-ry that will throw Light to show us where to go; O, the heart shall blessing know, When love shines in.
4. We may have un-fad-ing splendor, When love shines in, And a friend-ship true and ten-der, When love shines in. When earth vic-t'ries shall be won, And our life in Heav'n begun, There will be no need of sun, When love shines in.
Chorus
When love shines in,....... When love shines in,.......
When love shines in,...
When love shines in, When love shines in, When love shines in,....
How the heart is tuned to sing-ing, When love.. shines in;.....
When love shines in;......

When Love Shines In
When love shines in,....... When love shines in,..
When love shines in,........
When love shines in, When love shines in, When love shines in,...
Joy and peace to oth - ers bring-ing, When love shines in...
When love, when love shines in....
144
JOHN H. STOCKTON
Only Trust Him
JOHN H. STOCKTON
1. Come, ev - 'ry soul by sin op-pressed, There's mer - cy with the Lord,
2. For Je - sus shed His pre-cious blood, Rich bless-ings to be - stow;
3. Yes, Je - sus is the Truth, the Way, That leads you in - to rest:
4. Come, then, and join this ho - ly band, And on to glo - ry go,
And He will sure - ly give you rest By trust - ing in His word.
Plunge now in - to the crim - son flood That wash - es white as snow.
Be - lieve in Him with - out de - lay, And you are ful - ly blest.
To dwell in that ce - les - tial land, Where joys im - mor - tal flow.
1
2
On - ly trust Him, on-ly trust Him, On - ly trust Him now.
He will save you, He will save you, He will (Omit .....
save you now.

145 Whiter Than Snow

JAMES NICHOLSON — WILLIAM G. FISCHER

1. Lord Je-sus, I long to be per-fect-ly whole; I want Thee for-ev-er to
2. Lord Je-sus, look down from Thy throne in the skies, And help me to make a com-
3. Lord Je-sus, for this I most hum-bly en-treat, I wait, bless-ed Lord, at Thy
4. Lord Je-sus, Thou seest I pa-tient-ly wait, Come now, and with-in me a

live in my soul, Break down ev-'ry i-dol, cast out ev-'ry foe;
plete sac-ri-fice; I give up my-self, and what-ev-er I know,
cru-ci-fied feet; By faith, for my cleans-ing, I see Thy blood flow,
new heart cre-ate; To those who have sought Thee, Thou nev-er saidst "No,"

CHORUS.

Now wash me, and I shall be whit-er than snow. Whit-er than snow, yes,

whit-er than snow; Now wash me, and I shall be whit-er than snow.

Wonderful Story of Love

J. M. DRIVER J. M. DRIVER

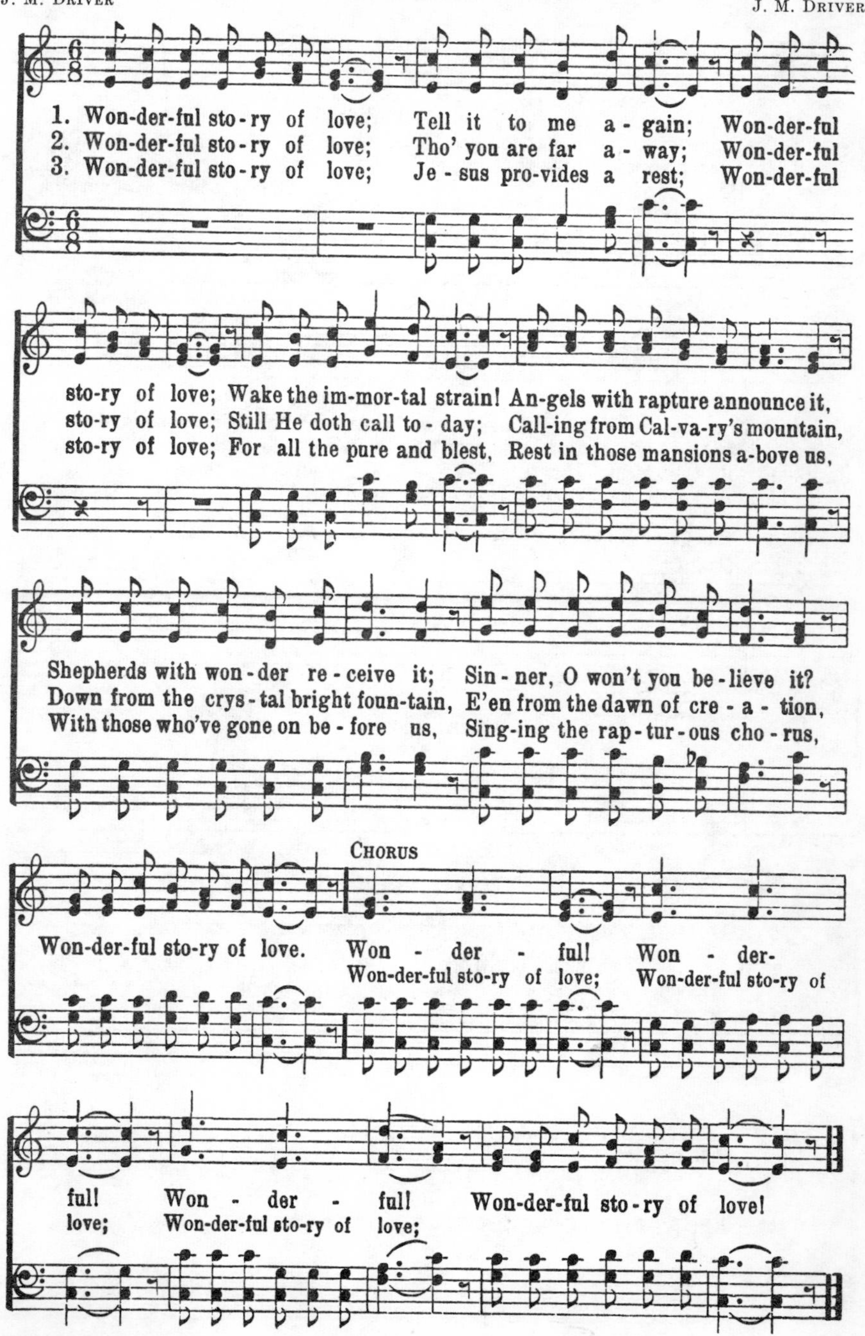
1. Won-der-ful sto-ry of love; Tell it to me a-gain; Won-der-ful
2. Won-der-ful sto-ry of love; Tho' you are far a-way; Won-der-ful
3. Won-der-ful sto-ry of love; Je-sus pro-vides a rest; Won-der-ful
sto-ry of love; Wake the im-mor-tal strain! An-gels with rapture announce it,
sto-ry of love; Still He doth call to-day; Call-ing from Cal-va-ry's mountain,
sto-ry of love; For all the pure and blest, Rest in those mansions a-bove us,
Shepherds with won-der re-ceive it; Sin-ner, O won't you be-lieve it?
Down from the crys-tal bright foun-tain, E'en from the dawn of cre-a-tion,
With those who've gone on be-fore us, Sing-ing the rap-tur-ous cho-rus,
Won-der-ful sto-ry of love.
CHORUS
Won - der - ful! Won - der- ful! Won - der - ful! Won-der-ful sto-ry of love!
Won-der-ful sto-ry of love; Won-der-ful sto-ry of love; Won-der-ful sto-ry of love;

147 Ye Must Be Born Again

WILLIAM T. SLEEPER — GEORGE C. STEBBINS

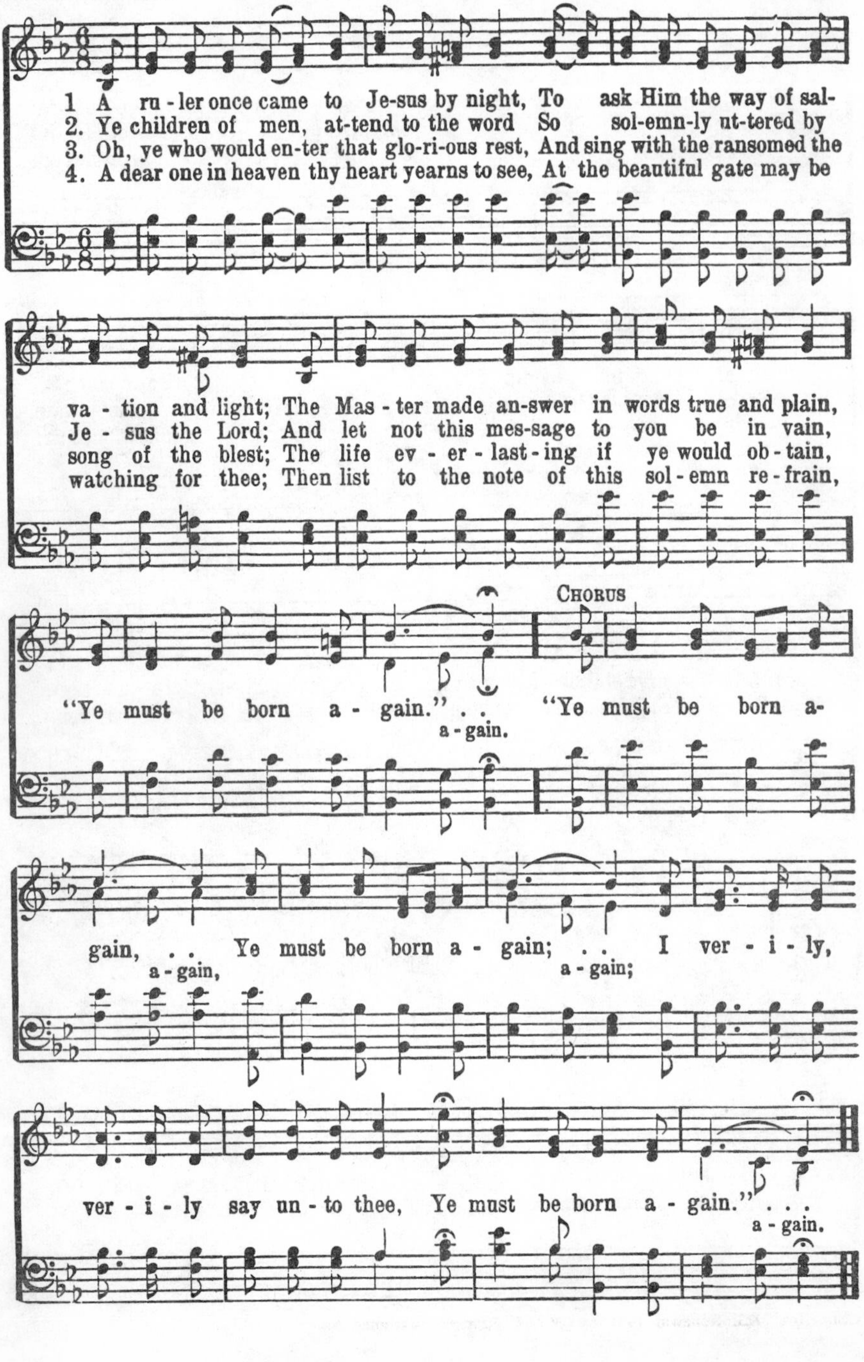

1 A ru-ler once came to Je-sus by night, To ask Him the way of sal-
2. Ye children of men, at-tend to the word So sol-emn-ly ut-tered by
3. Oh, ye who would en-ter that glo-ri-ous rest, And sing with the ransomed the
4. A dear one in heaven thy heart yearns to see, At the beautiful gate may be

va-tion and light; The Mas-ter made an-swer in words true and plain,
Je-sus the Lord; And let not this mes-sage to you be in vain,
song of the blest; The life ev-er-last-ing if ye would ob-tain,
watching for thee; Then list to the note of this sol-emn re-frain,

"Ye must be born a-gain." . . a-gain.

CHORUS

"Ye must be born a-gain, . . a-gain, Ye must be born a-gain; . . a-gain; I ver-i-ly, ver-i-ly say un-to thee, Ye must be born a-gain." . . . a-gain.

Great Is Thy Faithfulness 148

THOMAS O. CHISHOLM — WILLIAM M. RUNYAN

1. "Great is Thy faith-ful-ness," O God my Fa-ther, There is no shad-ow of
2. Sum-mer and win-ter, and spring-time and harvest, Sun, moon and stars in their
3. Par-don for sin and a peace that en-dur-eth, Thy own dear presence to
turn-ing with Thee; Thou chang-est not, Thy com-pas-sions, they fail not;
cours-es a-bove, Join with all na-ture in man-i-fold wit-ness,
cheer and to guide; Strength for to-day and bright hope for to-mor-row,
As Thou hast been Thou for-ev-er wilt be.
To Thy great faith-ful-ness, mer-cy and love.
Blessings all mine, with ten thou-sand be-side!
CHORUS
"Great is Thy faith-ful-ness!
Great is Thy faithfulness!" Morning by morning new mercies I see; All I have
needed Thy hand hath provided—"Great is Thy faithfulness," Lord, un-to me!
rall.

149 **Why Do I Sing About Jesus?**

ALBERT A. KETCHUM ALBERT A. KETCHUM

1. Deep in my heart there's a glad-ness, Je - sus has saved me from
2. On - ly a glimpse of His good-ness, That was suf-fi-cient for
3. He is the fair - est of fair ones, He is the Lil - y, the
sin! Praise to His name, what a Sav - iour! Cleans-ing with-
me; On - ly one look at the Sav - iour, Then was my
Rose; Riv - ers of mer - cy sur-round Him, Grace, love and
out and with - in.
spir - it set free.
pit - y He shows.
REFRAIN
Why do I sing a-bout Je - sus?
Why is He pre-cious to me?
He is my Lord and my
Sav - iour, Dy - ing, He set me free!
(set me free!)

He Took My Sins Away

Mrs. M. J. Harris — Mrs. M. J. Harris

1. I came to Je-sus, wea-ry, worn, and sad. He took my sins a-way, He
2. The load of sin was more than I could bear. He took them all a-way, He
3. No con-dem-na-tion have I in my heart. He took my sins a-way, He
4. If you will come to Je-sus Christ to-day, He'll take your sins a-way, He'll
took my sins a-way, And now His love has made my heart so glad. He
took them all a-way, And now on Him I roll my ev-'ry care. He
took my sins a-way, His per-fect peace He did to me im-part. He
take your sins a-way, And keep you hap-py in His love each day. He'll
took my sins a-way.
took my sins a-way.
took my sins a-way.
take your sins a-way.
CHORUS
He took my sins a-way, He
took my sins a-way, And keeps me sing-ing ev-'ry day!
I'm so glad He took my sins a-way. He took my sins a-way.

151 Wonderful, Wonderful Jesus

Anna B. Russell — Ernest O. Sellers

1. There is nev - er a day so drear - y, There is nev - er a night so long (so long), But the soul that is trust - ing Je - sus Will some-where find a song (a song).
2. There is nev - er a cross so heav - y, There is nev - er a weight of woe (of woe), But that Je - sus will help to car - ry Be- cause He lov - eth so (loves so).
3. There is nev - er a care or bur - den, There is nev - er a grief or loss (or loss), But that Je - sus in love will light - en When car - ried to the cross (the cross).
4. There is nev - er a guilt - y sin - ner, There is nev - er a wan-d'ring one (not one), But that God can in mer - cy par - don Thro' Je - sus Christ, His Son (His Son).
CHORUS.
Won - der-ful, won-der - ful Je - sus,
In the heart He im-plant-eth a song: . . . .
He plant-eth a song,
A song of de-liv-'rance, of cour - age, of strength, In the heart He im-plant - eth a song (a song).

Jesus, Lover of My Soul

Charles Wesley

Simeon B. Marsh

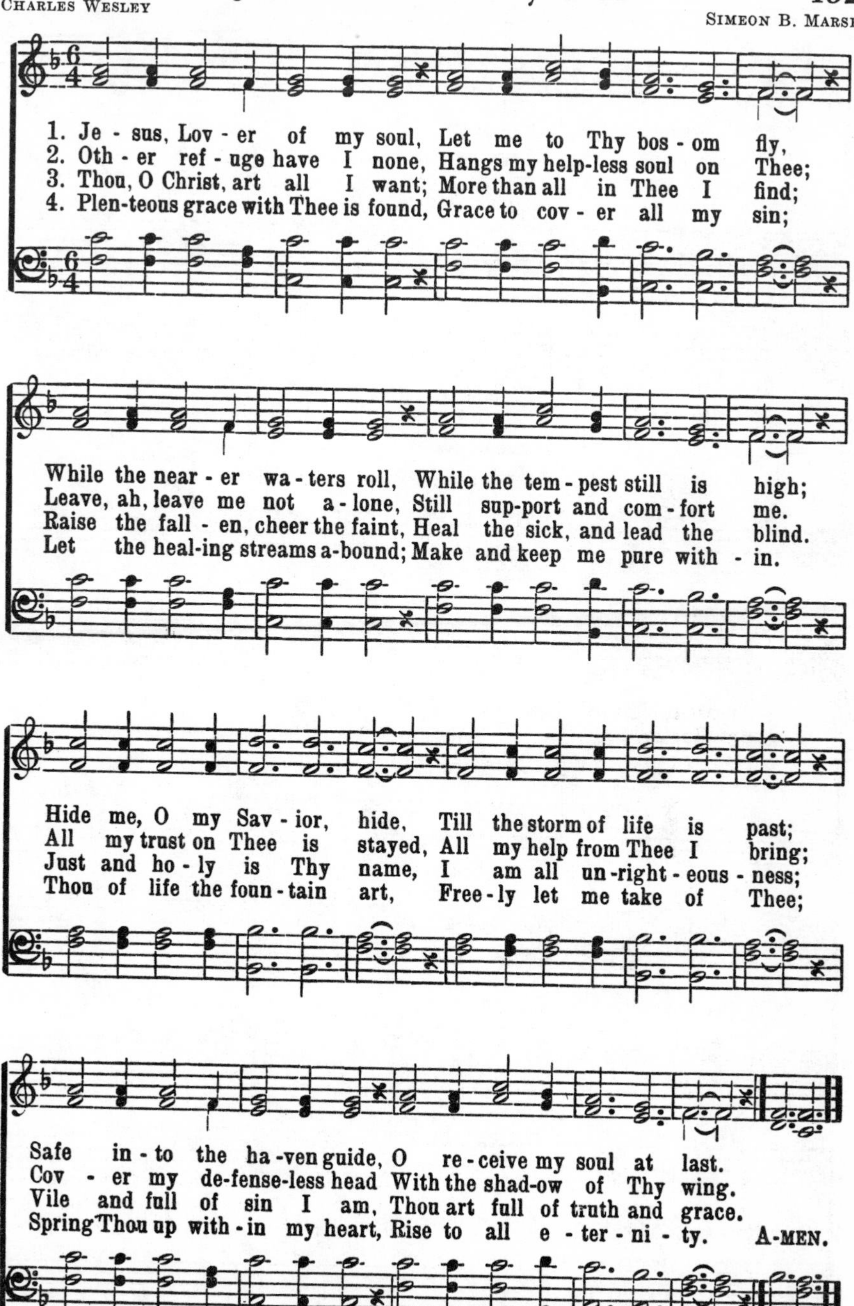
1. Je - sus, Lov - er of my soul, Let me to Thy bos - om fly,
2. Oth - er ref - uge have I none, Hangs my help-less soul on Thee;
3. Thou, O Christ, art all I want; More than all in Thee I find;
4. Plen-teous grace with Thee is found, Grace to cov - er all my sin;
While the near - er wa - ters roll, While the tem - pest still is high;
Leave, ah, leave me not a - lone, Still sup-port and com - fort me.
Raise the fall - en, cheer the faint, Heal the sick, and lead the blind.
Let the heal-ing streams a-bound; Make and keep me pure with - in.
Hide me, O my Sav - ior, hide, Till the storm of life is past;
All my trust on Thee is stayed, All my help from Thee I bring;
Just and ho - ly is Thy name, I am all un-right - eous - ness;
Thou of life the foun - tain art, Free - ly let me take of Thee;
Safe in - to the ha - ven guide, O re - ceive my soul at last.
Cov - er my de-fense-less head With the shad-ow of Thy wing.
Vile and full of sin I am, Thou art full of truth and grace.
Spring Thou up with - in my heart, Rise to all e - ter - ni - ty. A-MEN.

153 Only Jesus

AVIS B. CHRISTIANSEN LANCE B. LATHAM

1. I've found a ref - uge from life's care in Je - sus, I am
2. I've found a pre - cious joy in know-ing Je - sus, Nev - er
3. I've found a bless - ed hope di - vine in Je - sus, 'Tis a

hid - ing in His love di - vine; He ful - ly un - der-stands my
dreamed of in this world of woe; No clouds, how-ev - er dark, can
Day Star ev - er shin-ing bright; It fills my earth-ly way with

soul's deep long - ing, And He whis-pers soft - ly, "Thou art mine.".
dim the ra - diance Of the heav'n-ly light He doth be - stow.
heav'n-ly glo - ry, And it turns life's dark-ness in - to light.

REFRAIN

On - ly Je - sus! On - ly Je - sus! On - ly He can sat - is - fy;

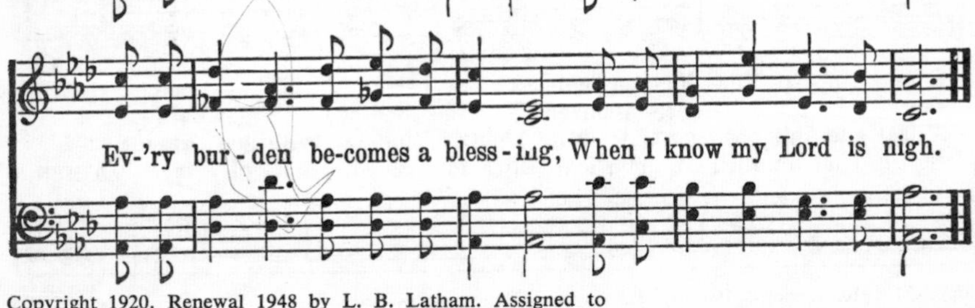
Ev-'ry bur - den be-comes a bless - ing, When I know my Lord is nigh.

Our Great Savior

J. Wilbur Chapman

Rowland W. Prichard
Arr. by Robert Harkness

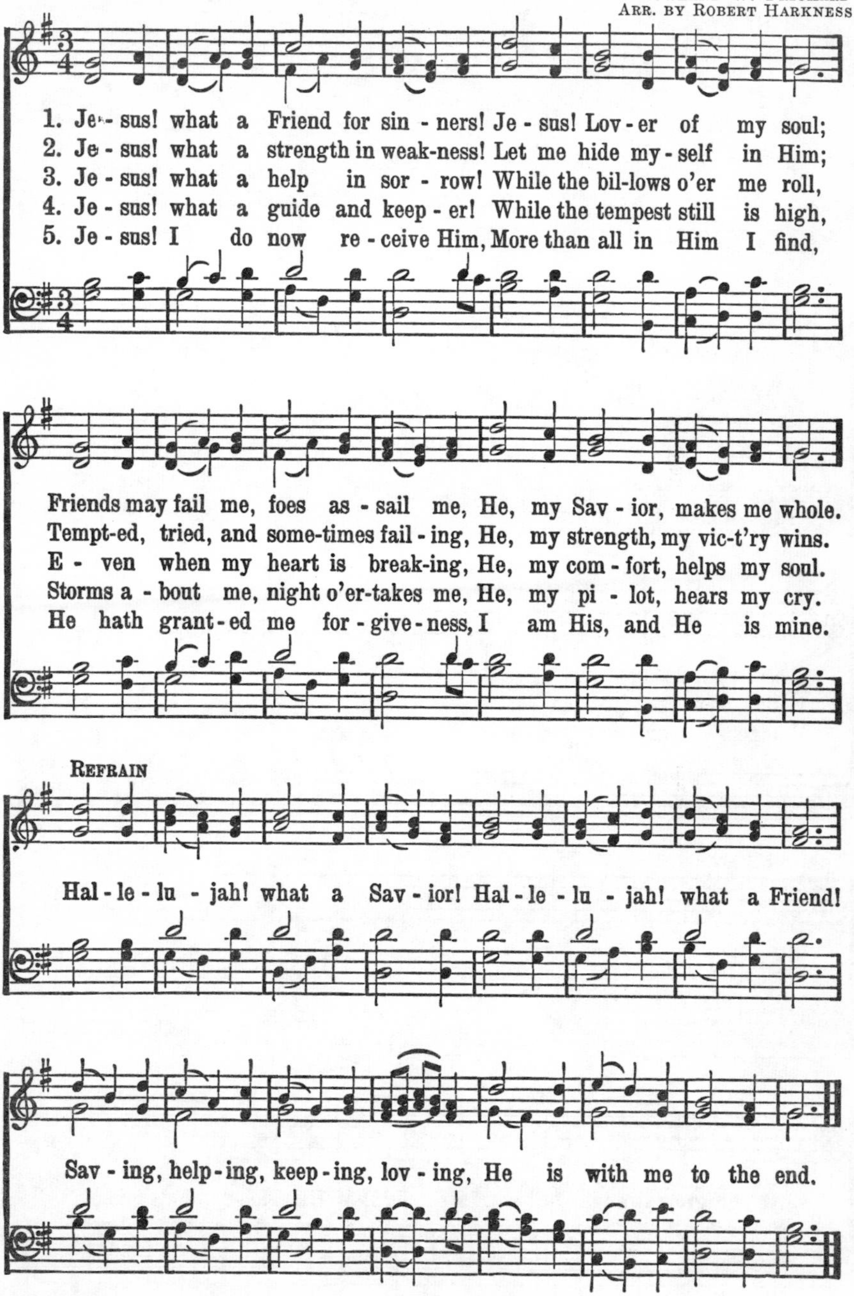

1. Je - sus! what a Friend for sin - ners! Je - sus! Lov - er of my soul;
2. Je - sus! what a strength in weak-ness! Let me hide my - self in Him;
3. Je - sus! what a help in sor - row! While the bil-lows o'er me roll,
4. Je - sus! what a guide and keep - er! While the tempest still is high,
5. Je - sus! I do now re - ceive Him, More than all in Him I find,

Friends may fail me, foes as - sail me, He, my Sav - ior, makes me whole.
Tempt-ed, tried, and some-times fail - ing, He, my strength, my vic-t'ry wins.
E - ven when my heart is break-ing, He, my com - fort, helps my soul.
Storms a - bout me, night o'er-takes me, He, my pi - lot, hears my cry.
He hath grant-ed me for - give - ness, I am His, and He is mine.

Refrain

Hal - le - lu - jah! what a Sav - ior! Hal - le - lu - jah! what a Friend!
Sav - ing, help - ing, keep - ing, lov - ing, He is with me to the end.

155 The Heavenly Vision

Helen H. Lemmel — Helen H. Lemmel

With expression
1. O soul, are you wea - ry and troub - led? No light in the dark-ness you see? There's light for a look at the Sav - ior, And life more a - bun-dant and free!
2. Thro' death in - to life ev - er - last - ing He passed, and we fol - low Him there; O - ver us sin no more hath do - min - ion— For more than con-qu'rors we are!
3. His word shall not fail you—He prom - ised; Be - lieve Him, and all will be well: Then go to a world that is dy - ing, His per - fect sal - va - tion to tell!
Refrain
Turn your eyes up-on Je - sus, Look full in His won - der - ful face; . . . . And the things of earth will grow strange-ly dim In the light of His glo - ry and grace.

The Light of the World Is Jesus

PHILIP P. BLISS PHILIP P. BLISS

1. The whole world was lost in the dark-ness of sin; The Light of the
2. No dark-ness have we who in Je - sus a - bide, The Light of the
3. Ye dwell-ers in dark-ness with sin-blind - ed eyes, The Light of the
4. No need of the sun-light in heav - en, we're told, The Light of the
world is Je - sus; Like sun - shine at noon - day His glo - ry shone in,
world is Je - sus; We walk in the Light when we fol - low our Guide,
world is Je - sus; Go, wash at His bid - ding, and light will a - rise,
world is Je - sus; The Lamb is the Light in the Cit - y of Gold,
CHORUS
The Light of the world is Je - sus. Come to the Light, 'tis
shin - ing for thee; Sweet-ly the Light has dawned up-on me; Once I was
blind, but now I can see; The Light of the world is Je - sus.

157 The Lily of the Valley

CHARLES W. FRY — ARR. FROM WILLIAM S. HAYS

1. I have found a friend in Je - sus, He's ev - ery-thing to me, He's the fair-est of ten thou-sand to my soul; The Lil - y of the Val - ley, in Him a - lone I see All I need to cleanse and make me ful-ly whole.
2. He all my griefs has tak - en, and all my sor-rows borne; In temp-ta - tion He's my strong and mighty tower; I have all for Him for-sak - en, and all my i - dols torn From my heart, and now He keeps me by His power.
3. He will nev - er, nev - er leave me, nor yet for-sake me here, While I live by faith and do His bless-ed will; A wall of fire a - bout me, I've noth-ing now to fear, With His man-na He my hun-gry soul shall fill.

D. S.—*Lil - y of the Val - ley, the Bright and Morn-ing Star, He's the fair - est of ten thou-sand to my soul.*

FINE

In sor - row He's my com - fort, in trou - ble He's my stay, He tells me ev - ery care on Him to roll: He's the
Though all the world for - sake me, and Sa - tan tempt me sore, Through Je - sus I shall safe - ly reach the goal: He's the
Then sweep-ing up to glo - ry to see His bless - ed face, Where riv - ers of de - light shall ev - er roll: He's the

D. S.

Hallelujah, What a Savior! 158

PHILIP P. BLISS — PHILIP P. BLISS

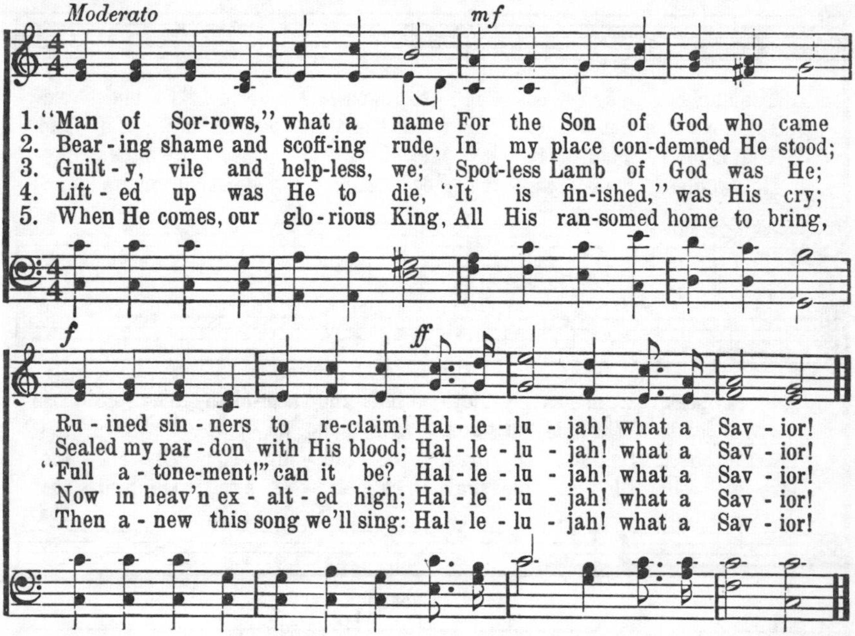

Moderato *mf*

1. "Man of Sorrows," what a name For the Son of God who came Ruined sinners to reclaim! Hallelujah! what a Savior!
2. Bearing shame and scoffing rude, In my place condemned He stood; Sealed my pardon with His blood; Hallelujah! what a Savior!
3. Guilty, vile and helpless, we; Spotless Lamb of God was He; "Full atonement!" can it be? Hallelujah! what a Savior!
4. Lifted up was He to die, "It is finished," was His cry; Now in heav'n exalted high; Hallelujah! what a Savior!
5. When He comes, our glorious King, All His ransomed home to bring, Then anew this song we'll sing: Hallelujah! what a Savior!

The Great Physician 159

WILLIAM HUNTER — JOHN H. STOCKTON

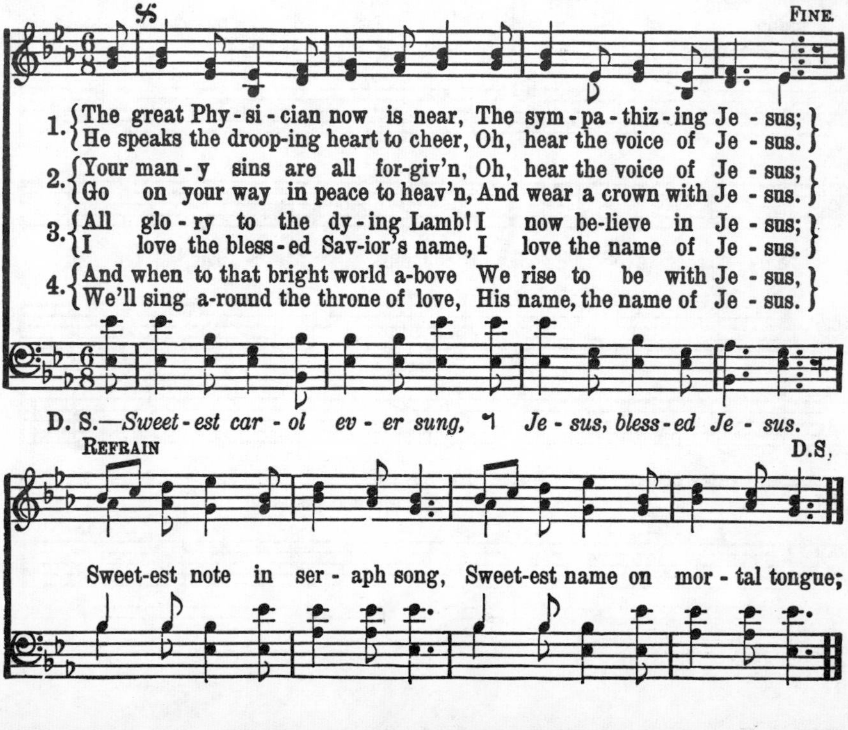

1. The great Physician now is near, The sympathizing Jesus;
He speaks the drooping heart to cheer, Oh, hear the voice of Jesus.
2. Your many sins are all forgiv'n, Oh, hear the voice of Jesus;
Go on your way in peace to heav'n, And wear a crown with Jesus.
3. All glory to the dying Lamb! I now believe in Jesus;
I love the blessed Savior's name, I love the name of Jesus.
4. And when to that bright world above We rise to be with Jesus,
We'll sing around the throne of love, His name, the name of Jesus.

FINE

REFRAIN

Sweetest note in seraph song, Sweetest name on mortal tongue;

D. S.—*Sweetest carol ever sung, Jesus, blessed Jesus.*

D.S.

160 The Name of Jesus

W. C. Martin Edmund S. Lorenz

1. The name of Je - sus is so sweet, I love its mu - sic
2. I love the name of Him whose heart Knows all my griefs and
3. That name I fond - ly love to hear, It nev - er fails my
4. No word of man can ev - er tell How sweet the name I
to re - peat; It makes my joys full and com-plete, The pre - cious
bears a part; Who bids all anx - ious fears de - part— I love the
heart to cheer, Its mu - sic dries the fall - ing tear; Ex - alt the
love so well; Oh, let its prais - es ev - er swell, Oh, praise the
The
Chorus
name of Je - sus. "Je - sus," oh, how sweet the name!
pre-cious name
"Je - sus," ev - 'ry day the same; "Je - sus," let all
saints pro - claim Its wor - thy praise for - ev - er.
Its wor - thy praise

The Unveiled Christ

161

N. B. Herrell — N. B. Herrell

mf
1. Once our bless-ed Christ of beau - ty Was veiled off from hu-man view;
2. Now He is with God the Fa - ther, In - ter-ced-ing there for you;
3. Ho - ly an-gels bow be - fore Him, Men of earth give prais-es due;
4. Thro'-out time and end-less a - ges, Heights and depths of love so true;
But thro' suff'ring, death and sor - row He has rent the veil in two.
For He is the might-y con-qu'ror Since He rent the veil in two.
For He is the well-be - lov - ed Since He rent the veil in two.
He a-lone can be the giv - er Since He rent the veil in two.
Chorus
f
cres.
O be-hold the Man of Sor - rows, O be-hold Him in plain view;
ff
p
Lo! He is the might-y con - qu'ror, Since He rent the veil in two.
ff
p
rit.
Lo! He is the might-y con - qu'ror, Since He rent the veil in two.

162 The Stranger of Galilee

LEILA N. MORRIS LEILA N. MORRIS

Solo or Quartet
1. In fan-cy I stood by the shore, one day, Of the beau-ti-ful murm'ring sea; . . . I saw the great crowds as they thronged the way Of the Stranger of Gal-i-lee; . . . I saw how the man who was blind from birth, In a
2. His look of com-pas-sion, His words of love, They shall nev-er for-got-ten be, . . . When sin-sick and helpless He saw me there, This Stranger of Gal-i-lee; . . . He show'd me His hand and His riv-en side, And He
3. I heard Him speak peace to the an-gry waves, Of that tur-bu-lent, rag-ing sea; . . . And lo! at His word are the wa-ters stilled, This Stranger of Gal-i-lee; . . . A peace-ful, a qui-et, and ho-ly calm, Now and
4. Come ye, who are driv-en, and tempest-tossed, And His gra-cious sal-va-tion see; . . . He'll qui-et life's storms with His "Peace, be still!" This Stranger of Gal-i-lee; . . . He bids me to go and the sto-ry tell What He
1. Of the beau-ti-ful murm'ring sea;
1. Of the Stran-ger of Gal-i-lee;

The Stranger of Galilee

mo-ment was made to see; . . . The lame was made whole by the matchless skill
whispered "It was for thee!" . . My bur-den fell off at the pierc-ed feet
ev - er a-bides with me; . . . He hold-eth my life in His might-y hands,
ev - er to you will be, . . . If on - ly you let Him with you a - bide,
1. mo - - ment was made to see;
Of the Stranger of Gal - i - lee.
Of the Stranger of Gal - i - lee.
This Stranger of Gal - i - lee.
This Stranger of Gal - i - lee. (4 v.)
CHORUS
And I felt I could love Him for-
Oh, my friend, won't you love Him for-
ev - - - - er, So gra-cious and ten-der was He! I
ev - - - - er? So gra-cious and ten-der was He! . . . . . Ac-
ev - er and ev - er, so ten - der was He!
rit.
a tempo
claimed Him that day as my Sav - ior, This Stranger of Gal - i - lee.
cept Him to-day as your Sav - ior, This Stranger of Gal - i - lee.
Lord and my Sav-ior,
cres.
rit. e dim.

163 Christ Is King

CHARLES R. SCOVILLE  DE LOSS SMITH

1. Come, friends sing, of the faith that's so dear to me, . . .
2. Cru - ci - fied, thus He suf-fered and bled for me, . . .
3. At His feet, on old Ol - i - vet's Hill they say, . . .

Re - vealed thro' God's Son, in Gal - i - lee; He brought
Death and the grave won sin's vic - to - ry; Then the
Cloud char - iots halt - ed, took Christ a - way; Then the

peace on earth and good will to the sons of men,
sky grew dark and the tem-ple veil rent in twain,
an - gels came and to wond'ring dis - ci - ples said

Go tell it to the world, her King reigns a - - gain.
Rocks rent, and an - gels came, for He lived a - - gain.
He'll come, and earth and sea shall yield up their dead.

Christ Is King

CHORUS Unison
I am so hap-py in Je - sus, Cap-tiv-i-ty's Cap-tor is
He; . . . . An-gels re-joice when a soul's saved, Some day we
like Him shall be, . . . Sor-row and joy have the same Lord,
cres.
Val-ley of shad-ows shall sing; . . . Death has its life, its door
Harmony
o-pens in heav-en e - ter-nal-ly, Christ is King . . . .

164 He Lives

ALFRED H. ACKLEY ALFRED H. ACKLEY

1. I serve a ris - en Sav-ior, He's in the world to-day; I know that He is
2. In all the world a-round me I see His lov-ing care, And tho' my heart grows
3. Re-joice, rejoice, O Christian, lift up your voice and sing E-ter - nal hal - le-
liv - ing, what-ev - er men may say; I see His hand of mer - cy, I
wea - ry I nev - er will de - spair; I know that He is lead - ing thro'
lu - jahs to Je - sus Christ the King! The Hope of all who seek Him, the
hear His voice of cheer, And just the time I need Him He's al-ways near.
all the storm-y blast, The day of His ap-pear-ing will come at last.
Help of all who find, None oth-er is so lov - ing, so good and kind.
REFRAIN Spirited
He lives, He lives, Christ Je-sus lives to - day! He walks with me and
He lives, He lives,
talks with me a-long life's nar-row way. He lives, He lives, sal-
He lives, He lives,

He Lives

rit. ff
va-tion to im - part! You ask me how I know He lives? He lives within my heart.
Jesus Never Fails
165
ARTHUR A. LUTHER
ARTHUR A. LUTHER
1. Earth-ly friends may prove un - true, Doubts and fears as - sail;
2. Tho' the sky be dark and drear, Fierce and strong the gale,
3. In life's dark and bit - ter hour Love will still pre - vail;
One still loves and cares for you: Je - sus nev - er fails.
nev - er fails.
Just re - mem - ber He is near, And He will not fail.
will not fail.
Trust His ev - er - last - ing pow'r, Je - sus will not fail.
will not fail.
CHORUS
Je - sus nev - er fails, Je - sus nev - er fails;
Heav'n and earth may pass a - way But Je - sus nev - er fails.

166 The Love of God

FREDERICK M. LEHMAN

FREDERICK M. LEHMAN
ARR. BY CLAUDIA L. MAYS

1. The love of God is great-er far Than tongue or pen can ev - er tell;
2. When hoar-y time shall pass a - way, And earth-ly thrones and king-doms fall;
3. Could we with ink the o-cean fill, And were the skies of parch-ment made,
It goes be-yond the high-est star, And reach-es to the low-est hell;
When men who here re-fuse to pray, On rocks and hills and moun-tains call;
Were ev - 'ry stalk on earth a quill, And ev-'ry man a scribe by trade;
The guilt - y pair, bowed down with care, God gave His Son to win;
God's love, so sure, shall still en - dure, All meas-ure - less and strong;
To write the love of God a - bove Would drain the o - cean dry;
His err - ing child He rec - on - ciled, And par-doned from his sin.
Re-deem-ing grace to Ad-am's race–The saints' and an - gels' song.
Nor could the scroll con-tain the whole, Tho' stretched from sky to sky.
CHORUS
Oh love of God, how rich and pure! How meas-ure - less and strong!

The Love of God

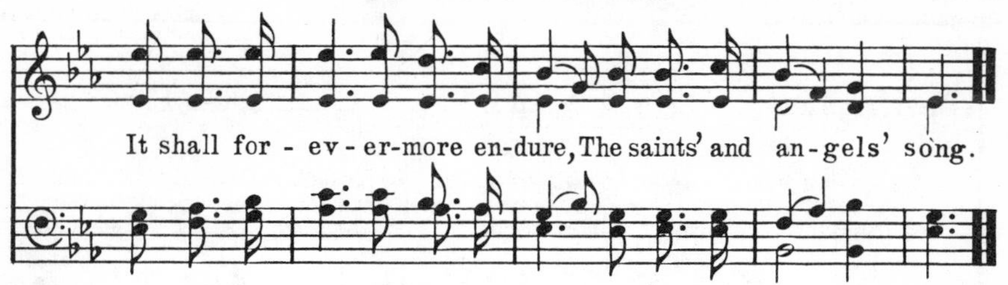
It shall for - ev - er-more en-dure, The saints' and an-gels' song.

I Long to Glorify Thee 167

RALPH MANCHEE HERMAN VOSS

1. Christ my Lord gave all for me, That from sin I might be free,
2. Christ my Lord a - rose and lives, O - ver all the vic-t'ry gives,
3. Christ my Lord will come one day, Take me home with Him to stay,

Now in me He lives a - gain; Glo - ry to His pre-cious Name.
Now in Him I live a - new, Praise His Name, I know 'tis true.
Then a-new His praise I'll sing; Reign with Him my Lord and King.

CHORUS

on-ly Thee.
I long to glo-ri-fy Thee, dear Lord, I long to glo-ri-fy Thee.

on - ly Thee.
In all I do, in all I say, I long to glo-ri-fy Thee.

168 Depth of Mercy! Can There Be

CHARLES WESLEY | WILLIAM B. BRADBURY

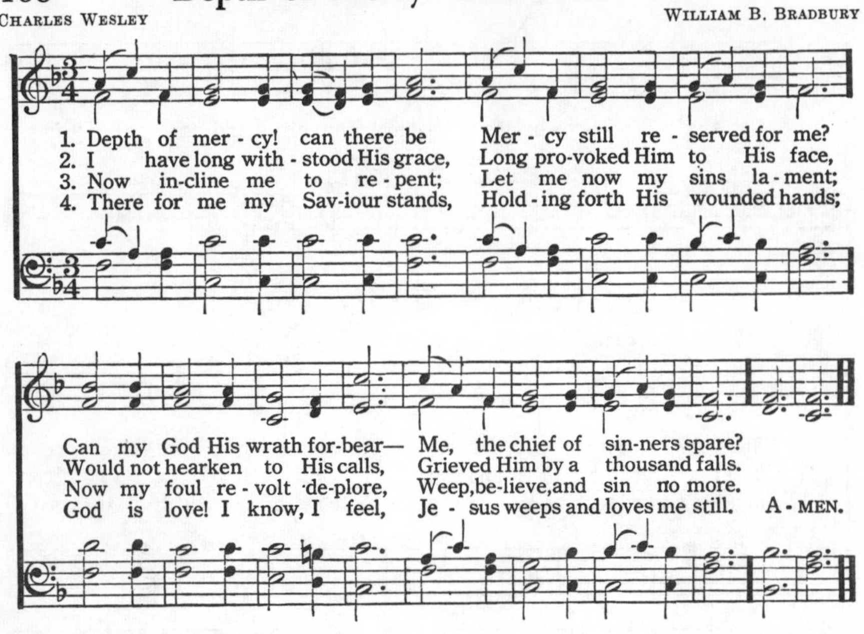
1. Depth of mer-cy! can there be Mer-cy still re-served for me?
2. I have long with-stood His grace, Long pro-voked Him to His face,
3. Now in-cline me to re-pent; Let me now my sins la-ment;
4. There for me my Sav-iour stands, Hold-ing forth His wounded hands;
Can my God His wrath for-bear— Me, the chief of sin-ners spare?
Would not hearken to His calls, Grieved Him by a thousand falls.
Now my foul re-volt de-plore, Weep, be-lieve, and sin no more.
God is love! I know, I feel, Je-sus weeps and loves me still. A-MEN.

169 Jesus, Thy Blood and Righteousness

NICOLAUS L. ZINZENDORF
TR. BY JOHN WESLEY | WILLIAM GARDINER'S "SACRED MELODIES"

1. Je-sus, Thy blood and right-eous-ness My beau-ty are, my glo-rious dress;
2. Bold shall I stand in Thy great day, For who aught to my charge shall lay?
3. Lord, I be-lieve Thy pre-cious blood, Which, at the mer-cy-seat of God,
4. Lord, I be-lieve were sin-ners more Than sands up-on the o-cean shore,

'Midst flaming worlds, in these ar-rayed, With joy shall I lift up my head.
Ful-ly ab-solved through these I am, From sin and fear, from guilt and shame.
For-ev-er doth for sin-ners plead, For me, e'en for my soul was shed.
Thou hast for all a ran-som paid, For all a full a-tone-ment paid. A-MEN.

Christ Returneth 170

H. L. TURNER JAMES McGRANAHAN

1. It may be at morn, when the day is a - wak-ing, When sunlight thro'
2. It may be at mid - day, it may be at twi-light, It may be, per-
3. While its hosts cry Hosanna, from heaven de-scend-ing, With glo - ri - fied
4. Oh, joy! oh, de - light! should we go with-out dy - ing, No sick-ness, no
dark - ness and shad - ow is break-ing, That Je - sus will come in the
chance, that the black-ness of mid-night Will burst in - to light in the
saints and the an - gels at - tend - ing, With grace on His brow, like a
sad - ness, no dread and no cry - ing, Caught up thro' the clouds with our
full - ness of glo - ry, To re - ceive from the world "His own."
blaze of His glo - ry, When Je - sus re - ceives "His own."
ha - lo of glo - ry, Will Je - sus re - ceive "His own."
Lord in - to glo - ry, When Je - sus re - ceives "His own."
CHORUS
O Lord Je - sus, how long, how long Ere we shout the glad song, Christ re-
rit.
turn-eth! Hal - le - lu - jah! hal - le - lu - jah! A - men, Hal - le - lu - jah! A - men.

171 He Is Coming Again

MABEL JOHNSTON CAMP

MABEL JOHNSTON CAMP

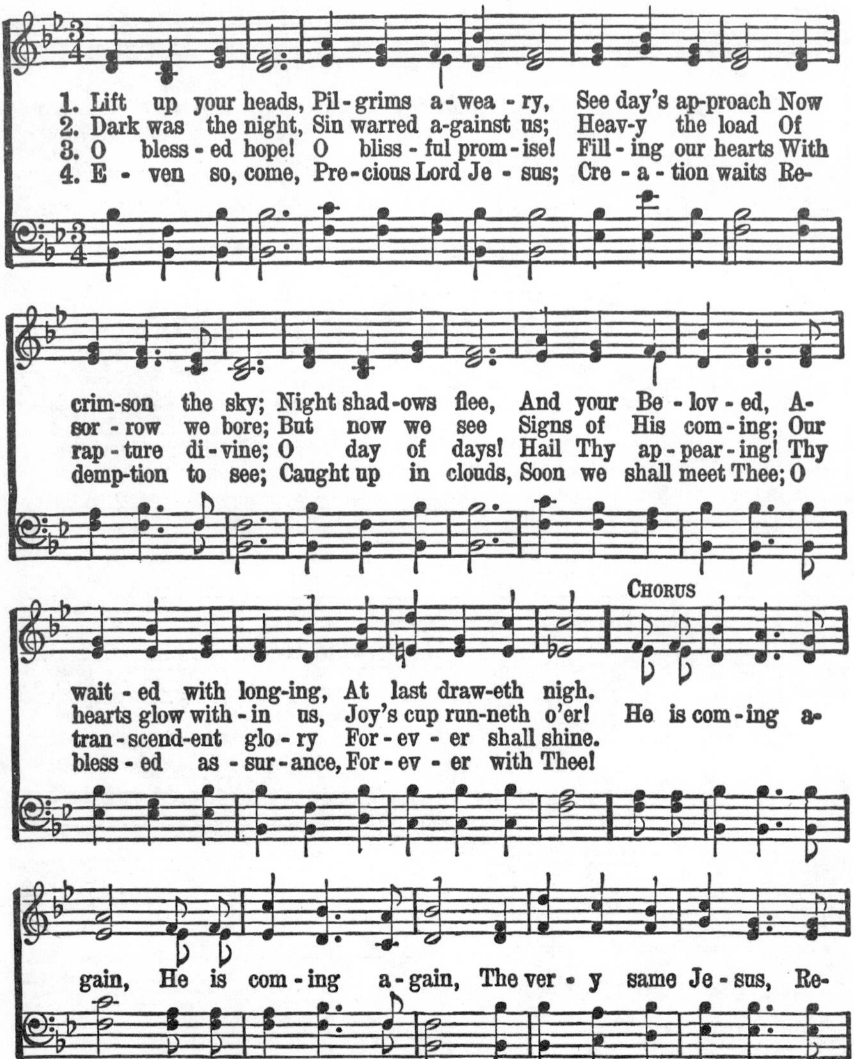

1. Lift up your heads, Pil-grims a-wea-ry, See day's ap-proach Now crim-son the sky; Night shad-ows flee, And your Be-lov-ed, A-wait-ed with long-ing, At last draw-eth nigh.

2. Dark was the night, Sin warred a-gainst us; Heav-y the load Of sor-row we bore; But now we see Signs of His com-ing; Our hearts glow with-in us, Joy's cup run-neth o'er!

3. O bless-ed hope! O bliss-ful prom-ise! Fill-ing our hearts With rap-ture di-vine; O day of days! Hail Thy ap-pear-ing! Thy tran-scend-ent glo-ry For-ev-er shall shine.

4. E-ven so, come, Pre-cious Lord Je-sus; Cre-a-tion waits Re-demp-tion to see; Caught up in clouds, Soon we shall meet Thee; O bless-ed as-sur-ance, For-ev-er with Thee!

CHORUS

He is com-ing a-gain, He is com-ing a-gain, The ver-y same Je-sus, Re-ject-ed of men; He is com-ing a-gain, He is com-ing a-gain, He is com-ing a-gain,

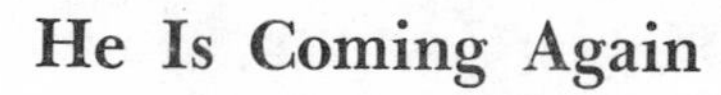
He Is Coming Again

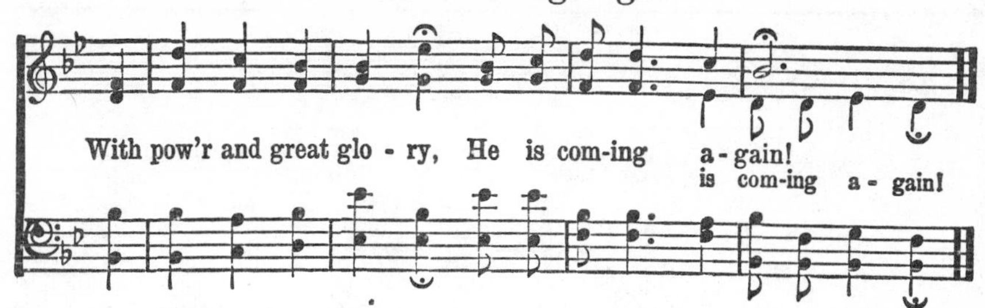
With pow'r and great glo - ry, He is com-ing a - gain!
is com-ing a - gain!

Is Thy Heart Right With God? 172

ELISHA A. HOFFMAN — ELISHA A. HOFFMAN

1. Have thy af-fec-tions been nailed to the cross? Is thy heart right with God?
2. Hast thou do - min-ion o'er self and o'er sin? Is thy heart right with God?
3. Is there no more con-dem-na-tion for sin? Is thy heart right with God?
4. Art thou now walk-ing in heaven's pure light? Is thy heart right with God?

Count-est thou all things for Je - sus but loss? Is thy heart right with God?
O - ver all e - vil with-out and with-in? Is thy heart right with God?
Does Je - sus rule in the tem - ple with-in? Is thy heart right with God?
Is thy soul wear-ing the gar-ment of white? Is thy heart right with God?

CHORUS

Is thy heart right with God, Washed in the crim - son flood,

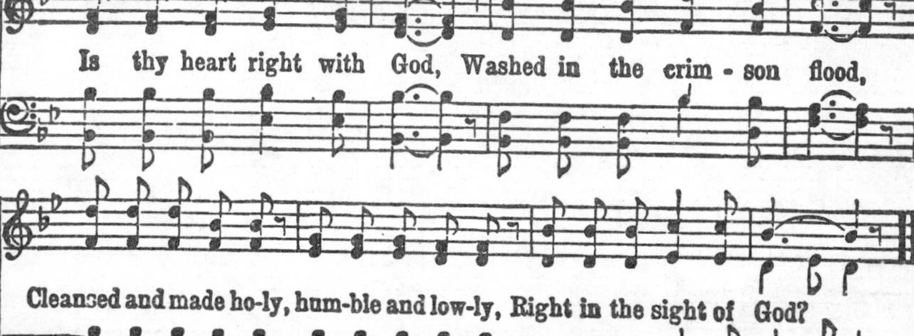
Cleansed and made ho-ly, hum-ble and low-ly, Right in the sight of God?

173 Jesus Is Coming Again

JOHN W. PETERSON | JOHN W. PETERSON

1. Mar-vel-ous mes-sage we bring, Glo-ri-ous car-ol we sing,
2. For-est and flow-er ex-claim, Moun-tain and mead-ow the same,
3. Stand-ing be-fore Him at last, Tri-al and trou-ble all past,

Won-der-ful word of the King— Je-sus is com-ing a-gain! (a-gain!)
All earth and heav-en pro-claim— Je-sus is com-ing a-gain! (a-gain!)
Crowns at His feet we will cast— Je-sus is com-ing a-gain! (a-gain!)

CHORUS

Com-ing a-gain, Com-ing a-gain;
May-be morn-ing, may-be noon, May-be eve-ning and may-be soon!

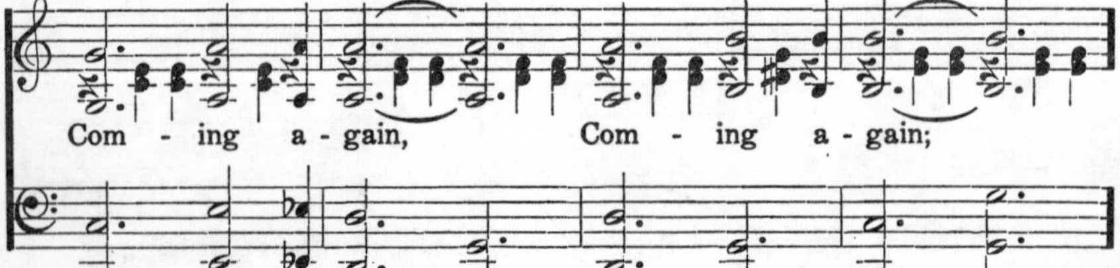
Com-ing a-gain, Com-ing a-gain;

Jesus Is Coming Again

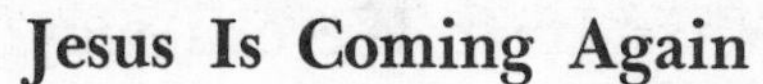

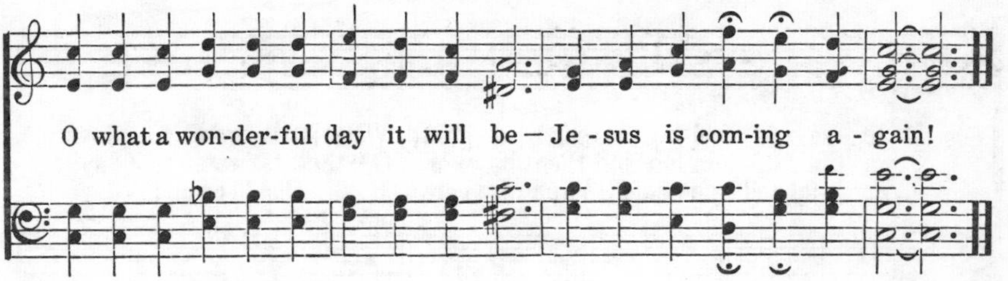
O what a won-der-ful day it will be — Je - sus is com-ing a - gain!

Have You Any Room for Jesus? 174

SOURCE UNKNOWN
ARR. BY DANIEL W. WHITTLE

C. C. WILLIAMS

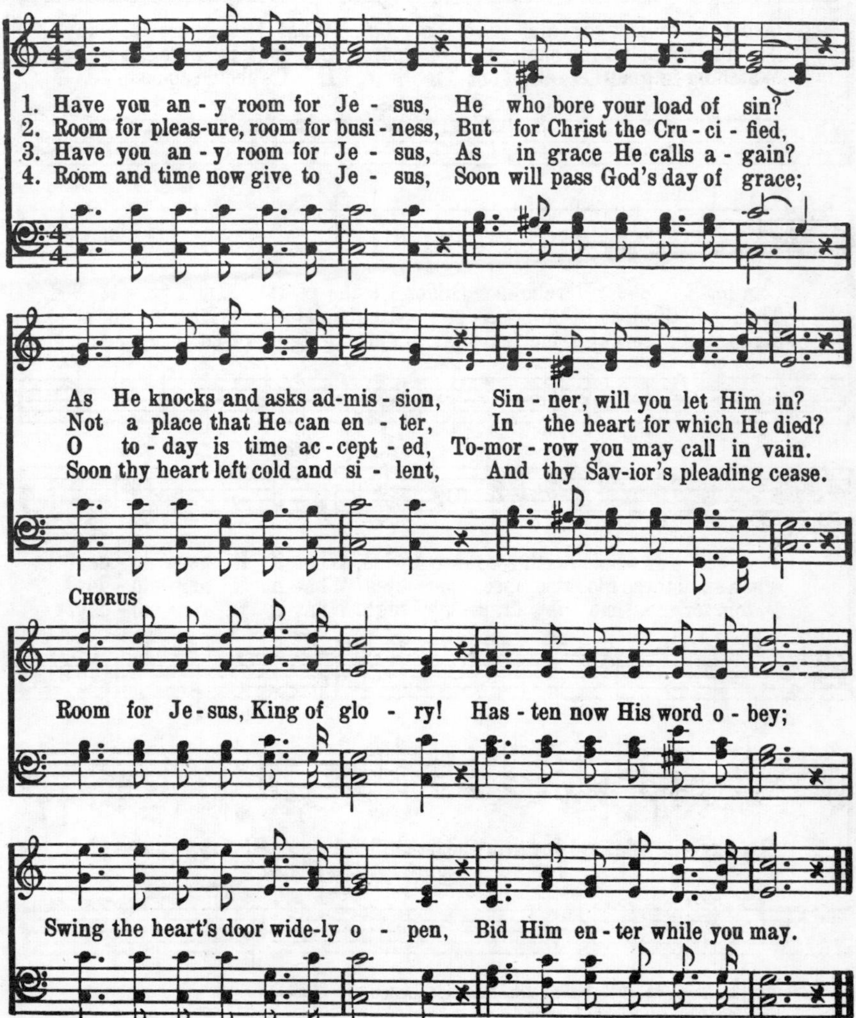
1. Have you an - y room for Je - sus, He who bore your load of sin?
2. Room for pleas-ure, room for busi - ness, But for Christ the Cru - ci - fied,
3. Have you an - y room for Je - sus, As in grace He calls a - gain?
4. Room and time now give to Je - sus, Soon will pass God's day of grace;
As He knocks and asks ad-mis - sion, Sin - ner, will you let Him in?
Not a place that He can en - ter, In the heart for which He died?
O to - day is time ac - cept - ed, To-mor - row you may call in vain.
Soon thy heart left cold and si - lent, And thy Sav-ior's pleading cease.
CHORUS
Room for Je - sus, King of glo - ry! Has - ten now His word o - bey;
Swing the heart's door wide-ly o - pen, Bid Him en - ter while you may.

175 What If It Were Today?

Leila N. Morris — Leila N. Morris

6/4
1. Je - sus is com-ing to earth a-gain, What if it were to - day?
2. Sa-tan's do-min-ion will then be o'er, O that it were to - day!
3. Faith-ful and true would He find us here If He should come to - day?
Com-ing in pow-er and love to reign, What if it were to - day?
Sor - row and sigh-ing shall be no more, O that it were to - day!
Watching in glad-ness and not in fear, If He should come to - day?
Com-ing to claim His cho - sen Bride, All the re-deemed and pu - ri - fied,
Then shall the dead in Christ a - rise, Caught up to meet Him in the skies,
Signs of His com - ing mul - ti - ply, Morning light breaks in east-ern sky,
rit.
a tempo
O - ver this whole earth scat - tered wide, What if it were to - day?
When shall these glo - ries meet our eyes? What if it were to - day?
Watch, for the time is draw - ing nigh, What if it were to - day?
Chorus
Glo - ry, glo - ry! Joy to my heart 'twill bring;.. Glo - ry, glo - ry!
Joy to my heart 'twill bring;

What If It Were Today?

When we shall crown Him King;... Glo-ry, glo-ry! Haste to pre-pare the
When we shall crown Him King; Haste to pre-
ritard.
way;.... Glo-ry, glo-ry! Je-sus will come some day.
pare the way;

Savior, More Than Life to Me 176

FANNY J. CROSBY WILLIAM H. DOANE

1. Sav-ior, more than life to me, I am cling-ing, cling-ing close to Thee;
2. Thro' this chang-ing world be-low, Lead me gen-tly, gen-tly as I go;
3. Let me love Thee more and more, Till this fleet-ing, fleet-ing life is o'er;
Fine
Let Thy pre-cious blood ap-plied, Keep me ev-er, ev-er near Thy side.
Trusting Thee, I can-not stray, I can nev-er, nev-er lose my way.
Till my soul is lost in love, In a bright-er, bright-er world a-bove.
Refrain
D. S.
Ev-'ry day, ev-'ry hour, Let me feel Thy cleans-ing pow'r;
Ev-'ry day and hour, ev-'ry day and hour,

177 God Be with You

JEREMIAH E. RANKIN — WILLIAM G. TOMER

1. God be with you till we meet a-gain; By His counsels guide, uphold you,
2. God be with you till we meet a-gain; 'Neath His wings protecting hide you,
3. God be with you till we meet a-gain; When life's perils thick confound you,
4. God be with you till we meet a-gain; Keep love's banner floating o'er you;
With His sheep se-cure-ly fold you; God be with you till we meet a-gain.
Dai-ly man-na still pro-vide you; God be with you till we meet a-gain.
Put His arms un-fail-ing round you; God be with you till we meet a-gain.
Smite death's threat'ning wave before you; God be with you till we meet a-gain.
CHORUS
Till we meet,.... till we meet, Till we meet at Je-sus' feet;
Till we meet, till we meet, till we meet;
Till we meet,.... till we meet, God be with you till we meet a-gain.
Till we meet, till we meet,

In the Service of the King

Alfred H. Ackley — Bentley D. Ackley

1. I am happy in the service of the King, I am happy, oh, so happy; I have peace and joy that nothing else can bring, In the service of the King.
2. I am happy in the service of the King, I am happy, oh, so happy; Thro' the sunshine and the shadow I can sing, In the service of the King.
3. I am happy in the service of the King, I am happy, oh, so happy; To His guiding hand forever I will cling, In the service of the King.
4. I am happy in the service of the King, I am happy, oh, so happy; All that I possess to Him I gladly bring, In the service of the King.

Chorus

In the service of the King, Ev'ry talent I will bring; I have peace and joy and blessing In the service of the King.

179 The Son of God Goes Forth to War

Reginald Heber — Henry S. Cutler

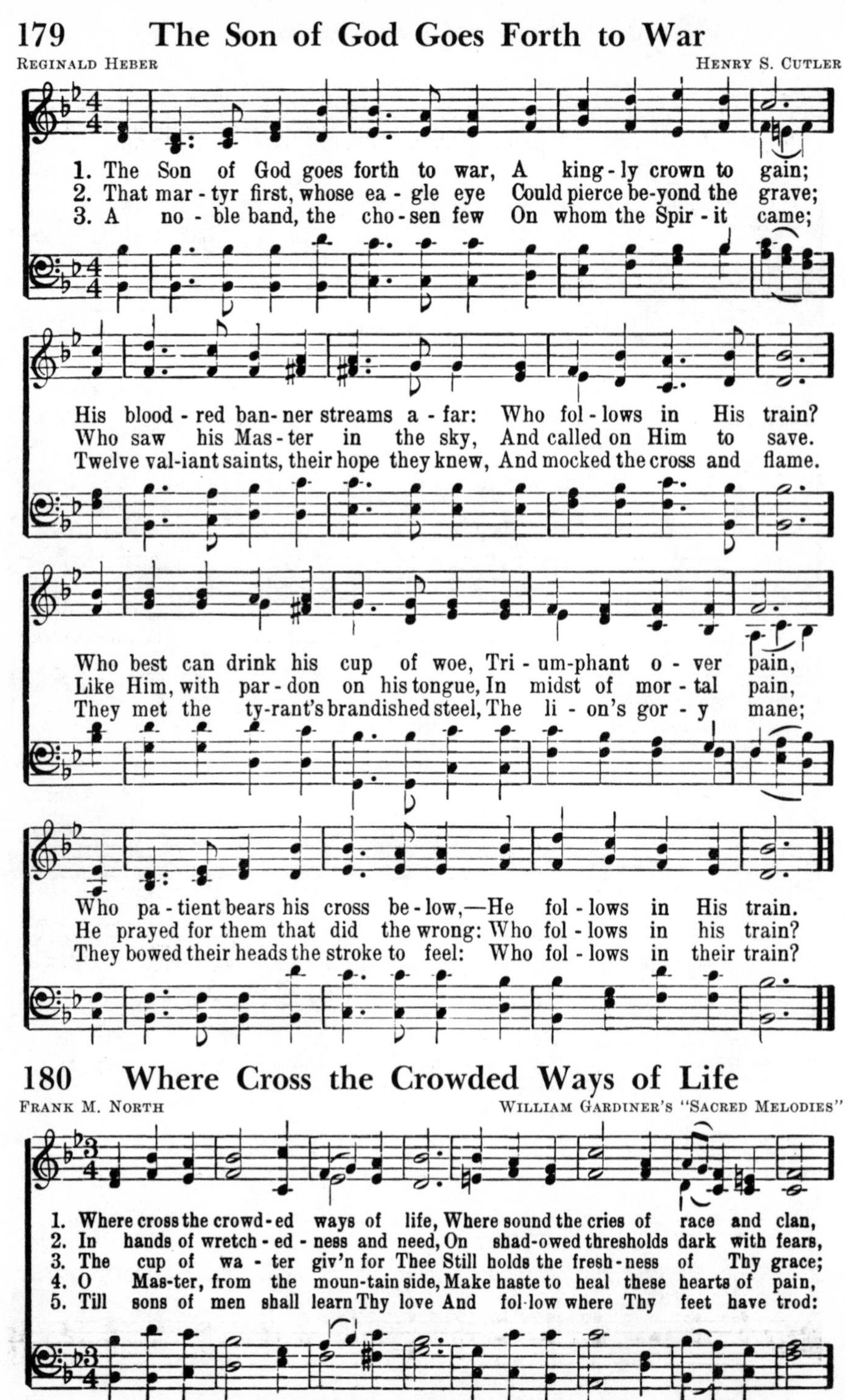
1. The Son of God goes forth to war, A king-ly crown to gain;
2. That mar-tyr first, whose ea-gle eye Could pierce be-yond the grave;
3. A no-ble band, the cho-sen few On whom the Spir-it came;
His blood-red ban-ner streams a-far: Who fol-lows in His train?
Who saw his Mas-ter in the sky, And called on Him to save.
Twelve val-iant saints, their hope they knew, And mocked the cross and flame.
Who best can drink his cup of woe, Tri-um-phant o-ver pain,
Like Him, with par-don on his tongue, In midst of mor-tal pain,
They met the ty-rant's brandished steel, The li-on's gor-y mane;
Who pa-tient bears his cross be-low,—He fol-lows in His train.
He prayed for them that did the wrong: Who fol-lows in his train?
They bowed their heads the stroke to feel: Who fol-lows in their train?
180 Where Cross the Crowded Ways of Life
Frank M. North
William Gardiner's "Sacred Melodies"
1. Where cross the crowd-ed ways of life, Where sound the cries of race and clan,
2. In hands of wretch-ed-ness and need, On shad-owed thresholds dark with fears,
3. The cup of wa-ter giv'n for Thee Still holds the fresh-ness of Thy grace;
4. O Mas-ter, from the moun-tain side, Make haste to heal these hearts of pain,
5. Till sons of men shall learn Thy love And fol-low where Thy feet have trod:

Where Cross the Crowded Ways of Life

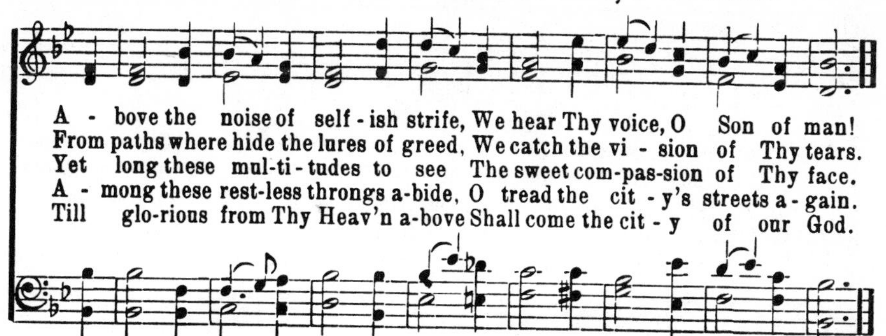
A - bove the noise of self - ish strife, We hear Thy voice, O Son of man!
From paths where hide the lures of greed, We catch the vi - sion of Thy tears.
Yet long these mul-ti-tudes to see The sweet com-pas-sion of Thy face.
A - mong these rest-less throngs a-bide, O tread the cit - y's streets a - gain.
Till glo-rious from Thy Heav'n a-bove Shall come the cit - y of our God.

Let the Lower Lights Be Burning 181

PHILIP P. BLISS

PHILIP P. BLISS

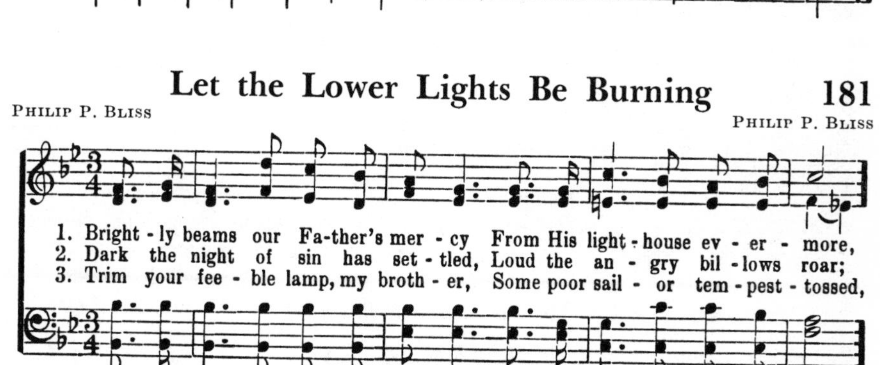
1. Bright - ly beams our Fa-ther's mer - cy From His light - house ev - er - more,
2. Dark the night of sin has set - tled, Loud the an - gry bil - lows roar;
3. Trim your fee - ble lamp, my broth - er, Some poor sail - or tem - pest - tossed,

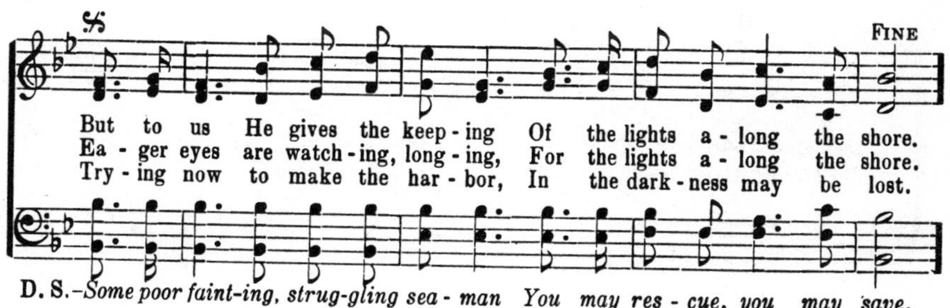
FINE
But to us He gives the keep - ing Of the lights a - long the shore.
Ea - ger eyes are watch - ing, long - ing, For the lights a - long the shore.
Try - ing now to make the har - bor, In the dark - ness may be lost.
D. S.–Some poor faint-ing, strug-gling sea - man You may res - cue, you may save.

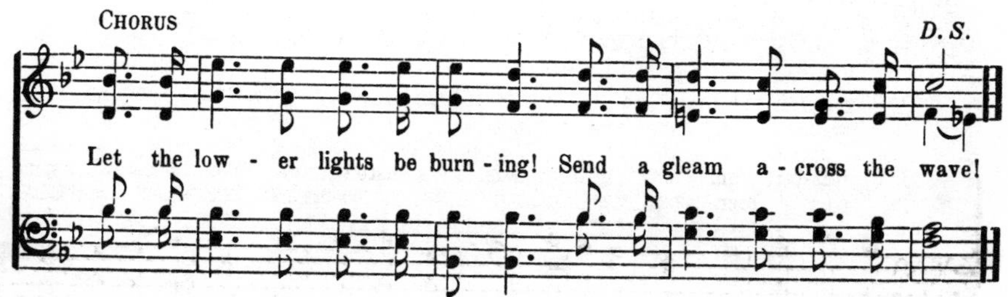
CHORUS
D. S.
Let the low - er lights be burn - ing! Send a gleam a - cross the wave!

182 My Savior's Love

CHARLES H. GABRIEL — CHARLES H. GABRIEL

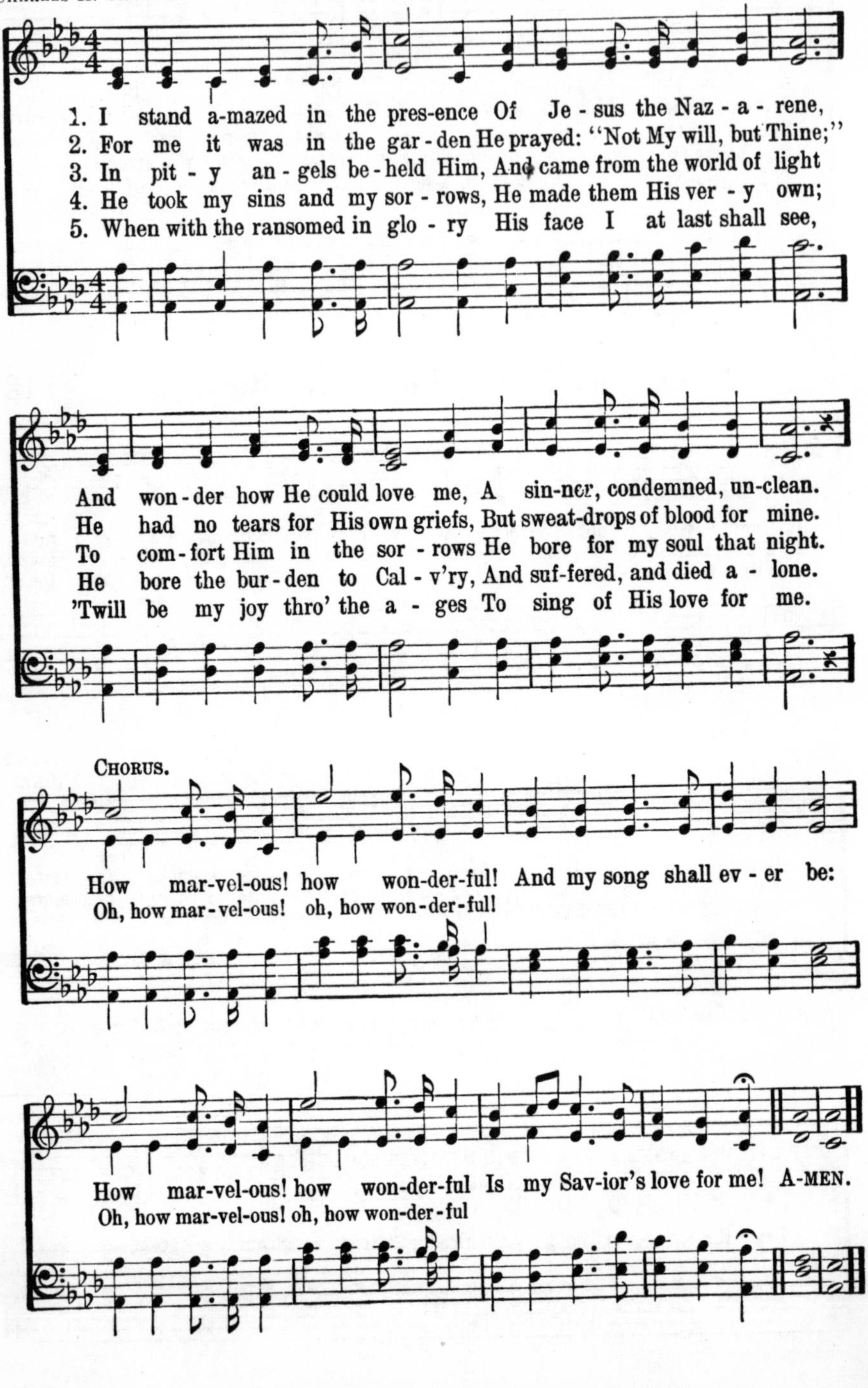

1. I stand amazed in the presence Of Jesus the Nazarene,
And wonder how He could love me, A sinner, condemned, unclean.

2. For me it was in the garden He prayed: "Not My will, but Thine;"
He had no tears for His own griefs, But sweat-drops of blood for mine.

3. In pity angels beheld Him, And came from the world of light
To comfort Him in the sorrows He bore for my soul that night.

4. He took my sins and my sorrows, He made them His very own;
He bore the burden to Calv'ry, And suffered, and died alone.

5. When with the ransomed in glory His face I at last shall see,
'Twill be my joy thro' the ages To sing of His love for me.

CHORUS.

How marvelous! how wonderful! And my song shall ever be:
(Oh, how marvelous! oh, how wonderful!)
How marvelous! how wonderful Is my Savior's love for me! AMEN.
(Oh, how marvelous! oh, how wonderful)

It Pays to Serve Jesus

FRANK C. HUSTON FRANK C. HUSTON

1. The serv-ice of Je-sus true pleas-ure af-fords, In Him there is joy with-out an al-loy; 'Tis heav-en to trust Him and rest on His words; It pays to serve Je-sus each day.
2. It pays to serve Je-sus what-e'er may be-tide, It pays to be true what-e'er you may do; 'Tis rich-es of mer-cy in Him to a-bide; It pays to serve Je-sus each day.
3. Tho' sometimes the shad-ows may hang o'er the way, And sor-rows may come to beck-on us home, Our pre-cious Re-deem-er each toil will re-pay; It pays to serve Je-sus each day.

CHORUS

It pays to serve Je-sus, it pays ev-'ry day, It pays ev-'ry step of the way; . . . . . (ev-'ry step of the way;) Tho' the pathway to glo-ry may sometimes be drear, You'll be hap-py each step of the way.

184

Make Me a Blessing

Ira B. Wilson — George S. Schuler

Slowly
1. Out in the high-ways and by-ways of life, Man-y are wea-ry and sad; . . . . . Car-ry the sunshine where darkness is rife,
are wea-ry and sad;
2. Tell the sweet sto-ry of Christ and His love, Tell of His pow'r to for-give; . . . . . Oth-ers will trust Him if on-ly you prove
His pow'r to for-give;
3. Give as 'twas giv-en to you in your need, Love as the Mas-ter loved you; . . . . . Be to the help-less a help-er in-deed,
the Mas-ter loved you;
rit.
Mak-ing the sor-row-ing glad. . . .
True, ev-'ry mo-ment you live. . . .
Un-to your mis-sion be true. . . .
Chorus Men or Unison
Make me a bless-ing,
Women
Make me a bless-ing, Out of my life . . . . may Je-
Out of my life
Men
rit.
sus shine; . . Make me a bless-ing, O Sav-ior,
Unison
Women

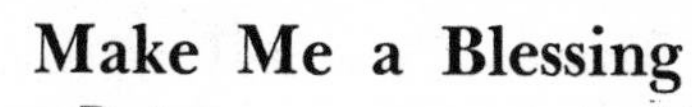

Make Me a Blessing

Parts *ad lib.*

I pray...... Make me a bless-ing to some-one to-day.
I pray Thee, my Sav-ior,

Tenors

185

Others

Charles D. Meigs — Roscoe S. Nickerson

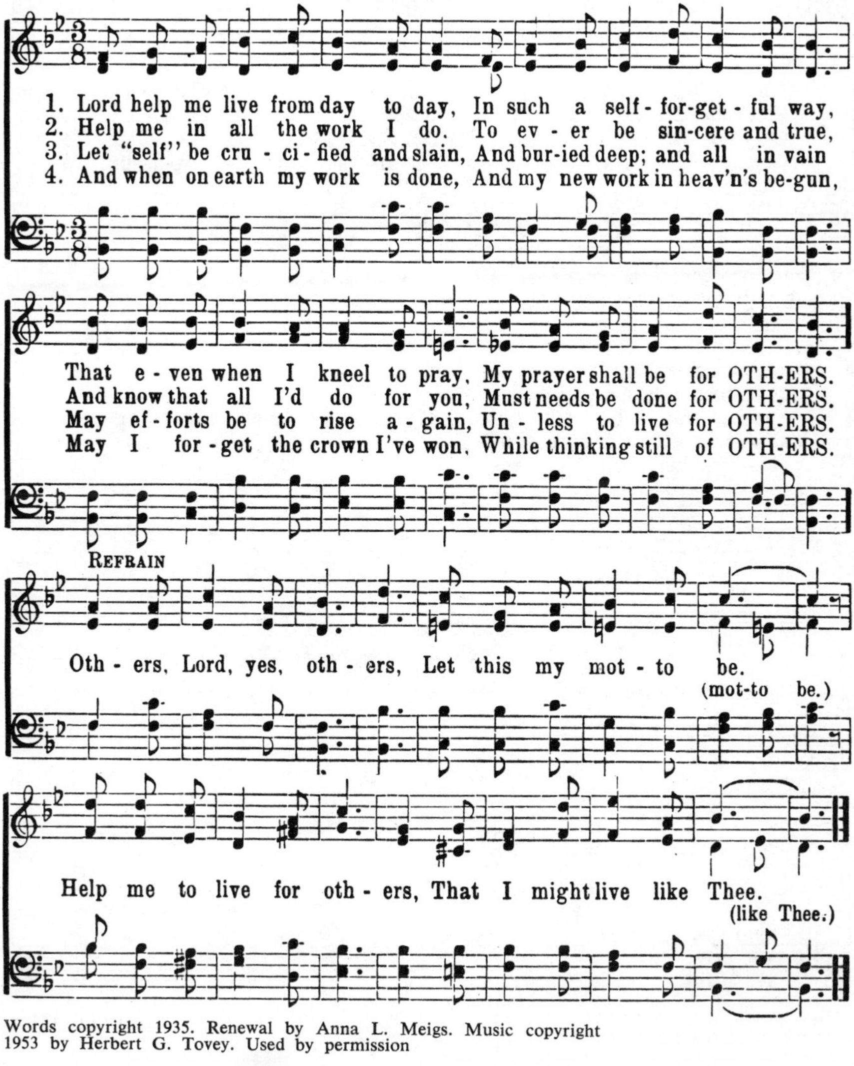

1. Lord help me live from day to day, In such a self-for-get-ful way,
2. Help me in all the work I do, To ev-er be sin-cere and true,
3. Let "self" be cru-ci-fied and slain, And bur-ied deep; and all in vain
4. And when on earth my work is done, And my new work in heav'n's be-gun,

That e-ven when I kneel to pray, My prayer shall be for OTH-ERS.
And know that all I'd do for you, Must needs be done for OTH-ERS.
May ef-forts be to rise a-gain, Un-less to live for OTH-ERS.
May I for-get the crown I've won, While thinking still of OTH-ERS.

Refrain

Oth-ers, Lord, yes, oth-ers, Let this my mot-to be. (mot-to be.)
Help me to live for oth-ers, That I might live like Thee. (like Thee.)

186 Make Me a Channel of Blessing

HARPER G. SMYTH — HARPER G. SMYTH

1. Is your life a chan-nel of bless-ing? Is the love of God flow-ing thro' you? Are you tell-ing the lost of the Sav-iour? Are you read-y His serv-ice to do?
2. Is your life a chan-nel of bless-ing? Are you bur-dened for those that are lost? Have you urged up-on those who are stray-ing, The Sav-iour who died on the cross?
3. Is your life a chan-nel of bless-ing? Is it dai-ly tell-ing for Him? Have you spo-ken the word of sal-va-tion To those who are dy-ing in sin?
4. We can-not be chan-nels of bless-ing If our lives are not free from known sin; We will bar-ri-ers be and a hin-drance To those we are try-ing to win.

CHORUS

Make me a chan-nel of bless-ing to-day,
Make me a chan-nel of bless-ing, I pray;
My life pos-sess-ing, my serv-ice bless-ing,
Make me a chan-nel of bless-ing to-day.

rit.

Will Jesus Find Us Watching? 187

FANNY J. CROSBY — WILLIAM H. DOANE

1. When Jesus comes to reward His servants, Whether it be noon or night, Faithful to Him will He find us watching, With our lamps all trimmed and bright?
2. If, at the dawn of the early morning, He shall call us one by one, When to the Lord we restore our talents, Will He answer thee—"Well done"?
3. Have we been true to the trust He left us? Do we seek to do our best? If in our hearts there is naught condemns us, We shall have a glorious rest.
4. Blessed are those whom the Lord finds watching. In His glory they shall share; If He shall come at the dawn or midnight, Will He find us watching there?
rit.
CHORUS
Oh, can we say we are ready, brother? Ready for the soul's bright home? Say, will He find you and me still watching, Waiting, waiting when the Lord shall come?

188 Glory to His Name

ELISHA A. HOFFMAN JOHN H. STOCKTON

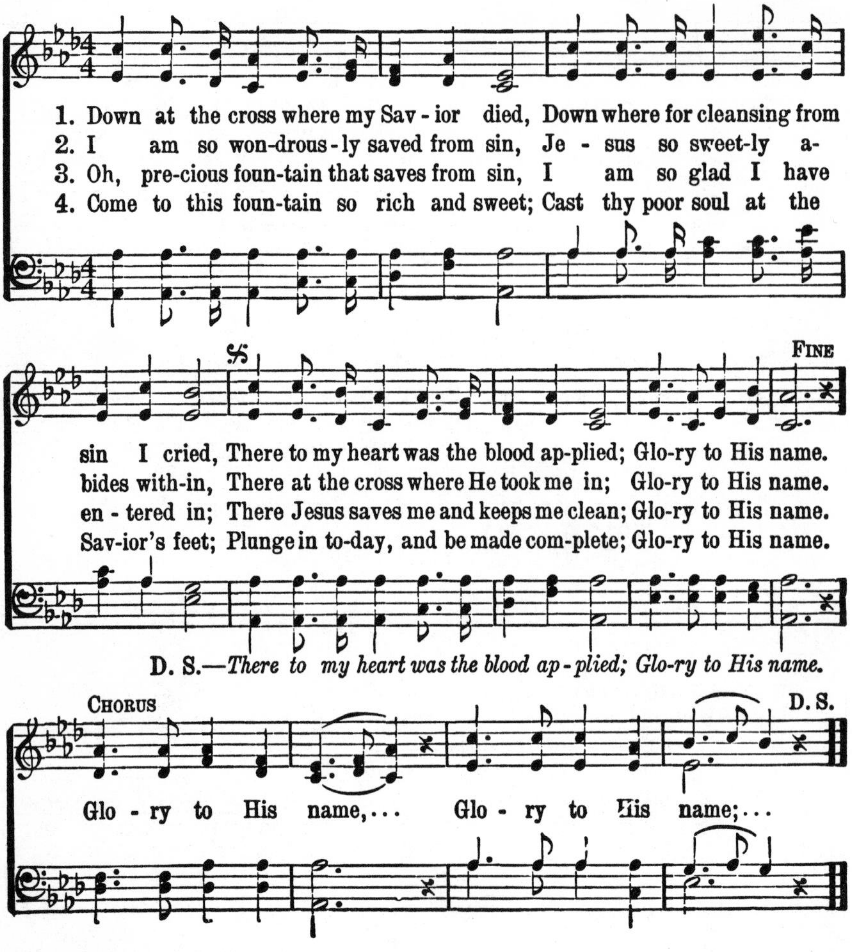

1. Down at the cross where my Sav - ior died, Down where for cleansing from
2. I am so won-drous - ly saved from sin, Je - sus so sweet-ly a-
3. Oh, pre-cious foun-tain that saves from sin, I am so glad I have
4. Come to this foun-tain so rich and sweet; Cast thy poor soul at the

FINE

sin I cried, There to my heart was the blood ap-plied; Glo-ry to His name.
bides with-in, There at the cross where He took me in; Glo-ry to His name.
en - tered in; There Jesus saves me and keeps me clean; Glo-ry to His name.
Sav-ior's feet; Plunge in to-day, and be made com-plete; Glo-ry to His name.

D. S.—*There to my heart was the blood ap - plied; Glo-ry to His name.*

CHORUS

Glo - ry to His name,... Glo - ry to His name;...

D. S.

189 Must Jesus Bear the Cross Alone?

THOMAS SHEPHERD GEORGE N. ALLEN

1. Must Je - sus bear the cross a - lone, And all the world go free?
2. The con - se - crat - ed cross I'll bear, Till death shall set me free,
3. Up - on the crys - tal pave-ment, down At Je - sus' pierc - ed feet,
4. O pre - cious cross! O glo - rious crown! O res - ur - rec - tion day!

Must Jesus Bear the Cross Alone?

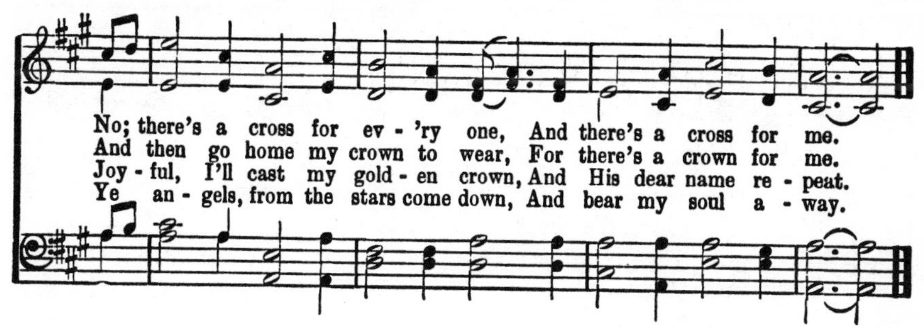

No; there's a cross for ev - 'ry one, And there's a cross for me.
And then go home my crown to wear, For there's a crown for me.
Joy - ful, I'll cast my gold - en crown, And His dear name re - peat.
Ye an - gels, from the stars come down, And bear my soul a - way.

Savior, Breathe an Evening Blessing 190

JAMES EDMESTON

GEORGE C. STEBBINS

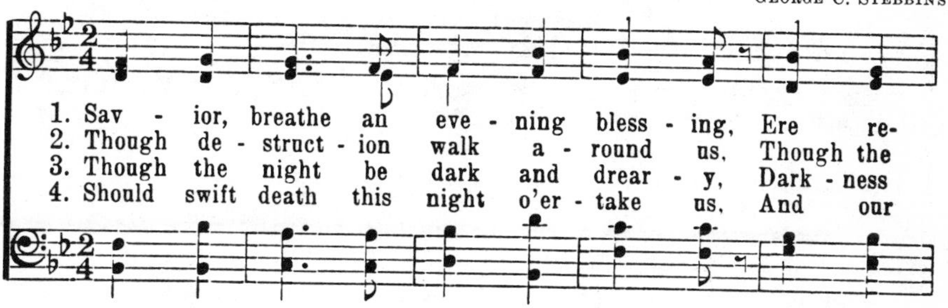

1. Sav - ior, breathe an eve - ning bless - ing, Ere re-
2. Though de - struct - ion walk a - round us, Though the
3. Though the night be dark and drear - y, Dark - ness
4. Should swift death this night o'er - take us, And our

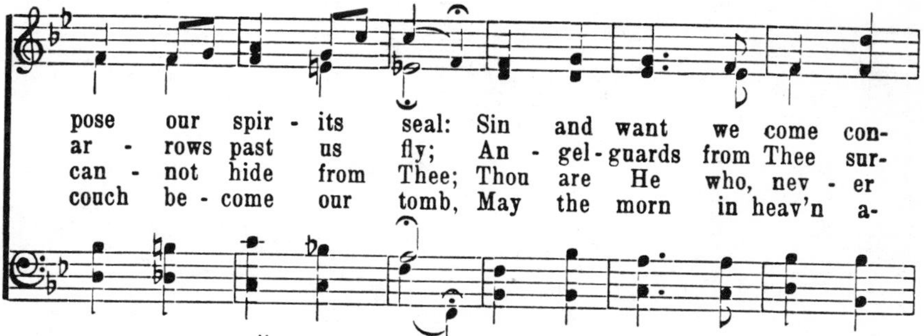

pose our spir - its seal: Sin and want we come con-
ar - rows past us fly; An - gel - guards from Thee sur-
can - not hide from Thee; Thou are He who, nev - er
couch be - come our tomb, May the morn in heav'n a-

rit.

fess - ing, Thou canst save and Thou canst heal.
round us, We are safe if Thou art nigh.
wea - ry, Watch - est where Thy peo - ple be.
wake us, Clad in bright and death-less bloom. A-MEN.

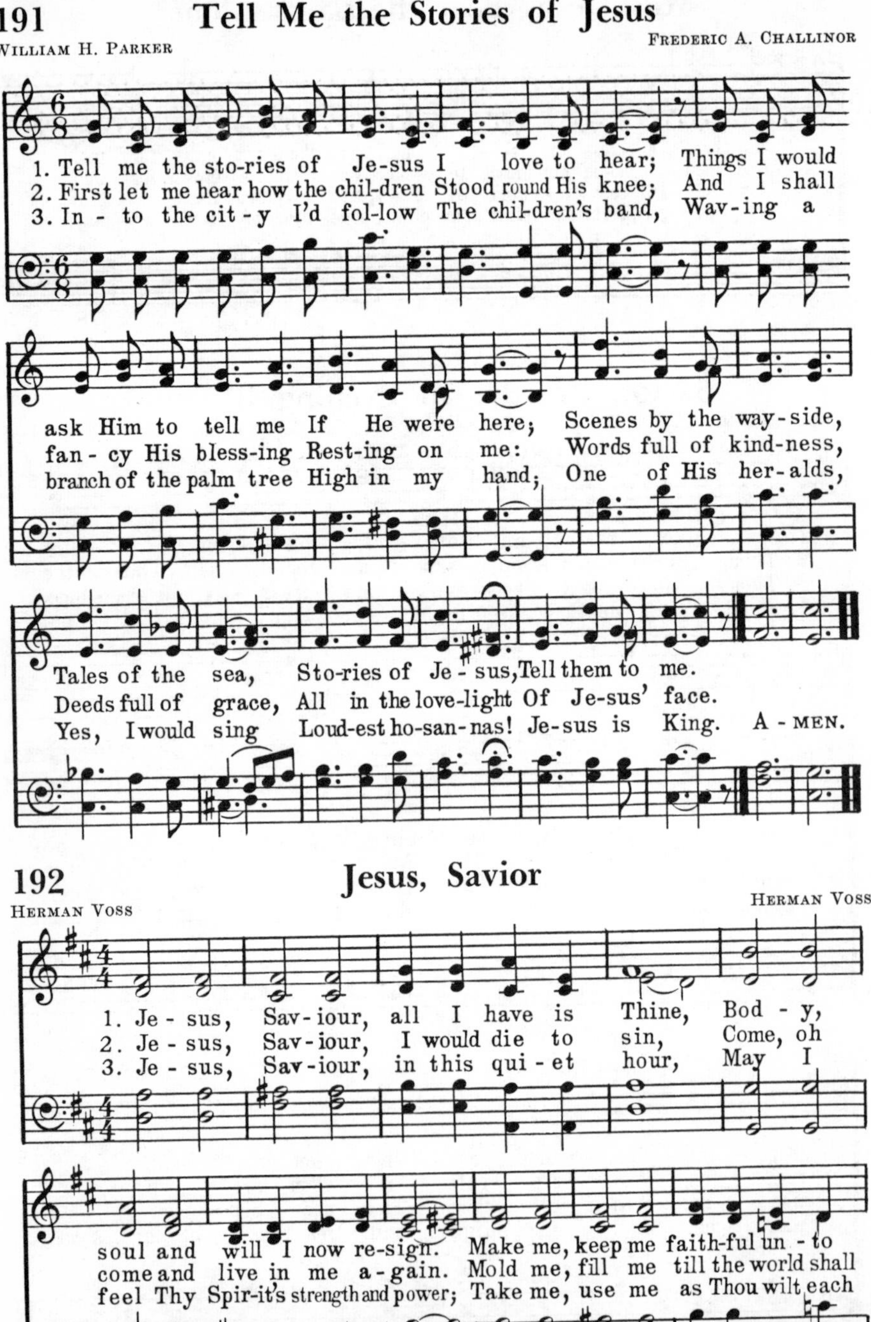
191 Tell Me the Stories of Jesus
William H. Parker
Frederic A. Challinor
1. Tell me the sto-ries of Je-sus I love to hear; Things I would
2. First let me hear how the chil-dren Stood round His knee; And I shall
3. In - to the cit - y I'd fol-low The chil-dren's band, Wav-ing a
ask Him to tell me If He were here; Scenes by the way-side,
fan - cy His bless-ing Rest-ing on me: Words full of kind-ness,
branch of the palm tree High in my hand; One of His her-alds,
Tales of the sea, Sto-ries of Je - sus, Tell them to me.
Deeds full of grace, All in the love-light Of Je-sus' face.
Yes, I would sing Loud-est ho-san-nas! Je-sus is King. A - men.
192 Jesus, Savior
Herman Voss
Herman Voss
1. Je - sus, Sav-iour, all I have is Thine, Bod - y,
2. Je - sus, Sav-iour, I would die to sin, Come, oh
3. Je - sus, Sav-iour, in this qui - et hour, May I
soul and will I now re-sign. Make me, keep me faith-ful un - to
come and live in me a-gain. Mold me, fill me till the world shall
feel Thy Spir-it's strength and power; Take me, use me as Thou wilt each

Jesus, Savior

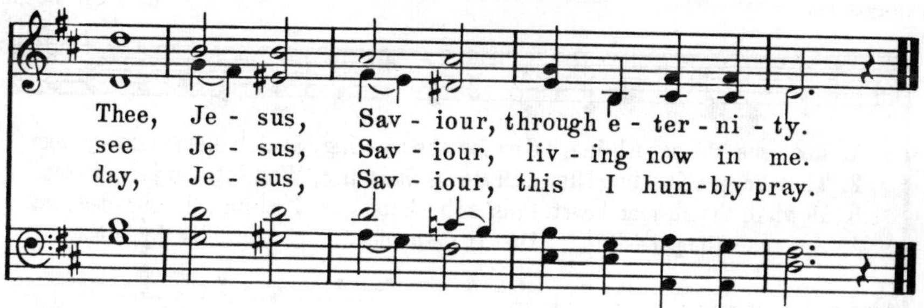

Thee, Je - sus, Sav - iour, through e - ter - ni - ty.
see Je - sus, Sav - iour, liv - ing now in me.
day, Je - sus, Sav - iour, this I hum - bly pray.

No Other Plea 193

LIDIE H. EDMUNDS

ARR. BY WILLIAM J. KIRKPATRICK

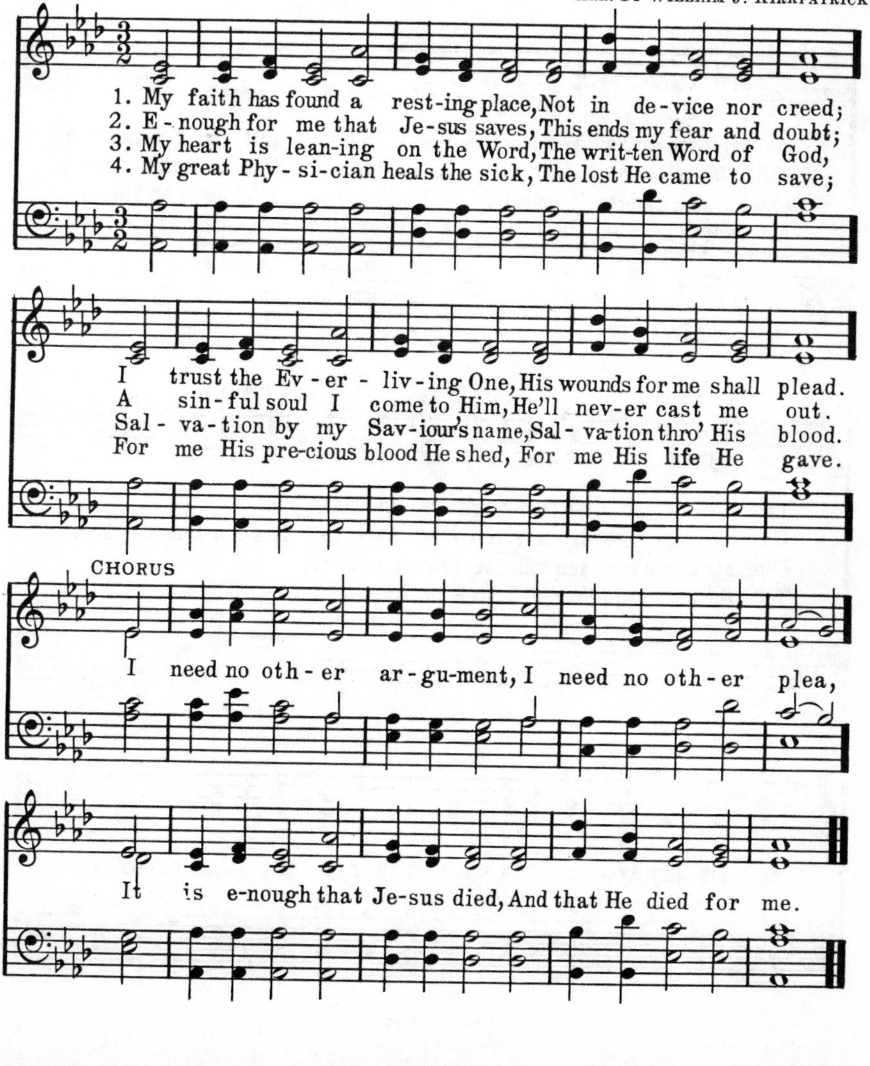

1. My faith has found a rest-ing place, Not in de-vice nor creed;
2. E-nough for me that Je-sus saves, This ends my fear and doubt;
3. My heart is lean-ing on the Word, The writ-ten Word of God,
4. My great Phy-si-cian heals the sick, The lost He came to save;

I trust the Ev-er-liv-ing One, His wounds for me shall plead.
A sin-ful soul I come to Him, He'll nev-er cast me out.
Sal-va-tion by my Sav-iour's name, Sal-va-tion thro' His blood.
For me His pre-cious blood He shed, For me His life He gave.

CHORUS

I need no oth-er ar-gu-ment, I need no oth-er plea,
It is e-nough that Je-sus died, And that He died for me.

194 Rescue the Perishing

FANNY J. CROSBY

WILLIAM H. DOANE

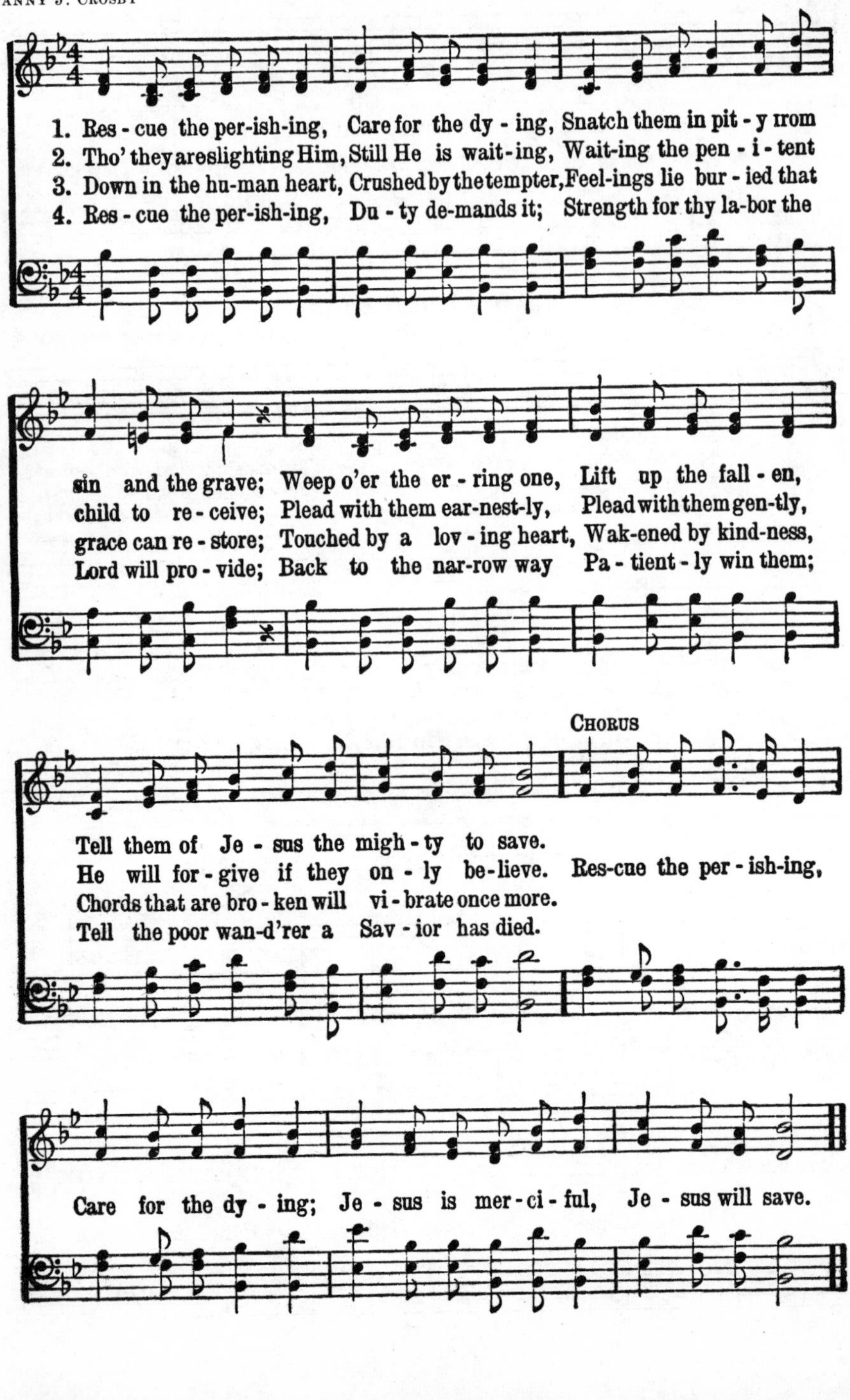

1. Res - cue the per-ish-ing, Care for the dy - ing, Snatch them in pit - y from sin and the grave; Weep o'er the er - ring one, Lift up the fall - en, Tell them of Je - sus the migh - ty to save.
2. Tho' they are slighting Him, Still He is wait-ing, Wait-ing the pen - i - tent child to re - ceive; Plead with them ear-nest-ly, Plead with them gen-tly, He will for - give if they on - ly be-lieve.
3. Down in the hu-man heart, Crushed by the tempter, Feel-ings lie bur - ied that grace can re - store; Touched by a lov - ing heart, Wak-ened by kind-ness, Chords that are bro - ken will vi - brate once more.
4. Res - cue the per-ish-ing, Du - ty de-mands it; Strength for thy la-bor the Lord will pro - vide; Back to the nar-row way Pa - tient - ly win them; Tell the poor wan-d'rer a Sav - ior has died.

CHORUS

Res-cue the per - ish-ing, Care for the dy - ing; Je - sus is mer - ci - ful, Je - sus will save.

A Passion for Souls

HERBERT G. TOVEY

FOSS L. FELLERS

1. Give me a pas - sion for souls, dear Lord, A pas - sion to save the lost;
2. Though there are dan-gers un-told and stern Con-front-ing me in the way,
3. How shall this pas - sion for souls be mine? Lord, make Thou the an-swer clear;
O that Thy love were by all a-dored, And wel-comed at an - y cost.
Will-ing - ly still would I go, nor turn, But trust Thee for grace each day.
Help me to throw out the old Life-Line To those who are strug-gling near.
CHORUS.
Je - sus, I long, I long to be win - ning Men who are
lost, and con - stant - ly sin - ning; O may this hour be
one of be - gin - ning The sto - ry of par - don to tell.

Help Somebody Today

CARRIE E. BRECK
CHARLES H. GABRIEL

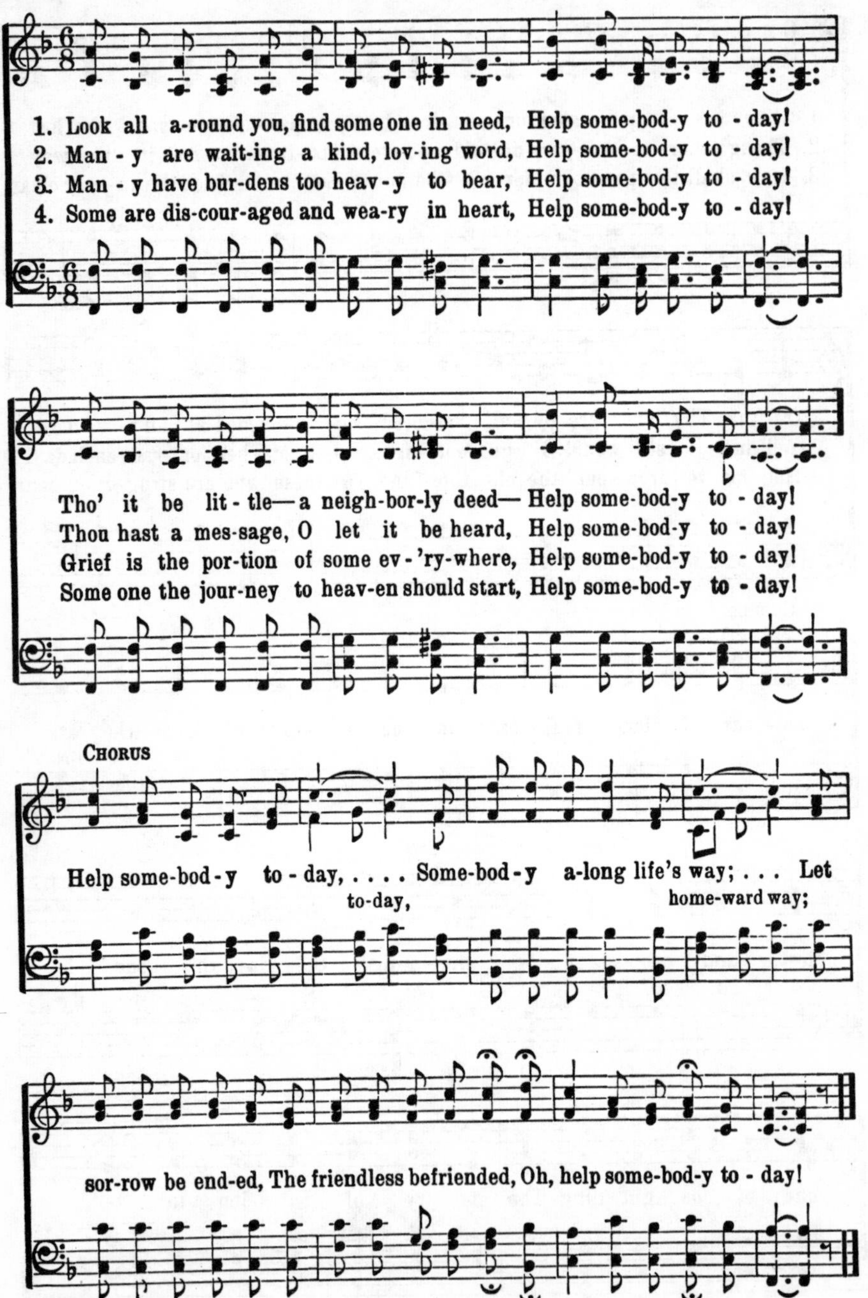
1. Look all a-round you, find some one in need, Help some-bod-y to - day!
2. Man - y are wait-ing a kind, lov-ing word, Help some-bod-y to - day!
3. Man - y have bur-dens too heav-y to bear, Help some-bod-y to - day!
4. Some are dis-cour-aged and wea-ry in heart, Help some-bod-y to - day!
Tho' it be lit-tle—a neigh-bor-ly deed— Help some-bod-y to - day!
Thou hast a mes-sage, O let it be heard, Help some-bod-y to - day!
Grief is the por-tion of some ev-'ry-where, Help some-bod-y to - day!
Some one the jour-ney to heav-en should start, Help some-bod-y to - day!
CHORUS
Help some-bod-y to - day, ... Some-bod-y a-long life's way; . . . Let
to-day,
home-ward way;
sor-row be end-ed, The friendless befriended, Oh, help some-bod-y to - day!

The Ninety and Nine

Elizabeth C. Clephane

Ira D. Sankey

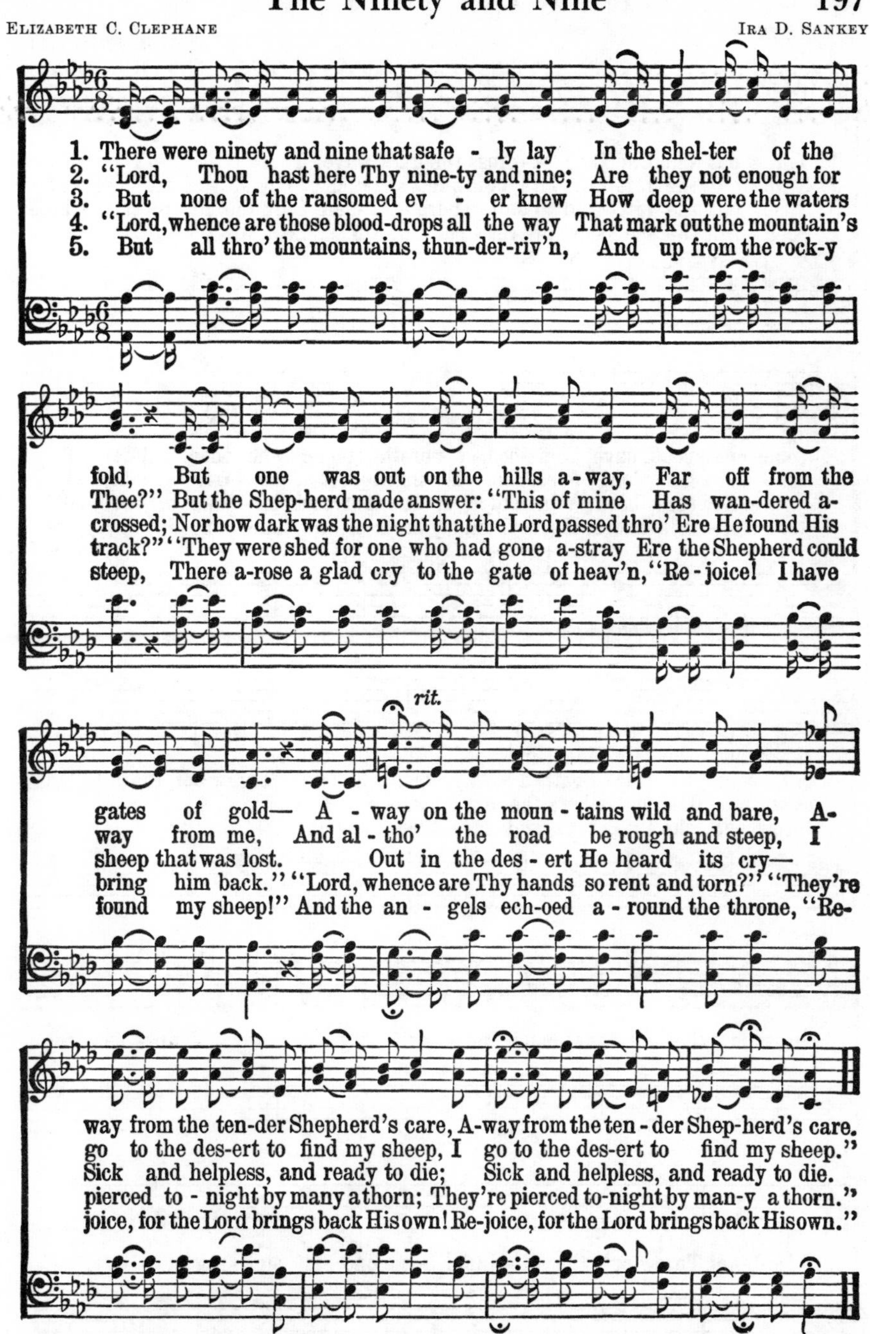
1. There were ninety and nine that safe - ly lay In the shel-ter of the
2. "Lord, Thou hast here Thy nine-ty and nine; Are they not enough for
3. But none of the ransomed ev - er knew How deep were the waters
4. "Lord, whence are those blood-drops all the way That mark out the mountain's
5. But all thro' the mountains, thun-der-riv'n, And up from the rock-y
fold, But one was out on the hills a-way, Far off from the
Thee?" But the Shep-herd made answer: "This of mine Has wan-dered a-
crossed; Nor how dark was the night that the Lord passed thro' Ere He found His
track?" "They were shed for one who had gone a-stray Ere the Shepherd could
steep, There a-rose a glad cry to the gate of heav'n, "Re - joice! I have
rit.
gates of gold— A - way on the moun - tains wild and bare, A-
way from me, And al - tho' the road be rough and steep, I
sheep that was lost. Out in the des - ert He heard its cry—
bring him back." "Lord, whence are Thy hands so rent and torn?" "They're
found my sheep!" And the an - gels ech-oed a - round the throne, "Re-
way from the ten-der Shepherd's care, A-way from the ten - der Shep-herd's care.
go to the des-ert to find my sheep, I go to the des-ert to find my sheep."
Sick and helpless, and ready to die; Sick and helpless, and ready to die.
pierced to - night by many a thorn; They're pierced to-night by man-y a thorn."
joice, for the Lord brings back His own! Re-joice, for the Lord brings back His own."

198 Throw Out the Life-Line

EDWARD S. UFFORD

EDWARD S. UFFORD
ARR. BY GEORGE C. STEBBINS

1. Throw out the Life-Line a-cross the dark wave, There is a broth-er whom some one should save; Some-bod-y's broth-er! oh, who then will dare To throw out the Life-Line, his per-il to share?
2. Throw out the Life-Line with hand quick and strong: Why do you tar-ry, why lin-ger so long? See! he is sink-ing; oh, has-ten to-day—And out with the Life-Boat! a-way, then, a-way!
3. Throw out the Life-Line to dan-ger-fraught men, Sink-ing in an-guish where you've nev-er been: Winds of temp-ta-tion and bil-lows of woe Will soon hurl them out where the dark wa-ters flow.
4. Soon will the sea-son of res-cue be o'er, Soon will they drift to e-ter-ni-ty's shore, Haste then, my broth-er, no time for de-lay, But throw out the Life-Line and save them to-day.

CHORUS

Throw out the Life-Line! Throw out the Life-Line! Some-one is drift-ing a-way; Throw out the Life-Line! Throw out the Life-Line! Some one is sink-ing to-day.

He's a Friend of Mine

JOHN H. SAMMIS

DANIEL B. TOWNER

1. Why should I charge my soul with care? The wealth of ev - 'ry mine
2. The sil - ver moon, the gold - en sun, The count - less stars that shine,
3. He dai - ly spreads a glo - rious feast, And at His ta - ble dine
4. And when He comes in bright ar - ray, And leads the conquering line,
Be - longs to Christ, God's Son and Heir, And He's a Friend of mine.
Are His a - lone, yes, ev - 'ry one, And He's a Friend of mine.
The whole cre - a - tion, man and beast, And He's a Friend of mine.
It will be glo - ry then to say, And He's a Friend of mine.
CHORUS
Yes, He's a Friend of mine, And He with me doth all things share;
Since all is Christ's, and Christ is mine, Why should I have a
care? For Je - sus is a Friend of mine....

200 A New Name in Glory

C. Austin Miles

1. I was once a sin-ner, but I came Par-don to re-ceive from my Lord: This was free-ly giv-en, and I found That He al-ways kept His word (kept His word).
2. I was hum-bly kneel-ing at the cross, Fear-ing naught but God's an-gry frown; When the heav-ens o-pened and I saw That my name was writ-ten down (writ-ten down).
3. In the Book 'tis writ-ten, "Saved by Grace," O the joy that came to my soul! Now I am for-giv-en, and I know By the blood I am made whole (am made whole).
Refrain
There's a new name writ-ten down in glo-ry,
And it's mine, O yes, it's mine!
And it's mine, yes, it's mine!
And the white-robed an-gels sing the sto-ry, "A sin-ner has come home."
has come home."
For there's a

A New Name in Glory
new name writ-ten down in glo-ry, And it's mine, O yes, it's mine!
And it's mine, yes, it's mine!
With my sins for-giv-en I am bound for heav-en, Nev-er-more to roam.
Come, Ye Disconsolate
201
Thomas Moore
Alt. by Thomas Hastings
Samuel Webbe
1. Come, ye dis-con-so-late, wher-e'er ye lan-guish; Come to the
2. Joy of the des-o-late, light of the stray-ing, Hope of the
3. Here see the bread of life; see wa-ters flow-ing Forth from the
mer-cy-seat, fer-vent-ly kneel; Here bring your wound-ed hearts,
pen-i-tent, fade-less and pure, Here speaks the Com-fort-er,
throne of God, pure from a-bove; Come to the feast of love;
here tell your an-guish; Earth has no sor-row that Heav'n can-not heal.
ten-der-ly say-ing, "Earth has no sor-row that Heav'n can-not cure."
come, ev-er know-ing Earth has no sor-row but Heav'n can re-move. A-men.

202 All Things in Jesus

HARRY D. LOES HARRY D. LOES

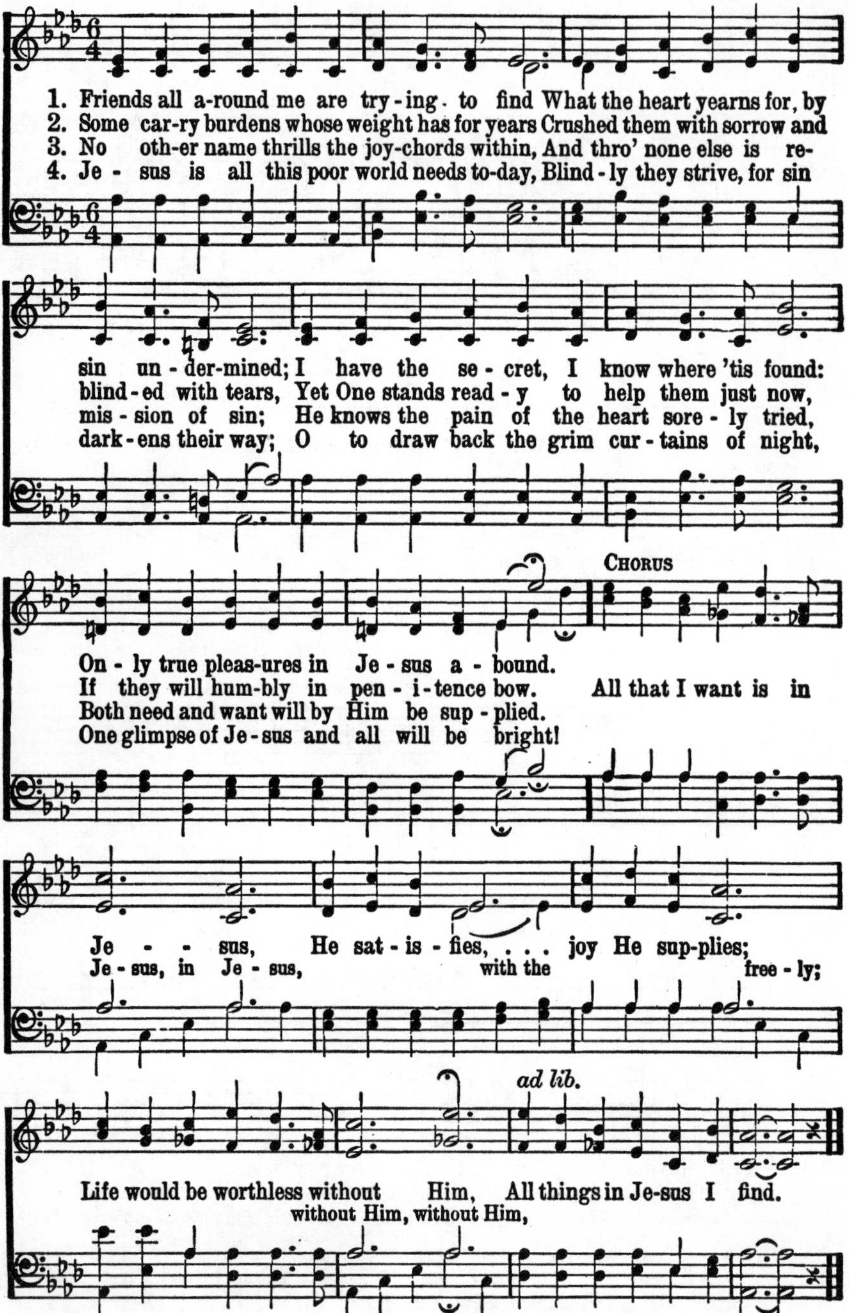

1. Friends all a-round me are try-ing to find What the heart yearns for, by
2. Some car-ry burdens whose weight has for years Crushed them with sorrow and
3. No oth-er name thrills the joy-chords within, And thro' none else is re-
4. Je-sus is all this poor world needs to-day, Blind-ly they strive, for sin

sin un-der-mined; I have the se-cret, I know where 'tis found:
blind-ed with tears, Yet One stands read-y to help them just now,
mis-sion of sin; He knows the pain of the heart sore-ly tried,
dark-ens their way; O to draw back the grim cur-tains of night,

On-ly true pleas-ures in Je-sus a-bound.
If they will hum-bly in pen-i-tence bow.
Both need and want will by Him be sup-plied.
One glimpse of Je-sus and all will be bright!

CHORUS

All that I want is in
Je - - sus, He sat-is-fies, . . . joy He sup-plies;
Je-sus, in Je-sus, with the free-ly;
Life would be worthless without Him, All things in Je-sus I find.
without Him, without Him,

ad lib.

Burdens Are Lifted at Calvary

John M. Moore — John M. Moore

1. Days are filled with sor-row and care, Hearts are lone-ly and drear;
Bur-dens are lift-ed at Cal-va-ry, Je-sus is ver-y near.

2. Cast your care on Je-sus to-day, Leave your wor-ry and fear;
Bur-dens are lift-ed at Cal-va-ry, Je-sus is ver-y near.

3. Trou-bled soul, the Sav-iour can see Ev-'ry heart-ache and tear;
Bur-dens are lift-ed at Cal-va-ry, Je-sus is ver-y near.

Chorus

Bur-dens are lift-ed at Cal-va-ry, Cal-va-ry, Cal-va-ry;
Bur-dens are lift-ed at Cal-va-ry, Je-sus is ver-y near.
ver-y near.

204 Christ Receiveth Sinful Men

ERDMANN NEUMEISTER
TR. BY EMMA F. BEVAN

JAMES MCGRANAHAN

1. Sin - ners Je - sus will re - ceive; Sound this word of grace to all
2. Come, and He will give you rest; Trust Him, for His word is plain;
3. Now my heart con - demns me not, Pure be - fore the law I stand;
4. Christ re - ceiv - eth sin - ful men, E - ven me with all my sin;
Who the heav'n - ly path - way leave, All who lin - ger, all who fall.
He will take the sin - ful - est; Christ re - ceiv - eth sin - ful men.
He who cleansed me from all spot, Sat - is - fied its last de - mand.
Purged from ev - 'ry spot and stain, Heav'n with Him I en - ter in.
REFRAIN
Sing it o'er. . . . . . . and o'er a - gain; . . . . . . Christ re -
Sing it o'er a - gain, Sing it o'er a - gain; Christ re -
ceiv - - - eth sin - ful men; . . . . . Make the mes - - - sage
ceiv - eth sin - ful men, Christ re - ceiv - eth sin - ful men; Make the message plain,
clear and plain: . . . . . . Christ re - ceiv - eth sin - ful men.
Make the mes - sage plain:

He Included Me

205

JOHNSON OATMAN, JR. HAMPTON H. SEWELL

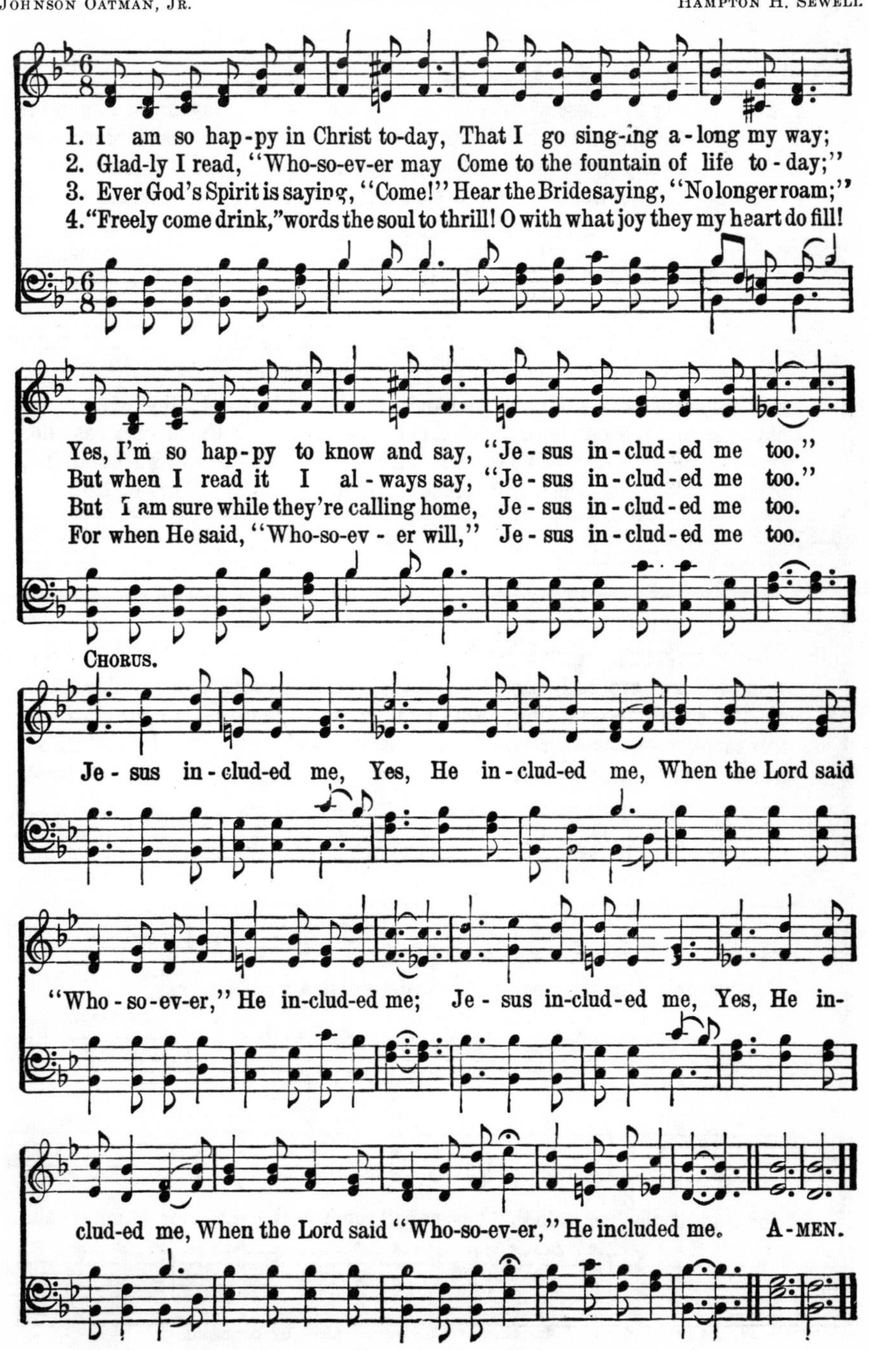
1. I am so hap-py in Christ to-day, That I go sing-ing a-long my way;
2. Glad-ly I read, "Who-so-ev-er may Come to the fountain of life to-day;"
3. Ever God's Spirit is saying, "Come!" Hear the Bride saying, "No longer roam;"
4. "Freely come drink," words the soul to thrill! O with what joy they my heart do fill!
Yes, I'm so hap-py to know and say, "Je-sus in-clud-ed me too."
But when I read it I al-ways say, "Je-sus in-clud-ed me too."
But I am sure while they're calling home, Je-sus in-clud-ed me too.
For when He said, "Who-so-ev-er will," Je-sus in-clud-ed me too.
CHORUS.
Je-sus in-clud-ed me, Yes, He in-clud-ed me, When the Lord said
"Who-so-ev-er," He in-clud-ed me; Je-sus in-clud-ed me, Yes, He in-
clud-ed me, When the Lord said "Who-so-ev-er," He included me.
A-MEN.

206 Dwelling in Beulah Land

C. Austin Miles | C. Austin Miles

1. Far a-way the noise of strife up-on my ear is fall-ing, Then I know the
2. Far be-low the storm of doubt up-on the world is beat-ing, Sons of men in
3. Let the storm-y breez-es blow, their cry can-not a-larm me; I am safe-ly
4. Viewing here the works of God, I sink in con-tem-pla-tion, Hearing now His
sins of earth be-set on ev-'ry hand: Doubt and fear and things of earth in
bat-tle long the en-e-my with-stand: Safe am I with-in the cas-tle
sheltered here, pro-tect-ed by God's hand: Here the sun is al-ways shin-ing,
bless-ed voice, I see the way He planned: Dwell-ing in the Spir-it, here I
vain to me are call-ing, None of these shall move me from Beu-lah Land.
of God's word re-treat-ing, Nothing then can reach me—'tis Beu-lah Land.
here there's naught can harm me, I am safe for-ev-er in Beu-lah Land.
learn of full sal-va-tion, Glad-ly will I tar-ry in Beu-lah Land.
Chorus
I'm liv-ing on the moun-tain, un-der-neath a cloud-less sky, I'm
Praise God!
drink-ing at the foun-tain that never shall run dry; O yes! I'm feasting on the

Dwelling in Beulah Land

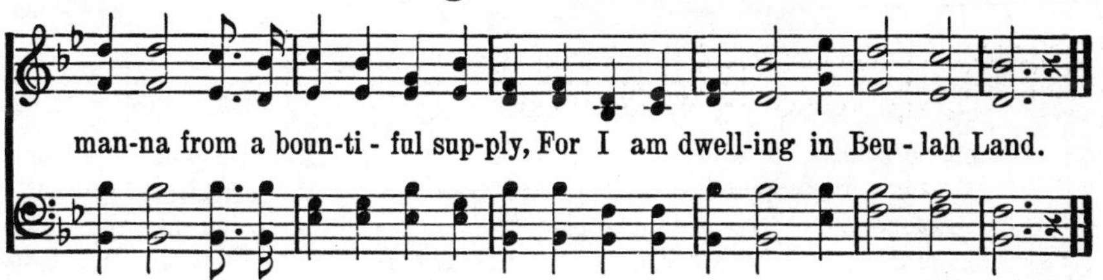
man-na from a boun-ti - ful sup-ply, For I am dwell-ing in Beu - lah Land.

Christ Liveth in Me

207

DANIEL W. WHITTLE JAMES MCGRANAHAN

1. Once far from God and dead in sin, No light my heart could see;
But in God's Word the light I found, Now Christ liv - eth in me.

2. As rays of light from yon - der sun, The flow'rs of earth set free,
So life and light and love came forth From Christ liv - ing in me.

3. As lives the flow'r with-in the seed, As in the cone the tree,
So, praise the God of truth and grace, His Spir-it dwell-eth in me.

4. With long - ing all my heart is filled, That like Him I may be,
As on the won - drous tho't I dwell That Christ liv - eth in me.

CHORUS

Christ liv - eth in me, Christ liv - eth in me,
Christ liv - eth in me, Christ liv - eth in me,
Oh! what a sal - va - tion this, That Christ liv - eth in me.

208 He Is So Precious to Me

CHARLES H. GABRIEL — CHARLES H. GABRIEL

1. So pre-cious is Je-sus, my Sav-ior, my King, His praise all the day long with rap-ture I sing; To Him in my weak-ness for strength I can cling,
2. He stood at my heart's door 'mid sunshine and rain, And pa-tient-ly wait-ed an en-trance to gain; What shame that so long He en-treat-ed in vain,
3. I stand on the moun-tain of bless-ing at last, No cloud in the heav-ens a shad-ow to cast; His smile is up-on me, the val-ley is past,
4. I praise Him be-cause He ap-point-ed a place Where, some day, thro' faith in His won-der-ful grace, I know I shall see Him—shall look on His face,
For He is so pre-cious to me.
CHORUS. Faster.
For He is so pre-cious to me, . . . so pre-cious to me,
For He is so pre-cious to me; . . . . so pre-cious to me;
'Tis Heav-en be-low
rit.
My Re-deem-er to know, For He is so pre-cious to me.
A-MEN.

He Lifted Me

Charles H. Gabriel — Charles H. Gabriel

1. In lov-ing-kind-ness Je-sus came My soul in mer-cy to re-claim,
2. He called me long be-fore I heard, Be-fore my sin-ful heart was stirred,
3. His brow was pierced with many a thorn, His hands by cru-el nails were torn,
4. Now on a high-er plane I dwell, And with my soul I know 'tis well;
And from the depths of sin and shame Thro' grace He lift-ed me. . . . . .
But when I took Him at His word, For-giv'n He lift-ed me. . . . . .
When from my guilt and grief, forlorn, In love He lift-ed me. . . . . .
Yet how or why, I can-not tell, He should have lift-ed me. . . . . .
He lift-ed me.
Chorus.
From sink-ing sand He lift-ed me, With ten-der hand He lift-ed me,
From shades of night to plains of light, Oh, praise His name, He lift-ed me!

210 A Child of the King

HARRIET E. BUELL — JOHN B. SUMMERS

1. My Fa-ther is rich in hous-es and lands, He hold-eth the wealth of the world in His hands! Of ru-bies and dia-monds, of sil-ver and gold, His cof-fers are full, He has rich-es un-told.
2. My Fa-ther's own Son, the Sav-ior of men, Once wan-dered on earth as the poor-est of them; But now He is plead-ing our par-don on high, That we may be His when He comes by and by.
3. I once was an out-cast stran-ger on earth, A sin-ner by choice, and an al-ien by birth; But I've been a-dopt-ed, my name's writ-ten down, An heir to a man-sion, a robe, and a crown.
4. A tent or a cot-tage, why should I care? They're build-ing a pal-ace for me o-ver there; Tho' ex-iled from home, yet, still I may sing: All glo-ry to God, I'm a child of the King.
REFRAIN
I'm a child of the King, A child of the King:
With Je-sus my Sav-ior I'm a child of the King.

A Shelter in the Time of Storm

211

Vernon J. Charlesworth
Arr. by Ira D. Sankey

Ira D. Sankey

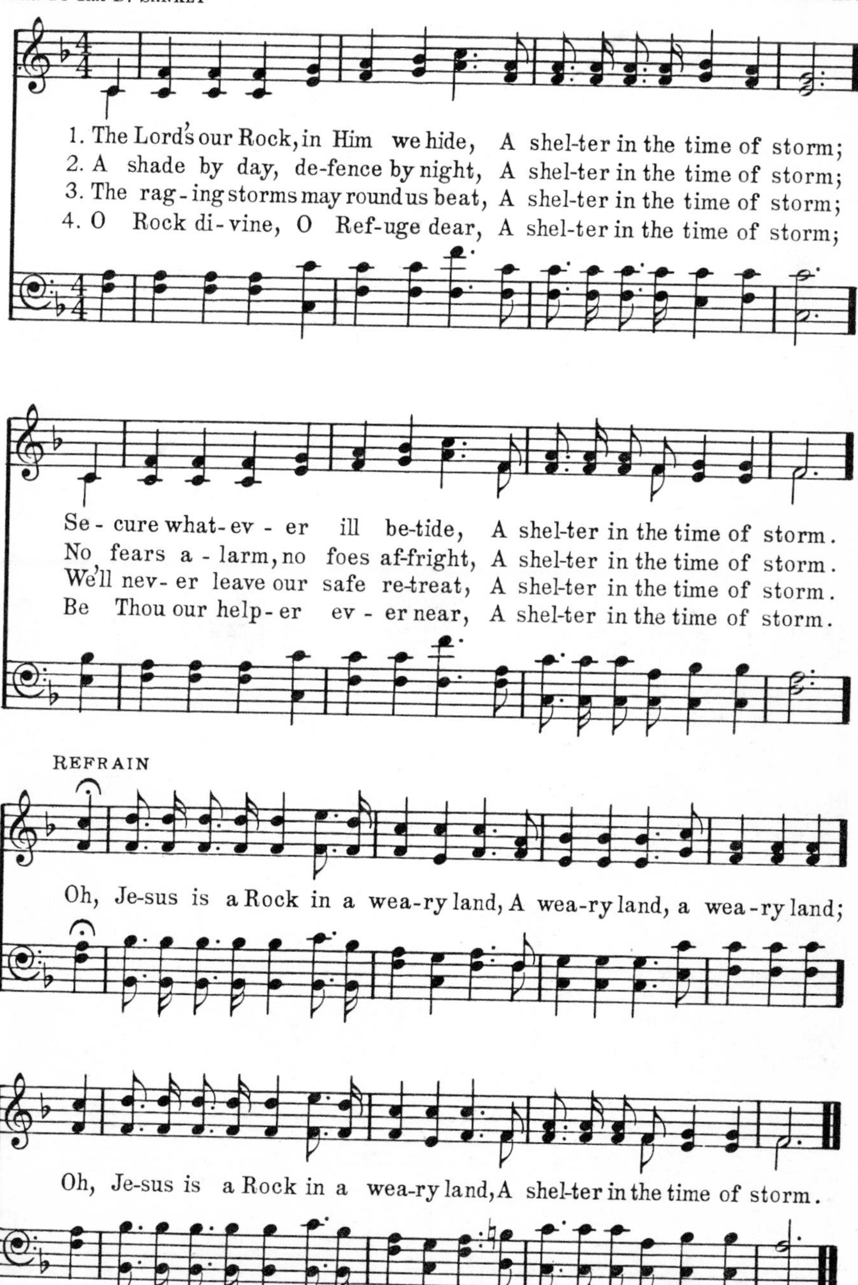

1. The Lord's our Rock, in Him we hide, A shel-ter in the time of storm;
2. A shade by day, de-fence by night, A shel-ter in the time of storm;
3. The rag-ing storms may round us beat, A shel-ter in the time of storm;
4. O Rock di-vine, O Ref-uge dear, A shel-ter in the time of storm;
Se-cure what-ev-er ill be-tide, A shel-ter in the time of storm.
No fears a-larm, no foes af-fright, A shel-ter in the time of storm.
We'll nev-er leave our safe re-treat, A shel-ter in the time of storm.
Be Thou our help-er ev-er near, A shel-ter in the time of storm.
Refrain
Oh, Je-sus is a Rock in a wea-ry land, A wea-ry land, a wea-ry land;
Oh, Je-sus is a Rock in a wea-ry land, A shel-ter in the time of storm.

212 I Belong to the King

Ida L. Reed

Maurice A. Clifton

1. I be-long to the King, I'm a child of His love, I shall dwell in His
2. I be-long to the King, and He loves me I know, For His mer-cy and
3. I be-long to the King, and His prom-ise is sure, That we all shall be
pal-ace so fair; For He tells of its bliss in yon heav-en a-bove, And His
kindness, so free, Are un-ceas-ing-ly mine, where-so-ev-er I go, And my
gathered at last In His king-dom a-bove, by life's wa-ters so pure, When this
chil-dren in splen-dor shall share.
ref-uge un-fail-ing is He.
life with its tri-als is past.
CHORUS
I be-long to the King, I'm a
child of His love, And He nev-er for-sak-eth His own; He will call me some
day to His pal-ace a-bove, I shall dwell by His glo-ri-fied throne.

I Know Whom I Have Believed

DANIEL W. WHITTLE

JAMES MCGRANAHAN

Moderato
1. I know not why God's won-drous grace To me He hath made known,
2. I know not how this sav-ing faith To me He did im-part,
3. I know not how the Spir-it moves, Con-vinc-ing men of sin,
4. I know not what of good or ill May be re-served for me,
5. I know not when my Lord may come, At night or noon-day fair,
Nor why un-wor-thy—Christ in love Re-deemed me for His own.
Nor how be-liev-ing in His Word Wrought peace within my heart.
Re-veal-ing Je-sus thro' the Word, Cre-at-ing faith in Him.
Of wea-ry ways or gold-en days, Be-fore His face I see.
Nor if I walk the vale with Him, Or "meet Him in the air."
CHORUS
But "I know whom I have be-liev-ed, and am per-suad-ed that He is
a-ble To keep that which I've committed Un-to Him a-gainst that day."

214 I Love Him Because He First Loved Me

FRANK E. ROUSH — J. E. STURGIS

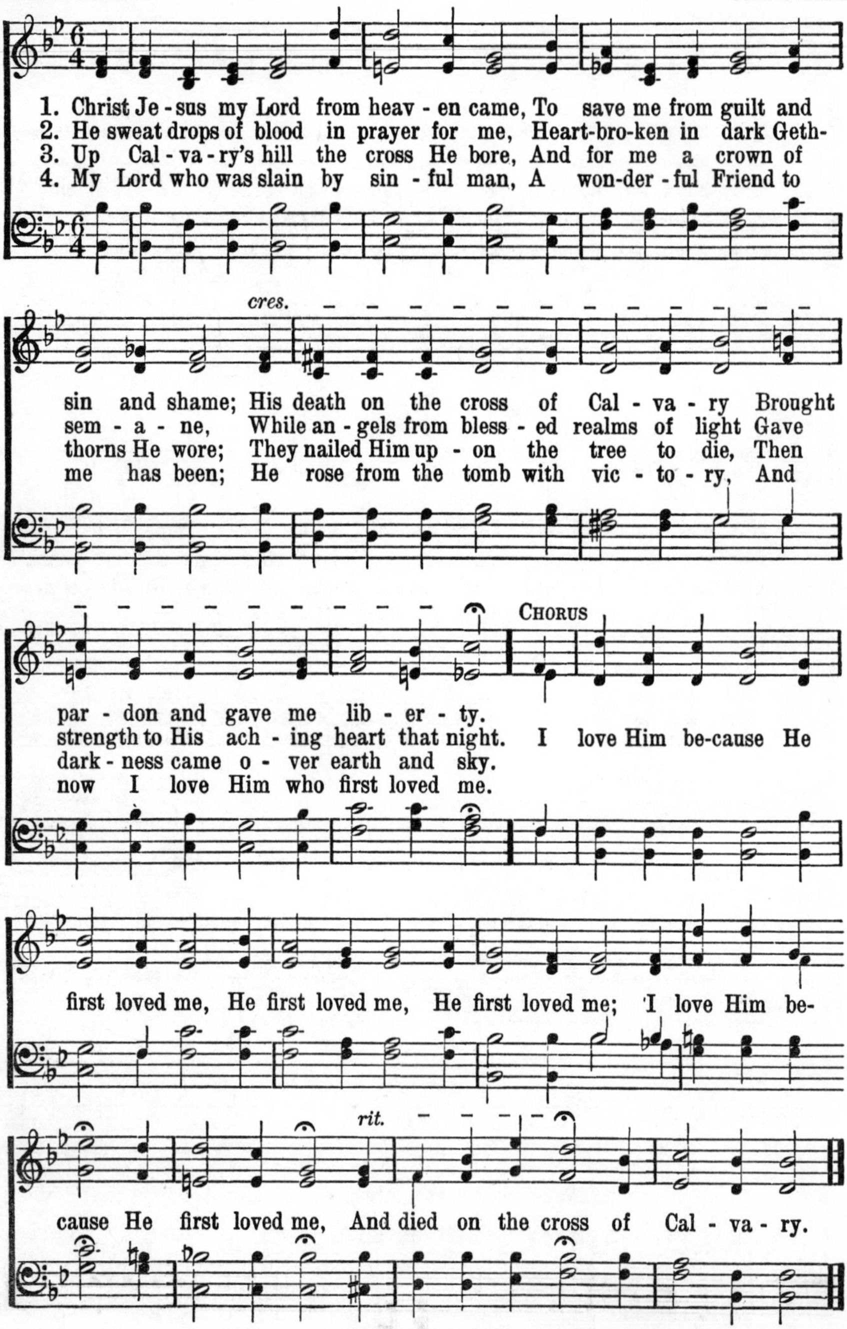

1. Christ Je - sus my Lord from heav - en came, To save me from guilt and sin and shame; His death on the cross of Cal - va - ry Brought par - don and gave me lib - er - ty.

2. He sweat drops of blood in prayer for me, Heart-bro-ken in dark Geth-sem - a - ne, While an - gels from bless - ed realms of light Gave strength to His ach - ing heart that night.

3. Up Cal - va - ry's hill the cross He bore, And for me a crown of thorns He wore; They nailed Him up - on the tree to die, Then dark - ness came o - ver earth and sky.

4. My Lord who was slain by sin - ful man, A won-der - ful Friend to me has been; He rose from the tomb with vic - to - ry, And now I love Him who first loved me.

cres.

CHORUS

I love Him be-cause He first loved me, He first loved me, He first loved me; I love Him be-cause He first loved me, And died on the cross of Cal - va - ry.

rit.

I Love to Tell the Story

A. Catherine Hankey — William G. Fischer

1. I love to tell the sto - ry Of un - seen things a - bove, Of Je - sus and His glo - ry, Of Je - sus and His love. I love to tell the sto - ry, Be-cause I know 'tis true; It sat - is - fies my longings As noth-ing else can do.
2. I love to tell the sto - ry, More won - der - ful it seems Than all the gold - en fan - cies Of all our gold-en dreams. I love to tell the sto - ry, It did so much for me; And that is just the rea - son I tell it now to thee.
3. I love to tell the sto - ry, 'Tis pleas - ant to re - peat What seems, each time I tell it, More won - der - ful - ly sweet. I love to tell the sto - ry, For some have nev - er heard The mes-sage of sal- va - tion From God's own ho - ly Word.
4. I love to tell the sto - ry, For those who know it best Seem hun - ger - ing and thirst-ing To hear it like the rest. And when, in scenes of glo - ry, I sing the new, new song, 'Twill be the old, old sto - ry That I have loved so long.
Chorus
I love to tell the sto - ry, 'Twill be my theme in glo-ry To tell the old, old sto - ry Of Jesus and His love.

216 I've Heard the King

Grant C. Tullar — Donald P. Hustad

1. I've heard the King! The King of heav-en! Nor can I e'er for-get the mu-sic of His voice. I've heard the King! His call I've answered. I've made the King of heav'n my ev-er-last-ing choice.
2. I've heard the King! The King of glo-ry; For whom my heart's door opened wide and He came in. I've heard the King! Oh, blessed hear-ing, His voice spoke peace and par-don for my guilt and sin.
3. I've heard the King! Oh, had I missed Him, My life for-ev-er-more could not re-gain the loss. From heav'n He came, the world to ran-som, And this He did one day on Calv-'ry's cru-el cross.
4. I've heard the King! and now I'm tell-ing To all the world the gos-pel of un-dy-ing love, That oth-ers too may catch the mu-sic His voice can bring, and find their way to heav'n above.
Chorus
He came to me, and with Him came a bless-ing. He spoke to me, and glo-ry filled my soul; His voice I heard, so charm-ing and so won-drous. I've heard the King, and hearing am made whole.
mp
f

Jesus Has Lifted Me!

Avis B. Christiansen

Haldor Lillenas

1. Out of the depths to the glo - ry a - bove, I have been lift - ed in won - der - ful love; From ev - 'ry fet - ter my spir - it is free— For Je - sus has lift - ed me! . . . .
2. Out of the world in - to heav - en - ly rest, In - to the land of the ran-somed and blest; There in the glo - ry with Him I shall be— For Je - sus has lift - ed me! . . . .
3. Out of my - self in - to Him I a - dore, There to a- bide in His love ev - er - more; Thro' end - less a - ges His glo - ry to see— My Je - sus has lift - ed me! . . . . lift - ed me!

Chorus

Je - sus has lift - ed me! . . . lift - ed me! Je - sus has lift - ed me! . . . lift - ed me! Out of the night in - to glo - ri-ous light, Yes, Je-sus has lift - ed me! . . . lift - ed me!

218 It's Just Like His Great Love

Edna H. Worrell — Clarence B. Strouse

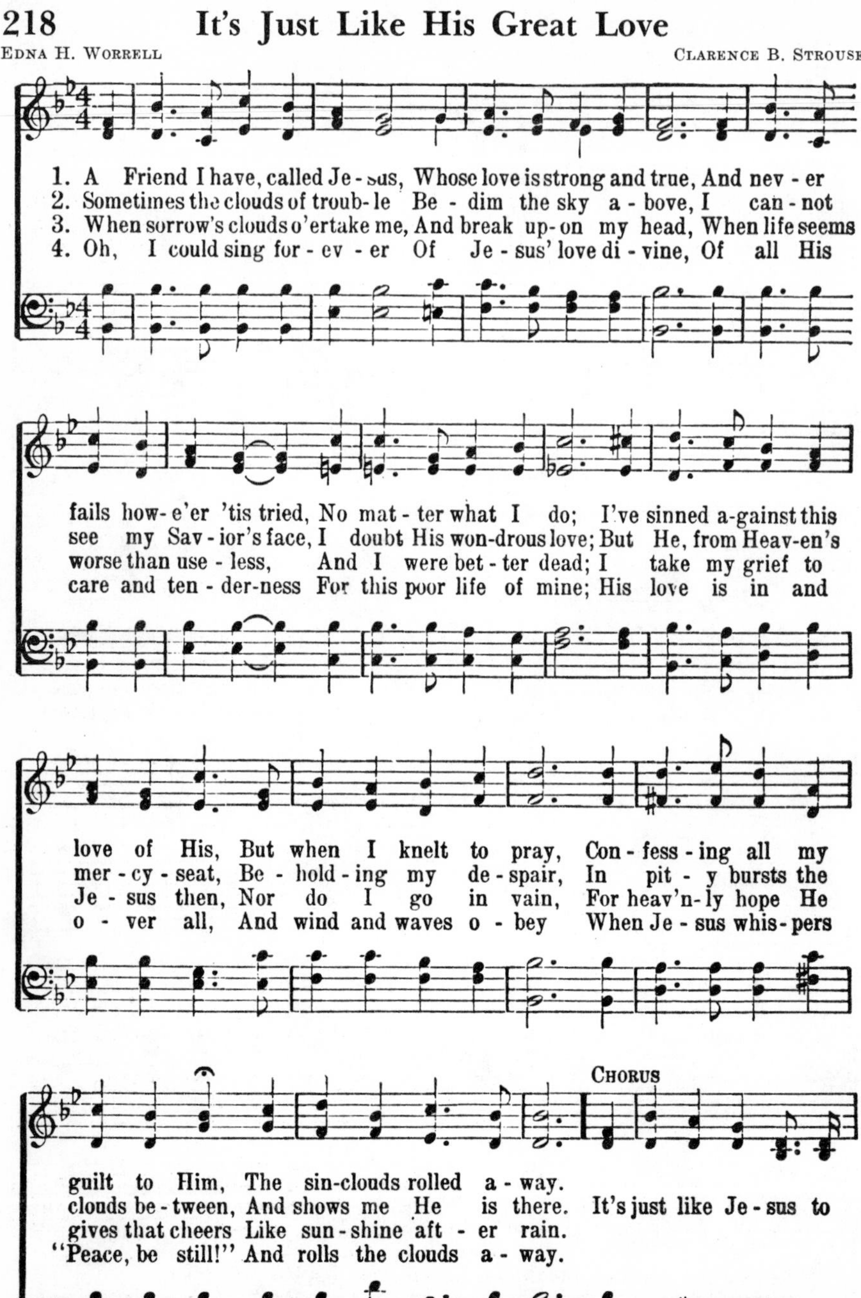

1. A Friend I have, called Je - sus, Whose love is strong and true, And nev - er
2. Sometimes the clouds of troub - le Be - dim the sky a - bove, I can - not
3. When sorrow's clouds o'ertake me, And break up - on my head, When life seems
4. Oh, I could sing for - ev - er Of Je - sus' love di - vine, Of all His
fails how - e'er 'tis tried, No mat - ter what I do; I've sinned a - gainst this
see my Sav - ior's face, I doubt His won - drous love; But He, from Heav - en's
worse than use - less, And I were bet - ter dead; I take my grief to
care and ten - der - ness For this poor life of mine; His love is in and
love of His, But when I knelt to pray, Con - fess - ing all my
mer - cy - seat, Be - hold - ing my de - spair, In pit - y bursts the
Je - sus then, Nor do I go in vain, For heav'n - ly hope He
o - ver all, And wind and waves o - bey When Je - sus whis - pers
guilt to Him, The sin - clouds rolled a - way.
clouds be - tween, And shows me He is there.
gives that cheers Like sun - shine aft - er rain.
"Peace, be still!" And rolls the clouds a - way.
CHORUS
It's just like Je - sus to

It's Just Like His Great Love

roll the clouds a - way, It's just like Je - sus to keep me day by day,
It's just like Je - sus all a - long the way, It's just like His great love.
219
He Leadeth Me
Joseph H. Gilmore
William B. Bradbury
1. He lead - eth, me O bless - ed tho't! O words with heav'nly comfort fraught!
2. Sometimes 'mid scenes of deepest gloom, Sometimes where Eden's bowers bloom,
3. Lord, I would clasp Thy hand in mine, Nor ev - er mur - mur nor re - pine,
4. And when my task on earth is done, When, by Thy grace, the vic-t'ry's won,
What-e'er I do, wher-e'er I be, Still 'tis God's hand that lead-eth me.
By wa - ters still, o'er trou-bled sea,—Still 'tis His hand that lead-eth me!
Con - tent, what-ev - er lot I see, Since 'tis my God that lead-eth me!
E'en death's cold wave I will not flee, Since God thro' Jor - dan lead-eth me.
Refrain
1
2
He lead-eth me, He lead-eth me! By His own hand He leadeth me!
His faithful foll'wer I would be, For by His hand He (Omit.....) leadeth me.

220 Jesus Is All the World to Me

Will H. Thompson

Will L. Thompson

1. Je - sus is all the world to me, My life, my joy, my all;
2. Je - sus is all the world to me, My Friend in tri - als sore;
3. Je - sus is all the world to me, And true to Him I'll be;
4. Je - sus is all the world to me, I want no bet - ter friend;
He is my strength from day to day, With - out Him I would fall.
I go to Him for bless-ings, and He gives them o'er and o'er.
Oh, how could I this Friend de - ny, When He's so true to me?
I trust Him now, I'll trust Him when Life's fleet - ing days shall end.
When I am sad, to Him I go, No oth - er one can
He sends the sun - shine and the rain, He sends the har - vest's
Fol - low - ing Him I know I'm right, He watch - es o'er me
Beau - ti - ful life with such a Friend; Beau - ti - ful life that
cheer me so; When I am sad He makes me glad, He's my Friend.
gold - en grain; Sun-shine and rain, har - vest of grain, He's my Friend.
day and night; Fol - low - ing Him, by day and night, He's my Friend.
has no end; E - ter - nal life, e - ter - nal joy, He's my Friend.
f
pp

Love Lifted Me

JAMES ROWE HOWARD E. SMITH

1. I was sink-ing deep in sin, Far from the peaceful shore, Ver - y deep-ly
2. All my heart to Him I give, Ev - er to Him I'll cling, In His bless-ed
3. Souls in dan-ger, look a-bove, Je - sus com-plete-ly saves; He will lift you
stained with-in, Sink-ing to rise no more; But the Mas - ter of the sea
pres - ence live, Ev - er His prais - es sing. Love so might-y and so true
by His love Out of the an - gry waves. He's the Mas - ter of the sea,
Heard my despairing cry, From the wa-ters lift - ed me, Now safe am I.
Mer-its my soul's best songs; Faith-ful, lov-ing serv-ice, too, To Him be - longs.
Bil-lows His will o - bey; He your Sav-ior wants to be—Be saved to - day.
CHORUS
Love lift-ed me! . . . . Love lift-ed me! . . . . When noth-ing
e - ven me! e - ven me!
else could help, Love lift - ed me. Love lift - ed me.
1
2

222 My Redeemer

PHILIP P. BLISS — JAMES MCGRANAHAN

1. I will sing of my Re-deem-er, And His won-drous love to me;
2. I will tell the won-drous sto-ry, How my lost es-tate to save,
3. I will praise my dear Re-deem-er, His tri-um-phant pow'r I'll tell,
4. I will sing of my Re-deem-er, And His heav'n-ly love to me;
On the cru-el cross He suf-fered, From the curse to set me free.
In His bound-less love and mer-cy, He the ran-som free-ly gave.
How the vic-to-ry He giv-eth O-ver sin, and death, and hell.
He from death to life hath bro't me, Son of God with Him to be.
CHORUS
Sing, oh, sing . . . . of my Re-deem-er,
of my Re-deem-er, Sing, oh, sing of my Re-deem-er,
With His blood . . . . He pur-chased me, ...
He pur-chased me, With His blood He pur-chased me,
On the cross . . . . He sealed my par-don,
He sealed my par-don, On the cross He sealed my par-don,

My Redeemer
Paid the debt, ... and made me free. . . . .
and made me free, and made me free.
223
He Will Answer Every Prayer
Mary Bernstecher
Daniel B. Towner
1. God has giv - en you His prom-ise, That He hears and an-swers prayer;
2. He will not with-hold one bless-ing, He will give you what is best;
3. He can hear the great pe - ti - tion, And the small - est, o - ver there;
4. Take to God your plans and fail-ures, An - y time and an - y - where;
He will heed your sup - pli - ca - tion, If you cast on Him your care.
God will an - swer by His Spir - it, Ev -'ry one who makes re - quest.
Un - to God pray with - out ceas - ing, He will an-swer ev -'ry prayer.
No one e'er has gone un-an-swered, For He an-swers ev -'ry prayer.
Chorus
He will an-swer ev - 'ry prayer, He will an-swer ev - 'ry prayer,
He will answer, answer ev'ry prayer, He will answer, answer ev'ry prayer,
Go to Him in faith be - liev-ing, He will an - swer ev - 'ry prayer.

No, Not One!

JOHNSON OATMAN, JR. GEORGE C. HUGG

1. There's not a friend like the low - ly Je - sus, No, not one! no, not one!
2. No friend like Him is so high and ho - ly, No, not one! no, not one!
3. There's not an hour that He is not near us, No, not one! no, not one!
4. Did ev - er saint find this Friend for-sake him? No, not one! no, not one!
5. Was e'er a gift like the Sav.-ior giv - en? No, not one! no, not one!

None else could heal all our soul's dis - eas - es, No, not one! no, not one!
And yet no friend is so meek and low - ly, No, not one! no, not one!
No night so dark but His love can cheer us, No, not one! no, not one!
Or sin - ner find that He would not take him? No, not one! no, not one!
Will He re - fuse us a home in heav - en? No, not one! no, not one!

CHORUS

Je - sus knows all a - bout our strug-gles, He will guide till the day is done;

There's not a friend like the low - ly Je - sus, No, not one! no, not one!

Only a Sinner

JAMES M. GRAY — DANIEL B. TOWNER

1. Naught have I got - ten but what I re-ceived; Grace hath be-stowed it since
2. Once I was fool - ish, and sin ruled my heart, Caus - ing my foot-steps from
3. Tears un - a-vail-ing, no mer - it had I; Mer - cy had saved me, or
4. Suf - fer a sin-ner whose heart o - ver-flows, Lov - ing his Sav - ior to
I have be-lieved; Boast-ing ex-clud - ed pride I a - base; I'm on - ly a
God to de - part; Je - sus hath found me hap - py my case; I now am a
else I must die; Sin had a-larmed me fear-ing God's face; But now I'm a
tell what he knows; Once more to tell it would I em-brace—I'm on - ly a
CHORUS
sin - ner saved by grace! On - ly a sin - ner saved by grace!
On - ly a sin - ner saved by grace! This is my sto - ry, to
God be the glo - ry,—I'm on - ly a sin - ner saved by grace!

226 Oh, How I Love Jesus

FREDERICK WHITFIELD | TRADITIONAL MELODY

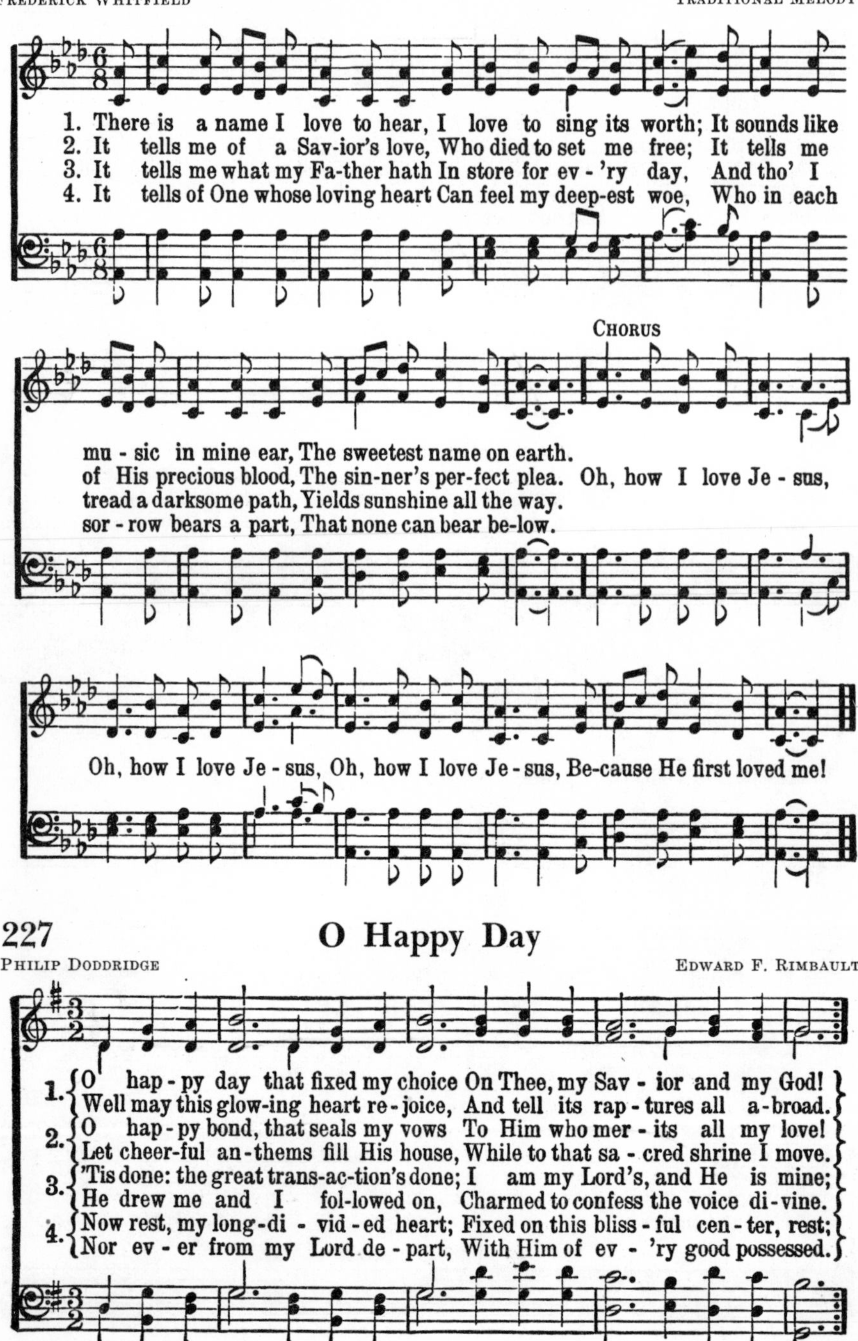
1. There is a name I love to hear, I love to sing its worth; It sounds like mu-sic in mine ear, The sweetest name on earth.
2. It tells me of a Sav-ior's love, Who died to set me free; It tells me of His precious blood, The sin-ner's per-fect plea.
3. It tells me what my Fa-ther hath In store for ev-'ry day, And tho' I tread a darksome path, Yields sunshine all the way.
4. It tells of One whose loving heart Can feel my deep-est woe, Who in each sor-row bears a part, That none can bear be-low.
CHORUS
Oh, how I love Je-sus,
Oh, how I love Je-sus, Oh, how I love Je-sus, Be-cause He first loved me!
227
O Happy Day
PHILIP DODDRIDGE
EDWARD F. RIMBAULT
1. O hap-py day that fixed my choice On Thee, my Sav-ior and my God!
Well may this glow-ing heart re-joice, And tell its rap-tures all a-broad.
2. O hap-py bond, that seals my vows To Him who mer-its all my love!
Let cheer-ful an-thems fill His house, While to that sa-cred shrine I move.
3. 'Tis done: the great trans-ac-tion's done; I am my Lord's, and He is mine;
He drew me and I fol-lowed on, Charmed to confess the voice di-vine.
4. Now rest, my long-di-vid-ed heart; Fixed on this bliss-ful cen-ter, rest;
Nor ev-er from my Lord de-part, With Him of ev-'ry good possessed.

O Happy Day
Fine
Hap - py day, hap - py day, When Je - sus washed my sins a - way!
D.S.
He taught me how to watch and pray, And live re - joic - ing ev - 'ry day;
We'll Work till Jesus Comes
228
Elizabeth Mills
William Miller
1. O land of rest, for thee I sigh! When will the mo-ment come When
2. To Je - sus Christ I fled for rest; He bade me cease to roam, And
3. I sought at once my Sav-iour's side, No more my steps shall roam; With
Chorus.
I shall lay my ar - mor by, And dwell in peace at home? We'll work till
lean for suc - cor on His breast Till He con-duct me home.
Him I'll brave death's chilling tide, And reach my heavenly home. We'll work
1
2
Je-sus comes, We'll work till Je-sus comes; And we'll be gath-ered home.
We'll work

229 Saved!

OSWALD J. SMITH — ROGER M. HICKMAN

1. Saved! saved! saved! my sins are all for - giv'n; Christ is mine! I'm on my way to heav'n; Once a guilt - - y sin-ner, lost, un-done, Now a child of God, saved thro' His Son.
2. Saved! saved! saved! by grace and grace a - lone; Oh, what won - drous love to me was shown, In my stead Christ Je - sus bled and died, Bore my sins, for me was cru - ci-fied.
3. Saved! saved! saved! oh, joy be-yond com-pare! Christ my life, and I His con-stant care; Yield - ing all and trust-ing Him a-lone, Liv - ing now each moment as His own.
CHORUS
Saved! I'm saved thro' Christ, my all in all; . . . . Saved! I'm saved, what-
my all in all;
ev - er may be - fall; He died up - on the cross for me, He bore the aw - ful

Saved!

rit.
pen - al - ty; And now I'm saved e - ter - nal - ly—I'm saved! saved! saved!

Now I Belong to Jesus 230

NORMAN J. CLAYTON NORMAN J. CLAYTON

1. Je - sus my Lord will love me for - ev - er, From Him no pow'r of e - vil can sev - er, He gave His life to ran-som my soul, Now I be-long to Him;
2. Once I was lost in sin's deg-ra-da-tion, Je - sus came down to bring me sal-va - tion, Lift-ed me up from sor-row and shame, Now I be-long to Him;
3. Joy floods my soul for Je-sus has saved me, Freed me from sin that long had en-slaved me, His pre-cious blood He gave to redeem, Now I be-long to Him;

CHORUS

Now I be-long to Je - sus, Je - sus be-longs to me, Not for the years of time a - lone, But for e - ter - ni - ty.

231 Saved, Saved!

Jack P. Scholfield — Jack P. Scholfield

1. I've found a friend who is all to me,.... His love is ev - er true; .... I love to tell how He lift - ed me.... And what His grace can do for you...
2. He saves me from ev - 'ry sin and harm,. Se-cures my soul each day; .... I'm lean - ing strong on His might-y arm;.. I know He'll guide me all the way...
3. When poor and need - y and all a - lone,... In love He said to me,........ "Come un - to me and I'll lead you home, To live with me e - ter - nal - ly."...
Chorus.
Saved .... by His pow'r di-vine, Saved .... to new life sub-lime!
Saved by His pow'r, Saved to new life,
rit.
Life now is sweet and my joy is com-plete, For I'm Saved, saved, saved!

Since I Have Been Redeemed

Edwin O. Excell   Edwin O. Excell

1. I have a song I love to sing, Since I have been re - deemed,
2. I have a Christ that sat - is - fies, Since I have been re - deemed,
3. I have a wit - ness bright and clear, Since I have been re - deemed,
4. I have a home pre-pared for me, Since I have been re - deemed,
Of my Re - deem-er, Sav - ior, King, Since I have been re - deemed.
To do His will my high - est prize, Since I have been re - deemed.
Dis - pel - ling ev - 'ry doubt and fear, Since I have been re - deemed.
Where I shall dwell e - ter - nal - ly, Since I have been re - deemed.
CHORUS.
Since I . . . . . have been re-deemed, Since I have been re-
Since I have been redeemed, Since I have been redeemed,
deemed, I will glo - ry in His name; Since I . . . . . have been re-
Since I have been redeemed, Since
deemed, I will glo - ry in my Sav - ior's name.
I have been re-deemed,

233 Since the Fullness of His Love Came In

Eliza E. Hewitt — Bentley D. Ackley

1. Once my way was dark and drear - y, For my heart was full of sin,
2. There is grace for all the low - ly, Grace to keep the trust-ing soul:
3. Let me spread a - broad the sto - ry, Oth - er souls to Je - sus win;
But the sky is bright and cheer-y, Since the full-ness of His love came in.
Pow'r to cleanse and make me ho - ly, Je - sus shall my yield-ed life con - trol.
For the cross is now my glo - ry, Since the full-ness of His love came in.
CHORUS
I can nev-er tell how much I love Him, I can nev-er tell His love for me;
For it pass-eth hu-man measure, Like a deep, unfathomed sea;
deep, unfathomed sea;
'Tis re-deeming love in Christ my Sav-ior, In my soul the heav'nly joys be-gin;

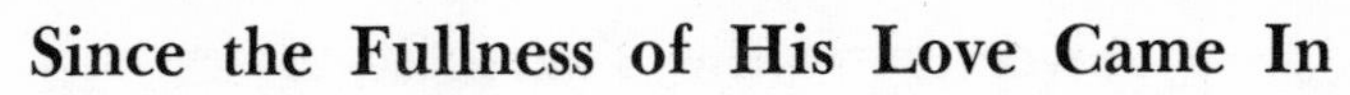
Since the Fullness of His Love Came In

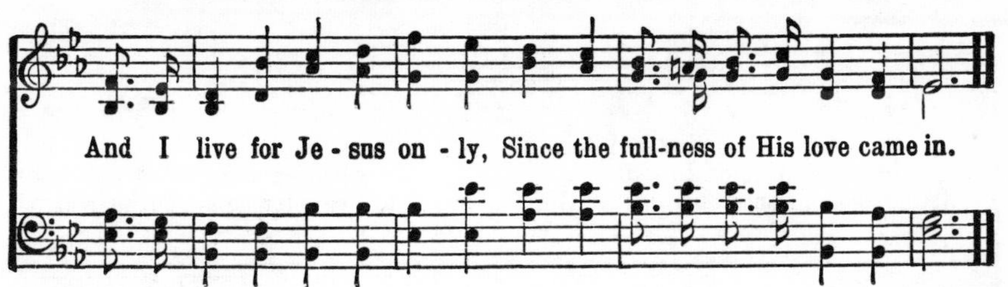
And I live for Je - sus on - ly, Since the full-ness of His love came in.

Jesus Loves Even Me 234

PHILIP P. BLISS PHILIP P. BLISS

1. I am so glad that our Fa - ther in heav'n Tells of His love in the
2. Tho' I for - get Him and wan - der a - way, Still He doth love me wher-
3. Oh, if there's on - ly one song I can sing, When in His beau - ty I

Book He has giv'n, Won - der - ful things in the Bi - ble I see;
ev - er I stray; Back to His dear lov - ing arms would I flee,
see the Great King, This shall my song in e - ter - ni - ty be:

This is the dear - est—that Je - sus loves me.
When I re - mem - ber that Je - sus loves me.
"Oh, what a won - der that Je - sus loves me!"

CHORUS.

I am so glad that Je - sus loves me, Je - sus loves me, Je - sus loves me; e - ven me.

235 Sweeter as the Years Go By

LEILA N. MORRIS — LEILA N. MORRIS

1. Of Je-sus' love that sought me, When I was lost in sin; Of wondrous grace that brought me Back to His fold a-gain; Of heights and depths of mer-cy, Far deep-er than the sea, And high-er than the heav-ens, My theme shall ev-er be.
2. He trod in old Ju-de-a Life's pathway long a-go; The peo-ple thronged a-bout Him, His sav-ing grace to know; He healed the bro-ken-heart-ed, And caused the blind to see; And still His great heart yearneth In love for e-ven me.
3. 'Twas wondrous love which led Him For us to suf-fer loss—To bear with-out a mur-mur The an-guish of the cross; With saints redeemed in glo-ry, Let us our voi-ces raise, Till heav'n and earth re-ech-o With our Re-deem-er's praise.
CHORUS
Sweet-er as the years go by,...... Sweet-er as the years go by; Rich-er, full-er, deep-er,
Sweet-er as the years go by, 'Tis sweet-er as the years go by;

Sweeter as the Years Go By

rit.
Je - sus' love is sweet - er, Sweet - er as the years go by.

Must I Go, and Empty-Handed? 236

CHARLES C. LUTHER GEORGE C. STEBBINS

1."Must I go, and emp - ty-hand - ed," Thus my dear Rɘ-deem - er meet?
2. Not at death I shrink nor fal - ter, For my Sav - ior saves me now;
3. O the years in sin - ning wast - ed, Could I but re - call them now,
4. O ye saints, a-rouse, be ear - nest, Up and work while yet 'tis day;

Not one day of serv - ice give Him, Lay no tro - phy at His feet?
But to meet Him emp - ty-hand - ed, Tho't of that now clouds my brow.
I would give them to my Sav - ior, To His will I'd glad - ly bow.
Ere the night of death o'er-take thee, Strive for souls while still you may.

CHORUS

"Must I go, and emp - ty-hand-ed?"Must I meet my Sav - ior so?
Not one soul with which to greet Him: Must I emp - ty-hand - ed go?

237 Tell Me the Story of Jesus

FANNY J. CROSBY
JOHN R. SWENEY

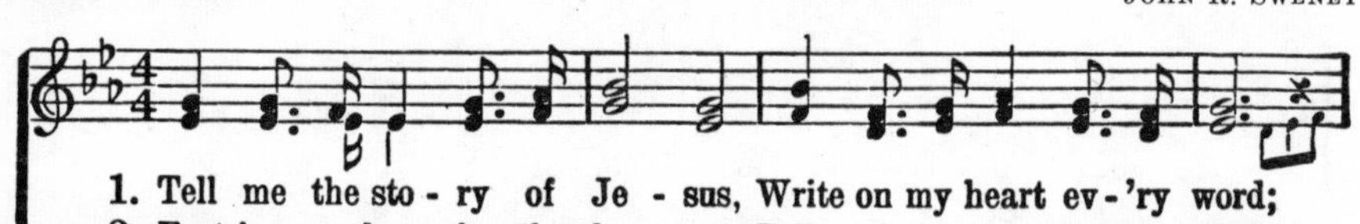

1. Tell me the sto - ry of Je - sus, Write on my heart ev - 'ry word;
2. Fast-ing a - lone in the des - ert, Tell of the days that are past,
3. Tell of the cross where they nailed Him, Writh-ing in an-guish and pain;

CHO.—*Tell me the sto - ry of Je - sus, Write on my heart ev - 'ry word;*

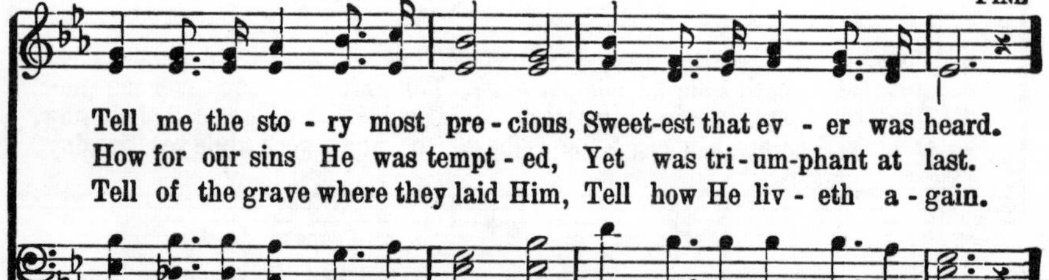

FINE

Tell me the sto - ry most pre - cious, Sweet-est that ev - er was heard.
How for our sins He was tempt - ed, Yet was tri - um-phant at last.
Tell of the grave where they laid Him, Tell how He liv - eth a - gain.

Tell me the sto - ry most pre - cious, Sweet-est that ev - er was heard.

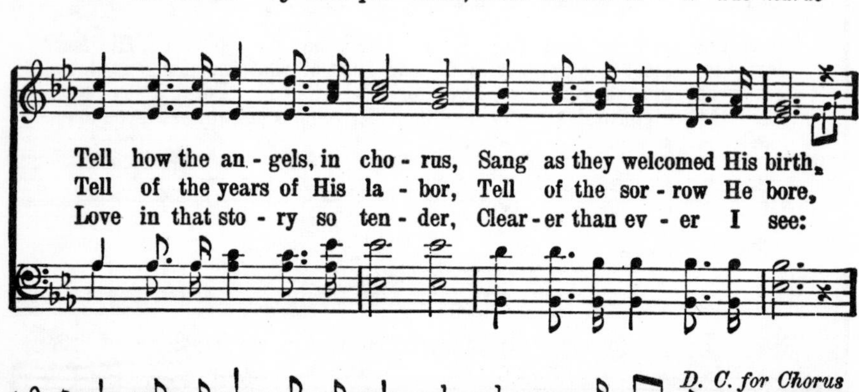

Tell how the an - gels, in cho - rus, Sang as they welcomed His birth,
Tell of the years of His la - bor, Tell of the sor - row He bore,
Love in that sto - ry so ten - der, Clear - er than ev - er I see:

D. C. for Chorus

"Glo - ry to God in the high - est! Peace and good ti - dings to earth."
He was de-spised and af - flict - ed, Home-less, re - ject - ed and poor.
Stay, let me weep while you whis - per, Love paid the ran - som for me.

"Whosoever" Meaneth Me

J. EDWIN MCCONNELL J. EDWIN MCCONNELL

1. I am hap - py to - day and the sun shines bright, The clouds have been
2. All my hopes have been raised, O His name be praised, His glo - ry has
3. O what won - der - ful love, O what grace di - vine, That Je - sus should

rolled a - way; For the Sav - ior said Who - so - ev - er will, May
filled my soul; I've been lift - ed up and from sin set free, His
die for me! I was lost in sin, for the world I pined, But

come with Him to stay (to stay).
blood hath made me whole (me whole).
now I am set free (set free).

CHORUS

"Who-so - ev - er," sure-ly mean-eth me,
Sure - ly mean-eth me, O sure - ly mean-eth me; "Who - so - ev - er,"
sure - ly mean - eth me, "Who - so - ev - er," mean-eth me.
mean - eth me.

239 I've Discovered the Way of Gladness

FLOYD W. HAWKINS FLOYD W. HAWKINS

1. Man-kind is search-ing ev-ery day In quest of some-thing new; But
2. I've found the Pearl of great-est price, "E-ter-nal life" so fair; 'Twas

I have found the "liv-ing way," The path of pleas-ures true.
through the Sav-iour's sac-ri-fice, I found this jew-el rare.

REFRAIN

LOWER VOICES HIGH VOICES

I've dis-cov-ered the way of glad-ness, I've dis-cov-ered the way of

LOWER VOICES DUET

joy, I've dis-cov-ered re-lief from sad-ness, 'Tis a hap-pi-ness with-out al-

PARTS

loy; I've dis-cov-ered the fount of bless-ing, I've dis-cov-ered the "Liv-ing

I've Discovered the Way of Gladness

Word", 'Twas the great-est of all dis-cov-er-ies When I found Je-sus my Lord.
Jesus, Revealed in Me
240
Gipsy Smith
E. Edwin Young
1. Christ, the Trans-form-ing Light, Touch-es this heart of mine,
2. Here, Lord, I bring my heart, My love, my strength, my will;
3. Life is no long-er mine, I yield it all to Thee;
4. Tri-um-phant peace is mine, Now Je-sus reigns with-in;
Pierc-ing the dark-est night, Mak-ing His glo-ry shine.
Cleanse me in ev-ery part, With all Thy Spir-it fill.
Fill me, that I may shine, Un-til Thy face I see.
He giv-eth joy di-vine, And vic-t'ry o-ver sin.
Refrain
Oh, to re-flect His grace, Caus-ing the world to see
His grace, to see
Love that will glow, till oth-ers shall know Je-sus, re-vealed in me.

241 'Tis So Sweet to Trust in Jesus
Louisa M. R. Stead
William J. Kirkpatrick
1. 'Tis so sweet to trust in Je-sus, Just to take Him at His Word; Just to rest up-on His prom-ise; Just to know, "Thus saith the Lord."
2. O how sweet to trust in Je-sus, Just to trust His cleans-ing blood; Just in sim-ple faith to plunge me 'Neath the heal-ing, cleans-ing flood!
3. Yes, 'tis sweet to trust in Je-sus, Just from sin and self to cease; Just from Je-sus sim-ply tak-ing Life and rest, and joy and peace.
4. I'm so glad I learned to trust Thee, Pre-cious Je-sus, Sav-ior, Friend; And I know that Thou art with me, Wilt be with me to the end.
Chorus
Je-sus, Je-sus, how I trust Him! How I've proved Him o'er and o'er!
p
Je-sus, Je-sus, pre-cious Je-sus! O for grace to trust Him more!
242 I Am Trusting Thee, Lord Jesus
Frances R. Havergal
Ethelbert W. Bullinger
1. I am trust-ing Thee, Lord Je-sus! Trust-ing on-ly Thee!
2. I am trust-ing Thee, Lord Je-sus! At Thy feet I bow,
3. I am trust-ing Thee to guide me: Thou a-lone shalt lead,
4. I am trust-ing Thee, Lord Je-sus! Nev-er let me fall!

I Am Trusting Thee, Lord Jesus

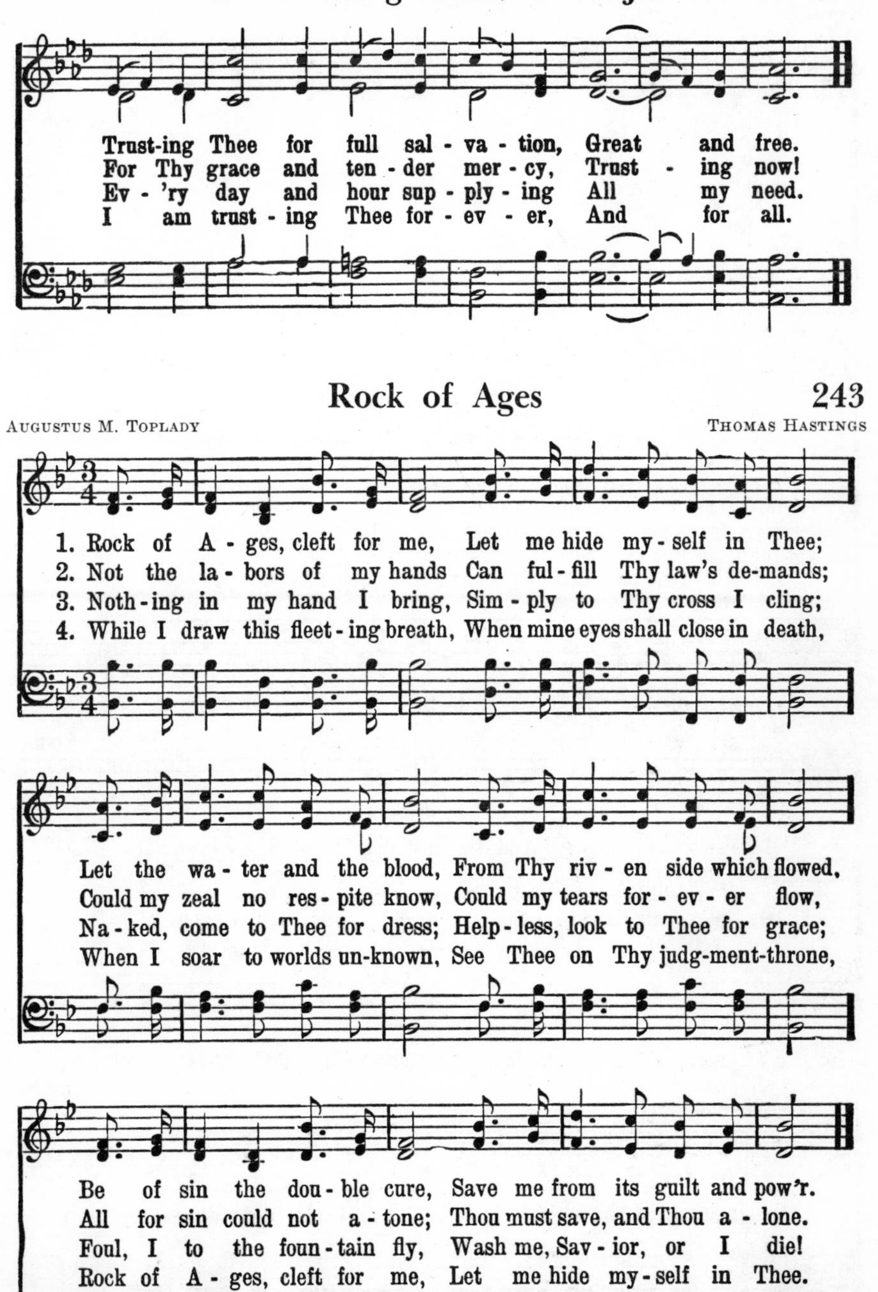
Trust-ing Thee for full sal - va - tion, Great and free.
For Thy grace and ten - der mer - cy, Trust - ing now!
Ev - 'ry day and hour sup - ply - ing All my need.
I am trust - ing Thee for - ev - er, And for all.
Rock of Ages
243
Augustus M. Toplady
Thomas Hastings
1. Rock of A - ges, cleft for me, Let me hide my - self in Thee;
2. Not the la - bors of my hands Can ful - fill Thy law's de-mands;
3. Noth - ing in my hand I bring, Sim - ply to Thy cross I cling;
4. While I draw this fleet - ing breath, When mine eyes shall close in death,
Let the wa - ter and the blood, From Thy riv - en side which flowed,
Could my zeal no res - pite know, Could my tears for - ev - er flow,
Na - ked, come to Thee for dress; Help - less, look to Thee for grace;
When I soar to worlds un-known, See Thee on Thy judg-ment-throne,
Be of sin the dou - ble cure, Save me from its guilt and pow'r.
All for sin could not a - tone; Thou must save, and Thou a - lone.
Foul, I to the foun - tain fly, Wash me, Sav - ior, or I die!
Rock of A - ges, cleft for me, Let me hide my - self in Thee.

244 The Haven of Rest

HENRY L. GILMOUR | GEORGE D. MOORE

1. My soul in sad ex - ile was out on life's sea, So
2. I yield - ed my - self to His ten - der em - brace, And
3. The song of my soul, since the Lord made me whole, Has
4. How pre - cious the thought that we all may re - cline, Like
5. Oh, come to the Sav - ior, He pa - tient - ly waits To

bur-dened with sin and dis - trest, Till I heard a sweet voice say-ing,
faith tak - ing hold of the Word, My fet - ters fell off, and I
been the old sto - ry so blest, Of Je - sus, who'll save who-so-
John the be - lov - ed and blest, On Je - sus' strong arm, where no
save by His pow - er di - vine; Come, an - chor your soul in the

D. S.—*The tem - pest may sweep o'er the*

FINE.

"Make me your choice;" And I en-tered the "Ha - ven of Rest!"
an - chored my soul; The "Ha-ven of Rest" is my Lord.
ev - er will have A home in the "Ha - ven of Rest!"
tem - pest can harm,— Se - cure in the "Ha - ven of Rest!"
"Ha - ven of Rest," And say, "My Be - lov - ed is mine."

wild, storm-y deep, In Je - sus I'm safe ev - er - more.

CHORUS | D. S.

I've anchored my soul in the "Ha-ven of Rest," I'll sail the wide seas no more;

Trusting Jesus

Edgar P. Stites — Ira D. Sankey

1. Sim - ply trust - ing ev - 'ry day, Trust - ing through a storm - y way;
2. Bright-ly doth His Spir - it shine In - to this poor heart of mine;
3. Sing - ing if my way is clear; Pray - ing if the path be drear;
4. Trust-ing Him while life shall last, Trust - ing Him till earth be past;
E - ven when my faith is small, Trust-ing Je - sus, that is all.
While He leads I can - not fall; Trust-ing Je - sus, that is all.
If in dan - ger, for Him call; Trust-ing Je - sus, that is all.
Till with - in the jas - per wall: Trust-ing Je - sus, that is all.
Chorus
Trust - ing as the mo - ments fly, Trust - ing as the days go by;
Trust - ing Him what - e'er be - fall, Trust - ing Je - sus, that is all.

246

Trust in the Lord

THOMAS O. CHISHOLM

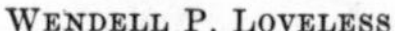

WENDELL P. LOVELESS

1. "Trust in the Lord with all thine heart," This is God's gra-cious com-mand;
"In all thy ways ac-know-ledge Him, So shalt thou dwell in the land."

2. "Trust in the Lord" who rul-eth all, See-eth all things as they are,
Be it a bird-ling in its nest, Or yon-der ut-ter-most star.

3. "Trust in the Lord" and peace-ful be, Fret not thy spir-it in vain,
What tho' the an-swer tar-ries long, Still shalt thou praise Him a-gain.

4. "Trust in the Lord"—His eye will guide All thro' the path-way a-head,
He hath re-deemed and He will keep, Trust Him and be not a-fraid.

REFRAIN

"Trust in the Lord," O trou-bled soul, Rest in the arms of His care; care, of His care; What-ev-er thy lot, It mat-ter-eth not, For noth-ing can trou-ble thee there;
"Trust in the Lord," O trou-bled soul, Noth-ing can trou-ble thee there.

He Hideth My Soul

FANNY J. CROSBY — WILLIAM J. KIRKPATRICK

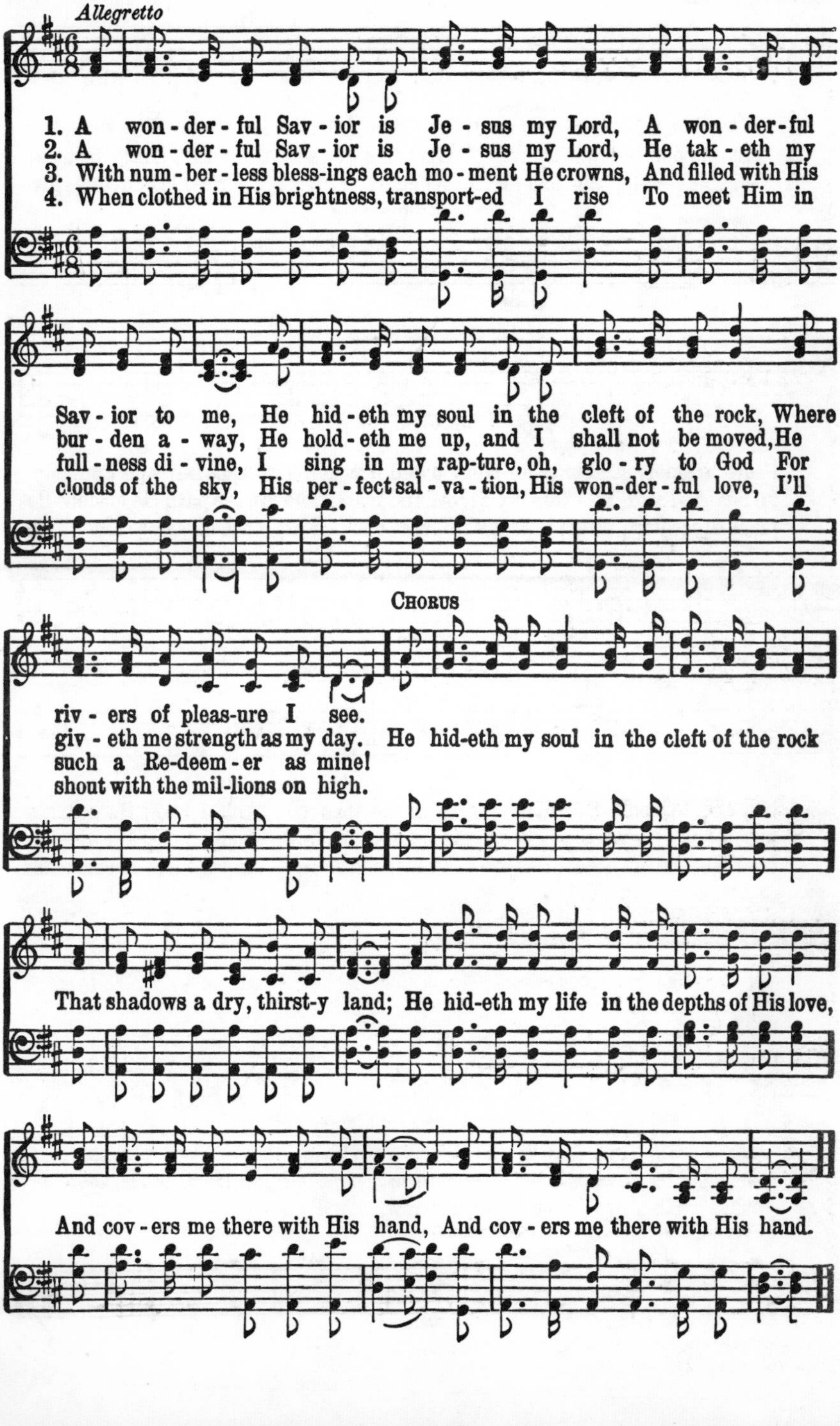

Allegretto

1. A won - der - ful Sav - ior is Je - sus my Lord, A won - der - ful
2. A won - der - ful Sav - ior is Je - sus my Lord, He tak - eth my
3. With num - ber - less bless-ings each mo - ment He crowns, And filled with His
4. When clothed in His brightness, transport-ed I rise To meet Him in

Sav - ior to me, He hid - eth my soul in the cleft of the rock, Where
bur - den a - way, He hold - eth me up, and I shall not be moved, He
full - ness di - vine, I sing in my rap - ture, oh, glo - ry to God For
clouds of the sky, His per - fect sal - va - tion, His won - der - ful love, I'll

riv - ers of pleas - ure I see.
giv - eth me strength as my day.
such a Re - deem - er as mine!
shout with the mil - lions on high.

CHORUS

He hid-eth my soul in the cleft of the rock

That shadows a dry, thirst-y land; He hid-eth my life in the depths of His love,

And cov - ers me there with His hand, And cov - ers me there with His hand.

248 His Eye Is on the Sparrow

CIVILLA D. MARTIN | CHARLES H. GABRIEL

1. Why should I feel discouraged, Why should the shadows come, Why should my heart be lonely And long for Heav'n and home, When Jesus is my portion? My constant Friend is He: His eye is on the spar-row, And I know He watches me; His eye is on the sparrow, And I know He watches me.
2. "Let not your heart be troubled," His ten-der word I hear, And rest-ing on His goodness, I lose my doubts and fears; Tho' by the path He leadeth But one step I may see: His eye is on the spar-row, And I know He watches me; His eye is on the sparrow, And I know He watches me.
3. When-ev-er I am temp-ted, When-ev-er clouds a - rise, When songs give place to sighing, When hope within me dies, I draw the clo-ser to Him, From care He sets me free; His eye is on the spar-row, And I know He cares for me; His eye is on the sparrow, And I know He cares for me.

His Eye Is on the Sparrow
Chorus.
I sing be-cause I'm hap-py (I'm hap-py), I sing because I'm free (I'm free),
rall.
For His eye is on the spar-row, And I know He watch-es me.
Precious Lord, Take My Hand
249
Thomas A. Dorsey
Arr. by Thomas A. Dorsey
Prayerfully
1. Pre-cious Lord, take my hand, Lead me on, help me stand; I am
2. When my way grows drear, Pre-cious Lord, lin-ger near; When my
tired, I am weak, I am worn; Thru the storm, thru the night, Lead me
life is al-most gone, Hear my cry, hear my call, Hold my
on to the light, Take my hand, pre-cious Lord, lead me home.
hand lest I fall; Take my hand, pre-cious Lord, lead me home.

250 I Know Who Holds Tomorrow

IRA STANPHILL IRA STANPHILL

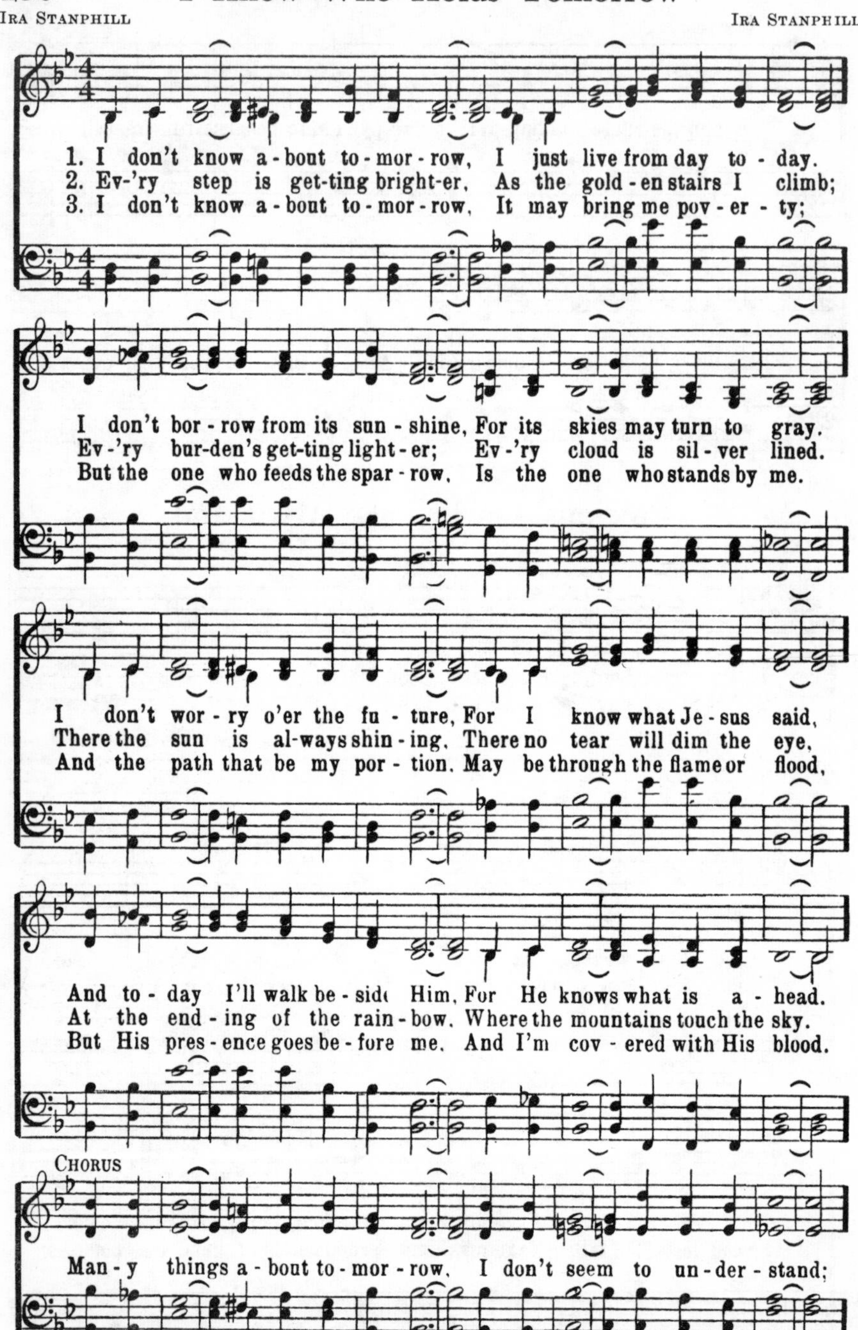
1. I don't know a - bout to - mor - row, I just live from day to - day.
2. Ev-'ry step is get-ting bright-er, As the gold - en stairs I climb;
3. I don't know a - bout to - mor - row, It may bring me pov - er - ty;
I don't bor - row from its sun - shine, For its skies may turn to gray.
Ev-'ry bur-den's get-ting light - er; Ev - 'ry cloud is sil - ver lined.
But the one who feeds the spar - row, Is the one who stands by me.
I don't wor - ry o'er the fu - ture, For I know what Je - sus said,
There the sun is al-ways shin - ing, There no tear will dim the eye,
And the path that be my por - tion, May be through the flame or flood,
And to - day I'll walk be - side Him, For He knows what is a - head.
At the end - ing of the rain - bow, Where the mountains touch the sky.
But His pres - ence goes be - fore me, And I'm cov - ered with His blood.
CHORUS
Man - y things a - bout to - mor - row, I don't seem to un - der - stand;

I Know Who Holds Tomorrow

But I know who holds to-mor - row, And I know who holds my hand.

In the Hollow of His Hand 251

WILLIAM M. RUNYAN | GEORGE S. SCHULER

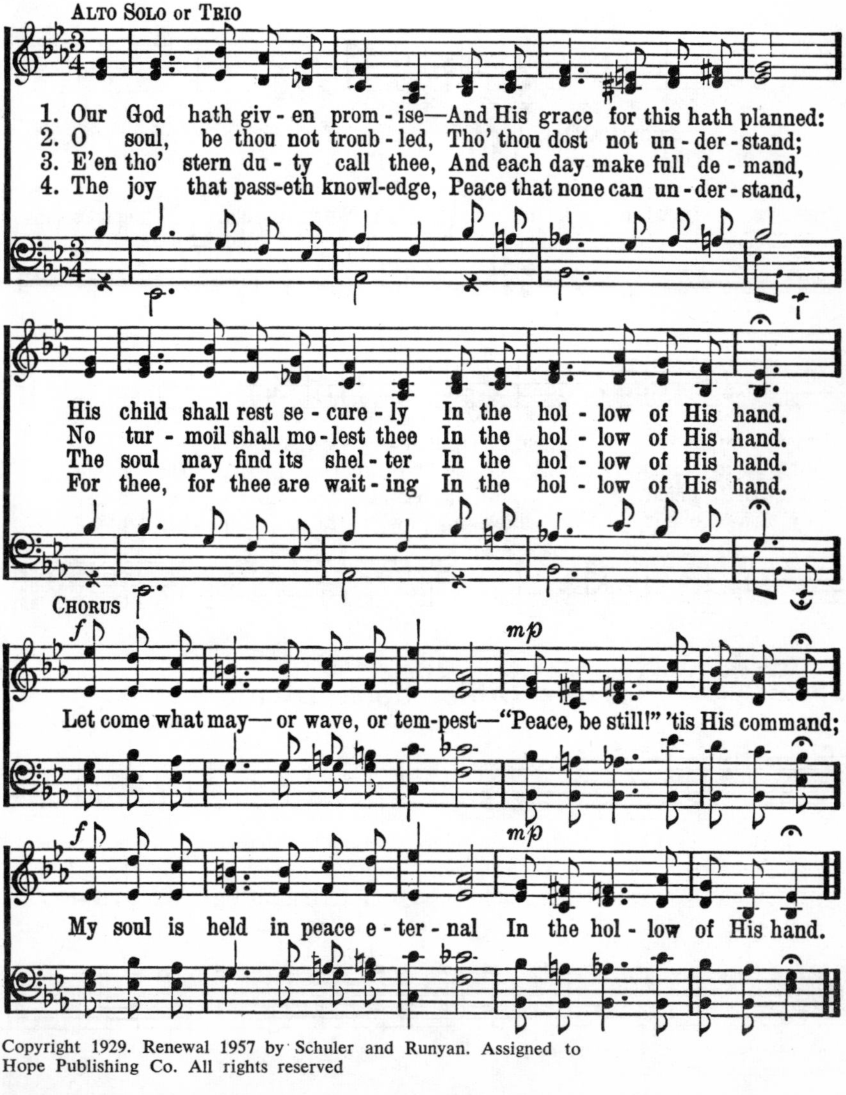

ALTO SOLO OR TRIO

1. Our God hath giv - en prom - ise—And His grace for this hath planned:
2. O soul, be thou not troub - led, Tho' thou dost not un - der - stand;
3. E'en tho' stern du - ty call thee, And each day make full de - mand,
4. The joy that pass-eth knowl-edge, Peace that none can un - der - stand,

His child shall rest se - cure - ly In the hol - low of His hand.
No tur - moil shall mo - lest thee In the hol - low of His hand.
The soul may find its shel - ter In the hol - low of His hand.
For thee, for thee are wait - ing In the hol - low of His hand.

CHORUS

f Let come what may— or wave, or tem-pest— *mp* "Peace, be still!" 'tis His command;

f My soul is held in peace e - ter - nal *mp* In the hol - low of His hand.

252 Cleanse Me

J. Edwin Orr — Maori Melody

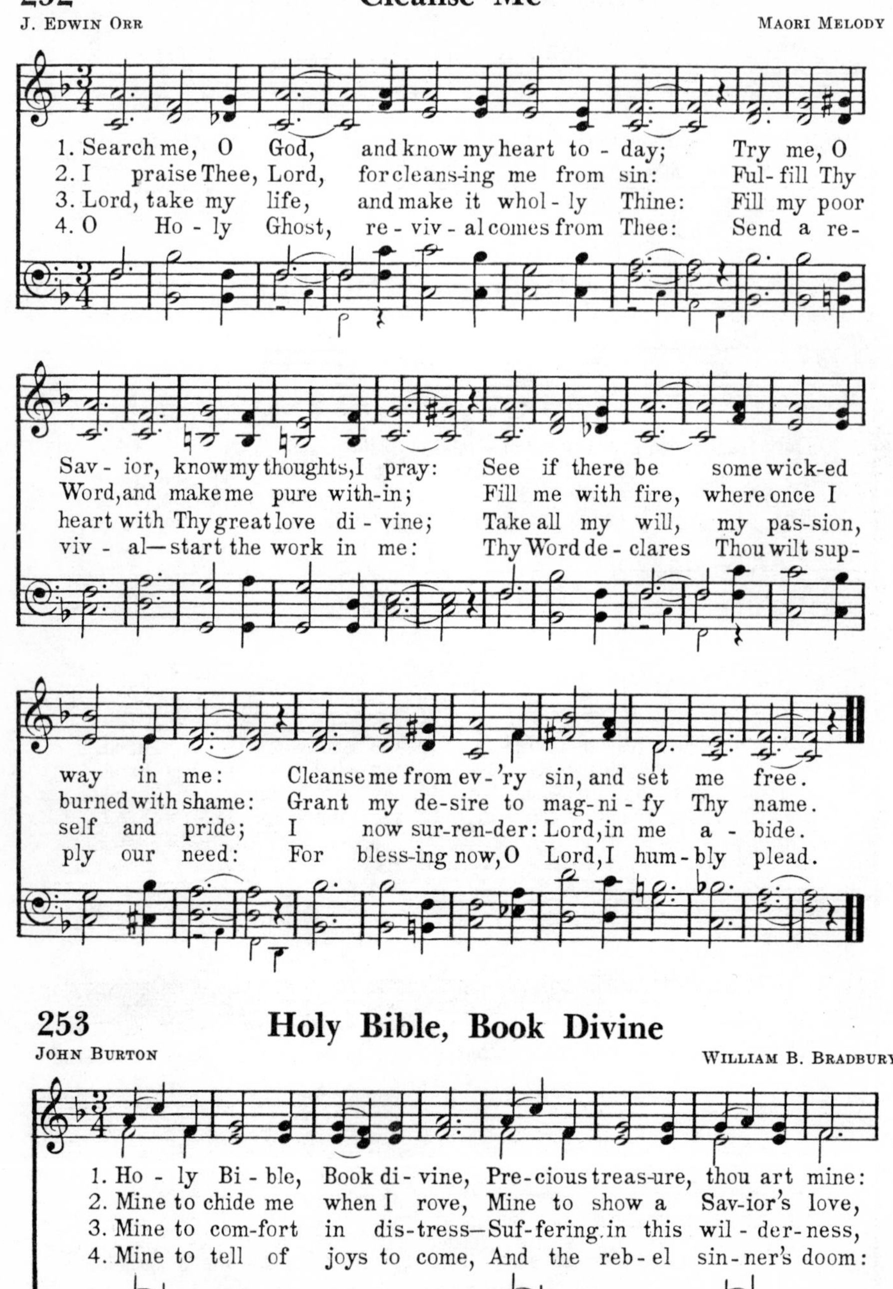

1. Search me, O God, and know my heart to - day; Try me, O
2. I praise Thee, Lord, for cleans-ing me from sin: Ful-fill Thy
3. Lord, take my life, and make it whol - ly Thine: Fill my poor
4. O Ho - ly Ghost, re - viv - al comes from Thee: Send a re-
Sav - ior, know my thoughts, I pray: See if there be some wick-ed
Word, and make me pure with-in; Fill me with fire, where once I
heart with Thy great love di - vine; Take all my will, my pas-sion,
viv - al—start the work in me: Thy Word de - clares Thou wilt sup-
way in me: Cleanse me from ev-'ry sin, and set me free.
burned with shame: Grant my de-sire to mag-ni - fy Thy name.
self and pride; I now sur-ren-der: Lord, in me a - bide.
ply our need: For bless-ing now, O Lord, I hum - bly plead.

253 Holy Bible, Book Divine

John Burton — William B. Bradbury

1. Ho - ly Bi - ble, Book di - vine, Pre - cious treas-ure, thou art mine:
2. Mine to chide me when I rove, Mine to show a Sav-ior's love,
3. Mine to com-fort in dis-tress—Suf-fering in this wil - der-ness,
4. Mine to tell of joys to come, And the reb - el sin - ner's doom:

Holy Bible, Book Divine

Mine to tell me whence I came, Mine to teach me what I am,
Mine thou art to guide and guard, Mine to pun-ish or re-ward,
Mine to show—by liv - ing faith— Man can tri-umph o - ver death,
O thou ho - ly Book di - vine, Pre-cious treas-ure, thou art mine.
Lord, Dismiss Us with Thy Blessing
254
JOHN FAWCETT, ASC.
ALT. BY GODFREY THRING
ARR. FROM A SICILIAN MELODY
1. Lord, dis - miss us with Thy bless-ing; Fill our hearts with joy and peace;
2. Thanks we give and ad - o - ra - tion For Thy gos - pel's joy - ful sound;
3. So that when Thy love shall call us, Sav-ior, from the world a - way,
Let us each, Thy love pos-sess-ing, Tri-umph in re - deem-ing grace:
May the fruits of Thy sal - va - tion In our hearts and lives a - bound:
Let no fear of death ap - pall us, Glad Thy sum - mons to o - bey:
O re - fresh us, O re - fresh us, Travel-ing through this wil-der-ness.
Ev - er faith-ful, Ev - er faith-ful To the truth may we be found.
May we ev - er, May we ev - er Reign with Thee in end-less day. A-MEN.

255

The Sands of Time

Anne Ross Cousin

Chretièn Urhan
Arr. by Edward F. Rimbault

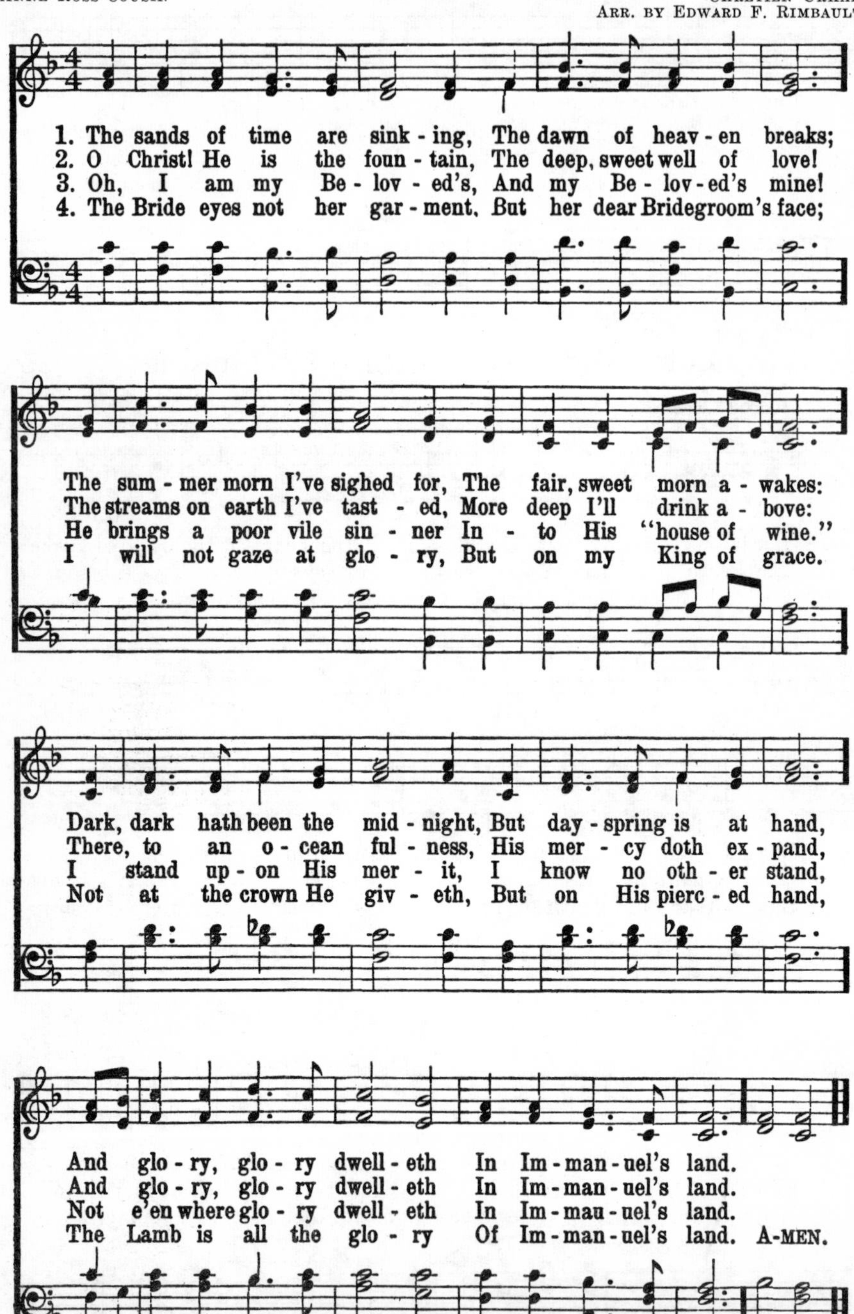
1. The sands of time are sink - ing, The dawn of heav - en breaks;
2. O Christ! He is the foun - tain, The deep, sweet well of love!
3. Oh, I am my Be - lov - ed's, And my Be - lov - ed's mine!
4. The Bride eyes not her gar - ment, But her dear Bridegroom's face;
The sum - mer morn I've sighed for, The fair, sweet morn a - wakes:
The streams on earth I've tast - ed, More deep I'll drink a - bove:
He brings a poor vile sin - ner In - to His "house of wine."
I will not gaze at glo - ry, But on my King of grace.
Dark, dark hath been the mid - night, But day - spring is at hand,
There, to an o - cean ful - ness, His mer - cy doth ex - pand,
I stand up - on His mer - it, I know no oth - er stand,
Not at the crown He giv - eth, But on His pierc - ed hand,
And glo - ry, glo - ry dwell - eth In Im - man - uel's land.
And glo - ry, glo - ry dwell - eth In Im - man - uel's land.
Not e'en where glo - ry dwell - eth In Im - mau - uel's land.
The Lamb is all the glo - ry Of Im - man - uel's land. A-men.

My Savior First of All

FANNY J. CROSBY | JOHN R. SWENEY

1. When my life-work is end-ed, and I cross the swell-ing tide, When the
2. Oh, the soul-thrill-ing rap-ture when I view His bless-ed face, And the
3. Oh, the dear ones in glo-ry, how they beck-on me to come, And our
4. Thro' the gates to the cit-y in a robe of spot-less white, He will
bright and glorious morning I shall see; I shall know my Re-deem-er when I
lus-ter of His kind-ly beaming eye; How my full heart will praise Him for the
part-ing at the riv-er I re-call; To the sweet vales of E-den they will
lead me where no tears will ev-er fall; In the glad song of a-ges I shall
reach the oth-er side, And His smile will be the first to wel-come me.
mer-cy, love, and grace, That pre-pare for me a man-sion in the sky.
sing my wel-come home; But I long to meet my Sav-ior first of all.
min-gle with de-light; But I long to meet my Sav-ior first of all.
CHORUS
I shall know . . Him, I shall know Him, And redeemed by His side I shall stand,
I shall know Him,
I shall know . . Him, I shall know Him By the print of the nails in His hand.
I shall know Him,

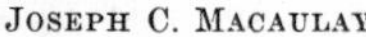

257 Gone, Yes, Gone Forevermore!

JOSEPH C. MACAULAY — JOHN F. WILSON

1. Now let songs of tri-umph swell loud and clear, loud and clear, Christ has con-quered sin and hell, sing it loud and clear. Once for us in mor-tal fray, Climbed He Cal-v'ry's rug-ged way. Praise Him now in glad-some lay; Sing it loud and clear!

2. Sins as black as death's dark shroud blot-ted out, blot-ted out! As the thick-est thun-der cloud, all are blot-ted out. From God's mem-o-ry e-rased– At such mer-cy stand a-mazed! Be His name for-ev-er praised; All are blot-ted out!

3. Far as east is from the west they are gone, they are gone. O, how rich-ly we are blest, for our sins are gone. In the deep, un-fath-omed sea They are cast, and we are free. Join our glo-rious ju-bi-lee– All our sins are gone!

REFRAIN

Gone, yes, gone for-ev-er-more! Ev-er-more! Ful-ly set-tled is the score! Since He purged my guilt-y stains, Not a spot re-mains; Not a spot re-mains;

Gone, Yes, Gone Forevermore!
Gone, yes, gone! Gone, yes, gone! Gone, yes, gone for-ev-er-more!
Who at My Door Is Standing?
258
Mary B. C. Slade
Asa B. Everett
1. Who at my door is stand-ing, Pa-tient-ly draw-ing near,
2. Lone-ly with-out He's stay-ing: Lone-ly with-in am I;
3. All through the dark hours drea-ry, Knock-ing a-gain is He;
4. Door of my heart, I has-ten! Thee will I o-pen wide.
En-trance with-in de-mand-ing? Whose is the voice I hear?
While I am still de-lay-ing, Will He not pass me by?
Je-sus, art Thou not wea-ry, Wait-ing so long for me?
Tho' He re-buke and chas-ten, He shall with me a-bide.
Refrain
Sweet-ly the tones are fall-ing: "O-pen the door for me!
If thou wilt heed My call-ing, I will a-bide with thee."

259 Living for Jesus

Thomas O. Chisholm

C. Harold Lowden

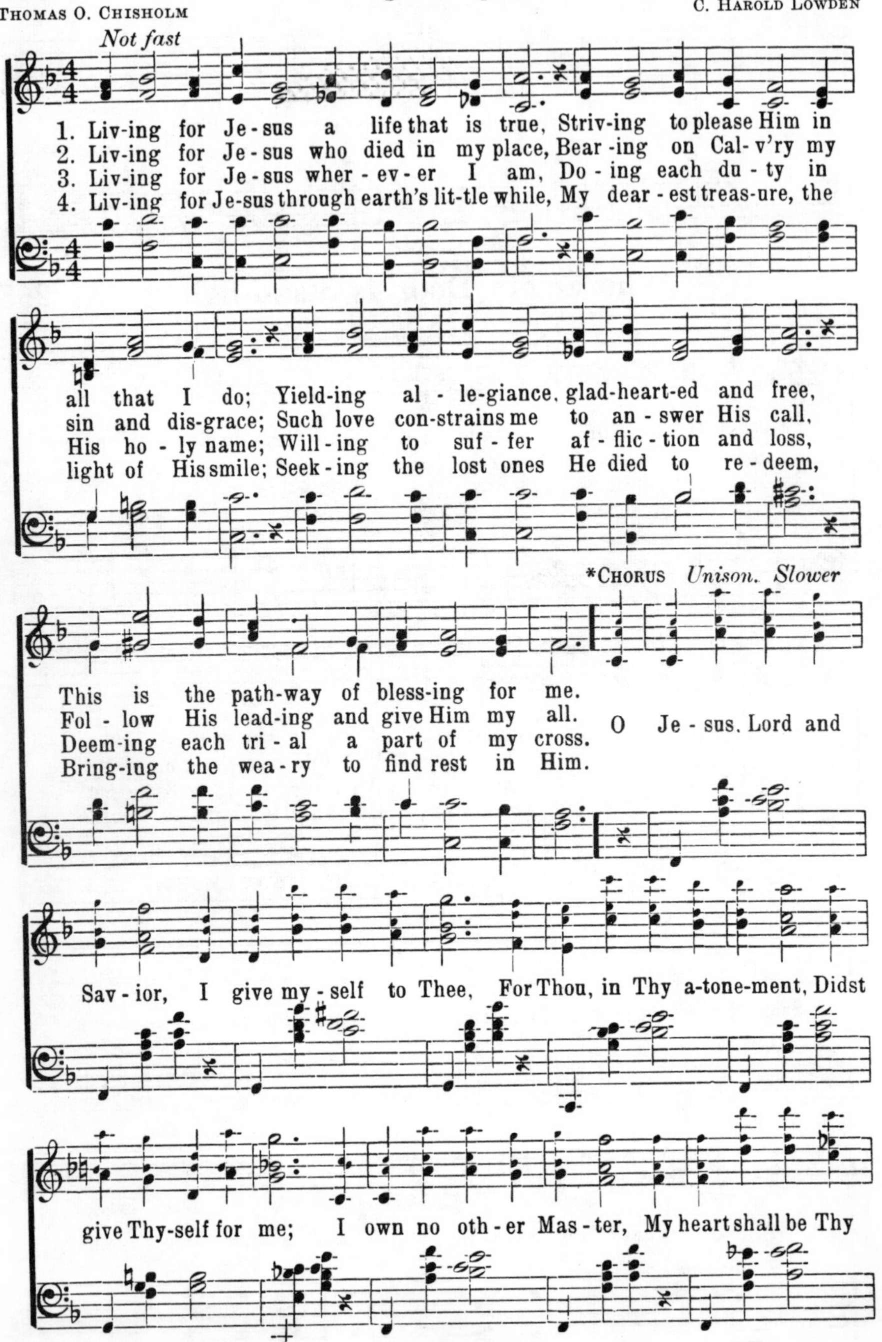
Not fast
1. Liv-ing for Je-sus a life that is true, Striv-ing to please Him in all that I do; Yield-ing al-le-giance, glad-heart-ed and free, This is the path-way of bless-ing for me.
2. Liv-ing for Je-sus who died in my place, Bear-ing on Cal-v'ry my sin and dis-grace; Such love con-strains me to an-swer His call, Fol-low His lead-ing and give Him my all.
3. Liv-ing for Je-sus wher-ev-er I am, Do-ing each du-ty in His ho-ly name; Will-ing to suf-fer af-flic-tion and loss, Deem-ing each tri-al a part of my cross.
4. Liv-ing for Je-sus through earth's lit-tle while, My dear-est treas-ure, the light of His smile; Seek-ing the lost ones He died to re-deem, Bring-ing the wea-ry to find rest in Him.
*CHORUS Unison. Slower
O Je-sus, Lord and Sav-ior, I give my-self to Thee, For Thou, in Thy a-tone-ment, Didst give Thy-self for me; I own no oth-er Mas-ter, My heart shall be Thy

Living for Jesus
rit.
throne, My life I give, hence-forth to live, O Christ, for Thee a - lone.
I Would Be True
260
Howard A. Walter
Joseph Yates Peek
1. I would be true, for there are those who trust me; I would be
2. I would be friend of all—the foe, the friend - less; I would be
3. I would be prayer - ful thru each bus - y mo - ment; I would be
pure, for there are those who care; I would be strong, for
giv - ing, and for - get the gift; I would be hum - ble,
con - stant - ly in touch with God; I would be tuned to
there is much to suf - fer; I would be brave, for there is
for I know my weak - ness; I would look up, and laugh, and
hear His slight - est whis - per; I would have faith to keep the
much to dare; I would be brave, for there is much to dare.
love, and lift; I would look up, and laugh, and love, and lift.
path Christ trod; I would have faith to keep the path Christ trod.

261 "Are Ye Able," Said the Master

Earl Marlatt — Harry S. Mason

1. "Are ye a - ble," said the Mas - ter, "To be cru - ci - fied with me?"
2. "Are ye a - ble" to re-mem - ber, When a thief lifts up his eyes,
3. "Are ye a - ble" when the shad-ows Close a-round you with the sod,
4. "Are ye a - ble?" Still the Mas - ter Whis-pers down e - ter - ni - ty,
"Yea," the stur - dy dream-ers an-swered, "To the death we fol - low Thee."
That his par-doned soul is wor - thy Of a place in par - a - dise?
To be-lieve that spir - it tri-umphs, To com-mend your soul to God?
And he - ro - ic spir - its an - swer Now, as then, in Gal - i - lee.
Refrain
"Lord, we are a - ble." Our spir - its are Thine. Re - mold them,
make us, Like Thee, di - vine. Thy guid - ing ra-diance A - bove us shall
be A bea - con to God, To love and loy - al - ty.

Higher Ground 262

Johnson Oatman, Jr. — Charles H. Gabriel

1. I'm press-ing on the up-ward way, New heights I'm gaining ev - 'ry day;
2. My heart has no de - sire to stay Where doubts a-rise and fears dis-may;
3. I want to live a - bove the world, Tho' Sa-tan's darts at me are hurled;
4. I want to scale the utmost height, And catch a gleam of glo - ry bright;

Still pray-ing as I'm on-ward bound, "Lord, plant my feet on high-er ground."
Tho' some may dwell where these abound, My prayer, my aim, is high-er ground.
For faith has caught the joy - ful sound, The song of saints on high-er ground.
But still I'll pray till Heav'n I've found, "Lord, lead me on to high-er ground."

Chorus

Lord, lift me up and let me stand, By faith, on Heav-en's ta - ble-land,

A high-er plane than I have found; Lord, plant my feet on high - er ground.

263 Bring Your Vessels, Not a Few

LEILA N. MORRIS | LEILA N. MORRIS

1. Are you look - ing for the full - ness of the bless-ing of the Lord
2. Bring your emp-ty earth - en ves - sels, clean thro' Je-sus' pre-cious blood,
3. Like the cruse of oil un-fail - ing is His grace for - ev - er-more,
In your heart and life to - day? Claim the prom-ise of your Fa-ther,
Come, ye need - y, one and all; And in hu-man con - se - cra-tion
And His love un-chang-ing still; And ac-cord - ing to His prom-ise
come ac - cord - ing to His word, In the bless - ed old-time way.
wait be - fore the throne of God, Till the Ho - ly Ghost shall fall.
with the Ho - ly Ghost and pow'r, He will ev - 'ry ves - sel fill.
CHORUS
He will fill your heart to-day to o - ver - flow - - - ing, As the
He will fill your heart to o - ver-flow-ing,
Lord commandeth you, "Bring your vessels, not a few;" He will fill your heart to-
He will fill

Bring Your Vessels, Not a Few
day to o - ver - flow - - - - ing With the Ho - ly Ghost and pow'r.
your heart to o - ver-flow-ing,
Something for Thee
264
Sylvanus D. Phelps
Robert Lowry
1. Sav - ior, Thy dy - ing love Thou gav - est me, Nor should I aught with-hold, Dear Lord, from Thee: In love my soul would bow, My heart ful-fill its vow, Some of-f'ring bring Thee now, Something for Thee.
2. At the blest mer - cy - seat, Plead-ing for me, My fee - ble faith looks up, Je - sus, to Thee: Help me the cross to bear, Thy wondrous love de - clare, Some song to raise, or prayer, Something for Thee.
3. Give me a faith - ful heart,—Like-ness to Thee,— That each de-part - ing day Hence-forth may see Some work of love be - gun, Some deed of kindness done, Some wand'rer sought and won, Something for Thee.
4. All that I am and have,—Thy gifts so free,— In joy, in grief, thro' life, Dear Lord, for Thee! And when Thy face I see, My ran-somed soul shall be, Thro' all e - ter - ni - ty, Something for Thee. A - MEN.

265 Draw Me Nearer

FANNY J. CROSBY
WILLIAM H. DOANE
1. I am Thine, O Lord, I have heard Thy voice, And it told Thy
2. Con-se-crate me now to Thy serv-ice, Lord, By the pow'r of
3. Oh, the pure de-light of a sin-gle hour That be-fore Thy
4. There are depths of love that I can-not know Till I cross the
love to me; But I long to rise in the arms of faith, And be
grace di-vine; Let my soul look up with a stead-fast hope, And my
throne I spend, When I kneel in prayer, and with Thee, my God, I com-
nar-row sea; There are heights of joy that I may not reach Till I
REFRAIN
clos-er drawn to Thee.
will be lost in Thine.
mune as friend with friend!
rest in peace with Thee.
Draw me near - er, near-er, bless-ed
near - er, near - er,
Lord, To the cross where Thou hast died; Draw me near-er, near-er,
near-er, bless-ed Lord, To Thy pre-cious, bleed-ing side.

I Need Jesus

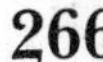

George O. Webster | Charles H. Gabriel

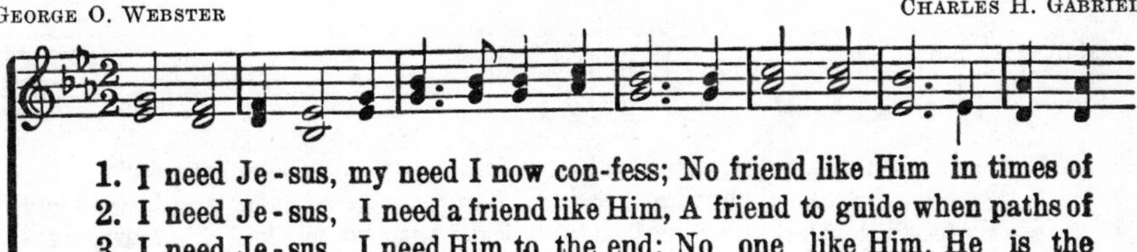
1. I need Je - sus, my need I now con-fess; No friend like Him in times of
2. I need Je - sus, I need a friend like Him, A friend to guide when paths of
3. I need Je - sus, I need Him to the end; No one like Him, He is the

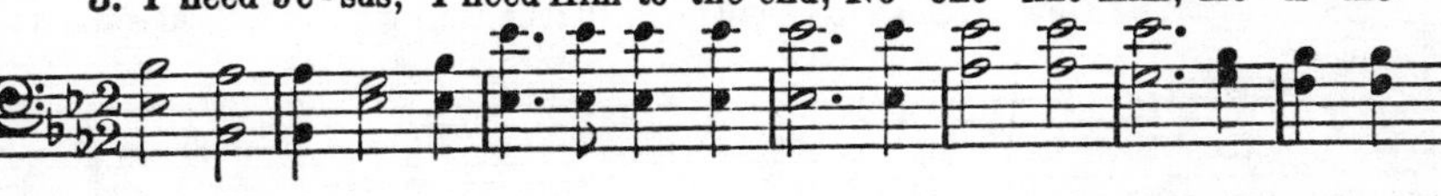

deep dis-tress; I need Je-sus, the need I glad-ly own; Tho' some may bear their
life are dim; I need Je-sus, when foes my soul assail; A - lone I know I
sin-ner's Friend; I need Je-sus, no oth-er friend will do; So constant, kind, so

Chorus
load a-lone, Yet I need Je - sus. I need Je - sus, I need Je-sus,
can but fail, So I need Je - sus.
strong and true, Yes, I need Je - sus. I need Je-sus with me, I need Je-sus always,

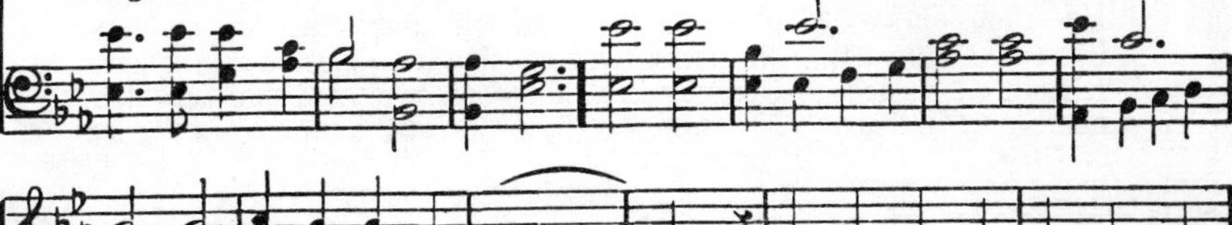
I need Je-sus ev-'ry day; . . . Need Him in the sunshine hour,
ev-'ry day;

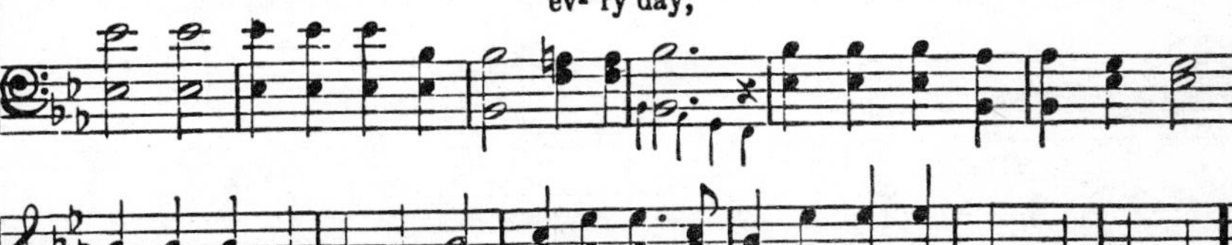
Need Him when the storm-clouds low'r; Ev'ry day a-long my way, Yes, I need Je-sus.

267 Nearer, Still Nearer

LEILA N. MORRIS LEILA N. MORRIS

1. Nearer, still nearer, close to Thy heart, Draw me, my Sav-ior, so precious Thou art; Fold me, O fold me close to Thy breast, Shel-ter me safe in that "Ha - ven of Rest," Shel-ter me safe in that "Ha - ven of Rest."
2. Nearer, still nearer, noth-ing I bring, Naught as an of-f'ring to Je - sus my King; On - ly my sin-ful, now contrite heart, Grant me the cleansing Thy blood doth im-part, Grant me the cleansing Thy blood doth im-part.
3. Nearer, still nearer, Lord, to be Thine, Sin, with its fol-lies, I glad-ly re-sign; All of its pleasures, pomp and its pride, Give me but Je - sus, my Lord cru-ci-fied, Give me but Je - sus, my Lord cru-ci-fied.
4. Nearer, still nearer, while life shall last, Till safe in glo-ry my an-chor is cast; Thro' endless a - ges, ev - er to be, Near-er, my Sav-ior, still near-er to Thee, Near-er, my Sav-ior, still near-er to Thee.

268 Revive Us Again

WILLIAM P. MACKAY JOHN J. HUSBAND

1. We praise Thee, O God! for the Son of Thy love, For Je-sus who
2. We praise Thee, O God! for Thy Spir - it of light, Who has shown us our
3. All glo - ry and praise to the Lamb that was slain, Who has borne all our
4. Re - vive us a - gain; fill each heart with Thy love; May each soul be re-

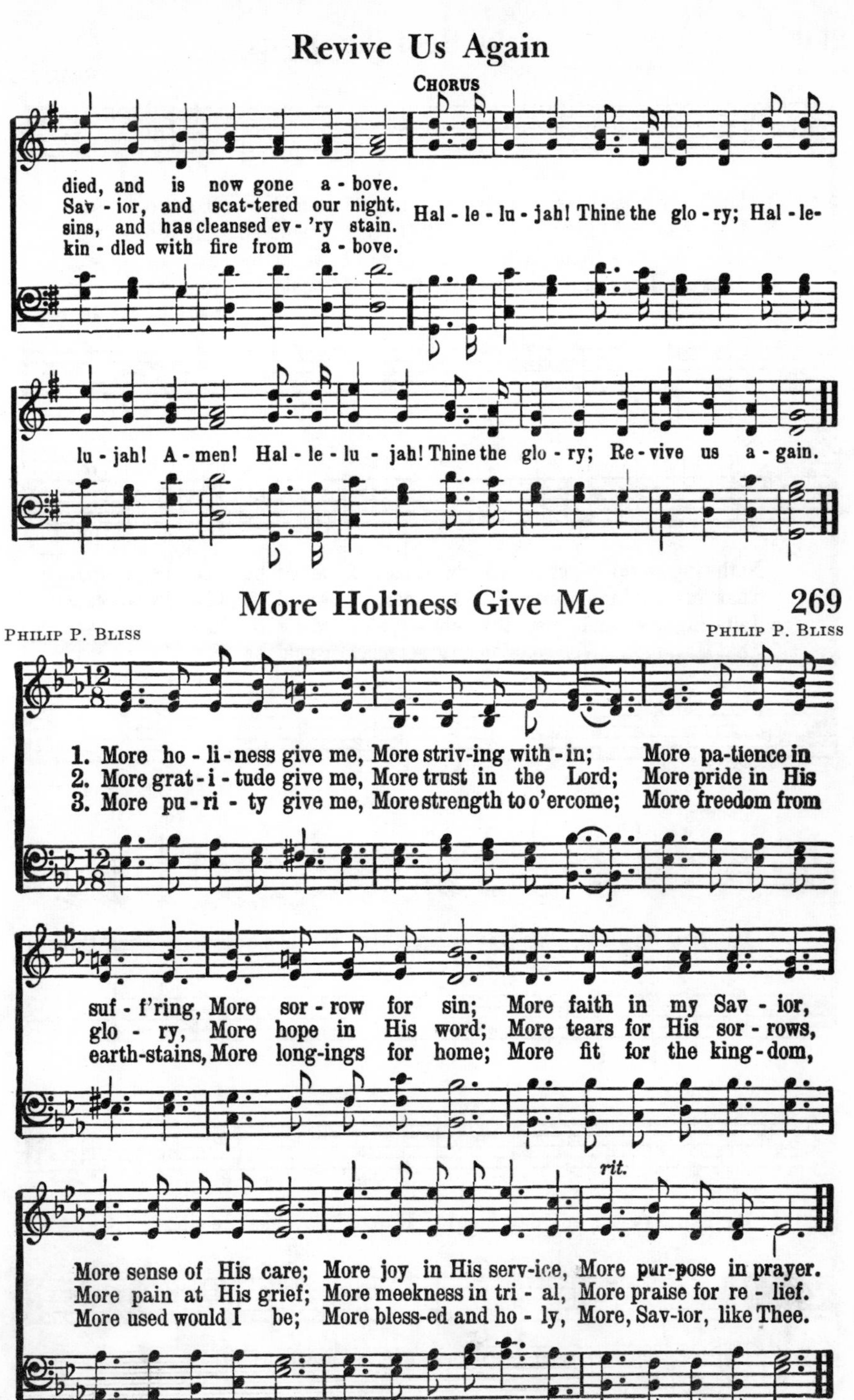
Revive Us Again
Chorus
died, and is now gone a - bove.
Sav - ior, and scat-tered our night.
sins, and has cleansed ev - 'ry stain.
kin - dled with fire from a - bove.
Hal - le - lu - jah! Thine the glo - ry; Hal - le-
lu - jah! A - men! Hal - le - lu - jah! Thine the glo - ry; Re - vive us a - gain.
More Holiness Give Me
269
Philip P. Bliss
Philip P. Bliss
1. More ho - li - ness give me, More striv-ing with - in; More pa-tience in
2. More grat - i - tude give me, More trust in the Lord; More pride in His
3. More pu - ri - ty give me, More strength to o'ercome; More freedom from
suf - f'ring, More sor - row for sin; More faith in my Sav - ior,
glo - ry, More hope in His word; More tears for His sor - rows,
earth-stains, More long-ings for home; More fit for the king - dom,
rit.
More sense of His care; More joy in His serv-ice, More pur-pose in prayer.
More pain at His grief; More meekness in tri - al, More praise for re - lief.
More used would I be; More bless-ed and ho - ly, More, Sav-ior, like Thee.

270

I Would Be Like Jesus

JAMES ROWE BENTLEY D. ACKLEY

1. Earth-ly pleas-ures vain-ly call me; I would be like Je - sus;
2. He has bro-ken ev - 'ry fet - ter, I would be like Je - sus;
3. All the way from earth to Glo - ry, I would be like Je - sus;
4. That in Heav-en He may meet me, I would be like Je - sus;
would be like Je - sus;
Noth-ing world-ly shall en-thrall me; I would be like Je - sus.
That my soul may serve Him bet - ter, I would be like Je - sus.
Tell - ing o'er and o'er the sto - ry, I would be like Je - sus.
That His words "Well done" may greet me, I would be like Je - sus.
would be like Je - sus.
CHORUS.
Be like Je - sus, this my song, In the home and in the throng;
Be like Je - sus, all day long! I would be like Je - sus. A - MEN.

Jesus, I My Cross Have Taken

HENRY F. LYTE

ASCRIBED TO WOLFGANG A. MOZART
ARR. BY HUBERT P. MAIN

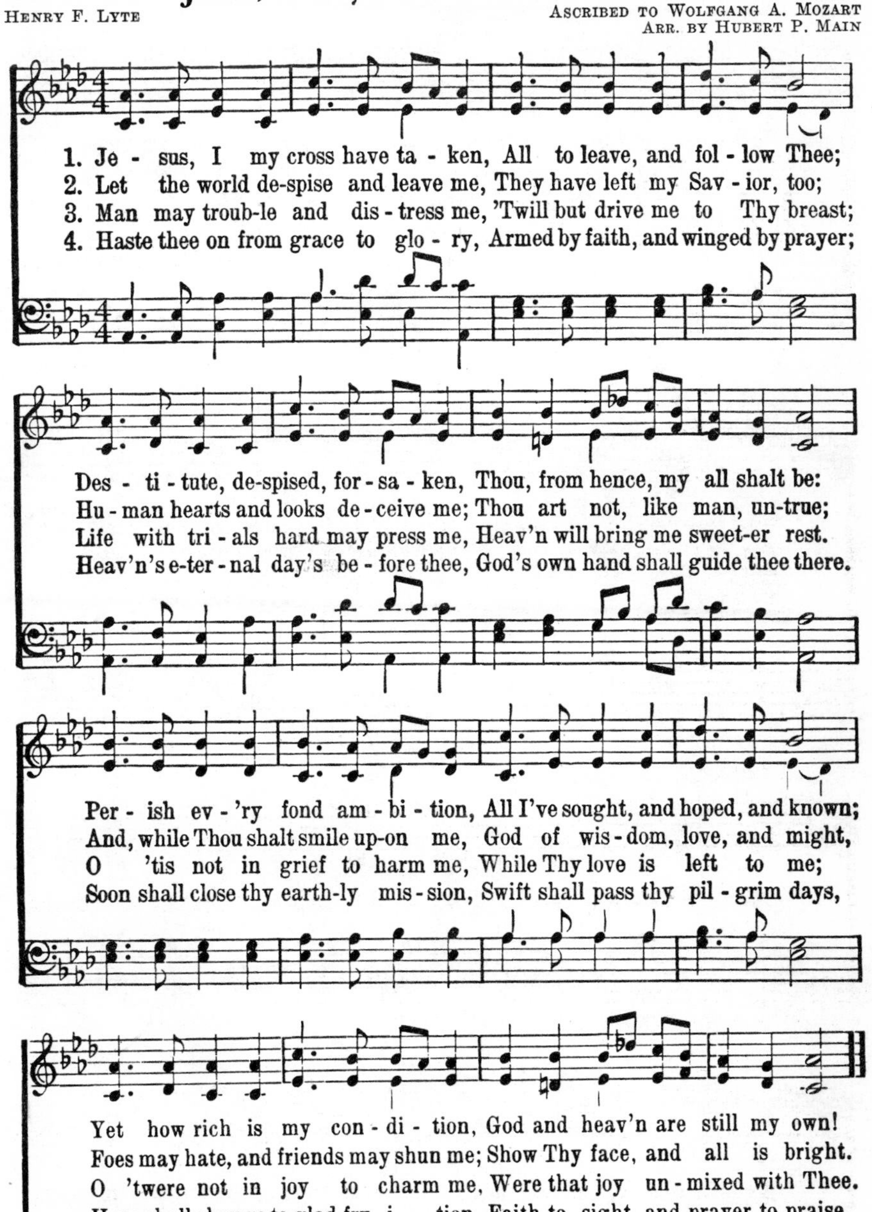
1. Je - sus, I my cross have ta - ken, All to leave, and fol - low Thee;
2. Let the world de-spise and leave me, They have left my Sav - ior, too;
3. Man may troub-le and dis - tress me, 'Twill but drive me to Thy breast;
4. Haste thee on from grace to glo - ry, Armed by faith, and winged by prayer;
Des - ti - tute, de-spised, for - sa - ken, Thou, from hence, my all shalt be:
Hu - man hearts and looks de - ceive me; Thou art not, like man, un-true;
Life with tri - als hard may press me, Heav'n will bring me sweet-er rest.
Heav'n's e-ter - nal day's be - fore thee, God's own hand shall guide thee there.
Per - ish ev - 'ry fond am - bi - tion, All I've sought, and hoped, and known;
And, while Thou shalt smile up-on me, God of wis - dom, love, and might,
O 'tis not in grief to harm me, While Thy love is left to me;
Soon shall close thy earth-ly mis - sion, Swift shall pass thy pil - grim days,
Yet how rich is my con - di - tion, God and heav'n are still my own!
Foes may hate, and friends may shun me; Show Thy face, and all is bright.
O 'twere not in joy to charm me, Were that joy un - mixed with Thee.
Hope shall change to glad fru - i - tion, Faith to sight, and prayer to praise.

272 Nearer, My God, to Thee

SARAH F. ADAMS

LOWELL MASON

1. Near - er, my God, to Thee, Near - er to Thee! E'en though it
2. Though like the wan - der - er, The sun gone down, Dark - ness be
3. There let the way ap - pear, Steps un - to Heav'n: All that Thou
4. Then, with my wak - ing tho'ts Bright with Thy praise, Out of my
5. Or if on joy - ful wing, Cleav - ing the sky, Sun, moon, and
be a cross That rais - eth me; Still all my song shall be,
o - ver me, My rest a stone; Yet in my dreams I'd be
send - est me, In mer - cy giv'n: An - gels to beck - on me,
ston - y griefs Beth - el I'll raise; So by my woes to be
stars for - got, Up - ward I fly, Still all my song shall be,
Near - er, my God, to Thee, Near - er, my God, to Thee, Near - er to Thee!
273 Lord, Speak to Me
FRANCES R. HAVERGAL
ROBERT SCHUMANN
1. Lord, speak to me, that I may speak In liv - ing ech - oes of Thy tone;
2. O teach me, Lord, that I may teach The pre - cious things Thou dost im - part;
3. O fill me with Thy full - ness, Lord, Un - til my ver - y heart o'er - flow
4. O use me, Lord, use e - ven me, Just as Thou wilt, and when, and where;

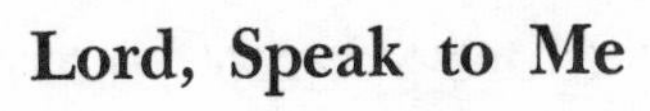

As Thou hast sought, so let me seek Thy err - ing chil - dren lost and lone.
And wing my words, that they may reach The hid-den depths of many a heart.
In kindling thought and glowing word, Thy love to tell, Thy praise to show.
Un - til Thy bless - ed face I see, Thy rest, Thy joy, Thy glo - ry share.

O Jesus, I Have Promised

274

JOHN E. BODE — ARTHUR H. MANN

1. O Je - sus, I have prom-ised To serve Thee to the end; Be Thou for-ev - er near me, My Mas-ter and my Friend: I shall not fear the bat - tle If Thou art by my side, Nor wan - der from the path-way If Thou wilt be my guide.

2. O let me feel Thee near me, The world is ev - er near; I see the sights that daz - zle, The tempting sounds I hear: My foes are ev - er near me, A-round me and with-in; But, Je - sus, draw Thou near-er, And shield my soul from sin.

3. O Je - sus, Thou hast promised To all who fol - low Thee, That where Thou art in glo - ry, There shall Thy servant be; And, Je-sus, I have promised To serve Thee to the end; O give me grace to fol - low My Mas - ter and my Friend.

275 More About Jesus

Eliza E. Hewitt — John R. Sweney

1. More a-bout Je-sus would I know, More of His grace to oth-ers show; More of His sav-ing full-ness see, More of His love who died for me.
2. More a bout Je-sus let me learn, More of His ho-ly will dis-cern; Spir-it of God, my teach-er be, Show-ing the things of Christ to me.
3. More a-bout Je-sus; in His word, Holding com-mun-ion with my Lord; Hear-ing His voice in ev-'ry line, Mak-ing each faith-ful say-ing mine.
4. More a-bout Je-sus on His throne, Rich-es in glo-ry all His own; More of His kingdom's sure in-crease; More of His com-ing, Prince of Peace.

Fine

D.S.—*More of His sav-ing full-ness see, More of His love who died for me.*

Refrain

More, more a-bout Je-sus, More, more a-bout Je-sus;

D. S.

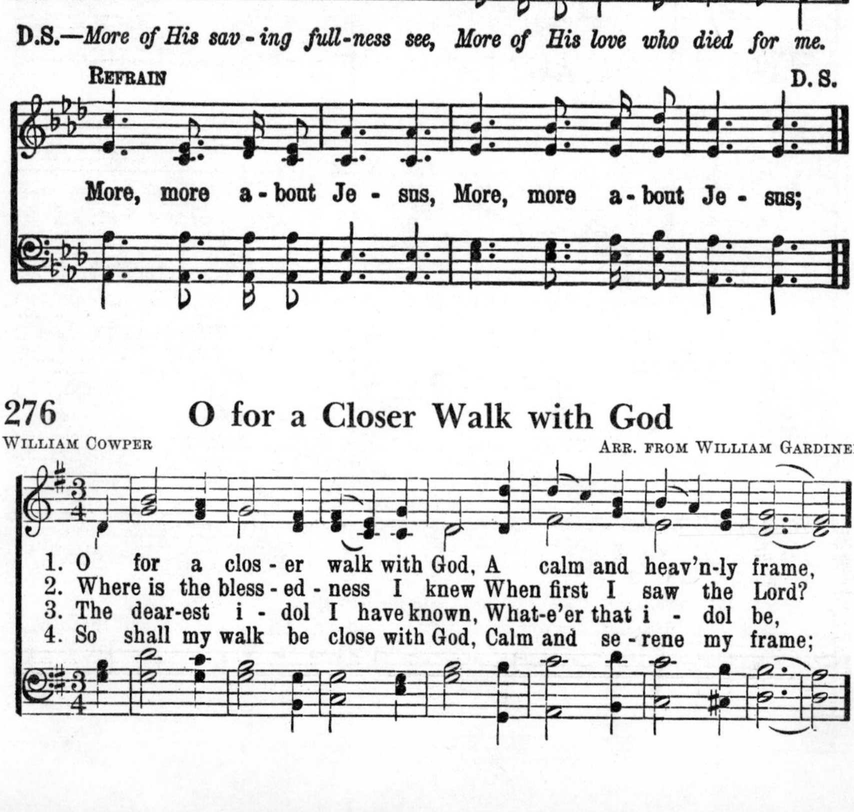

276 O for a Closer Walk with God

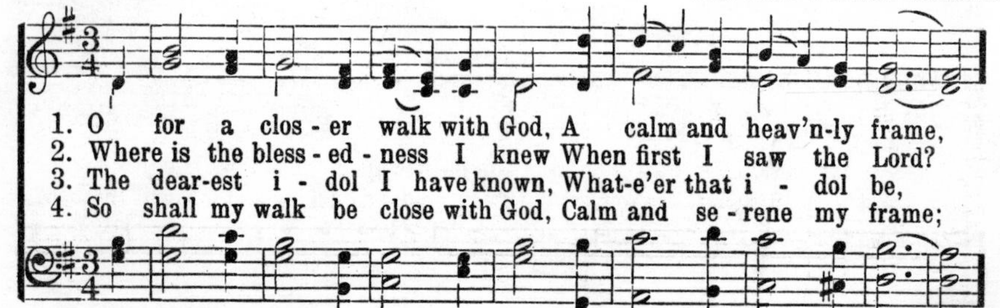
William Cowper
Arr. from William Gardiner
1. O for a clos-er walk with God, A calm and heav'n-ly frame,
2. Where is the bless-ed-ness I knew When first I saw the Lord?
3. The dear-est i-dol I have known, What-e'er that i-dol be,
4. So shall my walk be close with God, Calm and se-rene my frame;

O for a Closer Walk with God

A light to shine up - on the road That leads me to the Lamb!
Where is the soul - re - fresh-ing view Of Je - sus and His word?
Help me to tear it from Thy throne, And wor - ship on - ly Thee.
So pur - er light shall mark the road That leads me to the Lamb.
Lead, Kindly Light
277
John H. Newman
John B. Dykes
1. Lead, kindly Light, amid th'encircling gloom, Lead Thou me on! The night is
2. I was not ev-er thus, nor prayed that Thou Shouldst lead me on; I loved to
3. So long Thy pow'r hath blest me, sure it still Will lead me on O'er moor and
dark, and I am far from home; Lead Thou me on! Keep Thou my feet; I
choose and see my path; but now Lead Thou me on! I loved the gar - ish
fen, o'er crag and torrent, till The night is gone, And with the morn those
do not ask to see . . . The dis-tant scene; one step e - nough for me.
day, and, spite of fears, . . Pride ruled my will. Remember not past years!
an-gel fa - ces smile, . Which I have loved long since, and lost a - while!

278 Open My Eyes, That I May See

Clara H. Scott | Clara H. Scott

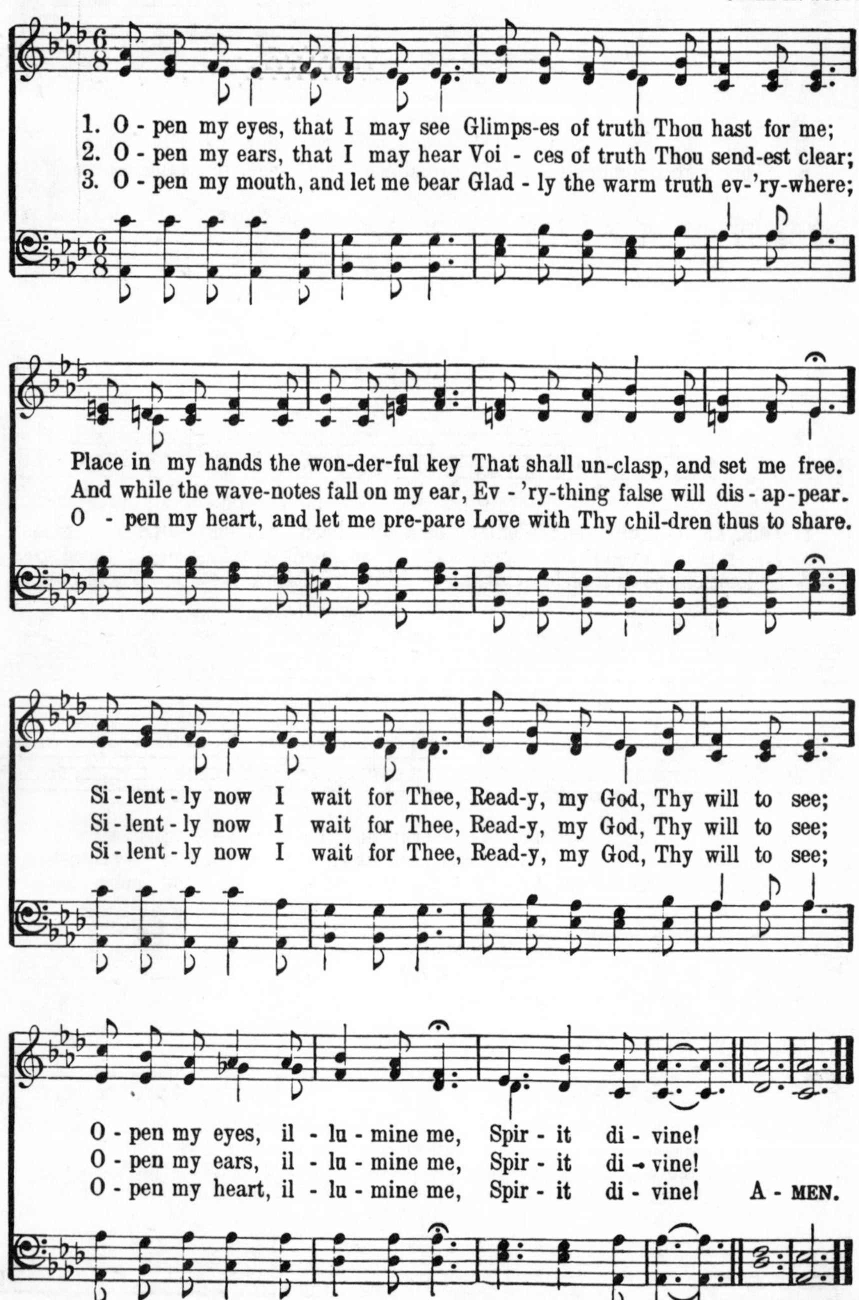
1. O - pen my eyes, that I may see Glimps-es of truth Thou hast for me;
2. O - pen my ears, that I may hear Voi - ces of truth Thou send-est clear;
3. O - pen my mouth, and let me bear Glad - ly the warm truth ev-'ry-where;
Place in my hands the won-der-ful key That shall un-clasp, and set me free.
And while the wave-notes fall on my ear, Ev - 'ry-thing false will dis - ap-pear.
O - pen my heart, and let me pre-pare Love with Thy chil-dren thus to share.
Si-lent-ly now I wait for Thee, Read-y, my God, Thy will to see;
Si-lent-ly now I wait for Thee, Read-y, my God, Thy will to see;
Si-lent-ly now I wait for Thee, Read-y, my God, Thy will to see;
O - pen my eyes, il - lu - mine me, Spir - it di - vine!
O - pen my ears, il - lu - mine me, Spir - it di - vine!
O - pen my heart, il - lu - mine me, Spir - it di - vine!
A - MEN.

There Shall Be Showers of Blessing

Daniel W. Whittle — James McGranahan

1. "There shall be show - ers of bless - ing:" This is the prom - ise of love;
2. "There shall be show - ers of bless - ing"—Pre - cious re - viv - ing a - gain;
3. "There shall be show - ers of bless - ing:" Send them up - on us, O Lord;
4. "There shall be show - ers of bless - ing:" Oh, that to - day they might fall,

There shall be sea - sons re - fresh - ing, Sent from the Sav - ior a - bove.
O - ver the hills and the val - leys, Sound of a - bun - dance of rain.
Grant to us now a re - fresh - ing, Come, and now hon - or Thy Word.
Now as to God we're con - fess - ing, Now as on Je - sus we call!

CHORUS

Show - - ers of bless - ing, Show - ers of bless - ing we need:
Show - ers, show - ers of bless - ing,

Mer - cy - drops round us are fall - ing, But for the show - ers we plead.

280 **More Like the Master**

CHARLES H. GABRIEL — CHARLES H. GABRIEL

1. More like the Mas-ter I would ev - er be, More of His meek-ness,
2. More like the Mas-ter is my dai - ly prayer; More strength to car-ry
3. More like the Mas-ter I would live and grow; More of His love to
more hu - mil - i - ty; More zeal to la - bor, more cour-age to be true,
cross-es I must bear; More ear-nest ef - fort to bring His kingdom in;
oth - ers I would show; More self-de - ni - al, like His in Gal - i - lee,
More con - se - cra - tion for work He bids me do. . . . . . Take Thou my
More of His Spir - it, the wan-der-er to win. . . . .
More like the Mas-ter I long to ev - er be. . . . . Take my heart, O
CHORUS.
rit.
heart, . . I would be Thine a-lone; . . Take Thou my heart . . and
take my heart, I would be Thine a-lone; Take my heart, O take my heart and
make it all Thine own; . . Purge me from sin, . . . O Lord, I now im-
make it all Thine own; Purge Thou me from ev'ry sin, O Lord, I

More Like the Master

plore, . . . Wash me and keep . . . me Thine for-ev - er - more.
now im-plore, Wash and keep, O wash and keep me Thine for-ev - er - more.
In the Hour of Trial
281
JAMES MONTGOMERY
SPENCER LANE
1. In the hour of tri - al, Je - sus, plead for me; Lest, by base de- ni - al, I de - part from Thee; When Thou see'st me wa - ver, With a look re - call; Nor for fear or fa - vor Suf - fer me to fall.
2. With for - bid- den pleas-ures Would this vain world charm; Or its sor - did treas-ures Spread to work me harm; Bring to my re-mem-brance Sad Geth- sem - a - ne, Or, in dark-er sem-blance, Cross-crowned Calvary.
3. Should Thy mer-cy send me Sor - row, toil, and woe; Or should pain at- tend me On my path be - low; Grant that I may nev - er Fail Thy hand to see; Grant that I may ev - er Cast my care on Thee.
4. When my last hour com - eth, Fraught with strife and pain, When my dust re- turn - eth To the dust a - gain; On Thy truth re - ly - ing Thro' that mor - tal strife; Lord, re-ceive me, dy - ing, To e - ter - nal life.
A-MEN.

282 More Love to Thee

ELIZABETH P. PRENTISS — WILLIAM H. DOANE

1. More love to Thee, O Christ, More love to Thee! Hear Thou the prayer I make On bend-ed knee; This is my ear-nest plea:
2. Once earth-ly joy I craved, Sought peace and rest; Now Thee a-lone I seek, Give what is best; This all my prayer shall be:
3. Let sor-row do its work, Send grief and pain; Sweet are Thy mes-sen-gers, Sweet their re-frain, When they can sing with me,
4. Then shall my lat-est breath Whis-per Thy praise; This be the part-ing cry My heart shall raise; This still its prayer shall be:

More love, O Christ, to Thee, More love to Thee, More love to Thee!

283 I'll Live for Him

RALPH E. HUDSON — C. R. DUNBAR

1. My life, my love, I give to Thee, Thou Lamb of God who died for me;
2. I now be-lieve Thou dost re-ceive, For Thou hast died that I might live;
3. O Thou who died on Cal-va-ry, To save my soul and make me free,

CHO. *I'll live for Him who died for me, How hap-py then my life shall be!*

I'll Live for Him
D. C. Chorus
Oh, may I ev - er faith - ful be, My Sav - ior and my God!
And now hence-forth I'll trust in Thee, My Sav - ior and my God!
I'll con - se - crate my life to Thee, My Sav - ior and my God!
I'll live for Him who died for me, My Sav - ior and my God!
Lord, I Hear of Showers of Blessing
284
Elizabeth Codner
William B. Bradbury
1. Lord, I hear of show'rs of bless - ing Thou art scat-t'ring full and free,
2. Pass me not, O ten - der Sav - ior! Let me love and cling to Thee;
3. Pass me not, O might - y Spir - it! Thou canst make the blind to see;
4. Love of God, so pure and changeless; Blood of Christ, so rich and free;
5. Pass me not! Thy lost one bring - ing, Bind my heart, O Lord, to Thee;
Show'rs the thirst - y land re - fresh - ing; Let some droppings fall on me—
I am long - ing for Thy fa - vor; Whilst Thou'rt calling, O call me.
Wit - ness - er of Je - sus' mer - it, Speak the word of pow'r to me.
Grace of God, so strong and bound - less; Mag - ni - fy them all in me.
While the streams of life are spring - ing, Bless - ing oth - ers, O bless me.
Chorus
E - ven me, e - ven me, Let Thy bless - ing fall on me.

285 Just When I Need Him Most

WILLIAM C. POOLE

CHARLES H. GABRIEL

1. Just when I need Him, Je - sus is near, Just when I fal - ter,
2. Just when I need Him, Je - sus is true, Nev - er for - sak - ing
3. Just when I need Him, Je - sus is strong, Bear - ing my bur - dens
4. Just when I need Him, He is my all, An - swer-ing when up-

just when I fear; Read - y to help me, read - y to cheer,
all the way thro'; Giv - ing for bur - dens pleas - ures a - new,
all the day long; For all my sor - row giv - ing a song,
on Him I call; Ten - der - ly watch - ing lest I should fall,

Just when I need Him most.

CHORUS.

Just when I need Him most,

Just when I need Him most; Je - sus is near to

com - fort and cheer, Just when I need Him most. A - MEN.

Anywhere with Jesus

286

Jessie B. Pounds — Daniel B. Towner

1. An - y-where with Je - sus I can safe - ly go; An - y-where He
2. An - y-where with Je - sus I am not a - lone; Oth - er friends may
3. An - y-where with Je - sus o - ver land and sea, Tell - ing souls in
4. An - y-where with Je - sus I can go to sleep, When the dark-'ning
leads me in this world be - low; An - y-where with-out Him dear-est
fail me, He is still my own; Tho' His hand may lead me o - ver
dark-ness of sal - va - tion free; Read - y as He sum-mons me to
shad-ows round a - bout me creep; Know-ing I shall wak - en nev - er
joys would fade; An - y-where with Je - sus I am not a - fraid.
drear - y ways, An - y-where with Je - sus is a house of praise.
go or stay, An - y-where with Je - sus when He points the way.
more to roam, An - y-where with Je - sus will be home, sweet home.
Chorus
An - y-where! an - y - where! Fear I can - not know;
An - y - where with Je - sus I can safe - ly go.

287 We Have an Anchor

PRISCILLA J. OWENS

WILLIAM J. KIRKPATRICK

1. Will your an-chor hold in the storms of life, When the clouds un-fold
2. It is safe-ly moored, 'twill the storm withstand, For 'tis well se-cured
3. It will firm-ly hold in the straits of fear, When the breakers have told
4. When our eyes be-hold thro' the gath-'ring night The cit-y of gold,

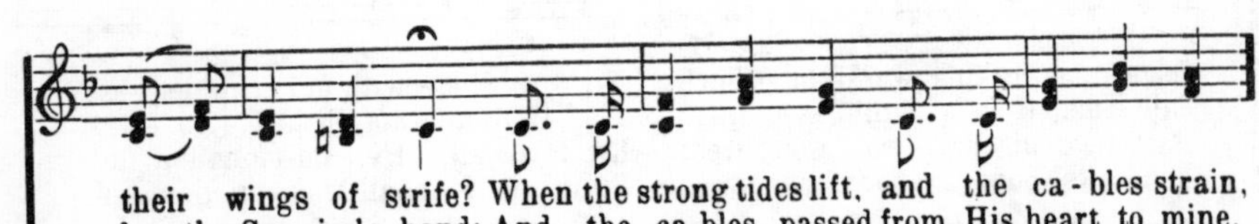

their wings of strife? When the strong tides lift, and the ca-bles strain,
by the Sav-ior's hand; And the ca-bles, passed from His heart to mine,
the reef is near; Tho' the tem-pest rave and the wild winds blow,
our har-bor bright, We shall an-chor fast by the heav'n-ly shore,

REFRAIN

Will your an-chor drift, or firm re-main?
Can de-fy that blast, thro' strength di-vine.
Not an an-gry wave shall our bark o'er-flow.
With the storms all past for-ev-er-more.

We have an an-chor that

keeps the soul Stead-fast and sure while the bil-lows roll, Fas-tened to the

We Have an Anchor

Rock which can - not move, Grounded firm and deep in the Sav - ior's love.

When I See My Savior

288

MAUD FRAZER

ROBERT HARKNESS

1. When I see my Sav - iour, hang - ing on Cal - va - ry,
2. I can see the blood - drops, red 'neath His thorn - y crown,
3. "Why hast thou for - sak - en?" list to that sad, sad moan!
Bear - ing there for sin - ners bit - ter - est ag - o - ny,
From the cru - el nail - wounds now they are fall - ing down;
Oh, His heart was bro - ken, suf - fer - ing there a - lone:
Grat - i - tude o'er-whelms me, makes mine eyes grow dim,
Lord, when I would wan - der from Thy love a - way,
Bro - ken then that mor - tals ne'er need cry in vain
All my ran - somed be - ing cap - tive is to Him.
Let me see those blood - drops shed for me that day.
For God's love and com - fort, in the hour of pain.

289 Blessed Assurance

FANNY J. CROSBY PHOEBE P. KNAPP

1. Bless-ed as - sur - ance, Je - sus is mine! Oh, what a fore - taste of
2. Per - fect sub-mis - sion, per-fect de - light, Vi-sions of rap - ture now
3. Per - fect sub-mis - sion, all is at rest, I in my Sav - ior am
glo - ry di - vine! Heir of sal - va - tion, pur-chase of God,
burst on my sight; An - gels de - scend - ing, bring from a - bove
hap - py and blest; Watching and wait - ing, look - ing a - bove,
Born of His Spir - it, washed in His blood.
Ech - oes of mer - cy, whis-pers of love.
Filled with His goodness, lost in His love.
CHORUS
This is my sto - ry, this is my
song, Prais-ing my Sav - ior all the day long; This is my sto - ry,
this is my song, Prais - ing my Sav - ior all the day long.

Each Step I Take

W. Elmo Mercer — W. Elmo Mercer

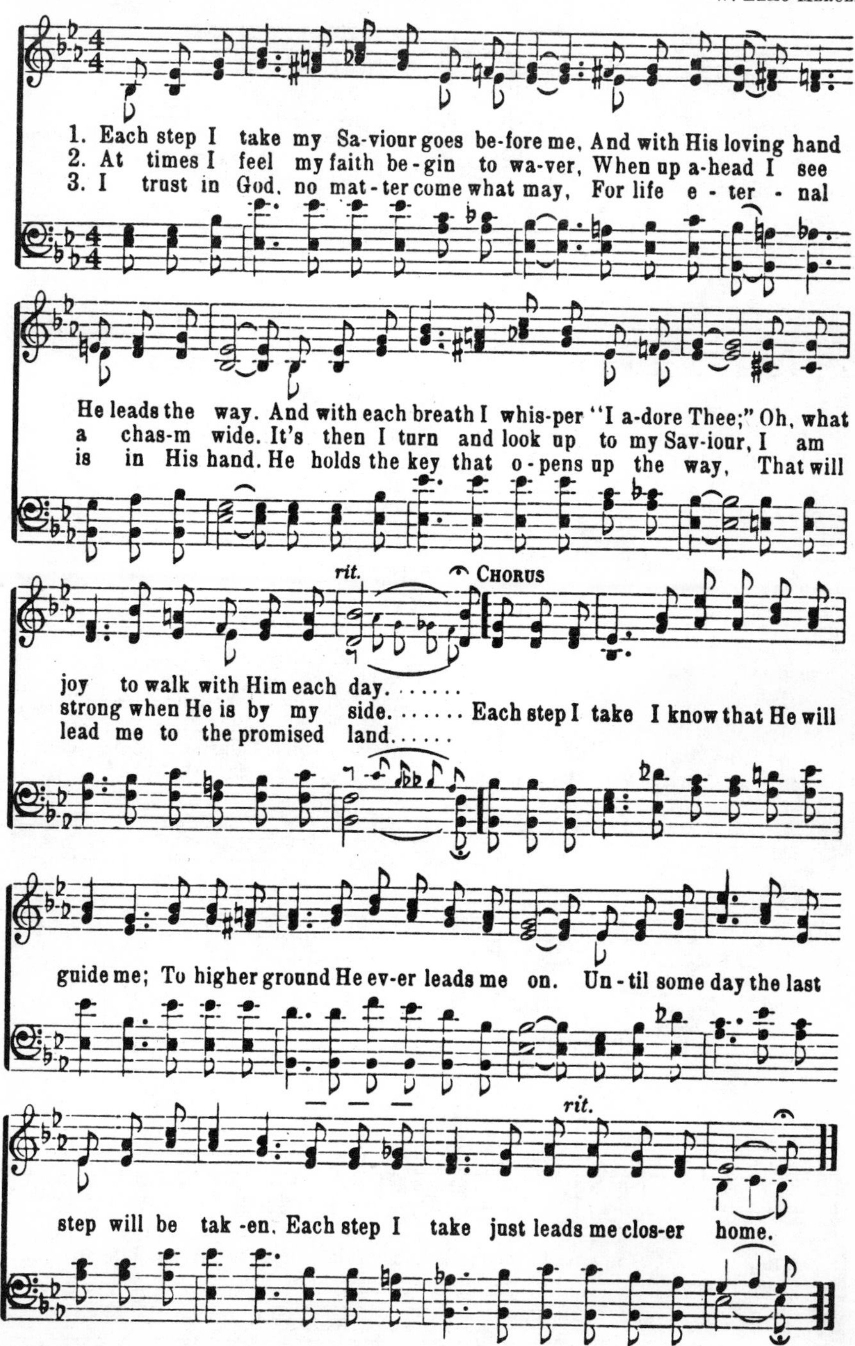
1. Each step I take my Sa-viour goes be-fore me, And with His loving hand
2. At times I feel my faith be-gin to wa-ver, When up a-head I see
3. I trust in God, no mat-ter come what may, For life e-ter-nal
He leads the way. And with each breath I whis-per "I a-dore Thee;" Oh, what
a chas-m wide. It's then I turn and look up to my Sav-iour, I am
is in His hand. He holds the key that o-pens up the way, That will
joy to walk with Him each day......
strong when He is by my side......
lead me to the promised land......
rit.
CHORUS
Each step I take I know that He will guide me; To higher ground He ev-er leads me on. Un-til some day the last step will be tak-en. Each step I take just leads me clos-er home.
rit.

291 My Anchor Holds

W. C. MARTIN, ALT. DANIEL B. TOWNER

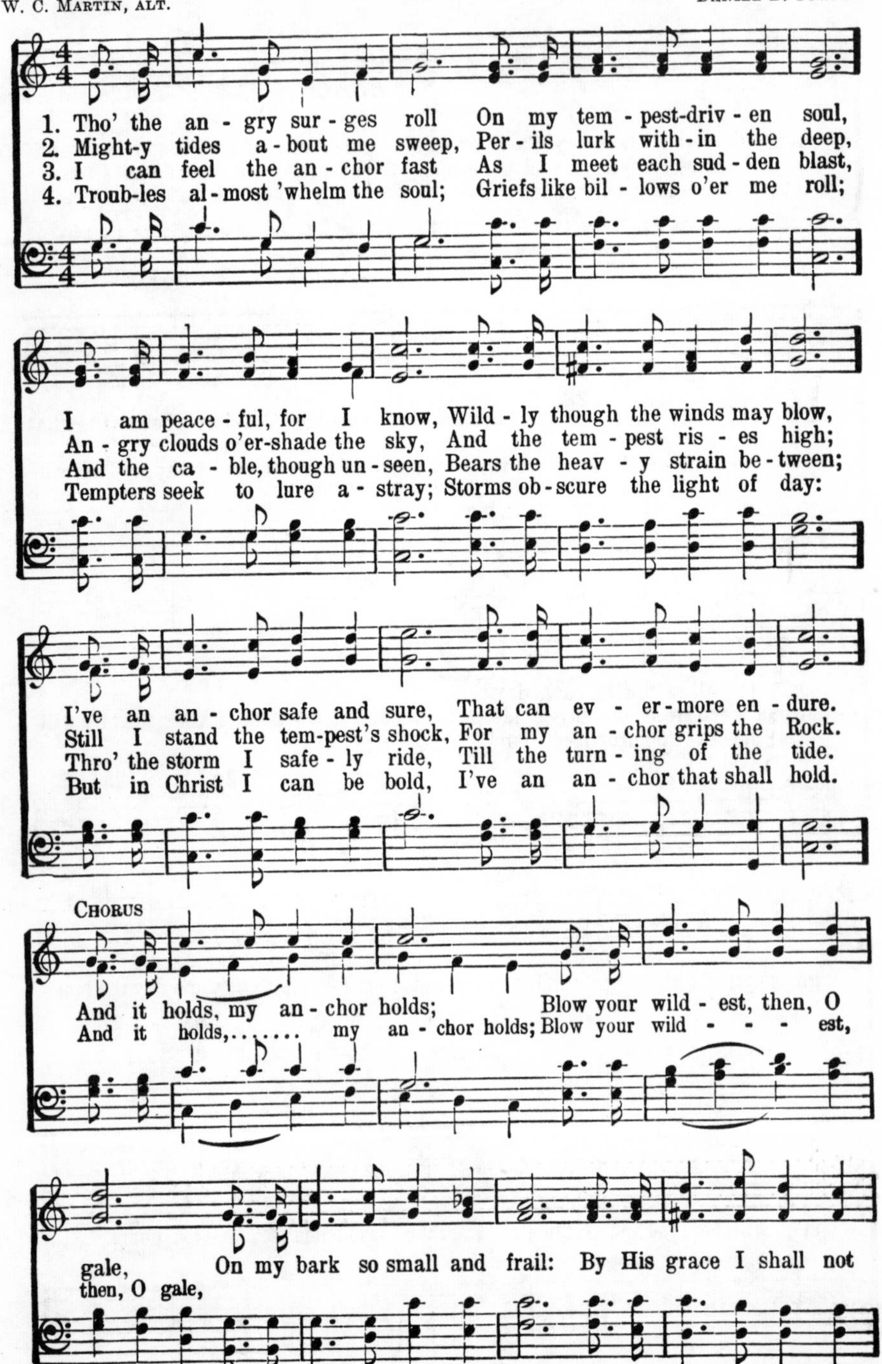
1. Tho' the an - gry sur - ges roll On my tem - pest-driv - en soul,
2. Might-y tides a - bout me sweep, Per - ils lurk with - in the deep,
3. I can feel the an - chor fast As I meet each sud - den blast,
4. Troub-les al - most 'whelm the soul; Griefs like bil - lows o'er me roll;
I am peace - ful, for I know, Wild - ly though the winds may blow,
An - gry clouds o'er-shade the sky, And the tem - pest ris - es high;
And the ca - ble, though un - seen, Bears the heav - y strain be - tween;
Tempters seek to lure a - stray; Storms ob - scure the light of day:
I've an an - chor safe and sure, That can ev - er - more en - dure.
Still I stand the tem-pest's shock, For my an - chor grips the Rock.
Thro' the storm I safe - ly ride, Till the turn - ing of the tide.
But in Christ I can be bold, I've an an - chor that shall hold.
CHORUS
And it holds, my an - chor holds; Blow your wild - est, then, O
And it holds,....... my an - chor holds; Blow your wild - - - est,
gale, On my bark so small and frail: By His grace I shall not
then, O gale,

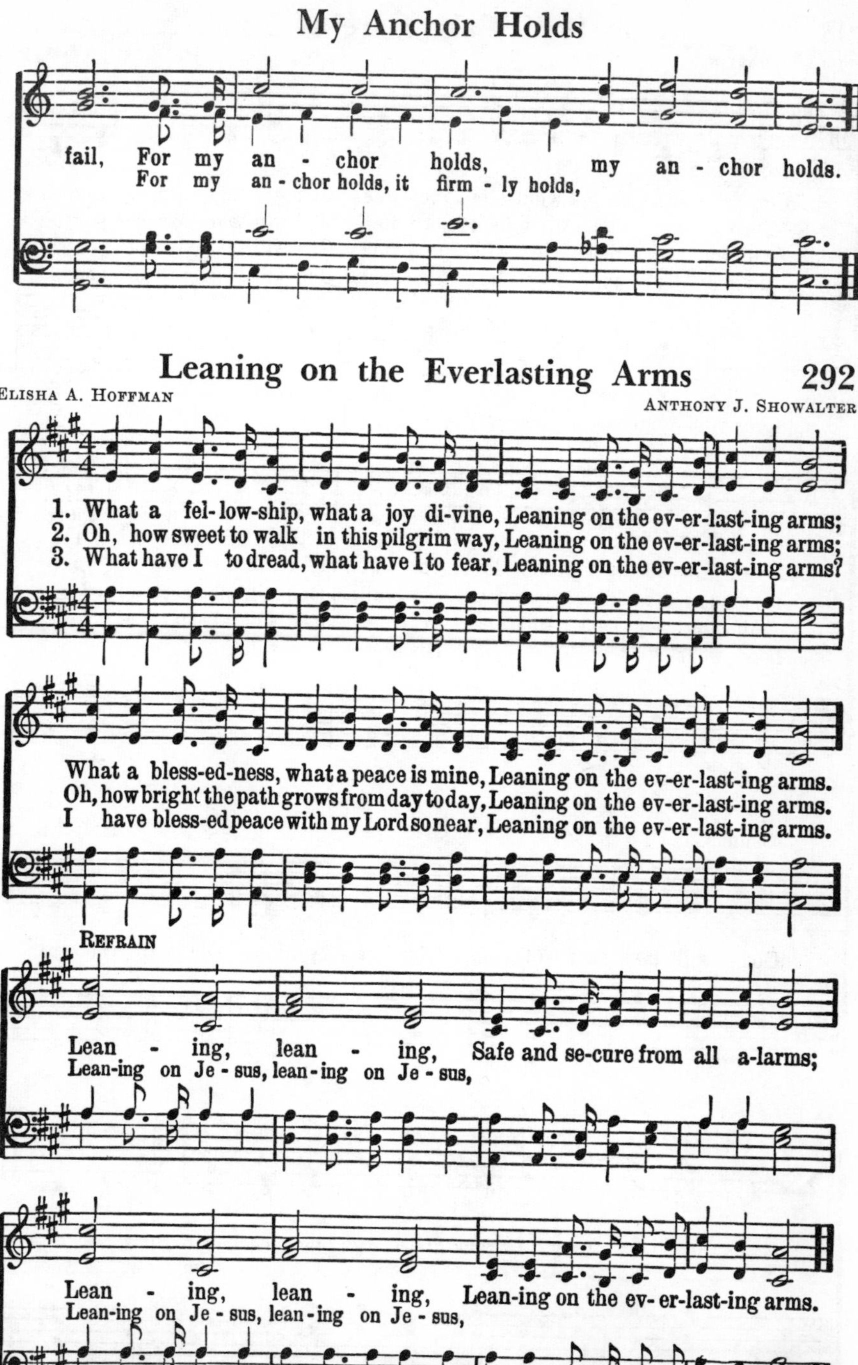
My Anchor Holds
fail, For my an - chor holds, my an - chor holds.
For my an - chor holds, it firm - ly holds,
Leaning on the Everlasting Arms
292
Elisha A. Hoffman
Anthony J. Showalter
1. What a fel-low-ship, what a joy di-vine, Leaning on the ev-er-last-ing arms;
2. Oh, how sweet to walk in this pilgrim way, Leaning on the ev-er-last-ing arms;
3. What have I to dread, what have I to fear, Leaning on the ev-er-last-ing arms?
What a bless-ed-ness, what a peace is mine, Leaning on the ev-er-last-ing arms.
Oh, how bright the path grows from day to day, Leaning on the ev-er-last-ing arms.
I have bless-ed peace with my Lord so near, Leaning on the ev-er-last-ing arms.
Refrain
Lean - ing, lean - ing, Safe and se-cure from all a-larms;
Lean-ing on Je - sus, lean-ing on Je - sus,
Lean - ing, lean - ing, Lean-ing on the ev- er-last-ing arms.
Lean-ing on Je - sus, lean-ing on Je - sus,

293 God Will Take Care of You

CIVILLA D. MARTIN — W. STILLMAN MARTIN

1. Be not dis - mayed what-e'er be - tide, God will take care of you;
Be - neath His wings of love a - bide, God will take care of you.

2. Thro' days of toil when heart doth fail, God will take care of you;
When dan-gers fierce your path as - sail, God will take care of you.

3. All you may need He will pro - vide, God will take care of you;
Noth - ing you ask will be de - nied, God will take care of you.

4. No mat - ter what may be the test, God will take care of you;
Lean, wear - y one, up - on His breast, God will take care of you.

CHORUS

God will take care of you, Thro' ev - 'ry day, O'er all the way;
He will take care of you, God will take care of you. . .
take care of you,

The Rock That Is Higher Than I 294

ERASTUS JOHNSON | WILLIAM G. FISCHER

1. O some-times the shadows are deep, And rough seems the path to the goal,
2. O sometimes how long seems the day, And sometimes how wea-ry my feet;
3. O near to the Rock let me keep, If bless-ings or sor-rows pre-vail;
And sorrows, sometimes how they sweep Like tempests down o - ver the soul!
But toil - ing in life's dust-y way, The Rock's blessed shadow, how sweet!
Or climb-ing the mountain way steep, Or walk - ing the shad-ow - y vale.
REFRAIN
O then to the Rock let me fly, To the
let me fly,
Rock that is high - er than I; O then to the
is high - er than I;
Rock let me fly, To the Rock that is high - er than I!
let me fly,

295 Jesus, I Come

WILLIAM T. SLEEPER GEORGE C. STEBBINS

1. Out of my bond-age, sor-row and night, Je-sus, I come, Je-sus, I come;
2. Out of my shame-ful fail-ure and loss, Je-sus, I come, Je-sus, I come;
3. Out of un - rest and ar - ro-gant pride, Je-sus, I come, Je-sus, I come;
4. Out of the fear and dread of the tomb, Je-sus, I come, Je-sus, I come;
In - to Thy free-dom, glad-ness and light, Je - sus, I come to Thee;
In - to the glo - rious gain of Thy cross, Je - sus, I come to Thee;
In - to Thy bless - ed will to a - bide, Je - sus, I come to Thee;
In - to the joy and light of Thy home, Je - sus, I come to Thee;
Out of my sick-ness in - to Thy health, Out of my want and in - to Thy wealth,
Out of earth's sorrows in-to Thy balm, Out of life's storms and in - to Thy calm,
Out of my - self to dwell in Thy love, Out of de-spair in-to rap-tures a-bove,
Out of the depths of ru - in un - told, In - to the peace of Thy sheltering fold,
Out of my sin and in - to Thy-self, Je - sus, I come to Thee.
Out of dis-tress to ju - bi - lant psalm, Je - sus, I come to Thee.
Up-ward for aye on wings like a dove, Je - sus, I come to Thee.
Ev - er Thy glo - rious face to be-hold, Je - sus, I come to Thee.

He Keeps Me Singing

296

Luther B. Bridgers — Luther B. Bridgers

1. There's within my heart a mel - o - dy Je - sus whis-pers sweet and low,
2. All my life was wrecked by sin and strife, Dis-cord filled my heart with pain,
3. Feast - ing on the rich - es of His grace, Resting 'neath His shelt'ring wing,
4. Tho' sometimes He leads thro' waters deep, Tri - als fall a - cross the way,
5. Soon He's com-ing back to wel-come me Far be - yond the star - ry sky;

Fear not, I am with thee, peace, be still, In all of life's ebb and flow.
Je - sus swept across the broken strings, Stirred the slumb'ring chords again.
Al - ways look-ing on His smil - ing face, That is why I shout and sing.
Tho' sometimes the path seems rough and steep, See His footprints all the way.
I shall wing my flight to worlds un-known, I shall reign with Him on high.

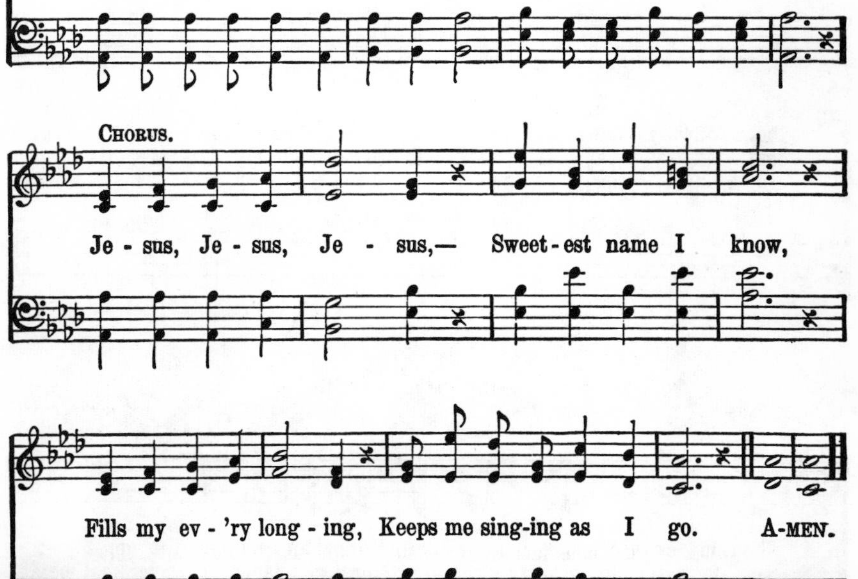
CHORUS.
Je - sus, Je - sus, Je - sus,— Sweet - est name I know,
Fills my ev - 'ry long - ing, Keeps me sing-ing as I go. A-MEN.

297 My Jesus, I Love Thee

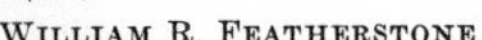
WILLIAM R. FEATHERSTONE — ADONIRAM J. GORDON

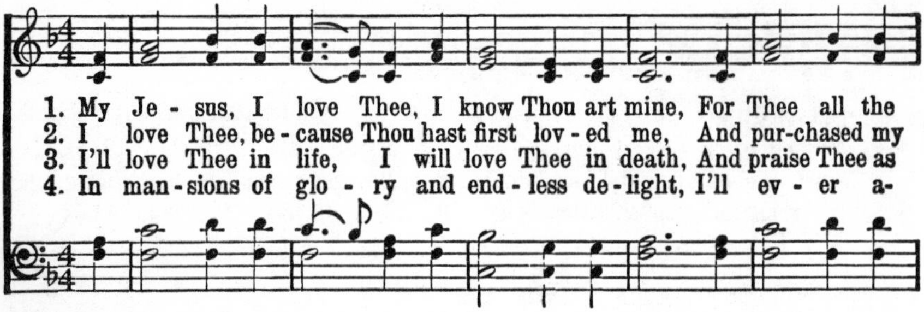

1. My Je - sus, I love Thee, I know Thou art mine, For Thee all the
2. I love Thee, be - cause Thou hast first lov - ed me, And pur-chased my
3. I'll love Thee in life, I will love Thee in death, And praise Thee as
4. In man - sions of glo - ry and end - less de - light, I'll ev - er a-

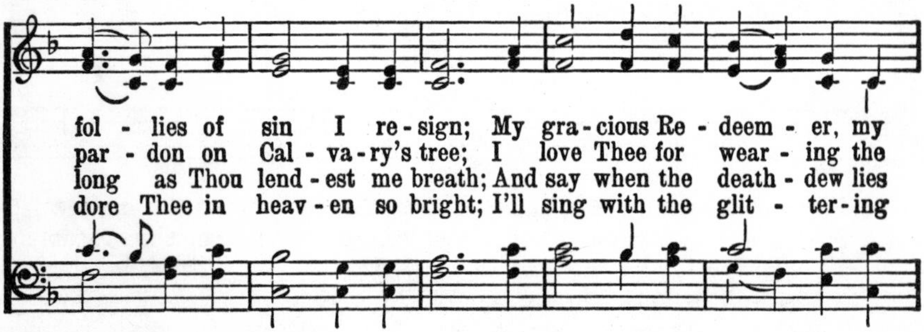

fol - lies of sin I re - sign; My gra - cious Re - deem - er, my
par - don on Cal - va - ry's tree; I love Thee for wear - ing the
long as Thou lend - est me breath; And say when the death - dew lies
dore Thee in heav - en so bright; I'll sing with the glit - ter - ing

Sav - ior art Thou; If ev - er I loved Thee, my Je - sus, 'tis now.
thorns on Thy brow: If ev - er I loved Thee, my Je - sus, 'tis now.
cold on my brow, If ev - er I loved Thee, my Je - sus, 'tis now.
crown on my brow, If ev - er I loved Thee, my Je - sus, 'tis now.

298 Close to Thee

FANNY J. CROSBY — SILAS J. VAIL

1. Thou, my ev - er - last - ing por - tion, More than friend or life to me;
2. Not for ease or world - ly pleas-ure, Nor for fame my prayer shall be;
3. Lead me thro' the vale of shad-ows, Bear me o'er life's fit - ful sea;

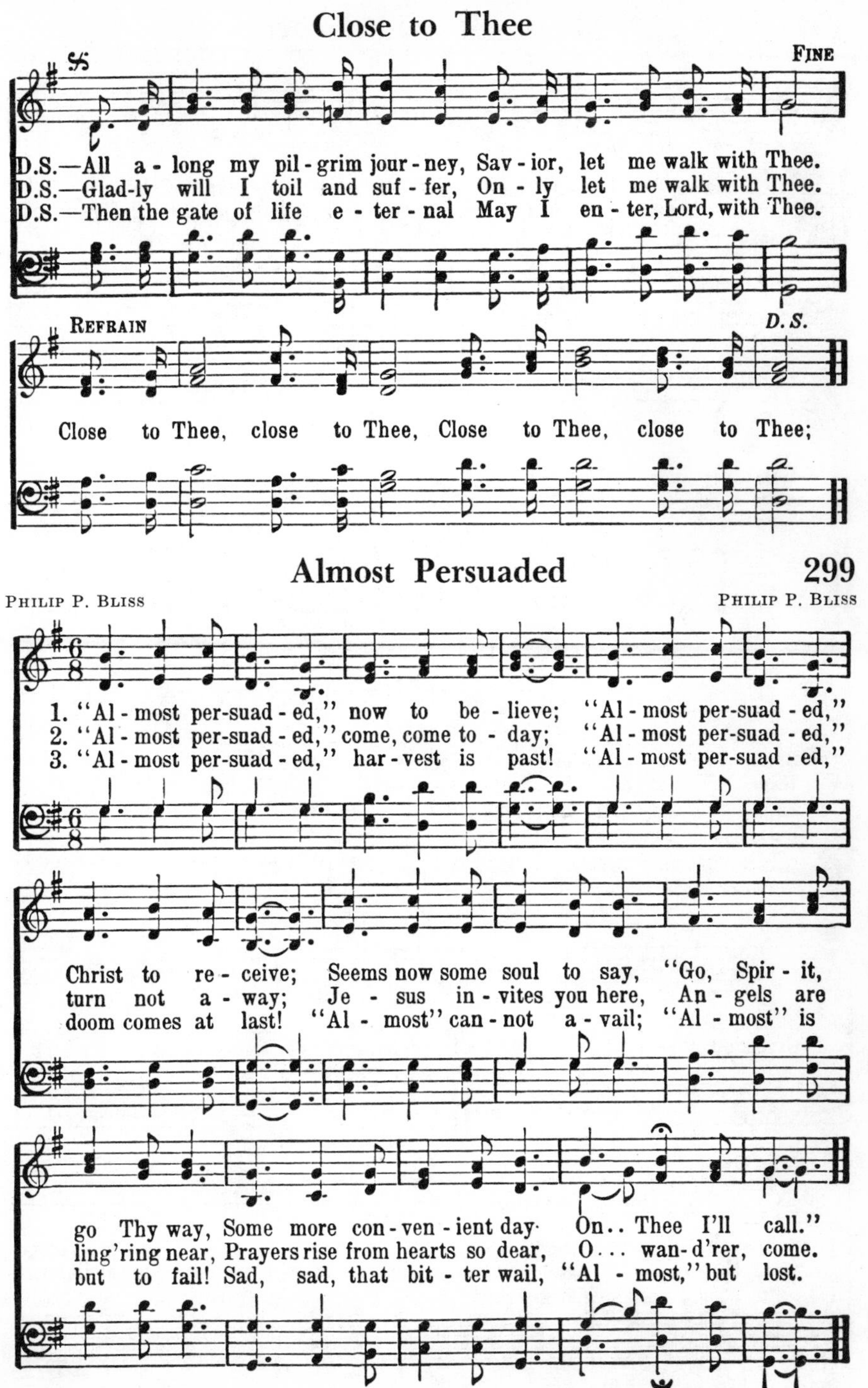
Close to Thee
FINE
D.S.—All a - long my pil - grim jour - ney, Sav - ior, let me walk with Thee.
D.S.—Glad-ly will I toil and suf - fer, On - ly let me walk with Thee.
D.S.—Then the gate of life e - ter - nal May I en - ter, Lord, with Thee.
REFRAIN
D.S.
Close to Thee, close to Thee, Close to Thee, close to Thee;
Almost Persuaded
299
PHILIP P. BLISS
PHILIP P. BLISS
1. "Al - most per-suad - ed," now to be - lieve; "Al - most per-suad - ed,"
2. "Al - most per-suad - ed," come, come to - day; "Al - most per-suad - ed,"
3. "Al - most per-suad - ed," har - vest is past! "Al - most per-suad - ed,"
Christ to re - ceive; Seems now some soul to say, "Go, Spir - it,
turn not a - way; Je - sus in - vites you here, An - gels are
doom comes at last! "Al - most" can - not a - vail; "Al - most" is
go Thy way, Some more con - ven - ient day On.. Thee I'll call."
ling'ring near, Prayers rise from hearts so dear, O... wan - d'rer, come.
but to fail! Sad, sad, that bit - ter wail, "Al - most," but lost.

300 Give Me Thy Heart

Eliza E. Hewitt | William J. Kirkpatrick

1. "Give me thy heart," says the Fa - ther a - bove, No gift so pre-cious to
2. "Give me thy heart," says the Sav - ior of men, Call-ing in mer - cy a-
3. "Give me thy heart," says the Spir - it di - vine, "All that thou hast, to my
Him as our love, Soft - ly He whis-pers wher - ev - er thou art,
gain and a - gain; "Turn now from sin, and from e - vil de - part,
keep - ing re - sign; Grace more a - bound-ing is mine to im - part,
"Grate - ful - ly trust me, and give me thy heart."
Have I not died for thee? give me thy heart."
Make full sur - ren - der and give me thy heart."
Chorus
"Give me thy heart,
p
Give me thy heart," Hear the soft whisper, wher-ev - er thou art; From this dark
rit.
world He would draw thee a-part, Speak-ing so ten-der-ly, "Give me thy heart."

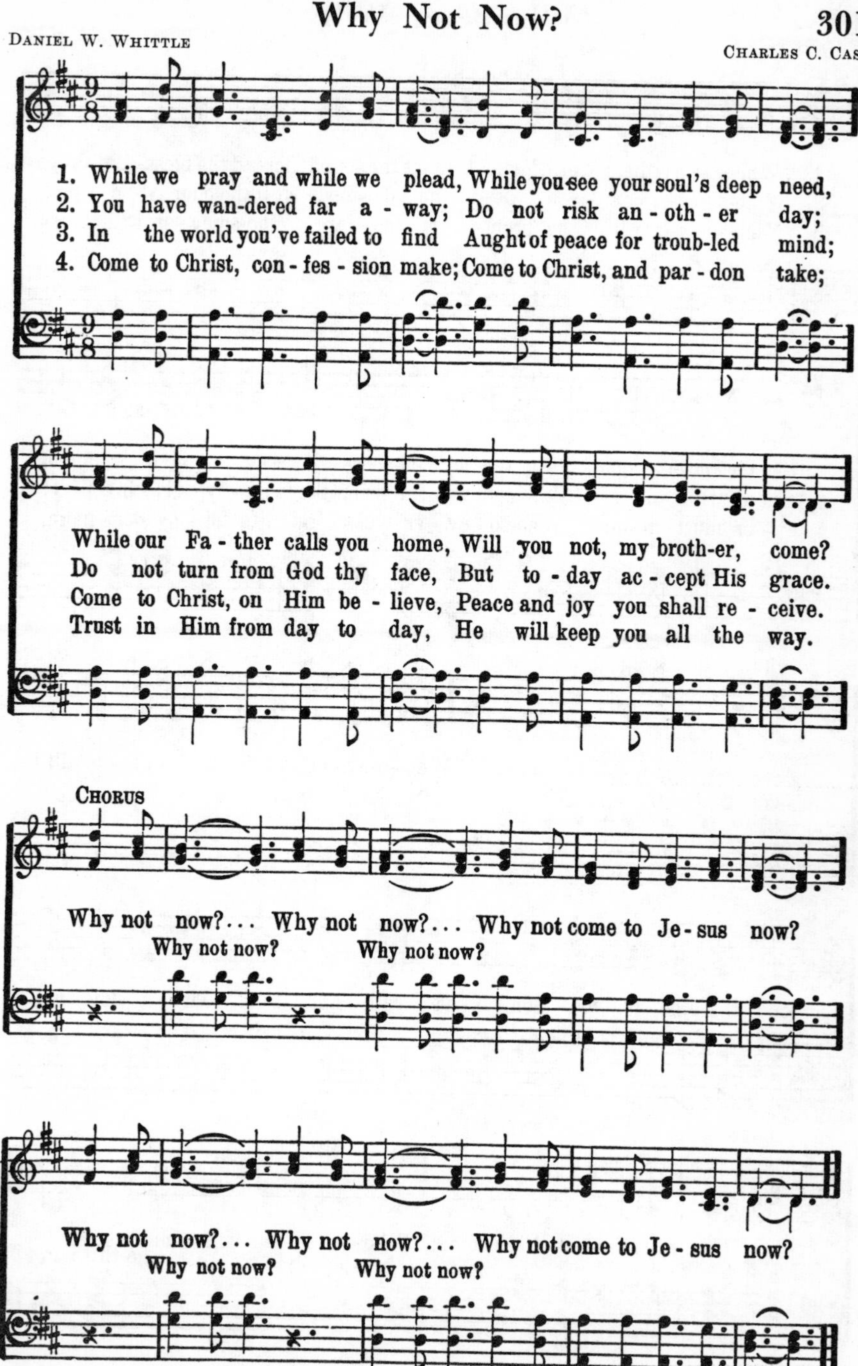
Why Not Now?
301
Daniel W. Whittle
Charles C. Case
1. While we pray and while we plead, While you see your soul's deep need,
2. You have wan-dered far a - way; Do not risk an - oth - er day;
3. In the world you've failed to find Aught of peace for troub-led mind;
4. Come to Christ, con - fes - sion make; Come to Christ, and par - don take;
While our Fa - ther calls you home, Will you not, my broth-er, come?
Do not turn from God thy face, But to - day ac - cept His grace.
Come to Christ, on Him be - lieve, Peace and joy you shall re - ceive.
Trust in Him from day to day, He will keep you all the way.
Chorus
Why not now?... Why not now?... Why not come to Je - sus now?
Why not now? Why not now?
Why not now?... Why not now?... Why not come to Je - sus now?
Why not now? Why not now?

302 "Whosoever Will"

Philip P. Bliss — Philip P. Bliss

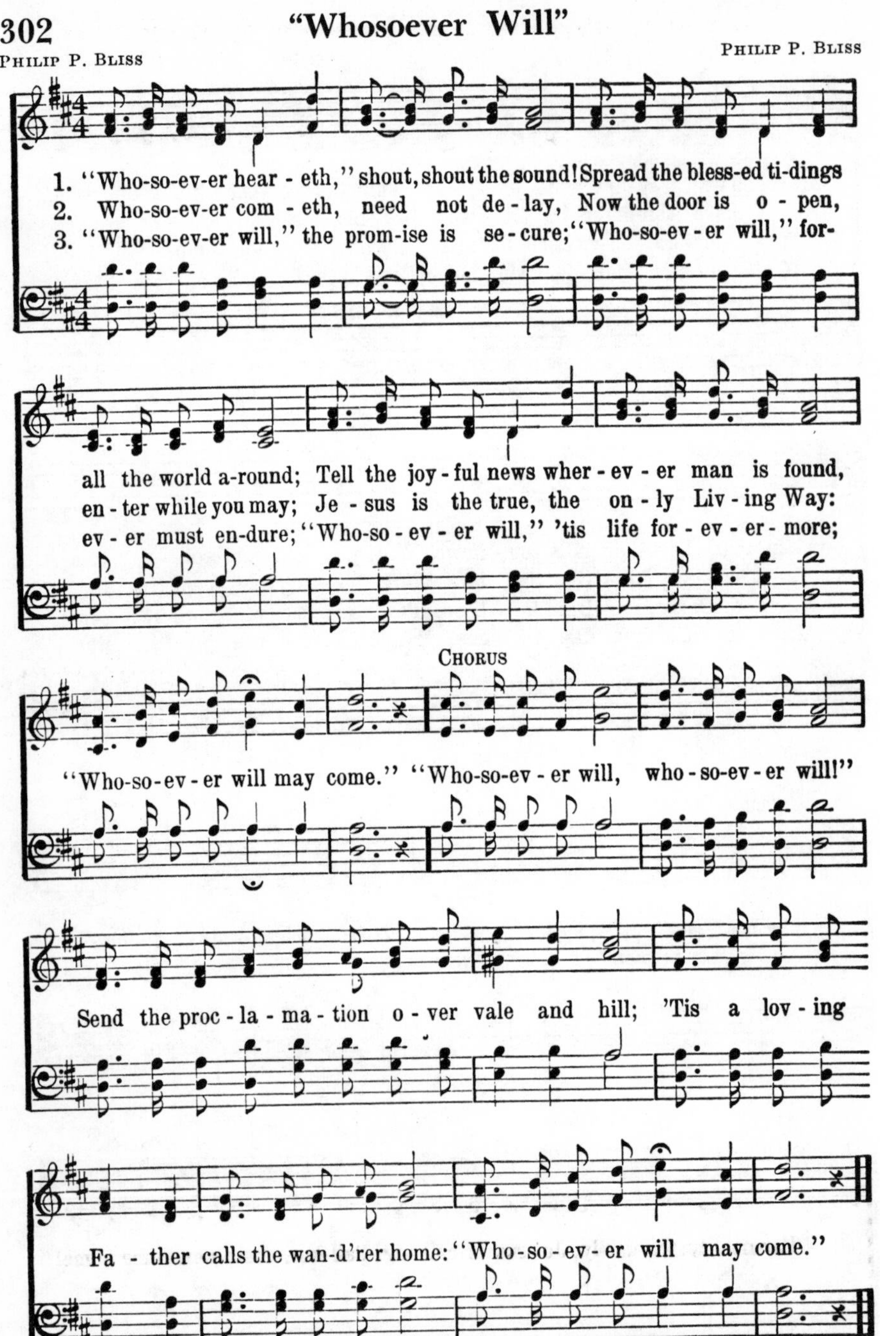
1. "Who-so-ev-er hear - eth," shout, shout the sound! Spread the bless-ed ti-dings
2. Who-so-ev-er com - eth, need not de - lay, Now the door is o - pen,
3. "Who-so-ev-er will," the prom-ise is se - cure; "Who-so-ev - er will," for-
all the world a-round; Tell the joy - ful news wher - ev - er man is found,
en - ter while you may; Je - sus is the true, the on - ly Liv - ing Way:
ev - er must en-dure; "Who-so - ev - er will," 'tis life for - ev - er - more;
Chorus
"Who-so-ev - er will may come." "Who-so-ev - er will, who - so-ev - er will!"
Send the proc - la - ma - tion o - ver vale and hill; 'Tis a lov - ing
Fa - ther calls the wan-d'rer home: "Who - so - ev - er will may come."

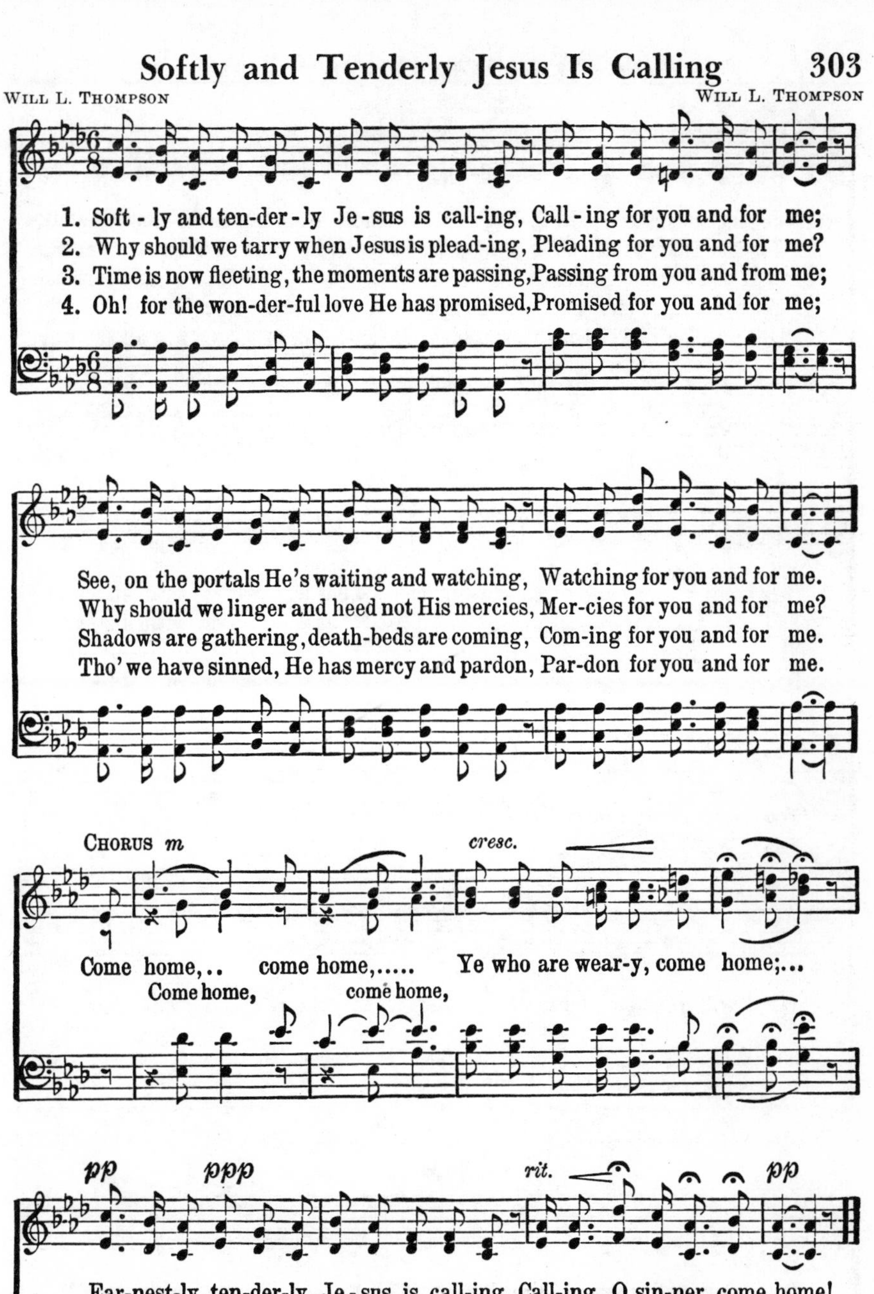
Softly and Tenderly Jesus Is Calling
303
Will L. Thompson
Will L. Thompson
1. Soft - ly and ten-der - ly Je - sus is call-ing, Call - ing for you and for me;
2. Why should we tarry when Jesus is plead-ing, Pleading for you and for me?
3. Time is now fleeting, the moments are passing, Passing from you and from me;
4. Oh! for the won-der-ful love He has promised, Promised for you and for me;
See, on the portals He's waiting and watching, Watching for you and for me.
Why should we linger and heed not His mercies, Mer-cies for you and for me?
Shadows are gathering, death-beds are coming, Com-ing for you and for me.
Tho' we have sinned, He has mercy and pardon, Par-don for you and for me.
Chorus
m
cresc.
Come home,.. come home,..... Ye who are wear-y, come home;...
Come home, come home,
pp
ppp
rit.
pp
Ear-nest-ly, ten-der-ly, Je - sus is call-ing, Call-ing, O sin-ner, come home!

304 What Will You Do with Jesus?

AUTHOR UNKNOWN

M. L. STOCKS

1. Je - sus is stand-ing in Pi-late's hall–Friendless, for-sak-en, be-trayed by all:
2. Je - sus is stand-ing on tri - al still, You can be false to Him if you will,
3. Will you e-vade Him as Pi-late tried? Or will you choose Him, what-e'er be-tide?
4. Will you, like Peter, your Lord de-ny? Or will you scorn from His foes to fly,
5. "Je - sus, I give Thee my heart to-day! Je-sus, I'll fol-low Thee all the way,

Heark-en! what mean-eth the sud-den call! What will you do with Je - sus?
You can be faith-ful thro' good or ill: What will you do with Je - sus?
Vain-ly you strug-gle from Him to hide: What will you do with Je - sus?
Dar-ing for Je - sus to live or die? What will you do with Je - sus?
Glad-ly o - bey-ing Thee!" will you say: "This will I do with Je - sus!"

CHORUS

What will you do with Je - sus? Neu-tral you can-not be;

Some day your heart will be ask - ing, "What will He do with me?"

Come to the Feast

Charles H. Gabriel

William A. Ogden

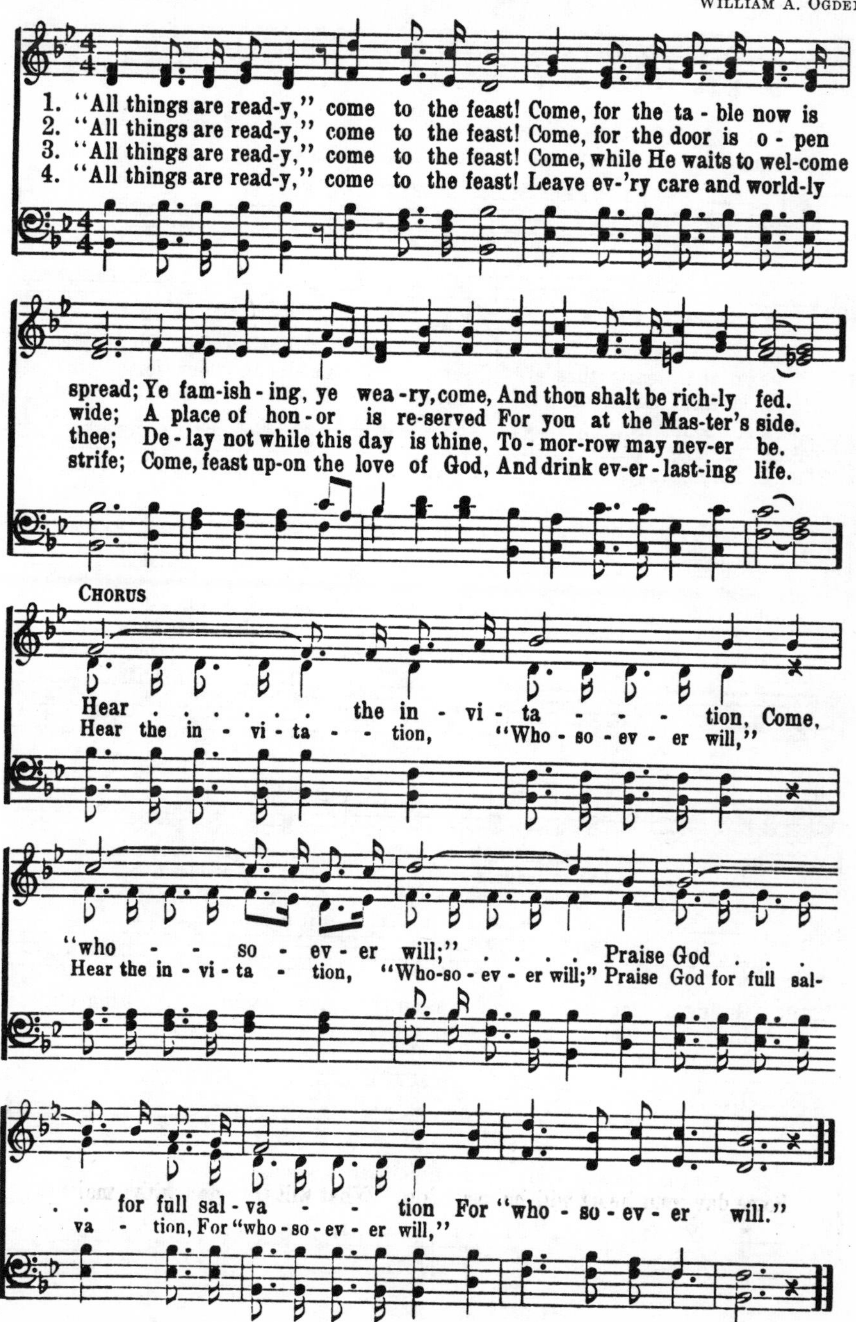
1. "All things are read-y," come to the feast! Come, for the ta - ble now is
2. "All things are read-y," come to the feast! Come, for the door is o - pen
3. "All things are read-y," come to the feast! Come, while He waits to wel-come
4. "All things are read-y," come to the feast! Leave ev-'ry care and world-ly
spread; Ye fam-ish - ing, ye wea - ry, come, And thou shalt be rich-ly fed.
wide; A place of hon - or is re-served For you at the Mas-ter's side.
thee; De - lay not while this day is thine, To - mor-row may nev-er be.
strife; Come, feast up-on the love of God, And drink ev-er - last-ing life.
Chorus
Hear . . . . the in - vi - ta - - - tion, Come,
Hear the in - vi - ta - - tion, "Who - so - ev - er will,"
"who - - so - ev - er will;" . . . . Praise God . . .
Hear the in - vi - ta - tion, "Who-so - ev - er will;" Praise God for full sal-
. . for full sal - va - - tion For "who - so - ev - er will."
va - tion, For "who - so - ev - er will,"

306 Seeking the Lost

William A. Ogden William A. Ogden

1. Seek-ing the lost, yes, kind-ly en-treat-ing Wan-der-ers on the moun-tain a-stray; "Come un-to Me," His mes-sage re-peat-ing, Words of the Mas-ter speak-ing to-day.
2. Seek-ing the lost and point-ing to Je-sus Souls that are weak and hearts that are sore, Lead-ing them forth in ways of sal-va-tion, Show-ing the path to life ev-er-more.
3. Thus I would go on mis-sions of mer-cy, Fol-low-ing Christ from day un-to day, Cheer-ing the faint and rais-ing the fall-en, Point-ing the lost to Je-sus, the Way.
Chorus
Go-ing a-far up-on the moun-tain,
In-to the fold of my Re-deem-er,
Go-ing a-far . . . . up-on the moun-tain, . . . Bring-ing the
In-to the fold . . . . of my Re-deem-er, . . . Je-sus, the
Bring-ing the wan-d'rer back a-gain, back a-gain,
Je-sus, the Lamb for sin-ners (Omit . . . . .) slain, for sin-ners slain,
wan - - - d'rer back a-gain . . .
Lamb . . . . for sin-ners (Omit . . .) slain. . . . .

Come to the Savior

GEORGE F. ROOT

GEORGE F. ROOT

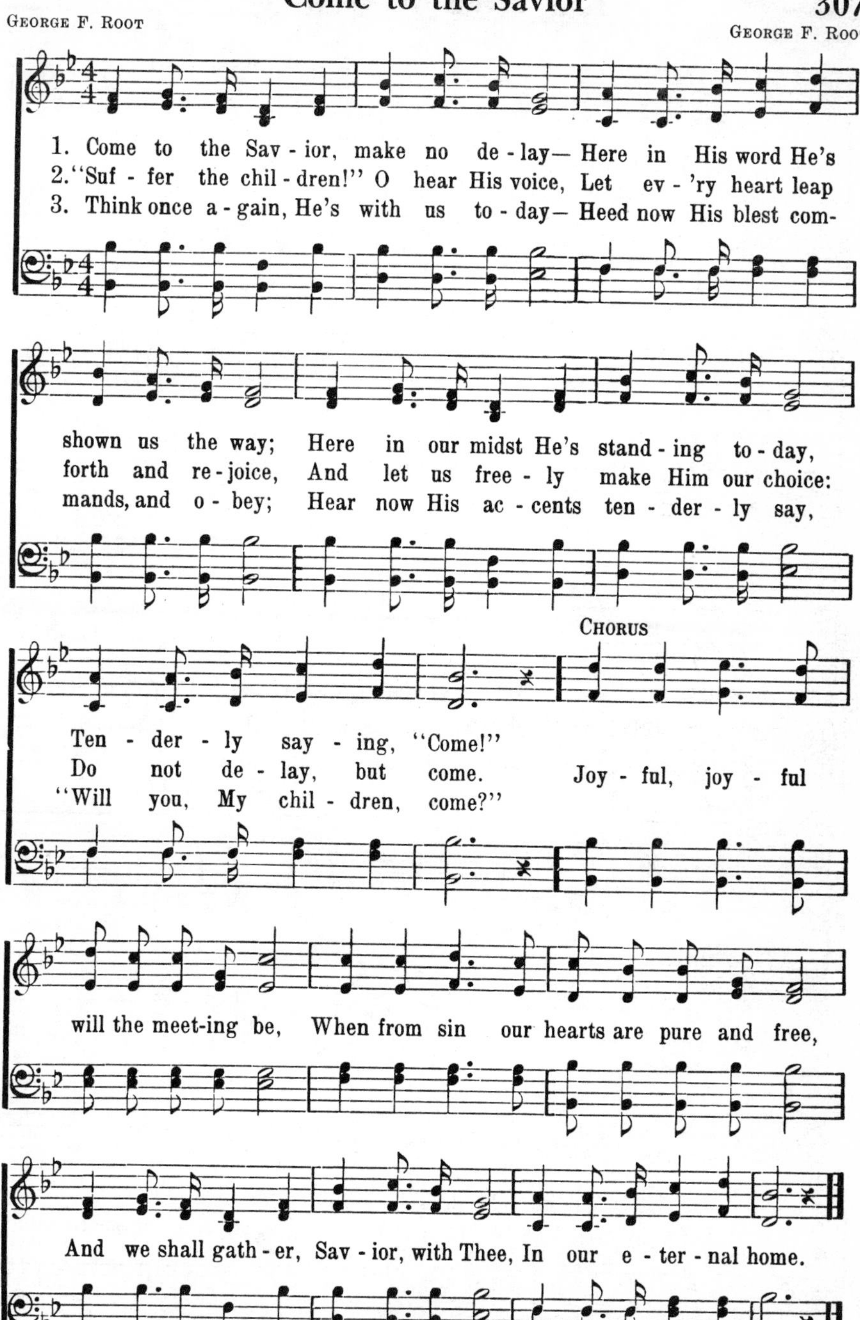
1. Come to the Sav - ior, make no de - lay— Here in His word He's
2. "Suf - fer the chil - dren!" O hear His voice, Let ev - 'ry heart leap
3. Think once a - gain, He's with us to - day— Heed now His blest com-
shown us the way; Here in our midst He's stand - ing to - day,
forth and re - joice, And let us free - ly make Him our choice:
mands, and o - bey; Hear now His ac - cents ten - der - ly say,
Ten - der - ly say - ing, "Come!"
Do not de - lay, but come.
"Will you, My chil - dren, come?"
CHORUS
Joy - ful, joy - ful
will the meet-ing be, When from sin our hearts are pure and free,
And we shall gath - er, Sav - ior, with Thee, In our e - ter - nal home.

308

The Savior Is Waiting

RALPH CARMICHAEL | RALPH CARMICHAEL

1. The Saviour is waiting to enter your heart, Why don't you let Him come in? There's nothing in this world to keep you apart, What is your answer to Him?

2. If you'll take one step t'ward the Saviour, my friend, You'll find His arms open wide; Receive Him, and all of your darkness will end, Within your heart He'll abide.

CHORUS

Time after time He has waited before, And now He is waiting again To see if you're willing to open the door, Oh, how He wants to come in.

Don't Turn the Savior Away 309

HARRY D. CLARKE

HARRY D. CLARKE
ARR. BY JOHN F. WILSON

1. The Sav-iour is call-ing, is call-ing for you, In ac-cents so ten-der, so
2. The Sav-iour is call-ing, why turn Him a-way? Sin's bur-den is heav-y, why
3. The Sav-iour is call-ing, O, can it be true That life ev-er-last-ing is
4. The Sav-iour is call-ing from Cal-va-ry's cross, Where He died to save you at

lov-ing and true, How can you re-fuse Him? O heed His sweet call! O,
long-er de-lay? O heart full of sor-row, there's com-fort to-day; O,
wait-ing for you? Come now and re-ceive Him, to Sa-tan say nay; O,
in-fi-nite cost; His heart there was bro-ken for you and for me; O,

REFRAIN

don't turn the Sav-iour a - way. Don't turn the Sav-iour a -

way from your heart, Don't turn the Sav-iour a - way from your heart;

O hear Him plead-ing, O list to His call, O, don't turn the Sav-iour a - way.

310 The Solid Rock

EDWARD MOTE — WILLIAM B. BRADBURY

1. My hope is built on noth-ing less Than Je-sus' blood and right-eous-ness;
2. When darkness veils His love - ly face, I rest on His un-chang-ing grace;
3. His oath, His cov - e-nant, His blood, Sup-port me in the whelm-ing flood;
4. When He shall come with trumpet sound, Oh, may I then in Him be found;

I dare not trust the sweet-est frame, But whol-ly lean on Je-sus' name.
In ev - 'ry high and storm - y gale, My an - chor holds with-in the veil.
When all a-round my soul gives way, He then is all my hope and stay.
Dressed in His right-eous-ness a - lone, Fault-less to stand be - fore the throne.

REFRAIN

On Christ, the sol - id Rock, I stand; All oth - er ground

is sink - ing sand, All oth - er ground is sink - ing sand.

Under His Wings

William O. Cushing — Ira D. Sankey

1. Un - der His wings I am safe - ly a - bid - ing; Tho' the night deep - ens and tem - pests are wild, Still I can trust Him; I know He will keep me; He has re - deemed me, and I am His child.
2. Un - der His wings, what a ref - uge in sor - row! How the heart yearn - ing - ly turns to His rest! Oft - en when earth has no balm for my heal - ing, There I find com - fort, and there I am blest.
3. Un - der His wings, O what pre - cious en - joy - ment! There will I hide till life's tri - als are o'er; Shel - tered, pro - tect - ed, no e - vil can harm me; Rest - ing in Je - sus I'm safe ev - er - more.
Chorus
Un - der His wings, un - der His wings, Who from His love can sev - er?
Un - der His wings my soul shall a - bide, Safe - ly a - bide for - ev - er.

312 Never Alone!

AUTHOR UNKNOWN

AUTHOR UNKNOWN
ARR. BY FRED JACKY

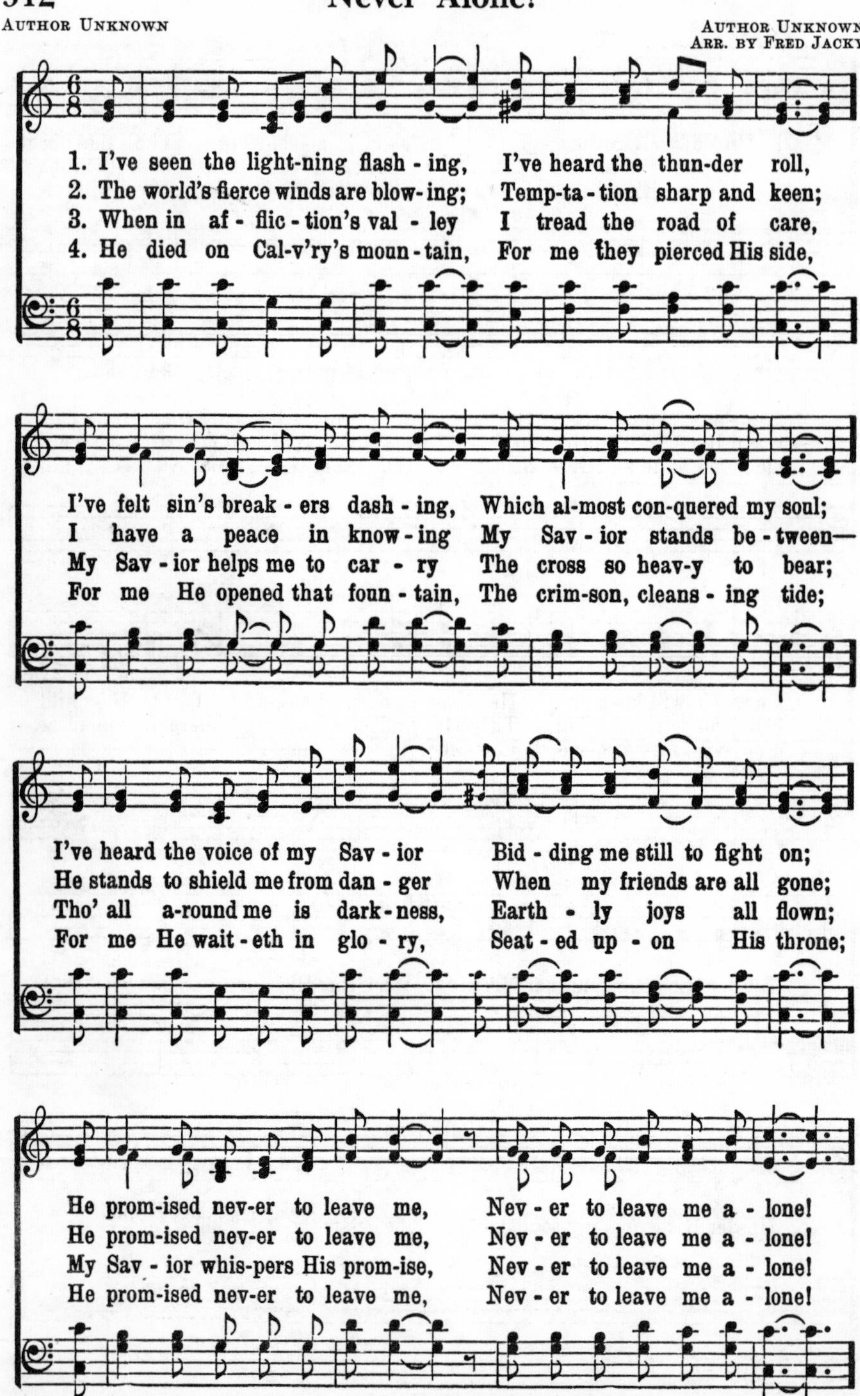
1. I've seen the light-ning flash - ing, I've heard the thun-der roll,
2. The world's fierce winds are blow-ing; Temp-ta - tion sharp and keen;
3. When in af - flic - tion's val - ley I tread the road of care,
4. He died on Cal-v'ry's moun - tain, For me they pierced His side,
I've felt sin's break - ers dash - ing, Which al-most con-quered my soul;
I have a peace in know - ing My Sav - ior stands be - tween—
My Sav - ior helps me to car - ry The cross so heav-y to bear;
For me He opened that foun - tain, The crim-son, cleans - ing tide;
I've heard the voice of my Sav - ior Bid - ding me still to fight on;
He stands to shield me from dan - ger When my friends are all gone;
Tho' all a-round me is dark - ness, Earth - ly joys all flown;
For me He wait - eth in glo - ry, Seat - ed up - on His throne;
He prom-ised nev-er to leave me, Nev - er to leave me a - lone!
He prom-ised nev-er to leave me, Nev - er to leave me a - lone!
My Sav - ior whis-pers His prom-ise, Nev - er to leave me a - lone!
He prom-ised nev-er to leave me, Nev - er to leave me a - lone!

Never Alone!
CHORUS
No, nev-er a - lone,......... No, nev-er a - lone, ... He prom-ised nev-er to
No, nev-er a - lone, No. no, nev-er a - lone,
leave me, He'll claim me for His own. No, nev-er a - lone,...... No, nev-er a-
No, nev-er a - lone, No, no,
lone,...... He prom-ised nev - er to leave me, Nev - er to leave me a - lone.
nev-er a - lone,
I Love Thy Kingdom, Lord
313
TIMOTHY DWIGHT
AARON WILLIAMS
1. I love Thy king - dom, Lord, The house of Thine a - bode,
2. I love Thy Church, O God! Her walls be - fore Thee stand,
3. For her my tears shall fall; For her my prayers as-cend;
4. Be - yond my high - est joy I prize her heav'n-ly ways,
5. Sure as Thy truth shall last, To Zi - on shall be giv'n
The Church our blest Re-deem-er saved With His own pre-cious blood.
Dear as the ap - ple of Thine eye, And grav - en on Thy hand.
To her my cares and toils be giv'n, Till toils and cares shall end.
Her sweet com-mun-ion, sol-emn vows, Her hymns of love and praise.
The bright-est glo-ries earth can yield, And bright - er bliss of heav'n. A-MEN.

314 His Mighty Hand

George W. Whitcomb | Albert S. Reitz

1. I am saved from sin, I have peace with-in, And I walk with Je - sus day by day; O His hand so strong holds me all day long, And with Him I will not go a-stray.
2. Man - y passed me by, heed-ing not my cry, But the Sav-iour heard and res-cued me; I was lost and blind, Je - sus was so kind, Lo, He touched my eyes and now I see.
3. There's a prom-ise sure and it shall en-dure, "Lo, I will be with thee all the way;" And tho' foes as - sail, I shall still pre - vail, For I know He helps me watch and pray.
4. There is sweet-er peace, there is per-fect peace, And my Fa-ther's word is won-drous dear; There is might-y pow'r for each try-ing hour, There is love that "cast-eth out all fear!"
REFRAIN
He will hold me with His might-y hand! He will hold me with His might-y hand! In temp-ta-tion He will help me stand! For He will hold me with His might-y hand.

I Never Walk Alone

Alfred H. Ackley Alfred H. Ackley

1. I nev-er walk a-lone, I have the Sav-iour, Who walks be-side me ev-ery-where I
2. I nev-er walk a-lone, in storm-y wea-ther, When winds of trou-ble sweep a-bout my
go; My heart re-joic-es in His lov-ing fa - vor, And
head; I know I'm safe, be-cause we are to - geth - er, And
all who will His sav-ing grace may know.
'round me His pro-tect-ing love is spread.
Refrain
I nev-er walk a-lone, Christ walks be-
side me, He is the dear-est Friend I've ev-er known, With such a Friend to
com-fort and to guide me, I nev-er, no, I nev-er walk a - lone.

316 The Nail-Scarred Hand

BAYLUS B. MCKINNEY BAYLUS B. MCKINNEY

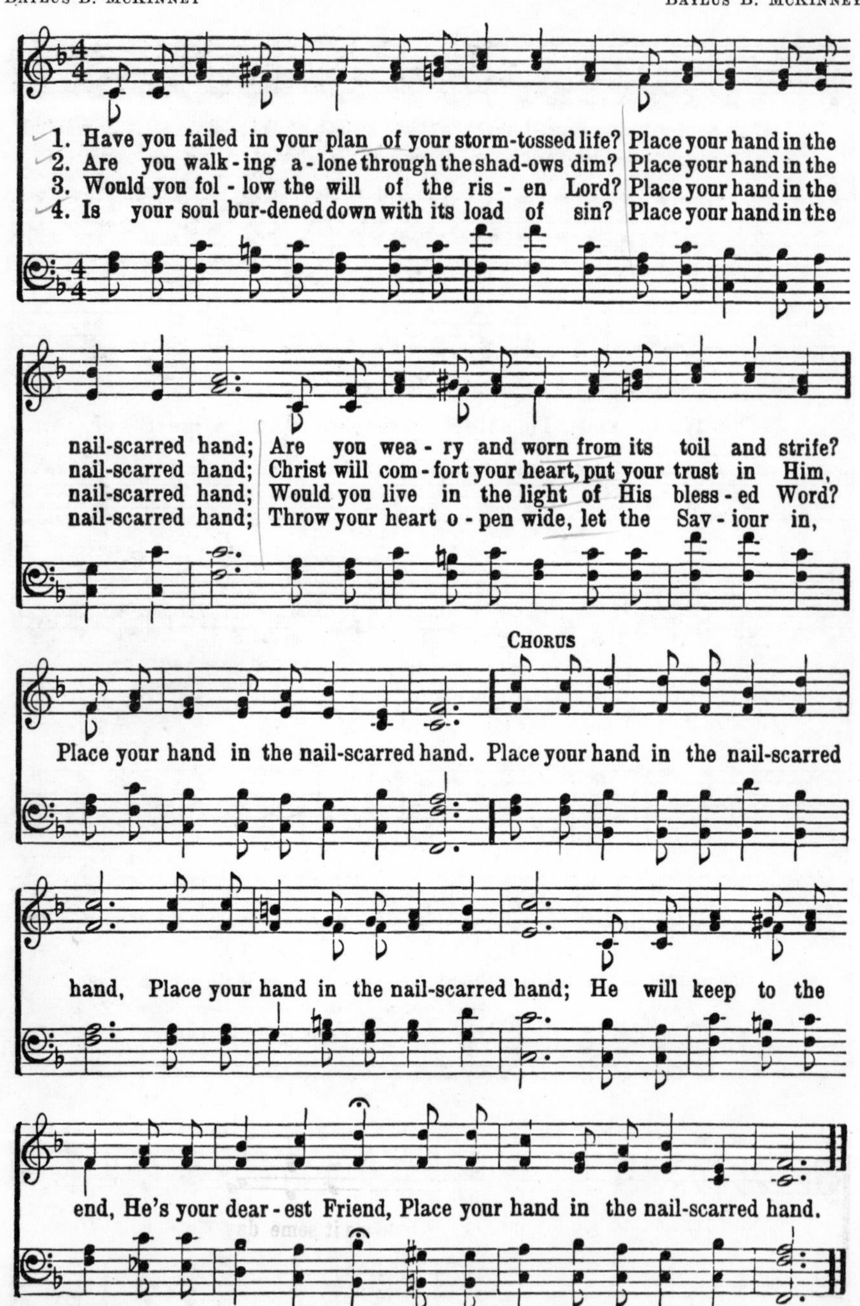
1. Have you failed in your plan of your storm-tossed life? Place your hand in the
2. Are you walk-ing a-lone through the shad-ows dim? Place your hand in the
3. Would you fol-low the will of the ris-en Lord? Place your hand in the
4. Is your soul bur-dened down with its load of sin? Place your hand in the
nail-scarred hand; Are you wea-ry and worn from its toil and strife?
nail-scarred hand; Christ will com-fort your heart, put your trust in Him,
nail-scarred hand; Would you live in the light of His bless-ed Word?
nail-scarred hand; Throw your heart o-pen wide, let the Sav-iour in,
Place your hand in the nail-scarred hand.
CHORUS
Place your hand in the nail-scarred hand, Place your hand in the nail-scarred hand; He will keep to the end, He's your dear-est Friend, Place your hand in the nail-scarred hand.

The Old Rugged Cross

GEORGE BENNARD GEORGE BENNARD

1. On a hill far a-way stood an old rug-ged cross, The em-blem of
2. Oh, that old rug-ged cross so de-spised by the world, Has a wondrous at-
3. In the old rug-ged cross, stained with blood so di-vine, A won-drous
4. To the old rug-ged cross I will ev-er be true, Its shame and re-
suf-f'ring and shame; And I love that old cross where the dear-est and best
trac-tion for me; For the dear Lamb of God left His glo-ry a-bove,
beau-ty I see; For 'twas on that old cross Je-sus suf-fered and died,
proach gladly bear; Then He'll call me some day to my home far a-way,
CHORUS
For a world of lost sin-ners was slain.
To bear it to dark Cal-va-ry.
To par-don and sanc-ti-fy me.
Where His glo-ry for-ev-er I'll share.
So I'll cher-ish the old rug-ged cross, the
cross, ... Till my tro-phies at last I lay down; I will cling to the
old rugged cross,
old rug-ged cross, ... And ex-change it some day for a crown.
cross, the old rug-ged cross,

Buried with Christ

T. Ryder — William J. Kirkpatrick

1. Bur - ied with Christ and raised with Him too, What is there left for
2. Ris - en with Christ my glo - ri - ous Head, Ho - li - ness now the
3. Liv - ing with Christ, who di - eth no more, Fol - low-ing Christ, who

me . . . to do? Sim - ply to cease from strug-gling and strife,
path-way I tread; Beau - ti - ful thought while walk-ing there - in,
go - eth be - fore; Not un - der law, I'm now un - der grace,

Sim - ply to walk in new-ness of life.
He that is dead is freed from all sin.
Sin is de-throned and Christ takes its place.

CHORUS

Bur - ied with Christ and dead un - to sin; Dy - ing but liv - ing, Je - sus with - in; Rul - ing and reign - ing day aft - er day, Guid-ing and keep-ing all of the way.

O Word of God Incarnate

319

William W. How

"Neuvermehrtes Meiningisches Gesangbuch"
Har. by Felix Mendelssohn-Bartholdy

1. O Word of God in - car - nate, O Wis - dom from on high,
2. The Church from her dear Mas - ter Re-ceived the gift di - vine,
3. It float - eth like a ban - ner Be - fore God's host un - furled;
4. O make Thy Church, dear Sav - ior, A lamp of pur - est gold,
O Truth un-changed, un-chang - ing, O Light of our dark sky;
And still that light she lift - eth O'er all the earth to shine.
It shin - eth like a bea - con A - bove the dark-'ning world.
To bear be - fore the na - tions Thy true light, as of old.
We praise Thee for the ra - diance That from the hal - lowed page,
It is the gold - en cask - et, Where gems of truth are stored;
It is the chart and com - pass That o'er life's surg - ing sea,
O teach Thy wan-d'ring pil - grims By this their path to trace,
A lan- tern to our foot-steps, Shines on from age to age.
It is the heav'n-drawn pic - ture Of Christ, the liv - ing Word.
'Mid mists and rocks and quick-sands, Still guides, O Christ, to Thee.
Till, clouds and dark - ness end - ed, They see Thee face to face. A-MEN.

320 Break Thou the Bread of Life

MARY ANN LATHBURY — WILLIAM F. SHERWIN

1. Break Thou the bread of life, Dear Lord, to me, As Thou didst
2. Bless Thou the truth, dear Lord To me— to me— As Thou didst
3. Thou art the bread of life, O Lord, to me, Thy ho - ly
4. O send Thy Spir - it, Lord, Now un - to me, That He may

break the loaves Be - side the sea; Be - yond the sa - cred page
bless the bread By Gal - i - lee; Then shall all bond- age cease,
Word the truth That sav - eth me; Give me to eat and live
touch my eyes, And make me see: Show me the truth con-cealed

I seek Thee, Lord; My spir - it pants for Thee, O liv - ing Word.
All fet - ters fall; And I shall find my peace, My All in All.
With Thee a - bove; Teach me to love Thy truth, For Thou art love.
With- in Thy Word, And in Thy book re-vealed I see the Lord.

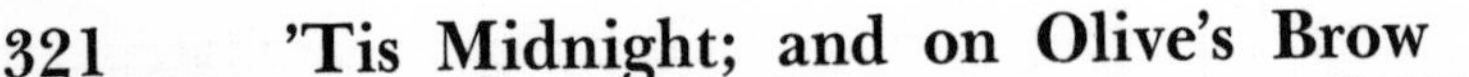

321 'Tis Midnight; and on Olive's Brow

WILLIAM B. TAPPAN — WILLIAM B. BRADBURY

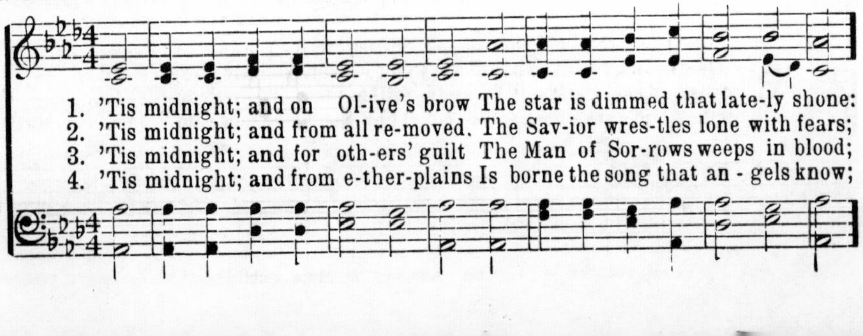

1. 'Tis midnight; and on Ol-ive's brow The star is dimmed that late-ly shone:
2. 'Tis midnight; and from all re-moved. The Sav-ior wres-tles lone with fears;
3. 'Tis midnight; and for oth-ers' guilt The Man of Sor-rows weeps in blood;
4. 'Tis midnight; and from e-ther-plains Is borne the song that an - gels know;

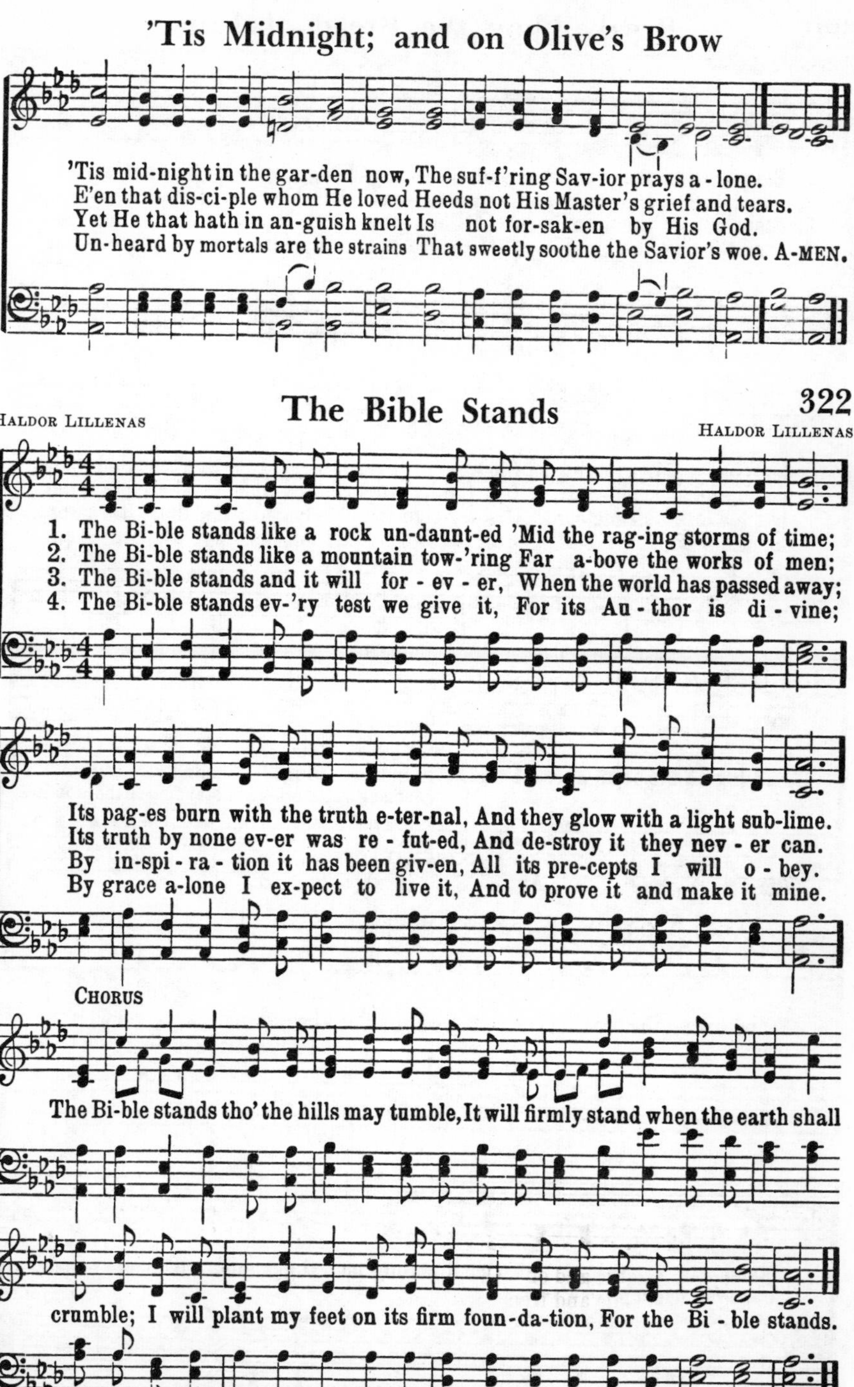
'Tis Midnight; and on Olive's Brow
'Tis mid-night in the gar-den now, The suf-f'ring Sav-ior prays a - lone.
E'en that dis-ci-ple whom He loved Heeds not His Master's grief and tears.
Yet He that hath in an-guish knelt Is not for-sak-en by His God.
Un-heard by mortals are the strains That sweetly soothe the Savior's woe. A-MEN.
322
The Bible Stands
HALDOR LILLENAS
HALDOR LILLENAS
1. The Bi-ble stands like a rock un-daunt-ed 'Mid the rag-ing storms of time;
2. The Bi-ble stands like a mountain tow-'ring Far a-bove the works of men;
3. The Bi-ble stands and it will for - ev - er, When the world has passed away;
4. The Bi-ble stands ev-'ry test we give it, For its Au - thor is di - vine;
Its pag-es burn with the truth e-ter-nal, And they glow with a light sub-lime.
Its truth by none ev-er was re - fut-ed, And de-stroy it they nev - er can.
By in-spi - ra - tion it has been giv-en, All its pre-cepts I will o - bey.
By grace a-lone I ex-pect to live it, And to prove it and make it mine.
CHORUS
The Bi-ble stands tho' the hills may tumble, It will firmly stand when the earth shall
crumble; I will plant my feet on its firm foun-da-tion, For the Bi - ble stands.

323

Standing on the Promises

R. KELSO CARTER | R. KELSO CARTER

1. Stand-ing on the prom-is-es of Christ my King, Thro' e-ter-nal a-ges
2. Stand-ing on the prom-is-es that can-not fail, When the howling storms of
3. Stand-ing on the prom-is-es of Christ the Lord, Bound to Him e-ter-nal-
4. Stand-ing on the prom-is-es I can-not fall, Lis-t'ning ev-'ry mo-ment
let His prais-es ring; Glo-ry in the high-est, I will shout and sing,
doubt and fear as-sail, By the liv-ing word of God I shall pre-vail,
ly by love's strong cord, O-ver-com-ing dai-ly with the Spir-it's sword,
to the Spir-it's call, Rest-ing in my Sav-ior, as my all in all,
CHORUS
Stand-ing on the prom-is-es of God. Stand - - ing, stand - - ing,
Standing on the promises, standing on the promises,
Stand-ing on the prom-is-es of God my Sav-ior; Stand - - ing,
Stand-ing on the prom-is-es,
stand - - ing, I'm stand-ing on the prom-is-es of God.
stand-ing on the prom-is-es,

Thy Word Have I Hid in My Heart

From Psalm 119
Adapted by Ernest O. Sellers

Ernest O. Sellers

1. Thy Word is a lamp to my feet, A light to my path al-way,
2. For-ev-er, O Lord, is Thy Word Es-tab-lished and fixed on high;
3. At morn-ing, at noon, and at night I ev-er will give Thee praise;
4. Thro' Him whom Thy Word hath foretold, The Sav-ior and Morn-ing Star,
To guide and to save me from sin, And show me the heav'n-ly way.
Thy faith-ful-ness un-to all men A-bid-eth for-ev-er nigh.
For Thou art my por-tion, O Lord, And shall be thro' all my days!
Sal-va-tion and peace have been bro't To those who have strayed a-far.
Chorus—Ps. 119: 11.
Thy Word have I hid in my heart (in my heart), That I might not
sin a-gainst Thee (a-gainst Thee); That I might not sin, That
ad lib.
I might not sin, Thy Word have I hid in my heart.

325 **Beautiful Words of Jesus**

Eliza E. Hewitt — Isaac H. Meredith

1. Beau-ti-ful words of Je-sus, Spo-ken so long a - go, Yet, as we sing them
2. Beau-ti-ful words of Je-sus, Cheering us, day by day; Throwing a gleam of
3. Beau-ti-ful words of Je-sus, To-kens of end-less rest, When, by and by, we
Duet. Ladies' Voices
o - ver, Dearer to us they grow, Calling the heav-y-la - den, Call-ing to hearts op-
sunshine Over a cloud-y way; Casting on Him the burden We are too weak to
en - ter In-to His presence blest; There shall we see His beauty, Meet with Him face to
All Voices
Chorus
pressed, "Come un-to me, ye wea - ry, Come, I will give you rest."
bear, He will give grace sufficient, He will re-gard our prayer. Hear the
face, There shall we sing His glory, Praising His matchless grace.
call . . . . of His voice, so sweet; . Bring your load . . . . to the
Sav - ior's feet; Lean your heart . . . on His lov - ing

breast,.. Come, O come and He will give you rest.....

Wonderful Words of Life

326

PHILIP P. BLISS PHILIP P. BLISS

1. Sing them o-ver a-gain to me, Won-der-ful words of Life;
Let me more of their beau-ty see, Won-der-ful words of Life.
Words of life and beau-ty, Teach me faith and du-ty:

2. Christ, the bless-ed One, gives to all, Won-der-ful words of Life;
Sin-ner, list to the lov-ing call, Won-der-ful words of Life.
All so free-ly giv-en, Woo-ing us to Heav-en:

3. Sweet-ly ech-o the gos-pel call, Won-der-ful words of Life;
Of-fer par-don and peace to all, Won-der-ful words of Life.
Je-sus, on-ly Sav-ior, Sanc-ti-fy for-ev-er:

REFRAIN

Beau-ti-ful words, won-der-ful words, Won-der-ful words of Life. Life.

327 Thy Word Is Like a Garden, Lord

EDWIN HODDER

GOTTFRIED W. FINK

1. Thy Word is like a gar - den, Lord, With flow - ers bright and fair;
And ev - 'ry one who seeks may pluck A love - ly clus - ter there.
Thy Word is like a deep, deep mine, And jew - els rich and rare
Are hid - den in its might - y depths For ev - 'ry search-er there.

2. Thy Word is like a star - ry host: A thou - sand rays of light
Are seen to guard the trav - el - er, And make his path-way bright.
Thy Word is like an ar - mor - y, Where sol-diers may re - pair,
And find, for life's long bat - tle - day, All need - ful weap-ons there.

3. Oh, may I love Thy pre-cious Word, May I ex - plore the mine,
May I its fra - grant flow - ers glean, May light up - on me shine!
Oh, may I find my ar - mor there! Thy Word my trust - y sword,
I'll learn to fight with ev - 'ry foe The bat - tle of the Lord.

Are You Washed in the Blood?

ELISHA A. HOFFMAN

ELISHA A. HOFFMAN

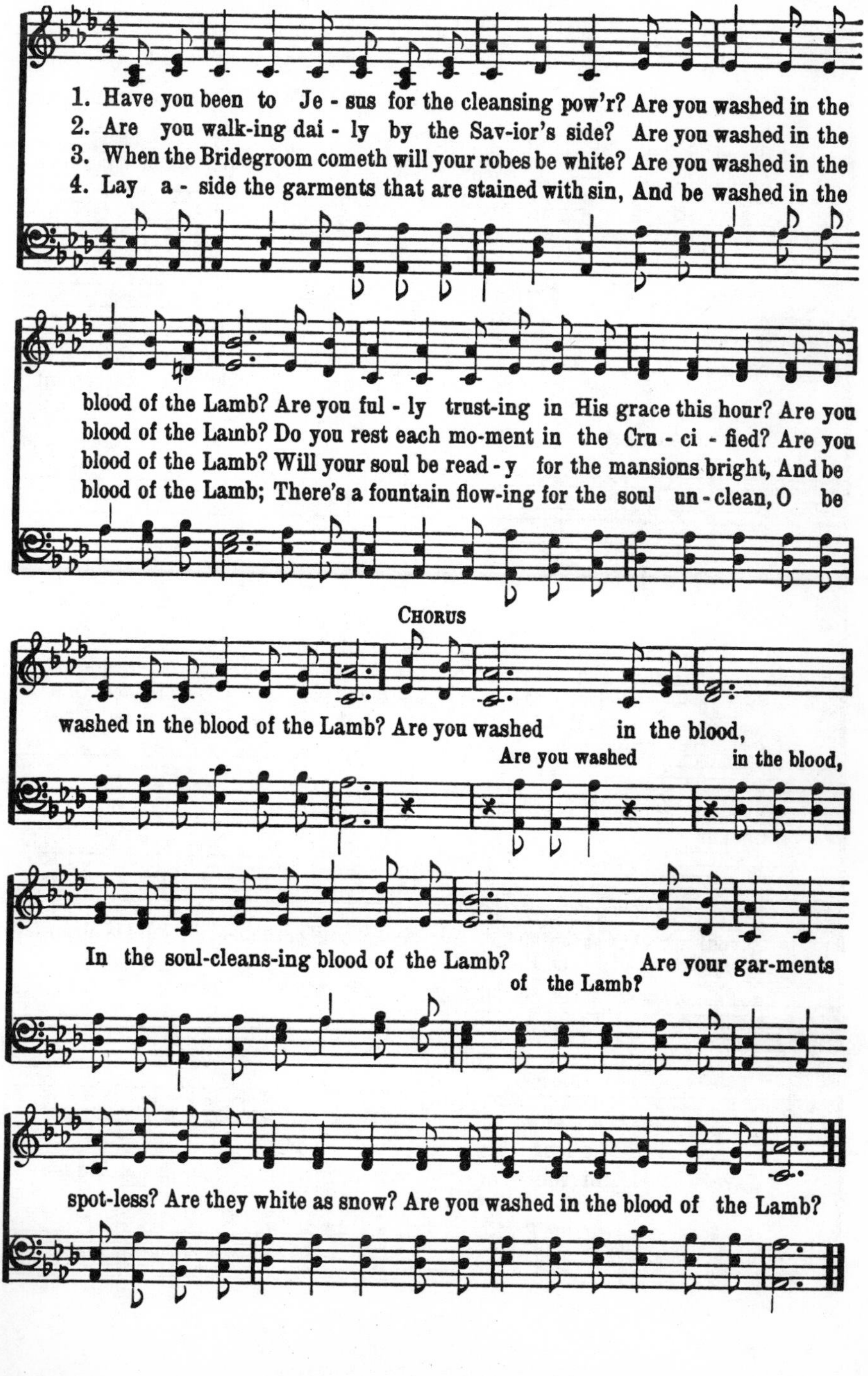

1. Have you been to Je - sus for the cleansing pow'r? Are you washed in the
2. Are you walk-ing dai - ly by the Sav-ior's side? Are you washed in the
3. When the Bridegroom cometh will your robes be white? Are you washed in the
4. Lay a - side the garments that are stained with sin, And be washed in the

blood of the Lamb? Are you ful - ly trust-ing in His grace this hour? Are you
blood of the Lamb? Do you rest each mo-ment in the Cru - ci - fied? Are you
blood of the Lamb? Will your soul be read - y for the mansions bright, And be
blood of the Lamb; There's a fountain flow-ing for the soul un-clean, O be

CHORUS

washed in the blood of the Lamb? Are you washed in the blood,
Are you washed in the blood,

In the soul-cleans-ing blood of the Lamb? Are your gar-ments
of the Lamb?

spot-less? Are they white as snow? Are you washed in the blood of the Lamb?

329 Saved by the Blood

S. J. Henderson

Daniel B. Towner

1. Saved by the blood of the Cru-ci-fied One! Now ran-somed from sin and a new work be-gun, Sing praise to the Fa-ther and praise to the Son, Saved by the blood of the Cru-ci-fied One!
2. Saved by the blood of the Cru-ci-fied One! The an-gels re-joic-ing be-cause it is done; A child of the Fa-ther, joint-heir with the Son, Saved by the blood of the Cru-ci-fied One!
3. Saved by the blood of the Cru-ci-fied One! The Fa-ther He spake, and His will it was done; Great price of my par-don, His own pre-cious Son; Saved by the blood of the Cru-ci-fied One!
4. Saved by the blood of the Cru-ci-fied One! All hail to the Fa-ther, all hail to the Son, All hail to-the Spir-it, the great Three in One! Saved by the blood of the Cru-ci-fied One!

CHORUS

Saved! .. saved! .. My sins are all pardoned, my guilt is all gone!
Glo-ry, I'm saved! glo-ry, I'm saved!
Saved! .. saved! .. I am saved by the blood of the Cru-ci-fied One!
Glo-ry, I'm saved! glo-ry, I'm saved!

There Is Power in the Blood

LEWIS E. JONES LEWIS E. JONES

1. Would you be free from the bur - den of sin? There's pow'r in the blood,
2. Would you be free from your pas-sion and pride? There's pow'r in the blood,
3. Would you be whit - er, much whiter than snow? There's pow'r in the blood,
4. Would you do serv - ice for Je - sus your King? There's pow'r in the blood,

pow'r in the blood; Would you o'er e - vil a vic - to - ry win? There's
pow'r in the blood; Come for a cleans-ing to Cal - va-ry's tide; There's
pow'r in the blood; Sin-stains are lost in its life - giv - ing flow; There's
pow'r in the blood; Would you live dai - ly His prais-es to sing? There's

won-der-ful pow'r in the blood.

CHORUS.

There is pow'r, there is pow'r, Wonder-working pow'r
In the blood of the Lamb; In the blood of the Lamb;
There is pow'r, there is pow'r,
Won - der - work - ing pow'r In the pre - cious blood of the Lamb.

331 When I See the Blood

JOHN FOOTE J. G. FOOTE

1. Christ our Re-deem - er died on the cross, Died for the sin - ner,
2. Chief-est of sin - ners, Je - sus will save; All He has prom-ised,
3. Judg-ment is com - ing, all will be there, Each one re - ceiv - ing
4. O great com-pas - sion! O bound-less love! O lov - ing kind - ness,
paid all his due; Sprin - kle your soul with the blood of the Lamb,
that He will do; Wash in the foun - tain o - pened for sin,
just - ly his due; Hide in the sav - ing sin-cleans-ing blood,
faith - ful and true! Find peace and shel - ter un - der the blood,
CHORUS
And I will pass, will pass o - ver you. When I see the
When I
blood, When I see the blood, When I see the
see the blood, When I see the blood, When I
rit.
blood, I will pass, I will pass o - ver you.
see the blood, o - ver you.

'Twas Jesus' Blood

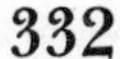

HARRY D. LOES — HARRY D. LOES

1. A sin-ner, lost, condemned was I, Doomed an e-ter-nal death to die;
2. I ne'er could be at peace with God, But for the cleansing, crimson flood,
3. No doubter's scorn or creed of man Can shake my faith in Cal-v'ry's plan;

But Je-sus died for me, He bore sin's pen-al-ty, On Cal-v'ry's hill was
No one but Christ could win A-tone-ment for all sin—He signed my par-don
His blood re-deemed my soul, It made me pure and whole; By faith my life in

lift-ed high.
with His blood.
Him be-gan.

CHORUS

'Twas Je-sus' blood...... that ransomed me.......
'Twas Jesus' blood that ransomed me,

From chains of sin He set me free........ While a-ges roll........
He set me free. While a-ges roll

my song shall be: .. ..'Twas Je-sus' blood that ransomed me......
My song shall be: ransomed me.

333 Yield Not to Temptation

Horatio R. Palmer — Horatio R. Palmer

1. Yield not to temp-ta - tion, For yield-ing is sin, Each vic - t'ry will help you Some oth - er to win; Fight man-ful - ly on - ward, Dark pas-sions sub-due, Look ev - er to Je - sus, He will car-ry you through.
2. Shun e - vil com-pan-ions, Bad lan-guage dis-dain, God's name hold in rev-'rence, Nor take it in vain; Be thought-ful and ear - nest, Kind-heart-ed and true, Look ev - er to Je - sus, He will car-ry you through.
3. To him that o'er-com-eth God giv-eth a crown, Thro' faith we shall con - quer, Though of - ten cast down; He who is our Sav - ior, Our strength will re - new, Look ev - er to Je - sus, He will car-ry you through.

Chorus

Ask the Sav - ior to help you, Com - fort, strengthen, and keep you, He is will - ing to aid you, He will car - ry you through.

He Died for Me

334

John Newton

Edwin O. Excell

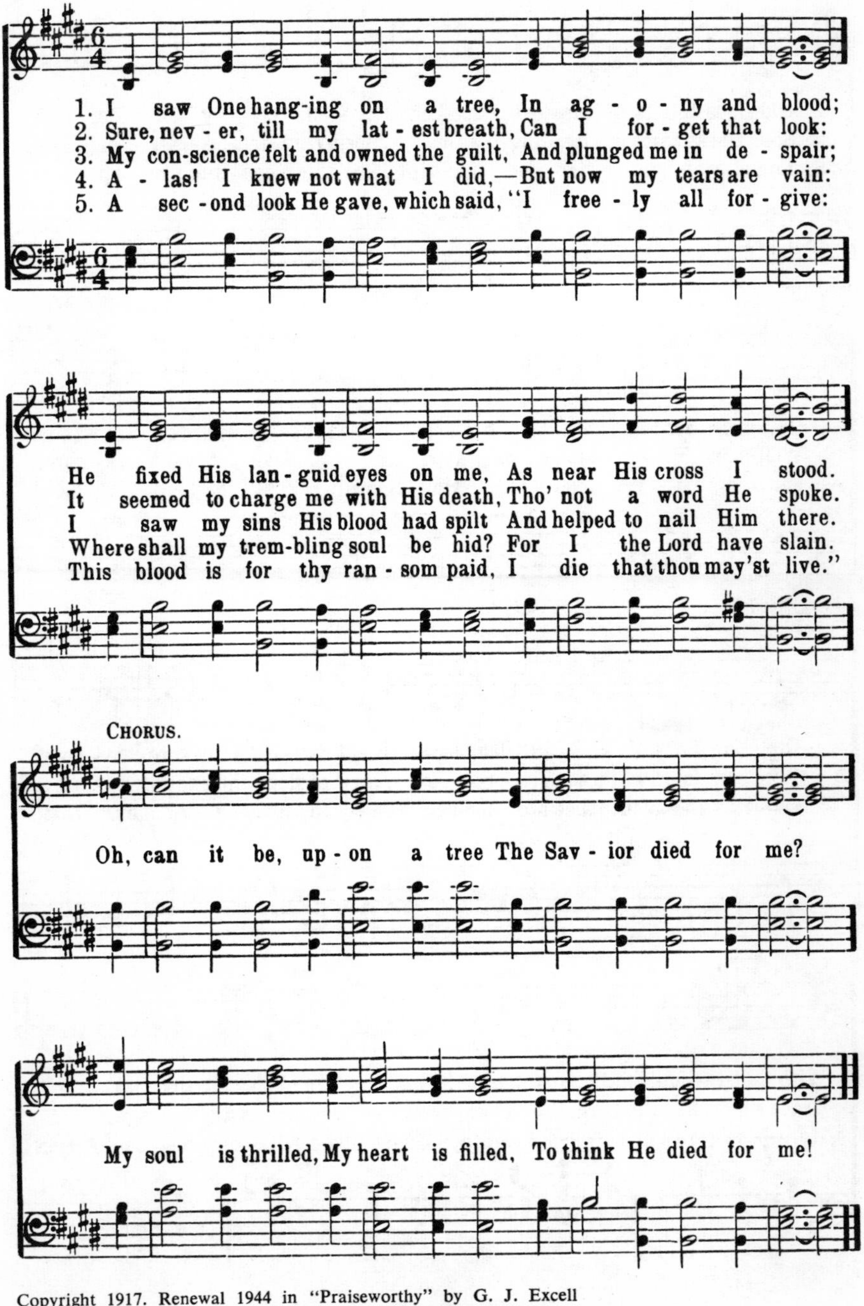

1. I saw One hang-ing on a tree, In ag - o - ny and blood;
He fixed His lan - guid eyes on me, As near His cross I stood.

2. Sure, nev - er, till my lat - est breath, Can I for - get that look:
It seemed to charge me with His death, Tho' not a word He spoke.

3. My con-science felt and owned the guilt, And plunged me in de - spair;
I saw my sins His blood had spilt And helped to nail Him there.

4. A - las! I knew not what I did,—But now my tears are vain:
Where shall my trem-bling soul be hid? For I the Lord have slain.

5. A sec - ond look He gave, which said, "I free - ly all for - give:
This blood is for thy ran - som paid, I die that thou may'st live."

Chorus.

Oh, can it be, up - on a tree The Sav - ior died for me?
My soul is thrilled, My heart is filled, To think He died for me!

335 Glorious Things of Thee Are Spoken

JOHN NEWTON | FRANZ JOSEPH HAYDN

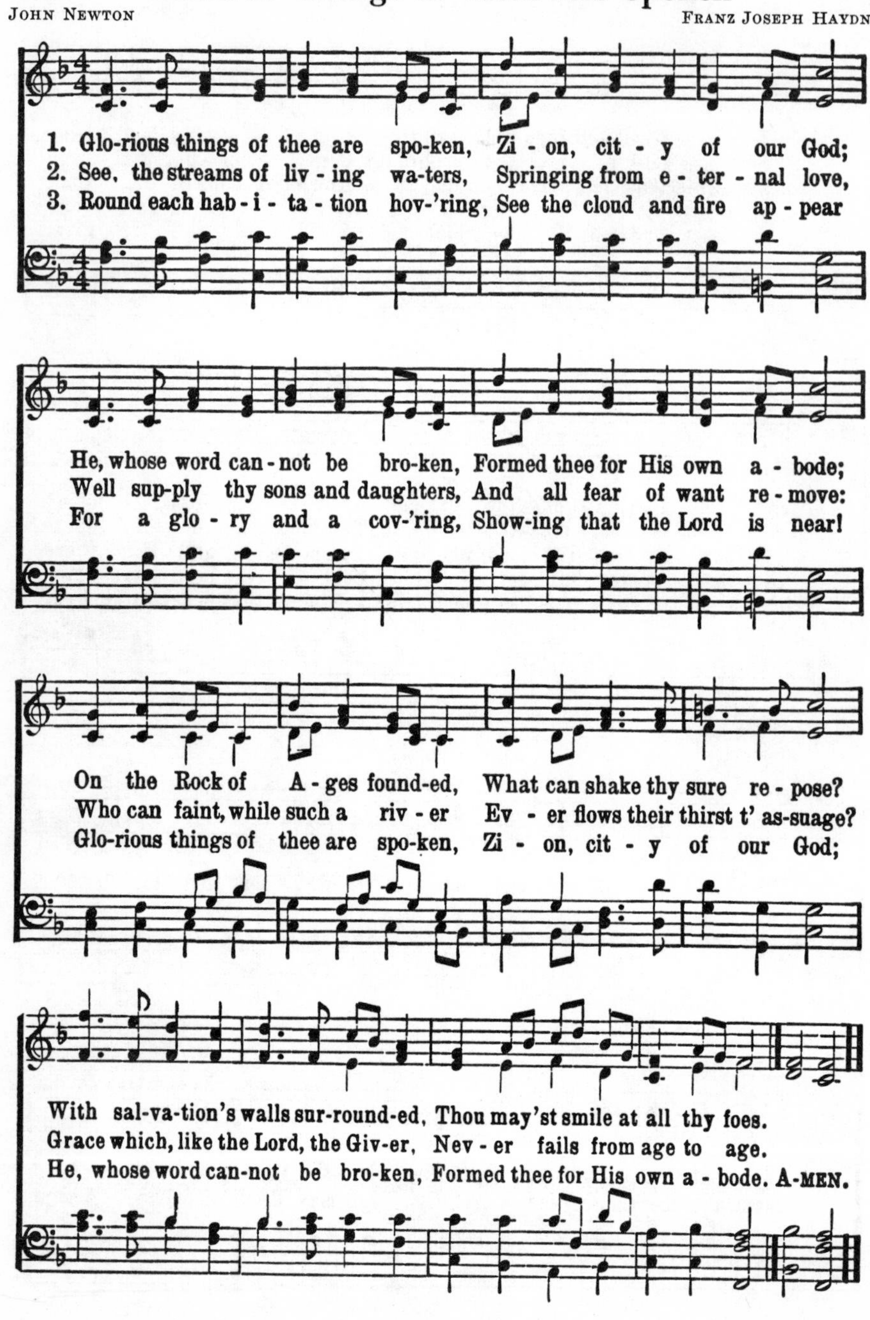
1. Glo-rious things of thee are spo-ken, Zi - on, cit - y of our God;
2. See, the streams of liv - ing wa-ters, Springing from e - ter - nal love,
3. Round each hab - i - ta - tion hov-'ring, See the cloud and fire ap - pear
He, whose word can - not be bro-ken, Formed thee for His own a - bode;
Well sup-ply thy sons and daughters, And all fear of want re - move:
For a glo - ry and a cov-'ring, Show-ing that the Lord is near!
On the Rock of A - ges found-ed, What can shake thy sure re - pose?
Who can faint, while such a riv - er Ev - er flows their thirst t' as-suage?
Glo-rious things of thee are spo-ken, Zi - on, cit - y of our God;
With sal-va-tion's walls sur-round-ed, Thou may'st smile at all thy foes.
Grace which, like the Lord, the Giv-er, Nev - er fails from age to age.
He, whose word can-not be bro-ken, Formed thee for His own a - bode. A-MEN.

The Church's One Foundation

Samuel J. Stone — Samuel S. Wesley

1. The Church-'s one foun - da - tion Is Je - sus Christ her Lord;
2. E - lect from ev - 'ry na - tion, Yet one o'er all the earth,
3. 'Mid toil and trib - u - la - tion, And tu - mult of her war,
4. Yet she on earth hath un - ion With God the Three in One,

She is His new cre - a - tion By wa - ter and the word:
Her char - ter of sal - va - tion, One Lord, one faith, one birth;
She waits the con - sum - ma - tion Of peace for - ev - er - more;
And mys - tic sweet com - mun - ion With those whose rest is won:

From Heav'n He came and sought her To be His ho - ly bride; With
One ho - ly name she bless - es, Par-takes one ho - ly food, And
Till, with the vi - sion glo - rious, Her long - ing eyes are blest, And
O hap - py ones and ho - ly! Lord, give us grace that we, Like

His own blood He bought her, And for her life He died.
to one hope she press - es, With ev - 'ry grace en - dued.
the great church vic - to - rious Shall be the church at rest.
them, the meek and low - ly, On high may dwell with Thee. A-MEN.

337 Lead Me to Calvary

Jennie E. Hussey — William J. Kirkpatrick

1. King of my life, I crown Thee now, Thine shall the glo - ry be;
2. Show me the tomb where Thou wast laid, Ten-der-ly mourned and wept;
3. Let me like Ma - ry, thro' the gloom, Come with a gift to Thee;
4. May I be will - ing, Lord, to bear Dai - ly my cross for Thee;
Lest I for - get Thy thorn-crowned brow, Lead me to Cal - va - ry.
An - gels in robes of light ar - rayed Guarded Thee whilst Thou slept.
Show to me now the emp - ty tomb, Lead me to Cal - va - ry.
E - ven Thy cup of grief to share, Thou hast borne all for me.
Chorus
Lest I for - get Geth-sem - a - ne; Lest I for - get Thine ag - o - ny;
Lest I for - get Thy love for me, Lead me to Cal - va - ry.

O Sacred Head, Now Wounded

Ascribed to Bernard of Clairvaux
Tr. (German) by Paul Gerhardt
Tr. (English) by James W. Alexander

Hans L. Hassler
Har. by J. S. Bach

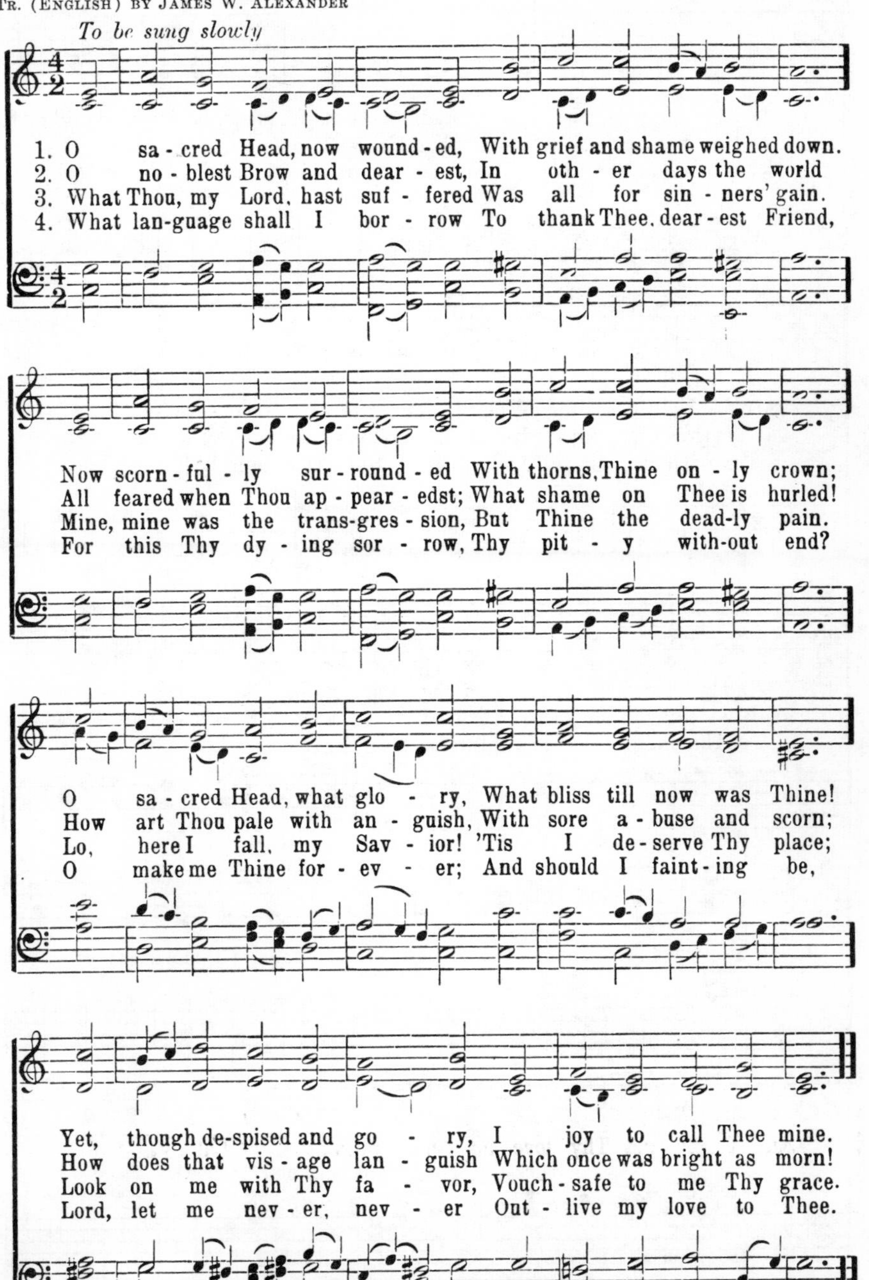

To be sung slowly
1. O sa - cred Head, now wound - ed, With grief and shame weighed down.
2. O no - blest Brow and dear - est, In oth - er days the world
3. What Thou, my Lord, hast suf - fered Was all for sin - ners' gain.
4. What lan-guage shall I bor - row To thank Thee, dear - est Friend,
Now scorn - ful - ly sur - round - ed With thorns, Thine on - ly crown;
All feared when Thou ap - pear - edst; What shame on Thee is hurled!
Mine, mine was the trans-gres - sion, But Thine the dead-ly pain.
For this Thy dy - ing sor - row, Thy pit - y with-out end?
O sa - cred Head, what glo - ry, What bliss till now was Thine!
How art Thou pale with an - guish, With sore a - buse and scorn;
Lo, here I fall, my Sav - ior! 'Tis I de - serve Thy place;
O make me Thine for - ev - er; And should I faint - ing be,
Yet, though de-spised and go - ry, I joy to call Thee mine.
How does that vis - age lan - guish Which once was bright as morn!
Look on me with Thy fa - vor, Vouch - safe to me Thy grace.
Lord, let me nev - er, nev - er Out - live my love to Thee.

339 **Surely Goodness and Mercy**

John W. Peterson
Alfred B. Smith

John W. Peterson

1. A pil-grim was I and a-wan-d'ring, In the cold night of
2. He re-stor-eth my soul when I'm wea-ry, He giv-eth me
3. When I walk thro' the dark lone-some val-ley, My Sav-ior will
sin I did roam, When Je-sus the kind Shep-herd found me,
strength day by day; He leads me be-side the still wa-ters,
walk with me there; And safe-ly His great hand will lead me
And now I am on my way home.
He guards me each step of the way.
To the man-sions He's gone to pre-pare.
CHORUS
Sure-ly good-ness and
mer-cy shall fol-low me All the days, all the days of my
life; Sure-ly good-ness and mer-cy shall fol-low

Surely Goodness and Mercy

D.C. ★ 3

me All the days, all the days of my life. And I shall

dwell in the house of the Lord for - ev - er, And I shall

feast at the ta-ble spread for me; Sure - ly good-ness

and mer-cy shall fol - low me All the days, all the

CODA (after last chorus only)

p *Slowly*

days of my life. All the days, all the days of my life.

★ Opt. D.C. The following section may be reserved for use with final chorus only.

340 There Is a Green Hill Far Away

Cecil F. Alexander | George C. Stebbins

1. There is a green hill far a - way, With-out a cit - y wall,
2. We may not know, we can - not tell What pains He had to bear;
3. He died that we might be for-giv'n, He died to make us good,
4. There was no oth - er good e-nough, To pay the price of sin;

Where the dear Lord was cru - ci - fied, Who died to save us all.
But we be-lieve it was for us He hung and suf-fered there.
That we might go at last to Heav'n, Saved by His pre - cious blood.
He on - ly could un - lock the gate Of Heav'n and let us in.

Chorus

Oh, dear - ly, dear - ly has He loved, And we must love Him, too;

rit . . .

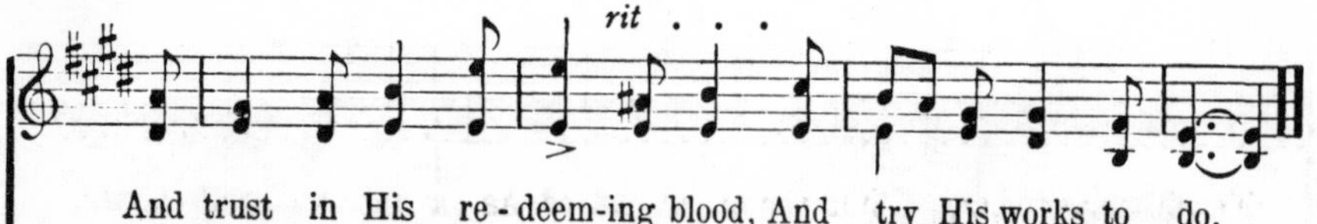

And trust in His re - deem-ing blood, And try His works to do.

As a Volunteer

W. S. Brown

Charles H. Gabriel

1. A call for loy-al sol-diers Comes to one and all; Sol-diers for the con-flict,
2. Yes, Jesus calls for soldiers Who are filled with pow'r, Soldiers who will serve Him
3. He calls you, for He loves you With a heart most kind, He whose heart was broken,
4. And when the war is o-ver, And the vic-t'ry won, When the true and faith-ful

Will you heed the call! Will you an-swer quick-ly, With a read-y cheer,
Ev-'ry day and hour; He will not for-sake you, He is ev-er near;
Bro-ken for man-kind; Now, just now He calls you, Calls in ac-cents clear,
Gath-er one by one, He will crown with glo-ry All who there ap-pear;

Chorus.

Will you be en-list-ed As a vol-un-teer? A vol-un-teer for Je-sus, A sol-dier

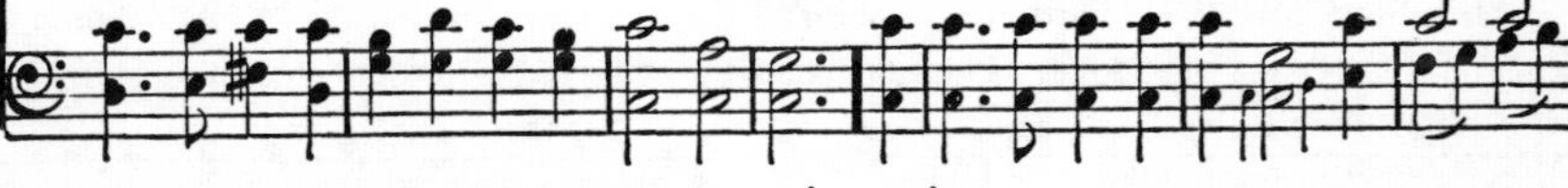

true! Oth-ers have enlisted, Why not you? Je-sus is the Cap-tain,
O why not?

We will nev-er fear; Will you be en-list-ed As a vol-un-teer? A-men.

342 Take Time to Be Holy

William D. Longstaff — George C. Stebbins

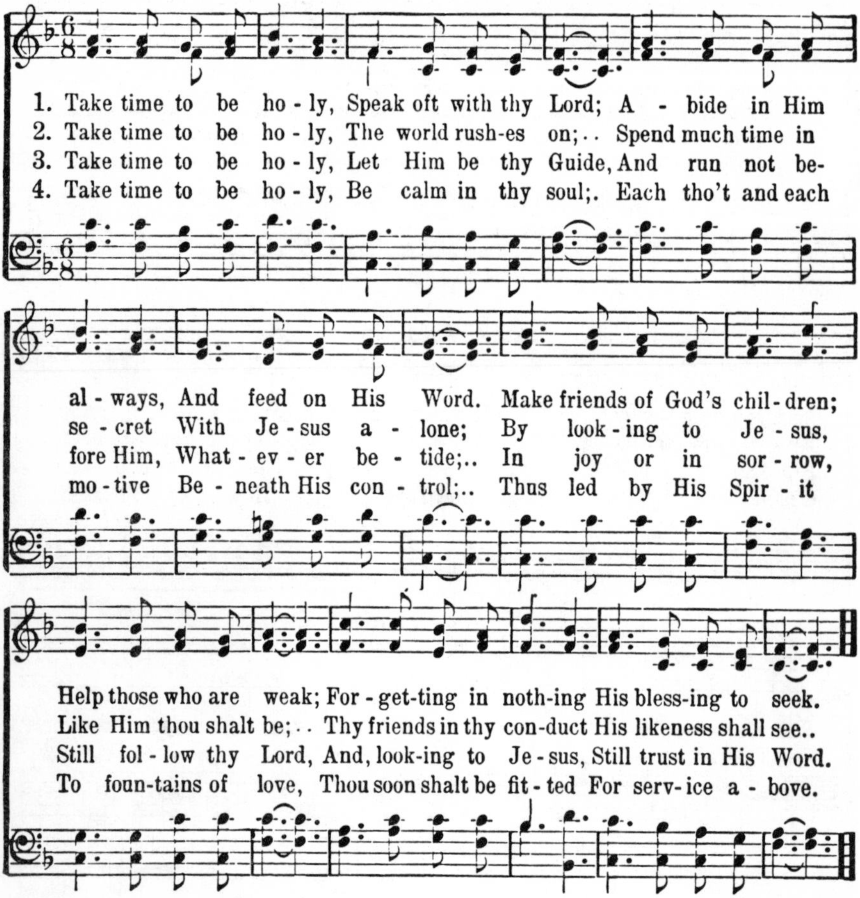

1. Take time to be ho - ly, Speak oft with thy Lord; A - bide in Him
2. Take time to be ho - ly, The world rush-es on;.. Spend much time in
3. Take time to be ho - ly, Let Him be thy Guide, And run not be-
4. Take time to be ho - ly, Be calm in thy soul;. Each tho't and each

al - ways, And feed on His Word. Make friends of God's chil - dren;
se - cret With Je - sus a - lone; By look - ing to Je - sus,
fore Him, What - ev - er be - tide;.. In joy or in sor - row,
mo - tive Be - neath His con - trol;.. Thus led by His Spir - it

Help those who are weak; For - get-ting in noth-ing His bless-ing to seek.
Like Him thou shalt be;.. Thy friends in thy con-duct His likeness shall see..
Still fol - low thy Lord, And, look-ing to Je - sus, Still trust in His Word.
To foun-tains of love, Thou soon shalt be fit - ted For serv- ice a - bove.

343 Jesus Calls Us

Cecil F. Alexander — William H. Jude

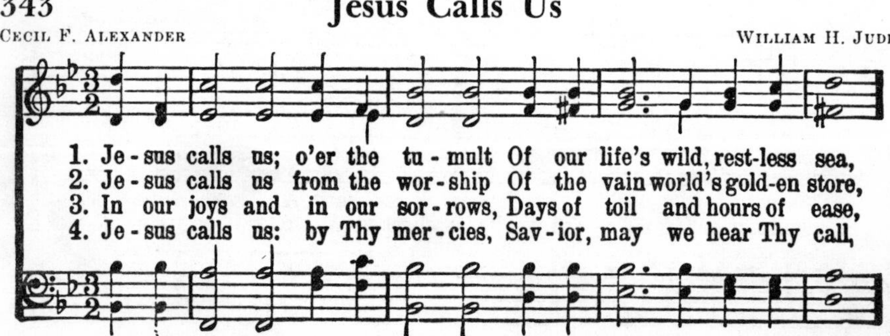
1. Je - sus calls us; o'er the tu - mult Of our life's wild, rest-less sea,
2. Je - sus calls us from the wor - ship Of the vain world's gold-en store,
3. In our joys and in our sor - rows, Days of toil and hours of ease,
4. Je - sus calls us: by Thy mer - cies, Sav - ior, may we hear Thy call,

Jesus Calls Us
Day by day His sweet voice sound-eth, Say-ing, "Chris-tian, fol - low Me."
From each i - dol that would keep us, Say-ing, "Chris-tian, love Me more."
Still He calls, in cares and pleasures, "Chris-tian, love Me more than these."
Give our hearts to Thy o - be-dience, Serve and love Thee best of all.
My Faith Looks Up to Thee
344
Ray Palmer
Lowell Mason
1. My faith looks up to Thee, Thou Lamb of Cal - va - ry,
2. May Thy rich grace im - part Strength to my faint - ing heart,
3. While life's dark maze I tread, And griefs a - round me spread,
4. When ends life's tran-sient dream, When death's cold, sul - len stream
Sav - ior di - vine! Now hear me while I pray, Take all my
My zeal in - spire; As Thou hast died for me, O may my
Be Thou my Guide; Bid dark - ness turn to day, Wipe sor - row's
Shall o'er me roll; Blest Sav - ior, then, in love, Fear and dis-
guilt a - way, O let me from this day Be whol - ly Thine!
love to Thee Pure, warm, and changeless be, A liv - ing fire!
tears a - way, Nor let me ev - er stray From Thee a - side.
trust re - move; O bear me safe a - bove, A ran - somed soul!

345 Hold the Fort

PHILIP P. BLISS — PHILIP P. BLISS

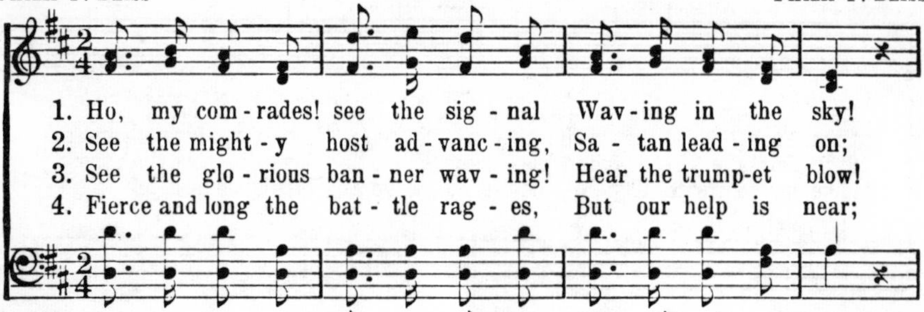

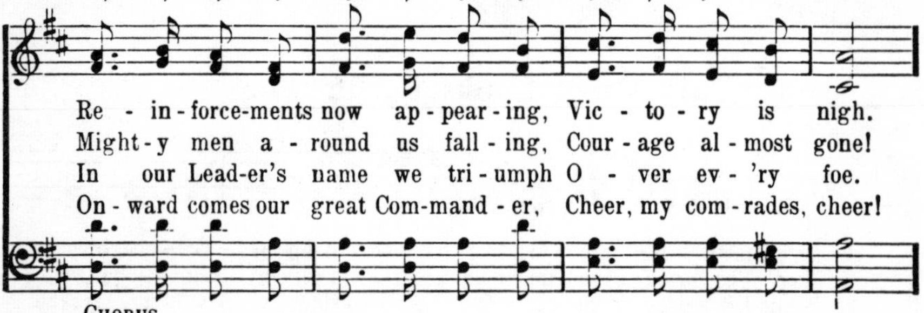

1. Ho, my comrades! see the signal Waving in the sky!
Reinforcements now appearing, Victory is nigh.

2. See the mighty host advancing, Satan leading on;
Mighty men around us falling, Courage almost gone!

3. See the glorious banner waving! Hear the trumpet blow!
In our Leader's name we triumph Over every foe.

4. Fierce and long the battle rages, But our help is near;
Onward comes our great Commander, Cheer, my comrades, cheer!

CHORUS
"Hold the fort, for I am coming," Jesus signals still;
Wave the answer back to heaven, "By Thy grace we will."

346 Fight the Good Fight

JOHN S. B. MONSELL — WILLIAM BOYD

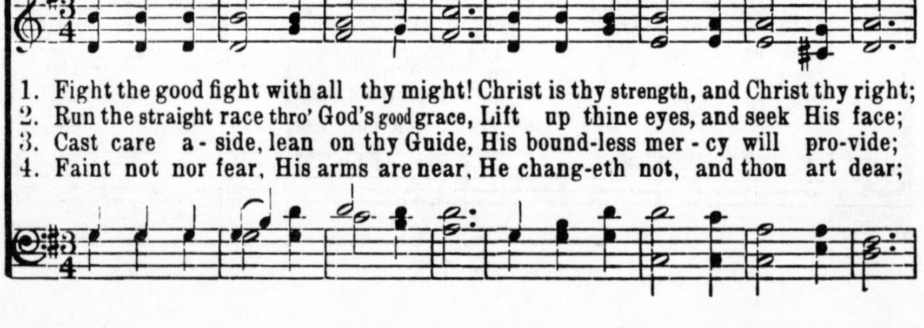

1. Fight the good fight with all thy might! Christ is thy strength, and Christ thy right;
2. Run the straight race thro' God's good grace, Lift up thine eyes, and seek His face;
3. Cast care aside, lean on thy Guide, His boundless mercy will provide;
4. Faint not nor fear, His arms are near, He changeth not, and thou art dear;

Fight the Good Fight
Lay hold on life, and it shall be Thy joy and crown e - ter - nal - ly.
Life with its way be-fore us lies, Christ is the path, and Christ the prize.
Trust, and thy trust-ing soul shall prove Christ is its life, and Christ its love.
On - ly be-lieve, and thou shalt see That Christ is all in all to thee. A-MEN.
Jesus Bids Us Shine
347
SUSAN WARNER
EDWIN O. EXCELL
1. Je - sus bids us shine, With a clear, pure light, Like a lit - tle
2. Je - sus bids us shine, First of all for Him; Well He sees and
3. Je - sus bids us shine, Then, for all a - round Man - y kinds of
4. Je - sus bids us shine, As we work for Him, Bring-ing those that
can - dle Burn - ing in the night; In this world of dark - ness
knows it If our light is dim; He looks down from heav - en,
dark-ness In this world a - bound— Sin, and want, and sor - row:
wan - der From the paths of sin; He will ev - er help us,
We must shine, You in your small cor - ner, And I in mine.
Sees us shine, You in your small cor - ner, And I in mine.
We must shine, You in your small cor - ner, And I in mine.
If we shine, You in your small cor - ner, And I in mine.

348 Give of Your Best to the Master

Howard B. Grose — Charlotte A. Bernard

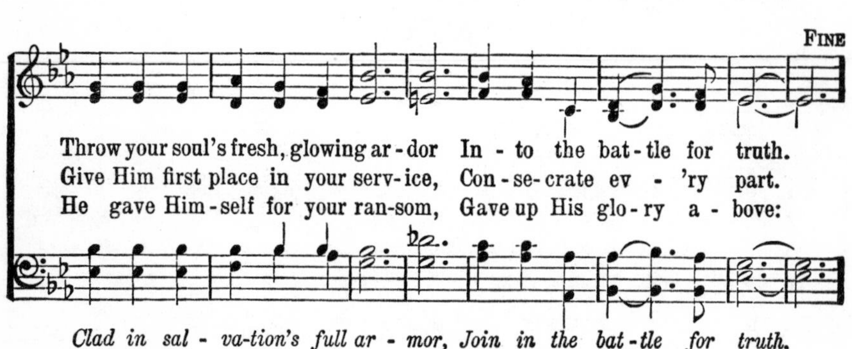

1. Give of your best to the Mas - ter; Give of the strength of your youth;
Throw your soul's fresh, glowing ar - dor In - to the bat - tle for truth.
Je - sus has set the ex - am - ple; Dauntless was He, young and brave;...
Give Him your loy - al de - vo - tion, Give Him the best that you have.....

2. Give of your best to the Mas - ter; Give Him first place in your heart;
Give Him first place in your serv - ice, Con - se - crate ev - 'ry part.
Give, and to you shall be giv - en; God His be - lov - ed Son gave;..
Grate - ful - ly seek - ing to serve Him, Give Him the best that you have.....

3. Give of your best to the Mas - ter; Naught else is wor - thy His love;
He gave Him - self for your ran - som, Gave up His glo - ry a - bove:
Laid down His life with - out mur - mur, You from sin's ru - in to save;...
Give Him your heart's ad - o - ra - tion, Give Him the best that you have.....

Ref.—Give of your best to the Mas - ter; Give of the strength of your youth;
Clad in sal - va - tion's full ar - mor, Join in the bat - tle for truth. Fine

rall. D. C.

I Am Resolved 349

PALMER HARTSOUGH — JAMES H. FILLMORE

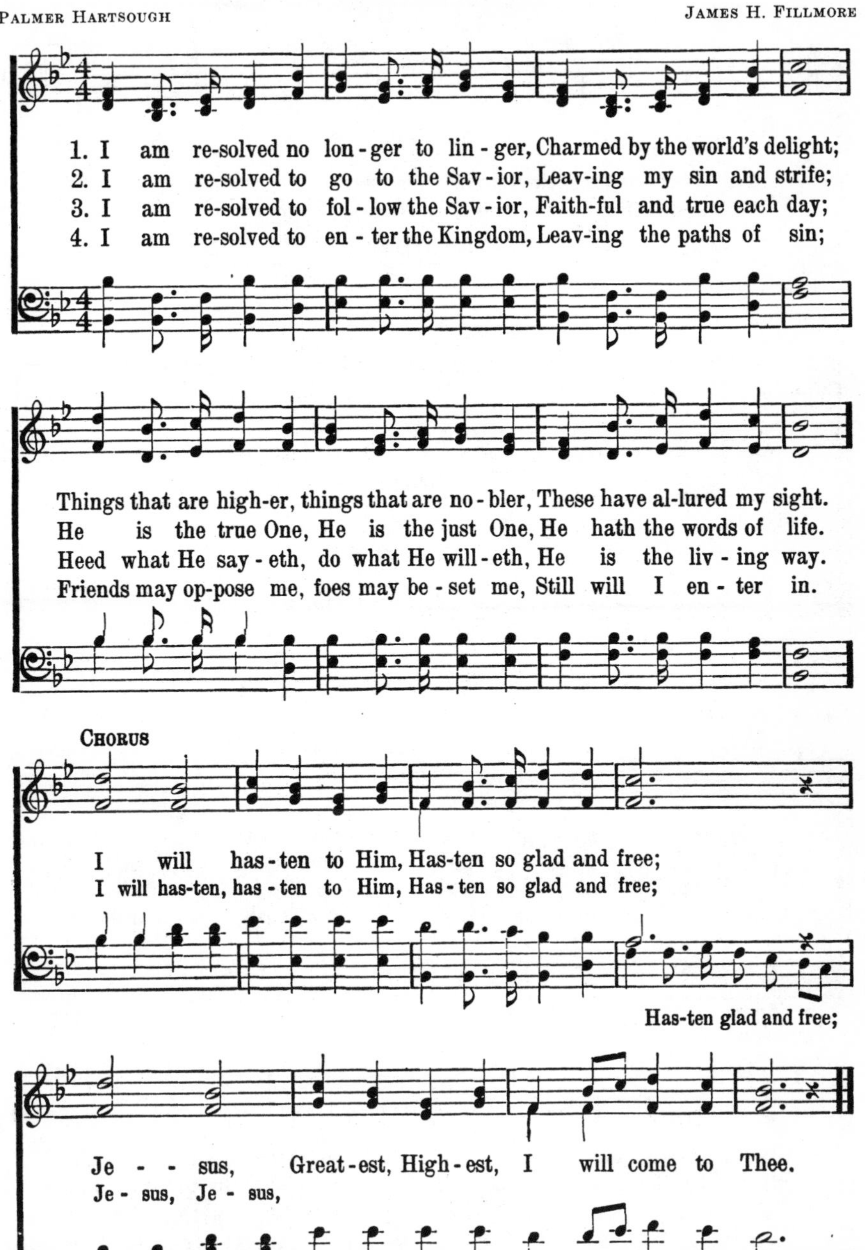

1. I am re-solved no lon-ger to lin-ger, Charmed by the world's delight;
2. I am re-solved to go to the Sav-ior, Leav-ing my sin and strife;
3. I am re-solved to fol-low the Sav-ior, Faith-ful and true each day;
4. I am re-solved to en-ter the Kingdom, Leav-ing the paths of sin;
Things that are high-er, things that are no-bler, These have al-lured my sight.
He is the true One, He is the just One, He hath the words of life.
Heed what He say-eth, do what He will-eth, He is the liv-ing way.
Friends may op-pose me, foes may be-set me, Still will I en-ter in.
CHORUS
I will has-ten to Him, Has-ten so glad and free;
I will has-ten, has-ten to Him, Has-ten so glad and free;
Has-ten glad and free;
Je - - sus, Great-est, High-est, I will come to Thee.
Je-sus, Je-sus,

350 My Soul, Be on Thy Guard
George Heath
Lowell Mason
1. My soul, be on thy guard; Ten thou-sand foes a - rise; The
2. O watch, and fight, and pray; The bat - tle ne'er give o'er; Re-
3. Ne'er think the vic - t'ry won, Nor lay thine ar - mor down; The
4. Fight on, my soul, till death Shall bring thee to thy God; He'll
hosts of sin are press - ing hard To draw thee from the skies.
new it bold - ly ev - 'ry day, And help di - vine im - plore.
work of faith will not be done, Till thou ob - tain the crown.
take thee, at thy part - ing breath, To His di - vine a - bode.
351 Rise Up, O Men of God
William P. Merrill
Aaron Williams
1. Rise up, O men of God! Have done with less - er things;
2. Rise up, O men of God! His king - dom tar - ries long;
3. Rise up, O men of God! The Church for you doth wait,
4. Lift high the cross of Christ! Tread where His feet have trod;
Give heart and mind and soul and strength To serve the King of kings.
Bring in the day of broth - er - hood And end the night of wrong.
Her strength un - e - qual to her task; Rise up, and make her great!
As broth - ers of the Son of man, Rise up, O men of God!

Words used by permission of "The Presbyterian Outlook," Richmond, Virginia 23219

In Times Like These

Ruth Caye Jones Ruth Caye Jones

1. In times like these you need a Sav - iour, In times like
2. In times like these you need the Bi - ble, In times like
3. In times like these I have a Sav - iour, In times like
these you need an an - chor; [D.S.] Be ver - y sure (Be ver - y sure),
these, oh, be not i - dle; [D.S.] Be ver - y sure (Be ver - y sure),
these, I have an an - chor; [D.S.] I'm ver - y sure (I'm ver - y sure),
Be ver - y sure (Be ver - y sure), Your an - chor holds
Be ver - y sure (Be ver - y sure), Your an - chor holds
I'm ver - y sure (I'm ver - y sure), My an - chor holds
and grips the Sol - id Rock!
and grips the Sol - id Rock!
and grips the Sol - id Rock!
Fine
Refrain
This Rock is Je - sus,
Yes, He's the One, This Rock is Je - sus,— The on - ly One;
D. S.

353 Onward, Christian Soldiers

SABINE BARING-GOULD ARTHUR S. SULLIVAN

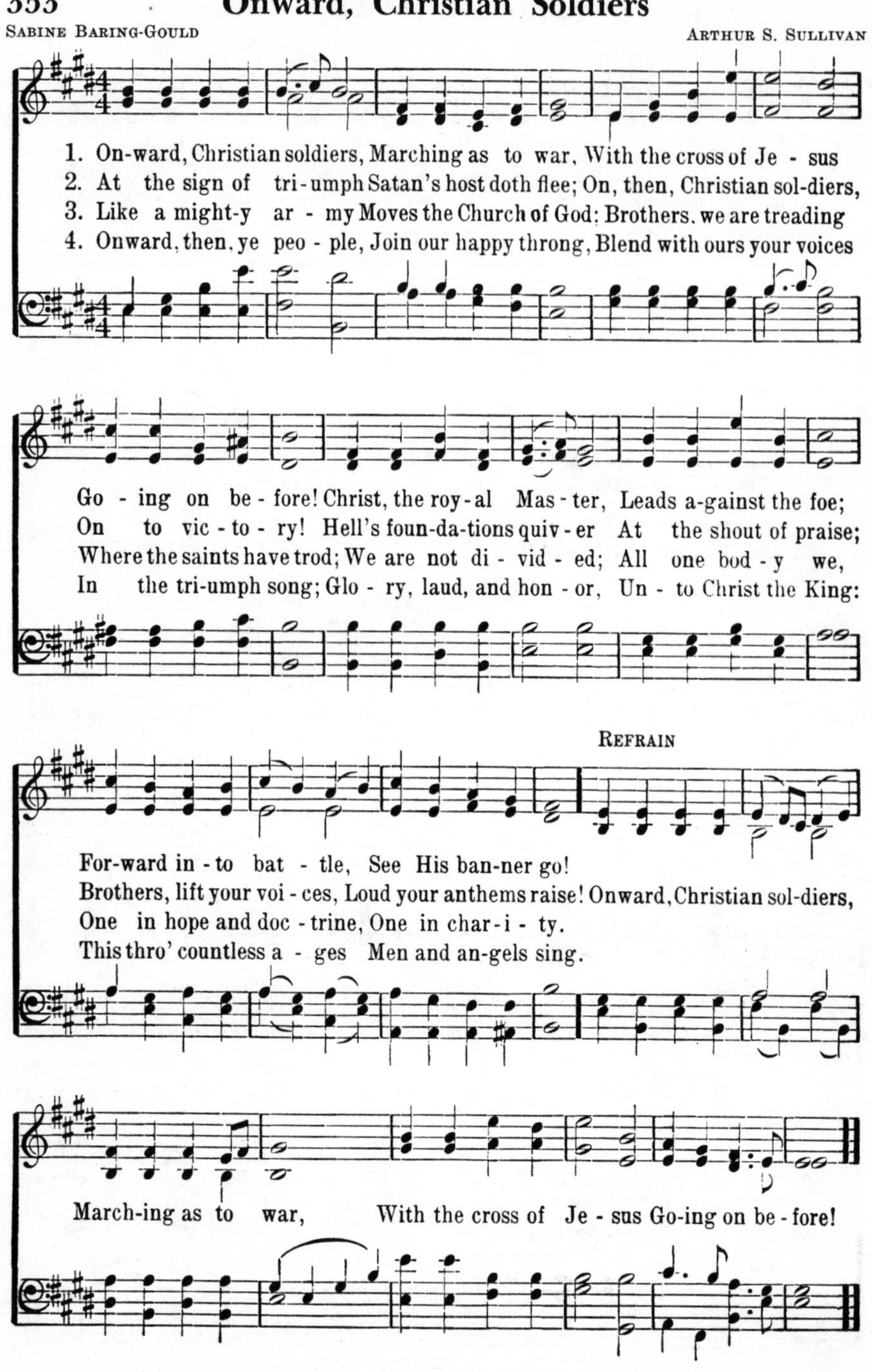
1. On-ward, Christian soldiers, Marching as to war, With the cross of Je - sus
2. At the sign of tri-umph Satan's host doth flee; On, then, Christian sol-diers,
3. Like a might-y ar - my Moves the Church of God: Brothers, we are treading
4. Onward, then, ye peo - ple, Join our happy throng, Blend with ours your voices
Go - ing on be - fore! Christ, the roy - al Mas - ter, Leads a-gainst the foe;
On to vic - to - ry! Hell's foun-da-tions quiv - er At the shout of praise;
Where the saints have trod; We are not di - vid - ed; All one bod - y we,
In the tri-umph song; Glo - ry, laud, and hon - or, Un - to Christ the King:
REFRAIN
For-ward in - to bat - tle, See His ban-ner go!
Brothers, lift your voi - ces, Loud your anthems raise! Onward, Christian sol-diers,
One in hope and doc - trine, One in char - i - ty.
This thro' countless a - ges Men and an-gels sing.
March-ing as to war, With the cross of Je - sus Go-ing on be - fore!

Into My Heart

Harry D. Clarke — Harry D. Clarke

1. Come in - to my heart, bless-ed Je - sus, Come in - to my heart, I pray;
2. Come in - to my heart, bless-ed Je - sus, I need Thee thro' life's drear-y way;
3. Come in - to my heart, bless-ed Je - sus, And take all my guilt a - way;
4. Come in - to my heart, bless-ed Je - sus, O cleanse and il - lu-mine my soul;
My soul is so troub-led and wea - ry, Come in - to my heart to - day.
The bur - den of sin is so heav - y, Come in - to my heart to stay.
Then spotless I'll stand in Thy pres-ence, When breaks Thine e-ter-nal day.
Fill me with Thy won-der-ful Spir - it, Come in and take full con - trol.
Chorus
In - to my heart, in - to my heart, Come in - to my heart, Lord Je - sus;
Come in to - day, Come in to stay, Come in - to my heart, Lord Je - sus.

355 Loyalty to Christ

E. TAYLOR CASSEL FLORA H. CASSEL

1. From o-ver hill and plain There comes the signal strain, 'Tis loy-al-ty, loy-al-ty,
2. O hear, ye brave, the sound That moves the earth around, 'Tis loy-al-ty, loy-al-ty,
3. Come, join our loy-al throng, We'll rout the giant wrong, 'Tis loy-al-ty, loy-al-ty,
4. The strength of youth we lay At Je-sus' feet to-day, 'Tis loy-al-ty, loy-al-ty,
loy-al-ty to Christ; Its mu-sic rolls a-long, The hills take up the song,
loy-al-ty to Christ; A-rise to dare and do, Ring out the watch-word true,
loy-al-ty to Christ; Where Satan's banners float We'll send the bu-gle note,
loy-al-ty to Christ; His gos-pel we'll pro-claim Thro'-out the world's domain,
CHORUS.
Of loy-al-ty, loy-al-ty, Yes, loy-al-ty to Christ. "On to vic-to-ry! On to
vic-to-ry!" Cries our great Commander; "On!" . . . We'll move at His command,
great Commander; "On!"
We'll soon possess the land, Thro' loyalty, loyalty, Yes, loy-al-ty to Christ. A-MEN.

Soldiers of Christ, Arise! 356

CHARLES WESLEY, ARR. GEORGE J. ELVEY

1. Sol - diers of Christ, a - rise, And put your ar - mor on,
2. Stand then in His great might, With all His strength en - dued,
3. Leave no un-guard - ed place, No weak - ness of the soul,

Strong in the strength which God sup-plies Through His e - ter - nal Son;
And take, to arm you for the fight, The pan - o - ply of God;
Take ev - 'ry vir - tue, ev - 'ry grace, And fort - i - fy the whole,

Strong in the Lord of hosts, And in His might - y pow'r,
That hav - ing all things done, And all your con - flicts past,
From strength to strength go on, Wres - tle and fight and pray,

Who in the strength of Je - sus trusts Is more than con - quer - or.
Ye may o'er-come through Christ a - lone, And stand en - tire at last.
Tread all the pow'rs of dark - ness down, And win the well-fought day.

357 Stand Up, Stand Up for Jesus

George Duffield — Adam Geibel

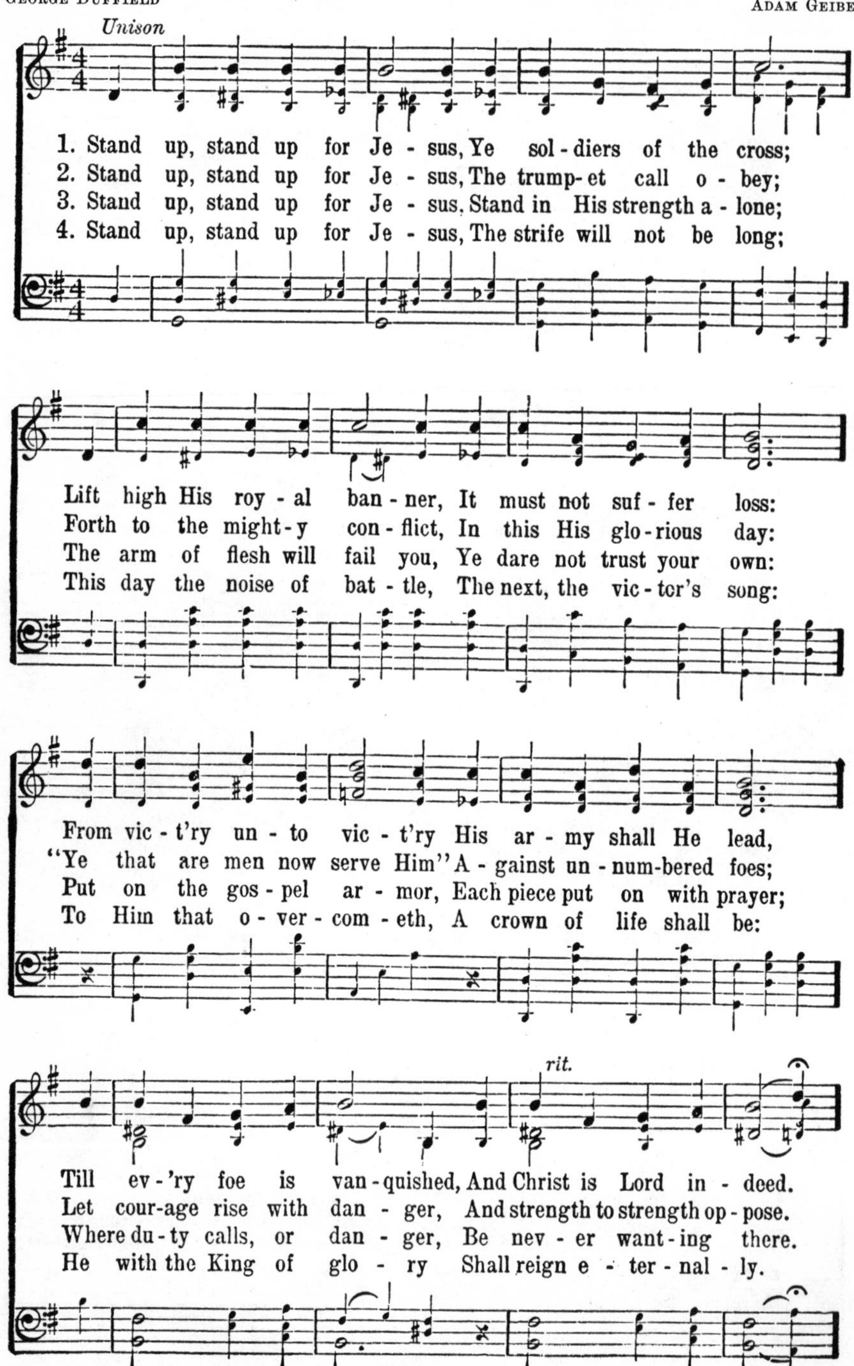

Unison
1. Stand up, stand up for Je - sus, Ye sol - diers of the cross;
2. Stand up, stand up for Je - sus, The trump - et call o - bey;
3. Stand up, stand up for Je - sus, Stand in His strength a - lone;
4. Stand up, stand up for Je - sus, The strife will not be long;
Lift high His roy - al ban - ner, It must not suf - fer loss:
Forth to the might - y con - flict, In this His glo - rious day:
The arm of flesh will fail you, Ye dare not trust your own:
This day the noise of bat - tle, The next, the vic - tor's song:
From vic - t'ry un - to vic - t'ry His ar - my shall He lead,
"Ye that are men now serve Him" A - gainst un - num - bered foes;
Put on the gos - pel ar - mor, Each piece put on with prayer;
To Him that o - ver - com - eth, A crown of life shall be:
rit.
Till ev - 'ry foe is van - quished, And Christ is Lord in - deed.
Let cour - age rise with dan - ger, And strength to strength op - pose.
Where du - ty calls, or dan - ger, Be nev - er want - ing there.
He with the King of glo - ry Shall reign e - ter - nal - ly.

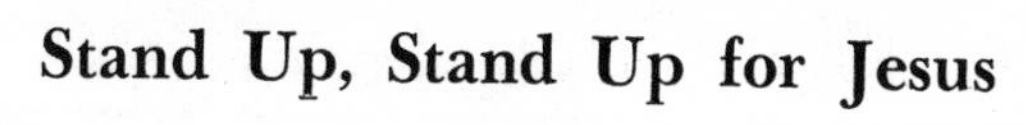
Stand Up, Stand Up for Jesus

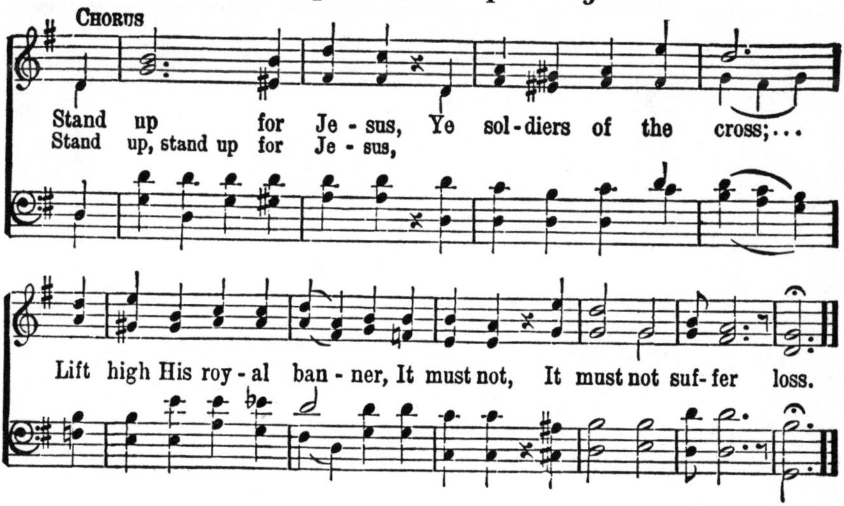

CHORUS

Stand up for Je - sus, Ye sol - diers of the cross;...
Stand up, stand up for Je - sus,
Lift high His roy - al ban - ner, It must not, It must not suf - fer loss.

Stand Up, Stand Up for Jesus 358

GEORGE DUFFIELD

GEORGE J. WEBB

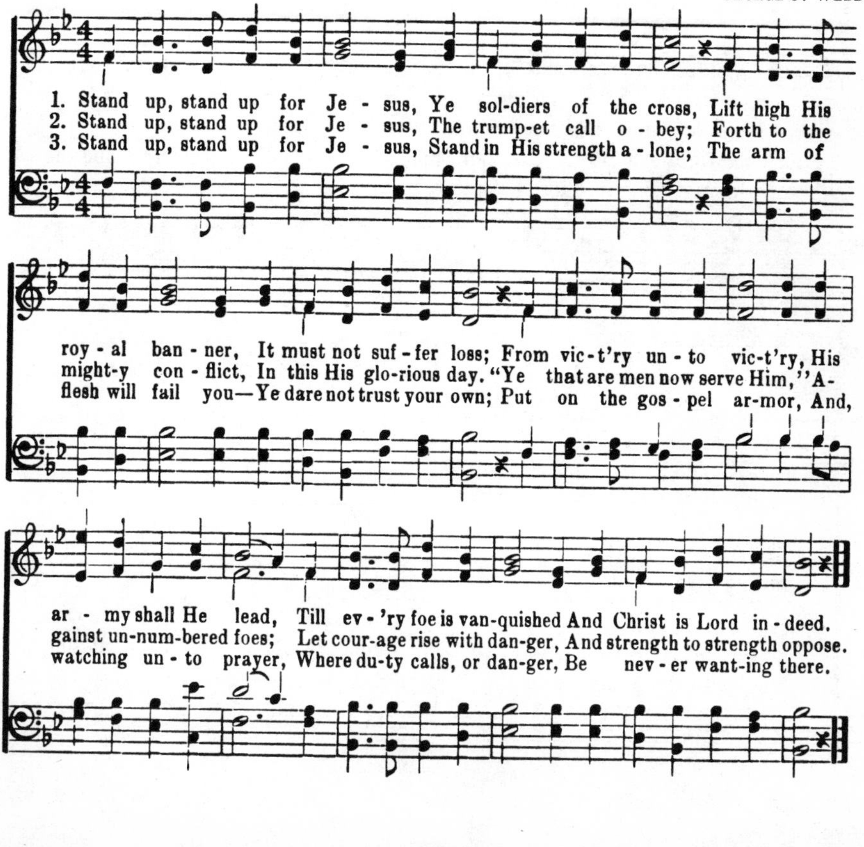

1. Stand up, stand up for Je - sus, Ye sol - diers of the cross, Lift high His roy - al ban - ner, It must not suf - fer loss; From vic - t'ry un - to vic - t'ry, His ar - my shall He lead, Till ev - 'ry foe is van - quished And Christ is Lord in - deed.

2. Stand up, stand up for Je - sus, The trump - et call o - bey; Forth to the might - y con - flict, In this His glo - rious day. "Ye that are men now serve Him," A - gainst un - num - bered foes; Let cour - age rise with dan - ger, And strength to strength oppose.

3. Stand up, stand up for Je - sus, Stand in His strength a - lone; The arm of flesh will fail you—Ye dare not trust your own; Put on the gos - pel ar - mor, And, watching un - to prayer, Where du - ty calls, or dan - ger, Be nev - er want - ing there.

359 Sound the Battle Cry

WILLIAM F. SHERWIN | WILLIAM F. SHERWIN

1. Sound the bat-tle cry! See, the foe is nigh; Raise the standard high For the Lord; Gird your ar-mor on, Stand firm, ev-'ry one; Rest your cause up-on His ho-ly word.
2. Strong to meet the foe, Marching on we go, While our cause we know, Must pre-vail; Shield and banner bright, Gleam-ing in the light; Bat-tling for the right We ne'er can fail.
3. O! Thou God of all, Hear us when we call, Help us one and all By Thy grace; When the bat-tle's done, And the vic-t'ry's won, May we wear the crown Be-fore Thy face.
CHORUS ff
Rouse, then, sol-diers, ral-ly round the ban-ner, Read-y, stead-y, pass the word a-long; On-ward, for-ward, shout a-loud Ho-san-na! Christ is Cap-tain of the might-y throng.

The Banner of the Cross

DANIEL W. WHITTLE

JAMES MCGRANAHAN

1. There's a roy - al ban - ner giv - en for dis-play To the sol- diers
2. Though the foe may rage and gath - er as the flood, Let the stand-ard
3. O - ver land and sea, wher-ev - er man may dwell, Make the glo - rious
4. When the glo - ry dawns—'tis draw-ing ver - y near—It is has-t'ning
3
of the King; As an en - sign fair we lift it up to-day,
be dis - played; And be-neath its folds, as sol - diers of the Lord,
ti - dings known; Of the crim - son ban - ner now the sto - ry tell,
day by day— Then be - fore our King the foe shall dis - ap-pear,
3
CHORUS
3
While as ran-somed ones we sing.
For the truth be not dis-mayed! March-ing on, . . . march-ing
While the Lord shall claim His own! on, on,
And the cross the world shall sway!
3
on, . . For Christ count ev - 'ry-thing but loss! . . . . . . And to
on, on, ev - 'ry-thing, ev - 'ry - thing but loss!
crown Him King, toil and sing 'Neath the ban - ner of the cross!
we'll Be - neath

361 Am I a Soldier of the Cross?

ISAAC WATTS — THOMAS A. ARNE

1. Am I a sol - dier of the cross, A fol-low'r of the Lamb?
2. Must I be car - ried to the skies On flow-'ry beds of ease,
3. Are there no foes for me to face? Must I not stem the flood?
4. Sure I must fight, if I would reign; In -crease my cour - age, Lord;

And shall I fear to own His cause, Or blush to speak His name?
While oth-ers fought to win the prize, And sailed thro' blood - y seas?
Is this vile world a friend to grace, To help me on to God?
I'll bear the toil, en - dure the pain, Sup - port - ed by Thy word.

362 A Charge to Keep I Have

CHARLES WESLEY — LOWELL MASON

1. A charge to keep I have, A God to glo - ri - fy;
2. To serve the pres - ent age, My call - ing to ful - fill;
3. Arm me with jeal - ous care, As in Thy sight to live,
4. Help me to watch and pray, And on Thy - self re - ly,

A nev - er - dy - ing soul to save, And fit it for the sky.
O may it all my pow'rs en-gage, To do my Mas - ter's will!
And O, Thy serv-ant, Lord, pre-pare, A strict ac-count to give!
As - sured, if I my trust be - tray, I shall for - ev - er die.

To the Work! 363

FANNY J. CROSBY WILLIAM H. DOANE

1. To the work! to the work! we are serv-ants of God, Let us fol - low the
2. To the work! to the work! let the hun - gry be fed; To the foun-tain of
3. To the work! to the work! there is la - bor for all; For the king-dom of
4. To the work! to the work! in the strength of the Lord, And a robe and a
path that our Mas - ter has trod; With the balm of His coun - sel our
life let the wea - ry be led; In the cross and its ban - ner our
dark-ness and er - ror shall fall; And the name of Je - ho - vah ex-
crown shall our la - bor re - ward, When the home of the faith - ful our
strength to re - new, Let us do with our might what our hands find to do.
glo - ry shall be, While we her - ald the ti - dings, "Sal - va - tion is free!"
alt - ed shall be, In the loud swell-ing cho - rus, "Sal - va - tion is free!"
dwell - ing shall be, And we shout with the ransomed, "Sal - va - tion is free!"
CHORUS
Toil-ing on, toil-ing on, Toil-ing on, toil-ing on;
Toil-ing on, toil-ing on, Toil-ing on, toil-ing on;
Let us hope, let us watch, And la - bor till the Mas-ter comes.
and trust, and pray,

364 True-Hearted, Whole-Hearted

FRANCES R. HAVERGAL | GEORGE C. STEBBINS

1. True-hearted, whole-hearted, faith-ful and loy - al, King of our lives, by Thy
2. True-hearted, whole-hearted, full - est al - le-giance Yielding henceforth to our
3. True-hearted, whole-hearted, Sav - ior all - glo-rious! Take Thy great pow-er and
grace we will be; Un-der the standard ex-alt-ed and roy - al, Strong in Thy
glo - ri - ous King; Val-iant en-deav-or and lov - ing o-be-dience, Free - ly and
reign there a - lone, O - ver our wills and af-fec-tions vic-to-rious, Free - ly sur-
strength we will bat-tle for Thee.
joy - ous - ly now would we bring.
ren-dered and whol-ly Thine own.
CHORUS
Peal out the watch-word! si - lence it nev-er!
Peal out the watch-word! si - lence it nev-er!
Song of our spir-its, re - joic - ing and free; Peal out the watch-word!
Song of our spir - its, re - joic-ing and free; Peal out the watch-word!
loy - al for-ev - er, King of our lives, by Thy grace we will be.
loy - al for - ev - er, King of our lives, by Thy grace we will be.

Trust and Obey

John H. Sammis

Daniel B. Towner

1. When we walk with the Lord In the Light of His Word What a glo - ry He
2. Not a shad-ow can rise, Not a cloud in the skies, But His smile quickly
3. Not a bur-den we bear, Not a sor-row we share, But our toil He doth
4. But we nev-er can prove The de-lights of His love Un-til all on the
5. Then in fel-low-ship sweet We will sit at His feet, Or we'll walk by His

sheds on our way! While we do His good-will, He a-bides with us still,
drives it a-way; Not a doubt or a fear, Not a sigh nor a tear,
rich-ly re-pay; Not a grief nor a loss, Not a frown or a cross,
al-tar we lay; For the fa-vor He shows, And the joy He be-stows,
side in the way; What He says we will do, Where He sends we will go,—

Chorus.

And with all who will trust and o - bey.
Can a-bide while we trust and o - bey.
But is blest if we trust and o - bey. Trust and o - bey, for there's no oth-er
Are for them who will trust and o - bey.
Nev-er fear, on-ly trust and o - bey.

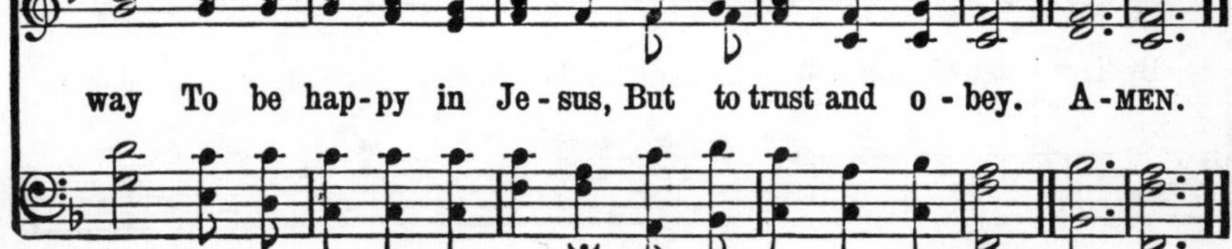
way To be hap-py in Je-sus, But to trust and o-bey. A-men.

366 Who Is on the Lord's Side?

FRANCES R. HAVERGAL | ARR. BY JOHN GOSS

1. Who is on the Lord's side? Who will serve the King? Who will be His help - ers
2. Not for weight of glo - ry, Not for crown and palm, En - ter we the ar - my,
3. Je - sus, Thou hast bought us, Not with gold or gem, But with Thine own life-blood,
4. Fierce may be the con - flict, Strong may be the foe, But the King's own ar - my

Oth - er lives to bring? Who will leave the world's side? Who will face the foe?
Raise the warrior psalm; But for love that claim-eth Lives for whom He died:
For Thy di - a - dem: With Thy blessing fill - ing Each who comes to Thee,
None can o - ver-throw: Round His standard rang-ing, Vic - t'ry to se - cure;

Who is on the Lord's side? Who for Him will go? By Thy call of mer - cy,
He whom Je - sus nam - eth Must be on His side. By Thy love constraining,
Thou hast made us will - ing, Thou hast made us free. By Thy grand redemption,
For His truth un-chang-ing Makes the tri - umph sure. Joy-ful - ly en - list - ing

By Thy grace di - vine, We are on the Lord's side, Sav - ior, we are Thine.

The Church in the Wildwood 367

WILLIAM S. PITTS | WILLIAM S. PITTS

1. There's a church in the val-ley by the wild-wood, No love-li-er spot in the dale; No place is so dear to my child-hood As the lit-tle brown church in the vale.
2. Oh, come to the church in the wild-wood, To the trees where the wild flow-ers bloom; Where the part-ing hymn will be chant-ed, We will weep by the side of the tomb.
3. How sweet on a clear Sun-day morn-ing, To list to the clear ring-ing bell; Its tones so sweet-ly are call-ing, Oh, come to the church in the vale.
4. From the church in the val-ley by the wild-wood, When day fades a-way in-to night, I would fain from this spot of my child-hood Wing my way to the man-sions of light.
D.S.—No spot is so dear to my child-hood As the lit-tle brown church in the vale.
FINE
CHORUS
Oh, come, come, come, come, come, come,
Come to the church in the wild - wood, Oh, come to the church in the vale;
come, come, come, come, come, come, come, come, come, come, come, come, come;
D.S.

368 If Jesus Had Not Come!

ALBERT C. NORTON — DONALD P. HUSTAD

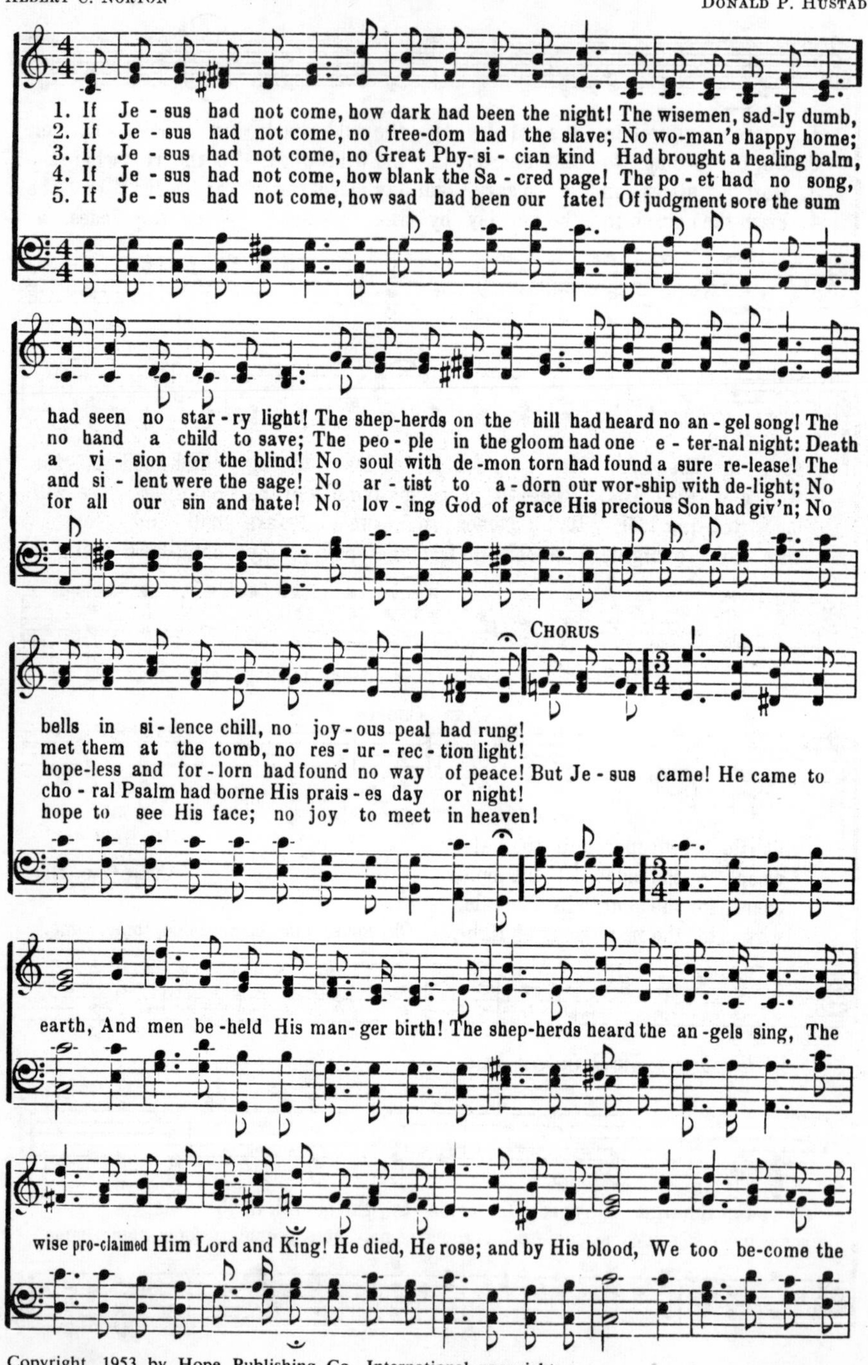
1. If Je - sus had not come, how dark had been the night! The wisemen, sad-ly dumb,
2. If Je - sus had not come, no free-dom had the slave; No wo-man's happy home;
3. If Je - sus had not come, no Great Phy- si - cian kind Had brought a healing balm,
4. If Je - sus had not come, how blank the Sa - cred page! The po - et had no song,
5. If Je - sus had not come, how sad had been our fate! Of judgment sore the sum
had seen no star - ry light! The shep-herds on the hill had heard no an - gel song! The
no hand a child to save; The peo - ple in the gloom had one e - ter-nal night: Death
a vi - sion for the blind! No soul with de-mon torn had found a sure re-lease! The
and si - lent were the sage! No ar - tist to a - dorn our wor-ship with de-light; No
for all our sin and hate! No lov - ing God of grace His precious Son had giv'n; No
bells in si - lence chill, no joy - ous peal had rung!
met them at the tomb, no res - ur - rec - tion light!
hope-less and for - lorn had found no way of peace!
cho - ral Psalm had borne His prais - es day or night!
hope to see His face; no joy to meet in heaven!
CHORUS
But Je - sus came! He came to
earth, And men be - held His man - ger birth! The shep-herds heard the an - gels sing, The
wise pro-claimed Him Lord and King! He died, He rose; and by His blood, We too be-come the

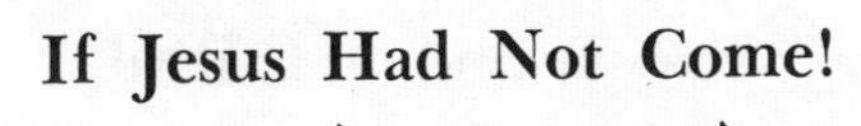
If Jesus Had Not Come!

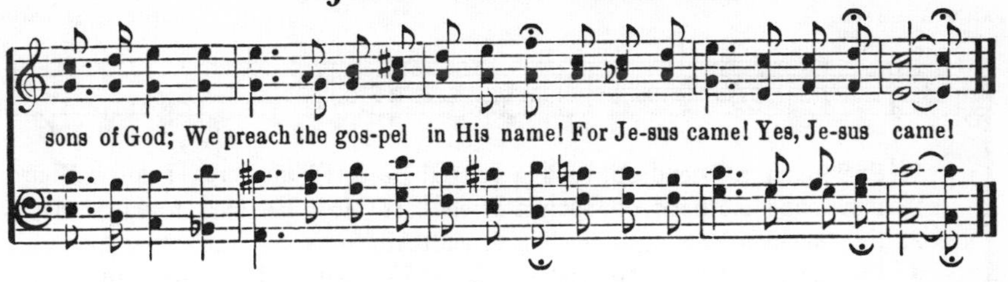
sons of God; We preach the gos-pel in His name! For Je-sus came! Yes, Je-sus came!

Wounded for Me

369

W. G. OVENS AND GLADYS W. ROBERTS

W. G. OVENS

1. Wound-ed for me, wound-ed for me, There on the cross
2. Dy - ing for me, dy - ing for me. There on the cross
3. Ris - en for me, ris - en for me, Up from the grave
4. Liv - ing for me, liv - ing for me, Up in the skies
5. Com - ing for me, com - ing for me, One day to earth

He was wound - ed for me; Gone my trans - gres - sions, and
He was dy - ing for me; Now in His death my re-
He has ris - en for me; Now ev - er - more from death's
He is liv - ing for me; Dai - ly He's plead - ing and
He is com - ing for me; Then with what joy His dear

now I am free, All be - cause Je - sus was wound-ed for me.
demp-tion I see, All be - cause Je - sus was dy - ing for me.
sting I am free, All be - cause Je - sus has ris - en for me.
pray - ing for me, All be - cause Je - sus is liv - ing for me.
face I shall see, Oh, how I praise Him! He's com - ing for me.

370 I've Found a Friend

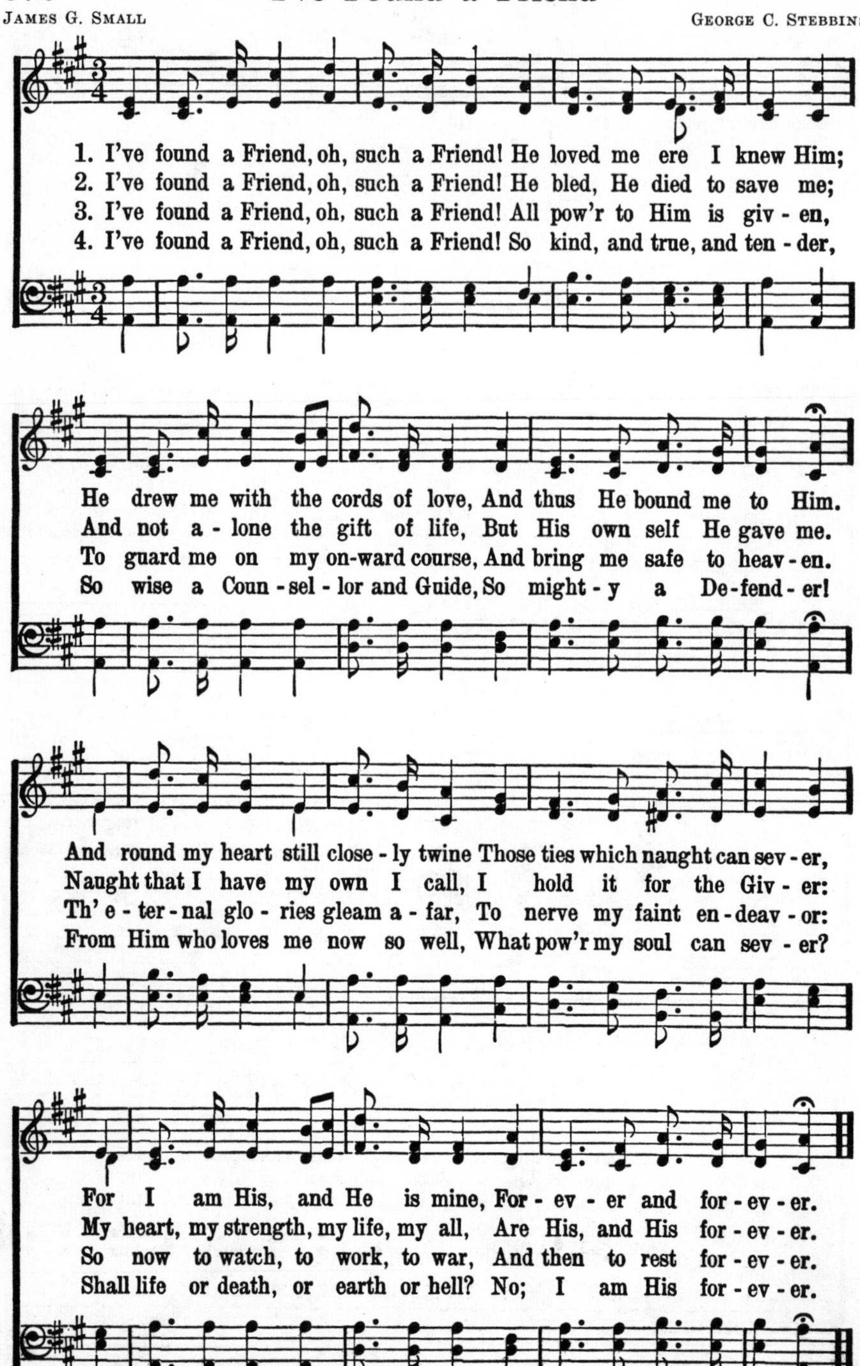
JAMES G. SMALL
GEORGE C. STEBBINS
1. I've found a Friend, oh, such a Friend! He loved me ere I knew Him;
2. I've found a Friend, oh, such a Friend! He bled, He died to save me;
3. I've found a Friend, oh, such a Friend! All pow'r to Him is giv - en,
4. I've found a Friend, oh, such a Friend! So kind, and true, and ten - der,
He drew me with the cords of love, And thus He bound me to Him.
And not a - lone the gift of life, But His own self He gave me.
To guard me on my on-ward course, And bring me safe to heav - en.
So wise a Coun - sel - lor and Guide, So might - y a De-fend - er!
And round my heart still close - ly twine Those ties which naught can sev - er,
Naught that I have my own I call, I hold it for the Giv - er:
Th' e - ter - nal glo - ries gleam a - far, To nerve my faint en - deav - or:
From Him who loves me now so well, What pow'r my soul can sev - er?
For I am His, and He is mine, For - ev - er and for - ev - er.
My heart, my strength, my life, my all, Are His, and His for - ev - er.
So now to watch, to work, to war, And then to rest for - ev - er.
Shall life or death, or earth or hell? No; I am His for - ev - er.

In Tenderness He Sought Me 371

W. Spencer Walton | Adoniram J. Gordon

1. In ten - der - ness He sought me, Wea - ry and sick with sin,
2. He washed the bleed - ing sin-wounds, And poured in oil and wine;
3. He point - ed to the nail - prints, For me His blood was shed,
4. I'm sit - ting in His pres - ence, The sun - shine of His face,
5. So while the hours are pass - ing, All now is per - fect rest;
And on His shoul-ders brought me Back to His fold a - gain. While
He whis-pered to as - sure me, "I've found thee, thou art Mine;" I
A mock - ing crown so thorn - y Was placed up - on His head: I
While with a - dor - ing won - der His bless - ings I re - trace. It
I'm wait - ing for the morn - ing, The bright-est and the best. When
an - gels in His pres - ence sang Un - til the courts of heav - en rang.
nev - er heard a sweet - er voice; It made my ach - ing heart re - joice!
won-dered what He saw in me, To suf - fer such deep ag - o - ny.
seems as if e - ter - nal days Are far too short to sound His praise.
He will call us to His side, To be with Him, His spot - less bride.
Chorus
Oh, the love that sought me! Oh, the blood that bought me! Oh, the grace that
brought me to the fold, Won-drous grace that brought me to the fold!

372 The King of Love My Shepherd Is

FROM PSALM 23
HENRY W. BAKER

JOHN B. DYKES

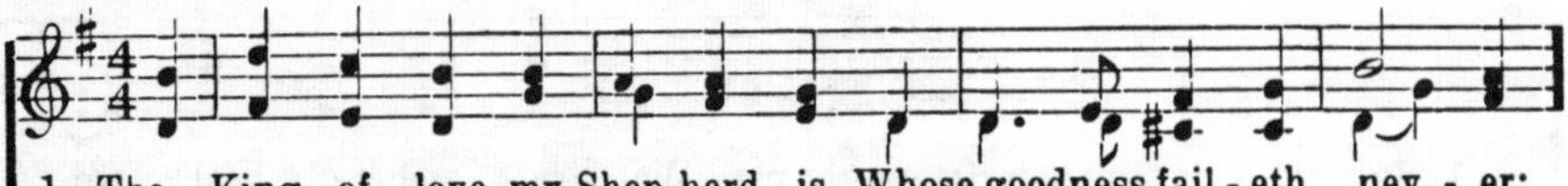

1. The King of love my Shep-herd is, Whose goodness fail-eth nev-er;
I noth-ing lack if I am His, And He is mine for-ev-er.

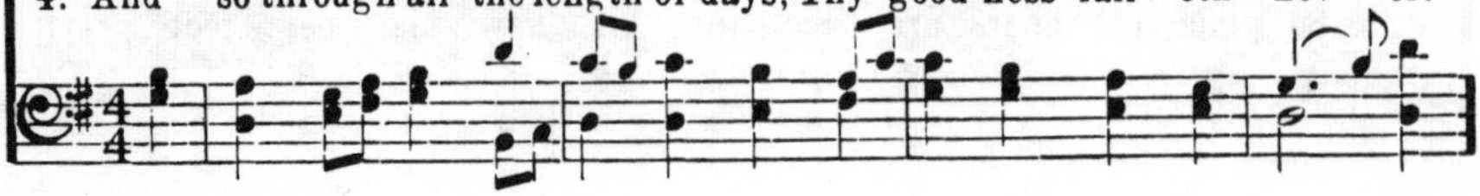

2. Where streams of liv-ing wa-ter flow My ran-somed soul He lead-eth,
And, where the ver-dant pas-tures grow, With food ce-les-tial feed-eth.

3. In death's dark vale I fear no ill With Thee, dear Lord, be-side me;
Thy rod and staff my com-fort still, Thy cross be-fore to guide me.

4. And so through all the length of days, Thy good-ness fail-eth nev-er:
Good Shep-herd, may I sing Thy praise With-in Thy house for-ev-er.

373 The Lord's My Shepherd

PSALM 23
"SCOTTISH PSALTER"

JESSIE S. IRVINE
HAR. BY DAVID GRANT

1. The Lord's my Shep-herd, I'll not want; He makes me down to lie
In pas-tures green; He lead-eth me The qui-et wa-ters by.

2. My soul He doth re-store a-gain. And me to walk, doth make,
With-in the paths of right-eous-ness, E'en for His own name's sake.

3. Yea, tho' I walk in death's dark vale, Yet will I fear no ill;
For Thou art with me, and Thy rod—And staff me com-fort still.

4. My ta-ble Thou hast fur-nish-ed In pres-ence of my foes:
My head Thou dost with oil a-noint, And my cup o-ver flows.

5. Good-ness and mer-cy all my life Shall sure-ly fol-low me,
And in God's house for ev-er-more My dwell-ing place shall be.

The Lord Is My Shepherd

PSALM 23
JAMES MONTGOMERY

THOMAS KOSCHAT
ARR. BY EDWIN O. EXCELL

1. The Lord is my Shep-herd, no want shall I know; I feed in green
2. Thro' the val-ley and shad-ow of death tho' I stray, Since Thou art my
3. In the midst of af - flic - tion my ta - ble is spread; With blessings un-
4. Let good-ness and mer - cy, my boun - ti - ful God, Still fol - low my
pas - tures, safe-fold - ed I rest; He lead - eth my soul where the
Guard-ian, no e - vil I fear; Thy rod shall de - fend me, Thy
meas-ured my cup run-neth o'er; With per-fume and oil Thou a-
steps till I meet Thee a - bove: I seek by the path which my
still wa - ters flow, Re - stores me when wan-d'ring, redeems when op-
staff be my stay; No harm can be - fall with my Com - fort - er
noint-est my head; O what shall I ask of Thy prov - i - dence
fore - fa - thers trod, Thro' the land of their so-journ, Thy king-dom of
pressed; Re - stores me when wan-d'ring, re - deems when op - pressed.
near; No harm can be - fall with my Com - fort - er near.
more? O what shall I ask of Thy prov - i - dence more?
love; Thro' the land of their so - journ, Thy king - dom of love.

375 Ivory Palaces

HENRY BARRACLOUGH HENRY BARRACLOUGH

1. My Lord has garments so wondrous fine, And myrrh their tex-ture fills;
2. His life had al - so its sor-rows sore, For al - oes had a part;
3. His gar-ments too were in cas - sia dipped, With healing in a touch;
4. In gar-ments glo - ri - ous He will come, To o - pen wide the door;

Its fragrance reached to this heart of mine, With joy my be - ing thrills.
And when I think of the cross He bore, My eyes with tear-drops start.
Each time my feet in some sin have slipped, He took me from its clutch.
And I shall en - ter my heav'nly home, To dwell for - ev - er - more.

CHORUS
DUET—*Slowly, softly, and with much expression*

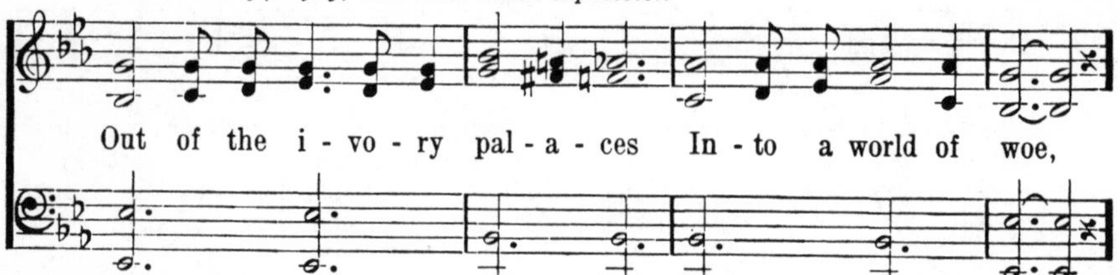

Out of the i - vo - ry pal - a - ces In - to a world of woe,

FULL CHORUS DUET—*Very softly*

On - ly His great e - ter - nal love.... Made my Sav - ior go.

What a Wonderful Savior!

Elisha A. Hoffman — Elisha A. Hoffman

1. Christ has for sin a-tone-ment made, What a won-der-ful Sav-ior!
We are re-deemed! the price is paid! What a won-der-ful Sav-ior!

2. I praise Him for the cleans-ing blood, What a won-der-ful Sav-ior!
That rec-on-ciled my soul to God; What a won-der-ful Sav-ior!

3. He cleansed my heart from all its sin, What a won-der-ful Sav-ior!
And now He reigns and rules there-in; What a won-der-ful Sav-ior!

4. He gives me o-ver-com-ing pow'r, What a won-der-ful Sav-ior!
And tri-umph in each try-ing hour; What a won-der-ful Sav-ior!

5. To Him I've giv-en all my heart, What a won-der-ful Sav-ior!
The world shall nev-er share a part; What a won-der-ful Sav-ior!

CHORUS

What a won-der-ful Sav-ior is Je-sus, my Je-sus!
What a won-der-ful Sav-ior is Je-sus, my Lord!

377 One Day!

J. Wilbur Chapman — Charles H. Marsh

1. One day when heav - en was filled with His prais - es, One day when sin was as black as could be, . . . Je - sus came forth to be born of a vir - gin—Dwelt amongst men, my ex - am - ple is He! . . .
2. One day they led Him up Cal - va - ry's moun-tain, One day they nailed Him to die on the tree; . . Suf - fer - ing an - guish, de - spised and re - ject - ed: Bear - ing our sins, my Re - deem - er is He! . . .
3. One day they left Him a - lone in the gar - den, One day He rest - ed, from suf - fer - ing free; . . An - gels came down o'er His tomb to keep vig - il; Hope of the hope - less, my Sav - ior is He! . . .
4. One day the grave could con - ceal Him no lon - ger, One day the stone rolled a - way from the door; . Then He a - rose, o - ver death He had con - quered; Now is as - cend - ed, my Lord ev - er - more! .
5. One day the trump - et will sound for His com - ing, One day the skies with His glo - ries will shine; Won - der - ful day, my be - lov - ed ones bring - ing; Glo - ri - ous Sav - ior, this Je - sus is mine! .
Chorus
Liv - ing, He loved me; dy - ing, He saved me; Bur - ied, He car - ried my sins far a - way; . . Ris - ing, He jus - ti - fied

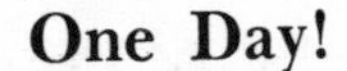
One Day!

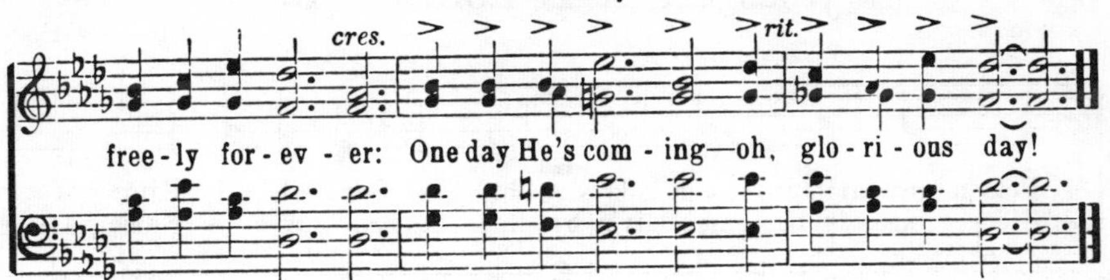
cres.
rit.
free-ly for-ev-er: One day He's com-ing—oh, glo-ri-ous day!

Take the Name of Jesus with You 378

Lydia Baxter — William H. Doane

1. Take the name of Je-sus with you, Child of sor-row and of woe;
It will joy and com-fort give you, Take it, then, wher-e'er you go.

2. Take the name of Je-sus ev-er, As a shield from ev-'ry snare;
If temp-ta-tions round you gath-er, Breathe that ho-ly name in prayer.

3. O the precious name of Je-sus! How it thrills our souls with joy,
When His lov-ing arms re-ceive us, And His songs our tongues em-ploy!

4. At the name of Je-sus bow-ing, Fall-ing pros-trate at His feet,
King of kings in Heav'n we'll crown Him, When our jour-ney is com-plete.

CHORUS

Pre-cious name, (Precious name,) O how sweet! (O how sweet!) Hope of earth and joy of Heav'n;
Pre-cious name, (Precious name,) O how sweet!... (O how sweet, how sweet!) Hope of earth and joy of Heav'n.

379 Jesus Christ Is Lord of All

DON WHITMAN | DON WHITMAN

1. Heav'n and earth pro-claim Je-sus Christ is Lord of all; King of
2. Glo - rious is His name Giv'n by God in heav'n a-bove. Name a -
Kings is He Whom an-gel hosts a - dore! Let men and na-tions bring
bove all names, And ev - er-more shall be. Come ev - 'ry knee, and bow,
Prais-es to Christ the King, Who o - ver all shall reign For-ev - er-more.
Come ev-'ry tongue, con-fess That Je-sus Christ is Lord E - ter-nal - ly.
CHORUS
WOMEN-UNISON or TWO PARTS
MEN-UNISON
Sing, my heart, oh praise His name; Je-sus Christ is Lord of all! Sing, ye
ALL PARTS
saints, His grace pro-claim; Je-sus Christ is Lord of all! At His
word the grave will o-pen, At His feet death's bonds will fall. King of

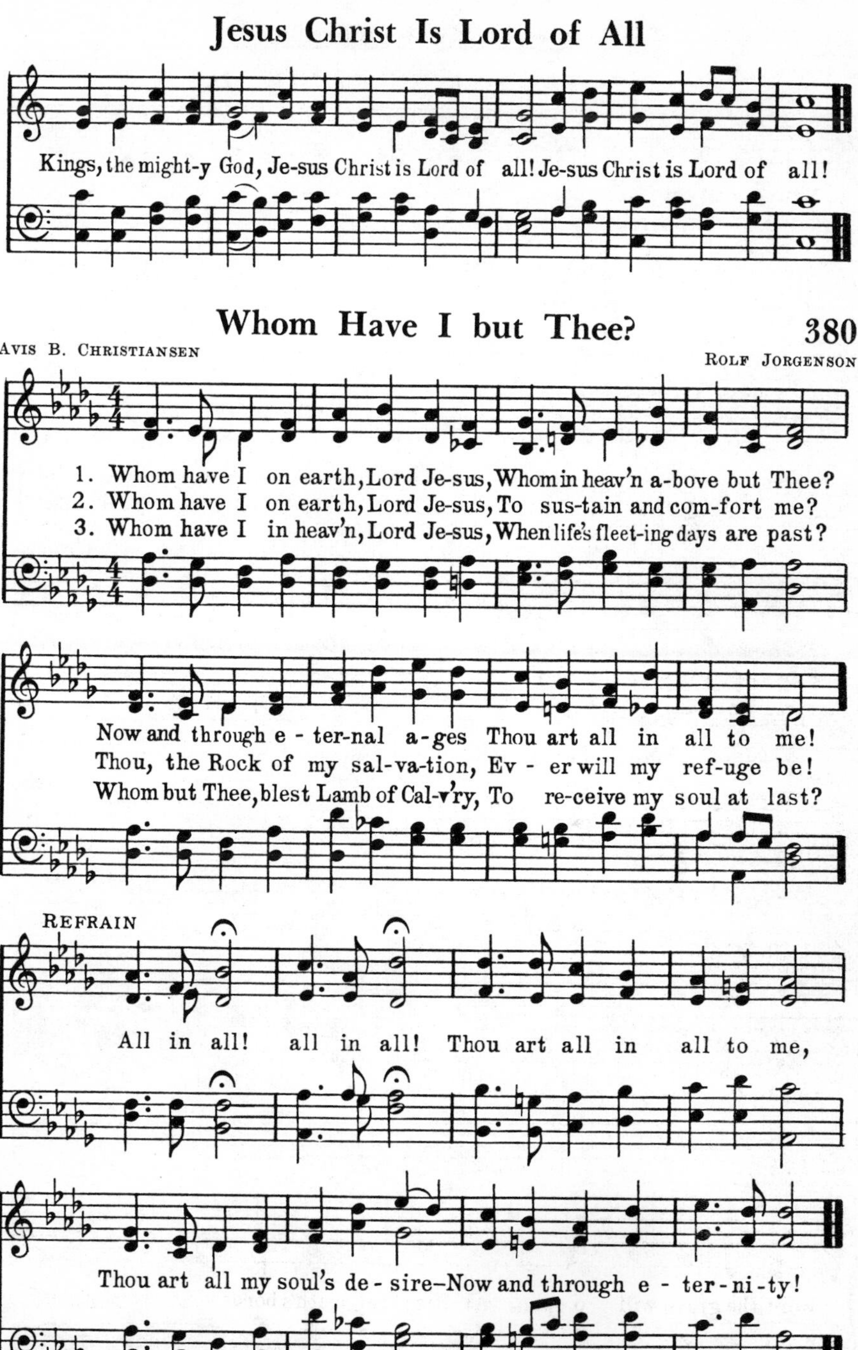
Jesus Christ Is Lord of All
Kings, the might-y God, Je-sus Christ is Lord of all! Je-sus Christ is Lord of all!
Whom Have I but Thee?
380
Avis B. Christiansen
Rolf Jorgenson
1. Whom have I on earth, Lord Je-sus, Whom in heav'n a-bove but Thee?
2. Whom have I on earth, Lord Je-sus, To sus-tain and com-fort me?
3. Whom have I in heav'n, Lord Je-sus, When life's fleet-ing days are past?
Now and through e-ter-nal a-ges Thou art all in all to me!
Thou, the Rock of my sal-va-tion, Ev-er will my ref-uge be!
Whom but Thee, blest Lamb of Cal-v'ry, To re-ceive my soul at last?
Refrain
All in all! all in all! Thou art all in all to me,
Thou art all my soul's de-sire—Now and through e-ter-ni-ty!

381 Jesus, Rose of Sharon

IDA A. GUIREY

CHARLES H. GABRIEL

1. Je-sus, Rose of Shar-on, bloom with-in my heart; Beau-ties of Thy
2. Je-sus, Rose of Shar-on, sweet-er far to me Than the fair-est
3. Je-sus, Rose of Shar-on, balm for ev-'ry ill, May Thy ten-der
4. Je-sus, Rose of Shar-on, bloom for-ev-er-more; Be Thy glo-ry
truth and ho-li-ness im-part, That wher-e'er I go my life may
flow'rs of earth could ev-er be, Fill my life com-plete-ly, add-ing
mer-cy's heal-ing pow'r dis-til For af-flict-ed souls of wea-ry,
seen on earth from shore to shore, Till the na-tions own Thy Sov'reign-
shed a-broad Fra-grance of the knowl-edge of the love of God.
more each day Of Thy grace di-vine and pur-i-ty, I pray.
bur-dened men, Giv-ing need-y mor-tals health and hope a-gain.
ty com-plete, Lay their hon-ors down and wor-ship at Thy feet.
REFRAIN
Je-sus, Rose of Shar-on,
Bless-ed Je-sus, Rose of Shar-on,
Bloom in ra-diance and in love with-in my heart.

We Gather Together

AUTHOR UNKNOWN
TR. BY THEODORE BAKER

NETHERLANDS FOLK SONG
ARR. BY EDWARD KREMSER

1. We gath - er to - geth - er to ask the Lord's bless - ing,
2. Be - side us to guide us, our God with us join - ing
3. We all do ex - tol Thee, Thou Lead - er in bat - tle,
He chas - tens and has - tens His will to make known;
Or - dain - ing, main - tain - ing His king - dom di - vine;
And pray that Thou still our De - fend - er wilt be.
The wick - ed op - press - ing cease them from dis - tress - ing,
So from the be - gin - ning the fight we were win - ning,
Let Thy con - gre - ga - tion es - cape trib - u - la - tion;
Sing prais - es to His name, He for - gets not His own.
Thou, Lord, wast at our side, — the glo - ry be Thine!
Thy name be ev - er praised. O Lord, make us free! A - MEN.

The first two stanzas should be sung in unison (alternately by the male and female voices if desired), and the last stanza in full harmony.

383 Leave It There

C. ALBERT TINDLEY C. ALBERT TINDLEY

Moderato
1. If the world from you with-hold of its sil - ver and its gold, And you
2. If your bod - y suf - fers pain and your health you can't re-gain, And your
3. When your en - e - mies as - sail and your heart be - gins to fail, Don't for-
4. When your youthful days are gone and old age is steal-ing on, And your
have to get a-long with mea-ger fare, Just re-mem-ber, in His word, how He
soul is al-most sink-ing in de-spair, Je-sus knows the pain you feel, He can
get that God in heav-en answers prayer; He will make a way for you and will
bod - y bends beneath the weight of care; He will nev - er leave you then, He'll go
feeds the lit - tle bird; Take your bur - den to the Lord and leave it there.
save and He can heal; Take your bur - den to the Lord and leave it there.
lead you safe - ly thro'; Take your bur - den to the Lord and leave it there.
with you to the end; Take your bur - den to the Lord and leave it there.
CHORUS
Leave it there, . . . leave it there, ... Take your bur-den to the
Leave it there, leave it there,
Lord and leave it there; . . . . If you trust and nev - er doubt, He will
leave it there;

Leave It There
sure-ly bring you out; Take your burden to the Lord and leave it there. . . . .
leave it there.
Does Jesus Care?
384
FRANK E. GRAEFF
J. LINCOLN HALL
1. Does Je-sus care when my heart is pained Too deep-ly for mirth and song;
2. Does Je-sus care when my way is dark With a name-less dread and fear?
3. Does Je-sus care when I've tried and failed To re-sist some temp-ta-tion strong;
4. Does Je-sus care when I've said "good-by" To the dear-est on earth to me,
As the burdens press, and the cares distress, And the way grows wea-ry and long?
As the daylight fades into deep night shades, Does He care e-nough to be near?
When for my deep grief I find no re-lief, Tho' my tears flow all the night long?
And my sad heart aches till it nearly breaks–Is it aught to Him? Does He see?
CHORUS
O yes, He cares; I know He cares, His heart is touched with my grief;
ad lib.
rit.
When the days are wea-ry, the long nights dreary, I know my Sav-ior cares.
He cares.

385

His Way with Thee

CYRUS S. NUSBAUM

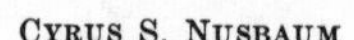

CYRUS S. NUSBAUM

1. Would you live for Je - sus, and be al-ways pure and good? Would you walk with
2. Would you have Him make you free, and fol-low at His call? Would you know the
3. Would you in His king-dom find a place of con-stant rest? Would you prove Him

Him with - in the nar-row road? Would you have Him bear your burden, car - ry
peace that comes by giv - ing all? Would you have Him save you, so that you need
true in prov - i - den-tial test? Would you in His serv - ice la - bor al-ways

all your load? Let Him have His way with thee.
nev - er fall? Let Him have His way with thee.
at your best? Let Him have His way with thee.

CHORUS.

His pow'r can make you what you ought to be; His blood can cleanse your heart and make you free; His love can fill your soul, and you will see 'Twas best for Him to have His way with thee.

rit.

A - MEN.

Nothing Between

C. ALBERT TINDLEY	C. ALBERT TINDLEY

1. Noth-ing be-tween my soul and the Sav-ior, Naught of this world's de-
2. Noth-ing be-tween, like world-ly pleas-ure, Hab-its of life though
3. Noth-ing be-tween, like pride or sta-tion, Self or friends shall
4. Noth-ing be-tween, e'en man-y hard tri-als, Tho' the whole world a-
lu-sive dream; I have re-nounced all sin-ful pleas-ure,
harm-less they seem, Must not my heart from Him e'er sev-er,
not in-ter-vene, Tho' it may cost me much trib-u-la-tion,
gainst me con-vene; Watching with prayer and much self-de-ni-al, I'll
Je-sus is mine; there's noth-ing be-tween.
He is my all; there's noth-ing be-tween.
I am re-solved; there's noth-ing be-tween.
tri-umph at last, with noth-ing be-tween.
CHORUS
Noth-ing be-tween my
soul and the Sav-ior, So that His bless-ed face may be seen; Noth-ing pre-
vent-ing the least of His fa-vor, Keep the way clear! Let nothing between.

387 Have Thine Own Way, Lord!

ADELAIDE A. POLLARD

GEORGE C. STEBBINS

Slowly

1. Have Thine own way, Lord! Have Thine own way! Thou art the
2. Have Thine own way, Lord! Have Thine own way! Search me and
3. Have Thine own way, Lord! Have Thine own way! Wound-ed and
4. Have Thine own way, Lord! Have Thine own way! Hold o'er my

Pot - ter; I am the clay Mould me and make me Aft - er Thy
try me, Mas-ter, to - day! Whit - er than snow, Lord, Wash me just
wea - ry, Help me, I pray! Pow - er—all pow - er—Sure - ly is
be - ing Ab - so - lute sway! Fill with Thy Spir - it Till all shall

will, While I am wait - ing, Yield - ed and still.
now, As in Thy pres - ence Hum - bly I bow.
Thine! Touch me and heal me, Sav - ior di - vine!
see Christ on - ly, al - ways, Liv - ing in me!

388 Take My Life, and Let It Be

FRANCES R. HAVERGAL

H. A. CÉSAR MALAN

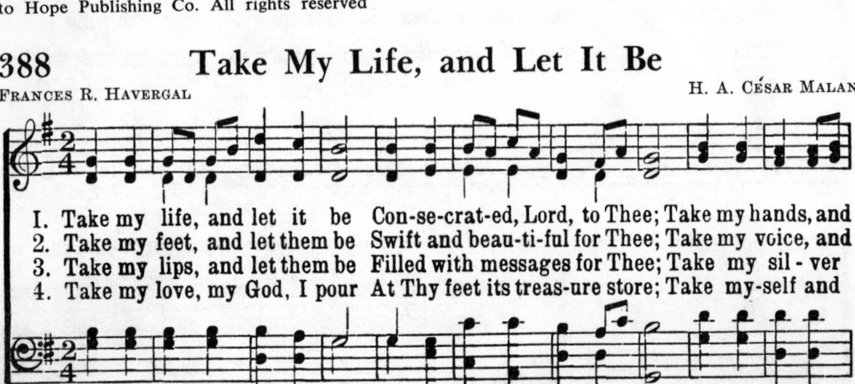
1. Take my life, and let it be Con-se-crat-ed, Lord, to Thee; Take my hands, and
2. Take my feet, and let them be Swift and beau-ti-ful for Thee; Take my voice, and
3. Take my lips, and let them be Filled with messages for Thee; Take my sil - ver
4. Take my love, my God, I pour At Thy feet its treas-ure store; Take my-self and

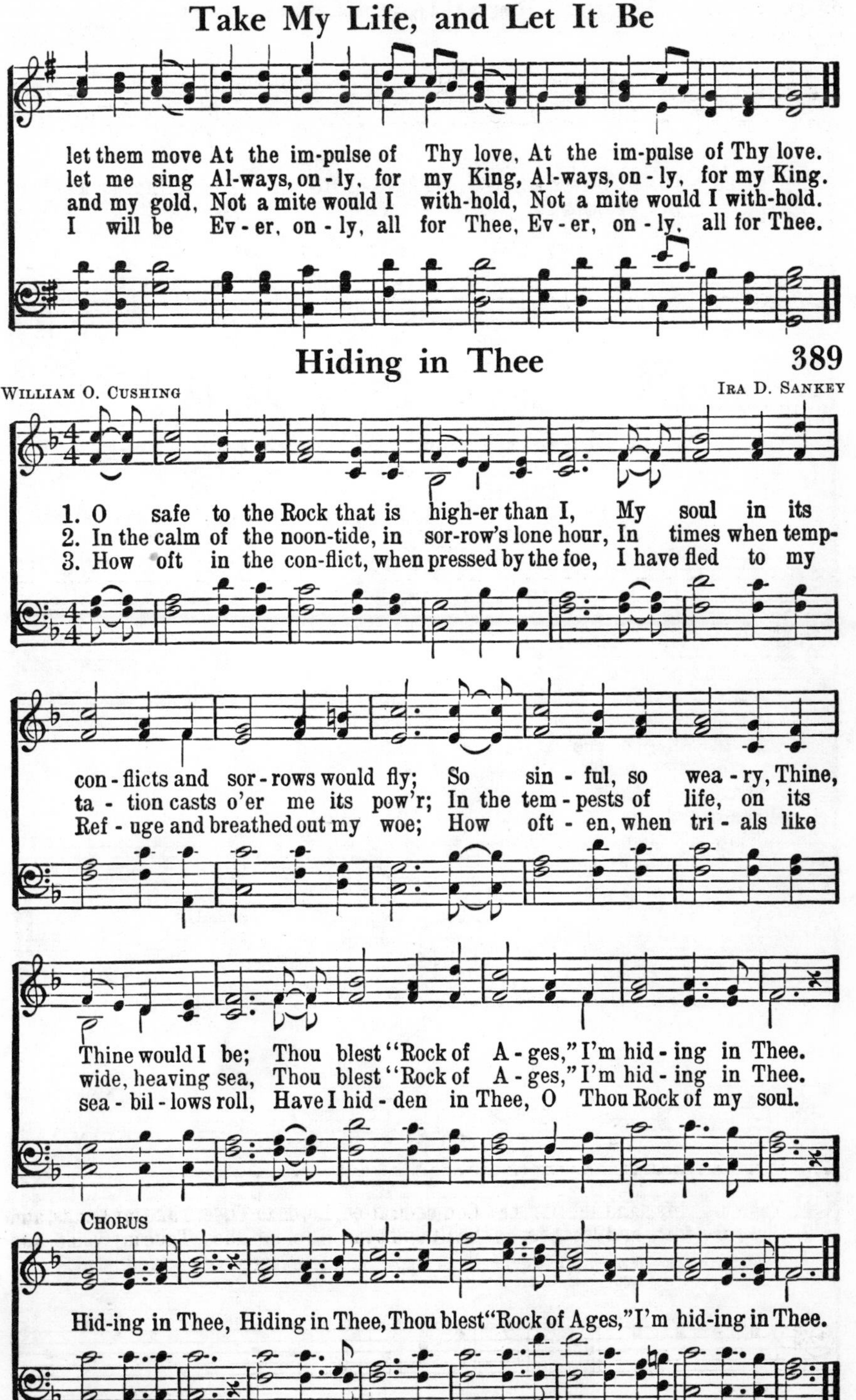
Take My Life, and Let It Be
let them move At the im-pulse of Thy love, At the im-pulse of Thy love.
let me sing Al-ways, on-ly, for my King, Al-ways, on-ly, for my King.
and my gold, Not a mite would I with-hold, Not a mite would I with-hold.
I will be Ev-er, on-ly, all for Thee, Ev-er, on-ly, all for Thee.
Hiding in Thee
389
William O. Cushing
Ira D. Sankey
1. O safe to the Rock that is high-er than I, My soul in its
2. In the calm of the noon-tide, in sor-row's lone hour, In times when temp-
3. How oft in the con-flict, when pressed by the foe, I have fled to my
con-flicts and sor-rows would fly; So sin-ful, so wea-ry, Thine,
ta-tion casts o'er me its pow'r; In the tem-pests of life, on its
Ref-uge and breathed out my woe; How oft-en, when tri-als like
Thine would I be; Thou blest "Rock of A-ges," I'm hid-ing in Thee.
wide, heaving sea, Thou blest "Rock of A-ges," I'm hid-ing in Thee.
sea-bil-lows roll, Have I hid-den in Thee, O Thou Rock of my soul.
Chorus
Hid-ing in Thee, Hiding in Thee, Thou blest "Rock of Ages," I'm hid-ing in Thee.

390 Is Your All on the Altar?

ELISHA A. HOFFMAN | ELISHA A. HOFFMAN

1. You have longed for sweet peace, and for faith to in-crease, And have ear-nest-ly,
2. Would you walk with the Lord, in the light of His Word, And have peace and con-
3. Oh, we nev - er can know what the Lord will be-stow Of the bless-ings for
4. Who can tell all the love He will send from a-bove, And how hap-py our
fer - vent-ly prayed; But you can-not have rest or be per-fect-ly blest
tent-ment al - way, You must do His sweet will, to be free from all ill,
which we have prayed, Till our bod - y and soul He doth ful - ly con-trol,
hearts will be made, Of the fel - low-ship sweet we shall share at His feet,
Un - til all on the al - tar is laid.
On the al - tar your all you must lay.
And our all on the al - tar is laid.
When our all on the al - tar is laid.
CHORUS
Is your all on the al - tar of
sac - ri - fice laid? Your heart, does the Spir-it con-trol? . . . You can on - ly be
blest and have peace and sweet rest, As you yield Him your bod - y and soul.

I Surrender All

Judson W. Van DeVenter

Winfield S. Weeden

1. All to Je-sus I sur-ren-der, All to Him I free-ly give;
2. All to Je-sus I sur-ren-der, Hum-bly at His feet I bow,
3. All to Je-sus I sur-ren-der, Make me, Sav-ior, whol-ly Thine;
4. All to Je-sus I sur-ren-der, Lord, I give my-self to Thee;
I will ev-er love and trust Him, In His pres-ence dai-ly live.
World-ly pleas-ures all for-sak-en, Take me, Je-sus, take me now.
Let me feel the Ho-ly Spir-it,— Tru-ly know that Thou art mine.
Fill me with Thy love and pow-er, Let Thy bless-ing fall on me.
Chorus
I sur-ren-der all, I sur-ren-der all.
I sur-ren-der all, I sur-ren-der all.
All to Thee, my bless-ed Sav-ior, I sur-ren-der all.

392 Savior, My Heart Is Thine

Author Unknown
Alt. by George C. Stebbins

George C. Stebbins

1. Sav - ior, my heart is Thine, Keep it for me; May ev - 'ry thought of mine Glo - ri - fy Thee. Glo - ri - fy Thee, Glo - ri - fy Thee; May ev - 'ry thought of mine Glo - ri - fy Thee.
2. Sav - ior, my will is Thine, Keep it for me; May ev - 'ry act of mine Be done for Thee. Be done for Thee, Be done for Thee; May ev - 'ry act of mine Be done for Thee.
3. Sav - ior, my life is Thine, Keep it for me; May ev - 'ry hour of mine Be lived for Thee. Be lived for Thee, Be lived for Thee; May ev - 'ry hour of mine Be lived for Thee.
4. Sav - ior, my all is Thine, Keep it for me; May all I have, O Lord, Be used for Thee. Be used for Thee, Be used for Thee; May all I have, O Lord, Be used for Thee.

393 Where He Leads Me

E. W. Blandy

John S. Norris

1. I can hear my Sav - ior call - ing, I can hear my Sav - ior call - ing,
2. I'll go with Him thro' the gar - den, I'll go with Him thro' the gar - den,
3. I'll go with Him thro' the judg-ment, I'll go with Him thro' the judg-ment,
4. He will give me grace and glo - ry, He will give me grace and glo - ry,
Ref. *Where He leads me I will fol - low, Where He leads me I will fol - low,*

Where He Leads Me

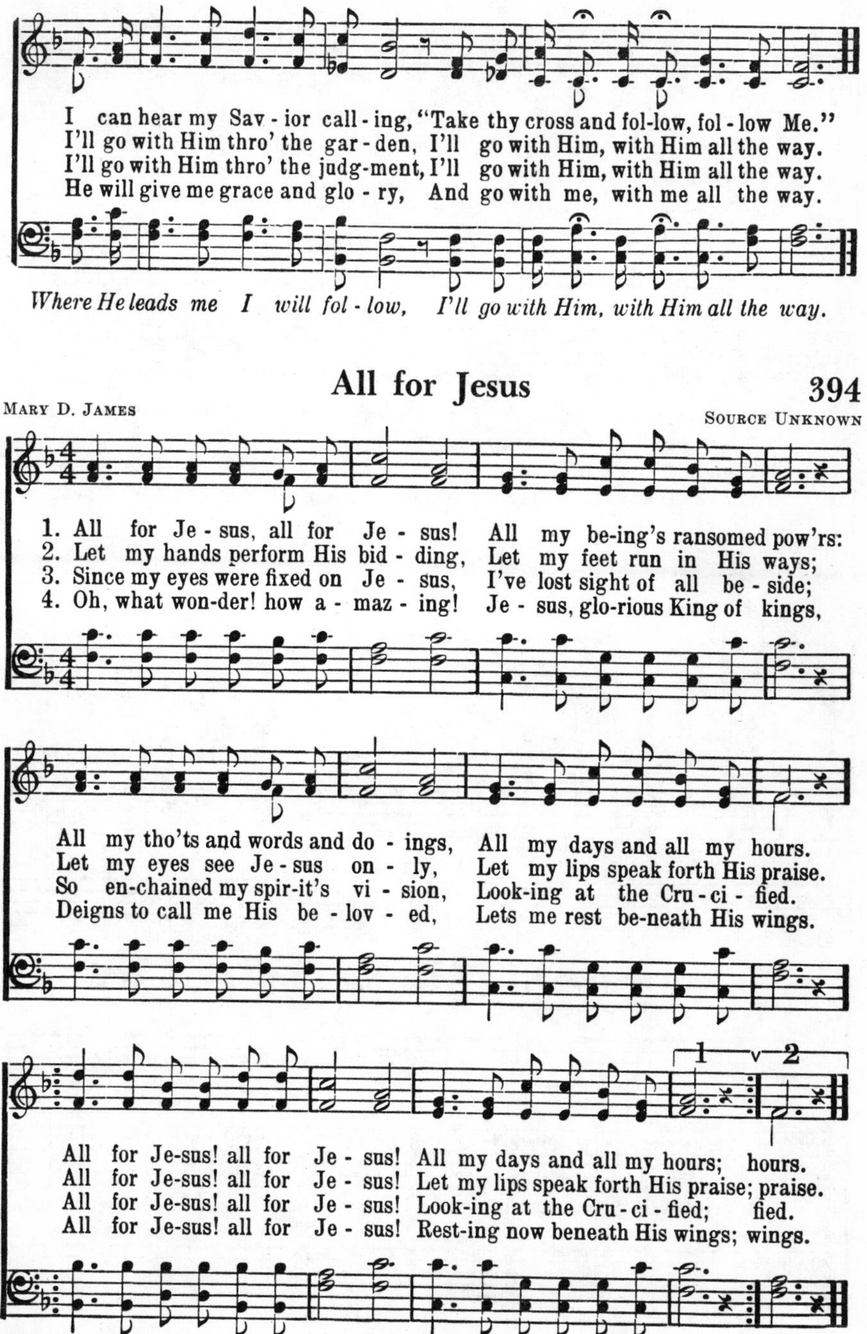
I can hear my Sav-ior call-ing, "Take thy cross and fol-low, fol-low Me."
I'll go with Him thro' the gar-den, I'll go with Him, with Him all the way.
I'll go with Him thro' the judg-ment, I'll go with Him, with Him all the way.
He will give me grace and glo-ry, And go with me, with me all the way.
Where He leads me I will fol-low, I'll go with Him, with Him all the way.
All for Jesus
394
Mary D. James
Source Unknown
1. All for Je-sus, all for Je-sus! All my be-ing's ransomed pow'rs:
2. Let my hands perform His bid-ding, Let my feet run in His ways;
3. Since my eyes were fixed on Je-sus, I've lost sight of all be-side;
4. Oh, what won-der! how a-maz-ing! Je-sus, glo-rious King of kings,
All my tho'ts and words and do-ings, All my days and all my hours.
Let my eyes see Je-sus on-ly, Let my lips speak forth His praise.
So en-chained my spir-it's vi-sion, Look-ing at the Cru-ci-fied.
Deigns to call me His be-lov-ed, Lets me rest be-neath His wings.
1
2
All for Je-sus! all for Je-sus! All my days and all my hours; hours.
All for Je-sus! all for Je-sus! Let my lips speak forth His praise; praise.
All for Je-sus! all for Je-sus! Look-ing at the Cru-ci-fied; fied.
All for Je-sus! all for Je-sus! Rest-ing now beneath His wings; wings.

395 **I Will Follow Thee**

JOHNSON OATMAN, JR. EDWIN O. EXCELL

1. Sav-iour, I will fol-low Thee; Thou art all the world to me;
2. Sav-iour, I will fol-low Thee, Tho' it lead me to the cross;
3. Sav-iour, I will fol-low Thee, Tho' it lead through toil and tears;
4. Sav-iour, I will fol-low Thee Till the toils of life are o'er;
Tho' the way I can-not see, Sav-iour, I will fol-low Thee.
Count-ing all things here but dross, Sav-iour, I will fol-low Thee.
Through the long and wea-ry years, Sav-iour, I will fol-low Thee.
Till I reach the Gold-en Shore, Sav-iour, I will fol-low Thee.
CHORUS
Fol-low Thee, I will fol-low Thee, Fol-low Thee,
Fol-low, I will fol-low Thee, fol-low Thee, Fol-low, I will fol-low
I will fol-low Thee, Fol-low till the day is done,
Thee, fol-low Thee,
Fol-low till the crown is won, Sav-iour, I will fol-low Thee.

I'll Put Jesus First in My Life

James D. Murch — James D. Murch

1. The world all a - bout me has now no al - lure: Its pleas-ures bring pain,
2. The Lord Je-sus died my sal - va-tion to win: He went in my stead
3. I know there's a home for the ran-somed and blest, When death is no more,
4. Tho' earth's trib-u - la-tions con-tin-ue each day, Tho' pleas-ures may call,
Its wis-dom is vain; I seek a foun-da-tion that's stead-fast and sure:
To Cal-v'ry and bled; Re-demp-tion im-pels me to give up all sin:
When strug-gle is o'er, For those who love Je-sus and give Him their best:
Tho' e - vil en-thrall, His grace will pro-tect me for - ev - er and aye:
CHORUS
I'll put Je-sus first in my life. In all that I say, In
all that I do, Thro'-out the world of toil and strife, By day and by
night, Thro' trust in His might, I'll put Je-sus first in my life.

397 If Jesus Goes with Me

C. AUSTIN MILES — C. AUSTIN MILES

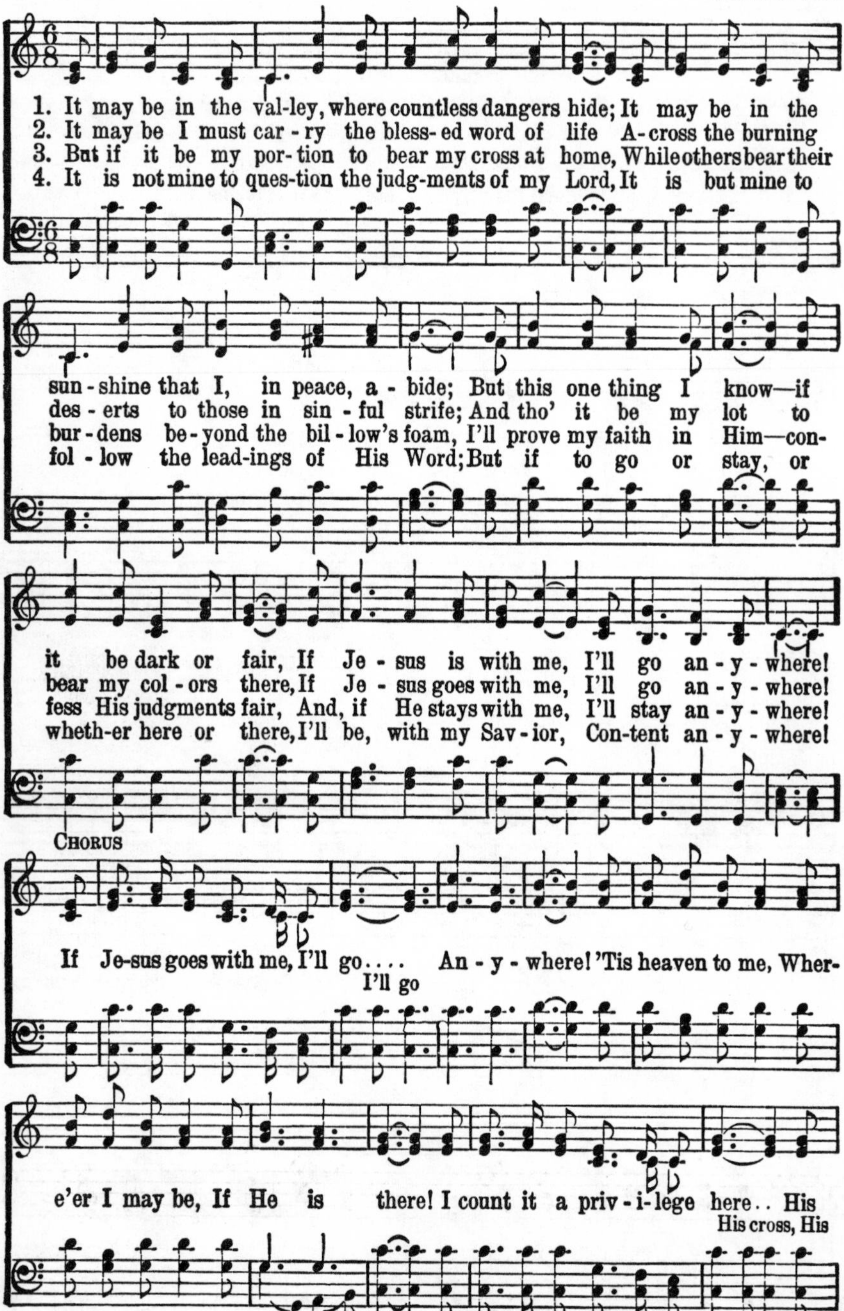

1. It may be in the val-ley, where countless dangers hide; It may be in the sun-shine that I, in peace, a-bide; But this one thing I know—if it be dark or fair, If Je-sus is with me, I'll go an-y-where!
2. It may be I must car-ry the bless-ed word of life A-cross the burning des-erts to those in sin-ful strife; And tho' it be my lot to bear my col-ors there, If Je-sus goes with me, I'll go an-y-where!
3. But if it be my por-tion to bear my cross at home, While others bear their bur-dens be-yond the bil-low's foam, I'll prove my faith in Him—con-fess His judgments fair, And, if He stays with me, I'll stay an-y-where!
4. It is not mine to ques-tion the judg-ments of my Lord, It is but mine to fol-low the lead-ings of His Word; But if to go or stay, or wheth-er here or there, I'll be, with my Sav-ior, Con-tent an-y-where!

CHORUS

If Je-sus goes with me, I'll go.... (I'll go) An-y-where! 'Tis heaven to me, Wher-e'er I may be, If He is there! I count it a priv-i-lege here.. (His cross, His) His

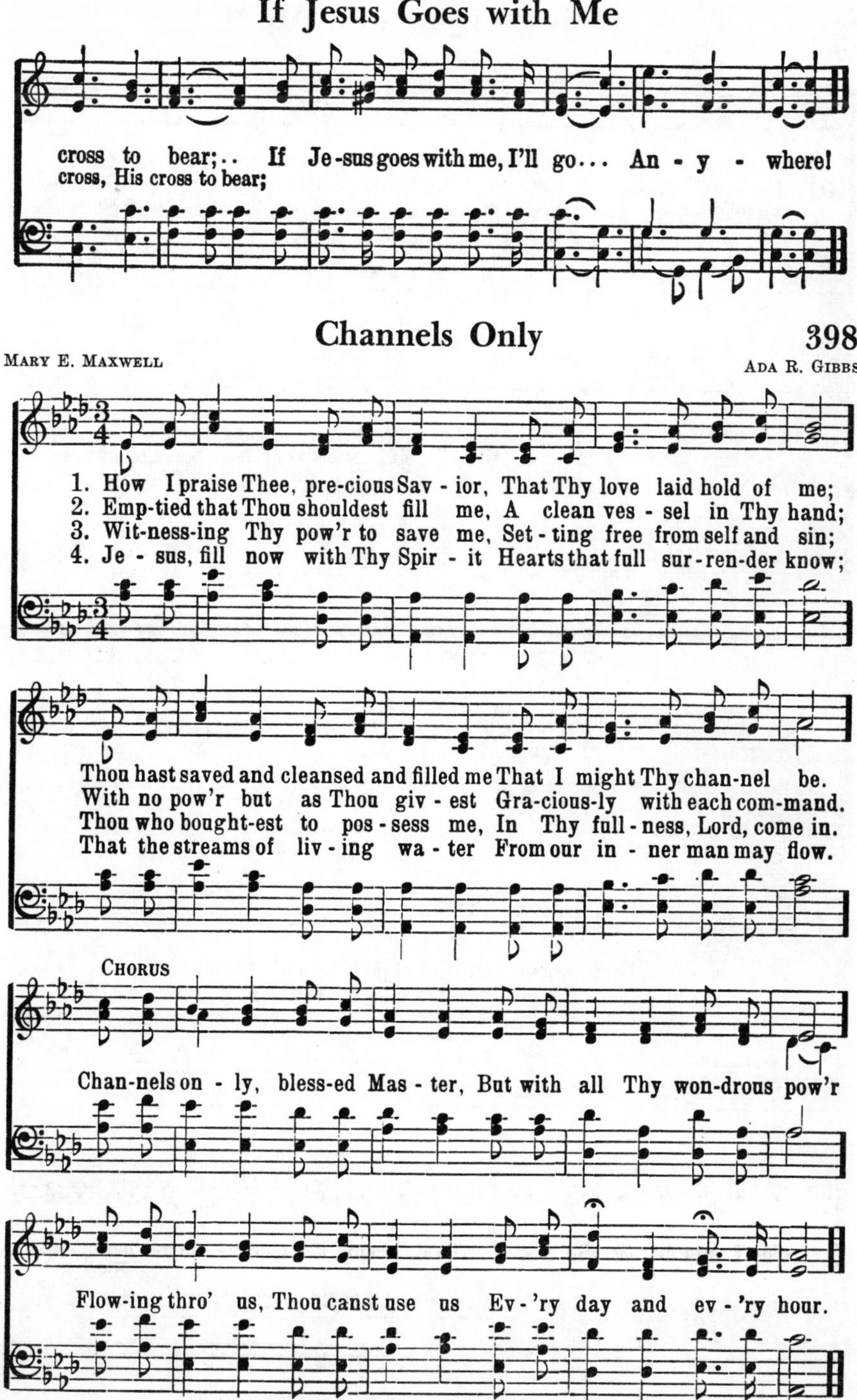
If Jesus Goes with Me
cross to bear;.. If Je-sus goes with me, I'll go... An - y - where!
cross, His cross to bear;
Channels Only
398
Mary E. Maxwell
Ada R. Gibbs
1. How I praise Thee, pre-cious Sav - ior, That Thy love laid hold of me;
2. Emp-tied that Thou shouldest fill me, A clean ves - sel in Thy hand;
3. Wit-ness-ing Thy pow'r to save me, Set-ting free from self and sin;
4. Je - sus, fill now with Thy Spir - it Hearts that full sur-ren-der know;
Thou hast saved and cleansed and filled me That I might Thy chan-nel be.
With no pow'r but as Thou giv - est Gra-cious-ly with each com-mand.
Thou who bought-est to pos-sess me, In Thy full-ness, Lord, come in.
That the streams of liv - ing wa - ter From our in - ner man may flow.
Chorus
Chan-nels on - ly, bless-ed Mas - ter, But with all Thy won-drous pow'r
Flow-ing thro' us, Thou canst use us Ev - 'ry day and ev - 'ry hour.

399 I'll Go Where You Want Me to Go

CHARLES H. GABRIEL CARRIE E. ROUNSEFELL

1. It may not be on the mountain's height, Or o - ver the storm - y sea;
2. Per-haps to - day there are lov - ing words Which Jesus would have me speak;
3. There's surely somewhere a low - ly place In earth's harvest-fields so wide,
It may not be at the bat - tle's front My Lord will have need of me;
There may be now, in the paths of sin, Some wand'rer whom I should seek.
Where I may la - bor thro' life's short day For Je - sus, the Cru - ci - fied.
But if by a still, small voice He calls To paths I do not know,
O Sav - ior, if Thou wilt be my Guide, Tho' dark and rug-ged the way,
So, trust-ing my all un - to Thy care, I know Thou lov - est me!
I'll answer, dear Lord, with my hand in Thine, I'll go where you want me to go.
My voice shall ech - o the mes-sage sweet, I'll say what you want me to say.
I'll do Thy will with a heart sin-cere, I'll be what you want me to be.
REFRAIN
I'll go where you want me to go, dear Lord, O'er mountain, or plain, or sea;

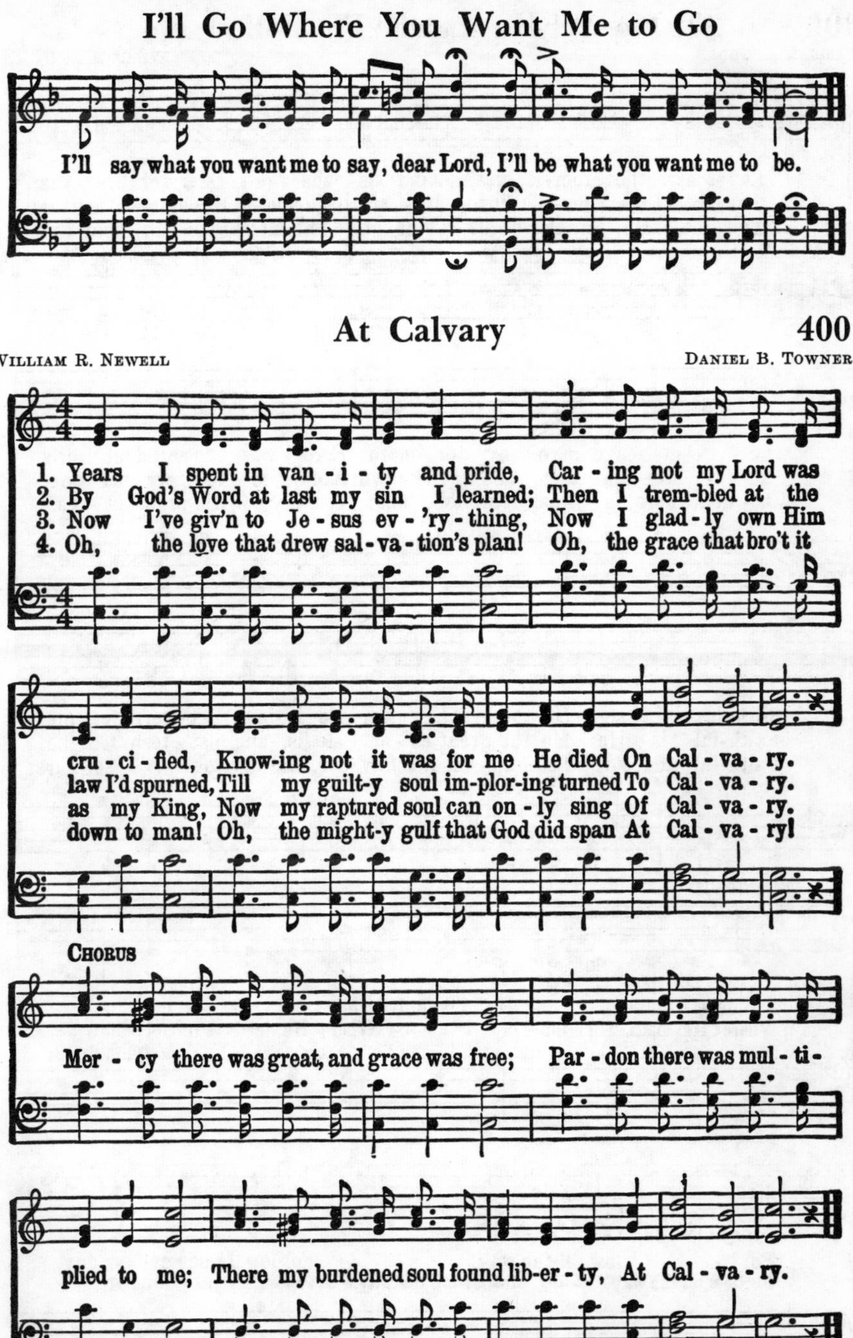
I'll Go Where You Want Me to Go
I'll say what you want me to say, dear Lord, I'll be what you want me to be.
At Calvary
400
William R. Newell
Daniel B. Towner
1. Years I spent in van - i - ty and pride, Car - ing not my Lord was
2. By God's Word at last my sin I learned; Then I trem-bled at the
3. Now I've giv'n to Je - sus ev - 'ry - thing, Now I glad - ly own Him
4. Oh, the love that drew sal - va - tion's plan! Oh, the grace that bro't it
cru - ci - fied, Know-ing not it was for me He died On Cal - va - ry.
law I'd spurned, Till my guilt - y soul im - plor - ing turned To Cal - va - ry.
as my King, Now my raptured soul can on - ly sing Of Cal - va - ry.
down to man! Oh, the might - y gulf that God did span At Cal - va - ry!
Chorus
Mer - cy there was great, and grace was free; Par - don there was mul - ti -
plied to me; There my burdened soul found lib - er - ty, At Cal - va - ry.

401 Where He Leads I'll Follow

WILLIAM A. OGDEN WILLIAM A. OGDEN

1. Sweet are the prom-is - es, Kind is the word, Dear-er far than
2. Sweet is the ten-der love Je - sus hath shown, Sweet-er far than
3. List to His lov-ing words, "Come un - to Me;" Wea - ry, heav - y-
an - y mes-sage man ev - er heard; Pure was the mind of Christ,
an - y love that mor - tals have known; Kind to the err - ing one,
la - den, there is sweet rest for thee; Trust in His prom - is - es,
Sin - less I see; He the great ex - am - ple is, and pat - tern for me.
Faith-ful is He; He the great ex - am - ple is, and pat - tern for me.
Faith-ful and sure; Lean up - on the Sav - ior, and thy soul is se - cure.
CHORUS
Where . . . . . . He leads I'll fol - - - - low,
Where He leads I'll fol - low, Where He leads I'll fol - low,
1
Fol - - - low all the way.
Fol-low all the way, yes, fol-low all the way.
2
Fol-low Je-sus ev-'ry day.

The Way of the Cross Leads Home

JESSIE B. POUNDS CHARLES H. GABRIEL

1. I must needs go home by the way of the cross, There's no oth - er
2. I must needs go on in the blood-sprinkled way, The path that the
3. Then I bid fare-well to the way of the world, To walk in it
way but this; I shall ne'er get sight of the Gates of Light,
Sav - ior trod, If I ev - er climb to the heights sub-lime,
nev - er - more; For my Lord says "Come," and I seek my home,
CHORUS.
If the way of the cross I miss.
Where the soul is at home with God. The way of the cross leads
Where He waits at the o - pen door.
home, The way of the cross leads home; It is
leads home, leads home;
sweet to know as I on-ward go, The way of the cross leads home.

403 He Wore a Crown of Thorns

WILLIAM M. RUNYAN — GEORGE S. SCHULER

1. 'Twas God's own Son who came to earth, Who chose to know a low - ly birth;
2. Won - der - ful, Coun-sel - lor was He, Matchless His grace; how could it be
3. Kind were the deeds that crowned each day, Gracious the words His lips would say.
4. Nev - er a-gain His brow shall know Pierc-ings of ag - o - ny and woe;
But, tho' a King of matchless worth, He wore a crown of thorns.
That, at the last, He wore for me That bitter crown of thorns?
While He pur-sued the fate - ful way To wear that crown of thorns.
But 'twas for us that, here be - low, He wore the crown of thorns.
CHORUS.
He wore a crown of thorns that I Might wear a crown of glo - ry!
He laid His heav'n-ly splendors by To bring me love's sweet sto-ry. In
pov - er - ty He walked life's way, In Ol - ive's gar-den bowed to pray;

He Wore a Crown of Thorns

He wore a crown of thorns that I Might wear a crown of glo - ry!

No One Understands Like Jesus 404

JOHN W. PETERSON JOHN W. PETERSON

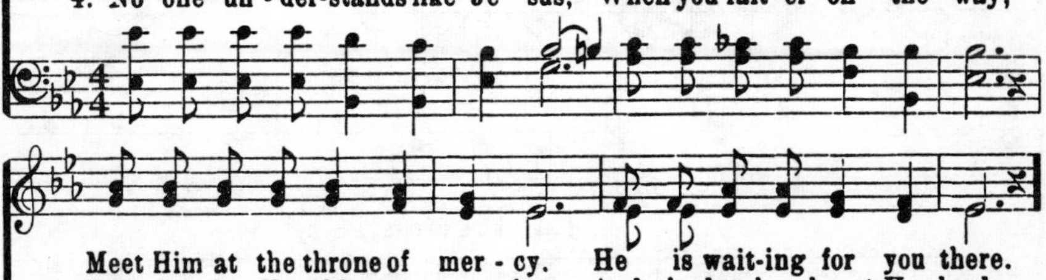
1. No one un - der-stands like Je - sus, He's a friend be-yond com-pare;
2. No one un - der-stands like Je - sus. Eve - ry woe He sees and feels;
3. No one un - der-stands like Je - sus, When the foes of life as - sail;
4. No one un - der-stands like Je - sus, When you falt-er on the way;
Meet Him at the throne of mer - cy. He is wait-ing for you there.
Ten - der-ly He whis-pers com - fort. And the bro-ken heart He heals.
You should nev-er be dis-cour-aged, Je - sus cares and will not fail.
Tho' you fail Him, sad - ly fail Him, He will par-don you to - day.

CHORUS
No one un - der-stands like Je - sus. When the days are dark and grim;

No one is so near, so dear as Je - sus, Cast your eve - ry care on Him.

405 Kneel at the Cross

CHARLES E. MOODY

CHARLES E. MOODY
ARR. BY WILLIAM J. FLOYD

1. Kneel at the cross, Christ will meet you there, Come while He waits for you; List to His voice, Leave with Him your care, And start your life a - new.
2. Kneel at the cross, There is room for all Who would His glo-ry share; Bliss there a-waits, Harm can ne'er be-fall Those who are an-chored there.
3. Kneel at the cross, Give your i-dols up, Look un - to realms a - bove; Turn not a way To life's spark-ling cup, Trust on-ly in His love.
REFRAIN
Kneel at the cross, (at the cross,) Leave ev - ery care, Kneel (oh kneel) at the cross, (at the cross,) Je - sus will meet you there. (meet you there.)

Come, Holy Spirit

406

LILY HEDMAN WELLS

KENNETH H. WELLS

1. Come, Ho-ly Spi-rit, heav'n-ly Dove, De-scend up-on my heart; Fill all my soul with per-fect love, Thy won-drous peace im - part.
2. Come, Ho-ly Spi-rit, cleans-ing fire, Thou pur - i - fy - ing Flame; Burn out the dross of base de - sire, And cleanse in Je - sus' name.
3. Come, Ho-ly Spi-rit, migh-ty pow'r I claim the prom-ised Word, That grace be mine each pass - ing hour, To wit - ness for my Lord.
CHORUS
Come, Ho - ly Spir - it, fill me now, My spir - it yearns for Thee;
With faith be-fore Thy throne I bow, And claim Thy Gift for me.

407 Near the Cross

FANNY J. CROSBY — WILLIAM H. DOANE

1. Jesus, keep me near the cross, There a precious fountain
Free to all— a healing stream, Flows from Cal-v'ry's mountain.

2. Near the cross, a trembling soul, Love and mercy found me;
There the Bright and Morning Star Sheds its beams around me.

3. Near the cross! O Lamb of God, Bring its scenes before me;
Help me walk from day to day, With its shadows o'er me.

4. Near the cross I'll watch and wait, Hoping, trusting ever,
Till I reach the golden strand, Just beyond the river.

CHORUS

In the cross, in the cross, Be my glory ever;
Till my raptured soul shall find Rest beyond the river.

408 In the Cross of Christ

JOHN BOWRING — ITHAMAR CONKEY

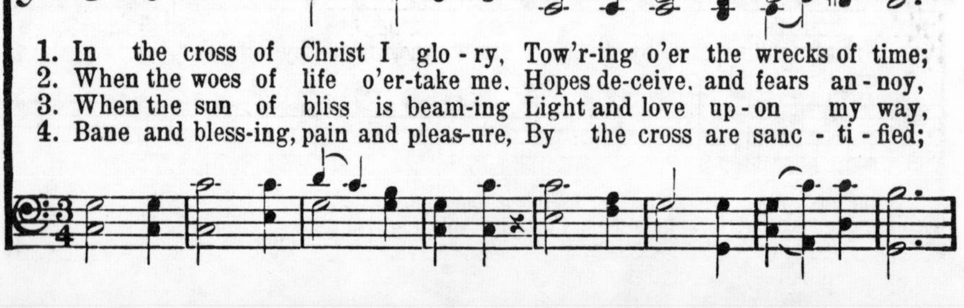

1. In the cross of Christ I glory, Tow'ring o'er the wrecks of time;
2. When the woes of life o'ertake me, Hopes deceive, and fears annoy,
3. When the sun of bliss is beaming Light and love upon my way,
4. Bane and blessing, pain and pleasure, By the cross are sanctified;

In the Cross of Christ
All the light of sa - cred sto - ry Gath-ers round its head sub-lime.
Nev - er shall the cross for - sake me: Lo! it glows with peace and joy.
From the cross the ra - diance streaming Adds more lus - ter to the day.
Peace is there that knows no meas-ure, Joys that thro' all time a - bide.
Nearer the Cross
409
Fanny J. Crosby
Phoebe P. Knapp
1. "Near-er the cross!" my heart can say, I am com-ing near - er, Near-er the
2. Near-er the Christian's mer-cy-seat, I am com-ing near - er, Feasting my
3. Near-er in prayer my hope as-pires, I am com-ing near - er, Deep-er the
cross from day to day, I am com-ing near - er; Near-er the cross where
soul on man - na sweet, I am com-ing near - er; Strong-er in faith, more
love my soul de-sires, I am com-ing near - er; Near-er the end of
Je - sus died, Near-er the fountain's crim-son tide, Near-er my Sav - ior's
clear I see Je - sus who gave Him-self for me; Near-er to Him I
toil and care, Near-er the joy I long to share, Near-er the crown I
wound-ed side, I am com-ing near - er, I am com-ing near - er.
still would be, Still I'm com-ing near - er, Still I'm com-ing near - er.
soon shall wear; I am com-ing near - er, I am com-ing near - er.

410 Ten Thousand Angels

RAY OVERHOLT — RAY OVERHOLT

Slowly, with much feeling

1. They bound the hands of Je-sus in the gar-den where He prayed; They
2. Up - on His pre-cious head they placed a crown of thorns; They
3. When they nailed Him to the cross, His moth-er stood near by; He
4. To the howl-ing mob He yield-ed; He did not for mer-cy cry. The

led Him thro' the streets in shame. They spat up-on the Sav-iour so
laughed and said, "Be-hold the King". They struck Him and they cursed Him and
said, "Wom-an, be-hold thy son!" He cried, "I thirst for wa-ter," but they
cross of shame He took a-lone. And when He cried, "It's fin-ished," He

pure and free from sin; They said, "Cru-ci-fy Him; He's to blame."
mocked His ho-ly name. All a-lone He suf-fered ev-'ry-thing.
gave Him none to drink. Then the sin-ful work of man was done.
gave Him-self to die; Sal-va-tion's won-drous plan was done.

CHORUS

Faster

He could have called ten thou-sand an-gels To de-stroy the world and set Him free. He could have called

the world

Ten Thousand Angels

rall.
ten thou-sand an - gels, But He died a - lone, for you and me.
a-lone,
Jesus Only, Let Me See
411
Oswald J. Smith
Daniel B. Towner
1. For sal - va - tion full and free, Pur-chased once on Cal - va - ry,
2. He my guide from day to day, As I jour-ney on life's way;
3. May my mod - el ev - er be Christ the Lord, and none save He,
4. He shall reign from shore to shore, His the glo - ry ev - er-more-
Christ a - lone shall be my plea- Je - sus! Je - sus on - ly.
Close be-side Him let me stay- Je - sus! Je - sus on - ly.
That the world may see in me Je - sus! Je - sus on - ly.
Heav'n and earth shall bow be-fore Je - sus! Je - sus on - ly.
CHORUS
Je - sus on - ly, let me see, Je - sus on - ly, none save He,
Then my song shall ev - er be- Je - sus! Je - sus on - ly!

412 We Would See Jesus

ANNA B. WARNER — FELIX MENDELSSOHN-BARTHOLDY

1. We would see Je - sus, for the shad-ows length-en A - cross this
2. We would see Je - sus, the great rock foun-da - tion, Where-on our
3. We would see Je - sus; oth - er lights are pal - ing, Which for long
4. We would see Je - sus; this is all we're need - ing; Strength, joy, and

lit - tle land-scape of our life; We would see Je - sus, our weak
feet were set by sov-'reign grace; Not life, nor death, with all their
years we have re - joiced to see; The bless-ings of our pil - grim-
will - ing-ness come with the sight; We would see Je - sus, dy - ing,

faith to strength-en For the last wea - ri - ness, the fi - nal strife.
ag - i - ta - tion, Can thence re - move us, if we see His face.
age are fail - ing; We would not mourn them, for we go to Thee.
ris - en, plead - ing; Then wel-come, day! and fare-well, mor - tal night!

413 When I Survey the Wondrous Cross

ISAAC WATTS — ARR. BY LOWELL MASON

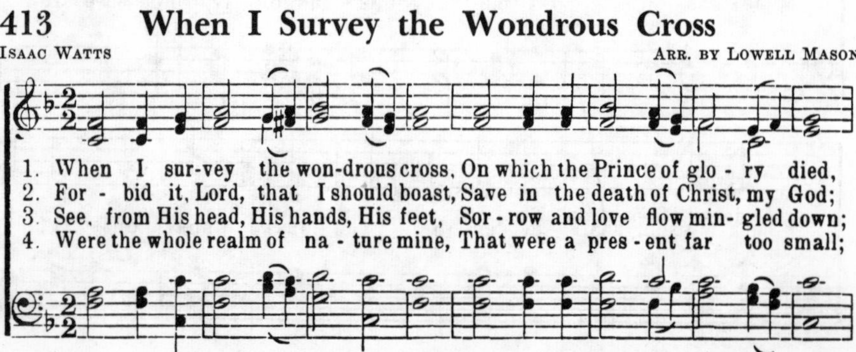

1. When I sur-vey the won-drous cross, On which the Prince of glo - ry died,
2. For - bid it, Lord, that I should boast, Save in the death of Christ, my God;
3. See, from His head, His hands, His feet, Sor - row and love flow min - gled down;
4. Were the whole realm of na - ture mine, That were a pres - ent far too small;

When I Survey the Wondrous Cross

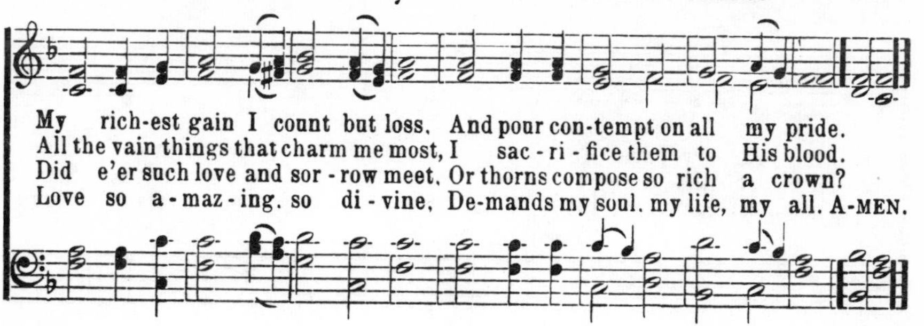
My rich-est gain I count but loss, And pour con-tempt on all my pride.
All the vain things that charm me most, I sac-ri-fice them to His blood.
Did e'er such love and sor-row meet, Or thorns compose so rich a crown?
Love so a-maz-ing, so di-vine, De-mands my soul, my life, my all. A-MEN.

Dear Lord and Father of Mankind 414

JOHN G. WHITTIER

FREDERICK C. MAKER

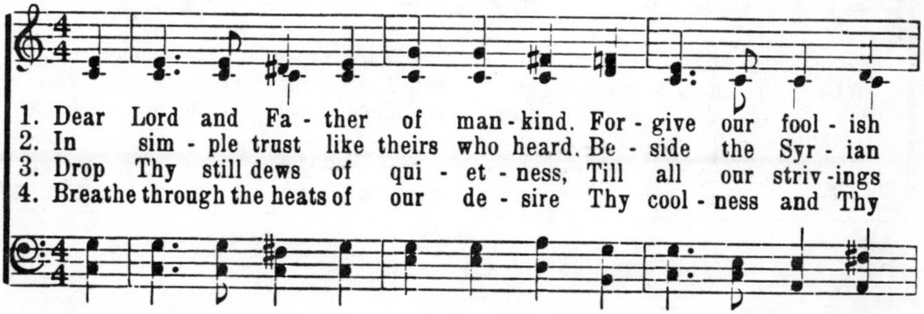

1. Dear Lord and Fa-ther of man-kind, For-give our fool-ish
2. In sim-ple trust like theirs who heard, Be-side the Syr-ian
3. Drop Thy still dews of qui-et-ness, Till all our striv-ings
4. Breathe through the heats of our de-sire Thy cool-ness and Thy

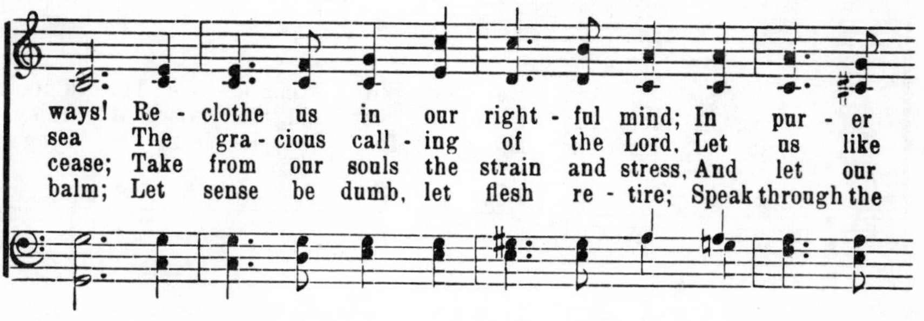

ways! Re-clothe us in our right-ful mind; In pur-er
sea The gra-cious call-ing of the Lord, Let us like
cease; Take from our souls the strain and stress, And let our
balm; Let sense be dumb, let flesh re-tire; Speak through the

lives Thy serv-ice find, In deep-er rev-'rence, praise.
them, with-out a word, Rise up and fol-low Thee.
or-dered lives con-fess The beau-ty of Thy peace.
earth-quake, wind, and fire, O still small voice of calm! A-MEN.

415 All Glory, Laud and Honor

THEODULPH OF ORLEANS
TR. BY JOHN M. NEALE

MELCHIOR TESCHNER

1. All glo - ry, laud and hon - or To Thee, Re - deem - er, King,
2. Thou art the King of Is - rael, Thou Da - vid's roy - al Son,
3. Thou didst ac - cept their prais - es; Ac - cept the prayers we bring,

To Whom the lips of chil - dren Made sweet ho - san - nas ring!
Who in the Lord's name com - est, The King and bless - ed One!
Who in all good de - light - est, Thou good and gra - cious King!

The peo - ple of the He - brews With palms be - fore Thee went;
To Thee, be - fore Thy pas - sion They sang their hymns of praise;
All glo - ry, laud and hon - or To Thee, Re - deem - er, King,

Our praise and prayer and an - thems Be - fore Thee we pre - sent.
To Thee, now high ex - alt - ed, Our mel - o - dy we raise.
To Whom the lips of chil - dren Made sweet ho - san - nas ring! A-MEN.

Christ Arose! 416

ROBERT LOWRY ROBERT LOWRY

1. Low in the grave He lay— Je - sus my Sav - ior! Wait-ing the com-ing day—
2. Vain-ly they watch His bed—Je - sus my Sav - ior! Vain-ly they seal the dead—
3. Death cannot keep his prey— Je - sus my Sav - ior! He tore the bars a - way—
REFRAIN Faster
Je - sus my Lord! Up from the grave He a - rose, (He a-rose,) With a
might-y tri-umph o'er His foes; (He a - rose!) He a - rose a Vic - tor from the
dark do - main, And He lives for - ev - er with His saints to reign. He a-
rose! He a - rose! Hal - le - lu - jah! Christ a - rose!
He a - rose! He a - rose!
rit.

417 Christ the Lord Is Risen Today

CHARLES WESLEY

ARR. FROM "LYRA DAVIDICA"

1. Christ the Lord is ris'n to - day, Al - - le - lu - ia!
2. Lives a - gain our glo - rious King: Al - - le - lu - ia!
3. Love's re - deem - ing work is done, Al - - le - lu - ia!
4. Soar we now, where Christ has led, Al - - le - lu - ia!

Sons of men and an - gels say: Al - - - le - lu - ia!
Where, O death, is now thy sting? Al - - - le - lu - ia!
Fought the fight, the bat - tle won; Al - - - le - lu - ia!
Fol - l'wing our ex - alt - ed Head; Al - - - le - lu - ia!

Raise your joys and tri - umphs high, Al - - - le - lu - ia!
Dy - ing once, He all doth save: Al - - - le - lu - ia!
Death in vain for - bids Him rise; Al - - - le - lu - ia!
Made like Him, like Him we rise; Al - - - le - lu - ia!

Sing, ye heav'ns, and earth re - ply. Al - - - le - lu - ia!
Where thy vic - to - ry, O grave? Al - - - le - lu - ia!
Christ has o - pened Par - a - dise. Al - - - le - lu - ia!
Ours the cross, the grave, the skies. Al - - - le - lu - ia!

Come, Ye Faithful, Raise the Strain

John of Damascus
Tr. by John M. Neale

Arthur S. Sullivan

1. Come, ye faithful, raise the strain Of triumphant gladness;
God hath brought His Israel Into joy from sadness.
Loosed from Pharaoh's bitter yoke Jacob's sons and daughters,
Led them with unmoistened foot Through the Red Sea waters.

2. 'Tis the Spring of souls today; Christ hath burst His prison,
And from three day's sleep in death As a sun hath risen.
All the Winter of our sins, Long and dark, is flying
From His light, to whom we give Laud and praise undying.

3. Now the queen of seasons, bright With the day of splendor,
With the royal feast of feasts, Comes its joy to render;
Comes to glad Jerusalem, Who with true affection
Welcomes in unwearied strains Jesus' resurrection.

4. Alleluia now to Thee, Christ, our King immortal,
Who hast passed the gates of death And the tomb's sealed portal;
Who, though never door unclose, In th'assembly standing,
Breathest on Thy friends the peace Past all understanding. Amen.

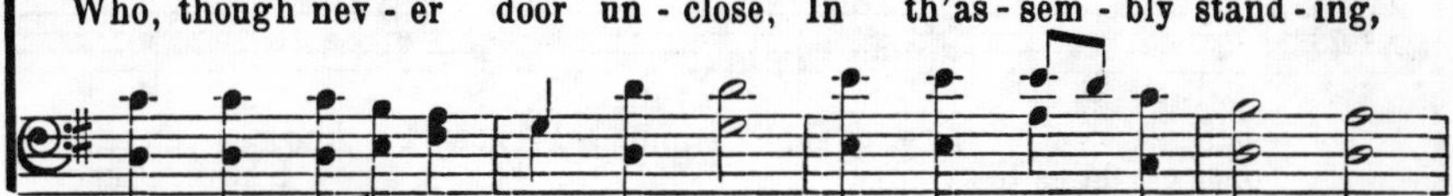

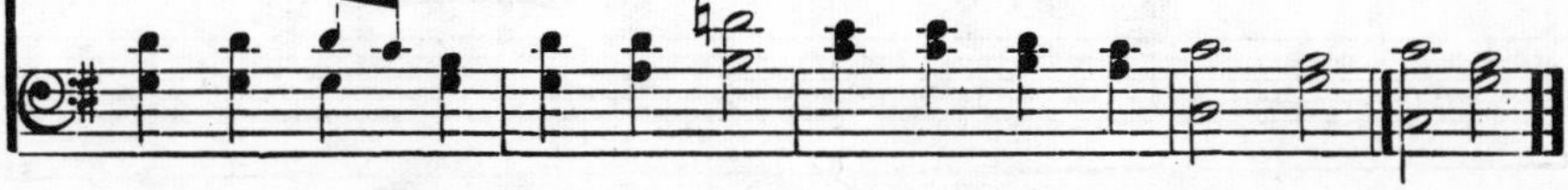

419 I Know That My Redeemer Liveth

JESSIE B. POUNDS JAMES H. FILLMORE

1. I know that my Redeemer liv-eth, And on the earth a-gain shall stand;
2. I know His promise never fail-eth, The word He speaks, it can-not die;
3. I know my mansion He prepareth, That where He is there I may be;
1. And on the earth again shall stand;
I know e-ter-nal life He giv-eth, That grace and pow'r are in His hand.
Tho' cruel death my flesh assaileth, Yet I shall see . . . . Him by and by.
O wondrous tho't, for me He careth, And He at last. . . . will come for me.
That grace and pow'r are in His hand.
CHORUS
I know, I know. . . . . . . that Je-sus liv-eth, And on the
I know, I know
earth. . . . . . . a-gain shall stand; I know, I know. . . . . . .
And on the earth
I know, I know
that life He giv-eth, That grace and pow'r. . . . . . are in His hand.
That grace and pow'r

Day Is Dying in the West

420

MARY A. LATHBURY — WILLIAM F. SHERWIN

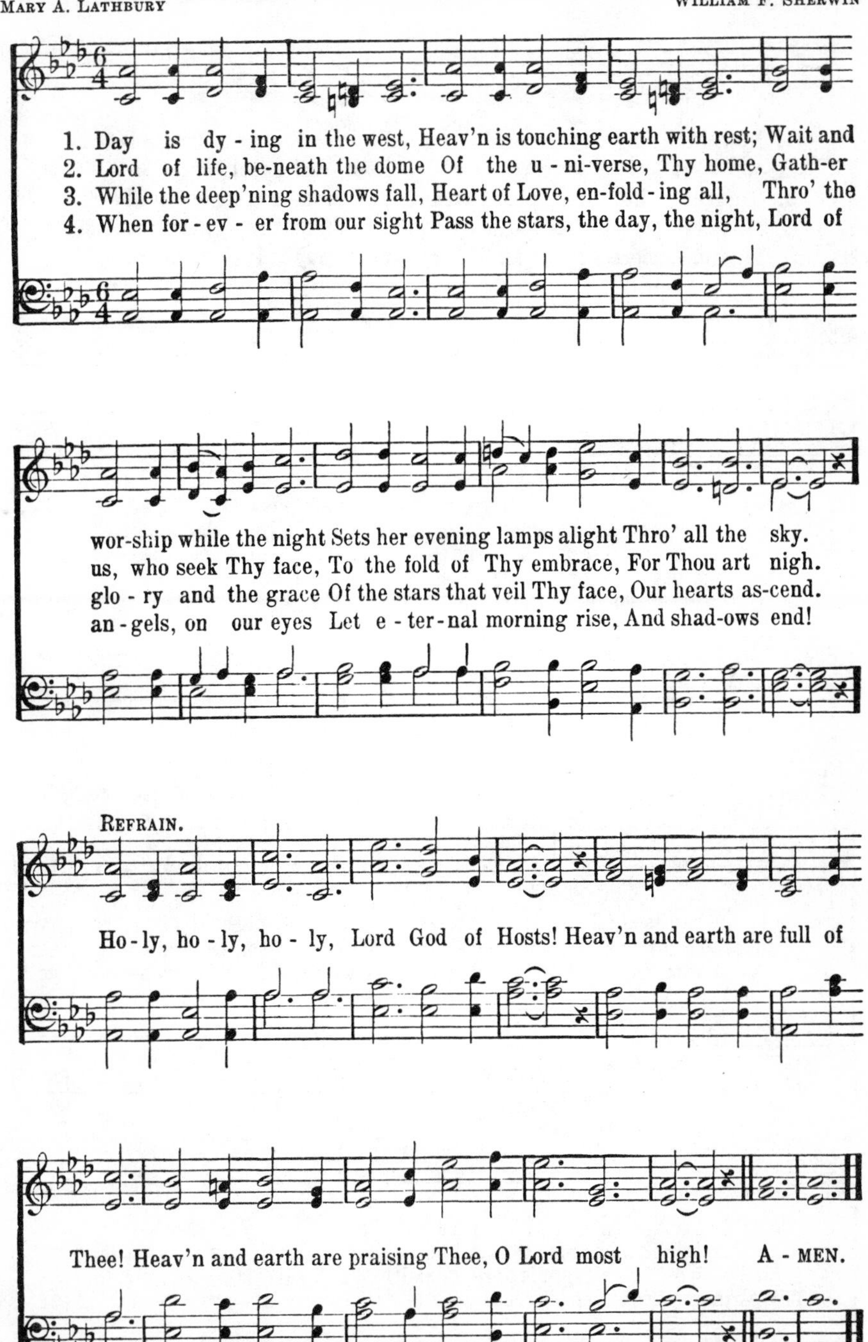
1. Day is dy - ing in the west, Heav'n is touching earth with rest; Wait and
2. Lord of life, be-neath the dome Of the u - ni-verse, Thy home, Gath-er
3. While the deep'ning shadows fall, Heart of Love, en-fold - ing all, Thro' the
4. When for - ev - er from our sight Pass the stars, the day, the night, Lord of
wor-ship while the night Sets her evening lamps alight Thro' all the sky.
us, who seek Thy face, To the fold of Thy embrace, For Thou art nigh.
glo - ry and the grace Of the stars that veil Thy face, Our hearts as-cend.
an - gels, on our eyes Let e - ter - nal morning rise, And shad-ows end!
REFRAIN.
Ho - ly, ho - ly, ho - ly, Lord God of Hosts! Heav'n and earth are full of
Thee! Heav'n and earth are praising Thee, O Lord most high! A - MEN.

421 Now the Day Is Over

SABINE BARING-GOULD — JOSEPH BARNBY

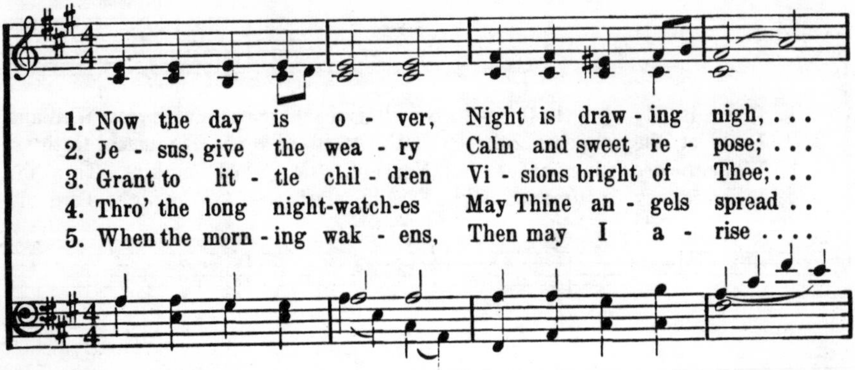

1. Now the day is o - ver, Night is draw - ing nigh, . . .
2. Je - sus, give the wea - ry Calm and sweet re - pose; . . .
3. Grant to lit - tle chil - dren Vi - sions bright of Thee; . . .
4. Thro' the long night-watch-es May Thine an - gels spread . .
5. When the morn - ing wak - ens, Then may I a - rise . . . .

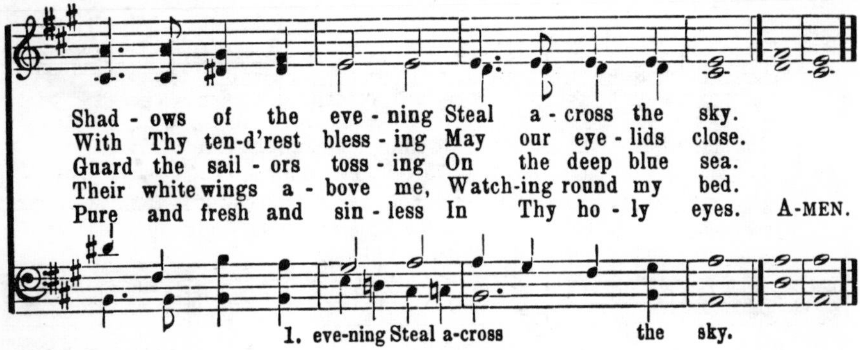

Shad - ows of the eve - ning Steal a - cross the sky.
With Thy ten-d'rest bless - ing May our eye - lids close.
Guard the sail - ors toss - ing On the deep blue sea.
Their white wings a - bove me, Watch-ing round my bed.
Pure and fresh and sin - less In Thy ho - ly eyes. A-MEN.

1. eve-ning Steal a-cross the sky.

422 Sun of My Soul

JOHN KEBLE — ADAPTED FROM "KATHOLISCHES GESANGBUCH"

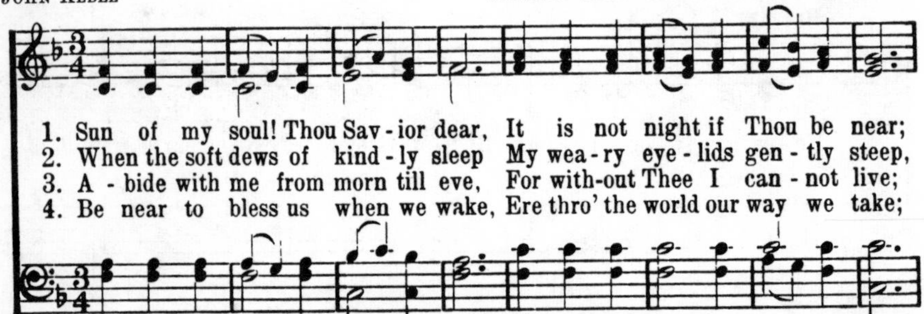

1. Sun of my soul! Thou Sav - ior dear, It is not night if Thou be near;
2. When the soft dews of kind - ly sleep My wea - ry eye - lids gen - tly steep,
3. A - bide with me from morn till eve, For with-out Thee I can - not live;
4. Be near to bless us when we wake, Ere thro' the world our way we take;

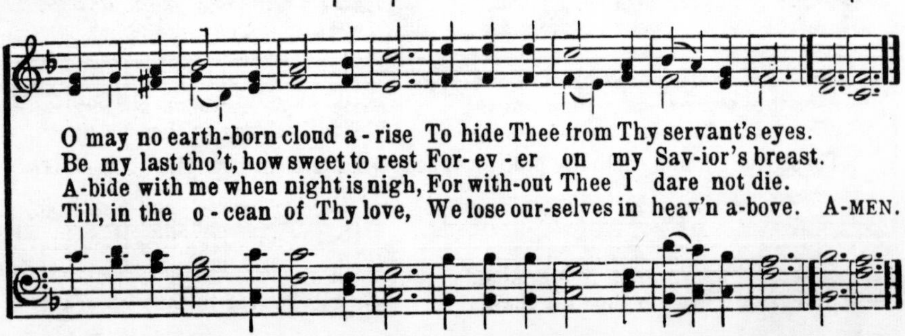

O may no earth-born cloud a - rise To hide Thee from Thy servant's eyes.
Be my last tho't, how sweet to rest For - ev - er on my Sav-ior's breast.
A-bide with me when night is nigh, For with-out Thee I dare not die.
Till, in the o - cean of Thy love, We lose our-selves in heav'n a-bove. A-MEN.

Faith of Our Fathers

FREDERICK W. FABER — HENRI F. HEMY, ALT. BY JAMES G. WALTON

1. Faith of our fa-thers! liv - ing still In spite of dung-eon, fire and sword:
2. Our fa-thers, chained in pri-sons dark, Were still in heart and conscience free:
3. Faith of our fa-thers, we still strive To win all na-tions un - to thee!
4. Faith of our fa-thers! we will love Both friend and foe in all our strife,

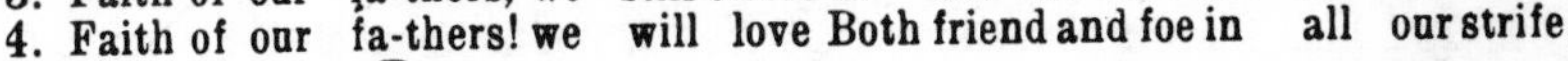

O how our hearts beat high with joy When-e'er we hear that glorious word!
How sweet would be their children's fate, If they, like them, could die for thee!
And thro' the truth that comes from God Mankind shall then in - deed be free:
And preach thee, too, as love knows how, By kind-ly words and virtuous life:

Faith of our fa-thers! ho - ly faith! We will be true to thee till death!
Faith of our fa-thers! ho - ly faith! We will be true to thee till death!
Faith of our fa-thers! ho - ly faith! We will be true to thee till death!
Faith of our fa-thers! ho - ly faith! We will be true to thee till death!

Faith of Our Mothers

424

TUNE-ABOVE

1 Faith of our mothers, living still
In cradle song and bedtime prayer;
In nursery lore and fireside love,
Thy presence still pervades the air:
Faith of our mothers, living faith!
We will be true to thee till death.

2 Faith of our mothers, loving faith,
Fount of our childhood's trust and grace,
Oh, may thy consecration prove
Source of a finer, nobler race:
Faith of our mothers, living faith,
We will be true to thee till death.

3 Faith of our mothers, guiding faith,
For youthful longing, youthful doubt,
How blurred our vision, blind our way,
Thy providential care without:
Faith of our mothers, guiding faith,
We will be true to thee till death.

4 Faith of our mothers, Christian faith,
In truth beyond our stumbling creeds,
Still serve the home and save the Church,
And breathe thy spirit thro' our deeds:
Faith of our mothers, Christian faith!
We will be true to thee till death.

Words by A. B. Patten

425 Faith Is the Victory!

John H. Yates — Ira D. Sankey

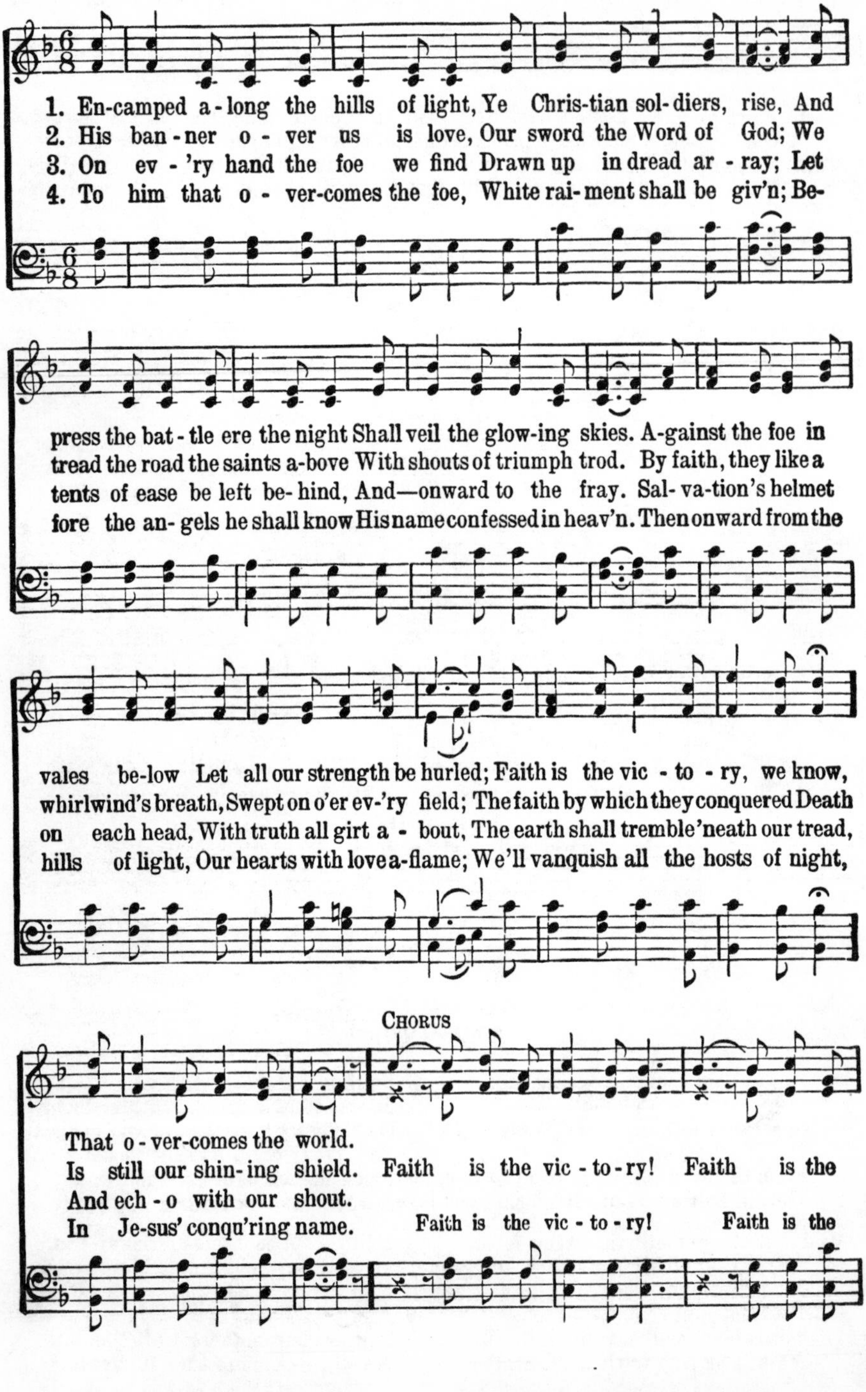

1. En-camped a-long the hills of light, Ye Chris-tian sol-diers, rise, And press the bat-tle ere the night Shall veil the glow-ing skies. A-gainst the foe in vales be-low Let all our strength be hurled; Faith is the vic-to-ry, we know, That o-ver-comes the world.

2. His ban-ner o-ver us is love, Our sword the Word of God; We tread the road the saints a-bove With shouts of triumph trod. By faith, they like a whirlwind's breath, Swept on o'er ev-'ry field; The faith by which they conquered Death Is still our shin-ing shield.

3. On ev-'ry hand the foe we find Drawn up in dread ar-ray; Let tents of ease be left be-hind, And—onward to the fray. Sal-va-tion's helmet on each head, With truth all girt a-bout, The earth shall tremble 'neath our tread, And ech-o with our shout.

4. To him that o-ver-comes the foe, White rai-ment shall be giv'n; Be-fore the an-gels he shall know His name confessed in heav'n. Then onward from the hills of light, Our hearts with love a-flame; We'll vanquish all the hosts of night, In Je-sus' conqu'ring name.

Chorus

Faith is the vic-to-ry! Faith is the

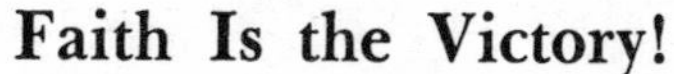
Faith Is the Victory!

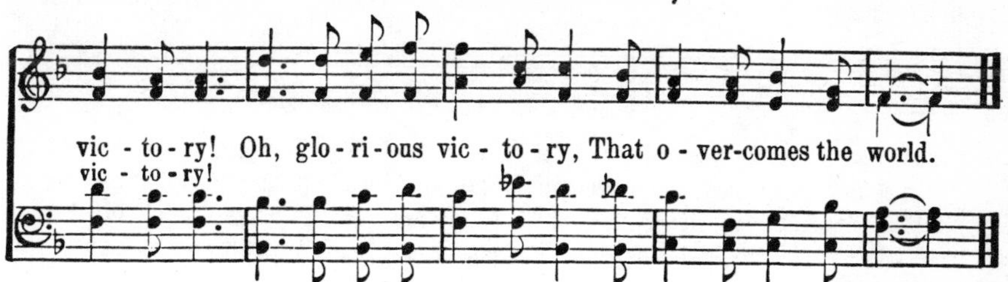
vic - to - ry! Oh, glo - ri - ous vic - to - ry, That o - ver-comes the world.
vic - to - ry!

Beneath the Cross of Jesus

ELIZABETH C. CLEPHANE

FREDERICK C. MAKER

1. Be - neath the cross of Je - sus I fain would take my stand,
The shad - ow of a might - y Rock With - in a wea - ry land;
A home with - in the wil - der - ness, A rest up - on the way,
From the burn - ing of the noon - day heat, And the bur - den of the day.

2. Up - on that cross of Je - sus Mine eye at times can see
The ver - y dy - ing form of One Who suf - fered there for me;
And from my smit - ten heart with tears Two won - ders I con - fess,
The won - ders of His glo - rious love, And my own worth - less - ness.

3. I take, O cross, thy shad - ow For my a - bid - ing - place;
I ask no oth - er sun - shine than The sun - shine of His face;
Con - tent to let the world go by, To know no gain nor loss,
My sin - ful self my on - ly shame, My glo - ry all the cross.

427 The Touch of His Hand on Mine

JESSIE B. POUNDS HENRY P. MORTON

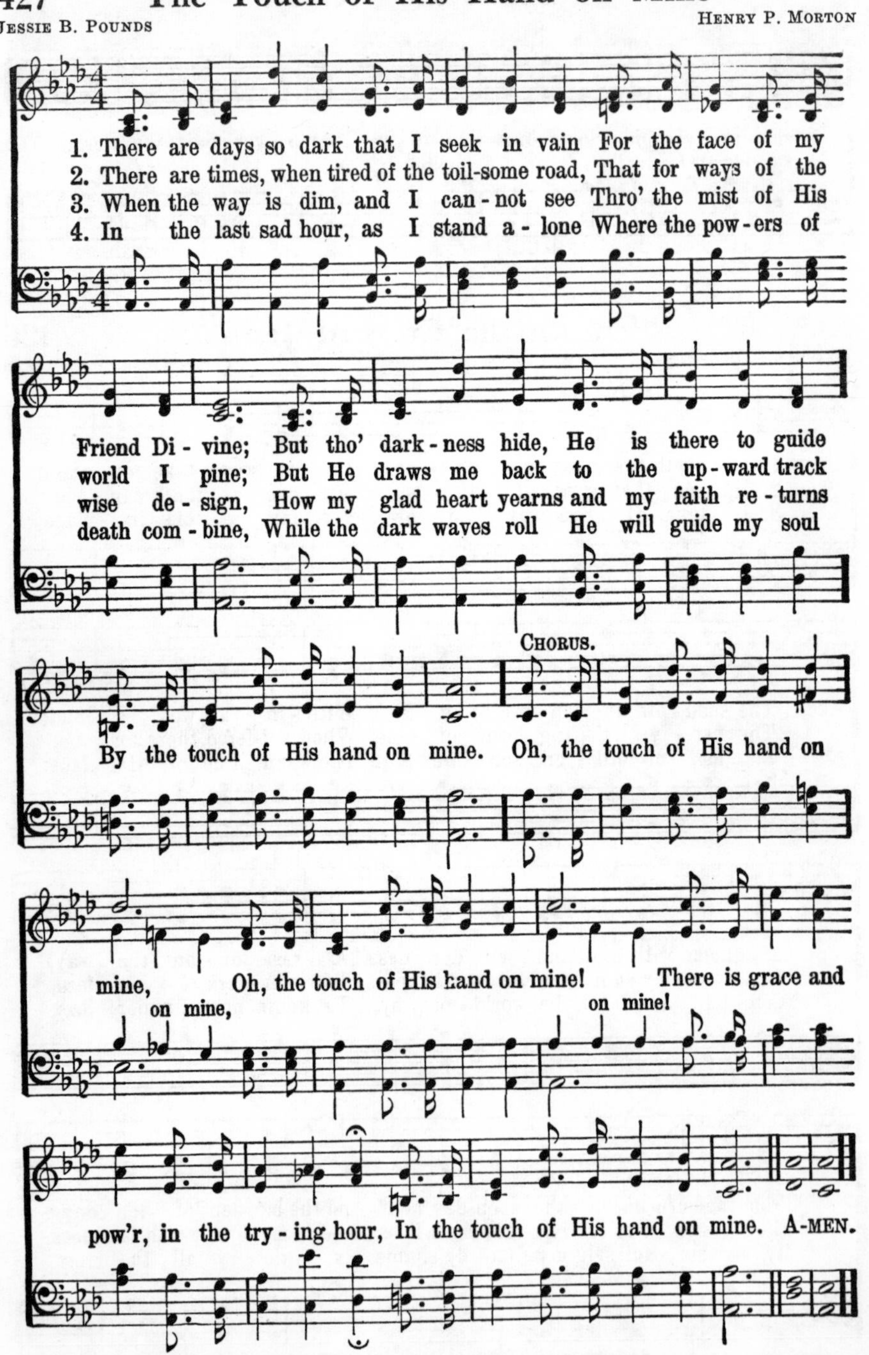
1. There are days so dark that I seek in vain For the face of my Friend Di - vine; But tho' dark - ness hide, He is there to guide By the touch of His hand on mine.
2. There are times, when tired of the toil-some road, That for ways of the world I pine; But He draws me back to the up-ward track
3. When the way is dim, and I can - not see Thro' the mist of His wise de - sign, How my glad heart yearns and my faith re - turns
4. In the last sad hour, as I stand a - lone Where the pow - ers of death com - bine, While the dark waves roll He will guide my soul
CHORUS.
Oh, the touch of His hand on mine, on mine, Oh, the touch of His hand on mine! on mine! There is grace and pow'r, in the try - ing hour, In the touch of His hand on mine. A-MEN.

In the Garden

C. AUSTIN MILES C. AUSTIN MILES

1. I come to the gar - den a - lone, While the dew is still on the
2. He speaks, and the sound of His voice Is so sweet the birds hush their
3. I'd stay in the gar - den with Him Tho' the night a - round me be
ros - es, And the voice I hear, Fall - ing on my ear, The
sing - ing, And the mel - o - dy That He gave to me, With-
fall - ing, But He bids me go; Thro' the voice of woe His
CHORUS
Son of God dis - clos - es.
in my heart is ring - ing. And He walks with me, and He
voice to me is call - ing.
talks with me, And He tells me I am His own; And the
joy we share as we tar - ry there, None oth - er has ev - er known.

429 O Master, Let Me Walk with Thee

WASHINGTON GLADDEN H. PERCY SMITH

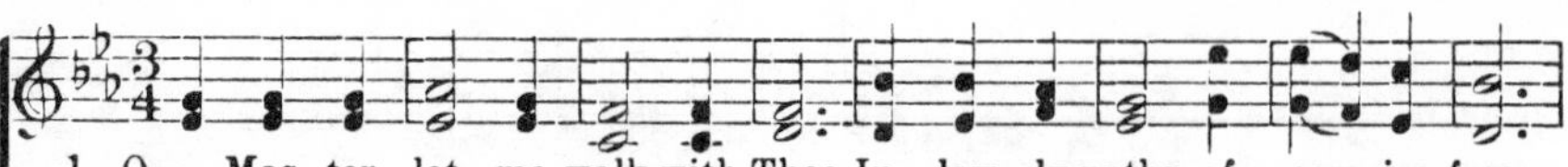

1. O Mas-ter, let me walk with Thee In low-ly paths of serv-ice free;
2. Help me the slow of heart to move By some clear, win-ning word of love;
3. Teach me Thy pa-tience! still with Thee In clos-er, dear-er com-pa-ny,
4. In hope that sends a shin-ing ray Far down the fu-ture's broad'ning way,

Tell me Thy se-cret; help me bear The strain of toil, the fret of care.
Teach me the way-ward feet to stay, And guide them in the homeward way.
In work that keeps faith sweet and strong, In trust that tri-umphs o-ver wrong.
In peace that on-ly Thou canst give, With Thee, O Mas-ter, let me live.

430 Blest Be the Tie That Binds

JOHN FAWCETT HANS G. NÄGELI
ARR. BY LOWELL MASON

1. Blest be the tie that binds Our hearts in Chris-tian love; The
2. Be-fore our Fa-ther's throne, We pour our ar-dent prayers; Our
3. We share our mu-tual woes, Our mu-tual bur-dens bear; And
4. When we a-sun-der part, It gives us in-ward pain; But

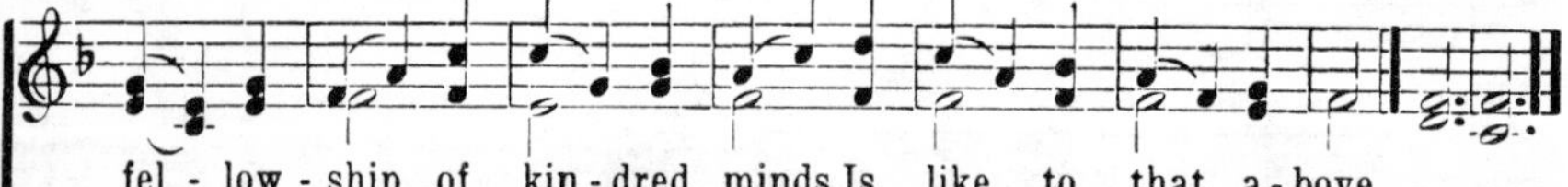

fel-low-ship of kin-dred minds Is like to that a-bove.
fears, our hopes, our aims are one, Our com-forts and our cares.
oft-en for each oth-er flows The sym-pa-thiz-ing tear.
we shall still be joined in heart, And hope to meet a-gain. A-MEN.

Follow On

W. O. Cushing — Robert Lowry

1. Down in the val-ley with my Sav-iour I would go, Where the flowers are
2. Down in the val-ley with my Sav-iour I would go, Where the storms are
3. Down in the val-ley, or up - on the moun-tain steep, Close be - side my
bloom-ing and the sweet wa-ters flow; Ev-ery-where He leads me I would
sweep-ing and the dark wa-ters flow; With His hand to lead me I will
Sav - iour would my soul ev - er keep; He will lead me safe - ly in the
fol - low, fol - low on, Walk-ing in His foot-steps till the crown be won.
nev - er, nev - er fear, Dan-ger can-not fright me if my Lord is near.
path that He has trod, Up to where they gath-er on the hills of God.
Refrain
Fol-low! fol-low! I would follow Je-sus! Anywhere, everywhere, I would follow on!
Fol-low! fol-low! I would follow Jesus! Everywhere He leads me I would follow on!

432 According to Thy Gracious Word

JAMES MONTGOMERY — HENRY W. GREATOREX'S COLLECTION

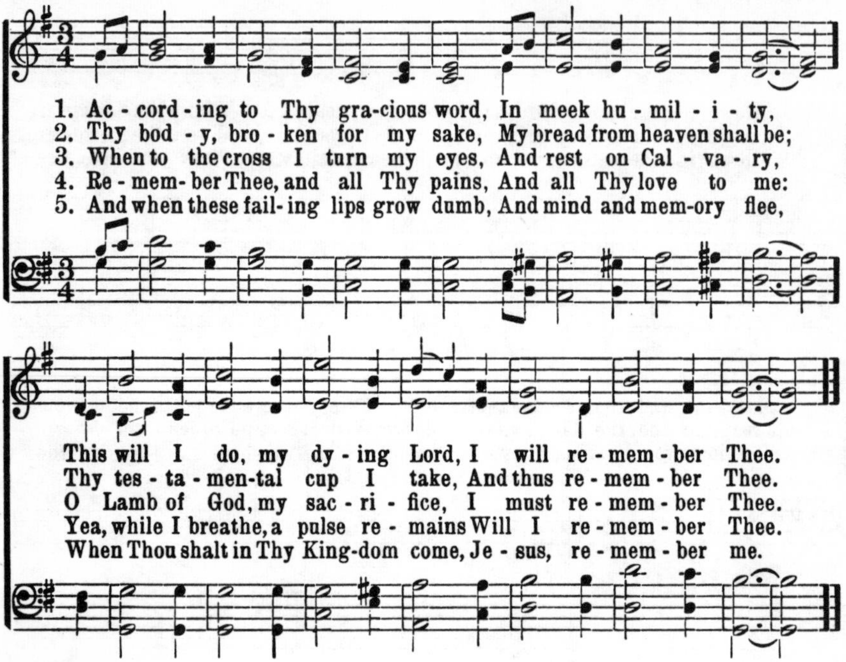

1. According to Thy gracious word, In meek humility,
This will I do, my dying Lord, I will remember Thee.

2. Thy body, broken for my sake, My bread from heaven shall be;
Thy testamental cup I take, And thus remember Thee.

3. When to the cross I turn my eyes, And rest on Calvary,
O Lamb of God, my sacrifice, I must remember Thee.

4. Remember Thee, and all Thy pains, And all Thy love to me:
Yea, while I breathe, a pulse remains Will I remember Thee.

5. And when these failing lips grow dumb, And mind and memory flee,
When Thou shalt in Thy Kingdom come, Jesus, remember me.

433 Bread of Heaven

JOSEPH CONDER — XAVIER SCHNYDER

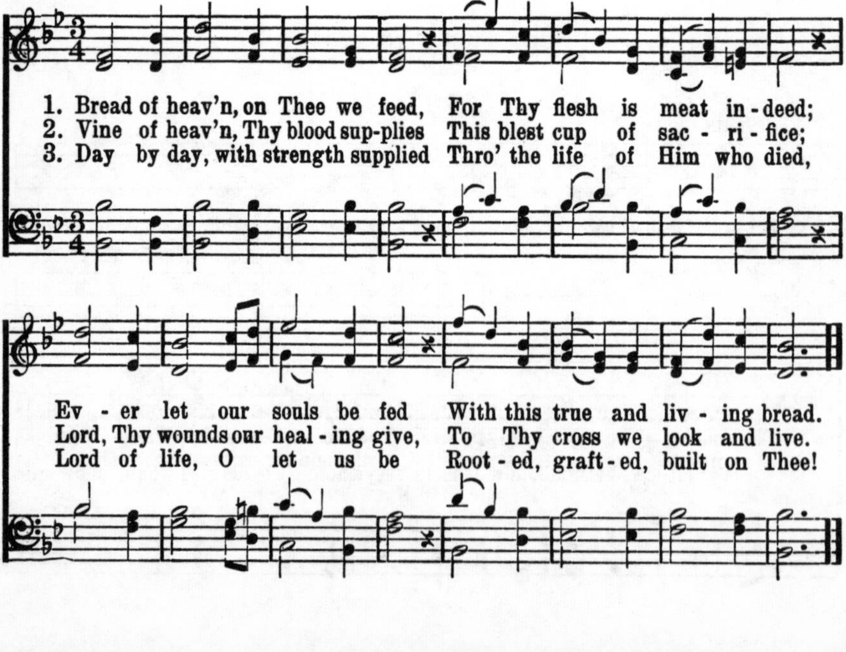

1. Bread of heav'n, on Thee we feed, For Thy flesh is meat indeed;
Ever let our souls be fed With this true and living bread.

2. Vine of heav'n, Thy blood supplies This blest cup of sacrifice;
Lord, Thy wounds our healing give, To Thy cross we look and live.

3. Day by day, with strength supplied Thro' the life of Him who died,
Lord of life, O let us be Rooted, grafted, built on Thee!

Communion Hymn

434

Charles McMillan

J. C. Blaker

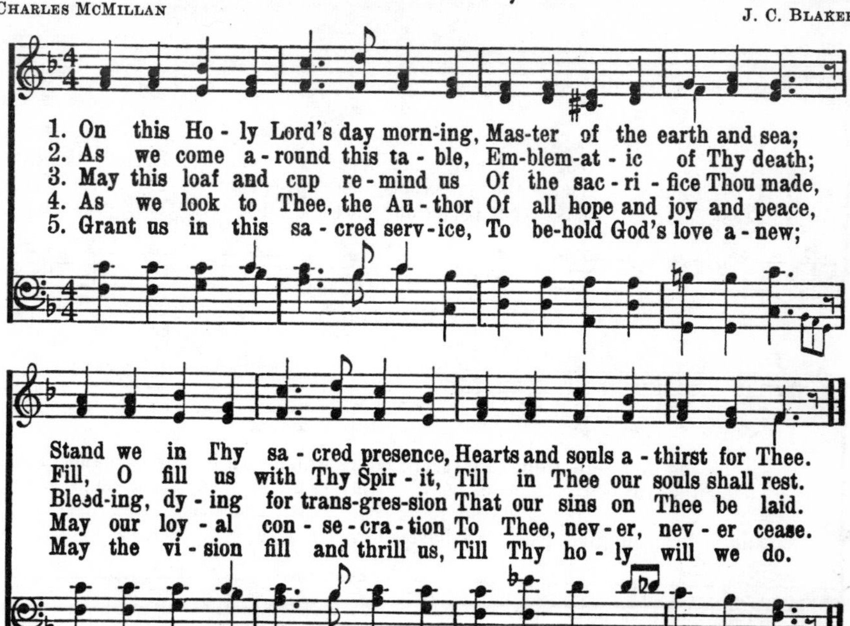

1. On this Ho - ly Lord's day morn-ing, Mas-ter of the earth and sea;
2. As we come a - round this ta - ble, Em-blem-at - ic of Thy death;
3. May this loaf and cup re - mind us Of the sac - ri - fice Thou made,
4. As we look to Thee, the Au - thor Of all hope and joy and peace,
5. Grant us in this sa - cred serv - ice, To be-hold God's love a - new;
Stand we in Thy sa - cred presence, Hearts and souls a - thirst for Thee.
Fill, O fill us with Thy Spir - it, Till in Thee our souls shall rest.
Bleed-ing, dy - ing for trans-gres-sion That our sins on Thee be laid.
May our loy - al con - se - cra - tion To Thee, nev - er, nev - er cease.
May the vi - sion fill and thrill us, Till Thy ho - ly will we do.

How Sweet the Name of Jesus Sounds

435

John Newton

Alexander R. Reinagle

1. How sweet the name of Je - sus sounds In a be - liev - er's ear!
2. It makes the wound-ed spir - it whole And calms the troub-led breast;
3. Dear name! the rock on which I build, My shield and hid - ing place;
4. Je - sus, my Shep-herd, Broth-er, Friend, My Proph - et, Priest and King,

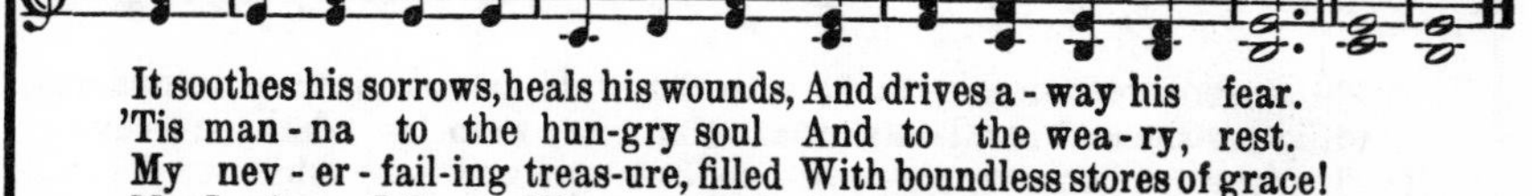

It soothes his sorrows, heals his wounds, And drives a - way his fear.
'Tis man - na to the hun-gry soul And to the wea - ry, rest.
My nev - er - fail-ing treas-ure, filled With boundless stores of grace!
My Lord, my Life, my Way, my End, Ac - cept the praise I bring. A - men.

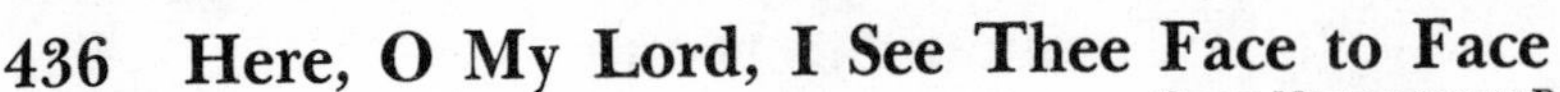

436 Here, O My Lord, I See Thee Face to Face

HORATIUS BONAR | FELIX MENDELSSOHN-BARTHOLDY

1. Here, O my Lord, I see Thee face to face; Here would I
touch and han - dle things un - seen; Here grasp with firm - er hand th' e-
ter - nal grace, And all my wea - ri - ness up - on Thee lean.

2. Here would I feed up - on the bread of God; Here drink with
Thee the roy - al wine of heav'n; Here would I lay a - side each
earth - ly load, Here taste a - fresh the calm of sin for - giv'n.

3. Too soon we rise; the sym - bols dis - ap - pear; The feast, tho'
not the love, is passed and gone; The bread and wine re-move, but
Thou art here— Near - er than ev - er—still my Shield and Sun.

4. Feast aft - er feast thus comes and pass - es by; Yet, pass - ing,
points to the glad feast a - bove—Giv - ing sweet fore - taste of the
fes - tal joy, The Lamb's great bri - dal feast of bliss and love.

437 Fling Out the Banner! Let It Float

GEORGE W. DOANE | JOHN B. CALKIN

1. Fling out the ban-ner, let it float Sky-ward and sea-ward, high and wide;
2. Fling out the ban-ner, heathen lands Shall see from far the glo-rious sight,
3. Fling out the ban-ner, sin-sick souls That sink and per - ish in the strife.
4. Fling out the ban-ner, let it float Sky-ward and sea-ward, high and wide,

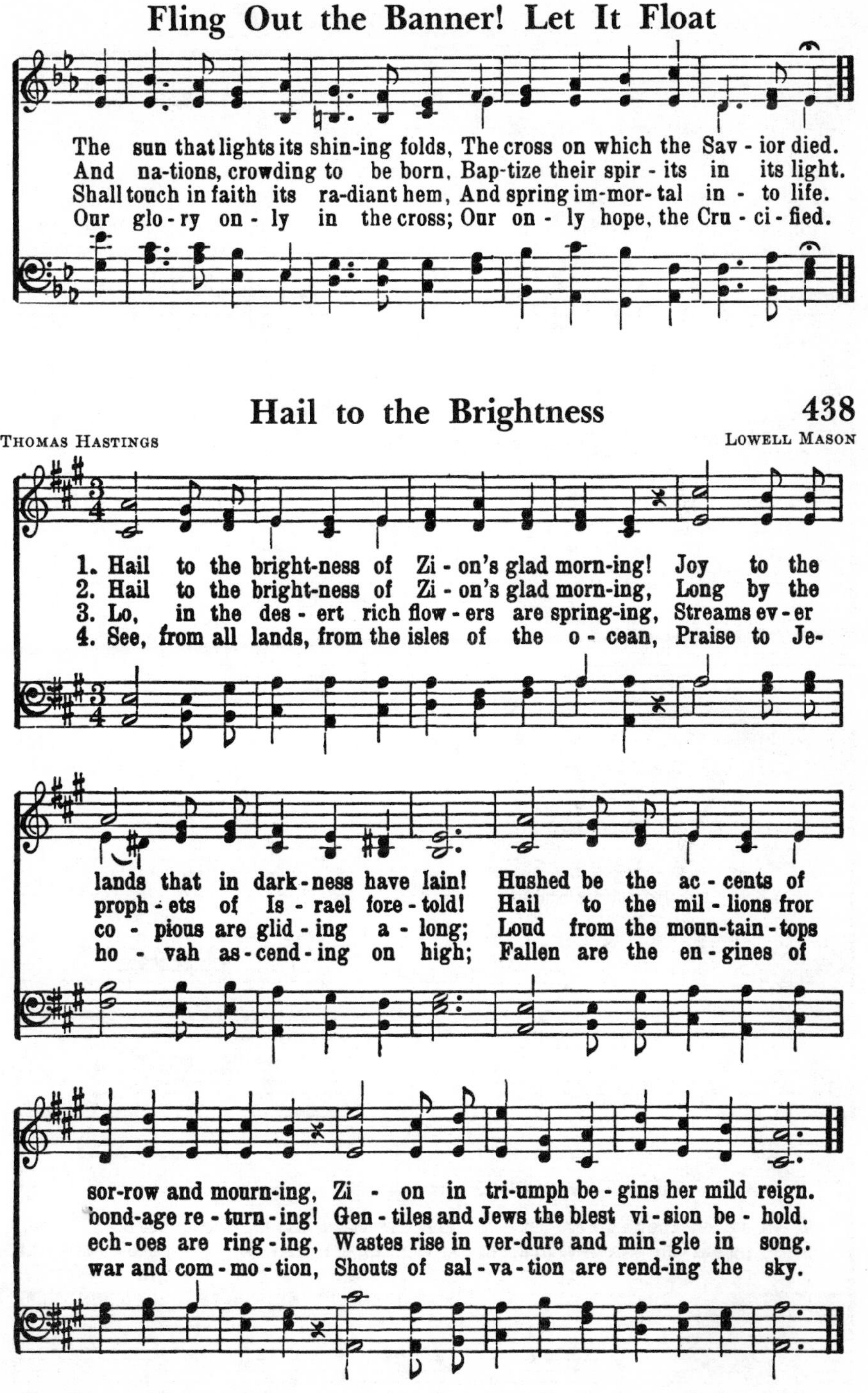
Fling Out the Banner! Let It Float
The sun that lights its shin-ing folds, The cross on which the Sav - ior died.
And na-tions, crowding to be born, Bap-tize their spir - its in its light.
Shall touch in faith its ra-diant hem, And spring im-mor-tal in - to life.
Our glo - ry on - ly in the cross; Our on - ly hope, the Cru - ci - fied.
Hail to the Brightness
438
Thomas Hastings
Lowell Mason
1. Hail to the bright-ness of Zi - on's glad morn-ing! Joy to the
2. Hail to the bright-ness of Zi - on's glad morn-ing, Long by the
3. Lo, in the des - ert rich flow - ers are spring-ing, Streams ev - er
4. See, from all lands, from the isles of the o - cean, Praise to Je-
lands that in dark - ness have lain! Hushed be the ac - cents of
proph - ets of Is - rael fore - told! Hail to the mil - lions from
co - pious are glid - ing a - long; Loud from the moun-tain - tops
ho - vah as-cend - ing on high; Fallen are the en - gines of
sor-row and mourn-ing, Zi - on in tri-umph be - gins her mild reign.
bond-age re - turn - ing! Gen - tiles and Jews the blest vi - sion be - hold.
ech - oes are ring - ing, Wastes rise in ver-dure and min - gle in song.
war and com - mo - tion, Shouts of sal - va - tion are rend-ing the sky.

439 This Do in Remembrance of Me

HELEN E. FROMM HELEN E. FROMM

1. The trial of the cross was ap - proach-ing With its bit-ter-ness, sor-row and
2. Then take of the bread to re - mem - ber That His bod-y was bro-ken for
3. The Sav-iour now liv-eth in glo - ry, Tri - um-phant o'er death and o'er
4. The Son of God gave to His chil-dren This to-ken in mem-'ry of

pain, When there in the up-per room, Je - sus Spoke
you; And drink of the cup to re - mem - ber His
sin; Un - til He shall come for His dear ones, Do
Him; Come, take of the bread of life free - ly, And

with His dis - ci - ples a - gain.
blood that was shed for you too.
this in re-mem-brance of Him.
let His blood cleanse you from sin.

CHORUS

This do in re-mem-brance of
Do this in re-mem-brance of

Me, This do in re-mem-brance of Me; The wine and the bread speak of
Him, Do this in re-mem-brance of Him; The wine and the bread speak of

blood that was shed; This do in re-mem-brance of Me.
blood that was shed; Do this in re-mem-brance of Him.

Macedonia

ANNE ORTLUND

HENRY S. CUTLER

1. The vis-ion of a dy-ing world Is vast be-fore our eyes;
2. The sav-age hugs his god of stone And fears de-scent of night;
3. To-day, as un-der-stand-ing's bounds Are stretch'd on ev-ery hand,
4. The warn-ing bell of judg-ment tolls, A-bove us looms the cross;
We feel the heart-beat of its need, We hear its fee-ble cries:
The cit-y dwell-er cring-es lone A-mid the gar-ish light:
O, clothe Thy Word in bright, new sounds, And speed it o'er the land;
A-round are ev-er-dy-ing souls-How great, how great the loss!
Lord Je-sus Christ, re-vive Thy church In this, her cru-cial hour!
Lord Je-sus Christ, a-rouse Thy church To see their mute dis-tress!
Lord Je-sus Christ, em-pow-er us To preach by ev-ery means!
O Lord, con-strain and move Thy church The glad news to im-part!
Lord Je-sus Christ, a-wake Thy church With Spir-it-giv-en pow'r.
Lord Je-sus Christ, e-quip Thy church With love and ten-der-ness.
Lord Je-sus Christ, em-bold-en us In near and dis-tant scenes.
And Lord, as Thou dost stir Thy church, Be-gin with-in my heart.

441 Go Ye into All the World

James McGranahan James McGranahan

1. Far, far a-way, in hea-then darkness dwell-ing, Mil-lions of souls for-
2. See o'er the world wide-o - pen doors in - vit - ing, Sol-diers of Christ, a-
3. "Why will ye die?" the voice of God is call-ing, "Why will ye die?" re-
4. God speed the day, when those of ev - 'ry na - tion "Glo - ry to God!" tri-
ev - er may be lost; Who, who will go, sal-va-tion's sto-ry tell-ing,
rise and en - ter in! Chris-tians, a-wake! your forc-es all u - nit - ing,
ech - o in His name; Je - sus hath died to save from death ap-pall-ing,
um-phant-ly shall sing; Ran-somed, redeemed, re - joic-ing in sal - va - tion,
Chorus
Look-ing to Je - sus, minding not the cost?
Send forth the gospel, break the chains of sin. "All pow'r is giv-en un - to Me,
Life and sal-va-tion therefore go pro-claim.
Shout Hal - le - lu - jah, for the Lord is King.
All pow'r is giv - en un - to Me, Go ye in - to all the world and
preach the gos - pel, And lo, I am with you al - way."

So Send I You

E. Margaret Clarkson — John W. Peterson

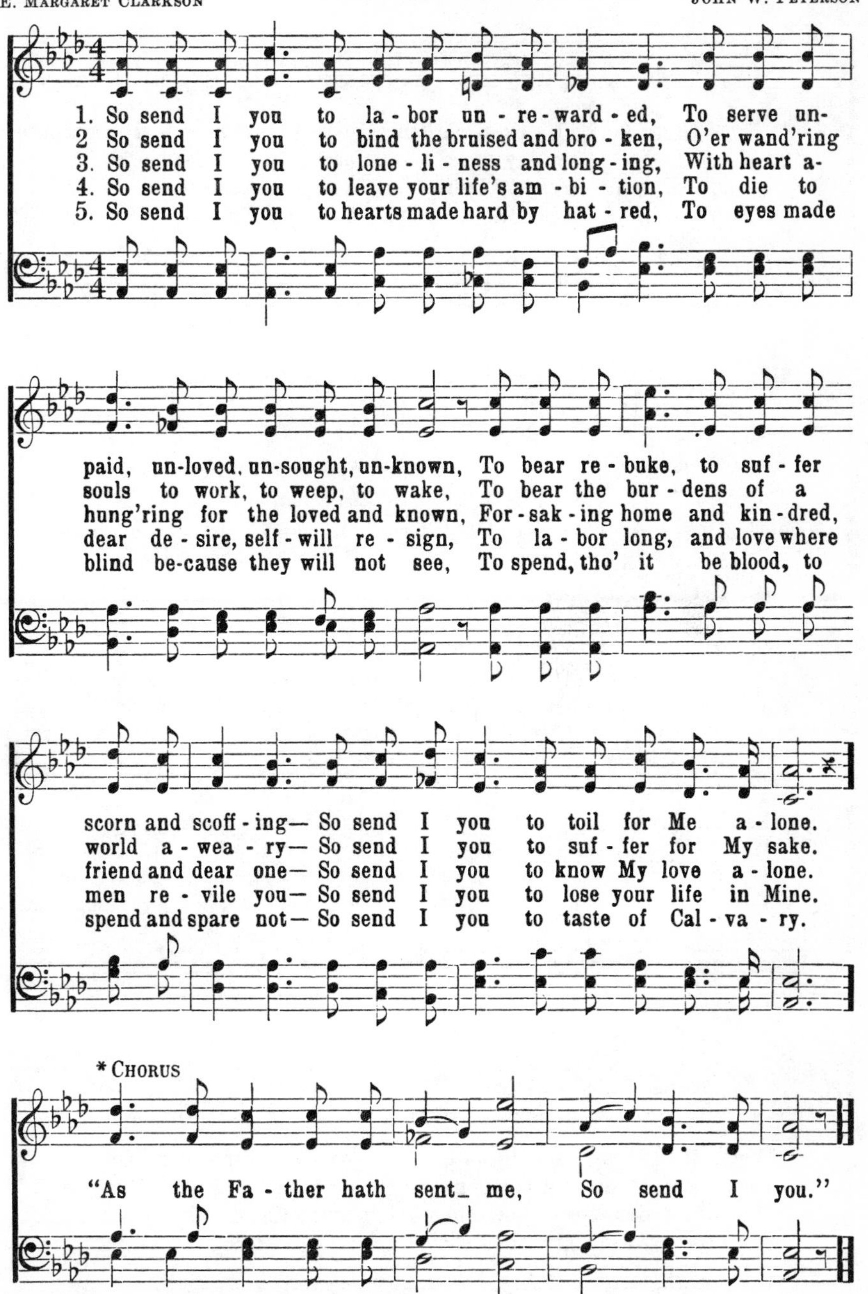
1. So send I you to la - bor un - re - ward - ed, To serve un-
2 So send I you to bind the bruised and bro - ken, O'er wand'ring
3. So send I you to lone - li - ness and long - ing, With heart a-
4. So send I you to leave your life's am - bi - tion, To die to
5. So send I you to hearts made hard by hat - red, To eyes made
paid, un-loved, un-sought, un-known, To bear re - buke, to suf - fer
souls to work, to weep, to wake, To bear the bur - dens of a
hung'ring for the loved and known, For - sak - ing home and kin - dred,
dear de - sire, self - will re - sign, To la - bor long, and love where
blind be-cause they will not see, To spend, tho' it be blood, to
scorn and scoff - ing— So send I you to toil for Me a - lone.
world a - wea - ry— So send I you to suf - fer for My sake.
friend and dear one— So send I you to know My love a - lone.
men re - vile you— So send I you to lose your life in Mine.
spend and spare not— So send I you to taste of Cal - va - ry.
* Chorus
"As the Fa - ther hath sent me, So send I you."

*Effective if sung only after the last verse.

443 From Greenland's Icy Mountains

Reginald Heber — Lowell Mason

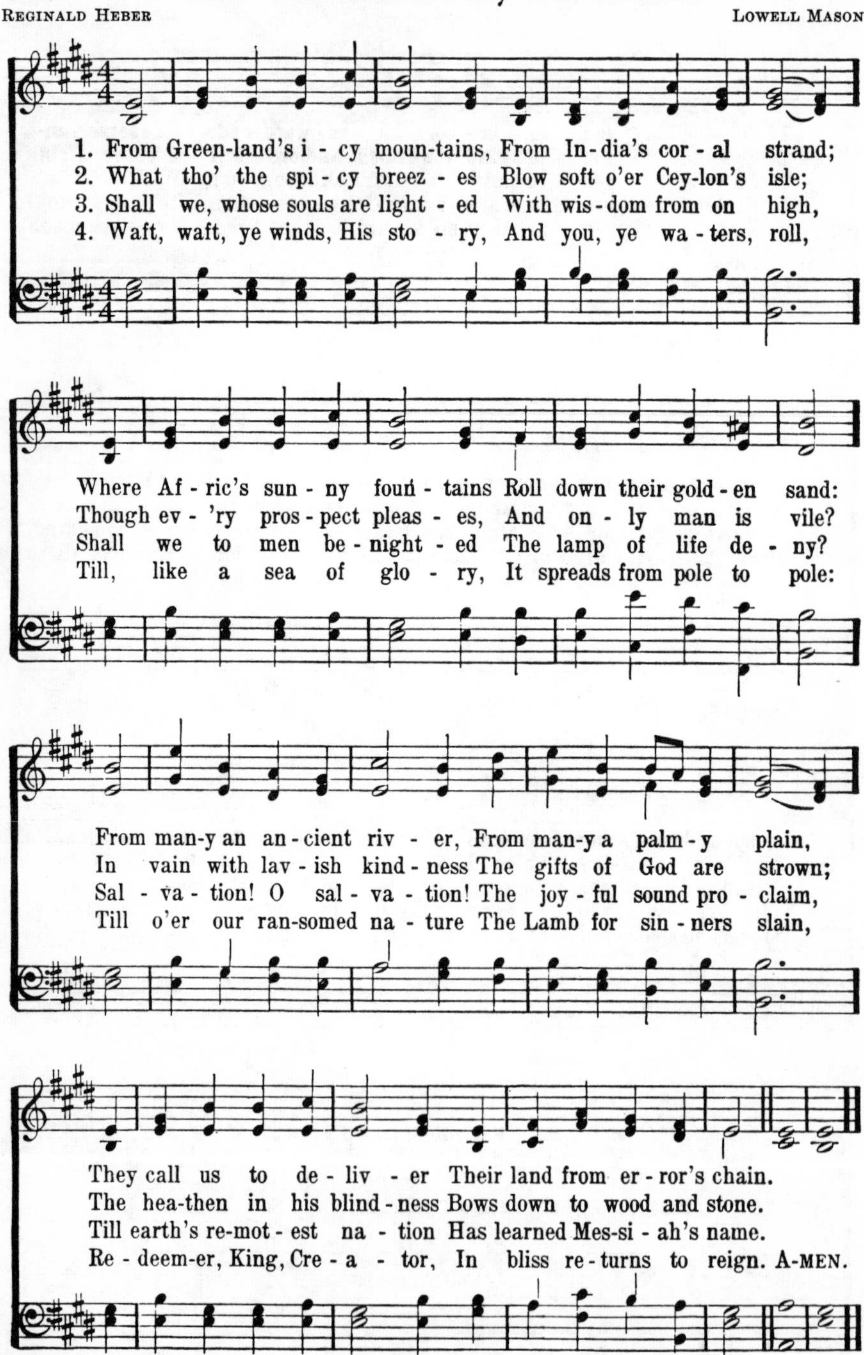
1. From Green-land's i - cy moun-tains, From In-dia's cor - al strand;
2. What tho' the spi - cy breez - es Blow soft o'er Cey-lon's isle;
3. Shall we, whose souls are light - ed With wis-dom from on high,
4. Waft, waft, ye winds, His sto - ry, And you, ye wa - ters, roll,
Where Af - ric's sun - ny foun - tains Roll down their gold - en sand:
Though ev - 'ry pros - pect pleas - es, And on - ly man is vile?
Shall we to men be - night - ed The lamp of life de - ny?
Till, like a sea of glo - ry, It spreads from pole to pole:
From man-y an an - cient riv - er, From man-y a palm - y plain,
In vain with lav - ish kind - ness The gifts of God are strown;
Sal - va - tion! O sal - va - tion! The joy - ful sound pro - claim,
Till o'er our ran-somed na - ture The Lamb for sin - ners slain,
They call us to de - liv - er Their land from er - ror's chain.
The hea-then in his blind - ness Bows down to wood and stone.
Till earth's re-mot - est na - tion Has learned Mes-si - ah's name.
Re - deem-er, King, Cre - a - tor, In bliss re - turns to reign. A-MEN.

Bringing In the Sheaves

KNOWLES SHAW

GEORGE A. MINOR

1. Sow-ing in the morn-ing, sow-ing seeds of kind-ness, Sow-ing in the noon-tide and the dew-y eve; Wait-ing for the har-vest, and the time of reap-ing, We shall come re-joic-ing, bring-ing in the sheaves.
2. Sow-ing in the sun-shine, sow-ing in the shad-ows, Fear-ing nei-ther clouds nor win-ter's chill-ing breeze; By and by the har-vest, and the la-bor end-ed, We shall come re-joic-ing, bring-ing in the sheaves.
3. Go-ing forth with weep-ing, sow-ing for the Mas-ter, Tho' the loss sus-tained our spir-it oft-en grieves; When our weep-ing's o-ver, He will bid us wel-come, We shall come re-joic-ing, bring-ing in the sheaves.
CHORUS
Bring-ing in the sheaves, bring-ing in the sheaves, We shall come re-joic-ing, bring-ing in the sheaves;
Bring-ing in the sheaves, bring-ing in the sheaves, We shall come re-joic-ing, bring-ing in the sheaves.
1
2

445 Jesus Saves

PRISCILLA J. OWENS — WILLIAM J. KIRKPATRICK

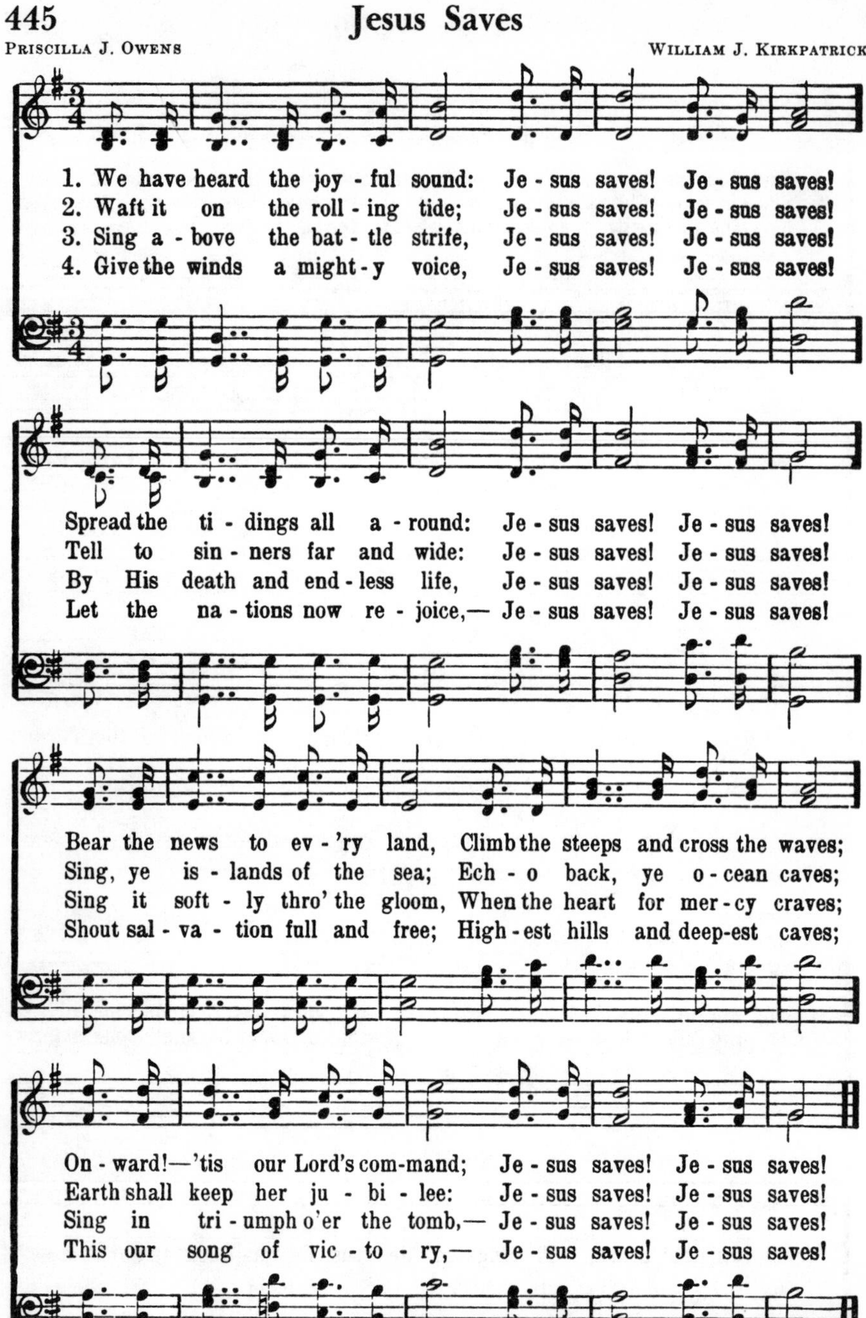

1. We have heard the joy - ful sound: Je - sus saves! Je - sus saves!
2. Waft it on the roll - ing tide; Je - sus saves! Je - sus saves!
3. Sing a - bove the bat - tle strife, Je - sus saves! Je - sus saves!
4. Give the winds a might - y voice, Je - sus saves! Je - sus saves!
Spread the ti - dings all a - round: Je - sus saves! Je - sus saves!
Tell to sin - ners far and wide: Je - sus saves! Je - sus saves!
By His death and end - less life, Je - sus saves! Je - sus saves!
Let the na - tions now re - joice,— Je - sus saves! Je - sus saves!
Bear the news to ev - 'ry land, Climb the steeps and cross the waves;
Sing, ye is - lands of the sea; Ech - o back, ye o - cean caves;
Sing it soft - ly thro' the gloom, When the heart for mer - cy craves;
Shout sal - va - tion full and free; High - est hills and deep-est caves;
On - ward!—'tis our Lord's com-mand; Je - sus saves! Je - sus saves!
Earth shall keep her ju - bi - lee: Je - sus saves! Je - sus saves!
Sing in tri - umph o'er the tomb,— Je - sus saves! Je - sus saves!
This our song of vic - to - ry,— Je - sus saves! Je - sus saves!

O Zion, Haste

446

Mary A. Thomson — James Walch

1. O Zi - on, haste, thy mis-sion high ful - fill - ing, To tell to all the
2. Be-hold how man - y thousands still are ly - ing, Bound in the dark-some
3. Pro-claim to ev - 'ry peo-ple, tongue and na - tion That God in Whom they
4. Give of thy sons to bear the mes-sage glo-rious; Give of thy wealth to

world that God is Light; That He who made all na-tions is not will - ing
pris - on-house of sin, With none to tell them of the Sav-ior's dy - ing,
live and move is love: Tell how He stooped to save His lost cre - a - tion,
speed them on their way; Pour out thy soul for them in prayer vic - to - rious;

Refrain

One soul should per - ish, lost in shades of night.
Or of the life He died for them to win. Pub - lish glad ti - dings,
And died on earth that man might live a - bove.
And all thou spend-est Je - sus will re - pay.

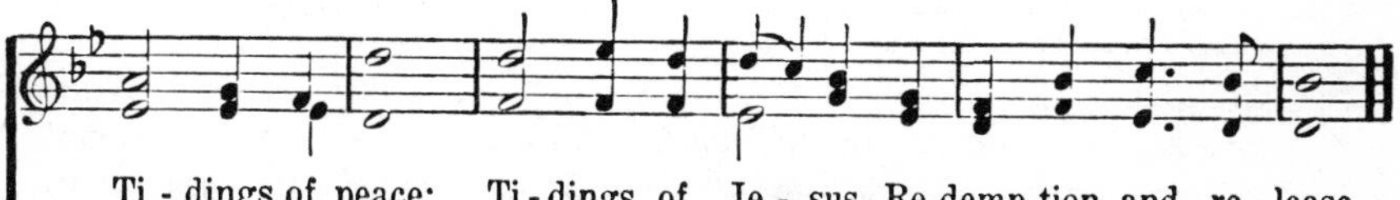

Ti - dings of peace; Ti - dings of Je - sus, Re-demp-tion and re - lease.

447 Send the Light

Charles H. Gabriel — Charles H. Gabriel

1. There's a call comes ring-ing o'er the rest-less wave, "Send the light! . . . Send the light!" There are souls to res-cue, there are souls to save, Send the light! . . .
2. We have heard the Mac-e-do-nian call to-day, "Send the light! . . . Send the light!" And a gold-en of-f'ring at the cross we lay, Send the light! . . .
3. Let us pray that grace may ev-'ry-where a-bound; Send the light! . . . Send the light! And a Christ-like spir-it ev-'ry-where be found, Send the light! . . .
4. Let us not grow wea-ry in the work of love, Send the light! . . . Send the light! Let us gath-er jew-els for a crown a-bove, Send the light! . . .

Send the light! Send the light!

Send the light! . . . Send the light! . . .

Send the light! Send the light!

REFRAIN

Send the light! . . . the bless-ed gos-pel light; Let it shine . . . from shore to shore! . . . . shine . . . for-ev-er-more. . . . .

Send the light! the bless-ed gos-pel light; Let it shine from shore to shore! Let it shine for-ev-er-more.

The Regions Beyond

Albert B. Simpson — Margaret M. Simpson

1. To the re-gions be-yond I must go, I must go, Where the sto-ry has nev-er been told(been told); To the mil-lions that never have heard of His love, I must tell the sweet sto-ry of old (of old).
2. To the hard-est of plac-es He calls me to go, Not think-ing of com-fort or ease (or ease); The world may pronounce me a dreamer, a fool, E - nough if the Mas-ter I please (I please).
3. Oh, ye that are spending your leisure and pow'rs In pleas-ures so fool-ish and fond(and fond); A - wake from your self-ish-ness, fol-ly and sin, And go to the re-gions be-yond (be-yond).
4. There are oth-er "lost sheep" that the Master must bring, And they must the mes-sage be told (be told); He sends me to gath-er them out of all lands, And wel-come them back to His fold(His fold).
Chorus With spirit
To the re - - gions be-yond I must go, I must go, Till the world, all the world, His sal-va - - - tion shall know.
I must go, I must go, To the re-gions be-yond I must go, Till the world, all the world, His sal-va-tion shall know, shall know.
rit.

449 We've a Story to Tell to the Nations

H. Ernest Nichol | H. Ernest Nichol

1. We've a sto - ry to tell to the na - tions That shall turn their hearts to the right,
A sto - ry of truth and mer - cy, A sto - ry of peace and light, A sto - ry of peace and light.

2. We've a song to be sung to the na - tions That shall lift their hearts to the Lord,
A song that shall con - quer e - vil And shat - ter the spear and sword, And shat - ter the spear and sword.

3. We've a mes - sage to give to the na - tions, That the Lord who reign - eth a - bove
Hath sent us His Son to save us, And show us that God is love, And show us that God is love.

4. We've a Sav - ior to show to the na - tions Who the path of sor - row hath trod,
That all of the world's great peo - ples Might come to the truth of God, Might come to the truth of God.

1. That shall turn their hearts to the right,

A sto - ry of peace and light.

Chorus

For the darkness shall turn to dawn - ing, And the dawn - ing to noonday bright,
And Christ's great kingdom shall come to earth, The kingdom of love and light.

rall.

O Beautiful for Spacious Skies

Katherine L. Bates — Samuel A. Ward

1. O beau - ti - ful for spa-cious skies, For am - ber waves of grain,
2. O beau - ti - ful for pil - grim feet, Whose stern, im-pas-sioned stress
3. O beau - ti - ful for he-roes proved In lib - er - at - ing strife,
4. O beau - ti - ful for pa-triot dream That sees be - yond the years
For pur - ple moun-tain maj - es - ties A - bove the fruit - ed plain!
A thor-ough-fare for free - dom beat A - cross the wil - der - ness!
Who more than self their coun-try loved, And mer - cy more than life!
Thine al - a - bas - ter cit - ies gleam, Undimmed by hu - man tears!
A - mer - i - ca! A - mer - i - ca! God shed His grace on thee,
A - mer - i - ca! A - mer - i - ca! God mend thine ev - 'ry flaw,
A - mer - i - ca! A - mer - i - ca! May God thy gold re - fine,
A - mer - i - ca! A - mer - i - ca! God shed His grace on thee,
And crown thy good with broth - er-hood From sea to shin - ing sea!
Con - firm thy soul in self - con-trol, Thy lib - er - ty in law!
Till all suc - cess be no - ble-ness And ev - 'ry gain di - vine!
And crown thy good with broth - er-hood From sea to shin - ing sea!

451

The Star-Spangled Banner

FRANCIS SCOTT KEY — AUTHOR UNKNOWN

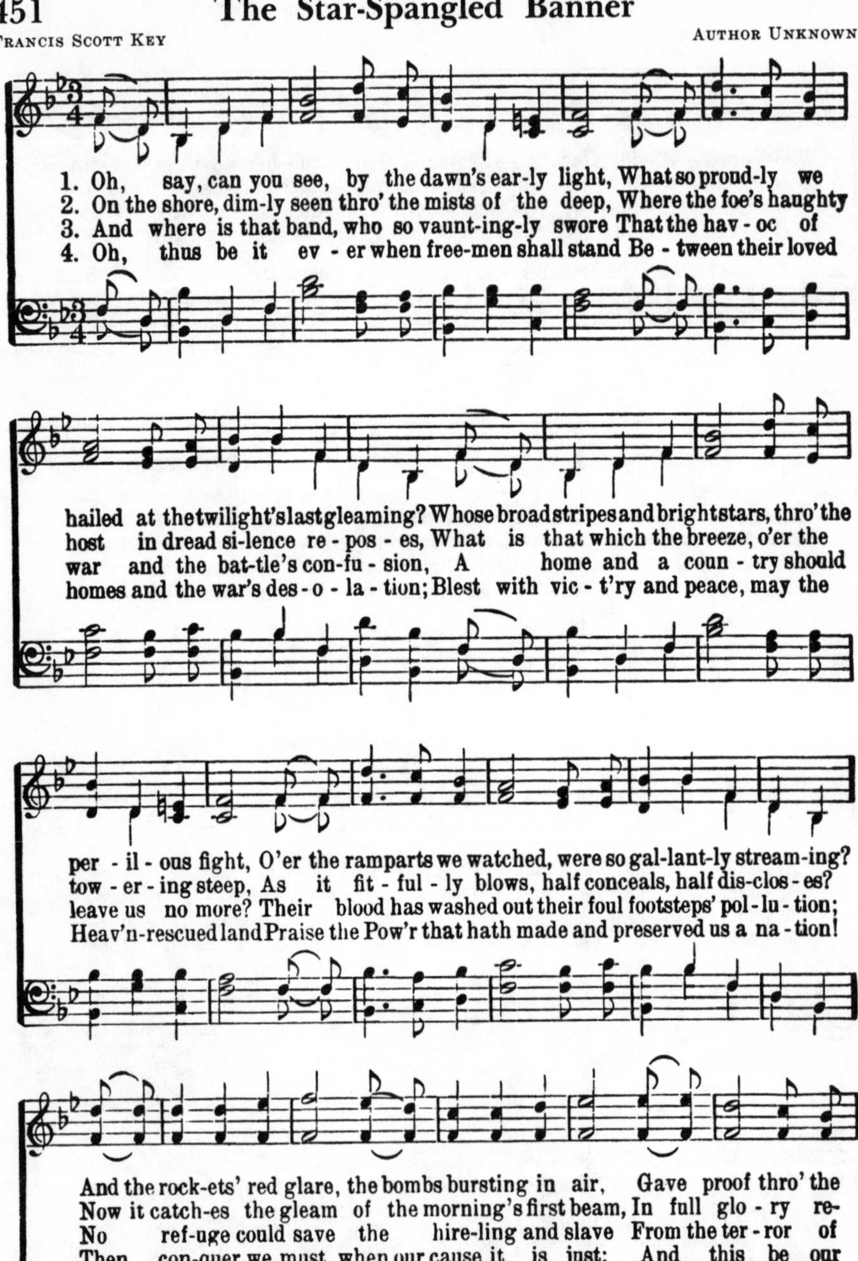
1. Oh, say, can you see, by the dawn's ear-ly light, What so proud-ly we
2. On the shore, dim-ly seen thro' the mists of the deep, Where the foe's haughty
3. And where is that band, who so vaunt-ing-ly swore That the hav-oc of
4. Oh, thus be it ev - er when free-men shall stand Be - tween their loved
hailed at the twilight's last gleaming? Whose broad stripes and bright stars, thro' the
host in dread si-lence re - pos - es, What is that which the breeze, o'er the
war and the bat-tle's con-fu - sion, A home and a coun - try should
homes and the war's des - o - la - tion; Blest with vic - t'ry and peace, may the
per - il - ous fight, O'er the ramparts we watched, were so gal-lant-ly stream-ing?
tow - er - ing steep, As it fit - ful - ly blows, half conceals, half dis-clos - es?
leave us no more? Their blood has washed out their foul footsteps' pol - lu - tion;
Heav'n-rescued land Praise the Pow'r that hath made and preserved us a na - tion!
And the rock-ets' red glare, the bombs bursting in air, Gave proof thro' the
Now it catch-es the gleam of the morning's first beam, In full glo - ry re-
No ref-uge could save the hire-ling and slave From the ter - ror of
Then con-quer we must, when our cause it is just; And this be our

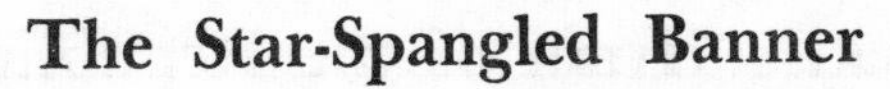

The Star-Spangled Banner

ff CHORUS

night that our flag was still there. Oh, say, does that star-span-gled
flect - ed, now shines on the stream: 'Tis the star-span-gled ban - ner; oh,
flight or the gloom of the grave. And the star-span-gled ban - ner in
mot - to: "In God is our trust!" And the star-span-gled ban - ner in

ban - ner yet wave O'er the land of the free, and the home of the brave?
long may it wave O'er the land of the free, and the home of the brave.
tri - umph doth wave O'er the land of the free, and the home of the brave.
tri - umph shall wave O'er the land of the free, and the home of the brave.

We Give Thee But Thine Own 452

WILLIAM W. HOW — MASON AND WEBB'S "CANTICA LAUDIS"

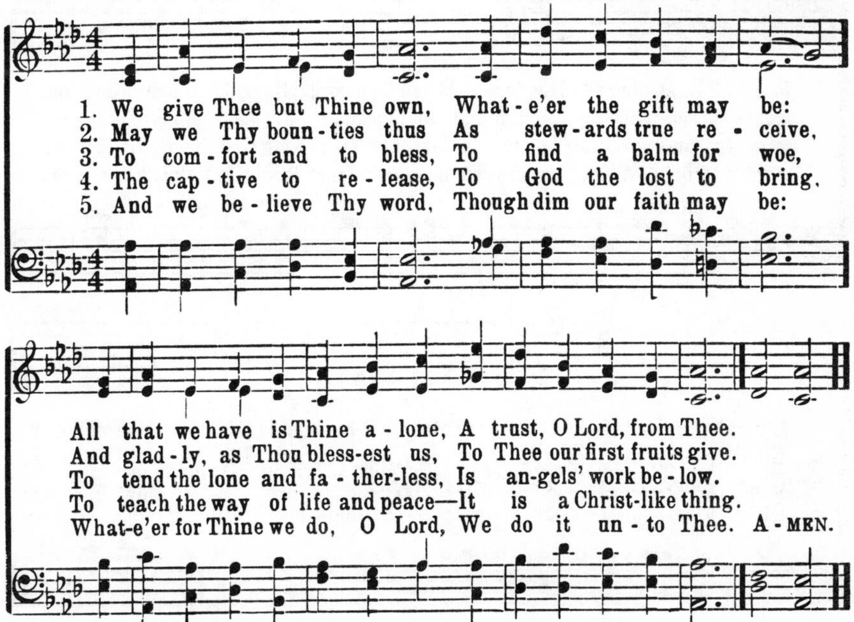

1. We give Thee but Thine own, What - e'er the gift may be:
2. May we Thy boun - ties thus As stew - ards true re - ceive,
3. To com - fort and to bless, To find a balm for woe,
4. The cap - tive to re - lease, To God the lost to bring,
5. And we be - lieve Thy word, Though dim our faith may be:

All that we have is Thine a - lone, A trust, O Lord, from Thee.
And glad - ly, as Thou bless-est us, To Thee our first fruits give.
To tend the lone and fa - ther-less, Is an-gels' work be - low.
To teach the way of life and peace—It is a Christ-like thing.
What-e'er for Thine we do, O Lord, We do it un - to Thee. A - MEN.

453 Battle Hymn of the Republic

JULIA WARD HOWE | WILLIAM STEFFE

1. Mine eyes have seen the glo - ry of the com - ing of the Lord; He is
2. I have seen Him in the watch-fires of a hun-dred circling camps; They have
3. He has sound-ed forth the trumpet that shall nev - er sound re-treat; He is
4. In the beau - ty of the lil - ies Christ was born a - cross the sea, With a

tram-pling out the vintage where the grapes of wrath are stored; He hath loosed the
build - ed Him an al - tar in the eve-ning dews and damps; I can read His
sift - ing out the hearts of men be - fore His judg-ment seat. O be swift, my
glo - ry in His bos - om that trans-fig-ures you and me; As He died to

fate - ful light-ning of His ter - ri-ble swift sword; His truth is march-ing on.
righteous sen-tence by the dim and flar-ing lamps; His day is march-ing on.
soul, to an-swer Him! be ju - bi-lant, my feet! Our God is march-ing on.
make men ho - ly, let us die to make men free; While God is march-ing on.

Glo-ry! glory, hal-le - lu-jah! Glory! glory, hal-le-lu-jah! His truth is marching on.
Glo-ry! glory, hal-le - lu-jah! Glory! glory, hal-le-lu-jah! His day is marching on.
Glo-ry! glory, hal-le - lu-jah! Glory! glory, hal-le-lu-jah! Our God is marching on.
Glo-ry! glory, hal-le - lu-jah! Glory! glory, hal-le-lu-jah! While God is marching on.

God of Our Fathers, Whose Almighty Hand 454

DANIEL O. ROBERTS — GEORGE W. WARREN

Trumpets, before each verse.

1. God of our fa - thers, whose al - might - y hand
Leads forth in beau - ty all the star - ry band
Of shin - ing worlds in splen - dor thro' the skies,
Our grate - ful songs be - fore Thy throne a - rise.

2. Thy love di - vine hath led us in the past,
In this free land by Thee our lot is cast;
Be Thou our rul - er, guard - ian, guide and stay,
Thy word our law, Thy paths our cho - sen way.

3. From war's a - larms, from dead - ly pes - ti - lence,
Be Thy strong arm our ev - er strong de - fense;
Thy true re - lig - ion in our hearts in - crease,
Thy boun - teous good - ness nour - ish us in peace.

4. Re - fresh Thy peo - ple on their toil - some way,
Lead us from night to nev - er - end - ing day;
Fill all our lives with love and grace di - vine,
And glo - ry, laud, and praise be ev - er Thine.

455 My Country, 'Tis of Thee
Samuel F. Smith
Author Unknown
1. My coun - try, 'tis of thee, Sweet land of lib - er - ty,
2. My na - tive coun - try, thee, Land of the no - ble, free,
3. Let mu - sic swell the breeze, And ring from all the trees
4. Our fa - thers' God, to Thee, Au - thor of lib - er - ty,
Of thee I sing: Land where my fa - thers died, Land of the
Thy name I love: I love thy rocks and rills, Thy woods and
Sweet free-dom's song: Let mor - tal tongues a - wake; Let all that
To Thee we sing: Long may our land be bright With free-dom's
pil - grim's pride, From ev - 'ry moun - tain side Let free - dom ring!
tem - pled hills; My heart with rap - ture thrills Like that a - bove.
breathe par-take; Let rocks their si - lence break, The sound pro - long.
ho - ly light; Pro - tect us by Thy might, Great God, our King!
456 O for a Thousand Tongues to Sing
Charles Wesley
Carl G. Glaser
Arr. by Lowell Mason
1. O for a thou-sand tongues to sing My great Re-deem - er's praise,
2. My gra-cious Mas - ter and my God, As - sist me to pro - claim,
3. Je - sus! the name that charms our fears, That bids our sor - rows cease;
4. He breaks the pow'r of can - celed sin, He sets the pris - 'ner free;
5. Hear Him, ye deaf; His praise, ye dumb, Your loosened tongues em - ploy;

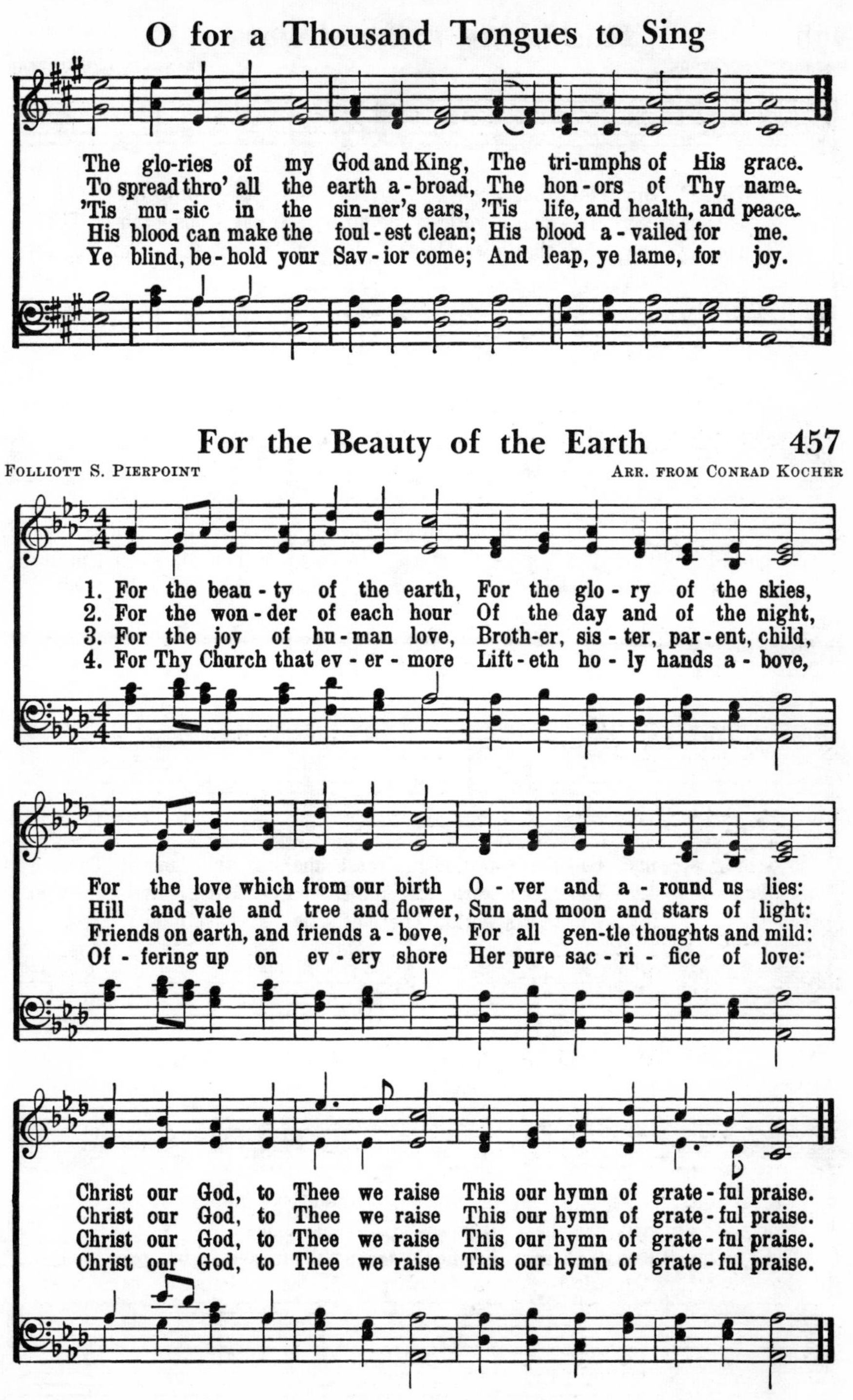
O for a Thousand Tongues to Sing
The glo-ries of my God and King, The tri-umphs of His grace.
To spread thro' all the earth a-broad, The hon-ors of Thy name.
'Tis mu-sic in the sin-ner's ears, 'Tis life, and health, and peace.
His blood can make the foul-est clean; His blood a-vailed for me.
Ye blind, be-hold your Sav-ior come; And leap, ye lame, for joy.
For the Beauty of the Earth
457
Folliott S. Pierpoint
Arr. from Conrad Kocher
1. For the beau-ty of the earth, For the glo-ry of the skies,
2. For the won-der of each hour Of the day and of the night,
3. For the joy of hu-man love, Broth-er, sis-ter, par-ent, child,
4. For Thy Church that ev-er-more Lift-eth ho-ly hands a-bove,
For the love which from our birth O-ver and a-round us lies:
Hill and vale and tree and flower, Sun and moon and stars of light:
Friends on earth, and friends a-bove, For all gen-tle thoughts and mild:
Of-fering up on ev-ery shore Her pure sac-ri-fice of love:
Christ our God, to Thee we raise This our hymn of grate-ful praise.
Christ our God, to Thee we raise This our hymn of grate-ful praise.
Christ our God, to Thee we raise This our hymn of grate-ful praise.
Christ our God, to Thee we raise This our hymn of grate-ful praise.

458 This Is My Father's World

Maltbie D. Babcock Franklin L. Sheppard

1. This is my Fa - ther's world, And to my lis - t'ning ears, All
2. This is my Fa - ther's world, The birds their car - ols raise, The
3. This is my Fa - ther's world, O let me ne'er for - get That

na - ture sings, and round me rings The mu - sic of the spheres.
morn-ing light, the lil - y white, De - clare their Ma - ker's praise.
though the wrong seems oft so strong, God is the Rul - er yet.

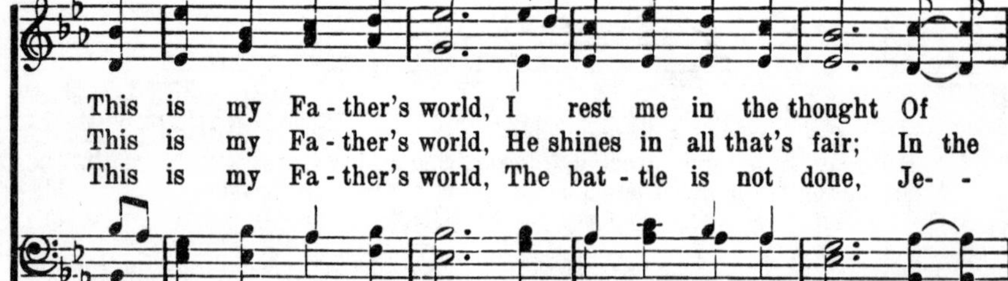

This is my Fa - ther's world, I rest me in the thought Of
This is my Fa - ther's world, He shines in all that's fair; In the
This is my Fa - ther's world, The bat - tle is not done, Je- -

rocks and trees, of . . skies and seas—His hand the won-ders wrought.
rus - tling grass I . . hear Him pass, He speaks to me ev - 'ry-where.
sus who died shall be sat - is - fied, And earth and heav'n be one. A-men.

Stepping in the Light

ELIZA E. HEWITT WILLIAM J. KIRKPATRICK

1. Try - ing to walk in the steps of the Sav-ior, Try - ing to fol - low our
2. Press-ing more close-ly to Him who is lead-ing, When we are tempted to
3. Walk-ing in foot-steps of gen - tle for-bear-ance, Foot-steps of faith-ful-ness,
4. Try - ing to walk in the steps of the Sav-ior, Up -ward, still upward we'll

Sav - ior and King; Shap - ing our lives by His bless - ed ex - am - ple,
turn from the way; Trust - ing the arm that is strong to de- fend us,
mer - cy and love, Look - ing to Him for the grace free - ly prom- ised,
fol - low our Guide; When we shall see Him, "the King in His beau - ty,"

Hap-py, how hap-py, the songs that we bring.
Hap-py, how hap-py, our prais - es each day.
Hap-py, how hap-py, our jour - ney a - bove.
Hap-py, how hap-py, our place at His side.

CHORUS

How beau-ti-ful to walk in the steps of the Sav - ior, Stepping in the light, Step-ping in the light; How beau - ti - ful to walk in the steps of the Sav - ior, Led in paths of light.

460 Room at the Cross for You

Ira F. Stanphill — Ira F. Stanphill

1. The cross up-on which Je-sus died Is a shel-ter in which we can
2. Tho' mil-lions have found Him a friend, And have turned from the sins they have
3. The hand of my Sav-iour is strong, And the love of my Sav-iour is
hide, And its grace so free is suf - fi-cient for me, And
sinned, The Sav-iour still waits to o - pen the gate And
long; Through sun-shine or rain, through loss or in gain, The
deep is its foun-tain, as wide as the sea.
wel-come a sin-ner be - fore it's too late.
blood flows from Cal-v'ry to cleanse ev-'ry stain.
CHORUS
There's room at the cross for
you, There's room at the cross for you; Tho' mil-lions have come, There's
still room for one, Yes, there's room at the cross for you.

O Perfect Love

DOROTHY F. GURNEY

JOSEPH BARNBY

1. O per-fect Love, all hu-man thought tran-scend-ing,
2. O per-fect Life, be Thou their full as-sur-ance
3. Grant them the joy which bright-ens earth-ly sor-row,
4. Hear us, O Fa-ther, gra-cious and for-giv-ing,
Low-ly we kneel in prayer be-fore Thy throne,
Of ten-der char-i-ty and stead-fast faith,
Grant them the peace which calms all earth-ly strife,
Through Je-sus Christ, Thy co-e-ter-nal Word,
That theirs may be the love which knows no end-ing,
Of pa-tient hope, and qui-et, brave en-dur-ance,
And to life's day the glo-rious, un-known mor-row
Who, with the Ho-ly Ghost, by all things liv-ing
Whom Thou for-ev-er-more dost join in one.
With child-like trust that fears nor pain nor death.
That dawns up-on e-ter-nal love and life.
Now and to end-less a-ges art a-dored. A-MEN.

462 Abide with Me

HENRY F. LYTE | WILLIAM H. MONK

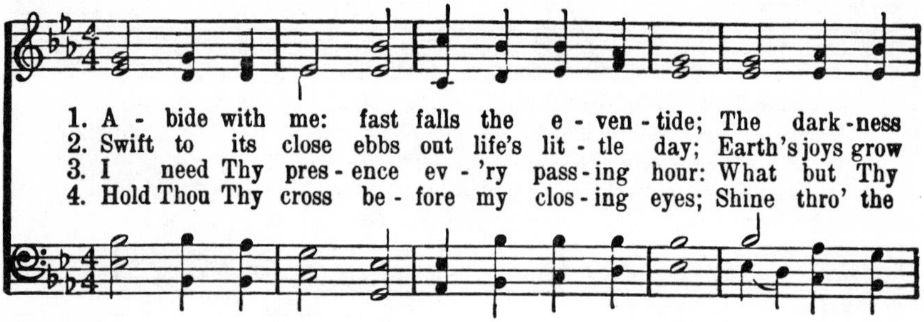

1. A - bide with me: fast falls the e - ven - tide; The dark - ness
2. Swift to its close ebbs out life's lit - tle day; Earth's joys grow
3. I need Thy pres - ence ev - 'ry pass - ing hour: What but Thy
4. Hold Thou Thy cross be - fore my clos - ing eyes; Shine thro' the

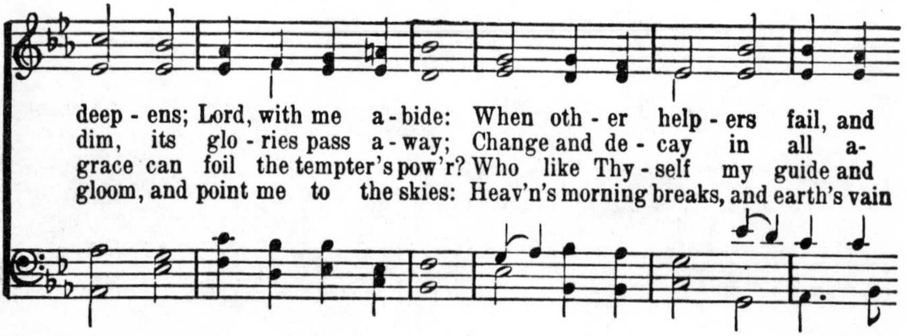

deep - ens; Lord, with me a - bide: When oth - er help - ers fail, and
dim, its glo - ries pass a - way; Change and de - cay in all a-
grace can foil the tempter's pow'r? Who like Thy - self my guide and
gloom, and point me to the skies: Heav'n's morning breaks, and earth's vain

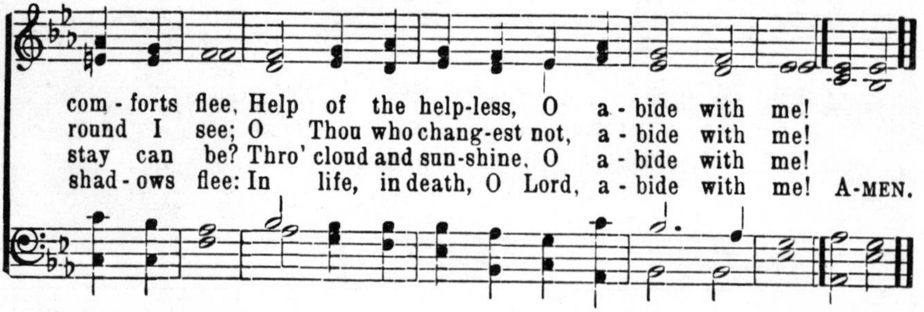

com - forts flee, Help of the help-less, O a - bide with me!
round I see; O Thou who chang-est not, a - bide with me!
stay can be? Thro' cloud and sun-shine, O a - bide with me!
shad - ows flee: In life, in death, O Lord, a - bide with me! A-MEN.

463 Jesus, the Very Thought of Thee

BERNARD OF CLAIRVAUX
TR. BY EDWARD CASWALL | JOHN B. DYKES

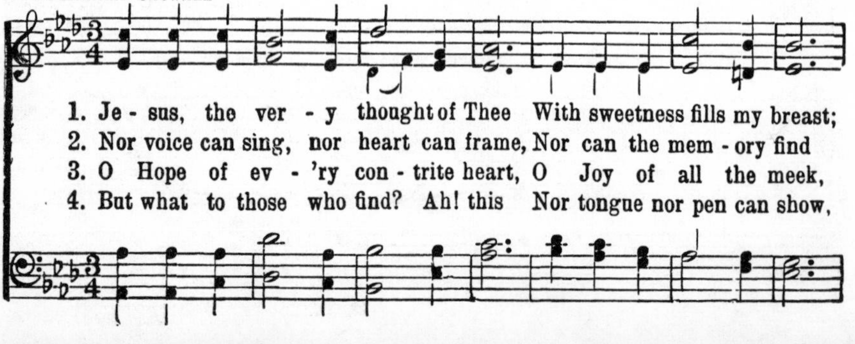

1. Je - sus, the ver - y thought of Thee With sweetness fills my breast;
2. Nor voice can sing, nor heart can frame, Nor can the mem - ory find
3. O Hope of ev - 'ry con - trite heart, O Joy of all the meek,
4. But what to those who find? Ah! this Nor tongue nor pen can show,

Jesus, the Very Thought of Thee

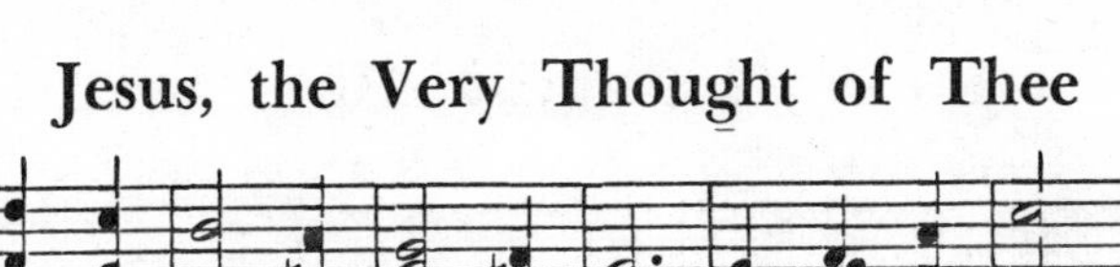

But sweet-er far Thy face to see, And in Thy pres-ence rest.
A sweet-er sound than Thy blest name, O Sav-ior of man-kind!
To those who fall, how kind Thou art! How good to those who seek!
The love of Je-sus, what it is None but His loved ones know.

Near to the Heart of God 464

CLELAND B. MCAFEE — CLELAND B. MCAFEE

1. There is a place of qui-et rest, Near to the heart of God,
2. There is a place of com-fort sweet, Near to the heart of God,
3. There is a place of full re-lease, Near to the heart of God,

A place where sin can-not mo-lest, Near to the heart of God.
A place where we our Sav-ior meet, Near to the heart of God.
A place where all is joy and peace, Near to the heart of God.

REFRAIN

O Je-sus, blest Re-deem-er, Sent from the heart of God,
Hold us, who wait be-fore Thee, Near to the heart of God.

465 I Am His, and He Is Mine

George W. Robinson — James Mountain

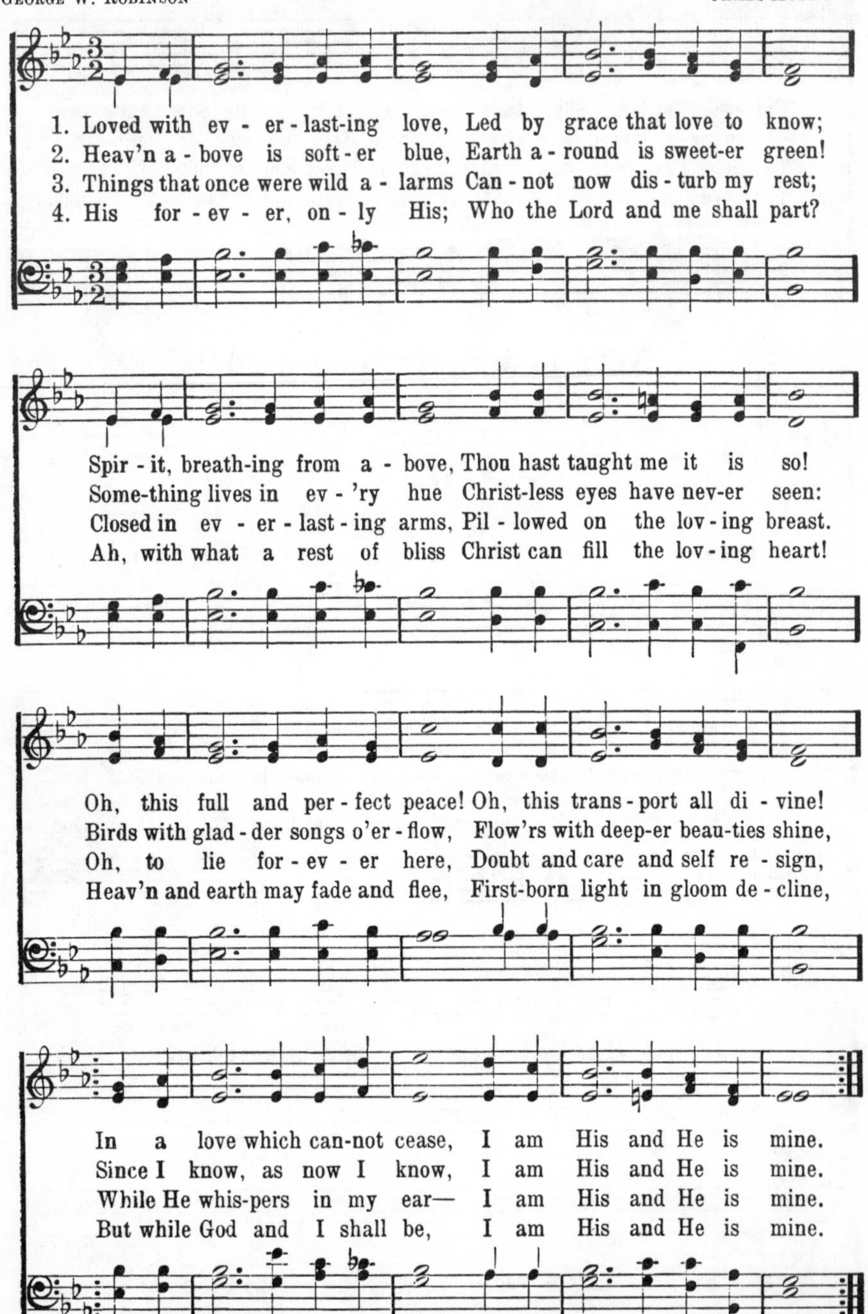
1. Loved with ev - er - last-ing love, Led by grace that love to know;
2. Heav'n a - bove is soft - er blue, Earth a - round is sweet-er green!
3. Things that once were wild a - larms Can - not now dis - turb my rest;
4. His for - ev - er, on - ly His; Who the Lord and me shall part?
Spir - it, breath-ing from a - bove, Thou hast taught me it is so!
Some-thing lives in ev - 'ry hue Christ-less eyes have nev-er seen:
Closed in ev - er - last - ing arms, Pil - lowed on the lov - ing breast.
Ah, with what a rest of bliss Christ can fill the lov - ing heart!
Oh, this full and per - fect peace! Oh, this trans - port all di - vine!
Birds with glad - der songs o'er - flow, Flow'rs with deep-er beau-ties shine,
Oh, to lie for - ev - er here, Doubt and care and self re - sign,
Heav'n and earth may fade and flee, First-born light in gloom de - cline,
In a love which can-not cease, I am His and He is mine.
Since I know, as now I know, I am His and He is mine.
While He whis-pers in my ear— I am His and He is mine.
But while God and I shall be, I am His and He is mine.

A Mighty Fortress Is Our God

466

MARTIN LUTHER
TR. BY FREDERICK H. HEDGE

MARTIN LUTHER

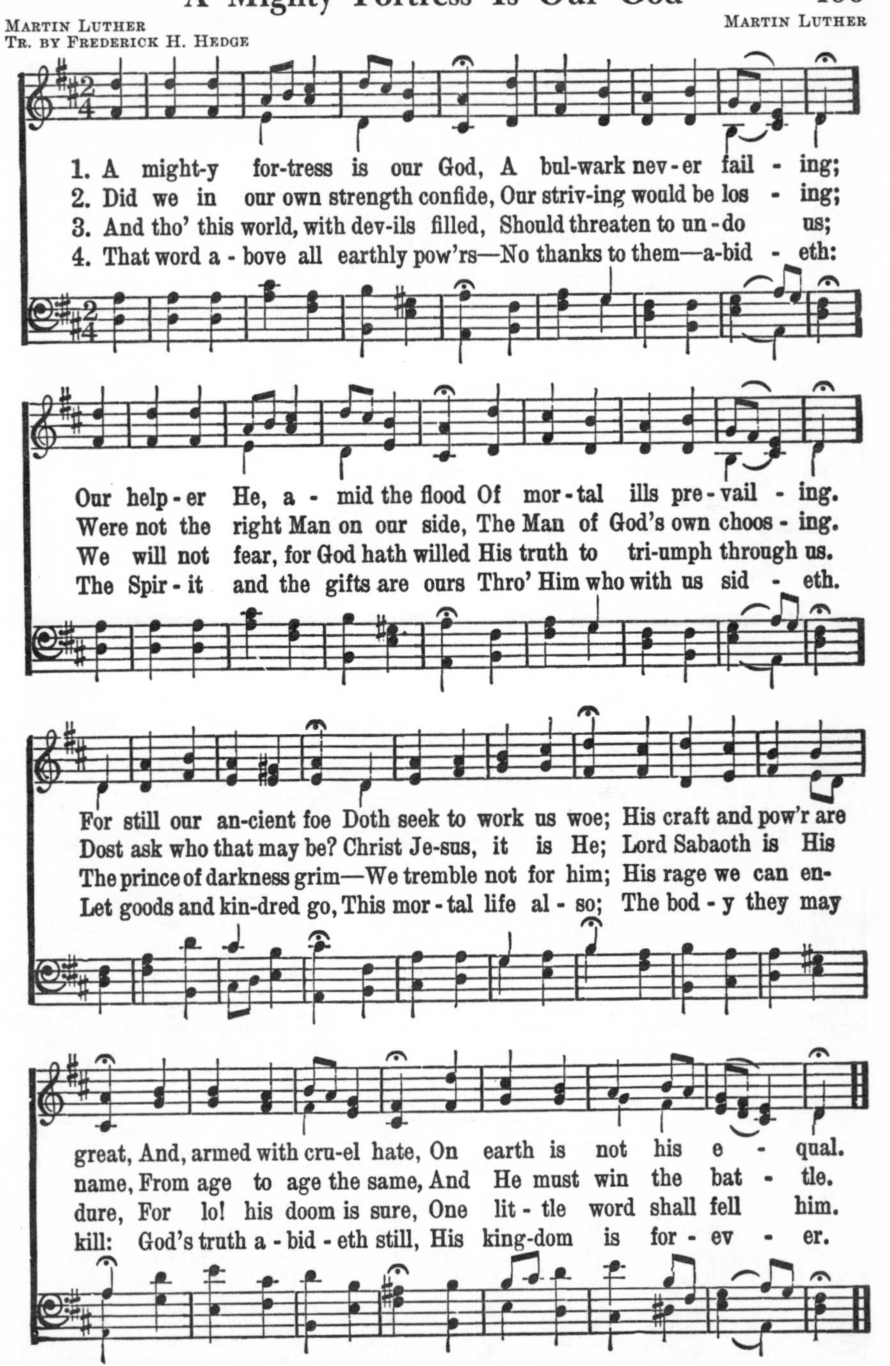

1. A mighty fortress is our God, A bulwark never failing;
2. Did we in our own strength confide, Our striving would be losing;
3. And tho' this world, with devils filled, Should threaten to undo us;
4. That word above all earthly pow'rs—No thanks to them—abideth:
Our helper He, amid the flood Of mortal ills prevailing.
Were not the right Man on our side, The Man of God's own choosing.
We will not fear, for God hath willed His truth to triumph through us.
The Spirit and the gifts are ours Thro' Him who with us sideth.
For still our ancient foe Doth seek to work us woe; His craft and pow'r are
Dost ask who that may be? Christ Jesus, it is He; Lord Sabaoth is His
The prince of darkness grim—We tremble not for him; His rage we can en-
Let goods and kindred go, This mortal life also; The body they may
great, And, armed with cruel hate, On earth is not his equal.
name, From age to age the same, And He must win the battle.
dure, For lo! his doom is sure, One little word shall fell him.
kill: God's truth abideth still, His kingdom is forever.

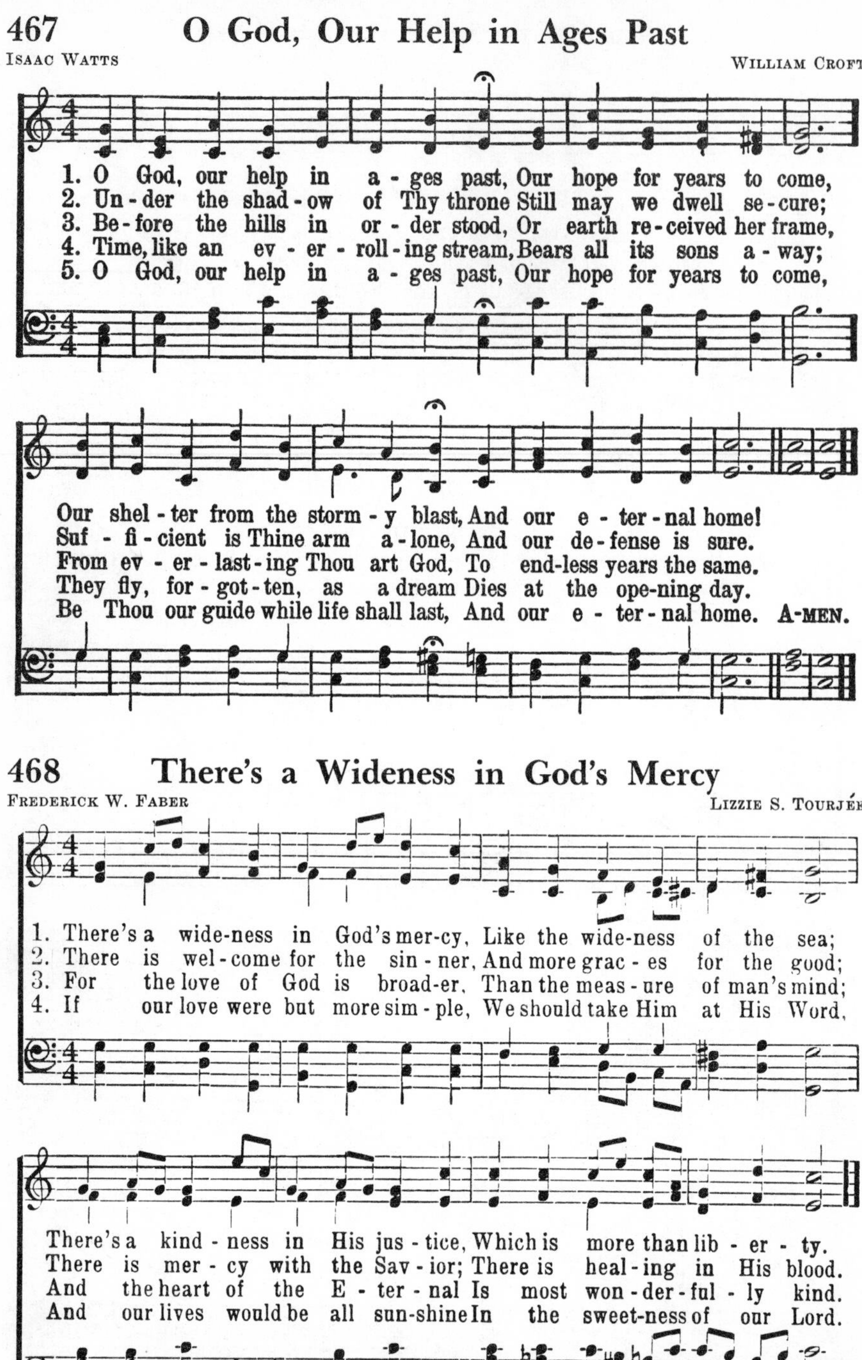

467 O God, Our Help in Ages Past
Isaac Watts
William Croft
1. O God, our help in a - ges past, Our hope for years to come,
2. Un - der the shad - ow of Thy throne Still may we dwell se - cure;
3. Be - fore the hills in or - der stood, Or earth re - ceived her frame,
4. Time, like an ev - er - roll - ing stream, Bears all its sons a - way;
5. O God, our help in a - ges past, Our hope for years to come,
Our shel - ter from the storm - y blast, And our e - ter - nal home!
Suf - fi - cient is Thine arm a - lone, And our de - fense is sure.
From ev - er - last - ing Thou art God, To end-less years the same.
They fly, for - got - ten, as a dream Dies at the ope-ning day.
Be Thou our guide while life shall last, And our e - ter - nal home. A-men.
468 There's a Wideness in God's Mercy
Frederick W. Faber
Lizzie S. Tourjée
1. There's a wide-ness in God's mer-cy, Like the wide-ness of the sea;
2. There is wel - come for the sin - ner, And more grac - es for the good;
3. For the love of God is broad-er, Than the meas - ure of man's mind;
4. If our love were but more sim - ple, We should take Him at His Word,
There's a kind - ness in His jus - tice, Which is more than lib - er - ty.
There is mer - cy with the Sav - ior; There is heal - ing in His blood.
And the heart of the E - ter - nal Is most won - der - ful - ly kind.
And our lives would be all sun-shine In the sweet-ness of our Lord.

Grace Greater Than Our Sin

469

Julia H. Johnston

Daniel B. Towner

1. Mar-vel-ous grace of our lov-ing Lord, Grace that ex-ceeds our
2. Sin and de-spair like the sea waves cold, Threat-en the soul with
3. Dark is the stain that we can-not hide, What can a-vail to
4. Mar-vel-ous, in-fi-nite, match-less grace, Free-ly be-stowed on
sin and our guilt, Yon-der on Cal-va-ry's mount out-poured,
in-fi-nite loss; Grace that is great-er, yes, grace un-told,
wash it a-way? Look! there is flow-ing a crim-son tide;
all who be-lieve; You that are long-ing to see His face,
There where the blood of the Lamb was spilt.
Points to the Ref-uge, the Might-y Cross.
Whit-er than snow you may be to-day.
Will you this mo-ment His grace re-ceive?
CHORUS
Grace, grace,
Mar-vel-ous grace,
God's grace, Grace that will par-don and cleanse with-in; Grace,
In-fi-nite grace,
Mar-vel-ous
grace, God's grace, Grace that is great-er than all our sin.
grace, In-fi-nite grace,

470 Wonderful Grace of Jesus

Haldor Lillenas — Haldor Lillenas

1. Won - der - ful grace of Je - sus, Great - er than all my sin; . .
2. Won - der - ful grace of Je - sus, Reach-ing to all the lost, . .
3. Won - der - ful grace of Je - sus, Reach-ing the most de - filed, . .
How shall my tongue de - scribe it, Where shall its praise be - gin? . . .
By it I have been pardoned, Saved to the ut - ter - most, . . .
By its trans-form-ing pow - er, Mak - ing him God's dear child, . .
Tak - ing a - way my bur - den, Set - ting my spir - it free; . .
Chains have been torn a - sun - der, Giv - ing me lib - er - ty; . . .
Pur - chas-ing peace and heav - en, For all e - ter - ni - ty; . . .
For the won - der - ful grace of Je - sus reach - es me.
For the won - der - ful grace of Je - sus reach - es me.
And the won - der - ful grace of Je - sus reach - es me.
Chorus
the matchless grace of Je-sus,
Won-der-ful the matchless grace of Je - - - sus, Deep-er than the

Wonderful Grace of Jesus

3 3
the roll-ing sea; Won - - - der - ful
might - y roll - ing sea;............... Higher than the mountain,
grace, all - suf - fi - - - - cient for
spar-kling like a foun - tain, All - suf - fi - cient grace for e - ven
3
me, for e - ven me, Broad - er than the scope of my trans-
me,................
gres - sions, Great - er far than all my sin and shame,..........
gres-sions, sing it! my sin and shame,
O mag - ni - fy the pre-cious name of Je - sus, Praise His name!

471 Saved by Grace

Fanny J. Crosby

George C. Stebbins
Arr. by Seymour Swets

1. Some day the sil - ver cord will break, And I no more as now shall sing;
2. Some day my earth - ly house will fall, I can-not tell how soon 'twill be;
3. Some day, when fades the gold-en sun Be-neath the ro - sy-tint-ed west,
4. Some day: till then I'll watch and wait, My lamp all trimmed and burning bright,
But oh, the joy when I shall wake With-in the pal-ace of the King!
But this I know—my All in All Has now a place in heav'n for me.
My blessed Lord will say, "Well done!" And I shall en-ter in - to rest.
That when my Sav - ior opes the gate, My soul to Him may take its flight.
Refrain
And I shall see Him face to face, And tell the sto-ry–Saved by grace;
shall see
to face,
And I shall see Him face to face, And tell the sto-ry—Saved by grace.
shall see
to face,
rit.

All the Way My Savior Leads Me 472

Fanny J. Crosby | Robert Lowry

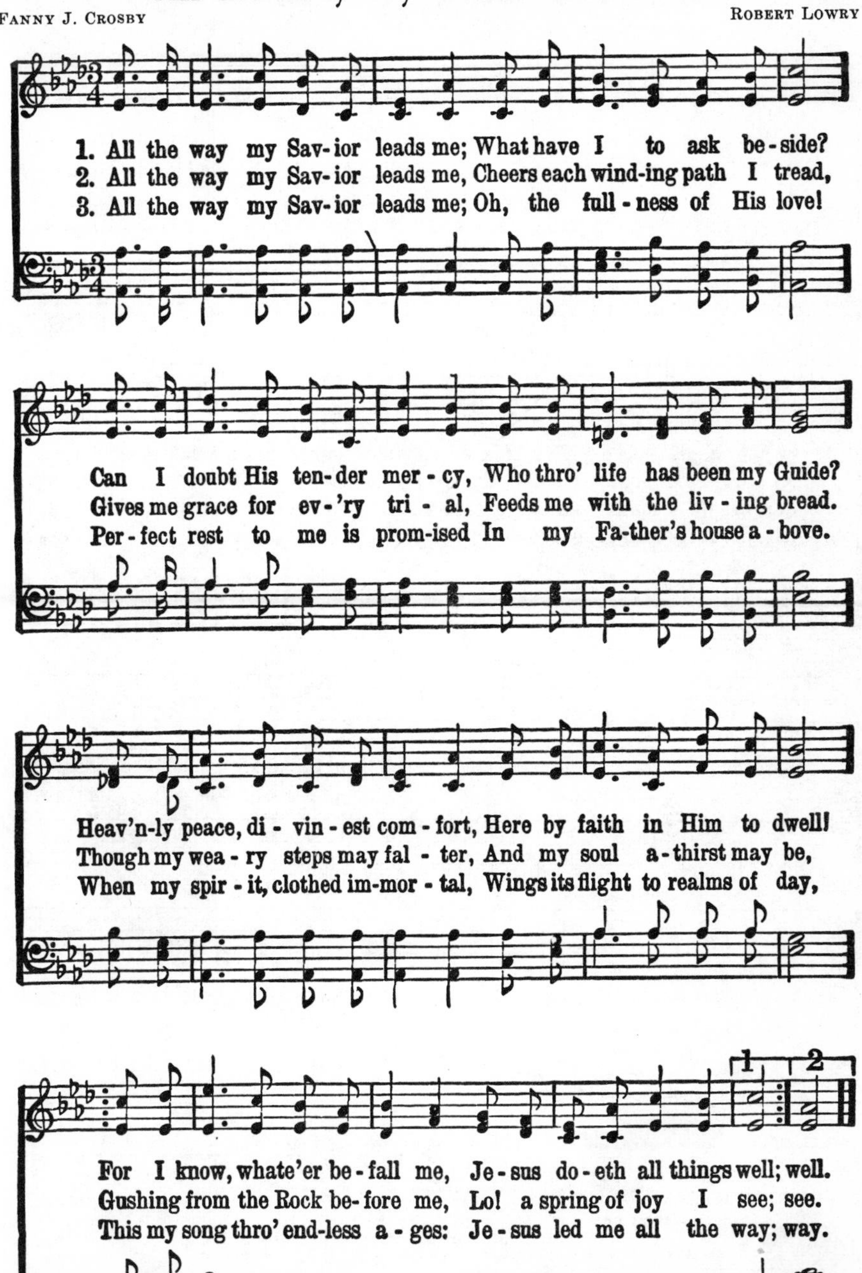
1. All the way my Sav-ior leads me; What have I to ask be-side?
2. All the way my Sav-ior leads me, Cheers each wind-ing path I tread,
3. All the way my Sav-ior leads me; Oh, the full-ness of His love!
Can I doubt His ten-der mer-cy, Who thro' life has been my Guide?
Gives me grace for ev-'ry tri-al, Feeds me with the liv-ing bread.
Per-fect rest to me is prom-ised In my Fa-ther's house a-bove.
Heav'n-ly peace, di-vin-est com-fort, Here by faith in Him to dwell!
Though my wea-ry steps may fal-ter, And my soul a-thirst may be,
When my spir-it, clothed im-mor-tal, Wings its flight to realms of day,
For I know, whate'er be-fall me, Je-sus do-eth all things well; well.
Gushing from the Rock be-fore me, Lo! a spring of joy I see; see.
This my song thro' end-less a-ges: Je-sus led me all the way; way.
1
2

473 God Leads Us Along

G. A. Young — G. A. Young

1. In shad - y, green pas-tures, so rich and so sweet. God leads His dear
2. Sometimes on the mount where the sun shines so bright, God leads His dear
3. Tho' sor - rows be - fall us, and Sa - tan op - pose, God leads His dear
4. A - way from the mire, and a - way from the clay, God leads His dear
chil-dren a - long; Where the wa-ter's cold flow bathes the wea-ry one's feet,
chil-dren a - long; Some - times in the val - ley, in dark-est of night,
chil-dren a - long; Through grace we can con-quer, de - feat all our foes,
chil-dren a - long; A - way up in glo - ry, e - ter - ni - ty's day,
CHORUS
God leads His dear chil-dren a - long. Some thro' the waters, some thro' the flood,
Some thro' the fire, but all thro' the blood; Some thro' great sor-row, but
God gives a song, In the night sea - son and all the day long.
rit.

What God Hath Promised 474

ANNIE JOHNSON FLINT
WILLIAM M. RUNYAN
1. God hath not prom-ised skies al-ways blue, Flow-er-strewn path-ways all our lives through; God hath not prom-ised sun with-out rain, Joy with-out sor-row, peace with-out pain.
2. God hath not prom-ised we shall not know Toil and temp-ta-tion, trou-ble and woe; He hath not told us we shall not bear Man-y a bur-den, man-y a care.
3. God hath not prom-ised smooth roads and wide, Swift, eas-y trav-el, need-ing no guide; Nev-er a moun-tain rock-y and steep, Nev-er a riv-er tur-bid and deep.
CHORUS
But God hath prom-ised strength for the day, Rest for the la-bor, light for the way, Grace for the tri-als, help from a-bove, Un-fail-ing sym-pa-thy, un-dy-ing love.

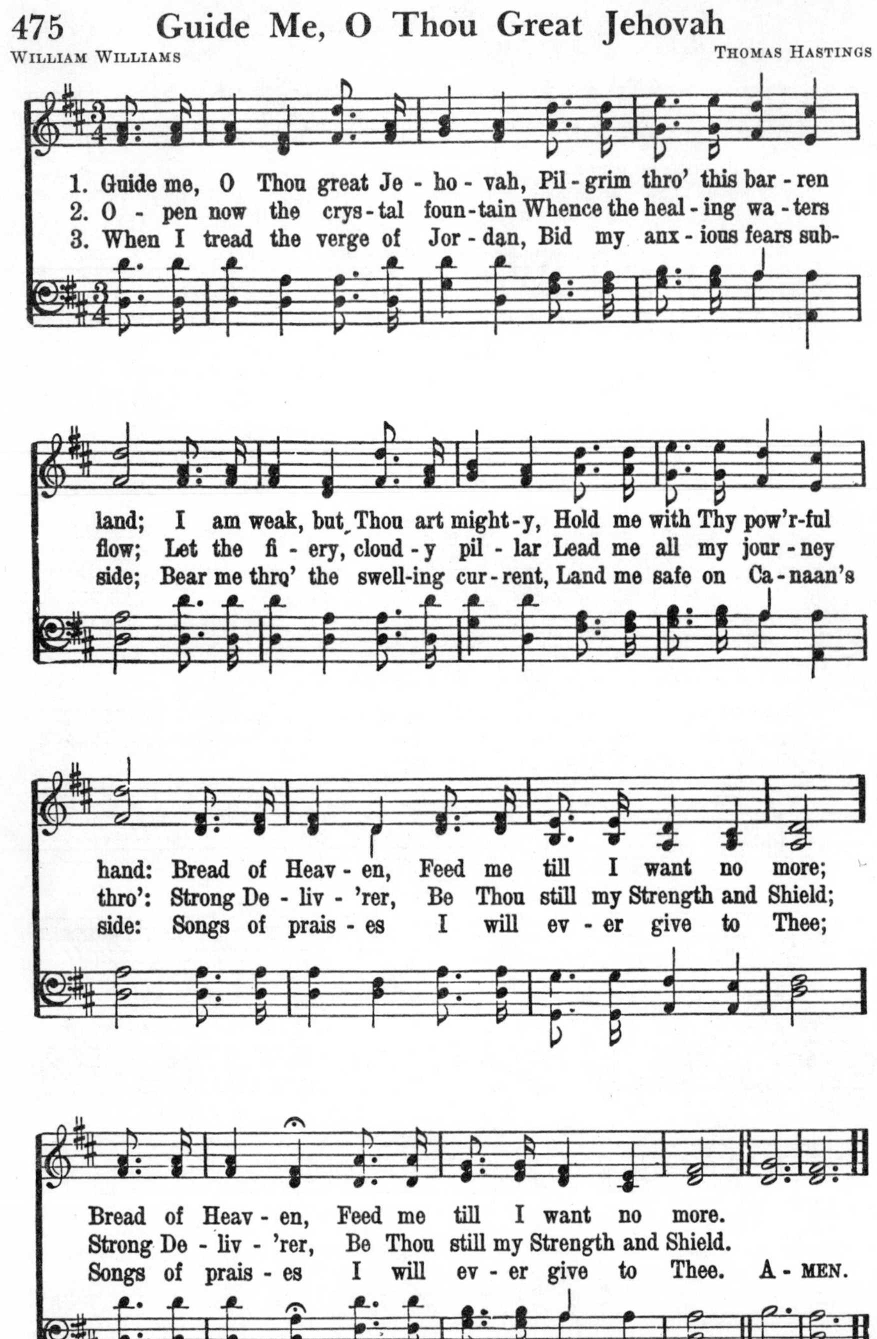
475 Guide Me, O Thou Great Jehovah
William Williams
Thomas Hastings
1. Guide me, O Thou great Je - ho - vah, Pil - grim thro' this bar - ren
2. O - pen now the crys - tal foun - tain Whence the heal - ing wa - ters
3. When I tread the verge of Jor - dan, Bid my anx - ious fears sub-
land; I am weak, but Thou art might - y, Hold me with Thy pow'r-ful
flow; Let the fi - ery, cloud - y pil - lar Lead me all my jour - ney
side; Bear me thro' the swell-ing cur - rent, Land me safe on Ca - naan's
hand: Bread of Heav - en, Feed me till I want no more;
thro': Strong De - liv - 'rer, Be Thou still my Strength and Shield;
side: Songs of prais - es I will ev - er give to Thee;
Bread of Heav - en, Feed me till I want no more.
Strong De - liv - 'rer, Be Thou still my Strength and Shield.
Songs of prais - es I will ev - er give to Thee. A - men.

Songs of Praises

WILLIAM WILLIAMS
GIPSY SMITH, 4

JOHN HUGHES
ARR. BY E. EDWIN YOUNG

1. Guide me, O Thou great Je - ho - vah, Pil - grim thro' this
2. O - pen now the crys - tal foun - tain, Whence the heal - ing
3. When I tread the verge of Jor - dan, Bid my anx - ious
4. Care and doubt - ing, gloom and sor - row, Fear and shame are
bar - ren land; I am weak, but Thou art might-y, Hold me with Thy
wa - ters flow; Let the fier - y, cloud-y pil - lar Lead me all my
fears sub-side; Bear me thro' the swell-ing cur-rent, Land me safe on
mine no more; Faith knows naught of dark to-mor-row, For my Sav - ior
pow'r-ful hand; Bread of heav-en, Bread of heav-en, Feed me till I
jour - ney thro'; Strong De - liv-'rer, Strong De - liv-'rer, Be Thou still my
Ca-naan's side; Songs of prais-es, Songs of prais-es, I will ev - er
goes be - fore; Songs of prais-es, Songs of prais-es, I will ev - er
want no more; Feed me till I want no more.
Un - til I want no more;
strength and shield; Be Thou still my strength and shield.
Be still my strength and shield;
give to Thee; I will ev - er give to Thee.
Will ev - er give to Thee;
give to Thee; I will ev - er give to Thee. A-MEN.
Will ev - er give to Thee;

477 Jesus, Savior, Pilot Me

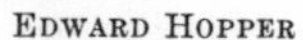

EDWARD HOPPER JOHN E. GOULD

1. Je - sus, Sav - ior, pi - lot me O - ver life's tem - pes-tuous sea;
2. As a moth - er stills her child, Thou canst hush the o - cean wild;
3. When at last I near the shore, And the fear - ful break-ers roar

Un-known waves be - fore me roll, Hid - ing rock and treacherous shoal;
Boisterous waves o - bey Thy will When Thou say'st to them "Be still!"
'Twixt me and the peace-ful rest, Then, while lean - ing on Thy breast,

Chart and com - pass came from Thee: Je - sus, Sav - ior, pi - lot me.
Won-drous Sov-'reign of the sea, Je - sus, Sav - ior, pi - lot me.
May I hear Thee say to me, "Fear not, I will pi - lot thee."

478 I Need Thee Every Hour

ANNIE S. HAWKS ROBERT LOWRY

1. I need Thee ev-'ry hour, Most gra - cious Lord; No ten - der voice like
2. I need Thee ev-'ry hour, Stay Thou near by; Temp-ta-tions lose their
3. I need Thee ev-'ry hour, In joy or pain; Come quick-ly and a-
4. I need Thee ev-'ry hour, Most Ho - ly One; O make me Thine in-

I Need Thee Every Hour

CHORUS
Thine Can peace af - ford.
pow'r When Thou art nigh. I need Thee, O I need Thee; Ev-'ry hour I
bide, Or life is vain.
deed, Thou bless-ed Son!

need Thee! O bless me now, my Sav - ior, I come to Thee!

I Am Not Skilled to Understand 479

DORA GREENWELL

WILLIAM J. KIRKPATRICK

1. I am not skilled to un-der-stand What God hath willed, what God hath planned;
2. I take Him at His word indeed: "Christ died for sin - ners," this I read;
3. That He should leave His place on high And come for sin - ful man to die,
4. Yea, liv - ing, dy - ing, let me bring My strength, my sol-ace from this spring:

I on - ly know at His right hand Is One who is my Sav-iour!
For in my heart I find a need Of Him to be my Sav-iour!
You count it strange? so once did I, Be - fore I knew my Sav-iour!
That He who lives to be my King Once died to be my Sav-iour!

480 Savior, Like a Shepherd Lead Us

"Hymns for the Young"
Asc. to Dorothy A. Thrupp

William B. Bradbury

1. Sav - ior, like a shep-herd lead us, Much we need Thy ten- der care;
2. We are Thine; do Thou be - friend us, Be the Guardian of our way;
3. Thou hast promised to re - ceive us, Poor and sin- ful though we be;
4. Ear - ly let us seek Thy fa - vor; Ear - ly let us do Thy will;
In Thy pleas-ant pas-tures feed us, For our use Thy folds pre-pare:
Keep Thy flock, from sin de - fend us, Seek us when we go a - stray:
Thou hast mer - cy to re - lieve us, Grace to cleanse, and pow'r to free:
Bless - ed Lord and on - ly Sav - ior, With Thy love our bos - oms fill:
Bless-ed Je - sus, Bless-ed Je - sus, Thou hast bought us, Thine we are;
Bless-ed Je - sus, Bless-ed Je - sus, Hear, O hear us when we pray;
Bless-ed Je - sus, Bless-ed Je - sus, Ear - ly let us turn to Thee;
Bless-ed Je - sus, Bless-ed Je - sus, Thou hast loved us, love us still;
Bless-ed Je - sus, Bless-ed Je - sus, Thou hast bought us, Thine we are.
Bless-ed Je - sus, Bless-ed Je - sus, Hear, O hear us when we pray.
Bless-ed Je - sus, Bless-ed Je - sus, Ear - ly let us turn to Thee.
Bless-ed Je - sus, Bless-ed Je - sus, Thou hast loved us, love us still.

Beulah Land

EDGAR P. STITES | JOHN R. SWENEY

1. I've reached the land of corn and wine, And all its rich-es free-ly mine;
2. My Sav-ior comes and walks with me, And sweet com-mun-ion here have we;
3. A sweet per-fume up-on the breeze Is borne from ev-er-ver-nal trees,
4. The zeph-yrs seem to float to me, Sweet sounds of Heaven's mel-o-dy,
Here shines undimmed one bliss-ful day, For all my night has passed a-way.
He gen-tly leads me by His hand, For this is Heav-en's bor-der-land.
And flow'rs, that nev-er-fad-ing grow, Where streams of life for-ev-er flow.
As an-gels with the white-robed throng Join in the sweet Re-demp-tion song.
CHORUS
O Beu-lah Land, sweet Beu-lah Land, As on thy high-est mount I stand,
I look a-way a-cross the sea, Where mansions are pre-pared for me, And
view the shin-ing glo-ry-shore,—My Heav'n, my home for-ev-er-more!

482 Sooner or Later

Lulu W. Koch — Wilbur E. Nelson

1. Soon-er or lat-er the skies will be bright, Tears will be all wiped a-way; Soon-er or lat-er, then com-eth the light, Night will be turned in-to day. (glad day.)
2. Soon-er or lat-er, our Lord knows the hour, He'll send His be-lov-ed Son; Soon-er or lat-er, in His might and pow'r, Our bat-tles all will be won. (be won.)
3. Soon-er or lat-er, yes, soon-er for some, Darkness will all then be past; Soon-er or lat-er our Sav-iour will come, With Him will your lot be cast? (be cast?)
CHORUS
Soon-er or lat-er cares will have flown, Sun-shine and glad-ness we'll see; we'll see; Soon-er or lat-er God call-eth His own, With Him for-ev-er to be. (to be.)

He the Pearly Gates Will Open

Fred Blom
Tr. by Nathaniel Carlson

Elsie Ahlwén

1. Love Di-vine, so great and won-drous, Deep and might-y, pure, sub-lime!
2. Like a dove when hunt-ed, frightened, As a wound-ed fawn was I;
3. Love Di-vine, so great and won-drous, All my sins He then for-gave!
4. In life's e-ven-tide, at twi-light, At His door I'll knock and wait;

Com-ing from the heart of Je-sus, Just the same thro' tests of time.
Bro-ken-heart-ed, yet He healed me, He will heed the sin-ner's cry.
I will sing His praise for-ev-er, For His blood, His pow'r to save.
By the pre-cious love of Je-sus I shall en-ter heav-en's gate.

Chorus

He the pear-ly gates will o-pen, So that I may en-ter in;

For He purchased my re-demp-tion And for-gave me all my sin.

484 He'll Understand and Say "Well Done"
Lucy E. Campbell
Lucy E. Campbell
Arr. by William J. Floyd
1. If when you give the best of your ser-vice, Tell-ing the
2. Mis-un-der-stood, the Sav-iour of sin-ners Hung on the
3. If when this life of la-bor is end-ed, And the re-
4. But if you try and fail in your try-ing, Hands sore and
world that the Sav-iour is come; Be not dis-mayed when men don't be-
cross; He was God's on-ly Son; Oh! hear Him call His Fa-ther in
ward of the race you have run; Oh! take the sweet rest pre-pared for
scarred from the work you've be-gun; Take up your cross, run quick-ly to
lieve you, He un-der-stands; He'll say, "Well done."
heav-en, "Let not my will, but Thine be done."
faith-ful, Will be His blest and fi-nal, "Well done."
meet Him, He'll un-der-stand; He'll say, "Well done."
CHORUS
Oh when I come to the end of my jour-ney, Wea-ry of
life and the bat-tle is won; Car-rying the staff and the

He'll Understand and Say "Well Done"

cross of re-demp-tion, He'll un-der-stand and say, "Well done."
Just a Closer Walk with Thee
485
Author Unknown
Arr. by William J. Floyd
1. I am weak but Thou art strong; (art strong;) Je-sus, keep me from all wrong;
2. Thro' this world of toil and snares, (and snares,) If I fal-ter Lord, who cares?
3. When my fee-ble life is o'er, (is o'er,) Time for me will be no more;
I'll be sat-is-fied as long (just as long) As I walk, let me walk close to Thee.
Who with me my bur-den shares (bur-den shares) None but Thee, dear Lord, none but Thee.
Guide me gent-ly, safe-ly o'er (safe-ly o'er) To Thy king-dom shore, to Thy shore.
Refrain
Just a clos-er walk with Thee, (with Thee) Grant it, Je-sus, is my plea,
Dai-ly walk-ing close to Thee, (to Thee,) Let it be, dear Lord, let it be.

486 Beyond the Sunset

VIRGIL P. BROCK — BLANCHE K. BROCK

1. Be-yond the sun - set, O bliss-ful morn - ing, When with our
2. Be-yond the sun - set no clouds will gath - er, No storms will
3. Be-yond the sun - set a hand will guide me To God, the
4. Be-yond the sun - set, O glad re - un - ion, With our dear

Sav - iour heav'n is be - gun. Earth's toiling end - ed, O glorious
threat - en, no fears an - noy; O day of glad - ness, O day un-
Fa - ther, whom I a - dore; His glorious pres - ence, His words of
loved ones who've gone be - fore; In that fair homeland we'll know no

dawn - ing; Be-yond the sun - set, when day is done.
end - ing, Be-yond the sun - set, e - ter - nal joy!
wel - come, Will be my por - tion on that fair shore.
par - ting, Bey-ond the sun - set for ev - er - more!

487 Amazing Grace

JOHN NEWTON — EARLY AMERICAN MELODY
ARR. BY EDWIN O. EXCELL

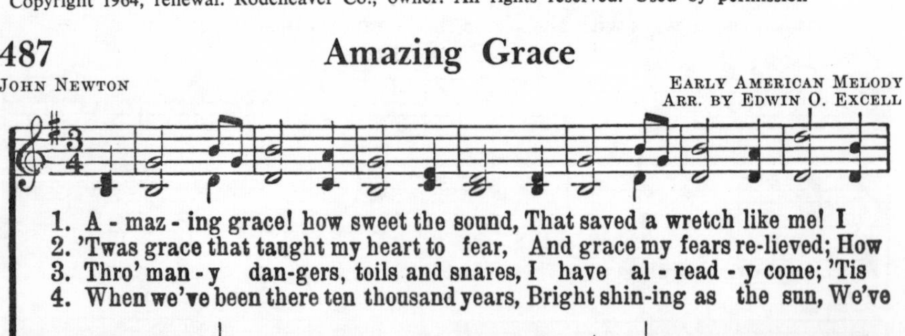
1. A - maz - ing grace! how sweet the sound, That saved a wretch like me! I
2. 'Twas grace that taught my heart to fear, And grace my fears re-lieved; How
3. Thro' man - y dan-gers, toils and snares, I have al - read - y come; 'Tis
4. When we've been there ten thousand years, Bright shin-ing as the sun, We've

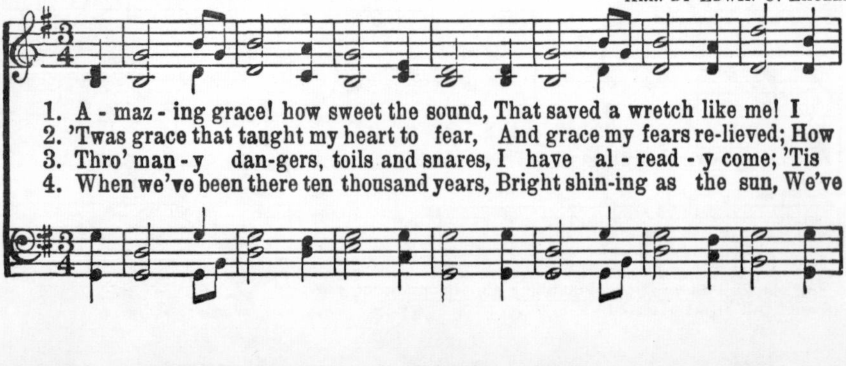

Amazing Grace

once was lost, but now am found, Was blind, but now I see.
pre - cious did that grace ap - pear The hour I first be-lieved!
grace hath bro't me safe thus far And grace will lead me home.
no less days to sing God's praise Than when we first be - gun.
I Shall Be Like Him
488
W. A. Spencer
W. A. Spencer
1. When I shall reach the more ex-cel-lent glo-ry, And all my tri-als are passed,
2. We shall not wait till the glo - ri-ous dawning Breaks on the vi-sion so fair,
3. More and more like Him, repeat the blest story, O - ver and o - ver a -gain,
I shall be like Him, O won-der-ful sto-ry! I shall be like Him at last.
Now we may welcome the heav-en-ly morning, Now we His image may bear.
Changed by His Spirit from glo-ry to glo-ry, I shall be sat - is - fied then.
Chorus
I shall be like Him, I shall be like Him, And in His beau - ty shall shine,
I shall be like Him, wondrously like Him, Je-sus, my Sav-iour di - vine.

489 Peace, Perfect Peace

EDWARD H. BICKERSTETH

GEORGE T. CALDBECK
ARR. BY CHARLES J. VINCENT

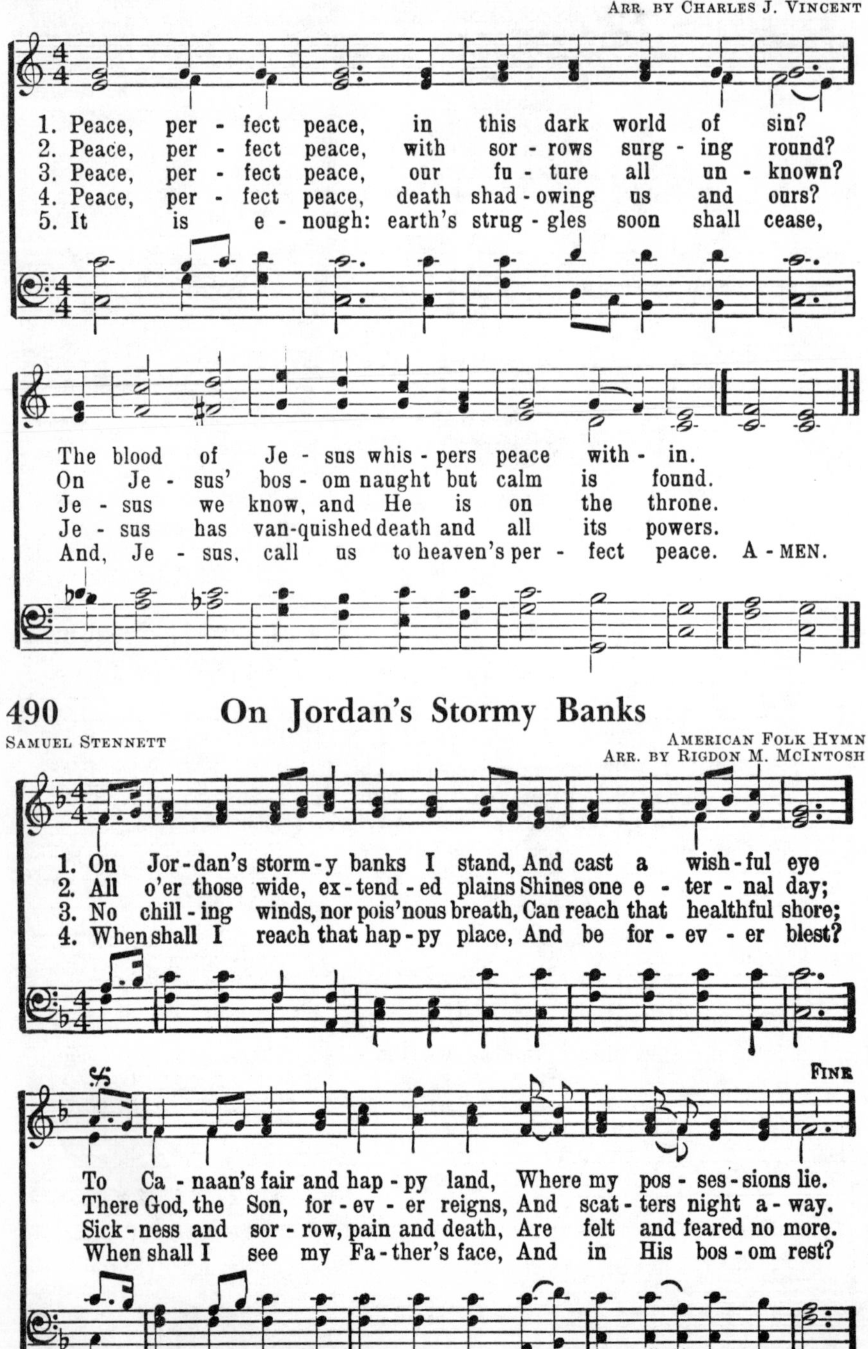
1. Peace, per - fect peace, in this dark world of sin?
2. Peace, per - fect peace, with sor - rows surg - ing round?
3. Peace, per - fect peace, our fu - ture all un - known?
4. Peace, per - fect peace, death shad - owing us and ours?
5. It is e - nough: earth's strug - gles soon shall cease,
The blood of Je - sus whis - pers peace with - in.
On Je - sus' bos - om naught but calm is found.
Je - sus we know, and He is on the throne.
Je - sus has van-quished death and all its powers.
And, Je - sus, call us to heaven's per - fect peace. A - MEN.
490 On Jordan's Stormy Banks
SAMUEL STENNETT
AMERICAN FOLK HYMN
ARR. BY RIGDON M. McINTOSH
1. On Jor-dan's storm-y banks I stand, And cast a wish-ful eye
2. All o'er those wide, ex-tend-ed plains Shines one e - ter - nal day;
3. No chill-ing winds, nor pois'nous breath, Can reach that healthful shore;
4. When shall I reach that hap-py place, And be for - ev - er blest?
FINE
To Ca-naan's fair and hap-py land, Where my pos-ses-sions lie.
There God, the Son, for-ev-er reigns, And scat-ters night a-way.
Sick-ness and sor-row, pain and death, Are felt and feared no more.
When shall I see my Fa-ther's face, And in His bos-om rest?
D.S.—O who will come and go with me? I am bound for the prom-ised land.

On Jordan's Stormy Banks

Refrain
D. S.
I am bound for the promised land, . . . I am bound for the promised land;
prom-ised land,

Shall We Gather at the River? 491

Robert Lowry
Robert Lowry
1. Shall we gath-er at the riv-er, Where bright an-gel feet have trod;
2. On the bos-om of the riv-er, Where the Sav-ior-King we own,
3. Ere we reach the shin-ing riv-er, Lay we ev-'ry bur-den down;
4. Soon we'll reach the shin-ing riv-er, Soon our pil-grim-age will cease;
With its crys-tal tide for-ev-er Flow-ing by the throne of God?
We shall meet, and sor-row nev-er,'Neath the glo-ry of the throne.
Grace our spir-its will de-liv-er, And pro-vide a robe and crown.
Soon our hap-py hearts will quiv-er With the mel-o-dy of peace.
Chorus
p
Yes, we'll gath-er at the riv-er, The beau-ti-ful, the beau-ti-ful riv-er,
Gath-er with the saints at the riv-er That flows by the throne of God.

492 No Night There

JOHN R. CLEMENTS HART P. DANKS

1. In the land of fade-less day Lies the "cit-y four-square,"
2. All the gates of pearl are made, In the "cit-y four-square,"
3. And the gates shall nev-er close To the "cit-y four-square,"
4. There they need no sun-shine bright, In that "cit-y four-square,"
It shall nev-er pass a-way, And there is "no night there."
All the streets with gold are laid, And there is "no night there."
There life's crys-tal riv-er flows, And there is "no night there."
For the Lamb is all the light, And there is "no night there."
CHORUS
mf
God shall "wipe a-way all tears;" There's no death, no pain, nor fears;
God shall "wipe a - way all tears;" There's no death, no pain, nor fears;
f
dim.
mf
And they count not time by years, For there is "no night there."
And they count not time by years, by years, For there is "no night..... there."

Face to Face

CARRIE E. BRECK GRANT C. TULLAR

1. Face to face with Christ, my Sav - ior, Face to face—what will it be?
2. On - ly faint - ly now I see Him, With the dark-ling veil be-tween,
3. What re-joic - ing in His pres - ence, When are ban-ished grief and pain;
4. Face to face! O bliss - ful mo - ment! Face to face—to see and know;

When with rap-ture I be - hold Him, Je - sus Christ who died for me.
But a bless - ed day is com - ing, When His glo - ry shall be seen.
When the crook-ed ways are straightened, And the dark things shall be plain.
Face to face with my Re-deem - er, Je - sus Christ who loves me so.

CHORUS

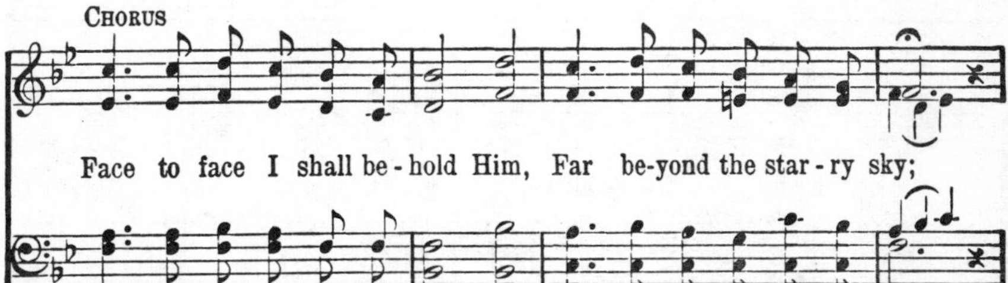

Face to face I shall be - hold Him, Far be-yond the star - ry sky;

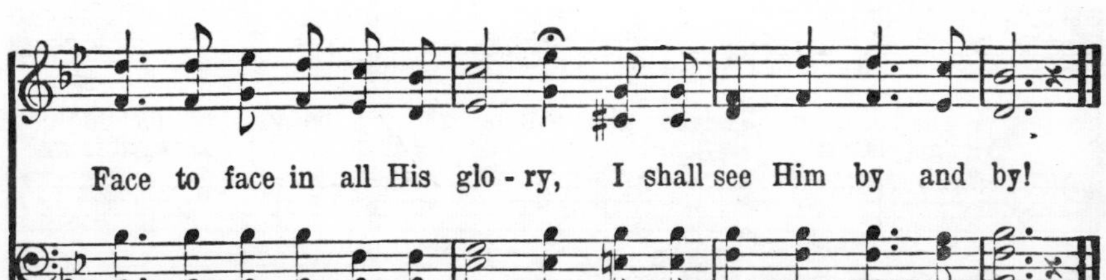

Face to face in all His glo - ry, I shall see Him by and by!

494 O That Will Be Glory

CHARLES H. GABRIEL CHARLES H. GABRIEL

1. When all my la-bors and tri-als are o'er, And I am safe on that beau-ti-ful shore, Just to be near the dear Lord I a-dore, Will thro' the a-ges be glo-ry for me. . . .
2. When, by the gift of His in-fi-nite grace, I am ac-cord-ed in Heav-en a place, Just to be there and to look on His face,
3. Friends will be there I have loved long a-go; Joy like a riv-er a-round me will flow; Yet, just a smile from my Sav-ior, I know,
rit.
CHORUS. Faster
O that will be glo-ry for me, Glo-ry for me, glo-ry for me; When by His grace I shall look on His face, That will be glo-ry, be glo-ry for me.
O . . . . . . that will be glo-ry for me, Glo-ry for me, glo-ry for me; . . . . .
rit.

Some Golden Daybreak

Carl A. Blackmore — Carl A. Blackmore

1. Some glo-rious morn-ing sor - row will cease, Some glo-rious morn-ing
2. Sad hearts will glad - den, all shall be bright, Good-bye for - ev - er
3. Oh, what a meet - ing, there in the skies, No tears nor cry - ing
all will be peace; Heart-aches all end - ed, school-days all done,
to earth's dark night; Changed in a mo - ment, like Him to be,
shall dim our eyes; Loved ones u - nit - ed e - ter - nal - ly,
rit.
CHORUS
Heav - en will o - pen— Je - sus will come.
Oh, glo-rious day-break, Je - sus I'll see, Some gold - en day-break
Oh, what a day-break that morn will be.
Je - sus will come; Some gold-en day-break, bat-tles all won, He'll shout the
vic - t'ry, break thro' the blue, Some gold-en day-break, for me, for you.

496 Some Time We'll Understand

Maxwell N. Cornelius — James McGranahan

1. Not now, but in the com-ing years, It may be in the bet-ter land,
2. We'll catch the broken thread a - gain, And fin - ish what we here be - gan;
3. We'll know why clouds instead of sun Were o - ver many a cherished plan;
4. God knows the way, He holds the key, He guides us with un - err - ing hand;

We'll read the meaning of our tears, And there, some time, we'll understand.
Heav'n will the mys-ter - ies ex - plain, And then, ah, then, we'll understand.
Why song has ceased when scarce begun; 'Tis there, some time, we'll understand.
Some time with tearless eyes we'll see; Yes, there, up there, we'll understand.

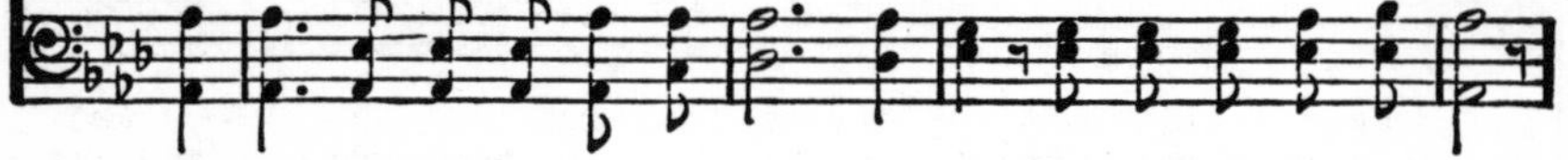

Chorus. *A little faster*

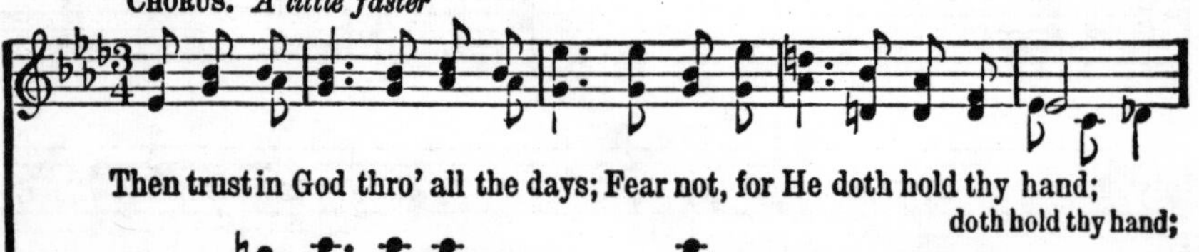
Then trust in God thro' all the days; Fear not, for He doth hold thy hand;
doth hold thy hand;

A tempo *cres.* *ad lib.*

Though dark thy way, still sing and praise, Some time, some time, we'll understand.

Sweet By and By

SANFORD F. BENNETT | JOSEPH P. WEBSTER

1. There's a land that is fair - er than day, And by faith we can
2. We shall sing on that beau - ti - ful shore The mel - o - di - ous
3. To our boun - ti - ful Fa - ther a - bove, We will of - fer our
see it a - far; For the Fa - ther waits o - ver the way, To pre-
songs of the blest, And our spir - its shall sor - row no more, Not a
trib - ute of praise, For the glo - ri - ous gift of His love, And the
CHORUS
pare us a dwell - ing-place there. In the sweet by and
sigh for the bless - ing of rest.
bless-ings that hal - low our days. In the sweet
by, We shall meet on that beau - ti - ful shore; In the
by and by, by and by,
sweet by and by, We shall meet on that beau - ti - ful shore.
In the sweet by and by,

498 We Shall See the King Some Day

LEWIS E. JONES LEWIS E. JONES

1. Tho' the way we jour - ney may be oft - en drear, We shall see the King some day (some day); On that bless-ed morn-ing clouds will dis-ap-pear;
2. Aft - er pain and an - guish, aft - er toil and care, We shall see the King some day (some day); Thro' the end-less a - ges joy and blessings share,
3. Aft - er foes are con-quered, aft - er bat - tles won, We shall see the King some day (some day); Aft - er strife is o - ver, aft - er set of sun,
4. There with all the loved ones who have gone be - fore, We shall see the King some day (some day); Sor - row past for - ev - er on that peace-ful shore,
We shall see the King some day.
CHORUS
We shall see the King some day (some day),
We will shout and sing some day (some day); Gath-ered round the throne,
When He shall call His own, We shall see the King some day.

Accepted in the Beloved

Civilla D. Martin — Wendell P. Loveless

1. "In the Be-lov-ed" ac-cept-ed am I, Ris-en, as-cend-ed, and seat-ed on high; Saved from all sin thro' His in-fi-nite grace, With the re-deemed ones ac-cord-ed a place.
2. "In the Be-lov-ed"–how safe my re-treat, In the Be-lov-ed ac-count-ed com-plete; "Who can con-demn me?" In Him I am free, Sav-ior and Keep-er for-ev-er is He.
3. "In the Be-lov-ed" I went to the tree, There, in His Per-son, by faith I may see In-fi-nite wrath roll-ing o-ver His head, In-fi-nite grace, for He died in my stead.
CHORUS
"In the Be-lov-ed," God's mar-vel-ous grace Calls me to dwell in this won-der-ful place; God sees my Sav-ior and then He sees me "In the Be-lov-ed," ac-cept-ed and free.

500 When the Roll Is Called Up Yonder

JAMES M. BLACK — JAMES M. BLACK

1. When the trumpet of the Lord shall sound, and time shall be no more, And the morning breaks, e-ter-nal, bright and fair; When the saved of earth shall gather o - ver on the oth-er shore, And the roll is called up yon-der, I'll be there.
2. On that bright and cloudless morning when the dead in Christ shall rise, And the glo - ry of His res - ur-rec-tion share; When His cho-sen ones shall gather to their home beyond the skies, And the roll is called up yon-der, I'll be there.
3. Let us la - bor for the Mas - ter from the dawn till set - ting sun, Let us talk of all His wondrous love and care; Then when all of life is o - ver, and our work on earth is done, And the roll is called up yon-der, I'll be there.

CHORUS.

When the roll . . . . . . is called up yon - - - - der, When the
When the roll is called up yon - der, I'll be there,

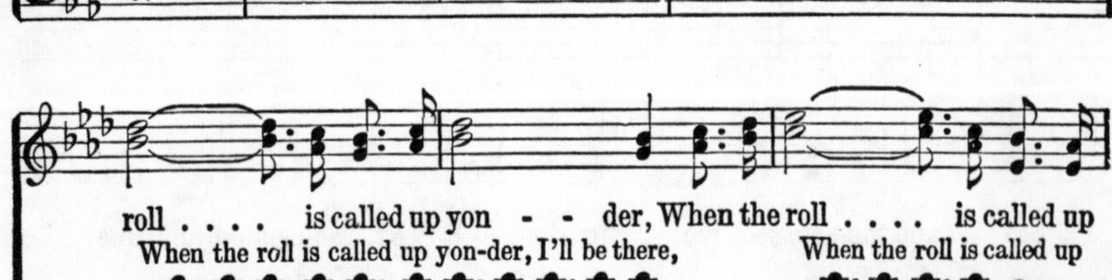
roll . . . . is called up yon - - der, When the roll . . . . is called up
When the roll is called up yon-der, I'll be there, When the roll is called up

When the Roll Is Called Up Yonder

yon - der, When the roll is called up yon - der, I'll be there.
When We All Get to Heaven
501
Eliza E. Hewitt
Emily D. Wilson
1. Sing the won-drous love of Je - sus, Sing His mer-cy and His grace;
2. While we walk the pil - grim pathway, Clouds will o - ver-spread the sky;
3. Let us then be true and faith-ful, Trust-ing, serv-ing ev - 'ry day;
4. On - ward to the prize be - fore us! Soon His beau-ty we'll be - hold;
In the man-sions bright and blessed, He'll pre-pare for us a place.
But when trav'ling days are o - ver, Not a shad-ow, not a sigh.
Just one glimpse of Him in glo - ry Will the toils of life re - pay.
Soon the pearl - y gates will o - pen, We shall tread the streets of gold.
for us a place.
Chorus
When we all get to heaven, What a day of re-joicing that will be!
When we all What a day of re-joicing that will be!
When we all see Je-sus, We'll sing and shout the vic-to-ry..........
When we all and shout the vic-to-ry.

502 Where the Gates Swing Outward Never

CHARLES H. GABRIEL — CHARLES H. GABRIEL

1. Just a few more days to be filled with praise, And to tell the
2. Just a few more years with their toil and tears, And the jour - ney
3. Tho' the hills be steep and the val - leys deep, With no flow'rs my
4. What a joy 'twill be when I wake to see Him for whom my
old, old sto - ry; Then, when twi - light falls, and my Sav - ior calls,
will be end - ed; Then I'll be with Him, where the tide of time
way a - dorn - ing; Tho' the night be lone and my rest a stone,
heart is burn - ing! Nev - er - more to sigh, nev - er - more to die—
CHORUS
I shall go to Him in glo - ry.
With e - ter - ni - ty is blend - ed. I'll ex-change my cross for a
Joy a - waits me in the morn - ing.
For that day my heart is yearn - ing.
star - ry crown, Where the gates swing out-ward nev - er; At His feet I'll
lay ev - 'ry bur - den down, And with Je - sus reign for - ev - er.

Will There Be Any Stars?

ELIZA E. HEWITT JOHN R. SWENEY

1. I am think-ing to-day of that beau-ti-ful land I shall reach when the sun go-eth down; When thro' wonderful grace by my Sav-ior I stand, Will there be an-y stars in my crown?
2. In the strength of the Lord let me la-bor and pray, Let me watch as a win-ner of souls; That bright stars may be mine in the glo-ri-ous day, When His praise like the sea-bil-low rolls.
3. Oh, what joy it will be when His face I be-hold, Liv-ing gems at His feet to lay down; It would sweeten my bliss in the cit-y of gold, Should there be an-y stars in my crown.
CHORUS.
Will there be an-y stars, an-y stars in my crown When at evening the sun go-eth down? . . . When I wake with the blest In the mansions of rest, Will there be an-y stars in my crown? . . A-MEN.
go-eth down?
an-y stars in my crown?

504 When We See Christ

Esther K. Rusthoi | Esther K. Rusthoi

1. Oft - times the day seems long, our tri - als hard to bear,
2. Some - times the sky looks dark with not a ray of light,
3. Life's day will soon be o'er, all storms for - ev - er past,
We're tempt - ed to com - plain, To mur - mur and de - spair;
We're tossed and driv - en on, No hu - man help in sight;
We'll cross the great di - vide To glo - ry — safe at last;
But Christ will soon ap - pear To catch His Bride a - way,
But there is one in heav'n Who knows our deep - est care,
We'll share the joys of heav'n—A harp, a home, a crown,
All tears for - ev - er o - ver In God's e - ter - nal day.
Let Je - sus solve your prob - lem, Just go to Him in pray'r.
The tempt - er will be ban - ished, We'll lay our bur - den down.
CHORUS
It will be worth it all when we see Je - sus, Life's trials will

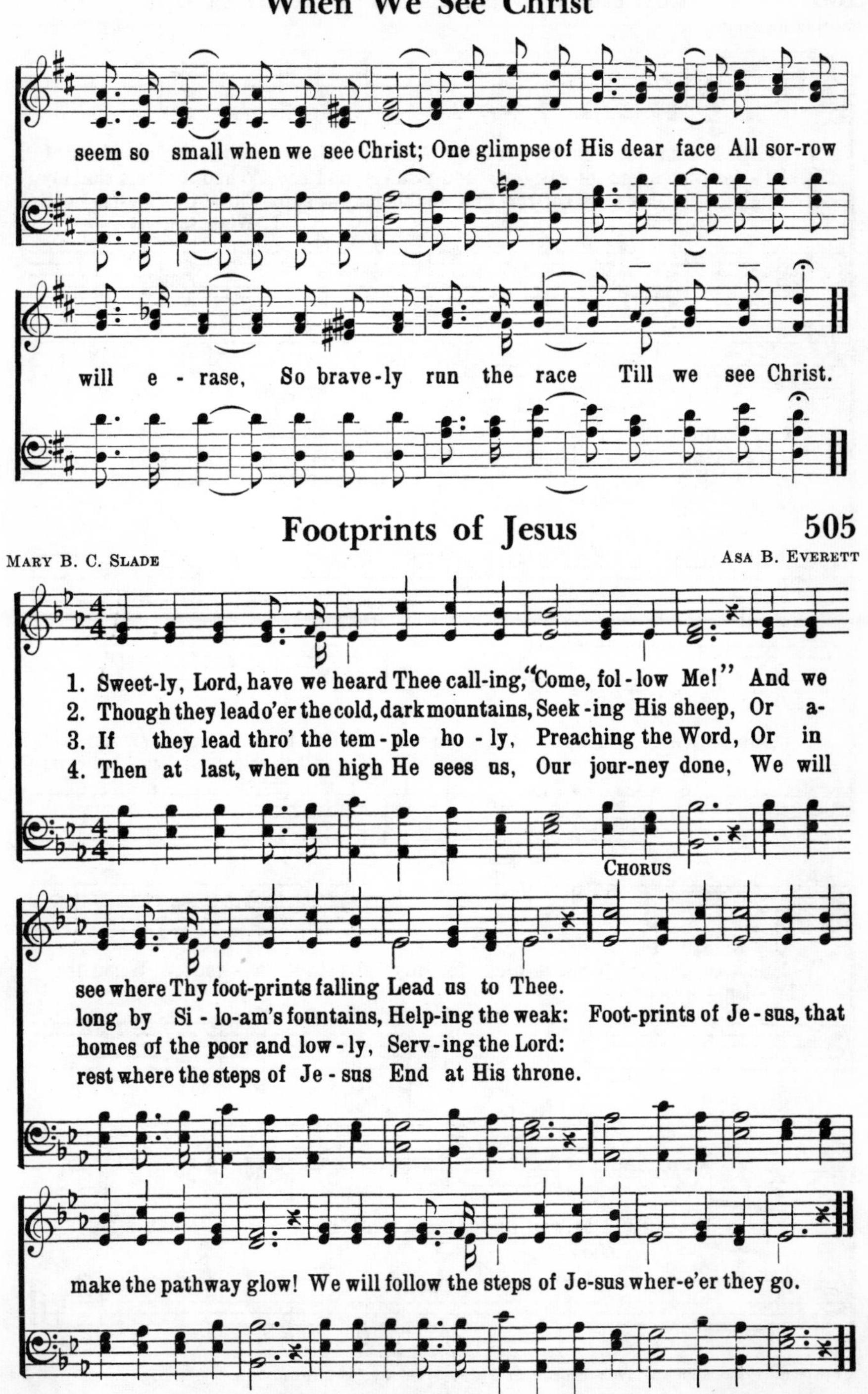
When We See Christ
seem so small when we see Christ; One glimpse of His dear face All sor-row
will e - rase, So brave-ly run the race Till we see Christ.
Footprints of Jesus
505
Mary B. C. Slade
Asa B. Everett
1. Sweet-ly, Lord, have we heard Thee call-ing, "Come, fol - low Me!" And we
2. Though they lead o'er the cold, dark mountains, Seek - ing His sheep, Or a-
3. If they lead thro' the tem - ple ho - ly, Preaching the Word, Or in
4. Then at last, when on high He sees us, Our jour-ney done, We will
see where Thy foot-prints falling Lead us to Thee.
long by Si - lo-am's fountains, Help-ing the weak:
homes of the poor and low - ly, Serv-ing the Lord:
rest where the steps of Je - sus End at His throne.
Chorus
Foot-prints of Je - sus, that
make the pathway glow! We will follow the steps of Je-sus wher-e'er they go.

506 I Won't Have to Cross Jordan Alone

THOMAS RAMSEY — CHARLES E. DURHAM

1. When I come to the riv-er at end-ing of day, When the last winds of
2. Of-ten-times I'm for-sak-en, and wea-ry and sad, When it seems that my
3. Tho' the bil-lows of sor-row and trouble may sweep, Christ the Sav-iour will
1. When the last
sor-row have blown; There'll be some-bod-y wait-ing to show me the way,
friends have all gone; There is one tho't that cheers me and makes my heart glad,
care for His own; Till the end of the jour-ney, my soul He will keep,
winds of sor-row have blown;
CHORUS
I won't have to cross Jor-dan a-lone. I won't have to cross Jor-dan a-
I won't have to cross
lone. . . . Je-sus died for my sins to a-tone; When the
Jor-dan a-lone,
SOLO ad lib.
PARTS
dark-ness I see, He'll be waiting for me, I won't have to cross Jordan a-lone.
Hum
Hum

Jerusalem the Golden

Bernard of Cluny
Tr. by John M. Neale

Alexander Ewing

1. Je - ru - sa - lem the gold - en, With milk and hon - ey blest,
2. They stand, those halls of Zi - on, All ju - bi - lant with song,
3. There is the throne of Da - vid; And there, from care re - leased,
4. O sweet and bless - ed coun - try, The home of God's e - lect!
Be - neath thy con - tem - pla - tion Sink heart and voice op - prest.
And bright with many an an - gel, And all the mar - tyr throng.
The song of them that tri - umph, The shout of them that feast;
O sweet and bless - ed coun - try That ea - ger hearts ex - pect!
I know not, O I know not What joys a - wait us there;
The Prince is ev - er in them, The day - light is se - rene;
And they, who with their Lead - er Have con-quered in the fight,
Je - sus, in mer - cy bring us To that dear land of rest;
What ra - dian - cy of glo - ry! What bliss be-yond com - pare!
The pas-tures of the bless - ed Are decked in glo-rious sheen.
For - ev - er and for - ev - er Are clad in robes of white.
Who art, with God the Fa - ther, And Spir - it, ev - er blest. A-MEN.

508 Now Thank We All Our God
Martin Rinkart
Tr. by Catherine Winkworth
Johann Crüger
Har. by Felix Mendelssohn-Bartholdy
1. Now thank we all our God, With heart and hands and voic - es,
2. O may this boun-teous God, Thro' all our life be near us,
3. All praise and thanks to God The Fa - ther now be giv - en,
Who won-drous things hath done, In whom His world re - joic - es;
With ev - er joy - ful hearts, And bless - ed peace to cheer us;
The Son and Him who reigns With Them in high - est heav - en;
Who from our moth - er's arms Hath blessed us on our way
And keep us in His grace, And guide us when per - plexed,
The one e - ter - nal God, Whom earth and heaven a - dore;
With count-less gifts of love, And still is ours to - day.
And free us from all ills In this world and the next.
For thus it was, is now, And shall be ev - er - more. A-MEN.

Come, Ye Thankful People, Come

HENRY ALFORD

GEORGE J. ELVEY

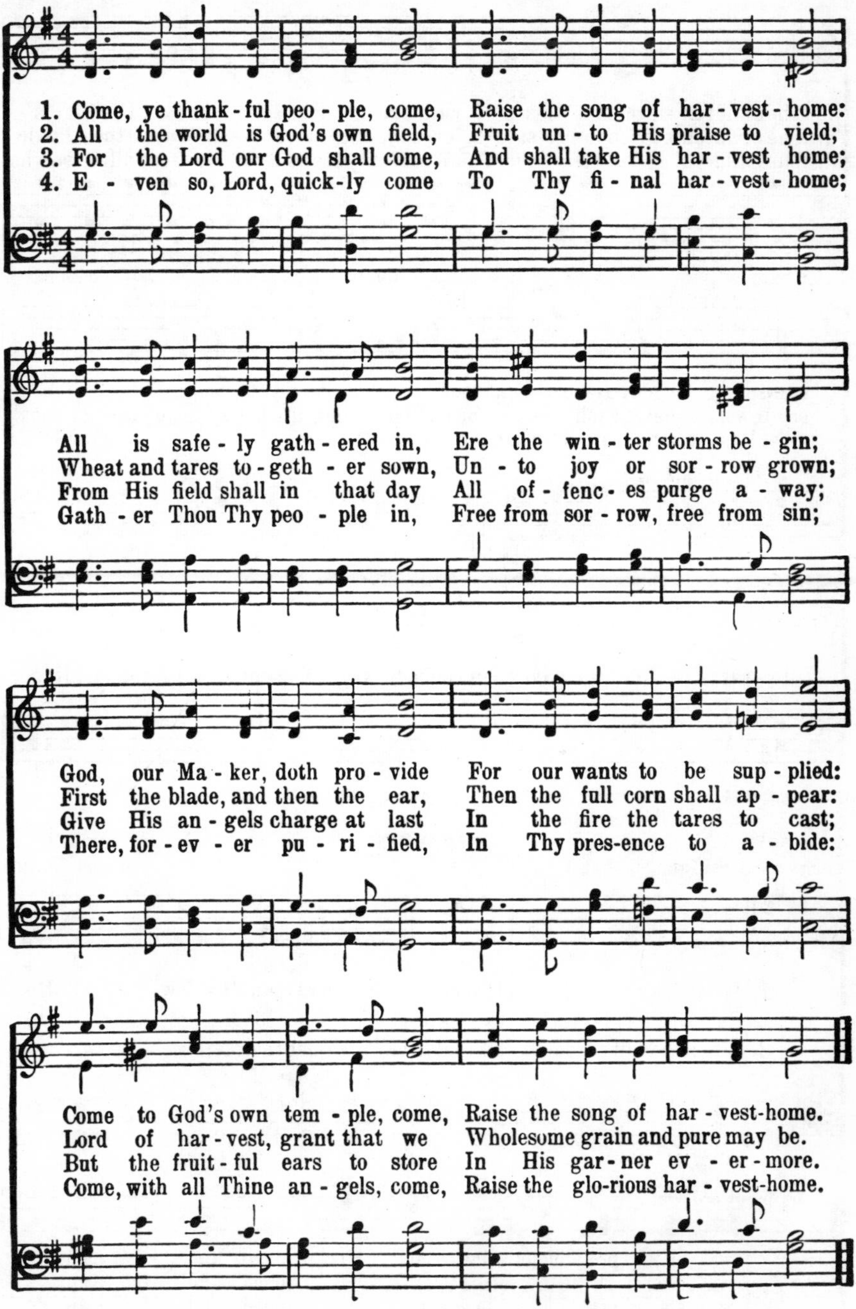

1. Come, ye thank - ful peo - ple, come, Raise the song of har - vest - home:
All is safe - ly gath - ered in, Ere the win - ter storms be - gin;
God, our Ma - ker, doth pro - vide For our wants to be sup - plied:
Come to God's own tem - ple, come, Raise the song of har - vest-home.

2. All the world is God's own field, Fruit un - to His praise to yield;
Wheat and tares to - geth - er sown, Un - to joy or sor - row grown;
First the blade, and then the ear, Then the full corn shall ap - pear:
Lord of har - vest, grant that we Wholesome grain and pure may be.

3. For the Lord our God shall come, And shall take His har - vest home;
From His field shall in that day All of - fenc - es purge a - way;
Give His an - gels charge at last In the fire the tares to cast;
But the fruit - ful ears to store In His gar - ner ev - er - more.

4. E - ven so, Lord, quick - ly come To Thy fi - nal har - vest - home;
Gath - er Thou Thy peo - ple in, Free from sor - row, free from sin;
There, for - ev - er pu - ri - fied, In Thy pres - ence to a - bide:
Come, with all Thine an - gels, come, Raise the glo - rious har - vest-home.

510 The Children's Friend Is Jesus

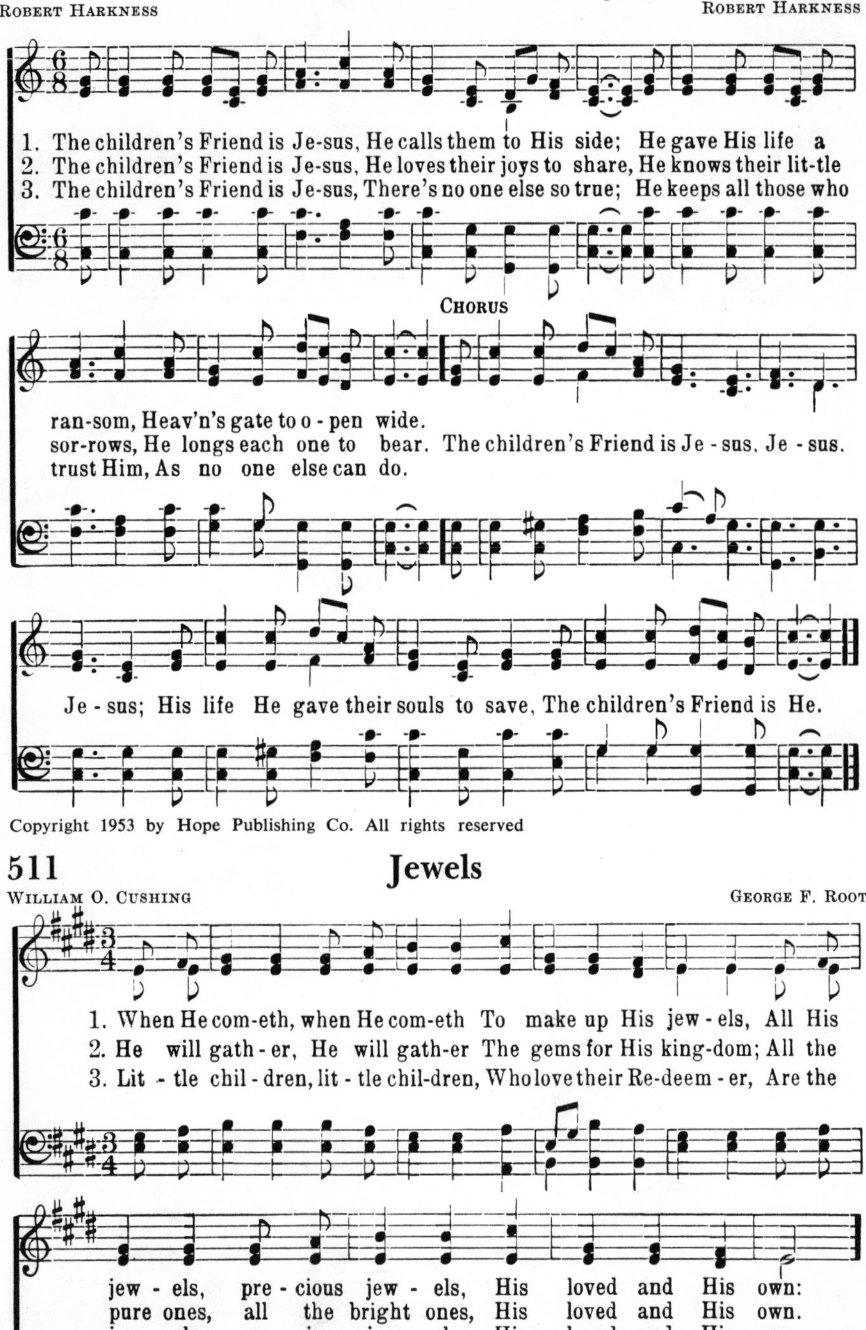
ROBERT HARKNESS
ROBERT HARKNESS
1. The children's Friend is Je-sus, He calls them to His side; He gave His life a
2. The children's Friend is Je-sus, He loves their joys to share, He knows their lit-tle
3. The children's Friend is Je-sus, There's no one else so true; He keeps all those who
CHORUS
ran-som, Heav'n's gate to o-pen wide.
sor-rows, He longs each one to bear. The children's Friend is Je - sus, Je - sus.
trust Him, As no one else can do.
Je - sus; His life He gave their souls to save, The children's Friend is He.
Copyright 1953 by Hope Publishing Co. All rights reserved
511
Jewels
WILLIAM O. CUSHING
GEORGE F. ROOT
1. When He com-eth, when He com-eth To make up His jew - els, All His
2. He will gath - er, He will gath-er The gems for His king-dom; All the
3. Lit - tle chil - dren, lit - tle chil-dren, Who love their Re-deem - er, Are the
jew - els, pre - cious jew - els, His loved and His own:
pure ones, all the bright ones, His loved and His own.
jew - els, pre - cious jew - els, His loved and His own.

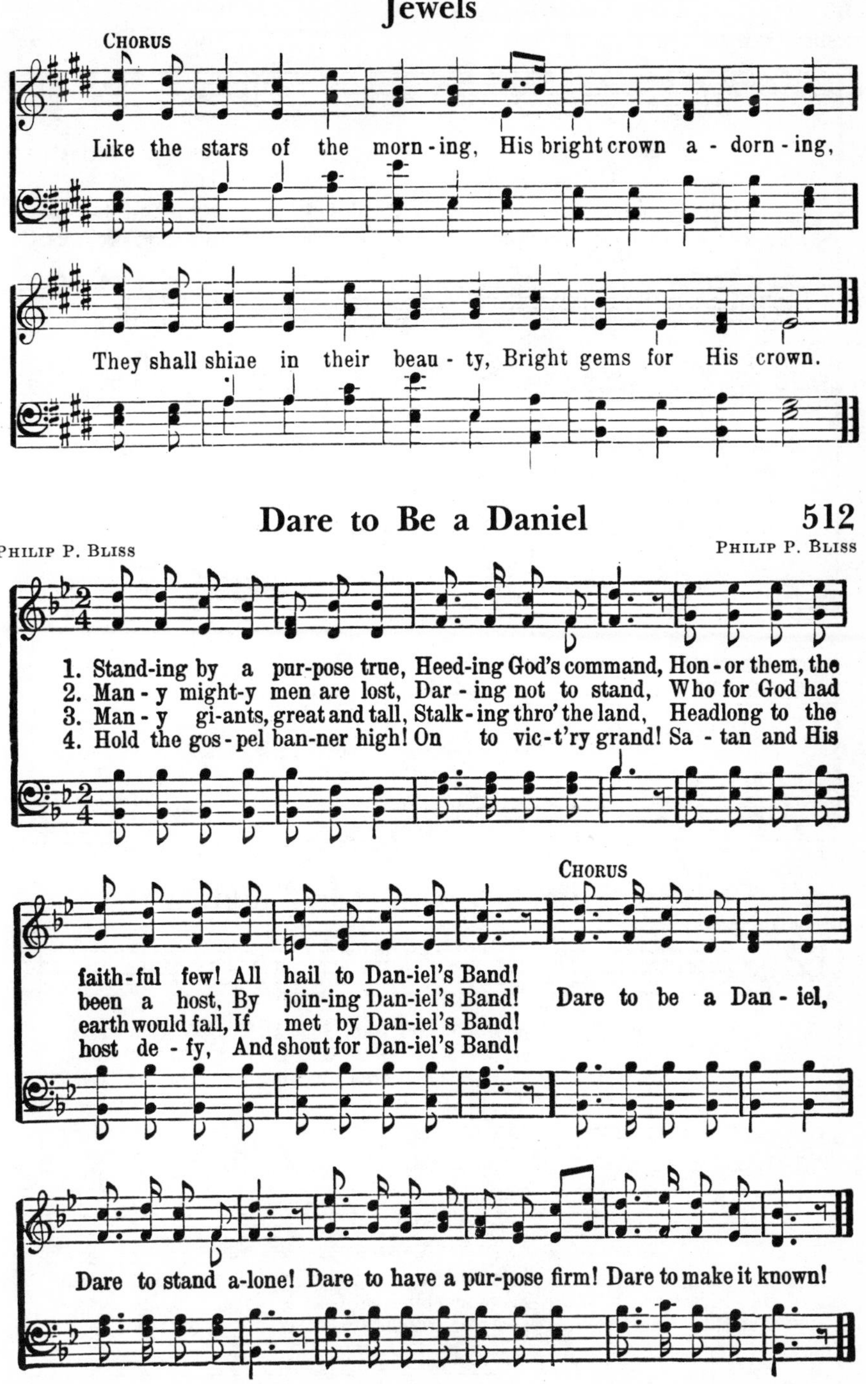
Jewels
Chorus
Like the stars of the morn-ing, His bright crown a-dorn-ing,
They shall shine in their beau-ty, Bright gems for His crown.
Dare to Be a Daniel
512
Philip P. Bliss
Philip P. Bliss
1. Stand-ing by a pur-pose true, Heed-ing God's command, Hon-or them, the faith-ful few! All hail to Dan-iel's Band!
2. Man-y might-y men are lost, Dar-ing not to stand, Who for God had been a host, By join-ing Dan-iel's Band!
3. Man-y gi-ants, great and tall, Stalk-ing thro' the land, Headlong to the earth would fall, If met by Dan-iel's Band!
4. Hold the gos-pel ban-ner high! On to vic-t'ry grand! Sa-tan and His host de-fy, And shout for Dan-iel's Band!
Chorus
Dare to be a Dan-iel,
Dare to stand a-lone! Dare to have a pur-pose firm! Dare to make it known!

513 Jesus Loves Me

ANNA B. WARNER, ALT.

WILLIAM B. BRADBURY

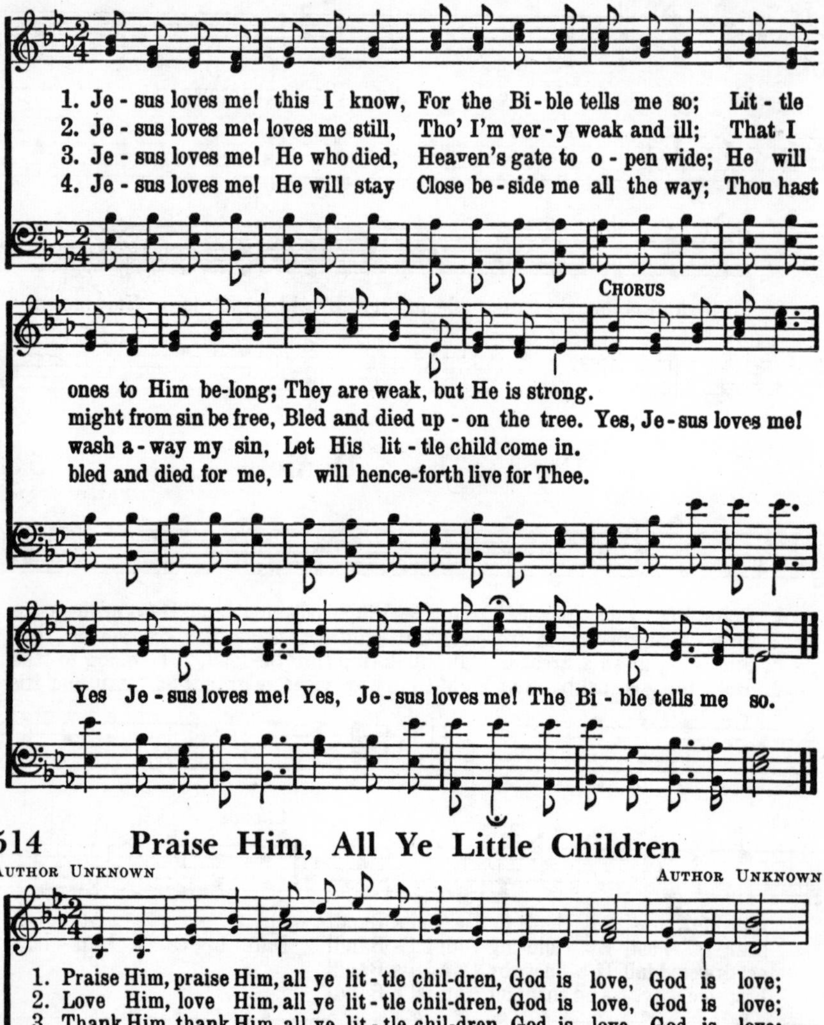

1. Je - sus loves me! this I know, For the Bi - ble tells me so; Lit - tle ones to Him be - long; They are weak, but He is strong.
2. Je - sus loves me! loves me still, Tho' I'm ver - y weak and ill; That I might from sin be free, Bled and died up - on the tree.
3. Je - sus loves me! He who died, Heaven's gate to o - pen wide; He will wash a - way my sin, Let His lit - tle child come in.
4. Je - sus loves me! He will stay Close be - side me all the way; Thou hast bled and died for me, I will hence - forth live for Thee.

CHORUS

Yes, Je - sus loves me! Yes Je - sus loves me! Yes, Je - sus loves me! The Bi - ble tells me so.

514 Praise Him, All Ye Little Children

AUTHOR UNKNOWN

AUTHOR UNKNOWN

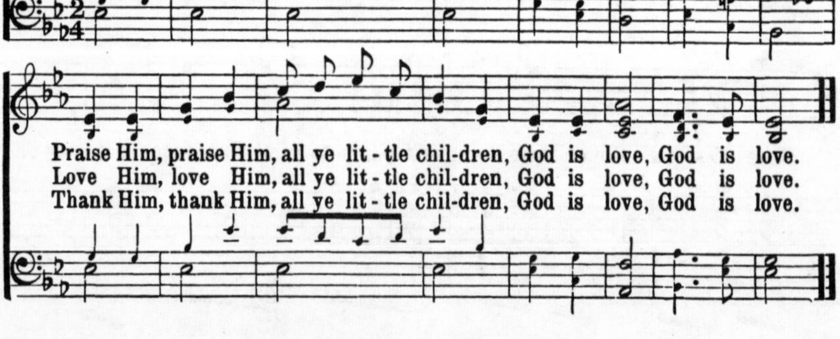

1. Praise Him, praise Him, all ye lit - tle chil - dren, God is love, God is love; Praise Him, praise Him, all ye lit - tle chil - dren, God is love, God is love.
2. Love Him, love Him, all ye lit - tle chil - dren, God is love, God is love; Love Him, love Him, all ye lit - tle chil - dren, God is love, God is love.
3. Thank Him, thank Him, all ye lit - tle chil - dren, God is love, God is love; Thank Him, thank Him, all ye lit - tle chil - dren, God is love, God is love.

I'll Be a Sunbeam

515

Nellie Talbot

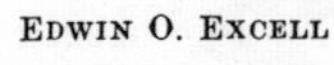
Edwin O. Excell

1. Je - sus wants me for a sun - beam, To shine for Him each day;
2. Je - sus wants me to be lov - ing, And kind to all I see;
3. I will ask Je-sus to help me To keep my heart from sin,
4. I'll be a sun-beam for Je - sus; I can if I but try;

In ev - 'ry way try to please Him, At home, at school, at play.
Showing how pleasant and hap - py His lit - tle one can be.
Ev - er re - flect-ing His good - ness, And al - ways shine for Him.
Serv-ing Him mo-ment by mo - ment, Then live with Him on high.

Chorus

A sun - beam, a sun - beam, Je - sus wants me for a sun - beam; A

sun - beam, a sun - beam, I'll be a sun-beam for Him.

516 Count Your Blessings

JOHNSON OATMAN, JR. EDWIN O. EXCELL

1. When up - on life's bil-lows you are tem - pest - tossed, When you are dis-
2. Are you ev - er bur-dened with a load of care? Does the cross seem
3. When you look at oth - ers with their lands and gold, Think that Christ has
4. So, a - mid the con-flict, whether great or small, Do not be dis-
cour-aged, think-ing all is lost, Count your man-y bless-ings, name them
heav - y you are called to bear? Count your man-y bless-ings, ev - 'ry
prom-ised you His wealth un - told; Count your man-y bless-ings, mon - ey
cour-aged, God is o - ver all; Count your man-y bless-ings, an - gels
one by one, And it will sur-prise you what the Lord hath done.
doubt will fly, And you will be sing - ing as the days go by.
can - not buy Your re-ward in heav-en, nor your home on high.
will at - tend, Help and com-fort give you to your jour - ney's end.
CHORUS.
Count your bless-ings, Name them one by one; Count your
Count your man-y bless - ings, Name them one by one; Count your man-y
bless-ings, See what God hath done; Count your bless-ings,
bless - ings, See what God hath done; Count your man-y bless - ings,

Count Your Blessings
rit.
a tempo
Name them one by one; Count your man-y blessings, See what God hath done.
What a Friend We Have in Jesus
517
JOSEPH SCRIVEN
CHARLES C. CONVERSE
1. What a Friend we have in Je - sus, All our sins and griefs to bear!
2. Have we tri - als and temp - ta - tions? Is there troub-le an - y - where?
3. Are we weak and heav-y - la - den, Cumbered with a load of care?—
What a priv - i - lege to car - ry Ev - 'ry-thing to God in prayer!
We should nev-er be dis - cour-aged, Take it to the Lord in prayer.
Pre - cious Sav-ior, still our ref - uge,—Take it to the Lord in prayer.
O what peace we oft - en for - feit, O what need-less pain we bear,
Can we find a friend so faith - ful Who will all our sor-rows share?
Do thy friends despise, for-sake thee? Take it to the Lord in prayer;
All be-cause we do not car - ry Ev - 'ry-thing to God in prayer!
Je - sus knows our ev - 'ry weak - ness, Take it to the Lord in prayer.
In His arms He'll take and shield thee, Thou wilt find a sol - ace there.

518 All Hail, Immanuel!

D. R. Van Sickle | Charles H. Gabriel

1. All hail to Thee, Im-man-u-el, We cast . . . our crowns be-fore Thee;
2. All hail to Thee, Im-man-u-el, The ran - somed hosts surround Thee;
3. All hail to Thee, Im-man-u-el, Our ris - - en King and Sav-ior!
Let ev-'ry heart o-bey Thy will, And ev - - - - 'ry voice a-
And earth-ly mon-archs clam-or forth Their Sov - - 'reign King to
Thy foes are van-quished, and Thou art Om-nip - - - - o-tent for-
dore Thee. In praise to Thee, our Sav-ior King, The vi-brant
crown Thee. While those re-deemed in a-ges gone, As-sem-bled
ev - er. Death, sin and hell no lon-ger reign, And Sa-tan's
chords of Heav-en ring, And ech-o back the might-y strain:
round the great white throne, Break forth in-to im-mor-tal song:
pow'r is burst in twain; E-ter-nal glo-ry to Thy Name:
ff
All hail! all hail! All hail! all hail! Im-man-u-el!
All hail! all hail!

All Hail, Immanuel!

Chorus.
Hail! . . . . . . Im-man-u-el! Im-man-u-el! Hail! . . . . . .
Hail to the King we love so well! Hail! Im - man-u - el! Hail to the King we love so well!
Hail! . . . . . .
Im-man-u-el! Im-man-u-el!
Hail! Im - man - u - el! Glo-ry and honor and majesty, Wisdom and power be
Hail! . . . . . . Glo - - ry and maj-es-ty, Wis - dom be
rit. . . . . Hail! . . . . Im-
un - to Thee, Now and ev - er - more! . . . Hail to the King we love so well!
man-u-el! Im-man-u-el! Hail! . . . . . . Im-man-u-el! Im-man-u-el!
Hail! Im - man - u - el! Hail to the King we love so well! Hail! Im - man - u - el!
Hail! . . . . . . Hail! . . . . . .
King of kings and Lord of lords, All hail, Im - man - u - el! A-MEN.

SCRIPTURE READINGS

The text used for the readings is the King James Version. The readings are arranged, generally, as follows: God the Father, life of Christ, the Holy Spirit, the church, and the Christian life. An Index to Scripture Readings is on page 498.

519 GOD THE CREATOR

In the beginning God created the heaven and the earth.

And the earth was without form, and void; and darkness was upon the face of the deep.

And the Spirit of God moved upon the face of the waters. And God said, Let there be light: and there was light.

And God saw the light, that it was good: and God divided the light from the darkness.

And God called the light Day, and the darkness he called Night.

And the evening and the morning were the first day. —Genesis 1:1-5.

By the word of the Lord were the heavens made; and all the host of them by the breath of his mouth.

He gathereth the waters of the sea together as an heap: he layeth up the depth in storehouses.

Let all the earth fear the Lord: let all the inhabitants of the world stand in awe of him.

For he spake, and it was done; he commanded, and it stood fast. —Psalm 33:6-9.

Let us come before his presence with thanksgiving, and make a joyful noise unto him with psalms.

For the Lord is a great God, and a great King above all gods.

In his hand are the deep places of the earth: the strength of the hills is his also.

The sea is his, and he made it: and his hands formed the dry land.

O come, let us worship and bow down: let us kneel before the Lord our maker.

For he is our God; and we are the people of his pasture, and the sheep of his hand. —Psalm 95:2-7.

520 GOD'S OMNISCIENCE

O Lord, thou hast searched me, and known me.

Thou knowest my downsitting and mine uprising, thou understandest my thought afar off.

Thou compassest my path and my lying down, and art acquainted with all my ways.

For there is not a word in my tongue, but, lo, O Lord, thou knowest it altogether.

Thou hast beset me behind and before, and laid thine hand upon me.

Such knowledge is too wonderful for me; it is high, I cannot attain unto it.

Whither shall I go from thy spirit? or whither shall I flee from thy presence?

If I ascend up into heaven, thou art there: if I make my bed in hell, behold, thou art there.

If I take the wings of the morning, and dwell in the uttermost parts of the sea;

Even there shall thy hand lead me, and thy right hand shall hold me.

If I say, Surely the darkness shall cover me; even the night shall be light about me.

Yea, the darkness hideth not from thee; but the night shineth as the

day: the darkness and the light are both alike to thee.

I will praise thee; for I am fearfully and wonderfully made: marvellous are thy works; and that my soul knoweth right well.

Search me, O God, and know my heart: try me, and know my thoughts: and see if there be any wicked way in me, and lead me in the way everlasting.

—Psalm 139:1-12, 14, 23, 24.

521 GOD'S CARE

I will lift up mine eyes unto the hills, from whence cometh my help.

My help cometh from the Lord, which made heaven and earth.

He will not suffer thy foot to be moved: he that keepeth thee will not slumber.

Behold, he that keepeth Israel shall neither slumber nor sleep.

The Lord is thy keeper: the Lord is thy shade upon thy right hand.

The sun shall not smite thee by day, nor the moon by night.

The Lord shall preserve thee from all evil: he shall preserve thy soul.

The Lord shall preserve thy going out and thy coming in from this time forth, and even for evermore.

—Psalm 121.

522 THE SHEPHERD PSALM

The Lord is my shepherd; I shall not want.

He maketh me to lie down in green pastures: he leadeth me beside the still waters.

He restoreth my soul: he leadeth me in the paths of righteousness for his name's sake.

Yea, though I walk through the valley of the shadow of death, I will fear no evil:

For thou art with me; thy rod and thy staff they comfort me.

Thou preparest a table before me in the presence of mine enemies:

Thou anointest my head with oil; my cup runneth over.

Surely goodness and mercy shall follow me all the days of my life: and I will dwell in the house of the Lord for ever. —Psalm 23.

523 DIVINE PROVIDENCE

I will bless the Lord at all times: his praise shall continually be in my mouth.

My soul shall make her boast in the Lord: the humble shall hear thereof, and be glad.

O magnify the Lord with me, and let us exalt his name together.

I sought the Lord, and he heard me, and delivered me from all my fears.

They looked unto him, and were lightened: and their faces were not ashamed.

This poor man cried, and the Lord heard him, and saved him out of all his troubles.

The angel of the Lord encampeth round about them that fear him, and delivereth them.

O taste and see that the Lord is good: blessed is the man that trusteth in him.

O fear the Lord, ye his saints: for there is no want to them that fear him.

The young lions do lack, and suffer hunger: but they that seek the Lord shall not want any good thing.

The righteous cry, and the Lord heareth, and delivereth them out of all their troubles.

The Lord is nigh unto them that

(*over*)

are of a broken heart; and saveth such as be of a contrite spirit.

Many are the afflictions of the righteous: but the Lord delivereth him out of them all.

The Lord redeemeth the soul of his servants: and none of them that trust in him shall be desolate.

—Psalm 34:1-10, 17-19, 22.

524 GOD'S COMMANDMENTS

I am the Lord thy God, which have brought thee out of the land of Egypt, out of the house of bondage. Thou shalt have no other gods before me.

Thou shalt not make unto thee any graven image, or any likeness of any thing that is in heaven above, or that is in the earth beneath, or that is in the water under the earth: thou shalt not bow down thyself to them, nor serve them:

Thou shalt not take the name of the Lord thy God in vain;

For the Lord will not hold him guiltless that taketh his name in vain.

Remember the sabbath day, to keep it holy. For in six days the Lord made heaven and earth, the sea, and all that in them is, and rested the seventh day:

Wherefore the Lord blessed the sabbath day, and hallowed it.

Honour thy father and thy mother: that thy days may be long upon the land which the Lord thy God giveth thee.

Thou shalt not kill.

Thou shalt not commit adultery.

Thou shalt not steal.

Thou shalt not bear false witness against thy neighbour.

Thou shalt not covet thy neighbour's house, thou shalt not covet thy neighbour's wife, nor his manservant, nor his maidservant, nor his ox, nor his ass, nor any thing that is thy neighbour's.

—Exodus 20:2-5, 7, 8, 11-17.

Thou shalt love the Lord thy God with all thy heart, and with all thy soul, and with all thy mind. This is the first and great commandment.

And the second is like unto it, Thou shalt love thy neighbour as thyself. On these two commandments hang all the law and the prophets. —Matthew 22:37-40.

525 WORSHIP OF GOD

O sing unto the Lord a new song: sing unto the Lord, all the earth.

Sing unto the Lord, bless his name; shew forth his salvation from day to day.

Declare his glory among the heathen, his wonders among all people.

For the Lord is great, and greatly to be praised: he is to be feared above all gods.

For all the gods of the nations are idols: but the Lord made the heavens.

Honour and majesty are before him: strength and beauty are in his sanctuary.

Give unto the Lord, O ye kindreds of the people, give unto the Lord glory and strength.

Give unto the Lord the glory due unto his name: bring an offering, and come into his courts.

O worship the Lord in the beauty of holiness: fear before him, all the earth.

Say among the heathen that the Lord reigneth: the world also shall be established that it shall not be moved: he shall judge the people righteously.

Let the heavens rejoice, and let the earth be glad;

Let the sea roar, and the fulness thereof. Let the field be joyful, and all that is therein:

Then shall all the trees of the wood rejoice before the Lord: for he cometh, for he cometh to judge the earth:

He shall judge the world with righteousness, and the people with his truth. —Psalm 96.

526 THANKSGIVING TO GOD

Bless the Lord, O my soul: and all that is within me, bless his holy name.

Bless the Lord, O my soul, and forget not all his benefits:

Who forgiveth all thine iniquities; who healeth all thy diseases;

Who redeemeth thy life from destruction; who crowneth thee with lovingkindness and tender mercies;

Who satisfieth thy mouth with good things; so that thy youth is renewed like the eagle's.

The Lord executeth righteousness and judgment for all that are oppressed.

He made known his ways unto Moses, his acts unto the children of Israel.

The Lord is merciful and gracious, slow to anger, and plenteous in mercy.

He will not always chide: neither will he keep his anger for ever.

He hath not dealt with us after our sins; nor rewarded us according to our iniquities.

For as the heaven is high above the earth, so great is his mercy toward them that fear him.

As far as the east is from the west, so far hath he removed our transgressions from us.

Like as a father pitieth his children, so the Lord pitieth them that fear him.

Bless the Lord, all his works in all places of his dominion: bless the Lord, O my soul. —Psalm 103:1-13, 22.

527 OBEDIENCE TO GOD

Thou hast commanded us to keep thy precepts diligently.

O that my ways were directed to keep thy statutes!

Then shall I not be ashamed, when I have respect unto all thy commandments.

I will praise thee with uprightness of heart, when I shall have learned thy righteous judgments.

I will keep thy statutes: O forsake me not utterly.

Wherewithal shall a young man cleanse his way? by taking heed thereto according to thy word.

With my whole heart have I sought thee: O let me not wander from thy commandments.

Thy word have I hid in mine heart, that I might not sin against thee.

Blessed art thou, O Lord: teach me thy statutes.

With my lips have I declared all the judgments of thy mouth.

I have rejoiced in the way of thy testimonies, as much as in all riches.

I will meditate in thy precepts, and have respect unto thy ways.

I will delight myself in thy statutes: I will not forget thy word.

Deal bountifully with thy servant, that I may live, and keep thy word.

Open thou mine eyes, that I may behold wondrous things out of thy law. —Psalm 119:4-18.

528 THE INCARNATE CHRIST

In the beginning was the Word, and the Word was with God, and the Word was God.

The same was in the beginning with God.

All things were made by him; and without him was not any thing made that was made.

In him was life; and the life was the light of men.

And the light shineth in darkness; and the darkness comprehended it not.

There was a man sent from God, whose name was John.

The same came for a witness, to bear witness of the Light, that all men through him might believe.

He was not that Light, but was sent to bear witness of that Light.

That was the true Light, which lighteth every man that cometh into the world.

He was in the world, and the world was made by him, and the world knew him not.

He came unto his own, and his own received him not.

But as many as received him, to them gave he power to become the sons of God, even to them that believe on his name:

Which were born, not of blood, nor of the will of the flesh, nor of the will of man, but of God.

And the Word was made flesh, and dwelt among us, (and we beheld his glory, the glory as of the only begotten of the Father,) full of grace and truth. —John 1:1-14.

For God so loved the world, that he gave his only begotten Son, that whosoever believeth in him should not perish, but have everlasting life.

For God sent not his Son into the world to condemn the world; but that the world through him might be saved. —John 3:16, 17.

529 THE SAVIOUR'S ADVENT

And there were in the same country shepherds abiding in the field, keeping watch over their flock by night.

And, lo, the angel of the Lord came upon them, and the glory of the Lord shone round about them: and they were sore afraid.

And the angel said unto them, Fear not: for, behold, I bring you good tidings of great joy, which shall be to all people.

For unto you is born this day in the city of David a Saviour, which is Christ the Lord.

And this shall be a sign unto you; Ye shall find the babe wrapped in swaddling clothes, lying in a manger.

And suddenly there was with the angel a multitude of the heavenly host praising God, and saying,

Glory to God in the highest, and on earth peace, good will toward men.

And it came to pass, as the angels were gone away from them into heaven, the shepherds said one to another,

Let us now go even unto Bethlehem, and see this thing which is come to pass, which the Lord hath made known unto us.

And they came with haste, and found Mary, and Joseph, and the babe lying in a manger.

And when they had seen it, they made known abroad the saying which was told them concerning this child.

And all they that heard it wondered at those things which were told them by the shepherds.

But Mary kept all these things, and pondered them in her heart.

And the shepherds returned, glorifying and praising God for all the things that they had heard and seen, as it was told unto them.
—Luke 2:8-20.

530 ADORATION OF THE MAGI

Now when Jesus was born in Bethlehem of Judaea in the days of Herod the king, behold, there came wise men from the east to Jerusalem, saying,

Where is he that is born King of the Jews? for we have seen his star in the east, and are come to worship him.

When Herod the king had heard these things, he was troubled, and all Jerusalem with him.

And when he had gathered all the chief priests and scribes of the people together, he demanded of them where Christ should be born.

And they said unto him, In Bethlehem of Judaea: for thus it is written by the prophet,

And thou Bethlehem, in the land of Juda, art not the least among the princes of Juda: for out of thee shall come a Governor, that shall rule my people Israel.

Then Herod, when he had privily called the wise men, enquired of them diligently what time the star appeared. And he sent them to Bethlehem, and said,

Go and search diligently for the young child; and when ye have found him, bring me word again, that I may come and worship him also.

When they had heard the king, they departed; and, lo, the star, which they saw in the east, went before them, till it came and stood over where the young child was.

When they saw the star, they rejoiced with exceeding great joy. And when they were come into the house, they saw the young child with Mary his mother, and fell down, and worshipped him:

And when they had opened their treasures, they presented unto him gifts; gold, and frankincense, and myrrh.

And being warned of God in a dream that they should not return to Herod, they departed into their own country another way. —Matthew 2:1-12.

531 BAPTISM OF JESUS

In those days came John the Baptist, preaching in the wilderness of Judaea, and saying,

Repent ye: for the kingdom of heaven is at hand.

For this is he that was spoken of by the prophet Esaias, saying, The voice of one crying in the wilderness, Prepare ye the way of the Lord, make his paths straight.

And the same John had his raiment of camel's hair, and a leathern girdle about his loins; and his meat was locusts and wild honey.

Then went out to him Jerusalem, and all Judaea, and all the region round about Jordan, and were baptized of him in Jordan, confessing their sins.

But when he saw many of the Pharisees and Sadducees come to his baptism, he said unto them,

O generation of vipers, who hath warned you to flee from the wrath

(over)

to come? Bring forth therefore fruits meet for repentance:

I indeed baptize you with water unto repentance: but he that cometh after me is mightier than I, whose shoes I am not worthy to bear: he shall baptize you with the Holy Ghost, and with fire:

Then cometh Jesus from Galilee to Jordan unto John, to be baptized of him.

But John forbad him, saying, I have need to be baptized of thee, and comest thou to me?

And Jesus answering said unto him, Suffer it to be so now: for thus it becometh us to fulfil all righteousness. Then he suffered him.

And Jesus, when he was baptized, went up straightway out of the water:

And, lo, the heavens were opened unto him, and he saw the Spirit of God descending like a dove, and lighting upon him:

And lo a voice from heaven, saying, This is my beloved Son, in whom I am well pleased.

—Matthew 3:1-8, 11, 13-17.

532 THE LAMB OF GOD

Who hath believed our report? and to whom is the arm of the Lord revealed?

For he shall grow up before him as a tender plant, and as a root out of a dry ground: he hath no form nor comeliness; and when we shall see him, there is no beauty that we should desire him.

He is despised and rejected of men; a man of sorrows, and acquainted with grief: and we hid as it were our faces from him; he was despised, and we esteemed him not.

Surely he hath borne our griefs, and carried our sorrows: yet we did esteem him stricken, smitten of God, and afflicted.

But he was wounded for our transgressions, he was bruised for our iniquities: the chastisement of our peace was upon him; and with his stripes we are healed.

All we like sheep have gone astray; we have turned every one to his own way; and the Lord hath laid on him the iniquity of us all.

He was oppressed, and he was afflicted, yet he opened not his mouth: he is brought as a lamb to the slaughter, and as a sheep before her shearers is dumb, so he openeth not his mouth.

He was taken from prison and from judgment: and who shall declare his generation? for he was cut off out of the land of the living: for the transgression of my people was he stricken.

And he made his grave with the wicked, and with the rich in his death; because he had done no violence, neither was any deceit in his mouth.

Yet it pleased the Lord to bruise him; he hath put him to grief: when thou shalt make his soul an offering for sin, he shall see his seed, he shall prolong his days, and the pleasure of the Lord shall prosper in his hand.

He shall see of the travail of his soul, and shall be satisfied: by his knowledge shall my righteous servant justify many; for he shall bear their iniquities.

Therefore will I divide him a portion with the great, and he shall divide the spoil with the strong; because he hath poured out his soul unto death: and he was numbered with the transgressors; and he bare the sin of many, and made intercession for the transgressors. —Isaiah 53.

533 THE LAST SUPPER

And the disciples did as Jesus had appointed them; and they made ready the passover.

Now when the even was come, he sat down with the twelve.

And as they did eat, he said, Verily I say unto you, that one of you shall betray me.

And they were exceeding sorrowful, and began every one of them to say unto him, Lord, is it I?

And he answered and said, He that dippeth his hand with me in the dish, the same shall betray me.

The Son of man goeth as it is written of him: but woe unto that man by whom the Son of man is betrayed! it had been good for that man if he had not been born.

Then Judas, which betrayed him, answered and said, Master, is it I? He said unto him, Thou hast said.

And as they were eating, Jesus took bread, and blessed it, and brake it, and gave it to the disciples, and said, Take, eat; this is my body.

And he took the cup, and gave thanks, and gave it to them, saying, Drink ye all of it; for this is my blood of the new testament, which is shed for many for the remission of sins.

But I say unto you, I will not drink henceforth of this fruit of the vine, until that day when I drink it new with you in my Father's kingdom.

—Matthew 26:19-29.

534 THE TRIUMPHAL ENTRY

And when they came nigh to Jerusalem, unto Bethphage and Bethany, at the mount of Olives, he sendeth forth two of his disciples, and saith unto them,

Go your way into the village over against you: and as soon as ye be entered into it, ye shall find a colt tied, whereon never man sat; loose him, and bring him.

And if any man say unto you, Why do ye this? say ye that the Lord hath need of him; and straightway he will send him hither.

And they went their way, and found the colt tied by the door without in a place where two ways met; and they loose him.

And certain of them that stood there said unto them, What do ye, loosing the colt?

And they said unto them even as Jesus had commanded: and they let them go.

And they brought the colt to Jesus, and cast their garments on him; and he sat upon him.

And many spread their garments in the way: and others cut down branches off the trees, and strawed them in the way.

And they that went before, and they that followed, cried, saying, Hosanna; Blessed is he that cometh in the name of the Lord:

Blessed be the kingdom of our father David, that cometh in the name of the Lord: Hosanna in the highest. And Jesus entered into Jerusalem, and into the temple.

—Mark 11:1-11.

And when he was come into Jerusalem, all the city was moved, saying, Who is this?

And the multitude said, This is Jesus the prophet of Nazareth of Galilee. —Matthew 21:10, 11.

535 CRUCIFIXION OF CHRIST

Then delivered he him therefore unto them to be crucified. And they took Jesus, and led him away.

(over)

And he bearing his cross went forth into a place called the place of a skull, which is called in the Hebrew Golgotha:

Where they crucified him, and two other with him, on either side one, and Jesus in the midst.

And Pilate wrote a title, and put it on the cross. And the writing was, JESUS OF NAZARETH THE KING OF THE JEWS.

Then the soldiers, when they had crucified Jesus, took his garments, and made four parts, to every soldier a part; and also his coat: now the coat was without seam, woven from the top throughout.

They said therefore among themselves, Let us not rend it, but cast lots for it, whose it shall be: . . . These things therefore the soldiers did.

Now there stood by the cross of Jesus his mother, and his mother's sister, Mary the wife of Cleophas, and Mary Magdalene.

When Jesus therefore saw his mother, and the disciple standing by, whom he loved, he saith unto his mother, Woman, behold thy son!

Then saith he to the disciple, Behold thy mother! And from that hour that disciple took her unto his own home.

After this, Jesus knowing that all things were now accomplished, that the scripture might be fulfilled, saith, I thirst.

Now there was set a vessel full of vinegar: and they filled a spunge with vinegar, and put it upon hyssop, and put it to his mouth.

When Jesus therefore had received the vinegar, he said, It is finished: and he bowed his head, and gave up the ghost.

—John 19:16-19, 23-30.

536 THE RISEN LORD

In the end of the sabbath, as it began to dawn toward the first day of the week, came Mary Magdalene and the other Mary to see the sepulchre.

And, behold, there was a great earthquake: for the angel of the Lord descended from heaven, and came and rolled back the stone from the door, and sat upon it.

And the angel answered and said unto the women, Fear not ye: for I know that ye seek Jesus, which was crucified.

He is not here: for he is risen, as he said. Come, see the place where the Lord lay.

And go quickly, and tell his disciples that he is risen from the dead; and, behold, he goeth before you into Galilee; there shall ye see him: lo, I have told you.

And they departed quickly from the sepulchre with fear and great joy; and did run to bring his disciples word.

And as they went to tell his disciples, behold, Jesus met them, saying, All hail. And they came and held him by the feet, and worshipped him.

Then said Jesus unto them, Be not afraid: go tell my brethren that they go into Galilee, and there shall they see me. —Matthew 28:1, 2, 5-10.

Then the same day at evening, being the first day of the week, when the doors were shut where the disciples were assembled for fear of the Jews, came Jesus and stood in the midst, and saith unto them, Peace be unto you.

And when he had so said, he shewed unto them his hands and his side. Then were the disciples glad, when they saw the Lord.

—John 20:19, 20.

537 THE GREAT COMMISSION

Then the eleven disciples went away into Galilee, into a mountain where Jesus had appointed them.

And when they saw him, they worshipped him: but some doubted.

And Jesus came and spake unto them, saying, All power is given unto me in heaven and in earth.

Go ye therefore, and teach all nations, baptizing them in the name of the Father, and of the Son, and of the Holy Ghost:

Teaching them to observe all things whatsoever I have commanded you: and, lo, I am with you alway, even unto the end of the world. —Matthew 28:16-20.

[Jesus] said unto them, Thus it is written, and thus it behoved Christ to suffer, and to rise from the dead the third day:

And that repentance and remission of sins should be preached in his name among all nations, beginning at Jerusalem.

And ye are witnesses of these things.

And, behold, I send the promise of my Father upon you: but tarry ye in the city of Jerusalem, until ye be endued with power from on high. —Luke 24:46-49.

They asked of him, saying, Lord, wilt thou at this time restore again the kingdom to Israel?

And he said unto them, It is not for you to know the times or the seasons, which the Father hath put in his own power.

But ye shall receive power, after that the Holy Ghost is come upon you:

And ye shall be witnesses unto me both in Jerusalem, and in all Judaea, and in Samaria, and unto the uttermost part of the earth.

And when he had spoken these things, while they beheld, he was taken up; and a cloud received him out of their sight. —Acts 1:6-9.

538 THE BEATITUDES

And seeing the multitudes, he went up into the mountain: and when he was set, his disciples came unto him:

And he opened his mouth, and taught them, saying,

Blessed are the poor in spirit: for theirs is the kingdom of heaven.

Blessed are they that mourn: for they shall be comforted.

Blessed are the meek: for they shall inherit the earth.

Blessed are they which do hunger and thirst after righteousness: for they shall be filled.

Blessed are the merciful: for they shall obtain mercy.

Blessed are the pure in heart: for they shall see God.

Blessed are the peacemakers: for they shall be called the children of God.

Blessed are they which are persecuted for righteousness' sake: for theirs is the kingdom of heaven.

Blessed are ye, when men shall revile you, and persecute you, and shall say all manner of evil against you falsely, for my sake.

Rejoice, and be exceeding glad: for great is your reward in heaven: for so persecuted they the prophets which were before you.

Ye are the light of the world.

Let your light so shine before men, that they may see your good works, and glorify your Father which is in heaven.

—Matthew 5:1-12, 14, 16.

539 THE VINE AND BRANCHES

I am the true vine, and my Father is the husbandman.

Every branch in me that beareth not fruit he taketh away: and every branch that beareth fruit, he purgeth it, that it may bring forth more fruit.

Now ye are clean through the word which I have spoken unto you.

Abide in me, and I in you. As the branch cannot bear fruit of itself, except it abide in the vine; no more can ye, except ye abide in me.

I am the vine, ye are the branches: He that abideth in me, and I in him, the same bringeth forth much fruit: for without me ye can do nothing.

If a man abide not in me, he is cast forth as a branch, and is withered; and men gather them, and cast them into the fire, and they are burned.

If ye abide in me, and my words abide in you, ye shall ask what ye will, and it shall be done unto you.

Herein is my Father glorified, that ye bear much fruit; so shall ye be my disciples.

These things have I spoken unto you, that my joy might remain in you, and that your joy might be full.

Ye are my friends, if ye do whatsoever I command you.

Henceforth I call you not servants; for the servant knoweth not what his lord doeth: but I have called you friends; for all things that I have heard of my Father I have made known unto you.

Ye have not chosen me, but I have chosen you, and ordained you, that ye should go and bring forth fruit, and that your fruit should remain: that whatsoever ye shall ask of the Father in my name, he may give it you. —John 15:1-8, 11, 14-16.

540 COMFORT FROM CHRIST

Let not your heart be troubled: ye believe in God, believe also in me.

In my Father's house are many mansions: if it were not so, I would have told you. I go to prepare a place for you.

And if I go and prepare a place for you, I will come again, and receive you unto myself; that where I am, there ye may be also.

And whither I go ye know, and the way ye know.

Thomas saith unto him, Lord, we know not whither thou goest; and how can we know the way?

Jesus saith unto him, I am the way, the truth, and the life: no man cometh unto the Father, but by me.

Philip saith unto him, Lord, shew us the Father, and it sufficeth us.

Jesus saith unto him, Have I been so long time with you, and yet hast thou not known me, Philip? he that hath seen me hath seen the Father; and how sayest thou then, Shew us the Father?

Believest thou not that I am in the Father, and the Father in me? the words that I speak unto you I speak not of myself: but the Father that dwelleth in me, he doeth the works.

Believe me that I am in the Father, and the Father in me: or else believe me for the very works' sake.

Verily, verily, I say unto you, He that believeth on me, the works that I do shall he do also; and greater works than these shall he do; because I go unto my Father.

Peace I leave with you, my peace I give unto you: not as the world giveth, give I unto you. Let not your heart be troubled, neither let it be afraid. —John 14:1-6, 8-12, 27.

541 THE HOLY SPIRIT

I will pray the Father, and he shall give you another Comforter, that he may abide with you for ever;

Even the Spirit of truth; whom the world cannot receive, because it seeth him not, neither knoweth him:

But ye know him; for he dwelleth with you, and shall be in you. I will not leave you comfortless: I will come to you.

Yet a little while, and the world seeth me no more; but ye see me: because I live, ye shall live also. —John 14:16-19.

But because I have said these things unto you, sorrow hath filled your heart.

Nevertheless I tell you the truth; It is expedient for you that I go away:

For if I go not away, the Comforter will not come unto you; but if I depart, I will send him unto you.

And when he is come, he will reprove the world of sin, and of righteousness, and of judgment:

Of sin, because they believe not on me;

Of righteousness, because I go to my Father, and ye see me no more;

Of judgment, because the prince of this world is judged.

I have yet many things to say unto you, but ye cannot bear them now.

Howbeit when he, the Spirit of truth, is come, he will guide you into all truth:

For he shall not speak of himself; but whatsoever he shall hear, that shall he speak: and he will shew you things to come.

He shall glorify me: for he shall receive of mine, and shall shew it unto you.

These things I have spoken unto you, that in me ye might have peace. In the world ye shall have tribulation: but be of good cheer; I have overcome the world. —John 16:6-14, 33.

542 THE HOLY SCRIPTURES

Knowing this first, that no prophecy of the scripture is of any private interpretation.

For the prophecy came not in old time by the will of man: but holy men of God spake as they were moved by the Holy Ghost. —2 Peter 1:20, 21.

All scripture is given by inspiration of God, and is profitable for doctrine, for reproof, for correction, for instruction in righteousness:

That the man of God may be perfect, throughly furnished unto all good works. —2 Timothy 3:16, 17.

Study to shew thyself approved unto God, a workman that needeth not to be ashamed, rightly dividing the word of truth. —2 Timothy 2:15.

For whatsoever things were written aforetime were written for our learning, that we through patience and comfort of the scriptures might have hope. —Romans 15:4.

For ever, O Lord, thy word is settled in heaven.

Thy word is a lamp unto my feet, and a light unto my path.

The entrance of thy words giveth light; it giveth understanding unto the simple.

Great peace have they which love thy law: and nothing shall offend them. —Psalm 119:89, 105, 130, 165.

543 TRUE WISDOM

Happy is the man that findeth wisdom, and the man that getteth understanding.

For the merchandise of it is better than the merchandise of silver, and the gain thereof than fine gold.

She is more precious than rubies: and all the things thou canst desire are not to be compared unto her.

Length of days is in her right hand; and in her left hand riches and honour.

Her ways are ways of pleasantness, and all her paths are peace.

She is a tree of life to them that lay hold upon her: and happy is every one that retaineth her.

The Lord by wisdom hath founded the earth; by understanding hath he established the heavens.

By his knowledge the depths are broken up, and the clouds drop down the dew.

My son, let not them depart from thine eyes: keep sound wisdom and discretion:

So shall they be life unto thy soul, and grace to thy neck.

Then shalt thou walk in thy way safely, and thy foot shall not stumble.

When thou liest down, thou shalt not be afraid: yea, thou shalt lie down, and thy sleep shall be sweet.

Be not afraid of sudden fear, neither of the desolation of the wicked, when it cometh.

For the Lord shall be thy confidence, and shall keep thy foot from being taken.

Trust in the Lord with all thine heart; and lean not unto thine own understanding.

In all thy ways acknowledge him, and he shall direct thy paths.
—Proverbs 3:13-26, 5, 6.

544 THE CHURCH

When Jesus came into the coasts of Caesarea Philippi, he asked his disciples, saying, Whom do men say that I the Son of man am?

And they said, Some say that thou art John the Baptist: some, Elias; and others, Jeremias, or one of the prophets.

He saith unto them, But whom say ye that I am?

And Simon Peter answered and said, Thou art the Christ, the Son of the living God.

And Jesus answered and said unto him, Blessed art thou, Simon Bar-jona: for flesh and blood hath not revealed it unto thee, but my Father which is in heaven.

And I say also unto thee, That thou art Peter, and upon this rock I will build my church; and the gates of hell shall not prevail against it. —Matthew 16:13-18.

Now therefore ye are no more strangers and foreigners, but fellowcitizens with the saints, and of the household of God;

And are built upon the foundation of the apostles and prophets, Jesus Christ himself being the chief corner stone;

In whom all the building fitly framed together groweth unto an holy temple in the Lord:

In whom ye also are builded together for an habitation of God through the Spirit. —Ephesians 2:19-22.

There is one body, and one Spirit, even as ye are called in one hope of your calling;

One Lord, one faith, one baptism, one God and Father of all, who is above all, and through all, and in you all. —Ephesians 4:4-6.

545 CHRISTIAN MINISTRY

Whosoever shall call upon the name of the Lord shall be saved. How then shall they call on him in whom they have not believed?

And how shall they believe in him of whom they have not heard?

And how shall they hear without a preacher?

And how shall they preach, except they be sent? —Romans 10:13-15.

For as we have many members in one body, and all members have not the same office: so we, being many, are one body in Christ, and every one members one of another.

Having then gifts differing according to the grace that is given to us, whether prophecy, let us prophesy according to the proportion of faith;

Or ministry, let us wait on our ministering:

Or he that teacheth, on teaching; or he that exhorteth, on exhortation.
—Romans 12:4-8.

As every man hath received the gift, even so minister the same one to another, as good stewards of the manifold grace of God. If any man speak, let him speak as the oracles of God;

If any man minister, let him do it as of the ability which God giveth: that God in all things may be glorified through Jesus Christ.
—1 Peter 4:10, 11.

546 CHRISTIAN UNITY

These words spake Jesus, and lifted up his eyes to heaven, and said, Father, the hour is come; glorify thy Son, that thy Son also may glorify thee:

I have manifested thy name unto the men which thou gavest me out of the world: thine they were, and thou gavest them me; and they have kept thy word.

I pray for them: I pray not for the world, but for them which thou hast given me; for they are thine.

And all mine are thine, and thine are mine; and I am glorified in them.

Neither pray I for these alone, but for them also which shall believe on me through their word; that they all may be one; as thou, Father, art in me, and I in thee,

That they also may be one in us: that the world may believe that thou hast sent me.
—John 17:1, 6, 9, 10, 20, 21.

Now I beseech you, brethren, by the name of our Lord Jesus Christ, that ye all speak the same thing, and that there be no divisions among you;

But that ye be perfectly joined together in the same mind and in the same judgment. —1 Corinthians 1:10.

With all lowliness and meekness, with longsuffering, forbearing one another in love;

Endeavouring to keep the unity of the Spirit in the bond of peace.

There is one body, and one Spirit, even as ye are called in one hope of your calling;

One Lord, one faith, one baptism, one God and Father of all, who is above all, and through all, and in you all. —Ephesians 4:2-6.

547 SIN AND FORGIVENESS

Blessed is the man that endureth temptation: for when he is tried, he shall receive the crown of life, which the Lord hath promised to them that love him.

Let no man say when he is

(*over*)

tempted, I am tempted of God: for God cannot be tempted with evil, neither tempteth he any man:

But every man is tempted, when he is drawn away of his own lust, and enticed.

Then when lust hath conceived, it bringeth forth sin: and sin, when it is finished, bringeth forth death.

—James 1:12-15.

But if we walk in the light, as he is in the light, we have fellowship one with another, and the blood of Jesus Christ his Son cleanseth us from all sin.

If we say that we have no sin, we deceive ourselves, and the truth is not in us.

If we confess our sins, he is faithful and just to forgive us our sins, and to cleanse us from all unrighteousness. —1 John 1:7-9.

Blessed is he whose transgression is forgiven, whose sin is covered.

Blessed is the man unto whom the Lord imputeth not iniquity, and in whose spirit there is no guile.

I acknowledged my sin unto thee, and mine iniquity have I not hid. I said, I will confess my transgressions unto the Lord; and thou forgavest the iniquity of my sin.

Many sorrows shall be to the wicked: but he that trusteth in the Lord, mercy shall compass him about.

Be glad in the Lord, and rejoice, ye righteous: and shout for joy, all ye that are upright in heart.

—Psalm 32:1, 2, 5, 10, 11.

548 LAW AND GOSPEL

Now we know that what things soever the law saith, it saith to them who are under the law:

That every mouth may be stopped, and all the world may become guilty before God.

Therefore by the deeds of the law there shall no flesh be justified in his sight: for by the law is the knowledge of sin.

But now the righteousness of God without the law is manifested, being witnessed by the law and the prophets;

Even the righteousness of God which is by faith of Jesus Christ unto all and upon all them that believe: for there is no difference:

For all have sinned, and come short of the glory of God;

Being justified freely by his grace through the redemption that is in Christ Jesus. —Romans 3:19-24.

But before faith came, we were kept under the law, shut up unto the faith which should afterwards be revealed.

Wherefore the law was our schoolmaster to bring us unto Christ, that we might be justified by faith.

But after that faith is come, we are no longer under a schoolmaster.

For ye are all the children of God by faith in Christ Jesus.

For as many of you as have been baptized into Christ have put on Christ. —Galatians 3:23-27.

Therefore being justified by faith, we have peace with God through our Lord Jesus Christ:

By whom also we have access by faith into this grace wherein we stand, and rejoice in hope of the glory of God. —Romans 5:1, 2.

549 GOD'S INVITATION

Ho, every one that thirsteth, come ye to the waters, and he that hath no money; come ye, buy, and eat;

yea, come, buy wine and milk without money and without price.

Wherefore do ye spend money for that which is not bread? and your labour for that which satisfieth not? hearken diligently unto me, and eat ye that which is good, and let your soul delight itself in fatness.

Incline your ear, and come unto me: hear, and your soul shall live; and I will make an everlasting covenant with you, even the sure mercies of David.

Seek ye the Lord while he may be found, call ye upon him while he is near:

Let the wicked forsake his way, and the unrighteous man his thoughts: and let him return unto the Lord, and he will have mercy upon him; and to our God, for he will abundantly pardon.

For my thoughts are not your thoughts, neither are your ways my ways, saith the Lord.

So shall my word be that goeth forth out of my mouth: it shall not return unto me void, but it shall accomplish that which I please, and it shall prosper in the thing whereto I sent it.

For ye shall go out with joy, and be led forth with peace: the mountains and the hills shall break forth before you into singing, and all the trees of the field shall clap their hands.

Instead of the thorn shall come up the fir tree, and instead of the brier shall come up the myrtle tree:

And it shall be to the Lord for a name, for an everlasting sign that shall not be cut off.

—Isaiah 55:1-3, 6-8, 11-13.

550 THE WAY OF LIFE

Blessed is the man that walketh not in the counsel of the ungodly, nor standeth in the way of sinners, nor sitteth in the seat of the scornful.

But his delight is in the law of the Lord; and in his law doth he meditate day and night.

And he shall be like a tree planted by the rivers of water, that bringeth forth his fruit in his season; his leaf also shall not wither; and whatsoever he doeth shall prosper.

The ungodly are not so: but are like the chaff which the wind driveth away.

Therefore the ungodly shall not stand in the judgment, nor sinners in the congregation of the righteous.

For the Lord knoweth the way of the righteous: but the way of the ungodly shall perish. —Psalm 1.

There is a way which seemeth right unto a man, but the end thereof are the ways of death.—Proverbs 14:12.

Trust in the Lord with all thine heart; and lean not unto thine own understanding.

In all thy ways acknowledge him, and he shall direct thy paths.

—Proverbs 3:5, 6.

Enter ye in at the strait gate: for wide is the gate, and broad is the way, that leadeth to destruction, and many there be which go in thereat:

Because strait is the gate, and narrow is the way, which leadeth unto life, and few there be that find it.

—Matthew 7:13, 14.

Jesus saith . . . I am the way, the truth, and the life: no man cometh unto the Father, but by me.

—John 14:6.

551 FAITH IN CHRIST

Now faith is the substance of things hoped for, the evidence of things not seen.

But without faith it is impossible to please him: for he that cometh

(*over*)

to God must believe that he is, and that he is a rewarder of them that diligently seek him. —Hebrews 11:1, 6.

And this is the will of him that sent me, that every one which seeth the Son, and believeth on him, may have everlasting life: and I will raise him up at the last day. —John 6:40.

For whatsoever is born of God overcometh the world: and this is the victory that overcometh the world, even our faith.

Who is he that overcometh the world, but he that believeth that Jesus is the Son of God?

And this is the record, that God hath given to us eternal life, and this life is in his Son.

These things have I written unto you that believe on the name of the Son of God; that ye may know that ye have eternal life, and that ye may believe on the name of the Son of God.

And we know that the Son of God is come, and hath given us an understanding, that we may know him that is true, and we are in him that is true, even in his Son Jesus Christ. This is the true God, and eternal life. —I John 5:4, 5, 11, 13, 20.

552 PRAYER OF PENITENCE

Have mercy upon me, O God, according to thy lovingkindness:

According unto the multitude of thy tender mercies blot out my transgressions.

Wash me throughly from mine iniquity, and cleanse me from my sin.

For I acknowledge my transgressions: and my sin is ever before me.

Against thee, thee only, have I sinned, and done this evil in thy sight: that thou mightest be justified when thou speakest, and be clear when thou judgest.

Behold, I was shapen in iniquity; and in sin did my mother conceive me.

Behold, thou desirest truth in the inward parts: and in the hidden part thou shalt make me to know wisdom.

Purge me with hyssop, and I shall be clean: wash me, and I shall be whiter than snow.

Make me to hear joy and gladness; that the bones which thou hast broken may rejoice.

Hide thy face from my sins, and blot out all mine iniquities.

Create in me a clean heart, O God; and renew a right spirit within me.

Cast me not away from thy presence; and take not thy holy spirit from me.

Restore unto me the joy of thy salvation; and uphold me with thy free spirit.

Then will I teach transgressors thy ways; and sinners shall be converted unto thee.

O Lord, open thou my lips; and my mouth shall shew forth thy praise. For thou desirest not sacrifice; else would I give it: thou delightest not in burnt offering.

The sacrifices of God are a broken spirit: a broken and a contrite heart, O God, thou wilt not despise. —Psalm 51:1-13, 15-17.

553 CONFESSION OF CHRIST

Whosoever shall confess that Jesus is the Son of God, God dwelleth in him, and he in God. —I John 4:15.

The word is nigh thee, even in thy

mouth, and in thy heart: that is, the word of faith, which we preach;

That if thou shalt confess with thy mouth the Lord Jesus, and shalt believe in thine heart that God hath raised him from the dead, thou shalt be saved.

For with the heart man believeth unto righteousness; and with the mouth confession is made unto salvation. —Romans 10:8-10.

Wherefore God also hath highly exalted him, and given him a name which is above every name: that at the name of Jesus every knee should bow, of things in heaven, and things in earth, and things under the earth;

And that every tongue should confess that Jesus Christ is Lord, to the glory of God the Father. —Philippians 2:9-11.

Whosoever shall confess me before men, him shall the Son of man also confess before the angels of God:

But he that denieth me before men shall be denied before the angels of God. —Luke 12:8, 9.

554 CHRISTIAN BAPTISM

And Jesus came and spake unto them, saying, All power is given unto me in heaven and in earth. Go ye therefore, and teach all nations,

Baptizing them in the name of the Father, and of the Son, and of the Holy Ghost: teaching them to observe all things whatsoever I have commanded you: and, lo, I am with you alway, even unto the end of the world. —Matthew 28:18-20.

Therefore we are buried with him by baptism into death: that like as Christ was raised up from the dead by the glory of the Father, even so we also should walk in newness of life.

For if we have been planted together in the likeness of his death, we shall be also in the likeness of his resurrection:

Knowing this, that our old man is crucified with him, that the body of sin might be destroyed, that henceforth we should not serve sin.

For he that is dead is freed from sin. Now if we be dead with Christ, we believe that we shall also live with him:

Knowing that Christ being raised from the dead dieth no more; death hath no more dominion over him. For in that he died, he died unto sin once: but in that he liveth, he liveth unto God.

Likewise reckon ye also yourselves to be dead indeed unto sin, but alive unto God through Jesus Christ our Lord. —Romans 6:4-11.

555 THE MIND OF CHRIST

If there be therefore any consolation in Christ, if any comfort of love, if any fellowship of the Spirit, if any bowels and mercies,

Fulfil ye my joy, that ye be likeminded, having the same love, being of one accord, of one mind.

Let nothing be done through strife or vainglory; but in lowliness of mind let each esteem other better than themselves.

Look not every man on his own things, but every man also on the things of others.

Let this mind be in you, which was also in Christ Jesus:

Who, being in the form of God, thought it not robbery to be equal with God:

But made himself of no reputation, and took upon him the form of a servant, and was made in the likeness of men:

(*over*)

And being found in fashion as a man, he humbled himself, and became obedient unto death, even the death of the cross.

Wherefore God also hath highly exalted him, and given him a name which is above every name:

That at the name of Jesus every knee should bow, of things in heaven, and things in earth, and things under the earth;

And that every tongue should confess that Jesus Christ is Lord, to the glory of God the Father.

For it is God which worketh in you both to will and to do of his good pleasure.

Do all things without murmurings and disputings: that ye may be blameless and harmless, the sons of God, without rebuke, in the midst of a crooked and perverse nation,

Among whom ye shine as lights in the world; holding forth the word of life. —Philippians 2:1-11, 13-16.

556 GROWTH IN GRACE

Grace and peace be multiplied unto you through the knowledge of God, and of Jesus our Lord,

According as his divine power hath given unto us all things that pertain unto life and godliness, through the knowledge of him that hath called us to glory and virtue:

Whereby are given unto us exceeding great and precious promises: that by these ye might be partakers of the divine nature, having escaped the corruption that is in the world through lust.

And beside this, giving all diligence, add to your faith virtue; and to virtue knowledge;

And to knowledge temperance; and to temperance patience; and to patience godliness;

And to godliness brotherly kindness; and to brotherly kindness charity.

For if these things be in you, and abound, they make you that ye shall neither be barren nor unfruitful in the knowledge of our Lord Jesus Christ.

But he that lacketh these things is blind, and cannot see afar off, and hath forgotten that he was purged from his old sins.

Wherefore the rather, brethren, give diligence to make your calling and election sure: for if ye do these things, ye shall never fall:

For so an entrance shall be ministered unto you abundantly into the everlasting kingdom of our Lord and Saviour Jesus Christ.

—2 Peter 1:2-11.

557 PRACTICAL CHRISTIANITY

I beseech you therefore, brethren, by the mercies of God, that ye present your bodies a living sacrifice, holy, acceptable unto God, which is your reasonable service.

And be not conformed to this world: but be ye transformed by the renewing of your mind, that ye may prove what is that good, and acceptable, and perfect, will of God.

For I say, through the grace given unto me, to every man that is among you, not to think of himself more highly than he ought to think; but to think soberly, according as God hath dealt to every man the measure of faith.

Let love be without dissimulation. Abhor that which is evil; cleave to that which is good.

Be kindly affectioned one to another with brotherly love; in honour preferring one another;

Not slothful in business; fervent in spirit; serving the Lord;

Rejoicing in hope; patient in tribulation; continuing instant in prayer;

Distributing to the necessity of saints; given to hospitality.

Bless them which persecute you: bless, and curse not.

Rejoice with them that do rejoice, and weep with them that weep.

Be of the same mind one toward another. Mind not high things, but condescend to men of low estate. Be not wise in your own conceits.

Recompense to no man evil for evil. Provide things honest in the sight of all men. If it be possible, as much as lieth in you, live peaceably with all men.

Dearly beloved, avenge not yourselves, but rather give place unto wrath: for it is written, Vengeance is mine; I will repay, saith the Lord.

Therefore if thine enemy hunger, feed him; if he thirst, give him drink: for in so doing thou shalt heap coals of fire on his head. Be not overcome of evil, but overcome evil with good. —Romans 12:1-3, 9-21.

558 TEMPERANCE

Wine is a mocker, strong drink is raging: and whosoever is deceived thereby is not wise. —Proverbs 20:1.

Who hath woe? who hath sorrow? who hath contentions? who hath babbling? who hath wounds without cause? who hath redness of eyes?

They that tarry long at the wine; they that go to seek mixed wine.
—Proverbs 23:29, 30.

For the flesh lusteth against the Spirit, and the Spirit against the flesh: and these are contrary the one to the other: so that ye cannot do the things that ye would.

But if ye be led of the Spirit, ye are not under the law.

Now the works of the flesh are manifest, which are these; Adultery, fornication, uncleanness, lasciviousness,

Idolatry, witchcraft, hatred, variance, emulations, wrath, strife, seditions, heresies, envyings, murders, drunkenness, revellings, and such like:

Of the which I tell you before, as I have also told you in time past, that they which do such things shall not inherit the kingdom of God.

But the fruit of the Spirit is love, joy, peace, longsuffering, gentleness, goodness, faith, meekness, temperance: against such there is no law.
—Galatians 5:17-23.

And whatsoever ye do in word or deed, do all in the name of the Lord Jesus, giving thanks to God and the Father by him.
—Colossians 3:17.

559 CHRISTIAN GIVING

Lay not up for yourselves treasures upon earth, where moth and rust doth corrupt, and where thieves break through and steal:

But lay up for yourselves treasures in heaven, where neither moth nor rust doth corrupt, and where thieves do not break through nor steal: for where your treasure is, there will your heart be also.
—Matthew 6:19-21.

Upon the first day of the week let every one of you lay by him in store, as God hath prospered him.
—1 Corinthians 16:2.

Therefore, as ye abound in every thing, in faith, and utterance, and

(over)

knowledge, and in all diligence, and in your love to us, see that ye abound in this grace also.

I speak not by commandment, but by occasion of the forwardness of others, and to prove the sincerity of your love.

For ye know the grace of our Lord Jesus Christ, that, though he was rich, yet for your sakes he became poor, that ye through his poverty might be rich. —2 Corinthians 8:7-9.

But this I say, He which soweth sparingly shall reap also sparingly; and he which soweth bountifully shall reap also bountifully.

Every man according as he purposeth in his heart, so let him give; not grudgingly, or of necessity: for God loveth a cheerful giver.

—2 Corinthians 9:6, 7.

560 CHRISTIAN ASSURANCE

As many as are led by the Spirit of God, they are the sons of God.

For ye have not received the spirit of bondage again to fear; but ye have received the Spirit of adoption, whereby we cry, Abba, Father.

The Spirit itself beareth witness with our spirit, that we are the children of God:

And if children, then heirs; heirs of God, and joint-heirs with Christ; if so be that we suffer with him, that we may be also glorified together.

For I reckon that the sufferings of this present time are not worthy to be compared with the glory which shall be revealed in us.

And we know that all things work together for good to them that love God, to them who are the called according to his purpose.

What shall we then say to these things? If God be for us, who can be against us?

He that spared not his own Son, but delivered him up for us all, how shall he not with him also freely give us all things?

Who shall separate us from the love of Christ? shall tribulation, or distress, or persecution, or famine, or nakedness, or peril, or sword?

Nay, in all these things we are more than conquerors through him that loved us.

For I am persuaded, that neither death, nor life, nor angels, nor principalities, nor powers, nor things present, nor things to come,

Nor height, nor depth, nor any other creature, shall be able to separate us from the love of God, which is in Christ Jesus our Lord.

—Romans 8:14-18, 28, 31, 32, 35, 37-39.

561 LOVE

Though I speak with the tongues of men and of angels, and have not love, I am become as sounding brass, or a tinkling cymbal.

And though I have the gift of prophecy, and understand all mysteries, and all knowledge;

And though I have all faith, so that I could remove mountains, and have not love, I am nothing.

And though I bestow all my goods to feed the poor, and though I give my body to be burned, and have not love, it profiteth me nothing.

Love suffereth long, and is kind; love envieth not; love vaunteth not itself, is not puffed up,

Doth not behave itself unseemly, seeketh not her own, is not easily provoked, thinketh no evil;

Rejoiceth not in iniquity, but rejoiceth in the truth;

Beareth all things, believeth all things, hopeth all things, endureth all things.

Love never faileth: but whether there be prophecies, they shall fail; whether there be tongues, they shall cease; whether there be knowledge, it shall vanish away.

For we know in part, and we prophesy in part.

But when that which is perfect is come, then that which is in part shall be done away.

When I was a child, I spake as a child, I understood as a child, I thought as a child: but when I became a man, I put away childish things.

For now we see through a glass, darkly; but then face to face: now I know in part; but then shall I know even as also I am known.

And now abideth faith, hope, love, these three; but the greatest of these is love. —1 Corinthians 13.

562 PRAYER

When ye pray, use not vain repetitions, as the heathen do: for they think that they shall be heard for their much speaking.

Be not ye therefore like unto them: for your Father knoweth what things ye have need of, before ye ask him.

After this manner therefore pray ye:

Our Father which art in heaven, Hallowed be thy name.

Thy kingdom come. Thy will be done in earth, as it is in heaven.

Give us this day our daily bread. And forgive us our debts, as we forgive our debtors.

And lead us not into temptation, but deliver us from evil:

For thine is the kingdom, and the power, and the glory, for ever. Amen. —Matthew 6:7-13.

Continue in prayer, and watch in the same with thanksgiving.
—Colossians 4:2.

Confess your faults one to another, and pray one for another, that ye may be healed. The effectual fervent prayer of a righteous man availeth much. —James 5:16.

Be careful for nothing; but in every thing by prayer and supplication with thanksgiving let your requests be made known unto God.

And the peace of God, which passeth all understanding, shall keep your hearts and minds through Christ Jesus. —Philippians 4:6, 7.

563 CIVIL POWER

Let every soul be subject unto the higher powers. For there is no power but of God: the powers that be are ordained of God.

Whosoever therefore resisteth the power, resisteth the ordinance of God: and they that resist shall receive to themselves damnation.

For rulers are not a terror to good works, but to the evil. Wilt thou then not be afraid of the power? do that which is good, and thou shalt have praise of the same:

For he is the minister of God to thee for good. But if thou do that which is evil, be afraid; for he beareth not the sword in vain: for he is the minister of God, a revenger to execute wrath upon him that doeth evil.

Wherefore ye must needs be subject, not only for wrath, but also for conscience sake.

For for this cause pay ye tribute also: for they are God's ministers, attending continually upon this very thing.

Render therefore to all their dues: tribute to whom tribute is

(*over*)

due; custom to whom custom; fear to whom fear; honour to whom honour.

Owe no man any thing, but to love one another: for he that loveth another hath fulfilled the law.

—Romans 13:1-8.

564 SPIRITUAL WARFARE

Finally, my brethren, be strong in the Lord, and in the power of his might.

Put on the whole armour of God, that ye may be able to stand against the wiles of the devil.

For we wrestle not against flesh and blood, but against principalities, against powers, against the rulers of the darkness of this world, against spiritual wickedness in high places.

Wherefore take unto you the whole armour of God, that ye may be able to withstand in the evil day, and having done all, to stand.

Stand therefore, having your loins girt about with truth, and having on the breastplate of righteousness;

And your feet shod with the preparation of the gospel of peace;

Above all, taking the shield of faith, wherewith ye shall be able to quench all the fiery darts of the wicked.

And take the helmet of salvation, and the sword of the Spirit, which is the word of God:

Praying always with all prayer and supplication in the Spirit, and watching thereunto with all perseverance and supplication for all saints.

—Ephesians 6:10-18.

The night is far spent, the day is at hand: let us therefore cast off the works of darkness, and let us put on the armour of light.

Let us walk honestly, as in the day; not in rioting and drunkenness, not in chambering and wantonness, not in strife and envying.

But put ye on the Lord Jesus Christ, and make not provision for the flesh, to fulfil the lusts thereof.

—Romans 13:12-14.

565 THE RETURN OF CHRIST

But I would not have you to be ignorant, brethren, concerning them which are asleep, that ye sorrow not, even as others which have no hope.

For if we believe that Jesus died and rose again, even so them also which sleep in Jesus will God bring with him.

For this we say unto you by the word of the Lord, that we which are alive and remain unto the coming of the Lord shall not prevent them which are asleep.

For the Lord himself shall descend from heaven with a shout, with the voice of the archangel, and with the trump of God: and the dead in Christ shall rise first:

Then we which are alive and remain shall be caught up together with them in the clouds, to meet the Lord in the air: and so shall we ever be with the Lord.

Wherefore comfort one another with these words.

But of the times and the seasons, brethren, ye have no need that I write unto you. For yourselves know perfectly that the day of the Lord so cometh as a thief in the night.

Therefore let us not sleep, as do others; but let us watch and be sober.

For they that sleep sleep in the night; and they that be drunken are drunken in the night.

But let us, who are of the day, be

sober, putting on the breastplate of faith and love; and for an helmet, the hope of salvation.

For God hath not appointed us to wrath, but to obtain salvation by our Lord Jesus Christ,

Who died for us, that, whether we wake or sleep, we should live together with him.

—1 Thessalonians 4:13—5:2, 6-10.

566 CHRIST AND IMMORTALITY

Now is Christ risen from the dead, and become the firstfruits of them that slept.

For since by man came death, by man came also the resurrection of the dead.

For as in Adam all die, even so in Christ shall all be made alive.

And so it is written, The first man Adam was made a living soul; the last Adam was made a quickening spirit.

The first man is of the earth, earthy: the second man is the Lord from heaven.

As is the earthy, such are they also that are earthy: and as is the heavenly, such are they also that are heavenly.

And as we have borne the image of the earthy, we shall also bear the image of the heavenly.

For this corruptible must put on incorruption, and this mortal must put on immortality.

So when this corruptible shall have put on incorruption, and this mortal shall have put on immortality, then shall be brought to pass the saying that is written, Death is swallowed up in victory.

O death, where is thy sting? O grave, where is thy victory?

The sting of death is sin; and the strength of sin is the law.

But thanks be to God, which giveth us the victory through our Lord Jesus Christ.

—1 Corinthians 15:20-22, 45, 47-49, 53-57.

567 THE JUDGMENT

And I saw a great white throne, and him that sat on it, from whose face the earth and the heaven fled away; and there was found no place for them.

And I saw the dead, small and great, stand before God; and the books were opened: and another book was opened, which is the book of life: and the dead were judged out of those things which were written in the books, according to their works.

And the sea gave up the dead which were in it; and death and hell delivered up the dead which were in them: and they were judged every man according to their works.

And death and hell were cast into the lake of fire. This is the second death.

And whosoever was not found written in the book of life was cast into the lake of fire.

—Revelation 20:11-15.

As therefore the tares are gathered and burned in the fire; so shall it be in the end of this world.

The Son of man shall send forth his angels, and they shall gather out of his kingdom all things that offend, and them which do iniquity;

And shall cast them into a furnace of fire: there shall be wailing and gnashing of teeth.

Then shall the righteous shine forth as the sun in the kingdom of their Father. Who hath ears to hear, let him hear. —Matthew 13:40-43.

568 THE NEW CREATION

And I saw a new heaven and a new earth: for the first heaven and the first earth were passed away; and there was no more sea.

And I John saw the holy city, new Jerusalem, coming down from God out of heaven, prepared as a bride adorned for her husband.

And I heard a great voice out of heaven saying, Behold, the tabernacle of God is with men, and he will dwell with them, and they shall be his people, and God himself shall be with them, and be their God.

And God shall wipe away all tears from their eyes; and there shall be no more death, neither sorrow, nor crying, neither shall there be any more pain: for the former things are passed away.

And he that sat upon the throne said, Behold, I make all things new. And he said unto me, Write: for these words are true and faithful.

And he said unto me, It is done. I am Alpha and Omega, the beginning and the end. I will give unto him that is athirst of the fountain of the water of life freely.

He that overcometh shall inherit all things; and I will be his God, and he shall be my son.

And he carried me away in the spirit to a great and high mountain, and shewed me that great city, the holy Jerusalem, descending out of heaven from God,

Having the glory of God: and her light was like unto a stone most precious, even like a jasper stone, clear as crystal;

And I saw no temple therein: for the Lord God Almighty and the Lamb are the temple of it.

And the city had no need of the sun, neither of the moon, to shine in it: for the glory of God did lighten it, and the Lamb is the light thereof.

And the nations of them which are saved shall walk in the light of it: and the kings of the earth do bring their glory and honour into it.

And the gates of it shall not be shut at all by day: for there shall be no night there.

And they shall bring the glory and honour of the nations into it.

And there shall in no wise enter into it any thing that defileth,

Neither whatsoever worketh abomination, or maketh a lie: but they which are written in the Lamb's book of life.

—Revelation 21:1-7, 10, 11, 22-27.

569 THE IDEAL MOTHER

Who can find a virtuous woman? for her price is far above rubies.

The heart of her husband doth safely trust in her, so that he shall have no need of spoil.

She will do him good and not evil all the days of her life.

She seeketh wool, and flax, and worketh willingly with her hands.

She is like the merchants' ships; she bringeth her food from afar.

She riseth also while it is yet night, and giveth meat to her household, and a portion to her maidens.

She considereth a field, and buyeth it: with the fruit of her hands she planteth a vineyard.

She girdeth her loins with strength, and strengtheneth her arms.

She perceiveth that her merchandise is good: her candle goeth not out by night.

She layeth her hands to the spindle, and her hands hold the distaff.

She stretcheth out her hand to the poor; yea, she reacheth forth her hands to the needy.

She is not afraid of the snow for her household: for all her household are clothed with scarlet.

She maketh herself coverings of tapestry; her clothing is silk and purple.

Her husband is known in the gates, when he sitteth among the elders of the land.

She maketh fine linen, and selleth it; and delivereth girdles unto the merchant.

Strength and honour are her clothing; and she shall rejoice in time to come.

She openeth her mouth with wisdom; and in her tongue is the law of kindness.

She looketh well to the ways of her household, and eateth not the bread of idleness.

Her children arise up, and call her blessed; her husband also, and he praiseth her.

Many daughters have done virtuously, but thou excellest them all.

Favour is deceitful, and beauty is vain: but a woman that feareth the Lord, she shall be praised.
—Proverbs 31:10-30.

570 CHRIST AND CHILDREN

At the same time came the disciples unto Jesus, saying, Who is the greatest in the kingdom of heaven? And Jesus called a little child unto him, and set him in the midst of them, and said,

Verily I say unto you, Except ye be converted, and become as little children, ye shall not enter into the kingdom of heaven.

Whosoever therefore shall humble himself as this little child, the same is greatest in the kingdom of heaven. And whoso shall receive one such little child in my name receiveth me.

But whoso shall offend one of these little ones which believe in me, it were better for him that a millstone were hanged about his neck, and that he were drowned in the depth of the sea.

Take heed that ye despise not one of these little ones; for I say unto you, That in heaven their angels do always behold the face of my Father which is in heaven.—Matthew 18:1-6, 10.

Whosoever shall receive one of such children in my name, receiveth me: and whosoever shall receive me, receiveth not me, but him that sent me.
—Mark 9:37.

And they brought young children to him, that he should touch them: and his disciples rebuked those that brought them.

But when Jesus saw it, he was much displeased, and said unto them, Suffer the little children to come unto me, and forbid them not: for of such is the kingdom of God.

Verily I say unto you, Whosoever shall not receive the kingdom of God as a little child, he shall not enter therein.

And he took them up in his arms, put his hands upon them, and blessed them.
—Mark 10:13-16.

Topical Index of Scripture Readings

TOPICAL INDEX

TOPICAL INDEX

TOPICAL INDEX

TOPICAL INDEX

TOPICAL INDEX

SANCTIFICATION

SECOND COMING

SECURITY

SERVICE

SERVICE MUSIC

Benedictions:

Call to Worship:

Doxologies:

Gloria Patri:

Offertory Responses:

Processionals:

SOCIAL RIGHTEOUSNESS

SOLOS

SORROW

SOUL WINNING

STEWARDSHIP

SUBMISSION

TEMPTATION

TESTIMONY

THANKFULNESS

TRIALS

TRINITY

TRUST

VICTORY

WARFARE, CHRISTIAN

WEDDING

WITNESSING

WORSHIP

YOUTH

GENERAL INDEX

GENERAL INDEX

GENERAL INDEX

GENERAL INDEX

2413

We Give Thee But Thine Own
William Walsham How
(Offertory Sentence)
Joseph Barnby
We give Thee but Thine own, What-e'er the gift may be; All
that we have is Thine a-lone, A trust, O Lord, from Thee. A-men.
Amens
1. Dresden Amen
pp cres.
A-men, A - - - men.
2. Threefold Amen
A-men, A-men, A - - - - men.
3. Sevenfold Amen
John Stainer
Slow and sustained
A - men, A - - - - - - men.
pp
cres.
f
A-men, A-men, A - - - men, A - - - men, A -
A - - - men, A - - - - men,
A - - - - - - men.
pp
ppp slower
- - - - men, A - - - - men, A - - men.
A - - men,